8037

Miroslav Prstojević

SARAJEVO
THE WOUNDED
CITY

Sarajevo
Yugoslavia

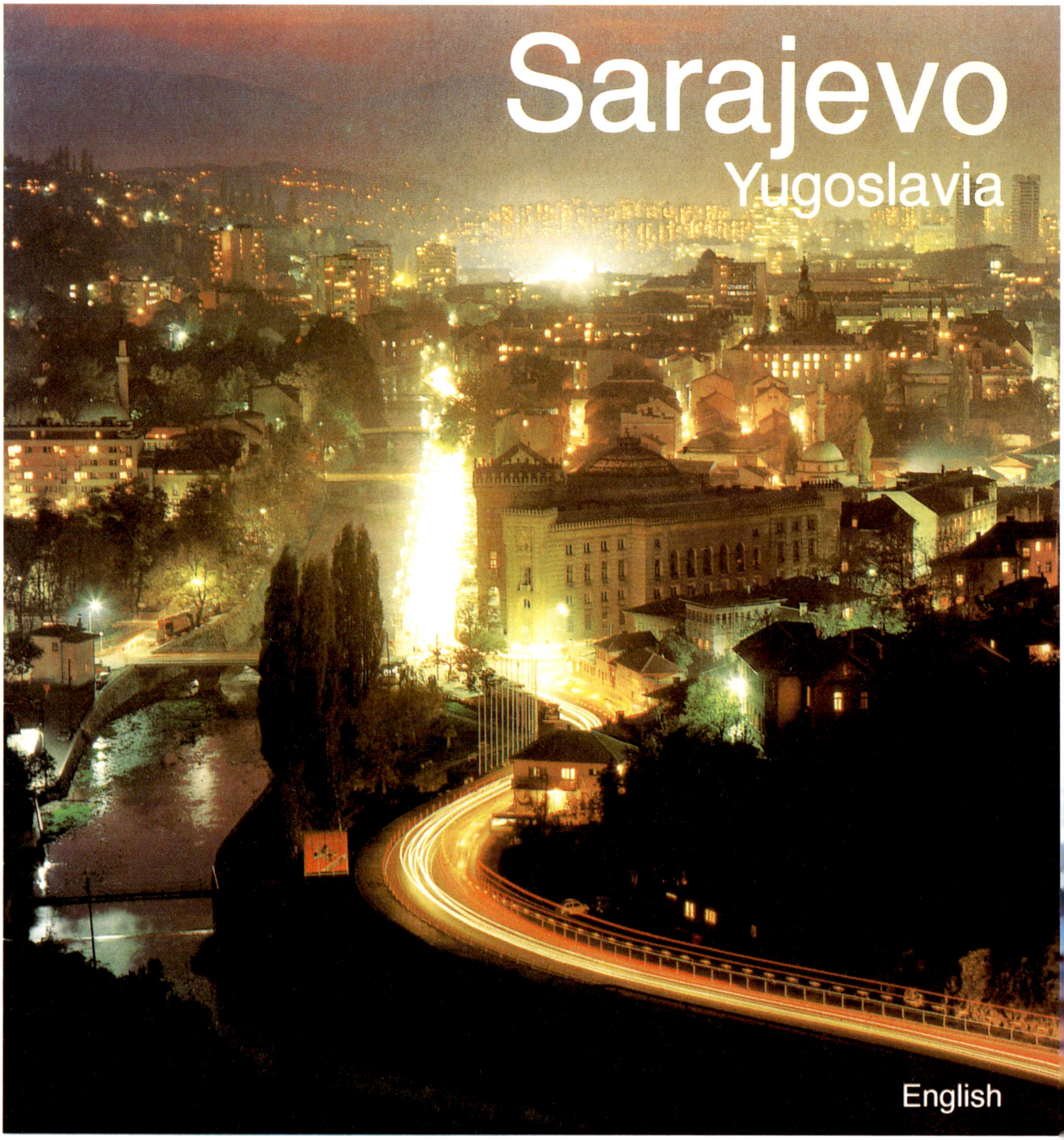

English

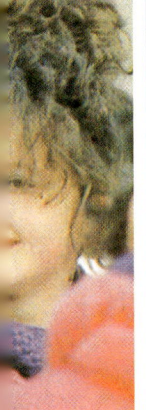

XIV Olympic Winter Games

SARAJEVO

Miroslav Prstojević

PHOTOS:

Emil GREBENAR
Senad GRUBELIĆ
Kemal H. HADŽIĆ
Milomir KOVAČEVIĆ
Danilo KRSTANOVIĆ
Rikard LARMA
Miroslav PRSTOJEVIĆ
Didije TORŠE
Miki UHERKA

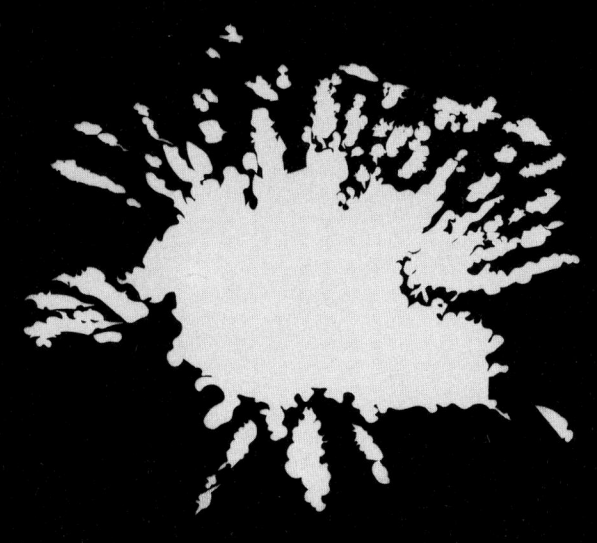

THE WOUNDED CITY

*"At many things
we shall remain amazed;
we all had our childhoods,
our stories and dreams
and a peaceful street by the river..."*
Hamid Dizdar

How to begin a story about a city which is being killed. The barrages are echoing. Shells are falling. They are buzzing over our heads. One of them riochets off the metal roof in the neighbourhood. In the wardrobe, among the bed linen and clothes, there is a new anti-aircraft bullet that came in last night. It bore a hole through the wall and lodged in the double chipboard of the wardrobe. You cannot pull it out by hand. As if it had been hammered in. It came to rest so high you can hang heavy military overcoats or winter coats on it. What is there in the bedroom? On the floor, bits of the room mortar, sand. Above the door, two new holes. On the beds, some clothes, books, pieces of furniture from the sitting room. They are safer here, they are further from the outer wall looking onto Poljine. It is from there that all the shells come. My building has received about fifty of them. The next building two fewer.

It is a December day. Tuesday. Here, all the days are the same. They are glued to one another. They stopped, but are still mercilessly oozing. They are slipping by.

Down, by the next building, a shell made a new crater last night. It is black. The asphalt layer is thick. My Škoda has two new holes in it. It has not got its rear window any more. Three side windows were broken some time ago. The windscreen was shattered. Two female neighbours were hit by shrapnel. One was hurt in an explosion and her cheek was cut. The other was hit in the foot. She had two toes amputated...

Who knows if one should start this story with something wise? This is my story about my city, about myself, my people, about those who are dear and those who are not.

The city is Sarajevo.

The poet whose verses start this story rests in a cemetery in the vicinity, some fifty paces from my room.

I know, now better than before, that there are some people, some events, some times which impress themselves on us, like a heated brand on a cow's flanks. There are some years that are remembered for happiness, pain, loneliness, success, or sorrow. In the calendars of our lives, we circle in red the birthdays of our beloved ones, graduation days, diplomas, handshakes, the first teeth of our sons or the first steps of our daughters, the time they started school, starry nights with black eyes of melancholy and a verse about a box waiting with maiden's gifts...

Pain also cuts its dates in. It does so in boldface, the colour of sorrow. Most frequently it does not fade. We curb it, but it disappears slowly.

Should I finish reading that poem of Hamid's from the beginning:

> "... And it seems to me that
> a dear smile is still hovering
> under the fig tree, behind the back door,
> Following his son's departure
> wishing him a lucky and safe night."

Does anything else exist except that April sentence: Will the war manage to separate us?

It is here that everything starts, or ends. In my temples echo Santayana's words: "Those who do not remember the past are condemned to live it again."

In Sarajevo, you can experience everything for the first time. It may also seem to you that you have seen it all somewhere before, to have already experienced it. Sarajevo is a city of its own memory. Former localities, even four millenia old, over which a string of medieval villages and settlements were built, intertwined into a city. It got rid of all the rural traces from its trappings. It did not walk that usual path from a kasaba (small town), a varoš (town) to a charshi (market, business centre). Here, a shekher (city) was immediately formed. A city was created, a big city whose name contains the word saraj (serai). This also means a court, a mansion, a villa and a residence, a settlement. There is, unlike elsewhere in etymology, no field, meadow or, fortress.

How many poets, travel writers and scientists walked about this city! They came to feel the East in the West, the West in the East, to stop over at a place where civilisations interwove, where parallel worlds lived for centuries, permeated one another, respected one another, relied on one another, inspired and stimulated one another. Many people came. Some stayed. Others left and came back. The city stood and remained in its place. They dedicated to it odes and verses of eternity. They furtively painted its contours on their canvasses. They did not harm it. It accepted all of those who came, offered them a home, gave them drink, kept them warm. It offered its welcoming hands through all those centuries even to those who burnt it. It forgave and gave them presents.

The shadows of Sarajevo rest under the veil of its past. To plunge into its history and feel the pulse of the past is to discover its wealth. Its message might be hidden in the words written on a stechak (medieval Bosnian tombstone):

> *"When I wanted to be –*
> *– then I was not..."*
> or
> *"Look at*
> *this stone –*
> *Whose might it have been?*
> *Whose is it now?*
> *Whose will it be?"*

There are still threads of the past, from the neolithic Butmir caves and mud huts with spiral ornaments on the pottery and unusual figurines, through the ancient Illyrian city ruins and the ruins of Debelo brdo, Zlatište, Soukbunar, the Roman bricks and mosaics of Marijin Dvor and Ilidža with scattered tombstone inscriptions, vague pages of the mediaeval Vrhbosna and Hodidjed to Sarajevo, its Ottoman centuries of power and construction, its four Austro-Hungarian decades, two world wars and down to the present day.

The panopticon of the city's age leads us to realise our love for it. Different pages were written about it, about us, our ancestors. Writing about Bosnia, the wise Meša Selimović, who lived until recently, said: "They are not angels or devils, but they can be both, they are good and evil, soft and tough, gentle and rude, frugal and prodigal, merry and sad, dissipated and shy, pleasant and awful. All sorts of people.

But, in one thing they have never changed: they love their homeland and they love freedom. They even prefer freedom to the homeland, they leave their homeland, as often happens, for the sake of freedom, the freedom as they perceive it."

Nobel Prize winner Ivo Andrić also made his observations about the Sarajevans. He spent his tempestuous but sentimental grammar school days in this city. Still after that he kept returning to it. One could say he never left it at all. He knew every path of it, every cul-de-sac, hill, cafe, cemetery and corner. For the soul of the Sarajevans he says that it breathes "selfconsciousness, enterprise, a wish to live fully and to gain wider horizons, with a veil of melancholy over all of these, a touch of some indefinite anxiety and historical caution about life and everything life brings."

Who knows, David Štrbac might be closest to us with his slyness, cunning, confusion, pathos and mockery. This, one might say, minor literary character with all the qualities of Petar Kočić says of himself: "It's difficult, very difficult, big-headed sir, to understand me."

Sarajevo, a city preserved for a life worthy of man, has preserved, in its life and creation, the measure of nature and naturality. It was and has remained open to the voices of the world, to travellers coming here and to those who settle in it. The unrestrictedness and the outstretched hands of its people, woven into its natural resources and building heritage, won over casual visitors with their charm. They got attached to the city itself and its people. They made those leaving it feel pain, like the Sarajevo poet from the 17th century, Nerkezi:

"My soul was affected by the sadness of leaving Sarajevo – the loss of my Sarajevo friends hurt me bitterly.

Here one seems to be able to live long – at thousands of places in Sarajevo there are fountains, the waters of life."

And then I come to that question:
Sarajevo?! What is it? Where is it?
Somewhere. It is that city on the television screens, in the radio news, in the newspapers.

Sarajevo is a story, laughter, song, tears, memories, the present, and the future.

The biggest game of roulette in the world is not in Monte Carlo. No, not in Las Vegas either. Nor have the Russians got it. All the roulette games of the world are tiny. The biggest casino is in Sarajevo. The year – 1992. The Stakes? Life.

All the adherents to microbiotics dream of having their own village. They got their own city in 1992. Its name is Sarajevo.

Sarajevo is the largest dartboard in the world.

This is the world's largest mousetrap. One cannot get out of it. The keys are held by UNPROFOR. The guards around are murderers incessantly shooting, shooting...

Sarajevo is a city of thin people.
Sarajevo is a city of the hungry.
Sarajevo was the city of the XIV Winter Olympic Games.

In this Olympic year, Sarajevo is a frozen city. Siberia, the Arctic, Alaska and the Antarctic have moved here.

Sarajevo is the world's biggest letterbox. It is being filled with letters and the postmen do not take them away. Letters do not go from here. They cannot come here.

Sarajevo used to have 600,000 inhabitants. Sarajevo does not know how many inhabitants it has today. In Sarajevo, you can die even when you do not want to. It happens hourly. It has been like this for months.

Sarajevo had the first electric tram in central Europe. It has not run since May 2nd. The tram traffic used to be second-hand green Washington ones. They became worn out. Prague trams ran in recent years.

The buses used to be London double deckers, green. They became red, home produced ones. They do not run any more. There is no petrol.

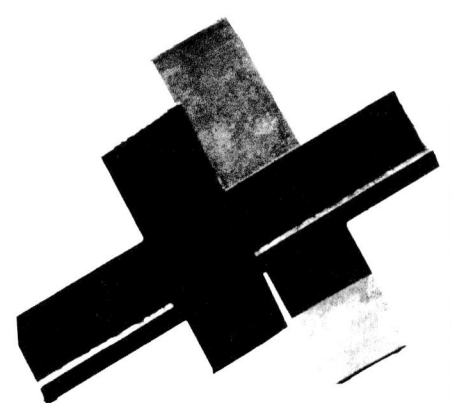

A cable car takes four passengers in each cabin from 530 metres above sea level to Mt Trebević at 1,570 metres above sea level. It has not run since April.

Sarajevo used to have around 10,000 taxis and cars. Today, there are 4 or 5 of them. Others have no fuel, there are no cars, they are not alive.

Sarajevo used to have telephones. Now they are silent. It is only connected with the world, after months of silence, via a few satellite lines. The city telephones do not work. They work only when the telephone exchange has electricity. Otherwise, they are silent.

Sarajevo has nothing.

Sarajevo exists.

Sarajevo is being destroyed, killed, devastated. Here the civilized world, an hour's flight from the centre of Europe, is singing its swan song. The world is worried, but does not really care. Sarajevo is disappearing. It has not existed since yesterday and it was not built to last until today. Is it a city showing what Europe will be like tomorrow? Is it, croaking like Poe's raven, showing the world the future with that ominous end:

"Never. Nevermore."

Welcome (while I am still here) to my city.

Sarajevo, year of our Lord (Satan) 1992.

One enters Sarajevo across a bridge. Unusual, but it is so. This city does not meet a traveller differently. It has been open for centuries. Sarajevo is a city that has no gates or doors. This is, perhaps, its centuries–long fate. Into it poured casual visitors, artisans and builders, priests and wise men, spies and tramps, dervishes and poets... To the east, Kozja ćuprija (Goat's Bridge), a slender stone bridge, is on guard. With its two eyes, rimmed with calcium deposits, it connects roads and meets, in the valley, both the River Miljacka and travellers. The western road leads across six bridge arches near Plandište. There one enters the city where the River Bosna is born. The waters of the Bosna here are cold, clear and good for drinking. The river comes out of a large mountain. It appears after a long, mysterious journey through Mt. Igman's dark womb. Drained through rocks, woods and earth covered with heavy snowdrifts, the water roars and foams up to the surface. It seethes. Its source is a well. It rushes to the north in torrents and gives its name to the country and its people.

Some thirty bridges of Sarajevo connect the city, form its backbone and are its life. Over their arches history has passed. Across them the present passes to tell the future about the past that we are becoming. Those bridges are also the outstretched hands of the banks which do not separate. The river is not their border. It is the city's amalgam. Through those arches, the patterns of the city quarters are woven. The stories about the city are thus formed. They say everything that is beautiful and cold.

Tracing this path of the past spanned by those bridges, we unwillingly go back three long centuries. The year is evil. Sarajevo still suffers from it. Prince and army commander Eugene of Savoy, the owner of the magnificent Vienna castle Belvedere, burnt down and looted the city. It is simply written: anno domini 1697. An anonymous poet, who was my and your ancestor, wrote:

"...
They came and burnt the beautiful shekher Sarajevo down.
Like cattle they drove the innocent people out,
They came and burnt the beautiful shekher Sarajevo down.

How many, how many Korans and countless other books,
How many mosques they burnt, altars pulled down!
The whole city from one end to the other they pulled down and devastated.
They came and burnt the beautiful shekher Sarajevo down.
...
Seen were even those ladies whose faces the sun did not see,
Barefoot and bareheaded they were driven.
Many of them of their happiness were deprived
They came and burnt the beautiful shekher Sarajevo down."

The poet did not write his name. The disaster was greater than his writings. It is unimportant who held that quill in some dark storeroom or on his lap in a houseless courtyard. He might have been shivering from the cold. It never rains but it pours. Misfortunes follow one another. It was late autumn at the end of the 17th century, and winter was cold, mountainous and long. Winters in Sarajevo are always mercilessly severe. He might have been warmed by the warmth of some dark eyes or a rosebush among the round pebbles of the courtyard. Perhaps. For a poet, there is always a love embrace or its evocation.

Another written record witnesses that it was not all to sink into oblivion. Again, a poet is the witness. Poets can fail, exaggerate, but they cannot lie. The heart cannot lie. He wrote his testimony in a simple way:

"...The sky turned into poison for us to drink, glass by glass. From day to day, it made our sorrow and rage grow bigger. It was the Lord's will that this beautiful city be burnt by the enemy, house by house.

Both the rich and the poor now cry, sighing. At the sight of it, the pain breaks my heart. See what the vineyards and lawns look like!

He who never reads books of love cannot understand such violence and Heaven's anger. Many who had huge fortunes now have need of a piece of bread.

The rich and the poor have now been made equal. Thousands of months will pass before we recover from this devastation. Imperial mosques and caravanserais have been pulled down. See what the bezistan (covered market) looks like!

...A sea of misfortune and hardship has flooded and engulfed us over our heads."

He also remained anonymous. He did not sign his testimony, either. But his words surpassed time. And they remained. The memory is long. It does not hurt any longer. The pain disappeared along with the tombs of the contemporaries. The memory and the verse remained. And the thoughts in my head about those three past centuries, too. Another testimony. The words written down shook off the dust of time. They revived, they rushed into the town five years before the anniversary. We are fresh witnesses to the eternity of the written. That wise Meša Selimović may have been right when he wrote: "Surprisingly, the Bosnian man has not got much sense of history and he remembers better the state than the event. But he remembers extremely well what one says and does; he remembers the good to repay it and the evil to avenge it, but he remembers the evil for his lifetime, the good for centuries, turning it into a myth and legend. (Keeping the memory of the remote Kulin Ban is touching; in his history there was so much evil that he does not easily forget that little bit of good.) However, history did not leave such a deep trace in anyone or determine him so much."

Here the decades, centuries, years overlap. Sarajevo raises itself, like a bridge, over its own history, hanging over epochs and strangely connecting the future with the past, the present with tomorrow and with yesterday. Sarajevo bridges, cultures, the Oriental too, the Austro-Hungarian times, modern times and times yet to come. Here are mixed domes, blossom, church bell towers, snow, dried up fountains, minarets, aluminium nets, streets paved with cobblestones, glass surfaces, wooden slippers, roofs, door knockers, satellite dishes, windows and top quality cameras. Sarajevo is a living museum. It has not got its own curator. You do not need a guide here, or a photosafari. It is enough to absorb its pictures, to inspire your soul and leave only to come back again. Photos and slides, metres of celluloid and audio records carry the memories on to others, to some remote cosy rooms. Seconds of the present life were stolen by those records where the new and the old were woven, nature and man's traces recorded for centuries.

Hurrying to commemorate three centuries since the Prince of Savoy's devastation, Sarajevo lived to see another bad year. The city was cut up by barricades and shelled, some of its quarters were occupied. It was on the way to total destruction, obliteration, ruin.

The murderous invasion of Eugene of Savoy made the Sarajevans build fortifications and towers, gates in the old part of the city – at Vratnik. The city was quite large even at that time, but it built its tower, as one might call it, on a hill, a city for defense. And it never used it! Its gates were open, its roads free, as well as the bridges up and down the river. Its heart, Baščaršija, remained outside the walls, unprotected. The whole city remained down. Up, within those walls, there were some houses, lanes and courtyards. The fortifications were built, it seems, more as a warning than in case of need. It did not even impose itself as a tower, a seat of someone in power, or as a castle, when it was built. A legend says that the cement was made from milk, eggs and salt. They would make it stronger. What symbolism! The stone was cut from tombstones. Stechaks and nishans (Muslim tombstones) were built into them. It might have been done to make the walls stronger, so that the dead would protect the living. Did those masons care about later writers who witnessed the obliteration of thousands of stechaks by wicked hands? "Only the people from Bosnia and Hum never disturbed those stones. The sleepers under the stones were good people," it is said. Following the golden thread of the inscriptions on the stechaks, Mak Dizdar wrote his inevitable pages of poetry. Inspired by the language and rhythm, poetic substance and vignettes carved into stone, he wrote:

> *"I beg you*
> *Do not disturb me*
> *Since I was as ye are now*
> *And ye shall be*
> *As*
> *I am."*

In that city there were guns, armies, ammunition and prisoners. The White Tower and the Yellow Tower, kulluks (hard and unpaid labour), day labourers... Here many ended their lives in chains. More ended their lives by the silk braid or sabre. Rebellions and rebels were crushed by the Istanbul authorities here, in the city which never loved them too much. The city was not of the sort that would be quiet and obedient. It preferred power to be further from it. Viziers did not stay here more than three nights, either. People lived more quietly and better by trading, travelling and creating their own future according to their own fancies. However, the city had to agree to be an administrative seat, tired of armies and wars. The Sarajevans were never proud of their vizier's seat. It was brought back here again by the powerful and inexorable Omer Pasha Latas in the middle of the last century. After that, Austria-Hungary had its seat in Sarajevo, as the centre of the province of Bosnia and Herzegovina. And it has remained so.

There might have been carved in Vratnik's cellars, somewhere in the dark, the words like the Blagaj inscription: "This was written by Vrsan Kosarić, a prisoner who was not happy."

The tower survived. Its name is Vratnik. It is a part of the city. Its name tells that it is a door. It does not say that it was bolted and that it was a door through which the city did not pulsate.

By the middle of the last century, a new epoch of the vizier's coming and the reforms of the Turkish Empire created a new fortress of the town. Modern life and a standing army needed accommodation. The Kršla barracks were built. Unusual, but so. It was built at a place called Begluk (Bey's Estate). The place is well-known for being the residence and seat of the founder of the city. There, a serai (court, palace) stood. It had stood there for centuries, renovated, extended. And it was not on an elevation, on a hill which dominates, but in a valley, by the river. In the city centre.

So, at that place, from 1854 to 1856 master Andrija Damjanov was building Kršla. Later he also built the Vizier's Palace (Konak) a little further to the east (1864). For his perfection of building, he was given, so they say, an order by the sultan and was entitled to carry a sabre. He was, probably, the same builder who built monuments in the Balkans, the best-known builder of his time. He is also known as Andrija Damjanović (Zagrafski). This Macedonian was also a painter, an engraver and a stonecutter. He built large Orthodox churches at Čajniče, and in Sarajevo and Mostar, as well. He also left some paintings behind, such as "Jesus on the Throne" in Mostar's Orthodox church with his own text.

Kršla, built in modern style for a contemporary army, dominated the city panorama. Later, the Austro-Hungarian Empire and Kingdom built its barracks around its ramparts and foundations. It was ceremonially opened in 1902. Until then, the old barracks was called Filipović's Barracks, after baron Josip Filipović, commander in chief of the occupation of Bosnia and Herzegovina and the bloodshed at the capture of Sarajevo in 1878. When its construction was completed, it was named the Franz Joseph Barracks.

New times needed new fortifications. They were called barracks. The powerful Austrian monarchy was looking for accommodation for its mob of soldiers. It was too heavy a burden for the city to provide accommodation in homes for that big army. Soon after they arrived, a 30-hectare plot was provided for the building of a large military camp on the outskirts of the city. It was called Filipović's Camp. Dull, grey buildings, boxlike, were built, scattered over a wide

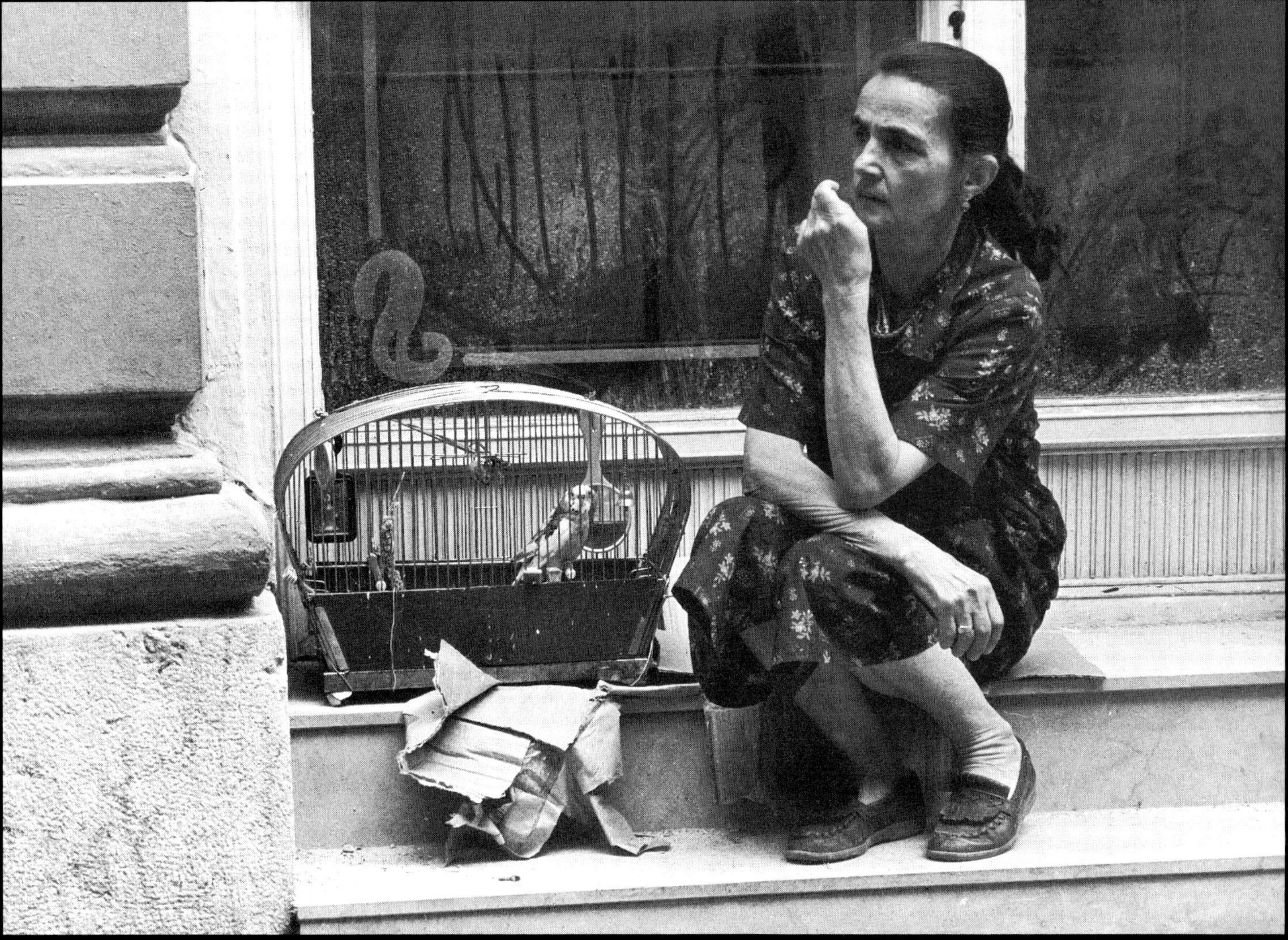

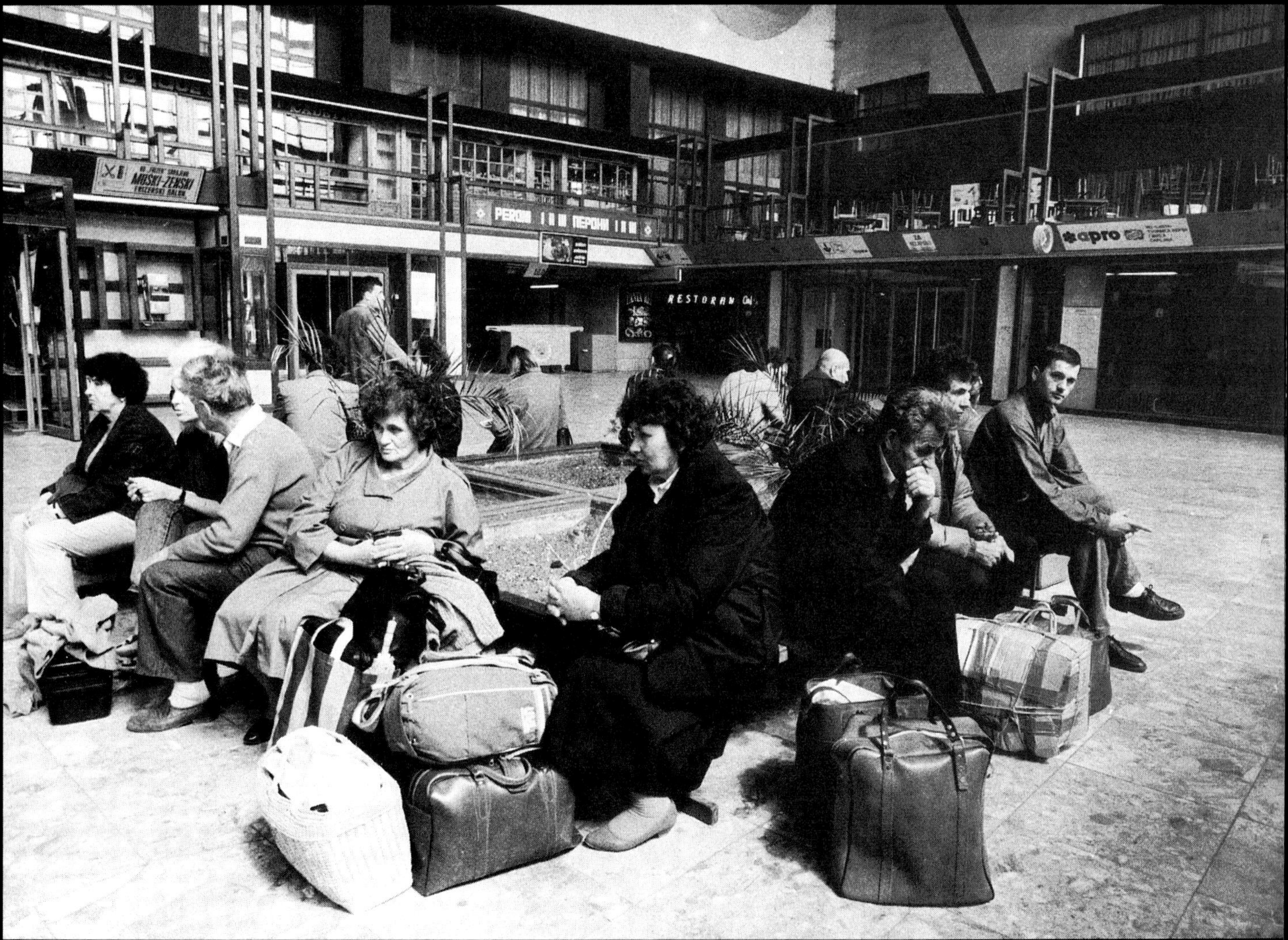
MUSKI-ZENSKI
PERONI
ПЕРОНИ
RESTORAN
apro

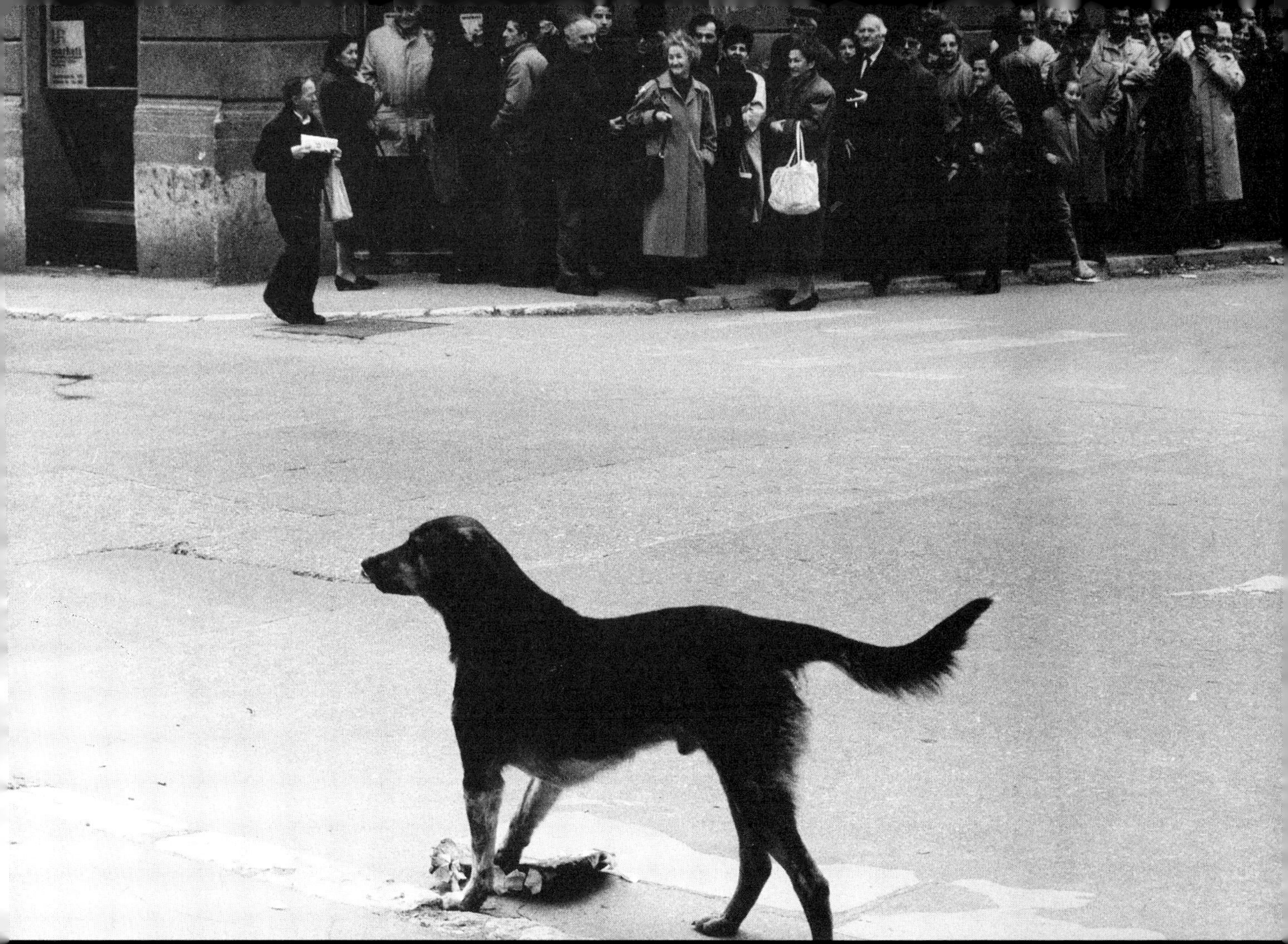

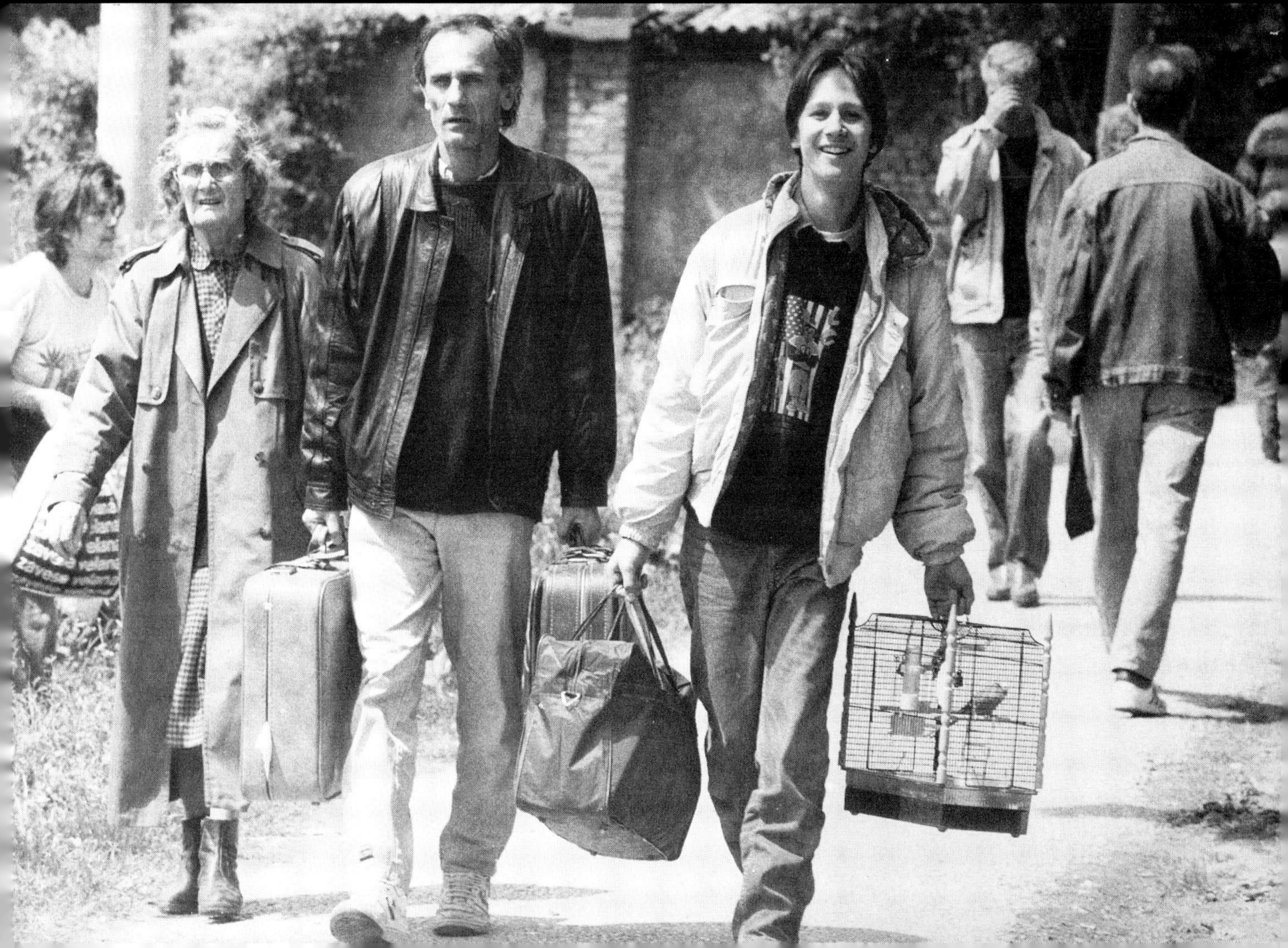

area. So at the end of the last century and at the beginning of this, there grew one of the biggest military complexes in the Balkans with dormitories, horse stables, gun sheds, drill grounds, and the inevitable military prison.

On the fringes of Vratnik, what irony, the barracks of the Prince of Savoy was built in 1914. On the city's dominating peak elevation a barracks named after the person who blackened the city by fire was planted. The Sarajevans did not even want to mention his name. They called it Jajce Barracks. It kept this name, although in recent decades it has borne the name of Gavrilo Princip. Jajce retained its name. It is remembered that in 1916, which was also a war year, the military hospital was moved here from Jajce, a medieval royal town in central Bosnia.

The first recruiting in Sarajevo was carried out peacefully on May 24, 1882. In Herzegovina, it was met with an uprising. How many more recruitments have taken place since then and for what different armies and wars!

The military building to the east of the Turkish Kršla – Platz Komande – dates from those days. The first modern structure in Sarajevo was also a military one. In 1880, The Officer's Hostel was built at a locality called Orta. Orta was also the name of an area in which there was a Catholic cathedral. In this place, there used to be a janissary seat, a janissary orta, i.e. a detachment of at least 400 soldiers. A military school, too – the Boy's Boarding School was a continuation of a Turkish lower military school. It was in the same Turkish building until 1890 near today's Railway Head Office. It was moved to Dobrovoljačka Street, to the so-called Zeleni mejdan (Green Field/Battlefield). There also was a considerably extended Military Hospital. The one from 1866 was too small. And so on to many more fortifications around the city, heaps of wasted money.

Barracks were built in the very heart of Sarajevo. Their names changed according to regimes and authorities. Their locations remained the same. They were for the defence and, one might say, the control of the city. Soldiers came and went serving their homeland. Officers advanced, moved, received awards and retired.

Austria-Hungary left marks that we live with. The wise Miroslav Krleža noticed people paying homage at the tomb of the poet Silvije Strahimir Kranjčević: "One should get accustomed to the Sarajevo valley, walled in by Austrian fortifications in a Portarthurian way, where one can still see the monograms of Franz Joseph's times in concrete on the mountains; one should imagine himself in that dusty Kranjčević's room in the Balkan Institute, leaf through the books in his poor library..." It might have had to build all of them, taught by the welcome of April 19, 1878. The progress of the regiments was bloody on that day, before victory was signalled on the Sarajevo fortress by the Imperial and Royal flag and a 101-gun salute. A contemporary wrote: "The

Sarajevans defended themselves with a desperate bravery (especially in the city's quarter between the Alipasha Mosque and the Military Hospital): each time, from each courtyard, even from the hospital, they fired at the companies; the women and young girls did not lag behind the men...

The battle for the capital lasted only six hours. During that short time, 56 young men and one officer were killed, 305 young men and nine officers were wounded, while two soldiers were lost."

That same Austro-Hungarian army and administration left Sarajevo without a shot being fired. By the narrow-gauge railway, a Serbian volunteer army arrived at Bistrik railway station from Višegrad, and then entered the city on November 6, 1918. A Serbian volunteer army. They were welcomed without a shot fired in resistance. With the end of the First World War, the Austro-Hungarian Monarchy disintegrated. The Kingdom of the Serbs, Croats and Slovenes, later the Kingdom of Yugoslavia, was created. At the beginning, it was a great hope for the peoples of the South Slavic countries. Soon, it disappointed many.

April 1941 saw the panicky disintegration and disappearance of the old Yugoslav army. The first day of the war, April 6, brought Sarajevo an air raid with a few bombs dropped. The royal government and the court, on their way to an exile without return, stopped over at Pale, 15 kilometres to the east of Sarajevo. Then, via Nikšić, the Karađorđević dynasty left forever. The generals signed the capitulation of the Kingdom of Yugoslavia in that very Pale. Then a German fascist mob of soldiers and quislings arrived. There followed four years of terror, arrests, murders, antifascist resistance and underground activities.

Then, again on April 6, but the year was 1945, partisan units were coming down from Vratnik. The People's Liberation Army was driving the invaders out. The liberators were being killed, but so were those fleeing. Sarajevo welcomed freedom with singing.

And then again, barracks were full. The army was there. It was a people's army. It changed with time. Everything changes. The city lives, pulsates and grows up, too.

Everything started again with the bridges. The River Miljacka witnessed the first bullets, victims and death. This time, they were not the centuries-old stone bridges of Sarajevo. They were the bridges of the new parts of the city. Barricades were put up near Kozja ćuprija (Goat's Bridge). At Ilidža, too. It was impossible to go further. At the barricades in the Grbavica suburb, just off the bridge near Ekonomska škola and Vodoprivreda, the first shots fired at the people rang out. Crowds of Sarajevans were halted by bullets. They rebelled against the barricades, divisions, the war-mongering, against the war whose burden and smell had been felt in the early months of 1992. Some hours later,

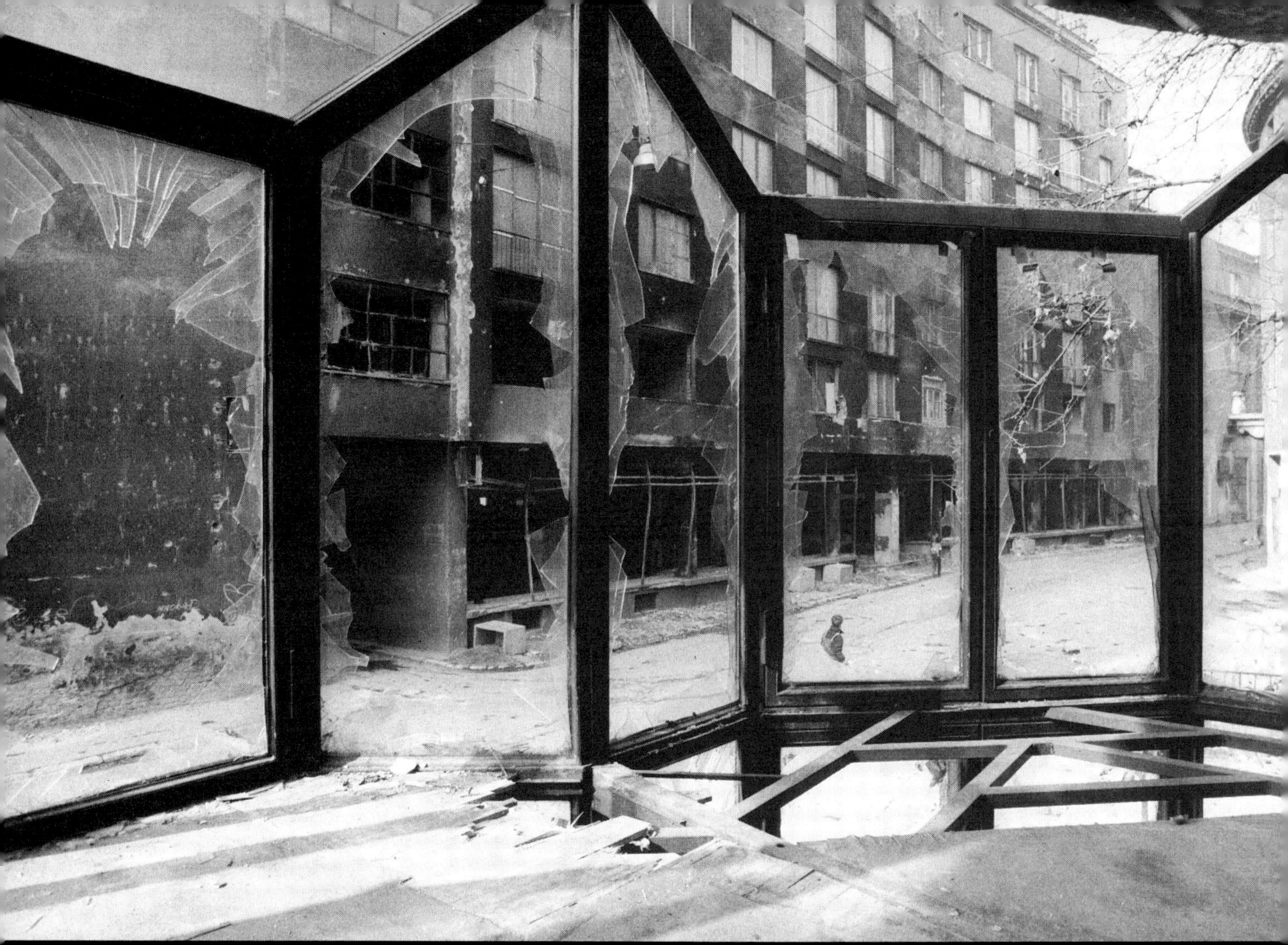

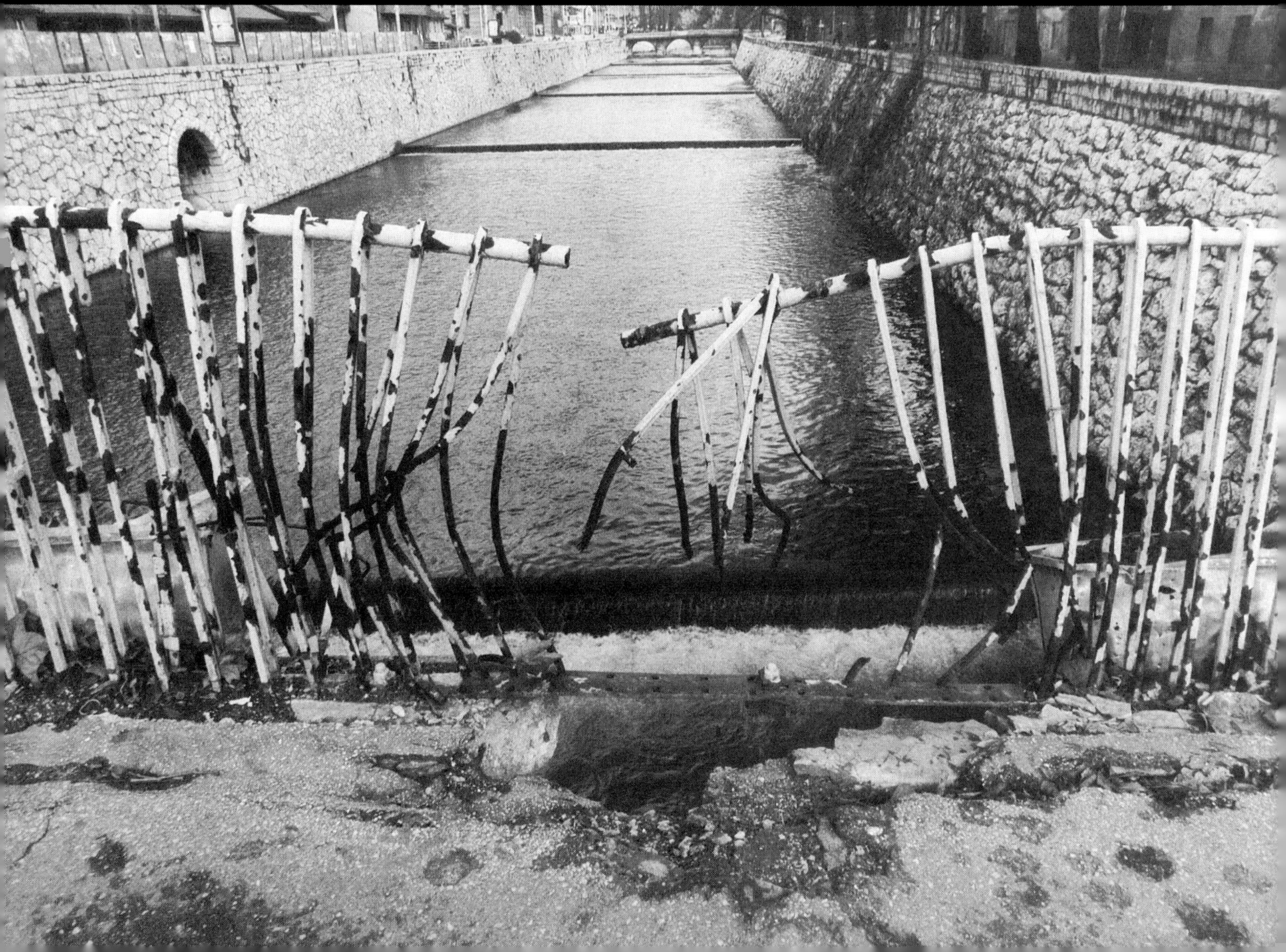

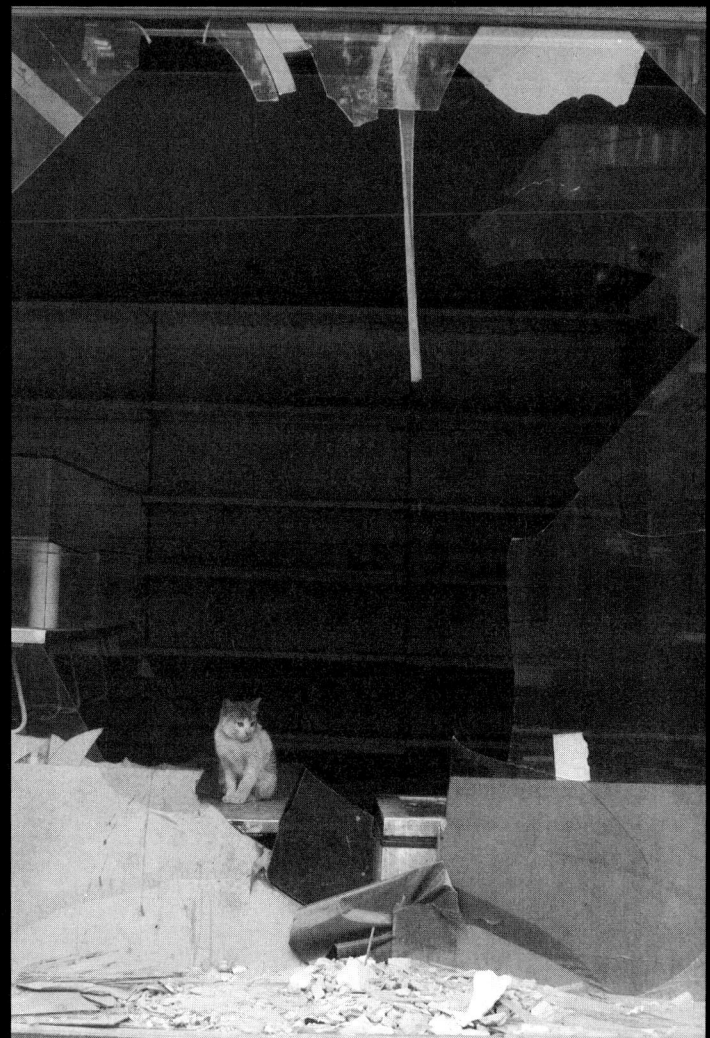

blood was shed on Vrbanja Bridge, just off the building of the Republic of Bosnia and Herzegovina's Parliament. From the next building, a concealed murderer shot a girl student, Suada Dilberović. She was marching in a procession of demonstrators. The girl's innocent blood, the blood of a future doctor, shed some fifteen paces in front of me and my fifteen-year-old daughter, changed the bridge's name. The procession of citizens was stopped by the roaring of rifle barrels. We wanted to join another procession of like-minded people who had been halted at Grbavica.

So we stopped. We stopped, embarrassed.

Sarajevo stopped.

We went back to the courtyard in front of the parliament building. We went into the great hall of the Republic of Bosnia and Herzegovina's parliament building, uninvited and breaking glass. Ministers fled through the nearest exit. They did not protect the people or supply them with microphones or loudspeakers to raise their voices outside the walls of the Assembly Building and seat of government. We went in and occupied the rostrum. The shots of the Serbian Democratic Party were ringing out at Grbavica. People talked, talked, talked. Demonstrations spontaneously sprang up. They decided to govern. They chose democracy. Students, doctors, workers, actors and teachers took their turns. Power rolled down the red woollen carpet going down the stairs of the parlaiment building. Sarajevo had its Petersburg Winter Palace in its Parliament.

History was in the making.

It was solemn, loud and emotional. Sarajevo was calling Bosnia and Herzegovina. Its echo could be heard.

In the afternoon of that April 5, the first shells fell on the city. The target was Bistrik. Time: 5.32 p.m. The first serail used to be there, the city's embryo. They also fell onto Kovači, a quarter below the Vratnik fortress. History seemed to be repeating itself. The city's most famous landmarks were being targeted.

The noose of the barricades had already strangled the city. It carved it up. The barracks became focuses, wasp's nests that should be eliminated, disturbed but not touched.

It was here that Sarajevo's hell began. The year 1992 went through its nine circles. Old Dante described Hell with those nine circles. From the beginning of April to the end of the year there were so many evil months, and each time we naively believed that we could not go further or deeper, that the end was near, that there was light at the end of the tunnel. Sarajevo was thus drawing its circles, circles, sinking and going on, on. In time, we realised it would last. We became aware that we were where we were, that we could not fall asleep and forget. We lived out, at least a great majority of us, that hellish year. We did not have to read Dante's "Divine Comedy". We lived to become in its best volume: "Hell". Mr Alighieri, I will have to tell you my story. I will take you round my circles. Pythagoras also begged Roman soldiers not to touch his. And they did not dare spoil his magic mathematical formulae. My circles were drawn by death, hunger, shells, bullets, crazy policies of evil, fear, hunger and camps.

I reached the end of the year 1992. Sarajevo too. It was not easy. Without it, it would be more difficult. It was here that I silently brooded over the verse of a poet stolen from a tombstone of mediaeval Bosnia:

"Let this be the last slave/who lost hope."

I did not lose hope in the long, sleepless nights while I was in the cellar, waiting for a shell looking for me too, mourning for a dead friend, for secret love, the columns of refugees, the expelled, the disgraced... In Andrić's "Ex Ponto" there is a part of each of us: "The worst misfortune and severest punishment in my life is that I am condemned to live alone."

But I was not alone.

Nor was Sarajevo alone. People were there. Everybody carried his own thoughts from "Ex Ponto", trudged through his circles of Hell and wrote his own Divine Comedy.

Historians will meticulously philosophise about the war chronicle. Contemporaries will be explaining in their memories what was happening to us. They will be witnesses to their own truths. We will be glad to understand the time we lived in without knowing it.

But, the year 1992 is both a chronicle, a record and a picture which is remembered. It leaves behind itself Sarajevo – a destroyed city, Bosnia and Herzegovina – depopulated, bloody, starved and for centuries barefoot, devastated and distraught.

It started with April. I believe even earlier. It lasted through the circles of the months of May, June, July, August, September, October, November and the whole of December.

It lasted.

CIRCLE ONE

JANUARY

Thursday, 2nd: *The first valid peace-treaty between the Serbs and the Croats signed under Cyrus Vance's sponsorship.*

FEBRUARY

Saturday, 29th: *A referendum of citizens on independence and sovereignty of Bosnia and Herzegovina. The Serbs are told by the Serbian Democratic Party to boycott the referendum. Attack on a wedding party at Baščaršija – one man killed. Tension in the city.*

MARCH

Sunday-Monday, 1st/2nd: *Barricades in Sarajevo after the polling stations close.*

Monday, 2nd: *The barricades cut off communications, starving the city.*

Tuesday, 3rd: *The referendum results announced. Out of a total number of 3,199,031 eligible voters in Bosnia and Herzegovina 1,997,664 or 63,4% of them voted. Among those who did vote 92,68% were in favour of an independent, sovereign and unified B-H. Only 0.19% voted against.*

I did not notice the entrance. I did not notice when or how I got in. Nowhere was it written: "Abandon all hope, ye who enter here!" I missed it, but somewhere, however, it must have been written, mustn't it? Searching for it in my mind later was in vain. There was nowhere that triumphal arch.

The first steps would have been impossible for Dante without Vergil. The Roman poet was his guide. I did not know that I had walked so deep. Contact with the darkness of time had blinded me. One takes time to adapt. Blindness is not caused by rubbing one's eyelids. I stamp my feet, crawl, grope around in some new, unknown room. A man, unaccustomed to the darkness, stops. He wants to step back, but he starts anew. Darkness. And only some black opaque dough. We were not even aware of the passing by of mythically silent Maro. We did not notice he was sailing on the River Acheron. Our dead spirits, believing themselves eternal, sailed without knowing where. There was no path. We walked in darkness. One could not go back. A slippery, steep path led downwards. One never goes back. It is man's nature to go forward, forward. Later, after walking through many circles of Hades, a friendly hand touched me. The good academician explained to me also what followed. He helped me not to look back. He repeated, in a professorial manner, his words from circle one: "I am afraid that many of us will not know how long all this will last."

Slowly, and unrestrainedly, we walked a full circle. The night shooting was repeated. During the day it was a nightmare behind us. We believed it was accidental, that somebody's unruliness was disturbing our peace. The whole of April was permeated with disbelief. The barricades carved up the city. During the day, they were removed. Rubbish skips were used as the barricades. They were pushed into the streets, and then moved aside. Road checkpoints were manned by reserve policemen or armed men, people from our neighbourhood. They searched our car boots. They only looked for weapons.

Nobody had stopped us for years. Now we are used to the checks. There was less and less petrol at petrol stations. After some time, there was no more left on the black market.

We avoided going out unnecessarily. We only went out to get the necessary groceries, to work and go back home. In the streets, there were more and more weapons. It gave one both hope and restlessness. After dark, people stayed in their cosy homes. The barricades were busy again at night. Bursts of fire, night shooting, could be heard. The radio news and newspapers reported on cars being taken away, cruel and faceless people masked by black socks with slits for their eyes and mouth.

The ring around the city was getting tighter. The system seemed innocent. The first barricades, the ones put up in

March, were crushed by a crowd of unarmed Sarajevans. A meeting of peace and readiness to live together crushed the obstacles on the roads, drove the terrorists out, plugged the barrels of their weapons. The all-national parliament was a strong expression of peace and the centuries-long existence of the country of Bosnia and Herzegovina.

We did not know whether there had been casualties at Vrbanja Bridge, just behind the parliament building or not. Whether a little thirteen-year-old girl had been killed or not. A young man, held unrealistically by his arms and legs like a sack, was being hurriedly carried just near me; there was a bloodstain on his thigh. A dark red colour was spreading over the white T-shirt. Dr. Ferid Selmanović, with his shirt and tie, treated the wound of Suvan Trumić, a young man from Brčko. Fifty-five-year-old Muhidin Šabanović tragically died here, too. You could also hear: "What they have done to us! Sarajevo is defending itself. Bosnia is defending itself, we shall win!" uttered by a wounded man. From the lips of Suada Dilberović, her last words resounded through Sarajevo: "Is this Sarajevo?"

The snipers from the Holiday Inn and other tall buildings fired into the people's revolt. They started the destruction with terror. From my diary I quote:

"There has been no authority for some time. As if it had been thrown out onto the pavement. It reminds me of a bag made of newspaper and filled with roast chestnut shells. There is no one to bend down, nobody to pick it up, or even to throw it somewhere.

The barricades and shots from the beginning of March are back in Sarajevo. Those disguised ones have again pulled their woollen peasant socks over their heads with the slits through which their eyes and mouths peep. They wave their machineguns and fire their bursts.

We withdraw again into our shelters. We sit and languish. TV and the radio, in turn, inform us about what is happening and where, what is being claimed and what is defended and by whom.

Something is in store. One has felt it for weeks behind us . . .

That March sentence from a French newspaper is being ominously applied. It was uttered by one of the organizers of the March barricades: "Sarajevo will soon become Belfast or Beirut."

We did not believe him. We did not accept that every birth is painful. Somebody had to cut the newborn infant's unbilical cord. It is not meant for strangling a foetus. Bosnia and Herzegovina is being born anew. It has been recognized by the international community. An all-national parliament is taking place.

Even then, I did not believe in the war. My friends did not take it seriously, either. Sarajevo was not prepared. It was surprised. It still believed the army. It had been

Thursday, 5th: *A peace gathering. Several tens of thousands of people in front of the Assembly of B-H.*

Saturday, 21st: *Anxiety among the citizens of Sarajevo caused by the increased movement of a large number of military vehicles. Artillery is found to have been deployed on the surrounding hills, turned in the direction of the city. Army units seen digging in.*

APRIL

Friday-Saturday, 3rd/4th: *Shooting around midnight. Masked men shoot at car drivers several times during the night. Barricades set up according to the instructions of the Serbian Democratic Party in the area of Vraca, Grbavica and Vrbanja bridge.*

Sunday, 5th: *Skirmishes all over the town. Seven dead and dozens of wounded. Masked terrorists shoot at peace processions at the blocked Grbavica and Vrbanja bridge. A student of medicine, Suada Dilberović, killed. Six wounded. A crowd of people forcibly enter the Assembly of B-H. They demand that something is done for peace by all means. The Prime Minister resigns in front of the people gathered in the Assembly Hall. An unsuccessful attempt by masked terrorists with white ribbons to capture some police stations. The terrorists attack the Police School at Vraca inflicting slight injuries on about 15 out of the 100 pupils of the school. The first shells fall on the city just after 4 p.m. The eastern parts of the town are hit by an 82 mm artillery piece firing from Lapišnica (near the Goat Bridge). Several people wounded. The airport of Sarajevo closes in the afternoon. The JNA seizes the airport.*

Monday, 6th: *Twelve dead and twenty-seven injured. The EC recognises Bosnia and Herzegovina. Sarajevo defends itself on the outskirts against the breakthrough of the terrorists into the town. A few shells fall onto the very heart of Baščaršija. At about 1.30 p.m. snipers fire from the "Holiday Inn" hotel and "UNIS" skyscrapers at about 100,000 citizens gathered at a meeting in front of the building of the Assembly of Bosnia and Herzegovina. Specialists from MUP (Interior Ministry Police) catch eight snipers in the hotel at about 2 p.m. The Hum TV-transmitter and RTV centre shelled. Cellars are turned into shelters.*

Tuesday, 7th: *About twenty bodies are in the mortuary. Drama in the Jarčedoli residential area: dead and wounded people, houses burnt down. The Presidency of the R B-H makes a decision about curfew in Sarajevo (from 10 p.m. to 6 a.m.) until the ongoing danger stops. Four disused cemeteries used again for burials of those who get killed every day. Crowds of people in food shops. No vegetables. Prices go up.*

Wednesday, 8th: *About thirty people injured by snipers or by stray bullets. Eastern parts of the city heavily shelled. The airport partly opened. Trains do not run after 7 p.m.*

Thursday, 9th: *The Presidency functioning as the Assembly decides to change the name of the Socialist Republic of Bosnia and Herzegovina into the Republic of Bosnia and Herzegovina. At the same*

a people's army for half a century. We believed, during those ominous shots into the citizens of Sarajevo, that the two military armoured vehicles, escorted by a police car, were hurrying to help us. How many lit up faces greeted our army with applause. It used to come to help. Where did it go? No, it knows best what to do. It is ours... And those two armoured vehicles just passed by. My friend and contemporary, Ekrem, a lieutenant colonel, started to cry in front of a TV screen at the headquarters watching how happy the people became when the soldiers arrived. He knew that they were hurrying, but only to the headquarters and the generals, with hot food containers, carrying dinner from a barracks in the vicinity. They were greeted with loud cheers while passing the old chestnut trees outside the Assembly Building. Those are the same trees at Marijin Dvor, along one of city's main arteries, where the Second World War fascists hanged about ten patriots, leaving the urinating corpses to swing, and "the torture houses with their fresh traces of the sadism of the ustasha criminals" in a mess. "Why does that stupid old Sarajevo woman cry for her rascal on the gallows," eternally wondered the old poet.

The Republic of Bosnia and Herzegovina was the world's biggest military camp. It became one, almost unnoticeably, in mid–1991 after the war in the western parts of the disintegrating Yugoslavia. Sarajevo became the centre of that camp, its newly created parade ground.

Columns of military vehicles had been moving round the city for months. Nobody dared to stop them. They were under military control. Later, big, heavy trucks with military escorts roared there. They were full of weaponry. We were silent about it. The army, good heavens, knows best what to do, we thought. We kept our eyes closed when several big trailers stopped in the city. They were full of military equipment and weaponry. The documents on the drivers said they were bananas! The army intervened and threatened. It protected them. The same was repeated until the April threat of an angry officer riding in an armoured vehicle that he would blast at a ten-storey skyscraper in the Otoka district. He was upset by a civilian road checkpoint.

No, I could not accept that the war pendulum was inexorably swinging over my head, too. I was helpless. So were my friends. It was happening for the first time to all of us. War probably comes so clumsily, and unrestrainedly. Some shook with the fear of tomorrow. Others were afraid of starvation. To others, it was clear that they had to flee, to go somewhere. To leave as soon as possible. They left without saying goodbye. Our neighbours and acquaintances sneaked out of the city. Women, children, mothers, whole families left. Their overstuffed bags which they pulled along the streets to the airport or the railway station looked like picnic bags. The most frequented place was the passport section at the police. They all wanted to get their trips out into the world certified, to take with them the document which is not left here. Some Anns, Maries, Sabinas left. We remained in the deserted streets worried about those leaving.

I was confused, I admit, by a young English lady of ours. She is ours because she has rested in a Sarajevo cemetery after living with us for more than four decades. Her name was Adelina Paulina Irby. Miss was prefixed to her name so that it became Miss Irby. In her time, the Turko-Serbo-Montenegrin war was being waged. Austria-Hungary was neutral. The war, devastation and starvation drove people from their homes. As early as 1876 Austria-Hungary fed over 100,000 Bosnian refugees and spent, as historians say, over two million florins or four million crowns. In 1878 contemporaries counted over 200,000 refugees from Bosnia and Herzegovina in Austria-Hungary. The total costs for three ... when money is spent and ... up to ten million florins or twenty million crowns for the powerful Austro-Hungarian Empire and Kingdom. Woven into those long columns of the wretched was the life story of a young English girl, her care, love and sacrifice for the refugees. As an expression of gratitude, candles were lit and bunches of fresh flowers were laid on her eight decades old tomb at Koševo cemetery until recently. It was unknown to me by whom. But I know she is the only one who did not send us her bill. She donated her money, and her property. She did not present her bill.

Words could not stop the columns of those leaving. They were not really leaving. They were going on a trip. They were going to return.

I still saw, from the tram that was still running, Uncle Aljoša in Brankova Street at Marijin Dvor. He walked with dignity, as usual. True, now he used a walking stick, stopping and looking in a shopwindow still full of bicycles and motorcycles. He was in my thoughts the whole of April, May and June. He was with me later, too, when the overcrowded convoys were leaving. I silently reviewed his life story. I reviewed the summary of my sports documentary about Aleksej P., a ninety-three-year-old from Marijin Dvor. A young Russian man struck by the October tempest set off on his journey as a refugee. He started out with friends from college, a private, civilian college for sons of the well-off and prominent families. His brothers and sisters supported the Red Army. He had a liking for it, too. His friends were inclined to the Whites. He set off naively with them. He thought: for a short while. His trip became a one way street. It seems to me that the wife and son of Trotsky, an intellectual, but a Red Army commander as well, were on the same path. This might be a story about some other Bolshevik dignitary. The trips usually ended in Istanbul. The funnel of the emigrants narrowed there. At the Bosphorus, they realized where they were. Many not even then.

time a warning is given of the immediate danger of war.

Friday, 10th: Schools closed until further notice. Regular and chartered flights for Belgrade. More than a thousand citizens leave the city. The Jewish community organizes the evacuation of 323 Jews. The first Children's Embassy appeals for help to evacuate children from threatened areas. Mortars fire at the slopes of Trebević. Banks open from 9 a.m. to 2 p.m. There is almost no money.

Saturday, 11th: The airport packed with passengers. Destruction of the town from the direction of Vraca.

Sunday, 12th: Shelling of Alipašino polje. Night gunfire in Grbavica. According to an official statement there are 17 killed and 172 injured people in Sarajevo since the beginning of the war till April 11.

Monday, 13th: Shelling of Mojmilo and Vojničko polje residential areas. "Nikola Tesla" primary school in Dobrinja on fire. The JNA grab weapons, equipment and ammunition from the Territorial Defence in the barracks in Faletići. Bread prices go up 50 per cent.

Tuesday, 14th: Two people killed, ten injured. Structures and vehicles of the Town Transport Company fired at with 120 mm shells. Twenty-four buses destroyed, forty damaged, thirty trams put out of service. The RTV centre fired at, as well. Trolleybuses stop running owing to shelling. New prices in shops.

Wednesday, 15th: Post arrives in the city after a fifteen-day delay. Shortage of fuel prevents long-distance bus transport. Hand grenades thrown at

"Osmice" boarding house. Machinegun fire at Zlatište.

Thursday, 16th: *Six people wounded, three killed. Crowds at the banks. The head office of the "Electrical Power Company of B-H" shelled. Oil supplies arrive. Buses leave for Ljubljana, Vienna and Germany. Cyrus Vance in Sarajevo: "The solution is not to be sought by means of arms, but by continuation of talks..."*

Friday, 17th: *Shelled are the Faculty of Natural Science and Mathematics and central and southern areas of the city. Three-hour street battles in Bratstvo i jedinstvo Street (Brotherhood and Unity Street). Shooting at Ilidža.*

Saturday, 18th: *The first plane with medicines, food and blankets lands in Sarajevo (American C-141 Hercules). Shells fired at the building of the Assembly of B-H and the Children's Embassy from Međaši. Also shelled were GRAS (Town Transport Co.), the railway worker's health centre, trolleybus depot, freight railway station, Institute of Geodesy, TV centre and the city heating plants. On the grounds of the "Pretis" factory in Vogošća five citizens are killed, 24 injured.*

Sunday, 19th: *Some big industrial plants are shelled and set on fire, such as "Vaso Miskin Crni", the Institute of Geodesy, "Kras", the hospital casualty department, TV centre and densely populated residential areas in the south-west of the city (Dobrinja, Vojničko polje, Mojmilo, Alipašino polje). City transport does not run any longer.*

Monday, 20th: *Shelled are Buća Potok, Hum and Stari grad. An attack on "Zrak" company repulsed. The*

My Aleksej P. reached Istanbul. He was eighteen. He could not go back. He did not know where to go. He went on. He disembarked in Split. In his pockets, there was no money, papers or school diplomas. He did not speak the language. The country was Slavic, the spirit too, but he was an alien. He stepped out of the column. He did not react to the calls of the other Russian imperial emigrants. He ignored the calls of the colonels, countesses and professors of music. He abandoned the cries and set off. It was not easy for him to work with gravel, a pickaxe and the tracks as a railway worker. He finished the first class of primary school. Then he completed his primary school education. He graduated from grammar school. He worked and studied. He graduated from university. He never had any news of his family. He could not even look for them. The Red Cross is a humanitarian organization, but not a salvation. He sent his letters to his Russian address. He did not know whether it still existed, whether anyone lived there. Then a new war, the Second World War, broke out. He lived it as an antifascist. After that, his friends, influential people, diplomats and ambassadors, tried to help him. Again nothing. Silence. He did not have his home address any more. There was no place to go back to. He got married and had a son when he was fifty. He seemed to have forgotten Russia. Only his wife Borka, a teacher of Russian, reminded him of his homeland by her work. He became a university professor of engineering. He retired with a pension honestly earned. Then, he took up a paintbrush and easel. And, suddenly, he painted winter, a sled drawn by horses with sleigh bells, Russian winter. He had a grandson, Boris. He was not too happy. He wanted a granddaughter. Then he had another grandson. Then he confessed that he wanted his surname to be forgotten, exterminated. He is not Russian any more. But perhaps he is.

Shells have started falling. Aleksej P. sits at home. He looks out of the window at his and my city. The grand piano that he bought at a brothel in 1945 is not in the room any longer. His son sold it a couple of years ago, and he was so good at playing it. His son made music which reminded him of his childhood, college and hot Russian tea. Only a guitar is left. Aleksej has not been able to hear it for some time, either.

Who knows how many Aleksejs will leave Sarajevo. How many memories will be related to that bag taken in April.

At that time, some other newspapers were already writing about jobless people, blue helmets, and red lanterns, about soup kitchens for refugees, about the fear of AIDS, about the second-class people. Gradually, the pavements of Ljubljana, Skopje, Zagreb, Belgrade, then Vienna, Paris, Trieste, Munich, Oslo, Hamburg, Istanbul... were crowded with Sarajevo. The passport section at the city

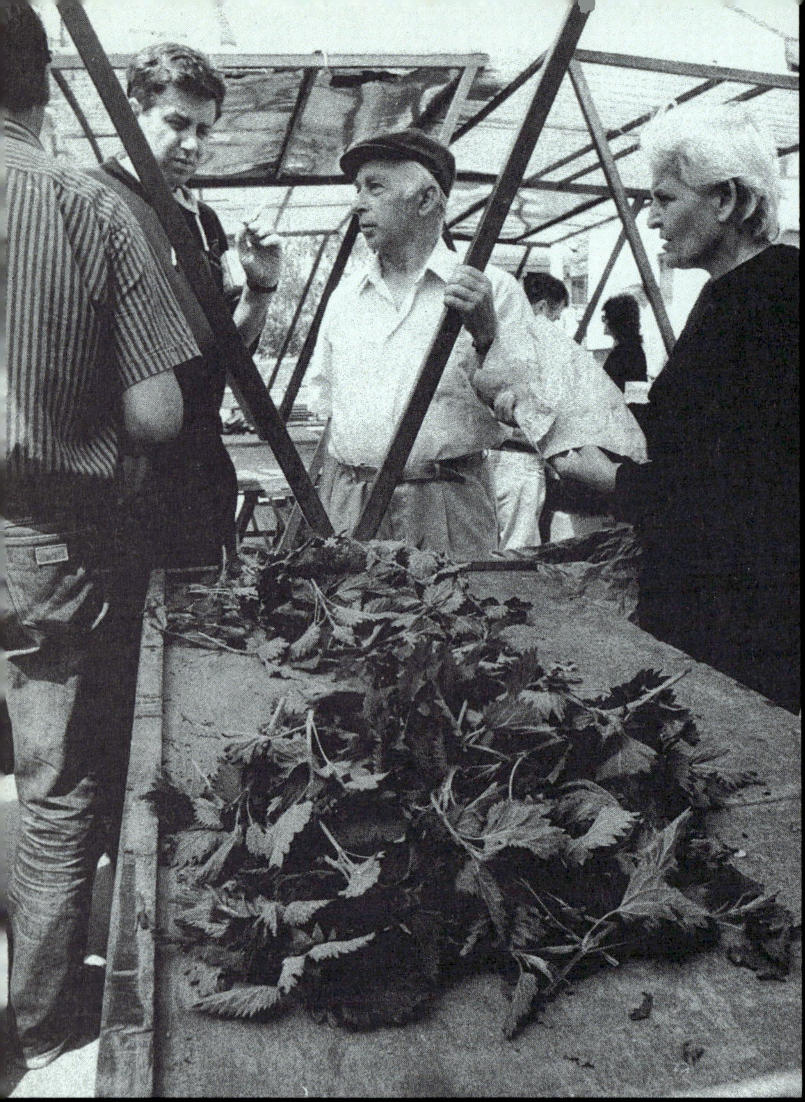

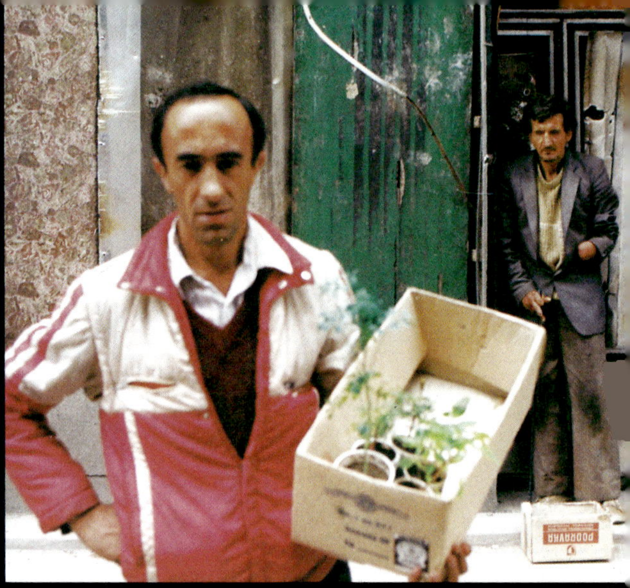

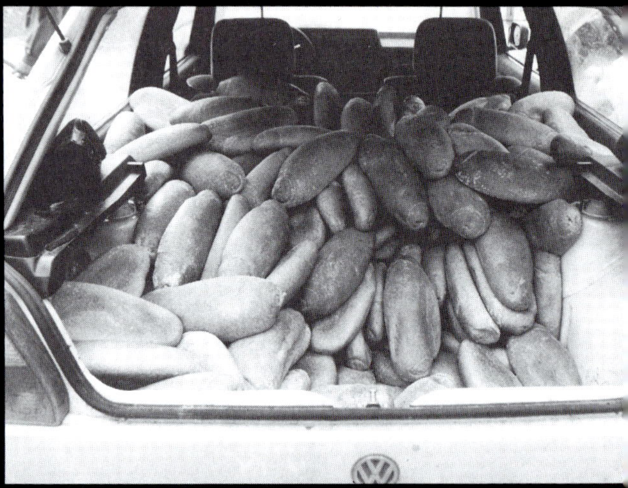

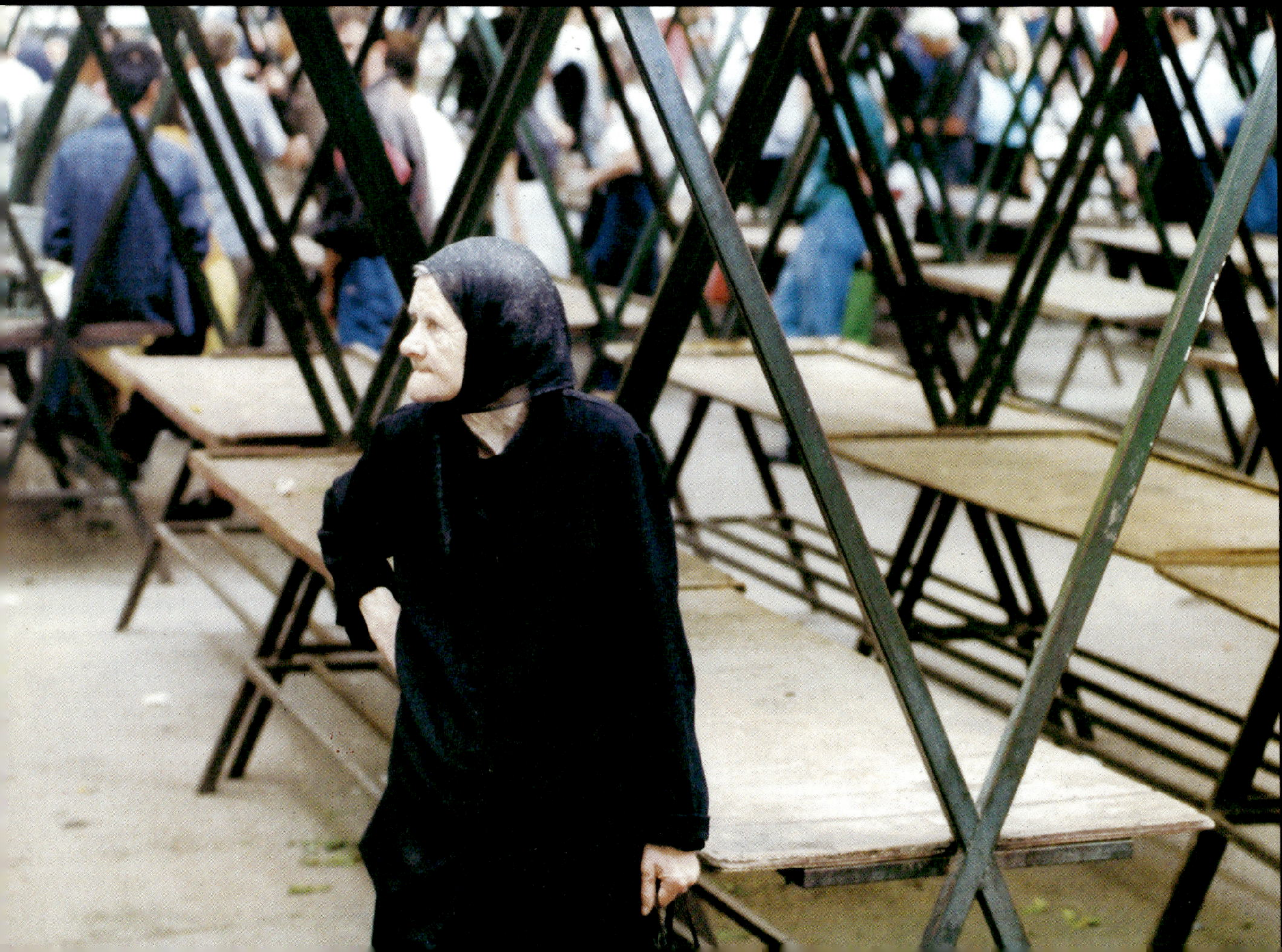

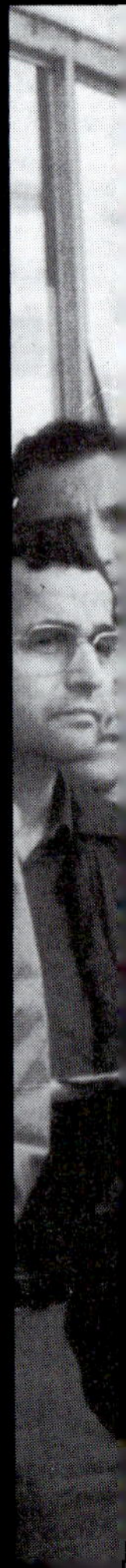

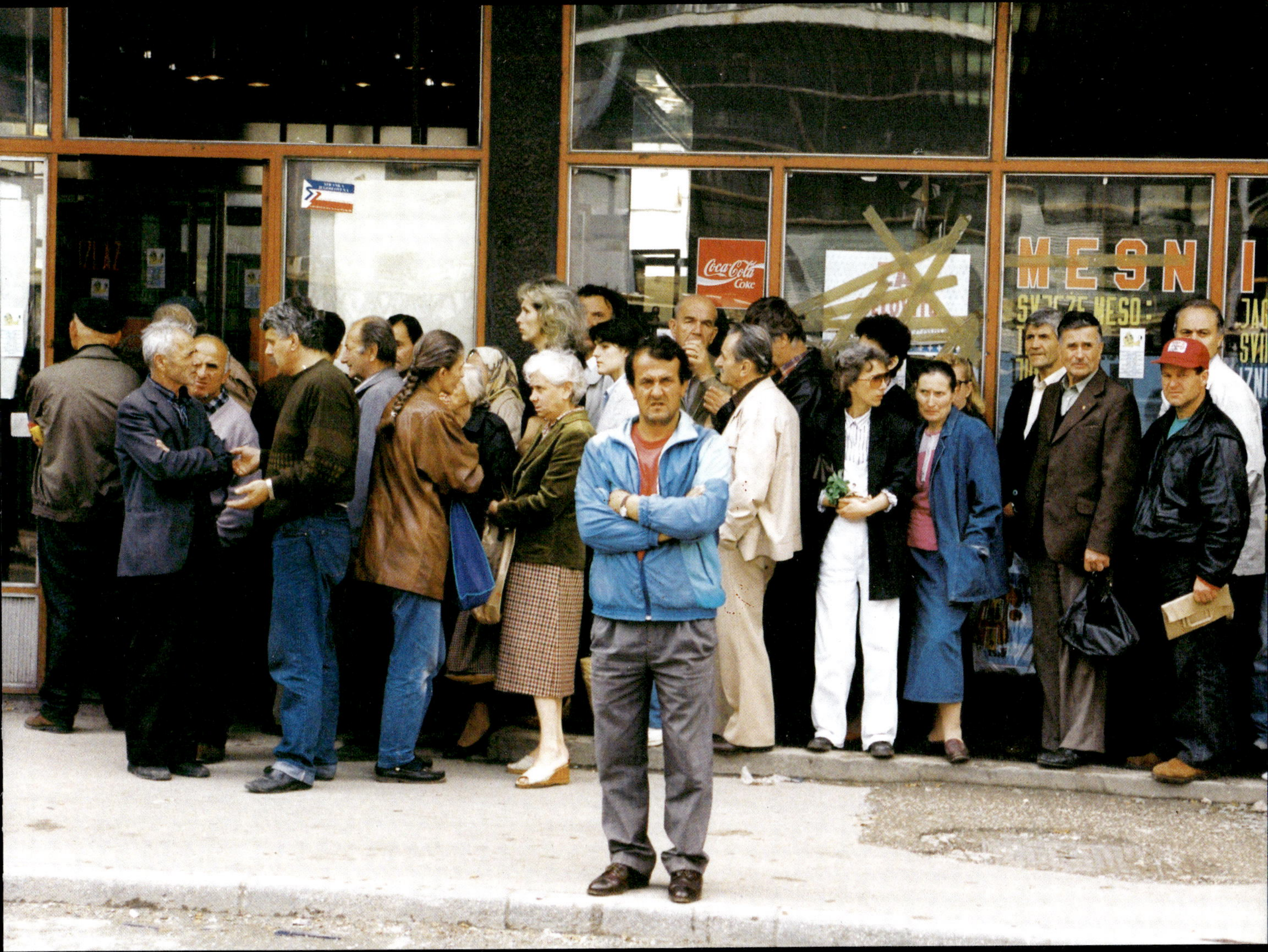
Coca-Cola
Coke
MESNI

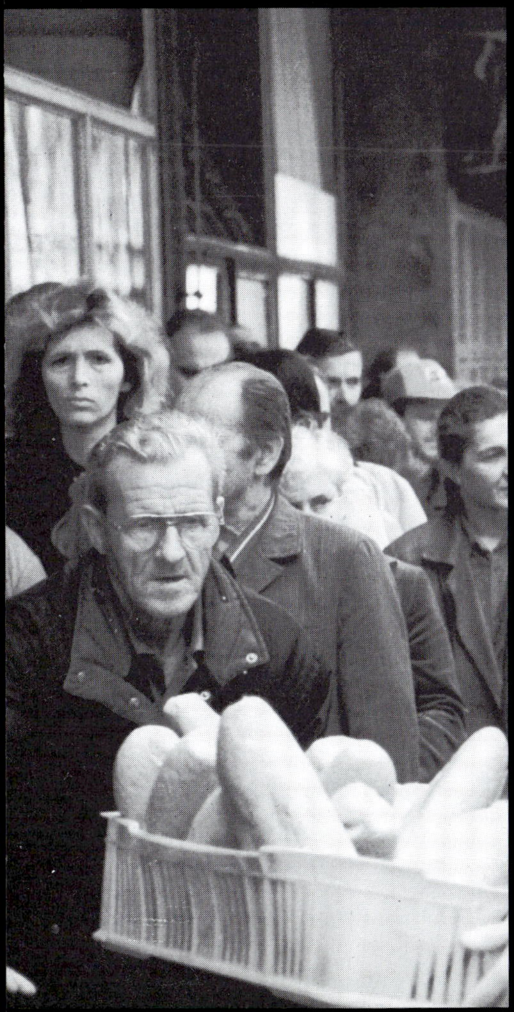

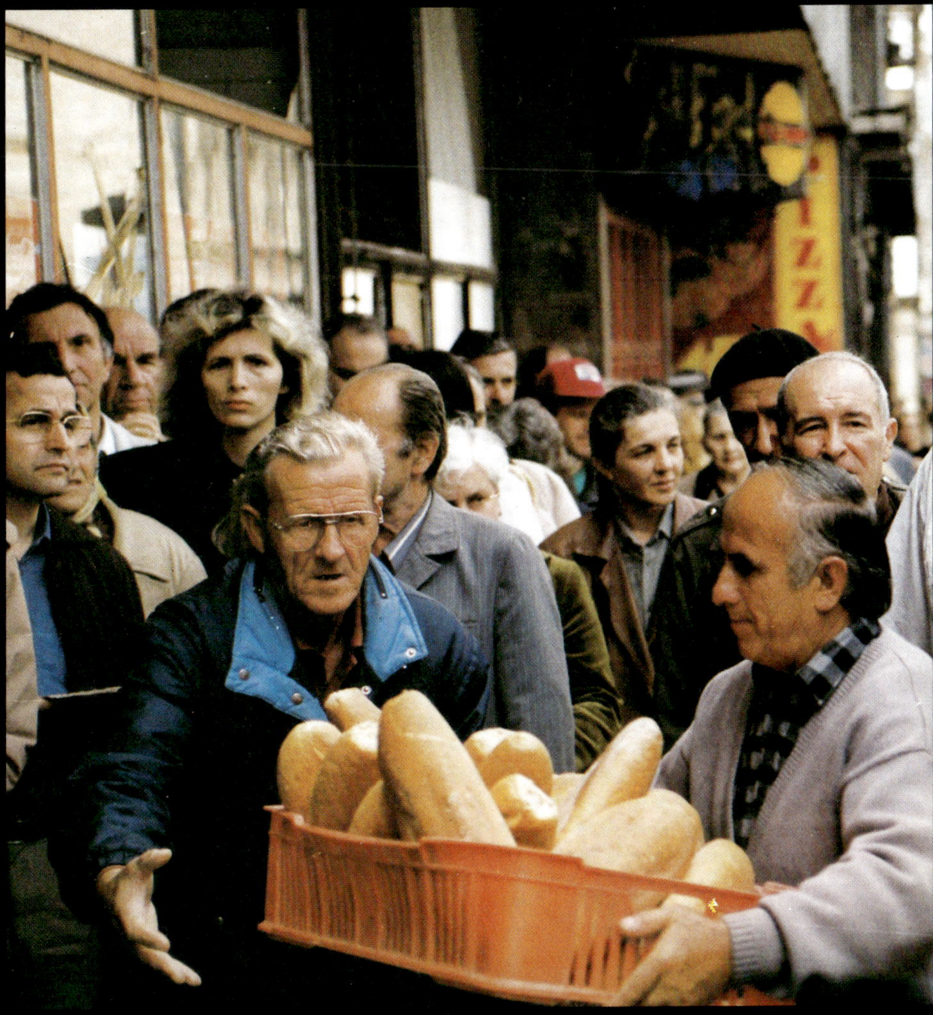

police station was crowded with applications, requests and urgency.

The city emptied daily.

On the station platforms of our twilight, our mothers wait. They go to the deserted tracks hoping for a train. There are no trains. They do not arrive. There are no bus timetables. Only local lines and tricksters are working. They skillfully move three empty matchboxes in circles with their dirty fingers. The onlookers have to guess where a little paper ball is. The stakes are not small. The gullible regularly win the first time, but later they are sure to lose and become penniless. Draftees and demobilized boys who have been waited for at home since August, wander about. They look for any connection to their destinations, to their families. Mothers ask about their sons who are not there.

There are not enough newspapers either. A dark-skinned shoeshine man swears aloud. Strong curses are aimed at the leaders, the generals, the war and the people. Uniformless officers daily leave the barracks. They leave yesterday's jobs, unhappy, disappointed and lost. They hurriedly try to obtain civilian documents. In the meantime, they do not go out into the streets, they do not answer the door. The first officer epaulets thrown away hang over rubbish bins. It still seems as if the war were happening to somebody else. All misfortunes happen to somebody else. All bad things belong to somebody else. It is hard to accept that the war is in us. We think it is enough to keep guard over our staircases. We guard the entrances to our houses. We believe that in this way we keep our places safe. We get to know our neighbours. The city is on guard. At night bursts of gunfire echo through the city. Explosions of hand grenades can be heard. Shells burst all around. In the distance, there is street infantry combat. We witness the war, but still from our armchairs in front of our TV sets. The war is still happening to somebody else. We are not very diligent in clearing our cellars and shelters. We gradually find out that there are shelters. We fit the first grids to our glass front doors. The suburb of Dobrinja sets a good example. It slowly becomes Alcatraz. We fill bags with sand, earth and gravel and put them at the windows of our basements. In Veliki park (Great Park) we read a warning note: MINES, We are surprised by the "White Eagles", (Serb paramilitaries) too, who are looting Grbavica and Ilidža, and who are attacking the city. We hear about Šešelj's and Arkan's men, about the Chetniks. We cannot place fascism at the end of the twentieth century. Slowly, incredibly slowly, we accept circle one of hell. We diligently black out our windows. We receive the news about light signals from flats with disbelief, about the blockade of the city, the snipers spreading death, about the cold-blooded murderers to whom it is all the same whether they shoot at a man or a child, a woman or a car.

railway line at Blažuj blown up. After a one-day break, the trams and buses run again.

Tuesday, 21st: *The symbol of Baščaršija – the Sebilj fountain – shelled. The Museum of the 14th Winter Olympic Games, recently the Gallery of Modern Art as well, set on fire.*

Wednesday, 22nd: *About 80 citizens wounded, two killed. An artillery attack on the city lasts from 1.30 to 5.50 a.m. The whole town is targeted. Heavy fighting at Ilidža, Sokolović Kolonija, Hrasnica, around the Ilidža hotels "Bosna" and "Serbia". "Energoinvest" factories at Stup shelled. "Unioninvest" building burnt down. The "MiG's" of the JNA attack the Hum TV transmitter and the area called Zlatište.*

Thursday, 23rd: *Thirteen people killed, seventy-seven injured. Artillery attacks on Butmir and Sokolović Kolonija. Shelling of Bistrik, Hrgić Street and Boguševac. Mr. Bernard Kouchner, Minister of Health of the French Government, delivered to Sarajevo by plane 5 tons of powdered milk, 5 tons of medicine and hospital supplies, two cars and a special-purpose vehicle. About a hundred mothers and children are evacuated to France by air.*

Friday, 24th: *Severe artillery attacks renewed on Butmir, Hrasnica and Sokolović Kolonija. The modern Institute of Agriculture at Butmir destroyed.*
At Ilidža 200 children and mothers from Hrasnica held prisoner.

Saturday, 25th: *TV relay station and post office communication relay on Trebević captured. Mass* emigration of army families goes on. Critical situation with medical supplies. Long queues for bread and in front of banks for money. Shelling of Mojmilo, Vasin han, Vojničko and Alipašino polje.

Sunday, 26th: Appeal from the Institute of Transfusion: "DONATE BLOOD". There are no flights. Railway transport halted near Blažuj by blowing up the lines.

Monday, 27th: The Presidency of the Republic B-H decides that JNA units must be withdrawn from Bosnia and Herzegovina. Heavy infantry firing; artillery and mortars fire at Butmir, Hrasnica and Sokolović Kolonija after 9 p.m. About 500 buildings are hit. Nine people dead and about a hundred wounded.

Tuesday, 28th: All payment operations between SR Yugoslavia and B-H stop. Hellish artillery attacks on Butmir, Hrasnica and Sokolović Kolonija.

Wednesday, 29th: Houses of the Airport residential area on fire. Artillery, mortars and machine guns fire at the city. Shells fall on Zlatište, Novo Sarajevo, Višnjik, Dobrinja, Alipašino polje, Novi Grad, Centre, Hrasnica, Butmir and Sokolović Kolonija. Damaged are the Mojmilo Sports Centre, primary schools "Pavle Goranin" and "Prvi maj", Novi Grad police station and the students' hostel in Nedžarići...

Thursday, 30th: Bosnia and Herzegovina has become the 52nd member of the Conference on Security and Cooperation in Europe (CSCE). The Maternity Hospital is without vaccines against tetanus and

Prices go up dizzily. Price tags are daily stuck on top of one another. Goods disappear from the shelves. People buy in enormous quantities. Food runs out first. So do the last boxes of those biscuits that nobody used to want. Alcohol runs out, cigarettes too. People buy everything. But everything is plundered as well. Shops are emptied by night during the strict curfew. The premises of former supermarkets, boutiques, greengrocers remain, but the goods do not. The largest firm in the city UPI, warns that during the two weeks of the blockade, their eighty-eight shops were demolished.

There is not enough bread. Queues stretch out. People stand and stamp their feet. Instead of the 130,000 litres of milk that the Sarajevans used to buy daily, the city gets only 10–18,000, and very often only 6–7,000. There is not enough money, either. There are long queues outside banks and post offices. People have to wait for their own money. Pensions are not paid out. German marks are bought on the street on the black market.

There is no blood at the Institute for Transfusiology, either. There is no medicine.

Everything runs out.

From time to time, there is no water, there is no electricity. We are warned about water pollution.

Kiosks are demolished and burgled, the goods stolen from them. There are robberies during the day, too. They do not wait for the veil of night. Journalists have become newspaperboys. There are no more kiosks. There are no more newsagents. There are no newspapers from other cities. We are in a mousetrap. Shells target the relay stations. The TV screens go black. The radio aerial gets shorter. Sarajevo is condemned. The die is cast.

The first prisoners of war return to Sarajevo on April 9. The teachers, instructors and director of the Police School at Vraca bear witness to the imprisonment they survived, the exchange of prisoners. I cannot accept what it means that policeman Nermin Levi had to eat his epaulets.

I ask him: "How?"

"Have you ever eaten a sheet of paper?"

"No."

"I have. And it was disgusting... I was forced to eat my epaulets. I chewed them, chewed and swallowed... Fortunately, I ate only half of them," he explains to me.

The geography lesson begins. I study the city's geography. I learn about the localities which are here, in the city, in the outskirts, which used to mean nothing to us. We learn daily about some new gun positions, some new target in the city, about the area they kill us from. From week to week, the whole year, we revise what we have learnt. There are victims in the same locations every day, and those who multiply the murders and destroy the city are at others. The majority of us did not know about the hills surrounding the

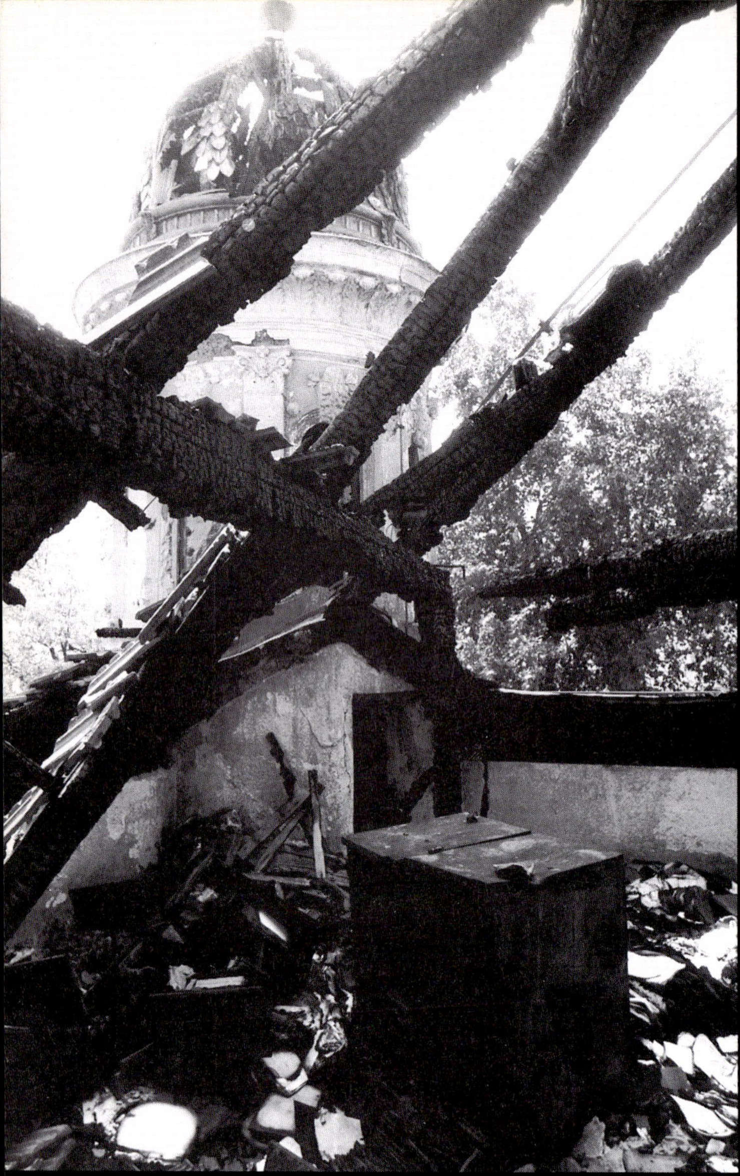
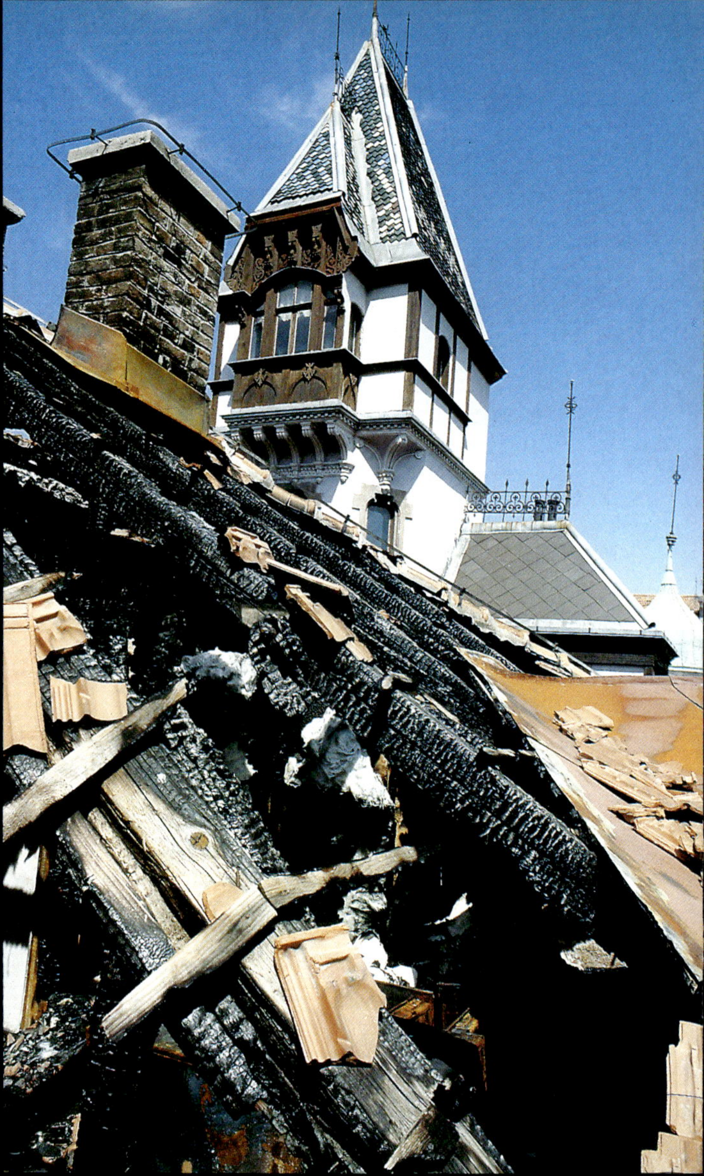
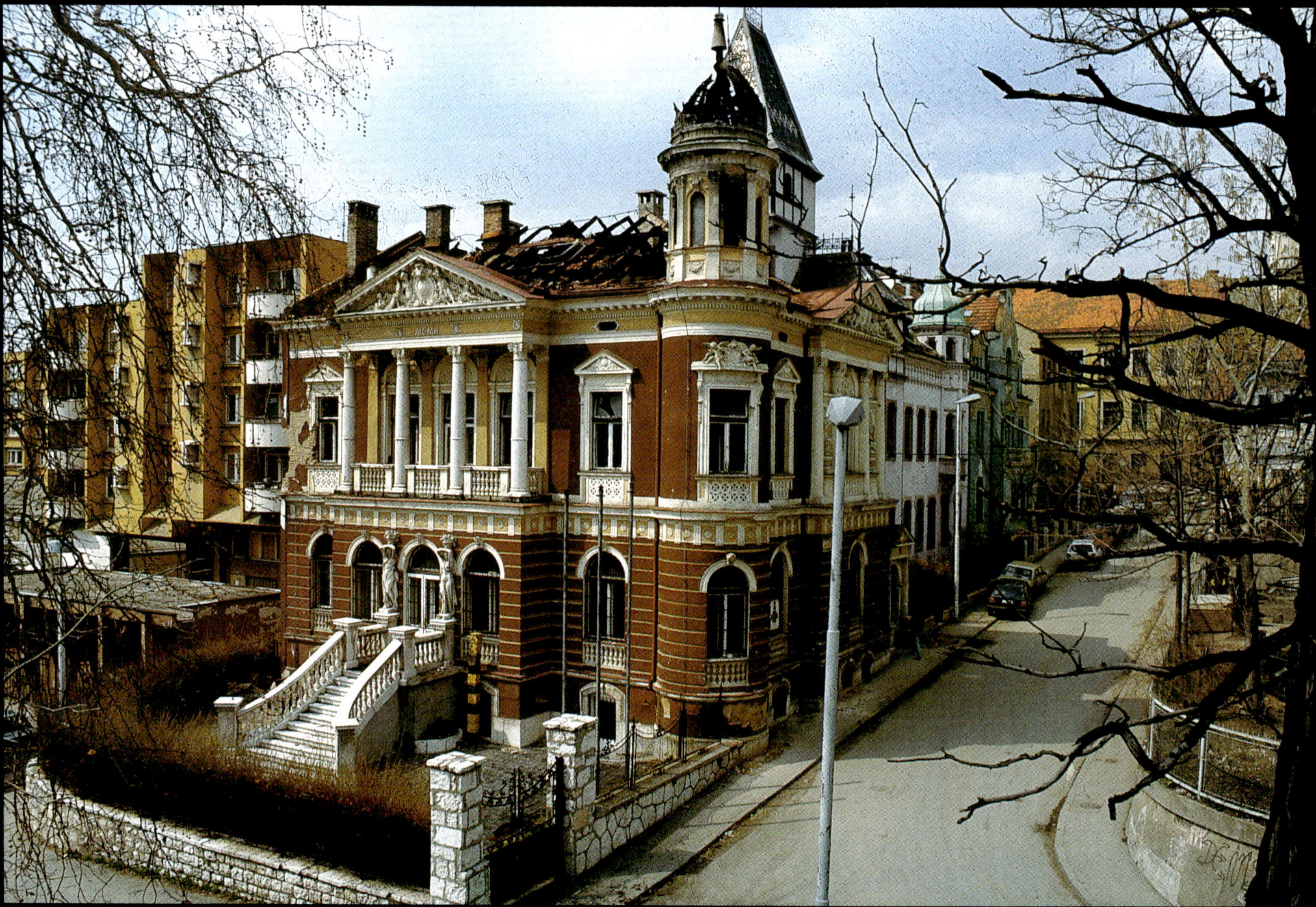

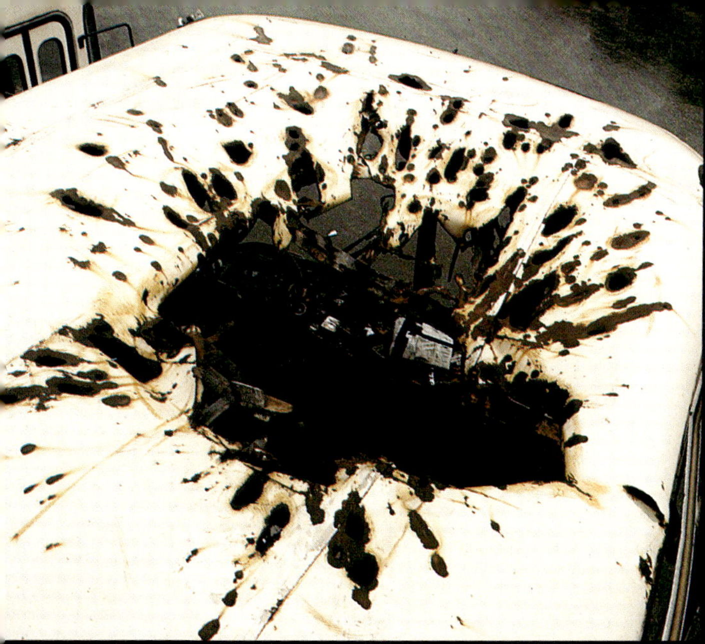

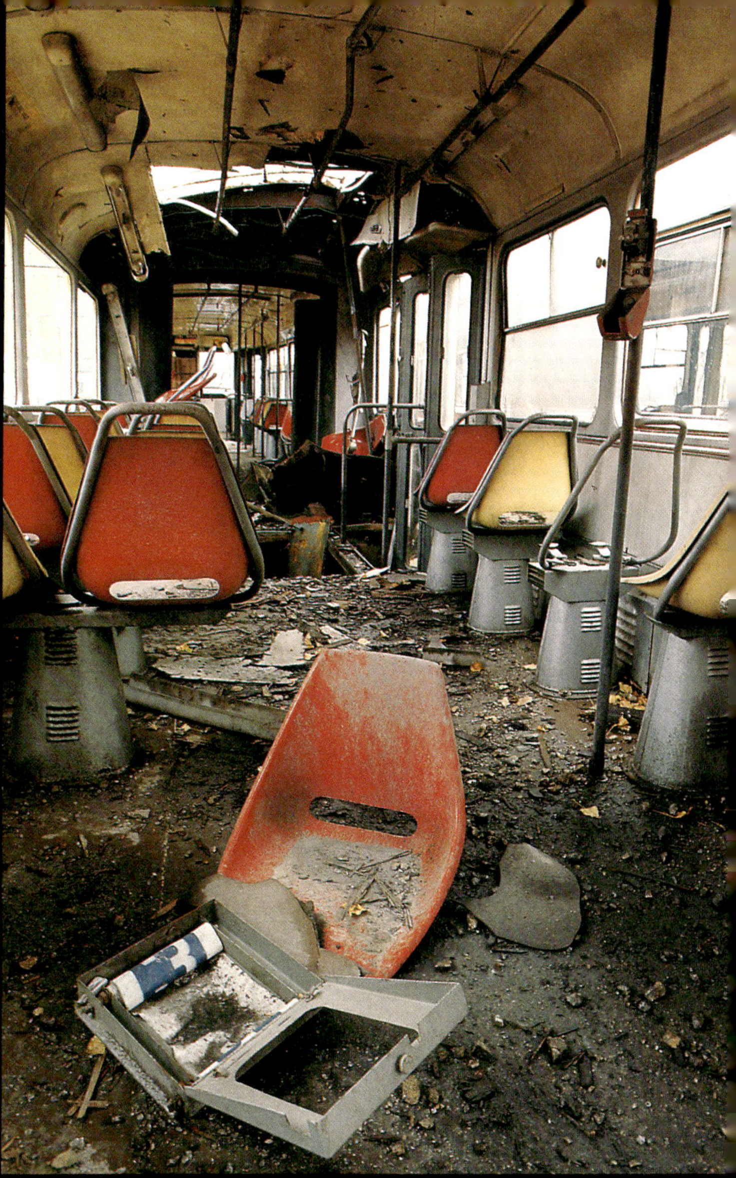

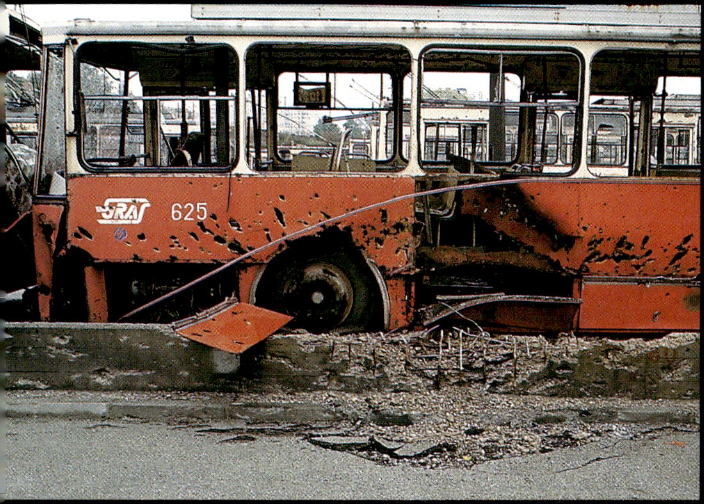
625

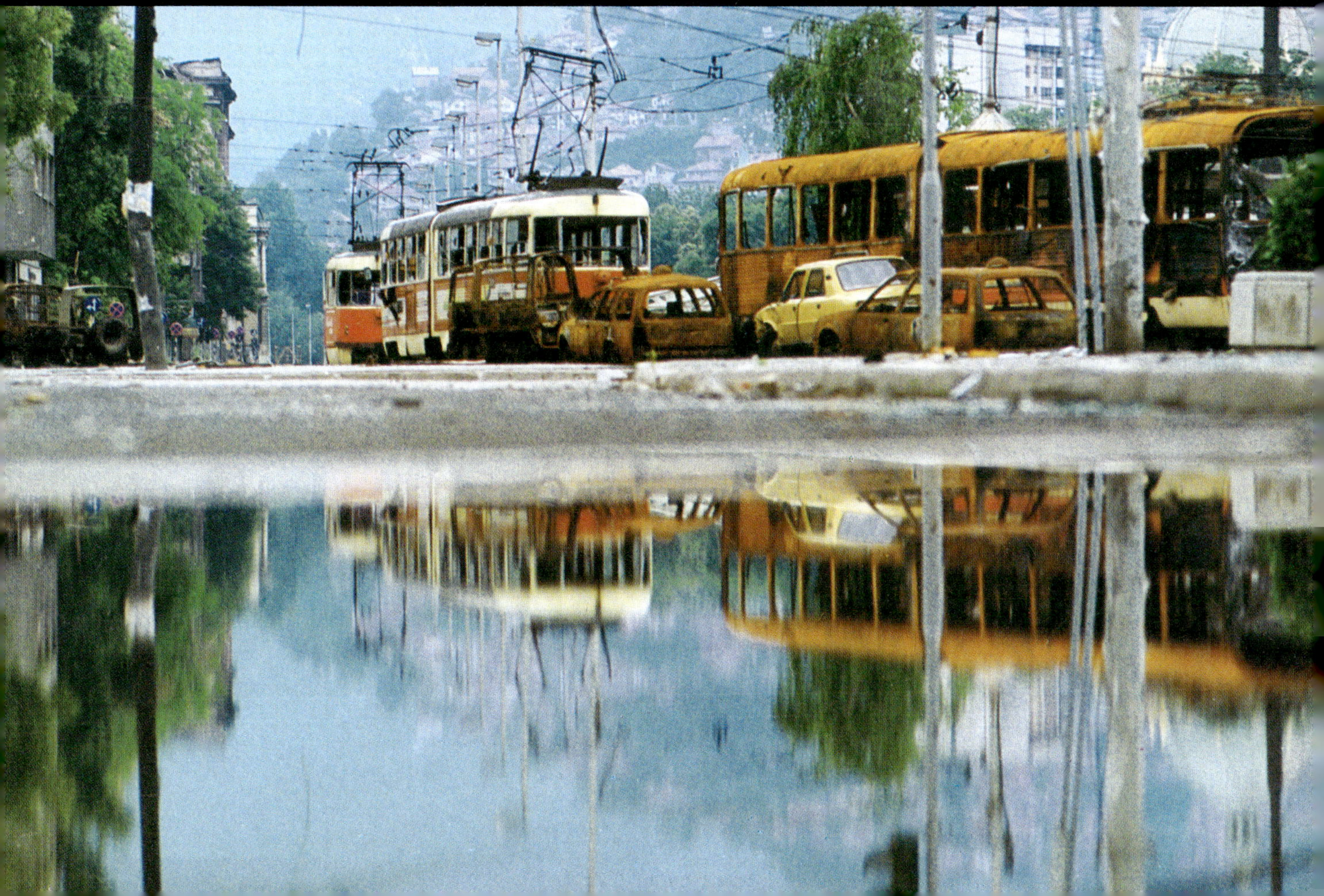

city, hamlets, gorges, valleys. The lesson of local geography was long, painful and it still lasts. I am not sure if we shall review the whole lesson at the end of the war and destruction. I believe we shall know it by heart. Never before did we have to study it for so long and so painfully.

We discover the targeted spots. We do not yet accept that it is done on purpose. We cannot understand that someone aims and destroys on purpose. They never stop. We imputed April 14 to a fool. 120 mm calibre shells were fired at the City Transport Company (GRAS). The city's communications were chosen as a target. Trams and buses were destroyed. We had to stop. We were used to wheels and rides. City dwellers do not walk. The city had to stop after the destruction of its transport; the barricades made postal traffic impossible as well. It started and then stopped again. There were difficulties with the telephone lines, too. They were cut off more and more frequently.

Appeals are the only thing that go into the world for sure. The voice of a shipwreck victim reaches the world. The destruction of the surrounding towns is a warning. Bosnia and Herzegovina is aflame. It is being destroyed. Sarajevo is chained. We still do not accept the war. We do not believe it is so serious.

Many people write to me. They call for sense, and ask for help and advice. Branko Mikulić, the head of the successful organization of the XIV Winter Olympic Games in Sarajevo in 1984, writes a letter. His message to Mr Antonio Samaranch is: "If you could see how ghostly this beautiful city looks now, you would be very sad, like us, the citizens of Sarajevo... I live with my family in Sarajevo. I am staying here." As if he felt the cataclysm which struck the Museum of the XIV Winter Olympics among the first structures. Thus burned down the villa designed by the architect Karl Paŕik in 1903 for the attorney Dr Nikola Mandić, just off from the city's main street. The skeleton of the corner tower and the roof structure stick out in ghostly fashion into the sky above the grimy façade. Here I copy a page from my April diary:

"The Museum of the Olympic Games has disappeared. In recent months, the authorities so eagerly tried to obtain possession of that building. Somebody's lustful desire for its disappearance came true in flames; somebody wanted us to forget the moments when Sarajevo climbed Olympus, or when we moved Olympus to the banks of the River Miljacka. Some did not like it when, at the beginning of February, the Museum of the XIV Olympic Games grew into a gallery of modern art housing the works of Milan Konjović, Safet Zec, Afan Ramić and Mersad Berber. Some in power, influential enough, did not mind taking it and giving it as a present, taking it away and dispensing it "like nobody's dowry". Now, we, the citizens of Sarajevo, have

tuberculosis. The worst night for Sarajevo so far. Heavily shelled are Širokača, Mahmutovac, Soukbunar, Zlatište, Komatin and Mala Brekuša. The Astronomical Observatory on Trebević seized.

MAY

Friday, 1st: *Milk provided only for hospitals. Forcible mobilization in Ilidža. Shelling at Rakovica, breaking into houses of Muslims and Croats, arrests, persecutions, looting. After 7 p.m. shells fall on Butmir, Ilidža, Hrasnica, Sokolović kolonija, the Airport residential area and the Stari grad (the Old Town) municipality.*

Saturday, 2nd: *Mortar shells and artillery barrages. After 12 a.m. fighting in the city centre, around the JNA Hall. Around 12.30 p.m. an infantry attack and the blowing up of the head post office building. A tram and about 10 cars hit at Skenderija burn. Street battles at Skenderija, Grbavica and around the theatre. At 3.40 p.m. sirens announce an air raid (the first one for 45 years). Fires at Đeka, Otoka, Shopping Centre and Grbavica. Shooting at Vogošća. Shelling of the old part of the town and west of the airport. Hit by artillery and mortar shells are: trade union building, the IRIS company (Computer Information System Engineering) situated in the*

old building of a power station which caught fire as well, St. Vinko's Church, the old Orthodox church, the Militia Hall, the main post office building, which also caught fire, the City Assembly, the Ministry of the Interior (the minister slightly injured), Trade Centre HEPOK, the main street – Marshall Tito Street (buildings of the National Bank, the department store ZEMA and "Kluz", a shop for ready made clothes), the TV Centre, the TV transmitter Hum (disrupting broadcasting), Višegrad Gate, the School of Economics, the buildings of the First Aid, Social Health Care, the School of Electrical Engineering, Electrical Power Company of B-H, the "Bristol", "Central" and "Beograd" hotels, the Upi Administrative building, Credit Bank (near the "Europe" hotel), Republic Institute of Statistics, the Assembly of B-H, the mosque in Hrasnica demolished... The President of the Presidency of the Republic of B-H, Alija Izetbegović, and the Vice-President of the Socialist Democratic Party, Mr Zlatko Lagumdžija, arrive from Lisbon at 7 p.m. They are both taken prisoner at the airport.

Sunday, 3rd: *Several dead people and 145 injured taken to hospitals during the last 24 hours. Shells fired at the Bey Mosque, the Baščaršija Mosque, Hanikah and M. Tito Street. In the burnt down building of the head Post Office 38,000 telephone connections and a computer system with 7,000 telephone lines are destroyed. Trams and trolleybuses do not run any longer. After a 24-hour captivity and a real drama over the captors, demands,*

not got this building either, and who knows whether anything has been saved in its depots..."

Little was saved after that unbridled fire and the firemen's water. One of the city's nooks, which we showed the world with pride, had been closed down by shells.

The "Unioninvest" high-rise office burned to the ground. Its concrete skeleton by Vrbanja Bridge sadly bears witness to a firm which successfully did business with the world, building in Africa, Asia and Europe. Fire destroyed the documentation designs, the projects on which people lived and by means of which they made progress into the future. The whole firm disappeared.

I am wandering in the dark; even the concern of my friends does not help. They ring up day and night. They ask questions. I help them comprehend what I am becoming aware of. So many questions. They multiply. For me, it is amazement, for many others pain after they realized that they had broken off with people they had known, loved and respected for decades. Some are leaving, some are staying. The airport is closed. The army has occupied it. The children, wives, husbands, and families of military personnel are leaving for Belgrade in military aircraft. Some go even further, much further. There are no buses. The trains run shorter and shorter distances. The shackles on the city's hands and feet get tighter. The noose is round our neck. How to explain to a friend of mine, by phone, the war that we are helplessly sinking into? For him, a literary and art critic, it means: "There are no dressed up women. There are no beautiful ones. No expensive perfumes. No good drinks. No luxury cigarettes." But what could I do with all of these before the curfew begins? I learnt about war and curfew from films. Now I live with it. After some time, it presents no handicap to me. I was in my room when night fell. How could I catch the truck with a trailer that drove past me along Obala Street towards Baščaršija? The day was sunny, an April day. The truck was crowded with tabuts (Muslim burial boards). It was hurrying. Never before had I seen these fir tabuts stacked on a lorry. There was a trailer as well. They were hurrying. They might not have been fir but beech tabuts. These lidless coffins must be for the Muslim cemetery "Bakije". But both the lorry and the trailer were full! The day was sunny and warm. Isn't it a custom only to carry men on tabuts to the cemetery, if women are being buried on them? How many of them were there?

In the very beginning, while we still were not aware of the dark of circle one of hell, the first defenders of the city were buried at Kovači cemetery. They were declared shekhids. The word means a Muslim who is killed as a hero for his faith. A shekhid is also a person killed without guilt, a martyr. There were many shekhid cemeteries in Bosnia and Herzegovina during the Ottoman Empire. They were respected. They are now being created anew.

I recalled a forgotten message from the past and an epitaph by an anonymous poet from 1121 Hegira:
"Oh, my eyes, weep blood, and let hundreds and thousands of sighs heave from the heart,
The structure of patience and steadiness is destroyed now...
From the gorge of transience it has gone into eternity..."

President Izetbegović and Mr Lagumdžija are freed. An accident in Dobrovoljačka Street with the army convoy going from its barracks. There are some dead and injured soldiers.

CIRCLE TWO

Monday, 4th: 30 new wounded taken to hospital, 8 killed. An appeal for military support from abroad. The Yugoslav People's Army, Serbia and Montenegro with their paramilitary forces and the SDS (Serbian Democratic Party) paramilitary forces are officially proclaimed by the Presidency of the Republic as aggressors on B-H. Battles at Vrbanja, Grbavica and Hrasno hill. Machinegun nests and snipers active from the Military Hospital. Shells fall on Hrasnica, Stari grad, Dobrinja, Sokolović kolonija, Marijin Dvor, the Assembly of the Republic and UNIS administrative buildings.

Tuesday, 5th: The dead are still in the streets. Shelled are the town hall and the old heart of Baščaršija. The "Mladost" kindergarten and "Unigradnja" company near the Cathedral set on fire. Hit by shells are the old Orthodox church, Višegrad City Gate, "Grbavica" stadium and Ciglane – a modern residential area.

Wednesday, 6th: The dead have still not been removed from the streets. Battles at Grbavica, Švrakino selo and

The club of the JNA, the former Officers' casino, was our Reichstag from 1933. Dimitrov and Göring were not there. Noon approached. It was sluggish. May Day was behind us. For the first time since 1945 it was not celebrated formally with flags, the early morning marches with music and flowers in festive mood. There were only a few feasts and gatherings outside houses, in courtyards and entrance halls in some quarters. Some hundred friends of mine – artisans, artists, retired policemen, workers, former diplomats, teachers and pensioners – gathered in the open-air restaurant "Šetalište". They did not want to renounce the decades-long tradition of celebrating the international workers' day. They celebrated it noisily, singing happily and with yellow graffiti on the kitchen wall of the restaurant that had been closed down a few months earlier by the municipal authorities. It said simply: "Long live May Day". It recalled 1886, Chicago and the bloody strike and a centennial tradition in Sarajevo.

I wrote in my diary for May 2nd: "I patiently sold newspapers outside an empty kiosk. On that sunny Sunday morning, I watched the JNA club and three covered trucks in front of it. They were some thirty metres across the street. They had never stood there before. They brought something. They may be taking or moving something. What will they do with those oil paintings by Ismet Mujezinović in the Concert Hall? They cannot be loaded on these trucks. A soldier peeped out from the club, went in and out, and one could guess that he was on guard. He was a teenager. He was 18–19. Then another soldier peeped out as well. They chatted, laughed with the girls who stopped while passing by. Three other men were civilians. They went back three times. They were taking drums, trombones and clarinets somewhere. The citizens of Sarajevo walked sluggishly on this hot, almost summer's day along the street from Drvenija Bridge. They went to the City Market only to find nothing. The luckier ones, on their way back, carried bunches of nettles or loaves of bread. They at least bought newspapers. Some twenty metres away, buses started off for the suburbs of Breka, Koševsko brdo and Novo gradsko groblje (the New City Cemetery). They had simply Cemetery on them. It has not been new for a long time. There were very few passengers. Departures were only every half hour.

"At 12.10 a.m. Act Two of the drama began. I heard the first shots looking towards that Austro-Hungarian officers' structure with its extraordinary concert hall. They were not a joke. They were not mere apparitions. They were not meant just to frighten. They were shooting at people. The three trucks loaded with furniture and worn out armchairs, as it transpired later, had been waiting for hours. They had been expecting an incident. After they had fired the first bullets in the club's lobby, the real firing started.

"And it did not stop.

"Outside the bohemian cafe "Cyrano de Bergerac", in the passage connecting Workers' University "Đuro Đaković" and Tito Street, guests sat indifferently at the covered tables. They did not care about the shots. They seemed to be somewhere far away. Along the crowded main street, passers-by walked hurriedly, children ran around, cars blew their horns in a wedding column drawing attention to 'just married'. A hundred metres away, war was being waged. But it was happening to somebody else.

"I got out of the tumult on the first corner. I went back to sell my newspapers by an empty kiosk near the National Theatre. I believed, calmed by those I met, that the recent shots had been only an incident. I did not care about Jasmina's calls to go home, to get away. She pointed out that she had been warned by some acquaintances of hers, as early as ten o'clock, to go home, to take the newspapers, that something was in store. We did not want to leave any copies unsold. We had only just become newspaperboys. And...

"In less than a quarter of an hour, the first armoured military vehicle rushed by. It drove towards Drvenija Bridge and the JNA club. It was followed by a military van and another armoured vehicle at top speed. They suddenly pulled up at the beginning of the street just near the Post Office and the National Theatre. Fierce firing started before they had properly stopped. Just like that: fierce firing. From the armoured vehicle, like in the most exciting action films, soldiers with helmets and in camouflage uniforms jumped out shooting; they were firing with their eyes fixed on the upper floors of the Main Post Office..."

Roaring firing, shell explosions, echoes of far away explosions... Circle Two of hell had started. It was deeper, steeper. I did not see you, Vergil. Had you, perhaps, replaced your Roman toga with the outfit of a warrior?

The Yugoslav People's Army was attacking Sarajevo. It had been in the city's centre for decades. Its barracks had stood firmly in the city's suburbs. And it attacked the city. Even had we wanted, we would not have been able to commit such mass suicide. The barrels of tanks, guns, mortars, and howitzers spat on Sarajevo. Their roaring refuted the statements made in March and April. Generals, in front of the TV cameras, had tried to convince us, looking straight at us, without even batting an eyelid, that they were ready to defend Sarajevo, that on the surrounding hills tanks were dug in for our defense, that they knew what to do and that they were holding routine military manoeuvres.

The horrible sights of charred corpses in the vicinity of the Municipal Assembly Building went round the world. They are fixed in our minds. A shell hit a tram and set it on fire. It burned down at the tram stop Skenderija, near a bridge upstream from Vrbanja Bridge. At that stop, the majority of passengers used to get off. It is here that young

Citizens from the captured part of Dobrinja taken to the "Kula" prison.

Thursday, 7th: *Shooting at Dobrinja. For six days nobody has left the house owing to heavy sniping.*

Friday, 8th: *Another fifty-one wounded in hospitals. Continuous attacks on Dobrinja, Hrasnica, Butmir, Sokolović kolonija, Mojmilo, Širokača, Bistrik and Švrakino selo.*

Saturday, 9th: *Terrorism at Grbavica – lootings, arrests and interrogations. The central parts of the city exposed to shelling.*

Sunday, 10th: *The Military Hospital moves out. Its name changes to the City Hospital. During the night (in the International Red Cross Week) the building of the Red Cross of B-H is completely demolished and burnt down. Shelling in western parts of the city. In "Centrotrans" depot 66 buses and 77 trucks are destroyed.*

Monday, 11th: *The Republic of Bosnia and Herzegovina issues a request to become a member of the UN. Nine dead and 54 injured. The city centre and the building of the Presidency of the Republic of B-H shelled. Infantry combat in Novo Sarajevo. Firing from the "Marshal Tito" barracks, which is in the very centre of the city and in the surrounding areas. Heavy fighting in the parts around the northern exit. The broadcasting of the YUTEL television channel "temporarily" stopped because "it has been reduced to the Sarajevo area". JNA Street becomes City Defenders' Street.*

Tuesday, 12th: *Three killed and 44 injured. The TV centre*

shelled. Street fighting in Dobrinja and Mojmilo. Twenty-seven tank shells filled with phosphorus fall on Stari grad, Marshal Tito, Strosmeyer and Lugavina Streets and on Vratnik and Bistrik. Burnt down are the Tabački mesjid (a place of worship below that of a mosque) and the Orthodox Metropolitan's Residence with its archives and library; St. Cyril and Methodius Church is damaged.

Wednesday, 13th: *The railway station, the "Bristol" hotel, the building of the "Electrical Power Company", the television relay station on Hum, Shopping Centre and the Primary School in Hrasno set on fire by shelling. The entire UPI Institute for Development and Research burnt down. Also burnt down are the Faculties of Agriculture and Forestry. The old people's home in which UNPROFOR is stationed at the moment is shelled.*

Thursday, 14th: *Twenty killed, 140 injured. Information not definite. Shelled are the Bey's Mosque, the "Sarajka" Department Store, the "Zora" chocolate company, the residence of UNPROFOR in an old people's home and the "Standard" factory of ŠIPAD furniture company. The old tobacco factory (now belonging to "Magros" and "Bosnasport" shops) burnt down. The Oriental Institute shelled and burnt down. On fire are the buildings of the "Electrical Power Company of B-H", "Social Care and Retirement Policy Administration of B-H". The building of the "Water Resources Management of B-H" is burnt down. The Catholic*

men waited for young girls to go out in the evening. It was the same at noon. Even when the tram was not late, you could see those impatiently glancing at their watches. They stood still when the tram arrived, pretending to be indifferent, uninterested.

Well, that tram stop had its tram in flames. The next one also caught fire. A young man in a yellow pullover jumped out of the rear door. The shooting and fire made him step back. I do not know even now if he succeeded in getting off. Armoured vehicles fierely spat fire. Two military jeeps and several cars were burning at the same time as the tram. The firing was hurricane-like. The wounded hid under the tram. A soldier crawled across the bridge towards "Skenderija"...

The Sarajevo tram stopped. All the trams in the city stopped. It was May 2nd. They did not start again. They have not run for the whole year. The day before that, the Sarajevo electric tram had celebrated its centenary. The first year when the trams were not drawn by horses was 1895. On May 1st of that year, the first electric bulbs had lit the streets and flats of Sarajevo. The "Grand" Hotel was opened ceremonially. It was luxuriously lit by electric lighting. The electric tram clanged along and set off on a tour of the city. For the past ninety-seven years it had never stopped. It ran transporting passengers with bowler hats, in pantaloons (dimije), with baskets full of groceries, schoolbags, in peasant shoes (opanci), and straw hats... There was not even the horse-drawn tram as a replacement. Since its first trip on January 1st, 1885, a century had passed.

Sarajevo is tramless. The stopped trams look unreal on the banks of the Miljacka today, at the beginning of the current year. Through mist and in decades-long memory, they come to meet us. They are about to arrive. And the burned out ones, drilled by bullets, are rusting away at Skenderija Bridge. Tomo Masarik Bridge is the next one upstream. It comes after the Vrbanja and Skenderija bridges. We call it "Two Fishermen's", after a well-known restaurant-tavern. By this bridge, which we also call the Post Office Bridge, there was a big fire in Sarajevo that day. The Post Office was in flames and was gutted.

I tear a page out of my diary: "Sarajevo has not got a Post Office any more. It is still unbelievable that that huge, almost eternal three-storey building on the bank of the Miljacka has been destroyed by shells and fire. The month of May has caused misfortunes to all of us, as well as to the Sarajevo Main Post Office. The main telephone exchange with all its 45,000 lines has been burned up."

We are cut off from the world and from ourselves. How strong was the anxiety and happiness our grandmothers feel about the postman, waiting for him to appear at the end of the street or to ring the doorbell unexpectedly!

The four carrier pigeons, facing Trebević and sadly

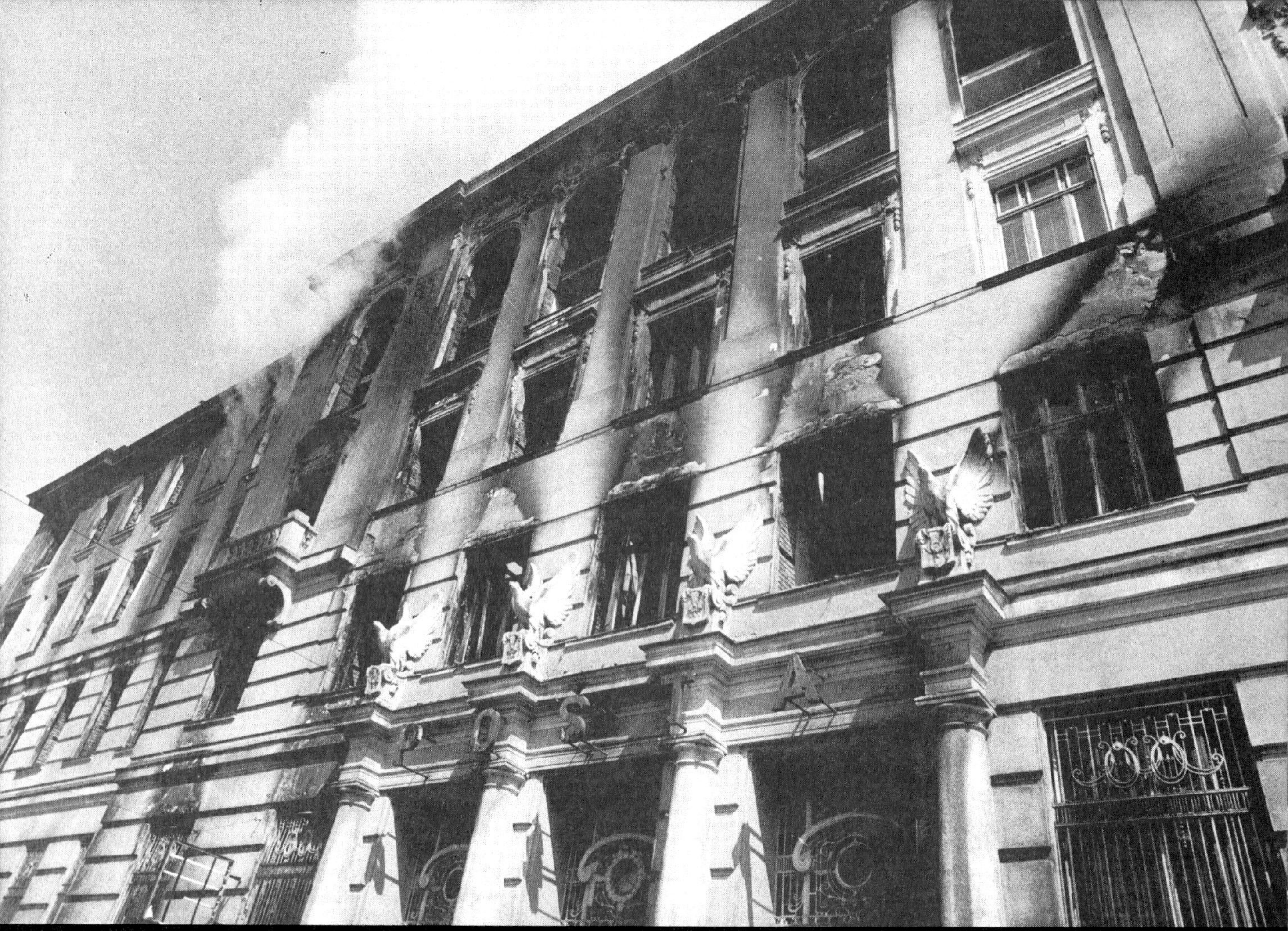
POSTA

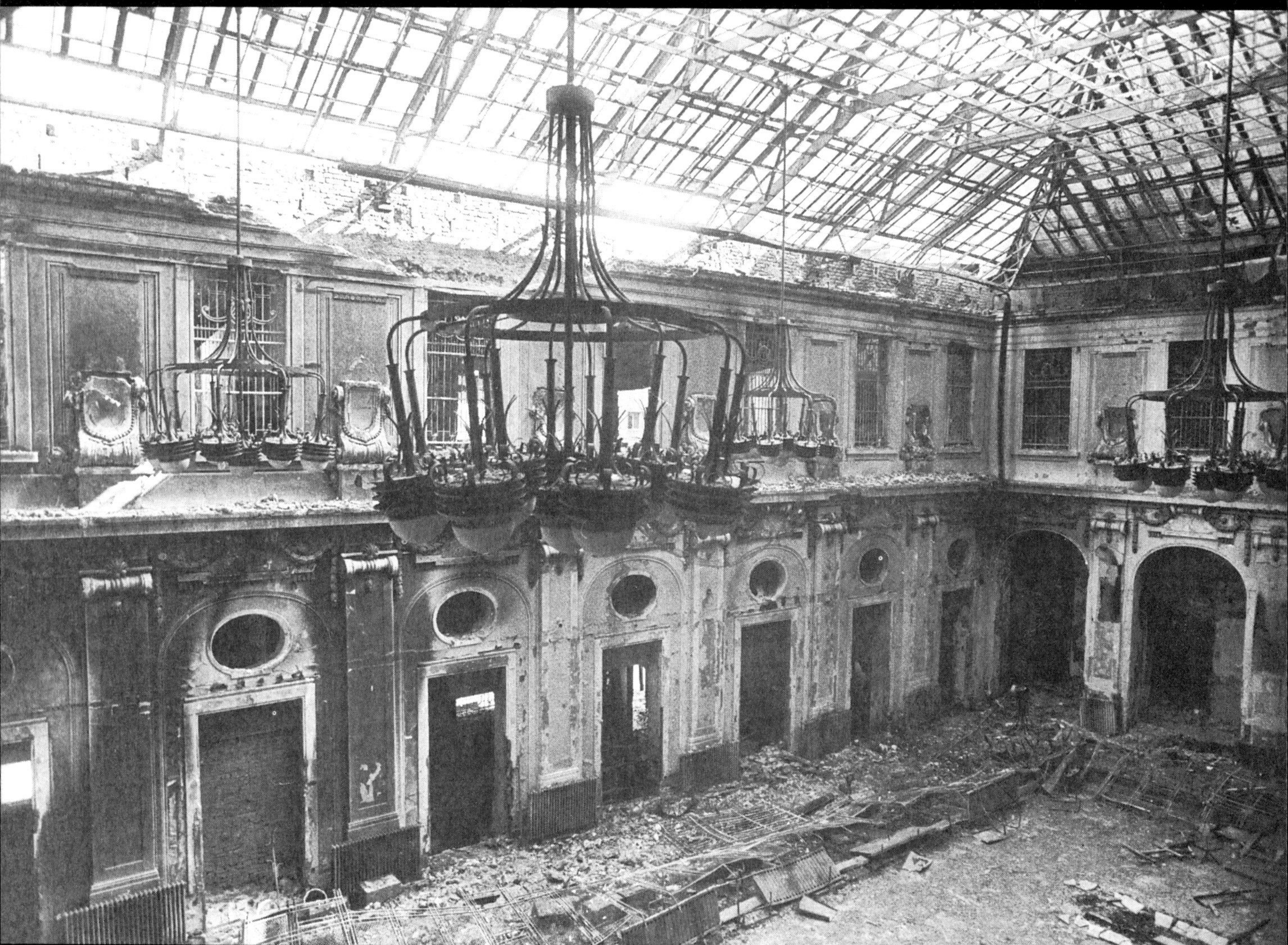

SARAJEVO – THE WOUNDED CITY

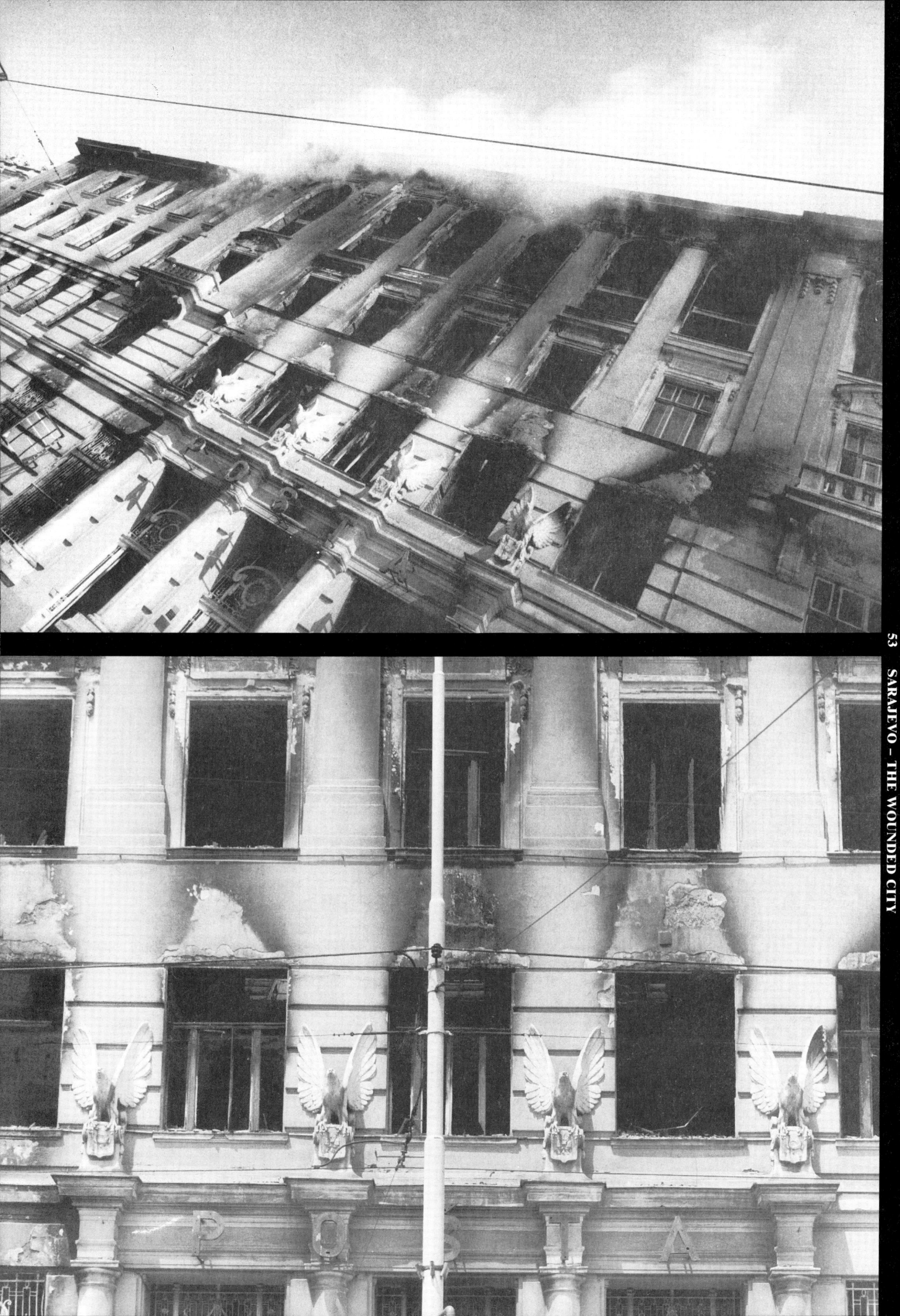

looking at those with Nero's destructive instinct, are nailed to the front of the Main Post Office, having no possibility ever to fly. Nobody empties the two letterboxes by the entrance door, either. This has lasted for days, unfortunately and shamefully for the whole world. A letter to my son may have stayed in them. I do not know if and when my telephone will ring, either. Who, only yesterday, believed that we would be deprived of that common civilizational invention by such a merciless and criminal plan?

Dark and too sad is this spring in Sarajevo and Bosnia. Dark smoke has been rising for days from the Post Office fire. The remains of the remains were burned down as if, with their disagreeable symbolism, emphasizing May 2nd of this anno domini, all the gods seem to have abandoned us. Sooty walls, charred beams and the ghostly looks of debris annulled that significant May of 1913, when the Military Post Office and Telegraph was ceremonially opened with music, the presence of authorities, post office clerks and happy citizens, the pride and embellishment of Sarajevo and the country of Bosnia and Herzegovina.

Today it is impossible to enter the ground floor of the great Post Office hall with its windows for different purposes, from posting letters to paying money, saving deposits, newspaper subscriptions, parcel handling, poste restante and stamp collecting, designed in the secession style. They were well-preserved and beautiful until the fire broke out, as if they had been recently built. In the past, a big clock which used to decorate the central part of the hall had disappeared. A big colour picture of the emperor and king Franz Joseph I had also disappeared without a trace as well as the coats of arms of the Austro-Hungarian successor countries. Even if they had remained, the fire would have destroyed them. Above the entrance, in golden letters, it was engraved that this large building was designed by Josip noble Vancaš, the architect who in his fruitful career built as many as 240 structures. It did not say that he was doing it between 1907 and 1910, and that he had started his fruitful thirty-five-year engagement in Sarajevo as a twenty-four-year-old architect who had been entrusted with the designs for the Cathedral and Land's Government Palace by the powerful minister Benjamin Kalaj.

These days it is difficult to write about many things. It is even more difficult to post what you write. Once, during World War One, which was also cruel, the post printed postcards with ready-written texts – messages: I AM ALIVE AND WELL, for those who were not able to write. In Sarajevo, there are no letters today, this ugly and sad spring. There are no postcards, either, while picture postcards of the city are not even stolen from the broken kiosks. They are also documents on this time. In the square outside the "Sarajka" department store, there is a letterbox pierced through by shrapnel...

church at Stup is shelled and set on fire. St. Vinko's Church demolished by shells. Shelling of Hrasnica, Dobrinja, Alipašino, Vojničko polje, Butmir and Sokolović kolonija. "Shopping Centre" at Grbavica on fire.

Friday, 15th: Black smoke comes from the "Zora" sweets factory. Shells fall on "Bitumenka" and the headquarters of the UNPROFOR in the PTT Engineering building. Fighting at Mojmilo and Vojničko polje, the primary "Simon Bolivar" school set on fire by shells.

Saturday, 16th: Heavy shelling again of Stari grad, Otoka, Dobrinja and Koševsko brdo. Shooting from the "Marshal Tito" and "Viktor Bubanj" barracks. Firing at the City Hospital (formerly the Military Hospital). Tanks fire at Dobrinja, which is without water and electricity. New factories on fire: "Zora", "Standard" and "Trgosirovina". The old tobacco factory and Independent TV "Good Vibrations" demolished. The psychiatric hospital "Jagomir" taken by SDS terrorists and 113 patients from the ward for the treatment of alcoholics thrown out in their pyjamas.

Sunday, 17th: 13 people killed and 94 wounded. Fighting on Vrbanja Bridge and in Pofalići. The newspaper publishing and printing house "Oslobođenje" shelled.

Monday, 18th: A 10-kilometre-long convoy of displaced people sets off in the direction of Split organized by the Children's Embassy. It is stopped at Ilidža by "Serbian authorities". Forcible *eviction from Grbavica and Dobrinja Four. A fire at the airport. Mortar shells fired from Lapišnica at a convoy of humanitarian aid and the mission of the International Red Cross at the entrance to Vratnik. Some people killed or wounded. About ten tons of medicines and medical supplies destroyed.*

Tuesday, 19th: *From this day on, the Yugoslav People's Army (JNA) is proclaimed as an occupying force in Bosnia and Herzegovina. There is a danger of outbreaks of typhoid fever, diphtheria and hepatitis.*

Wednesday, 20th: *Women and children from the halted convoy bound for Split are just a pawn in political games. About thirty babies and mothers are returned to the town.*

Thursday, 21st: *The captured convoy of women and children bound for Split finally arrive in Kiseljak and Travnik. The "Zetra" Olympic sports hall burnt down after shelling.*

Friday, 22th: *The Republic of Bosnia and Herzegovina becomes a member of the UN. Since April 6th about 20,000 children have been evacuated from Sarajevo by the Children's Embassy "Međaši".*

Saturday, 23rd: *The Secondary School of Economics hit by a shell and set on fire. Battles at Hrasno and around the "Grbavica" stadium. The Assembly of B-H and the "Holiday Inn" hotel shelled. The name of Vrbanja bridge changes to Suada Dilberović bridge. The Interior Ministry appeals to the B-H Public Prosecutor's Office to bring criminal charges against the following citizens of Bosnia and Herzegovina: Radovan Karadžić, Nikola*

A memory of its model – the Post Office Savings Bank in Vienna, designed by Otto Wagner, goes together with the Main Post Office which was built in the secession style. The story about the first telegraph in Sarajevo merges with it. The year was 1858. The connection with Istanbul was established via Novi Pazar. I cannot free myself from the same diary page: "The citizens of Sarajevo, finally and irrefutably, got telephones for private communications on November 16, 1898." So, the telephone as a means of communication was introduced in Bosnia and Herzegovina as the last postal activity. A century later, it was among the first things to disappear in flames. Sarajevo has had public telephones since 1894. The German journalist Henrik Renner noted that lists of telephone numbers had existed since 1889, that even "concerts were covered by telephone"; so "on Emperor Franz Joseph's birthday, the national anthem was broadcast to all the garrisons that did not have their own orchestras." Director of the Post and Telegraph, Cimponeri, spoke on the occasion of the formal opening of the main telephone exchange fitted in the house of the outstanding citizen Petar Petrović Petrakija, vice-administrator of the municipality, at 51 Franz Joseph Street (until recently called JNA Street, and now the City Defenders' Street), at 8 o'clock. A few telephone subscribers who had their telephones connected listened to him, and the attorney Fischer, from his telephone number 51, thanked the director for his efforts and the blessing which they had brought.

Who knows when and whether those dear yellow letter-boxes which reached the land of Bosnia with the occupying army in 1878 and appeared, to the amazement of our ancestors, at postal relays, in barracks, post offices and elsewhere, will work ever again? Shall I be able to post a letter, to send a message that I am alive and well, soon or at all, in this way when I cannot do it by telephone?

It was like hell. The city echoed to the sound of detonations. The swollen boil of war burst in the centre of Sarajevo. The city was mercilessly fired on.

The Post Office burned. Black, dense smoke rose into the sky. Shots from the building resounded. In Tito Street, after making a decision not to spend the night in the passage next to the Court, just near the petrol station and the burning Post Office, I ran over pieces of broken glass. The "Zema" department store was damaged by a missile. Those were the first bricks crushed on the pavement that I saw. The corner of the main street gaped shrieking. As if some powerful monster, some awakened leviathan, had torn that dignified, grey façade, eight decades old. As if it had waited to show the bricks from Sarajevo's brick kilns, the frailty of the century and of the city. The stone relief on the front of the National Bank was shelled, too. We can only guess the name and surname of the Russian who chiselled it. In a corner of the relief, as was appropriate, V. Zagorodnik

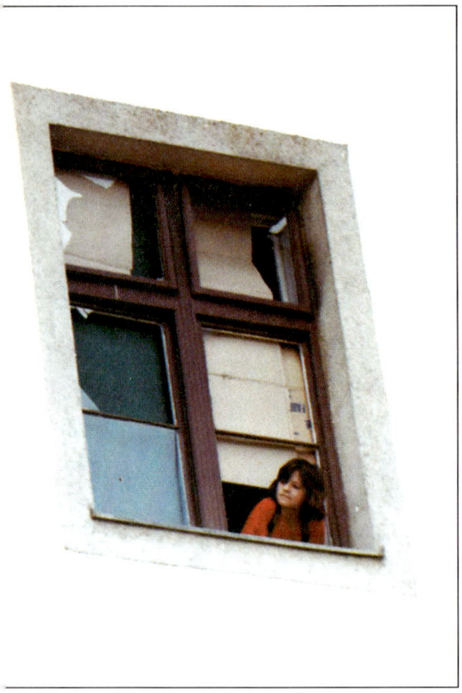
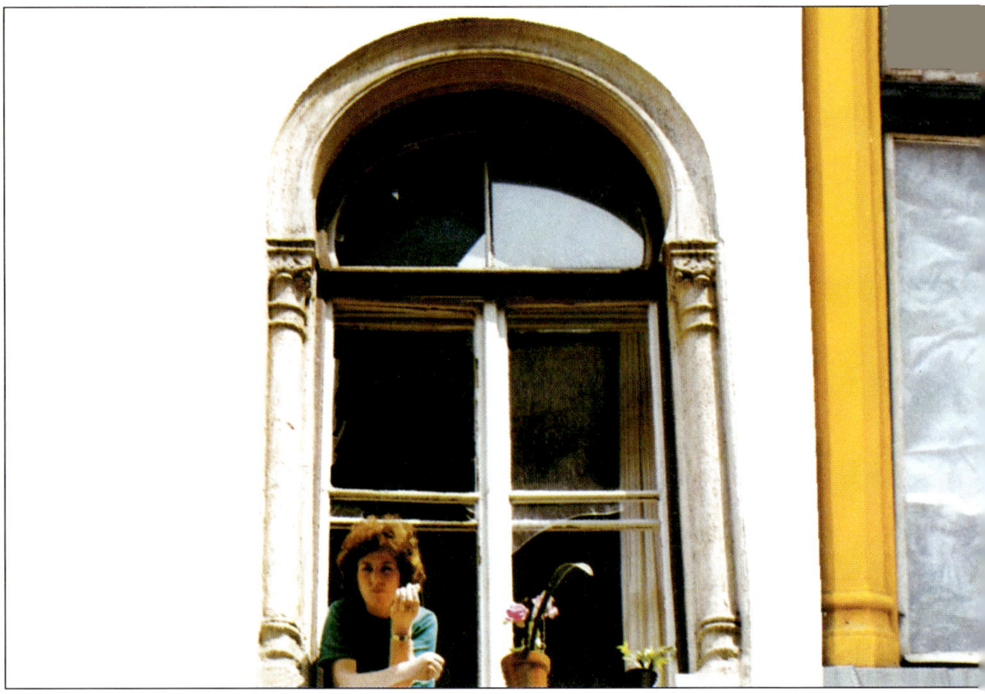
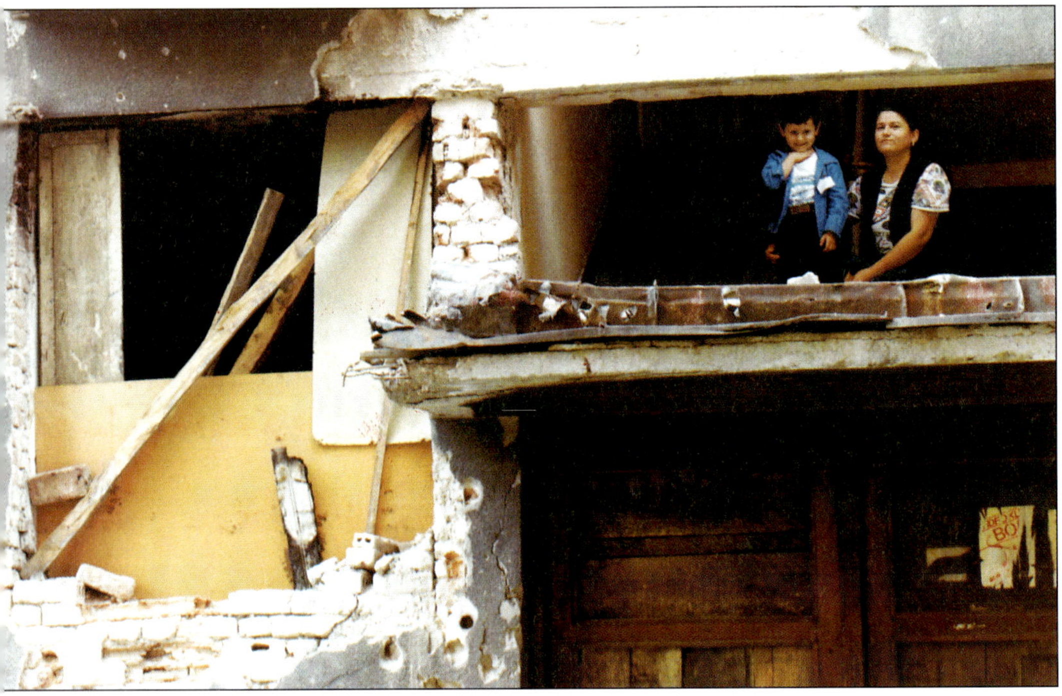
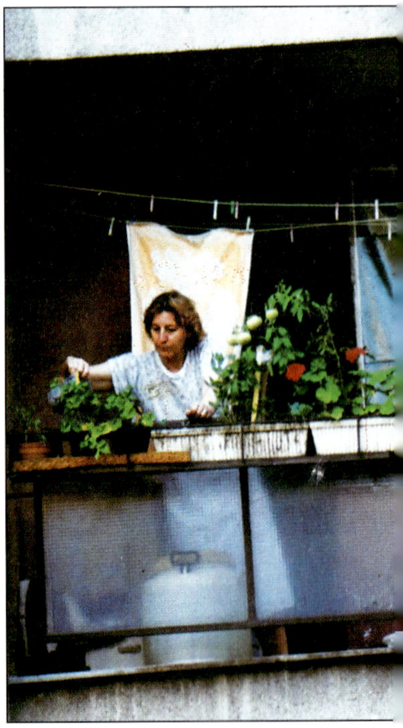
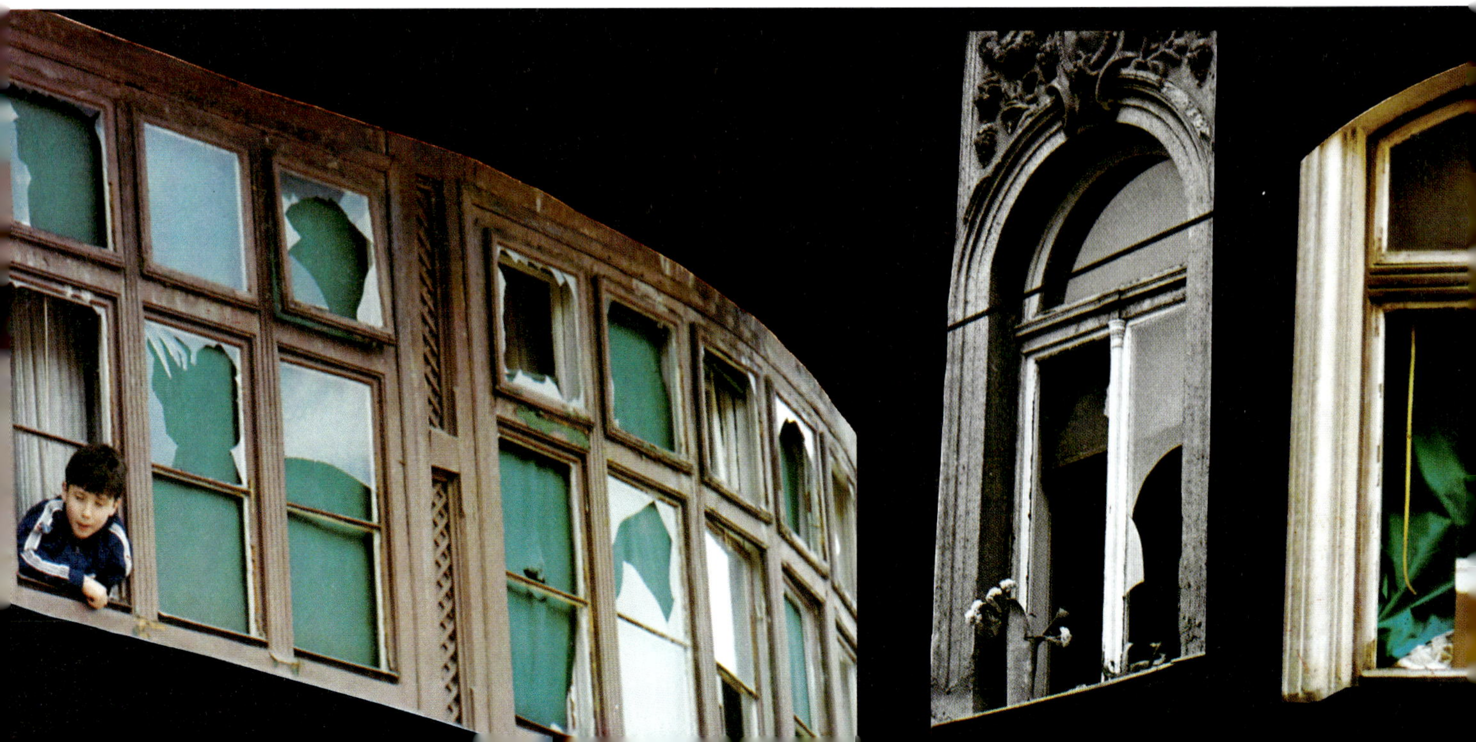

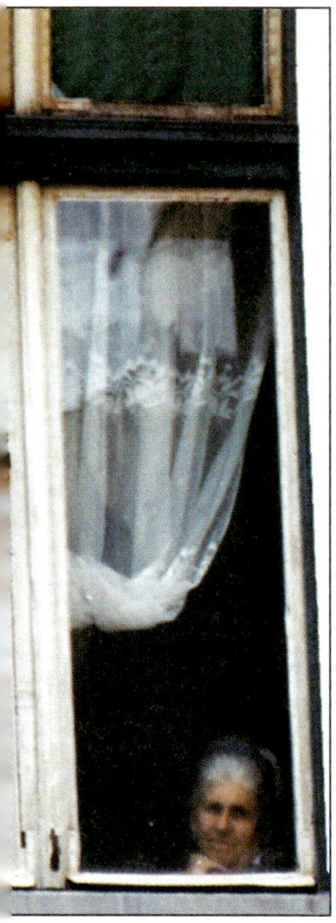
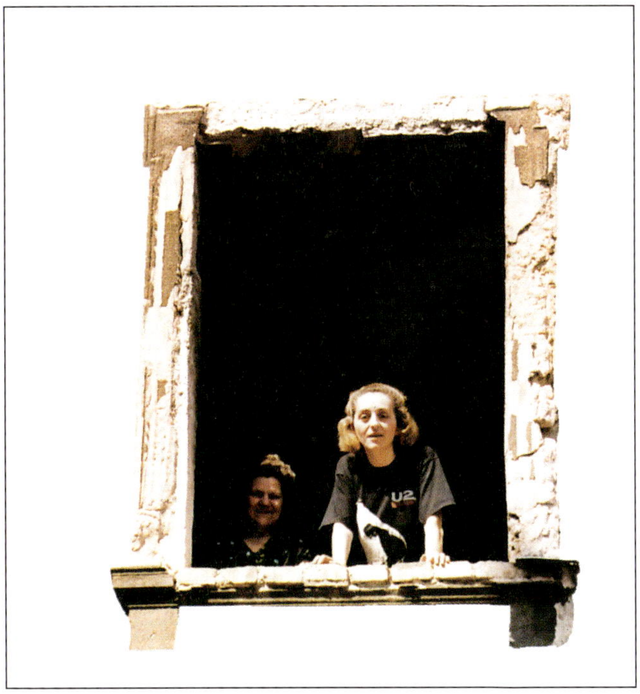
U2
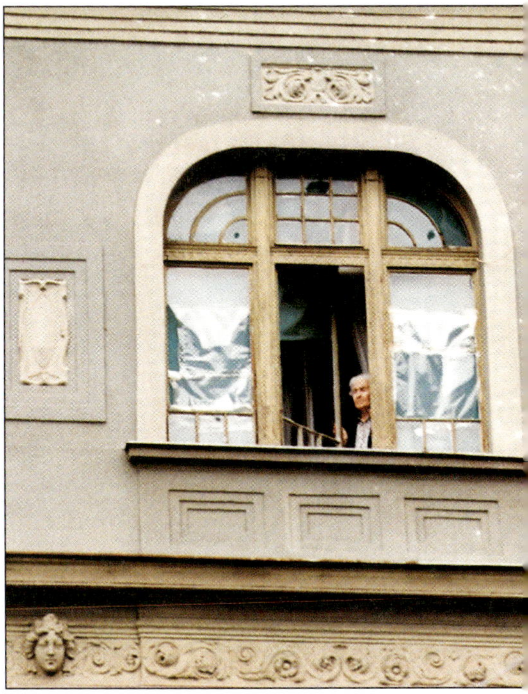
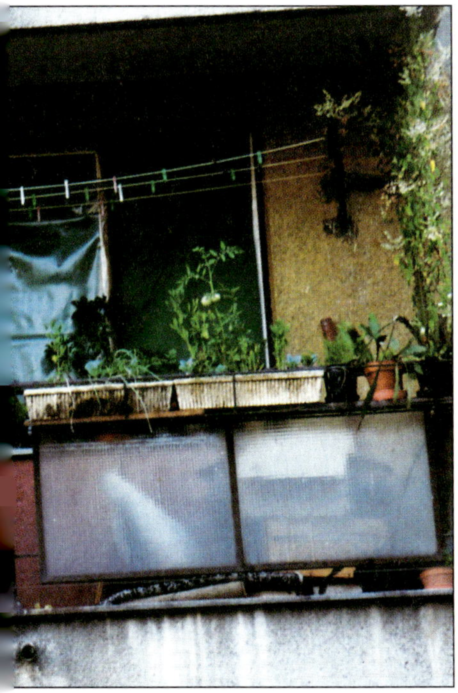
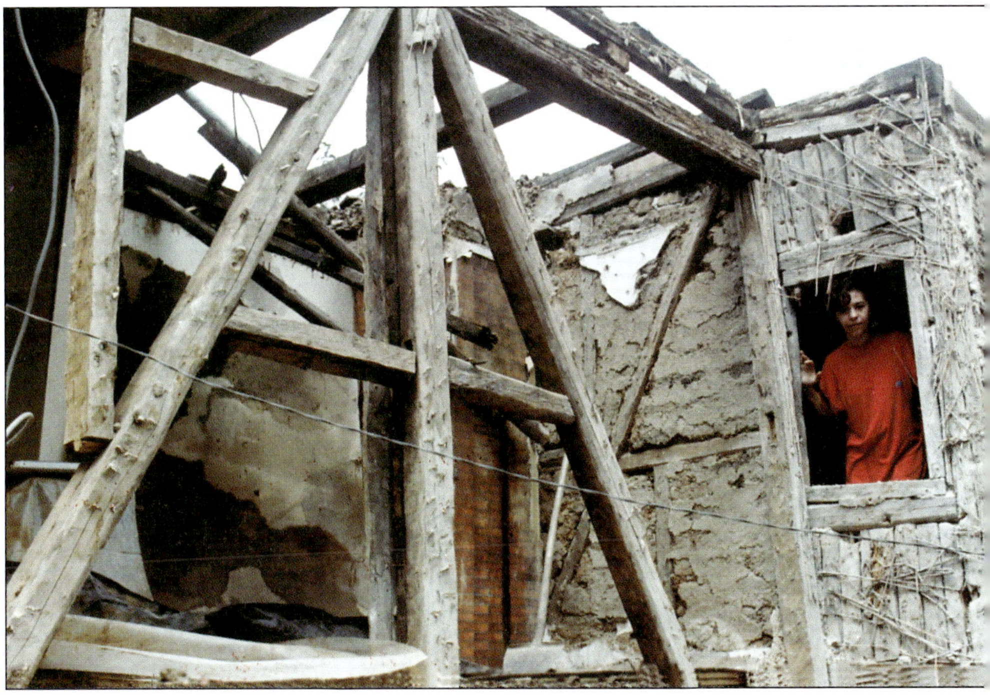
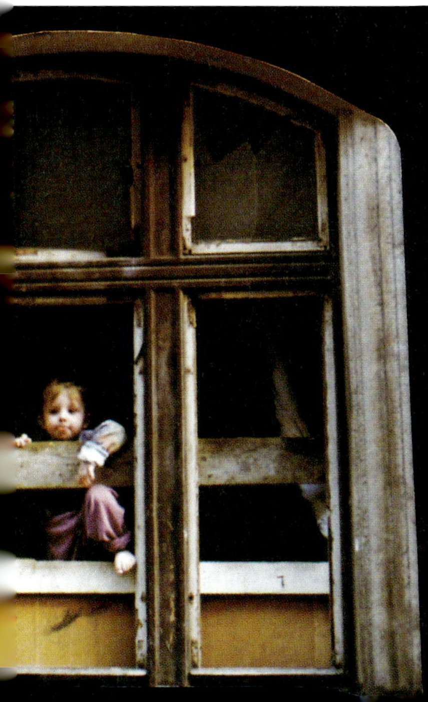
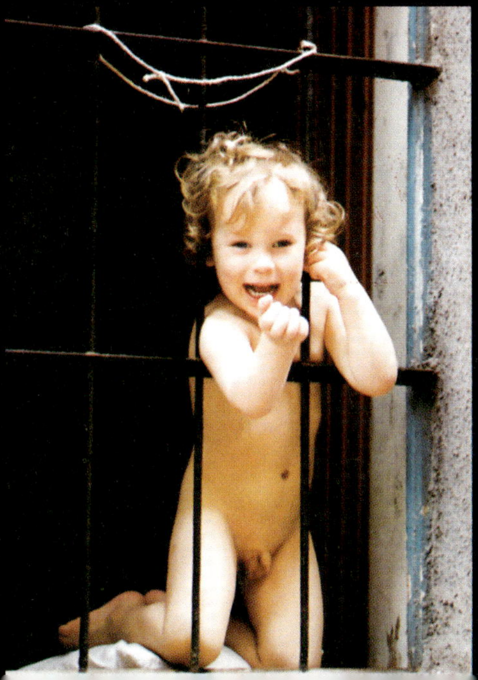
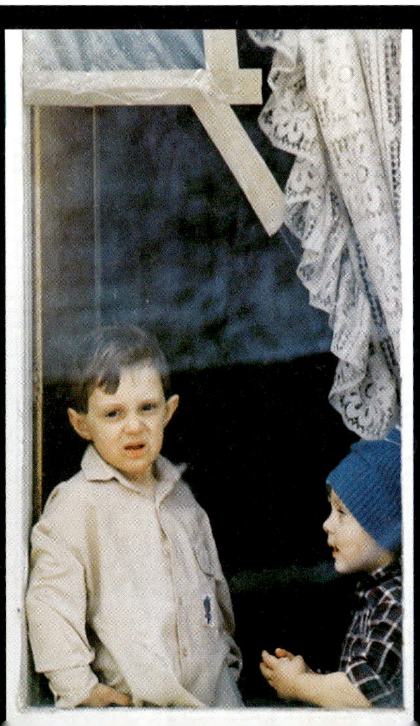

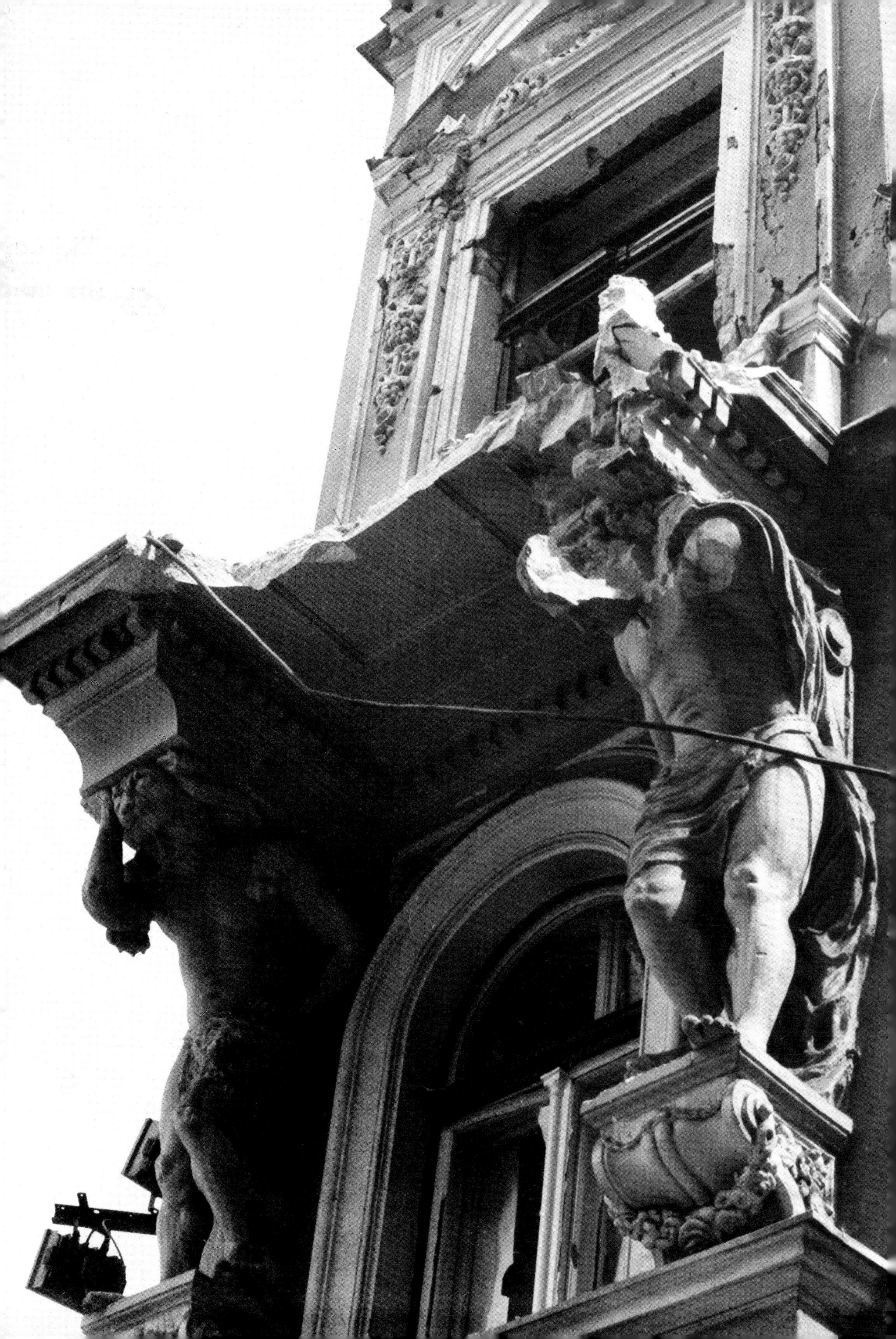

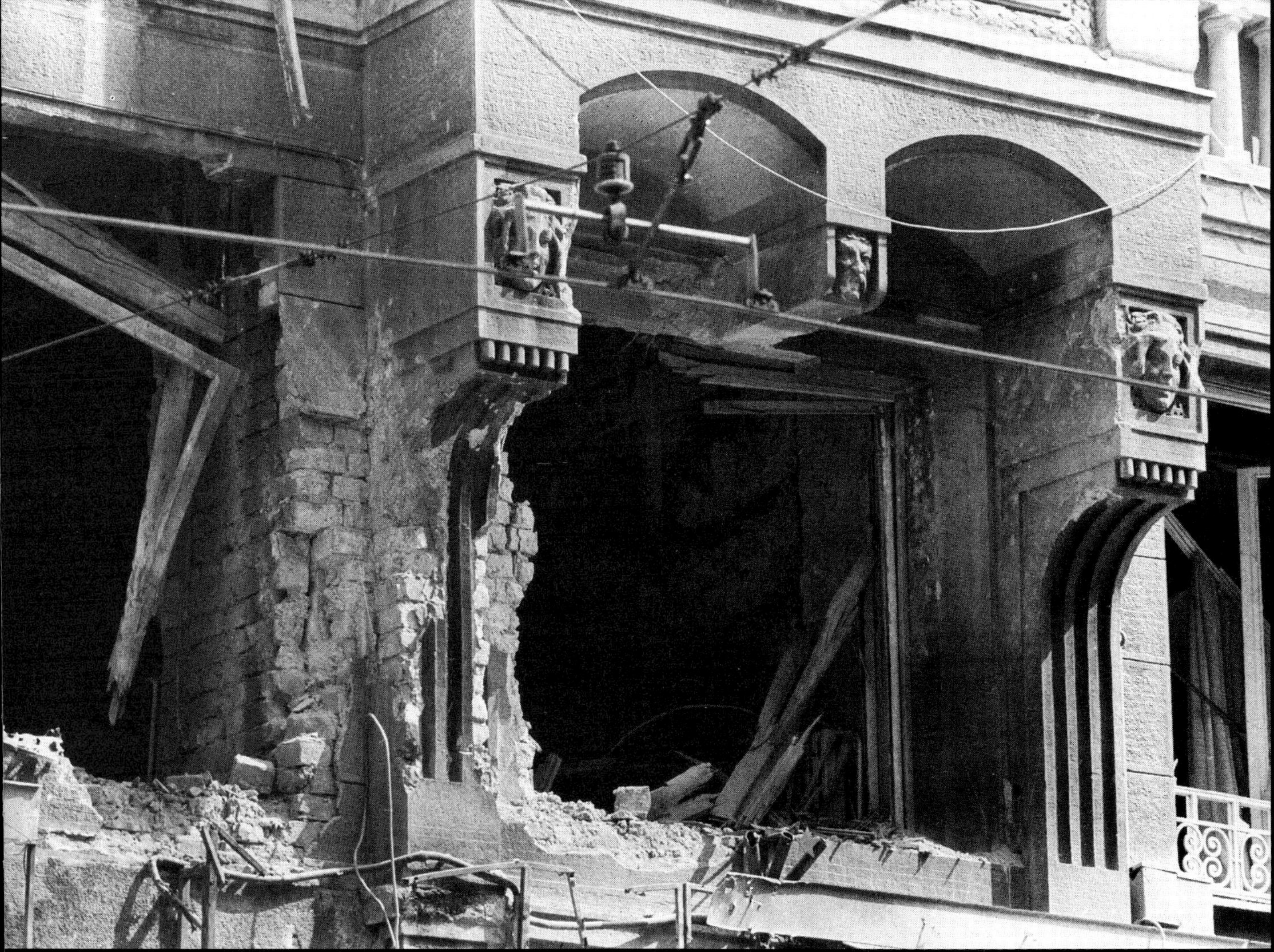

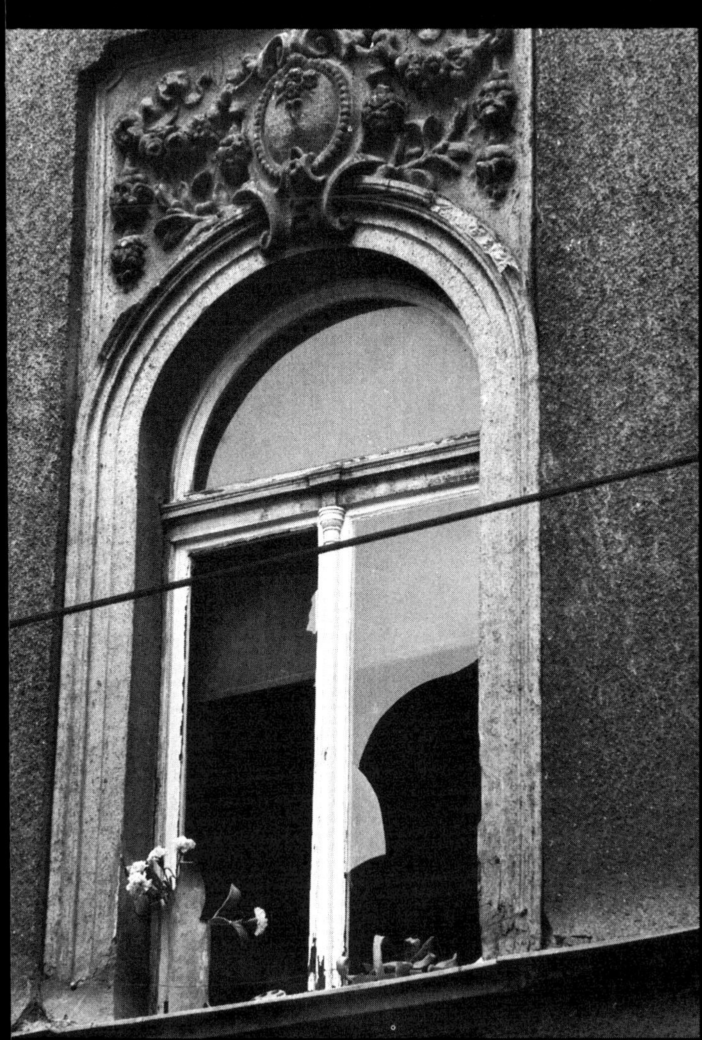

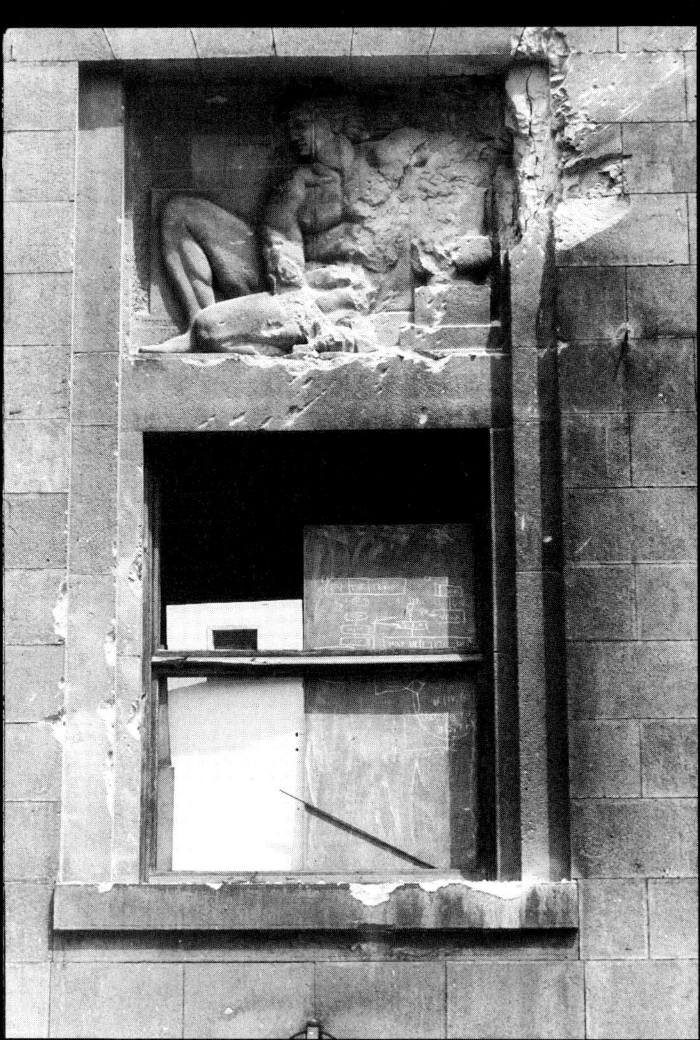

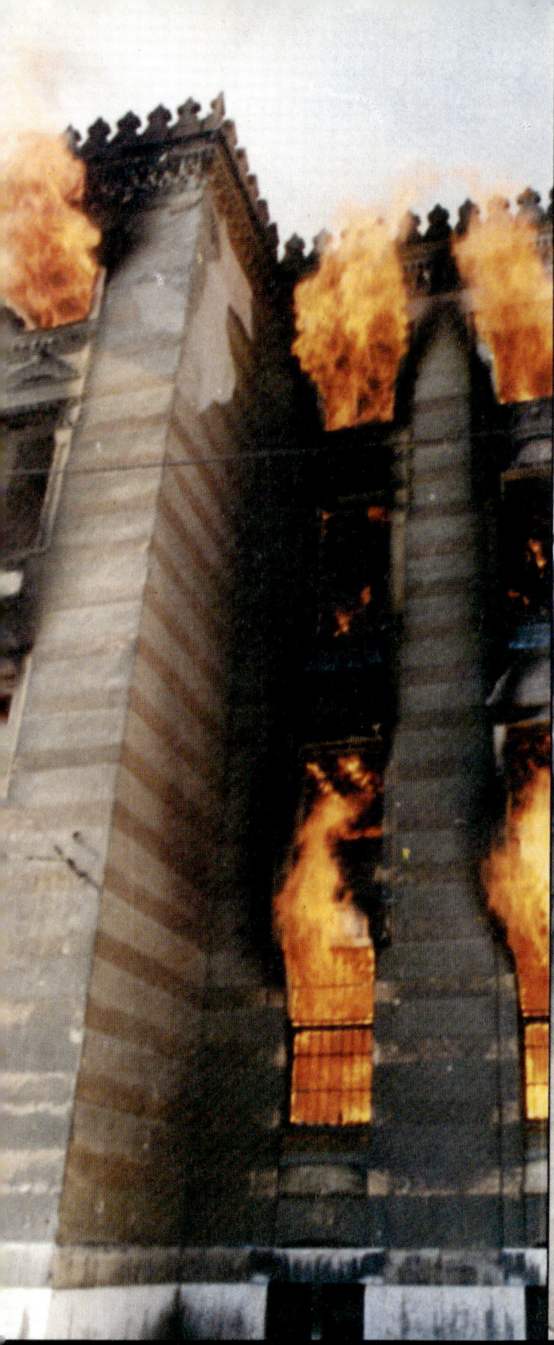
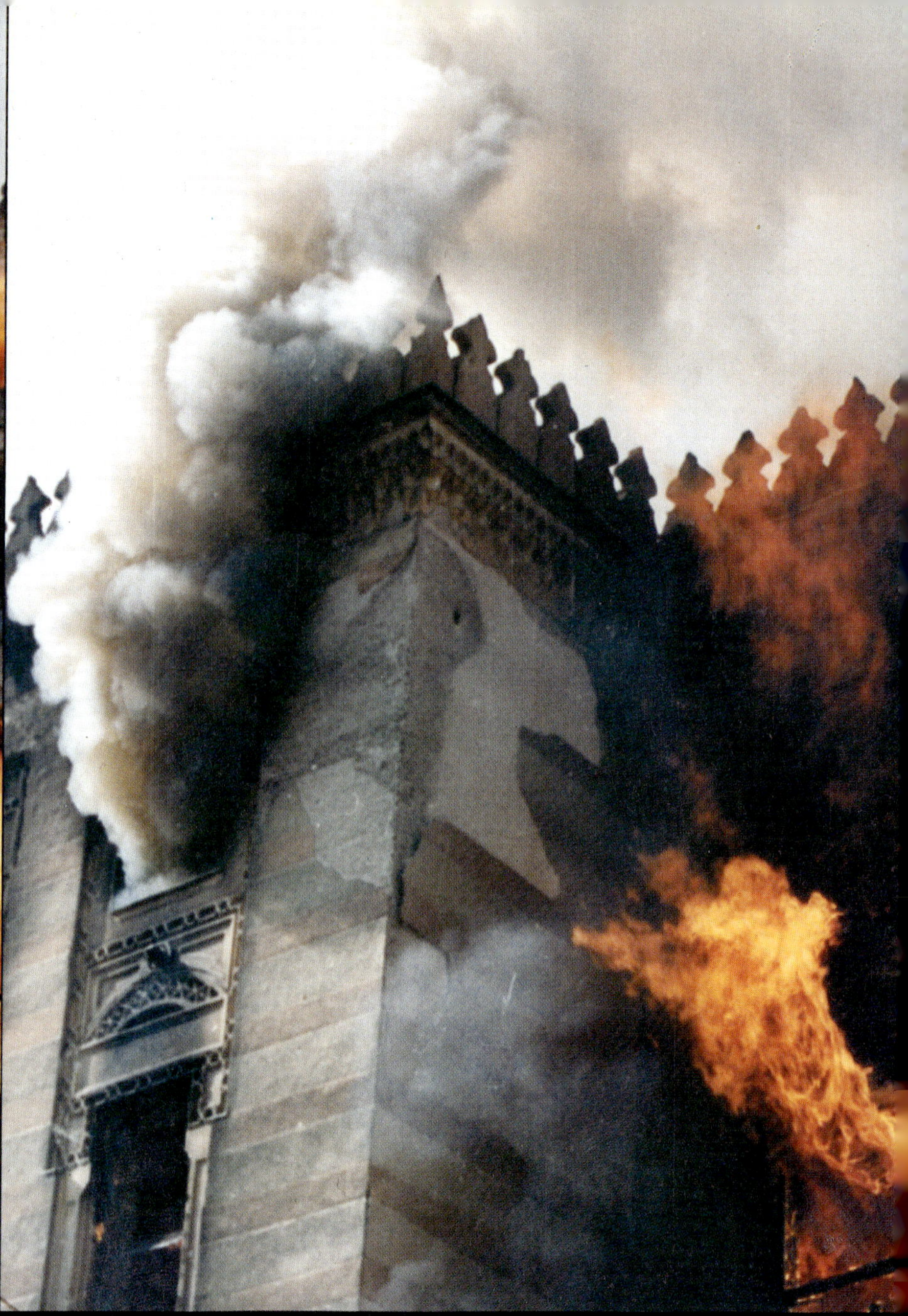
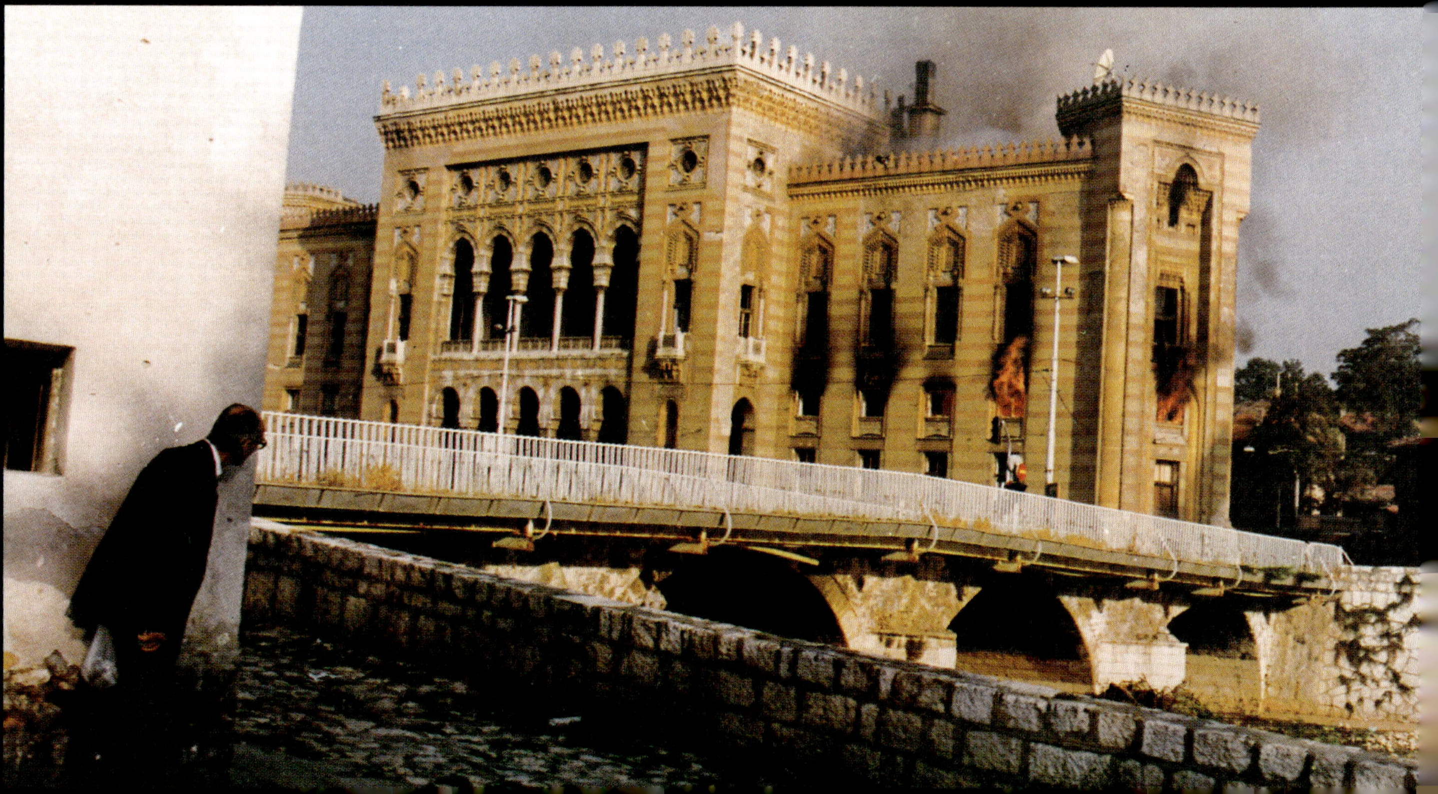

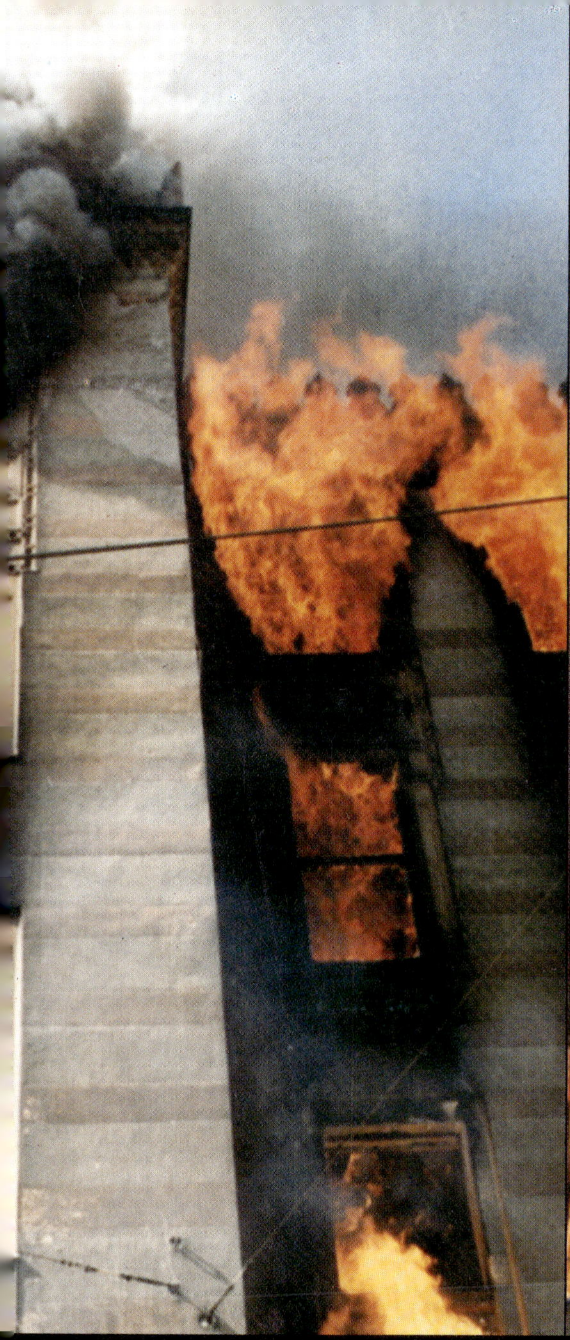

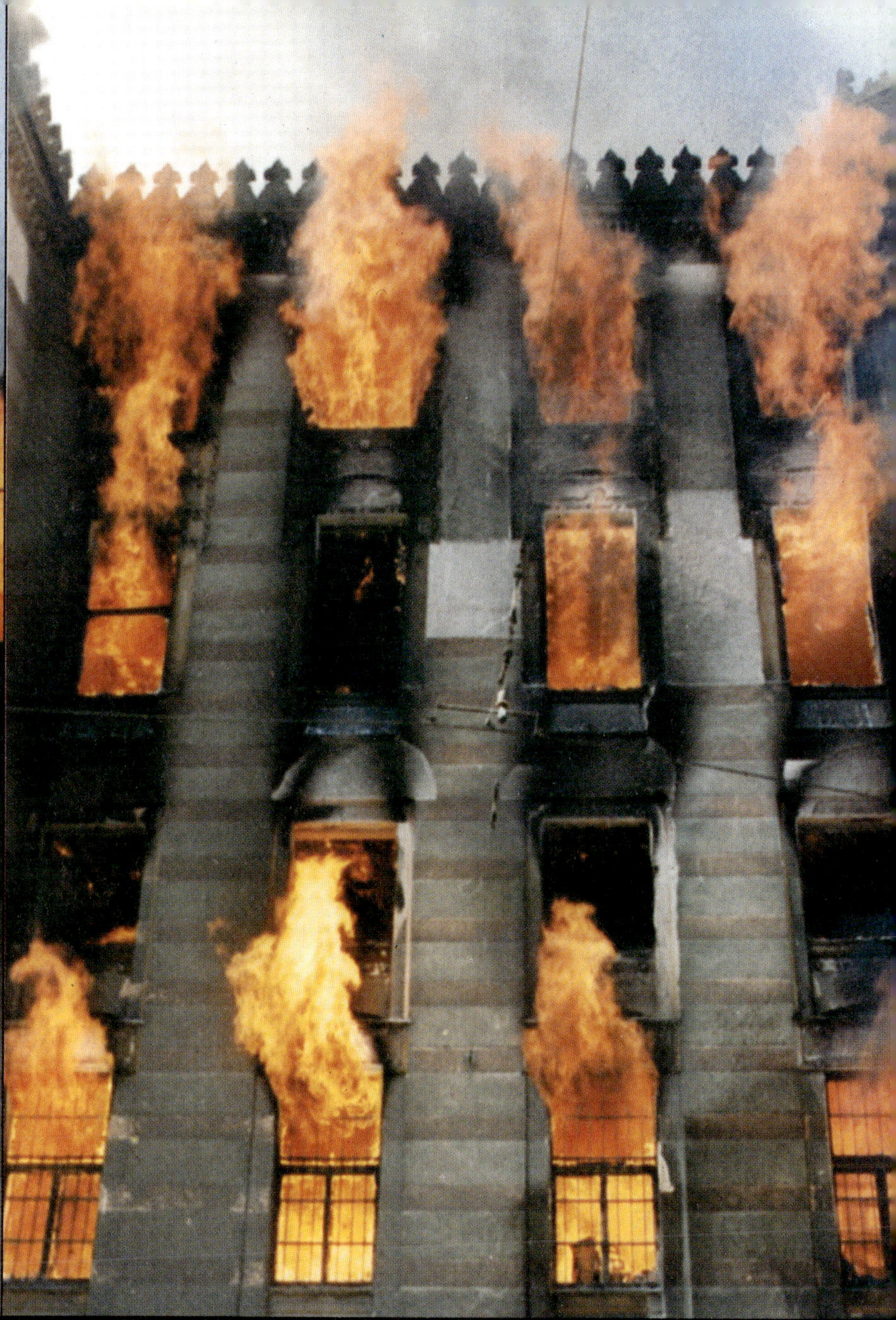

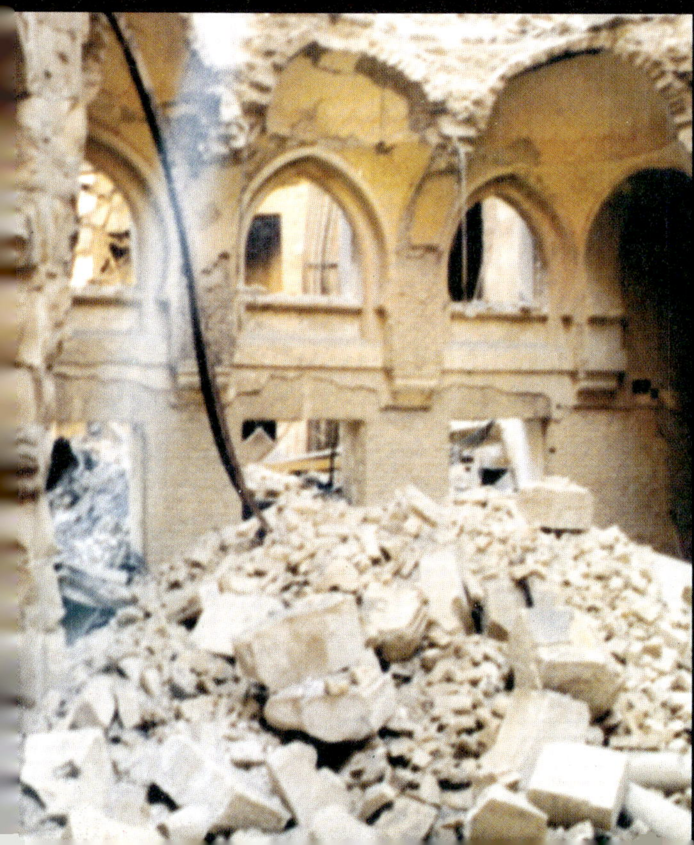

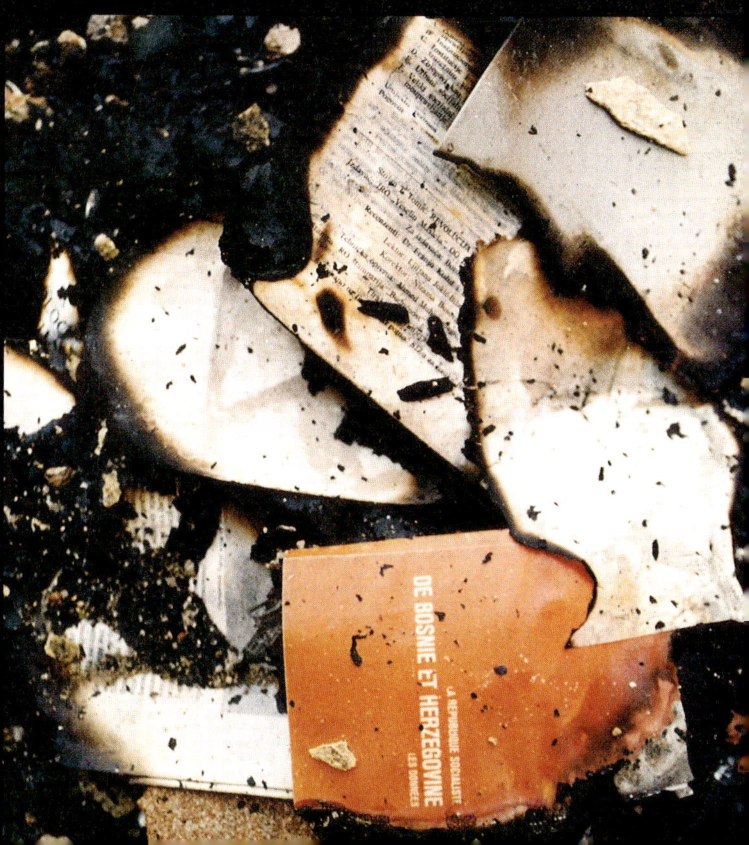
DE BOSNIE ET HERZEGOVINE

signed his name and wrote the year 1930. Historians of architecture wrote down that the Mortgage Bank had been erected in 1929 according to the design of the architect Milan Zlatović. We know little about the reliefs. On the front of today's National Bank, there are two, while on the sides, somewhere at the top, there is a series of stone reliefs. The designer seemed to repeat Jože Plečnik's words: "A front without ornaments is like a man who never smiles."

The main street was deserted. It looked like an ugly dream. Lovely day, sunshine, and the streets without people. There are no cars! No trams! The traffic lights work! Green and red go on and off alternately. At the entrance to the National Bank, two bronze sculptures stand guard in a dignified way. They are not frightened.

The war started fiercely, noisily and painfully. On the bank of the Miljacka, the Old Electric Power Station is ablaze after being shelled. The Municipal Assembly building took four shells. They shell the First Aid Building. Shells hit the TV Building. The Hum relay is shelled. TV broadcasting is cut off. Fire breaks out on Mount Hum. Detonations resound. These are not pictures from faraway Beirut, Dubrovnik or Vukovar. Sarajevo roars, burns, it is demolished. rovnik or Vukovar. Sarajevo roars, burns, is demolished. The target is the whole city. Its vital structures rank highest A large hole gapes in the building near the "eternal fire", above the well-supplied ready-made fashion shop "Kluz". They shoot mercilessly and hit the buildings of Elektroprivreda, Kreditna banka, hotels, the seat of the Ministry of Home Affairs, the buildings of Social and Old Age Insurance, the Republican Assembly, the Republican Institute for Statistics... Everything is a target. We are all targets to be destroyed. The plan is to kill the city's life, cut off telephone lines, TV programmes, electricity, to exterminate life. Places of worship are not spared the shells, either. St. Vinko Church, the Old Orthodox Church, the Hrasnica Mosque receive their share of shells. Fires break out at every step. Sarajevo burns. Fire brigades rush. They cannot decide where to go first. There are not enough fire engines, firemen or hoses. All the fires break out at the same time. The shooting goes on and a loud threat pierces of the bones of the Aerodrom suburb: "Do not put them out! We are going to kill you all! To kill! To kill! To kill! Do not put them out! Do not put them out!"

The first sirens sound the air raid alarm. Many of us did not notice any difference in the sounding of the alarms. Until yesterday, those signals for the air raid alert were mere schematic nonsense. Somebody else will need them.

Another drama on the TV news. It goes on the whole night. It goes on the following day. The President of the Presidency of the Republic of Bosnia and Herzegovina has been kidnapped! He has ended his trip back from the interrupted Lisbon peace talks at Lukavica barracks. The

Koljević, Biljana Plavšić, Velibor Ostojić and Vojislav Maksimović.

Sunday, 24th: Four people killed, fifty-seven wounded. An army convoy of 50 vehicles (personnel carriers, off-road vehicles and field kitchens) and 300 people leave the "Viktor Bubanj" barracks.

Monday, 25th: Shelling again, most severe in the Buća potok and Otoka residential areas. A formal session of the Socialist Democratic Party held on the occasion of the 100th anniversary of Josip Broz Tito's birth. An unsigned text on the jubilee on page three of "Oslobođenje" ends with the following: "He died on May 4th, 1980 at the age of 88. The whole world was at his funeral. His life was hard, but eventful and rich. History will judge his work. Some of the judgements have already been formed."

Tuesday, 26th: The town is shocked: the Maternity Hospital "Zehra Muidović" is hit by tank and mortar fire. There are 130 women and 70 new-born babies in the hospital. Traumatology Clinic shelled as well.

Wednesday, 27th: A crime is committed at 9.55 a.m. in front of the city market. An 82-mm shell kills 17 people and 156 are wounded while queueing for bread. There are children among them buying ice cream. Three babies die because after the cataclysm in the Maternity Hospital they have to be taken out of incubators. Most severely attacked by tank and mortar projectiles are the Dobrinja and Mojmilo residential areas and the "Oslobođenje" building. Nevertheless, the newspaper of that name is still being published...

Thursday, 28th: One person killed, 76 wounded. The "Marshal Tito" barracks set on fire by mortar shells from Vraca. Three people injured by shells fired at the building of the Presidency of the Republic of B-H.

Friday, 29th: The night of the great fires. Apart from rocket launchers, mortars, self-propelled guns and tanks are also used. The minaret and the roof of the Magribija mosque are damaged; also damaged and set on fire are the buildings of the Supreme Court and the Youth Hall. Hit by shells are the City Hospital (the former Military hospital), UNPROFOR headquarters, the cathedral, the Institute of Hygiene, the "Feroelektro" Company, "Oslobođenje", blocks of flats in Danijel Ozmo, King Tomislav, Kata Govorušić, Đuro Đaković, Skerlić, Hasan Kikić streets and the residential areas Vojničko polje, Mojmilo, Dobrinja, Butmir, Pofalići, Koševsko brdo and Bistrik. Eleven flats in Vojničko polje burning. The ŽTP Company is renamed the B-H Railways. The commander of the Territorial Defence Command of B-H declares general mobilization in ten Sarajevo municipalities.

Saturday, 30th: Shortage of "A" and "O" blood groups. Twenty shells fall on GRAS (the City Transport Company). Three trams totally destroyed and 17 damaged. Six trolleybuses destroyed and the same number damaged. Attacks on the Maternity Hospital, the "Jezero" hospital, Pionirska dolina, "Feroelektro", Baščaršija and the JAT tower block. Shooting from the "Marshal Tito" barracks. Banks closed – no money. Sixty-eight long-distance power lines of the high-

highest officer of the Yugoslav People's Army in the Republic that refused hospitality to that army has captured the President of the State. From the sinking ship, the commander in chief was rescuing himself by temporarily arresting somebody else. Yugoslav Lieutenant General Milutin Kukanjac remained in the mousetrap of all the mousetraps. The city became a mousetrap controlled by gun, tank and many other barrels from the surrounding hills. The military command and the general stayed in the city. The city was not taken in a couple of hours. The general captured himself. The game of hide and seek was over. He had to leave. He was freeing himself by threatening the confinement of President Izetbegović. The drama of freeing the head of state and his exchange for the general, who was fleeing with trucks loaded with armchairs, flowerpots, lamps and carpets, lasted for twenty-four hours.

On the way as the departing army left, there were again dead and wounded, burned trucks.

Time lost its sense. At once, but somehow gradually, the hours and weeks disappeared. There was a hole in which day and night were the same: long, dull and impersonal. They were worthless. Time fled the city as well. It was taken from us.

Many things we could not do without were no longer important. We were without our dearest ones, without friends and aquaintances. Some left, others set off on the road without return, along which only flowers are laid and yellow wax candles lit.

My telephone fell silent at 4.00 p.m. A little before that I used it to say I did not know when I would come home, that I might not be able to come. Then I ran across the streets and crossroads, I climbed up the stairs on the steep streets and hurried to a friend's at Breka. I ran risks. It was different up there. Columns of smoke rose into the sky. Explosions echoed all around. It was somewhere else. It was happening to others. The upper part of the city amphitheatre listened to the life down in a faraway arena. People sat, relaxed or worried, indisputably inquisitive, waiting. It was peaceful around them. There was peace in some enclaves in the city. Elsewhere, there were echoes, roars and fire. People counted the dead and wounded. They got confused with the figures.

The war slowly permeated the city with its smell, destroying it.

We still did not believe that all this could have happened, could have happened to us. We did not accept being condemned to extermination. We wondered. We evaded reality. The fiery language of Bosnia's past was felt by ours. However, how could we accept that all the worst was happening just to us, that we had to walk that Circle Two of hell, that even old Dante could not have described the hell of Sarajevo. We could only live as we did yesterday. The only thing I could do was to try to go beyond myself. The message was: Put on a smile and cover your sorrow with it.

How difficult it was, every new day in Sarajevo, to watch the people with suitcases, plastic bags or bundles. Everything they took with them was in there, everything that they could take, everything that was left after the shelling. Tearstained, confused, scared people arrived with the same bundles, driven out of their homes. Those were not some faraway television pictures. It was our life. Anathema became our fate. My friend Ivan, an outstanding writer, put only his toothbrush in his denim shirt pocket. His neighbour, the accountant Fadil, just came in a jogging suit. They had only three hundred metres of the street, a bridge and a few minutes to survive. They left their lives, memories, manuscripts, books, clothes and photographs behind. Many did not have time even to look back.

I wonder if we all remember equally well those ships crowded with Vietnamese who were fleeing, leaving, who did not want, or did not have, anything to take with them. Broken relationships became more and more numerous, SOS messages followed one another on the air waves of Radio Sarajevo. The messages were from those who could get through to the studio. All they said was: "We are well... I am alive and well." Messages were broadcast one after another for hours. There were two thousand messages a day. Only six or seven hundred could be broadcast. It went on for days and nights. This programme, which has continued throughout the war, is called: "messages of a personal character". Sons called mothers, fathers called children, brothers and relatives, informing them about life and death. It echoed long into the night: Save our souls. Save our souls. SOS, SOS... The radio was the only voice which connected the separated, cured the dumbness of ignorance. Morse's call to a ship or aircraft in danger, codified at the beginning of this century, has become man's call today. Are cities entitled to ask for help? Radio hams started work. Their love and persistance became a cure for many lost and grieving ones.

We walked on pieces of broken glass. The dead lay in the streets. They lay there for days. They were visited by stray dogs. We moved to the basements. We started living in shelters or basements entrances. We avoided crossroads. We ran across them. Everywhere we came across a warning written more or less skillfully – SNIPER! We were fired on even by shells with poison gas. Shells were fired at hospitals, cemeteries, hearses and ambulances. The city became emptier and emptier. There were no more cafes, shops or places where our friends used to meet. They all, suddenly, disappeared.

One could not leave Sarajevo. One could not come to Sarajevo. The trams stopped on May 2nd. They burned out at their stops. The railway station burned out, and it was big,

voltage network out of action. According to a warning by the Electrical Power Industry Board of B-H there is a serious threat of blackouts. The UN Security Council adopts Resolution 757 introducing general and wide-ranging sanctions against Serbia and Montenegro, urgently to stop the aggression on B-H, to withdraw the JNA and other units deployed in B-H, to deblock roads and Sarajevo airport for the delivery of humanitarian aid to the citizens of B-H, to stop the ethnic cleansing.

Sunday, 31st: *A relatively peaceful day. Shells fall from Hreša and Borije on Sedrenik and Baščaršija. Four people killed, thirty-seven wounded. The Government of B-H sends a letter to the UN Security Council with a request for humanitarian aid and their support to free all the parts of the state, establish the rule of law and punish those who have committed atrocities.*

JUNE

Monday, 1st: *Shells and missiles fall on Grbavica and Dolac Malta, the "Oslobođenje" building, the old part of the city, around the post office in Novo Sarajevo, the tobacco factory, the "Bristol" hotel, the market place in Hrasno and Alipašino polje. The Trinity Church at Dolac Malta damaged. Shelled are Butmir, Bistrik, Sedrenik, the students' hostel at Bjelave and the building of the Faculty of Philosophy.*

Tuesday, 2nd: *There have been eight people killed and forty nine injured in the last 24 hours. Banknotes of 1000 and 500 dinars withdrawn in December and January are in circulation again, marked with the seal of the National*

Bank of B-H. An attempt by the Children's Embassy and UNPROFOR to deliver six tons of food and medicine to Dobrinja citizens ends tragically. The bus driver is killed and his companion seriously injured. Negotiations on lifting the blockade of Sarajevo airport. Shelling of Koševsko brdo, Vratnik and the Bare residential area. 200 litres of fuel provided for power units in the Maternity Hospital.

Wednesday, 3rd: *Artillery firing at Marijin Dvor, central and old parts of the city and western residential areas. Infantry fighting around the "Jezero" hospital and at Pero Kosorić Square. Hit by shells are the building of the Presidency, the "Sarajka" department store, the "Europe" hotel, Sarači street at Baščaršija. A bus belonging to "Koševo" hospital staff fired at from the Jewish cemetery: one person killed, four injured. A group of entrepreneurs and businessmen issue wanted notices for General Ratko Mladić and Radovan Karadžić promising anyone who "finds, brings and hands them over" 4 million and 3 million German marks respectively. An initiative of shop owners from Baščaršija and abroad to offer an award of 5 kilograms of gold to the person who kills Radovan Karadžić or Ratko Mladić. Owing to poor communications with Pale, the exchange of prisoners at Stup delayed. Tickets for rationing on basic foods in use from today.*

Thursday, 4th: *Firing from Vraca and Jewish cemetery at Marijin Dvor, the City Hospital, a bus of the City Transport. The town hall hit by shells. The Olympic Committee of B-H formed.*

beautiful; they say it was the biggest one in the Balkans and, according to some, even in Europe. Buses could not leave, either. The halted trams will wait for their passengers for a long time. Passengers became pedestrians. There were fewer and fewer cars in the streets. You could not buy petrol or oil any more. We were becoming cityless.

Down the millenia, I called out to Aristotle. He taught: "The man without his city is either a beast or a god." It did not help.

Everywhere only death, funerals, tears, despair, smoke, fire, debris and destruction.

On May 1st, the official public holiday, the last announcement of job vacancies was published by the Employment Exchange in the newspapers. Nobody was looking for workers. We all were redundant. The economy stopped. Firms closed down. Twenty-five days later, it was obvious even from the newspapers that starvation threatened the city, that the dark was coming in. There were no blood reserves. The citizens were given coupons to survive. We were given "ration cards" for basic foods. It was the only way we would be buying flour, sugar, cooking oil, fat, pastry, rice, butter, margarine, milk, meat products and milk products. The card contained the selling outlet, the registration number of the household and the number of people in the family. There were people who did succeed in buying something. All we could get was flour and sugar, but not more than once.

The introductory lecture delivered in May by Dr Pascal Satirovski from the Medau Observatory in Paris was no consolation, either. At the Academy of Sciences and Arts of Macedonia, he said: "All wars, from the French Revolution until now have been waged during a period of sunspots and eruptions. That period is nearing its end, it ends next year, so I hope that the war will then stop, too."

The mortuaries were crowded. At the beginning of May there were no burials. There were no obituaries on May 3, 4, 5, 15, 16... The last burial at Bare cemetery was on May 11th. In Dobrinja, they started burying the dead outside their houses. Coffins were made from wardrobes. Being unable to bury a dead man who lay for days in his flat, his neighbours, the radio announced, put a plaster cast over him. The corpse started to decay. They made a plaster mummy on the front lawn. The lawns around the houses turned into narrow cemeteries. Burials took place under fire, at night. From the Old People's Home at Nedžarići, there came a cry for help. Eight corpses had lain next to the living for days. Nobody managed to come to pick them up. We very often only said: "We buried him in the absence of his relatives who were not able to come." The Lav cemetery, which, for decades, had been overgrown by grass, was again used. Cemeteries gradually die. Here they revive. The green carpet, little by little, but faster and faster, faded away. On May 10th, we had burials there after more than a quarter of a century. On May 10th, we had the first barricades there. It was closed down in 1965. In 1992 it was put back into service.

Destinies and dramas are being knitted together. Greek tragedies are the real life in Sarajevo. We are living them. Our dearest ones are being killed. In a newspaper of the 19th, I came across the obituary of Srbo's father. There was no photograph. Uncle Milan, son of Aleksandar, Petronijević died on 16th. The obituary says:

"Date of burial will be announced later.

The bereaved son"

I was deeply hurt. Death always hurts. The loss of loved ones is not measured by the number of years they lived. I know how attached he and Srbo were to each other. They had been tied to each other for years. I find a telephone I can make a call from. I dial the number in the "Shopping Centre". Silence. I dial again. I keep dialling. Always the same silence. Nobody answers. I inquire about Srbo and his father's death. He passed away in hospital. His heart did not endure the age. Srbo was cut off in Grbavica at the beginning of May. The father was dying in hospital. The son did not manage to cross the bridge. We did not have the telephone any longer. We have not been able to get in touch with him since that destructive May 2nd.

There was no notice about the funeral the next day. Not even the day after. I learnt, waiting for a newspaper notice, that the dear old eighty-year-old had been buried by a nurse Fatima. She succeeded in contacting Srbo. She could not get to the burial area of the Petronijević family. Srbo could not come, either. He was not able to see his father's grave. His cousin Boban, after a week, found out about the death and the funeral. He found the grave, arranged the heaped clay and then laid a bunch of flowers on it.

In the city, there were no wreaths. Flower shops were not open, either. People picked flowers from balcony flowerpots, neighbours' gardens, and parks.

I tear away a May page:

"It roared last night. The shells echoed somewhere in the east, behind Koševo. The Old Town must have been 'paying tribute' to those from Lapišnica, Borija, Hreša and Trebević. How much madness there must be in those crazed nights' fireworks and detonations. On the radio, they talked about the wounds of Butmir, Sokolović and Hrasnica. From somewhere far away, at night, there came some western sounds of death.

A starry night, sounds we are not used to, and waiting. We wait for something. We wish for all this to pass soon, to become just an ugly dream.

But, it goes on.

"It goes on.

Friday, 5th: The "Marshal Tito" barracks evacuated without a single bullet fired. In the evening Baščaršija, Bistrik, Pero Kosorić Square, Dobrinja shelled. An infantry attack on Dobrinja. "Ljubljanska banka", "Jelavica" warehouse, the "Oslobođenje" building on fire. From 7.30 p.m. to 9 p.m. several hundred shells fall on the city. The first war posters appear. Since the beginning of the war 150,000 shells and missiles have been fired at Sarajevo. That is 2,500 a day. The shells fired at the city could fill 250 trucks making a convoy ten kilometres long.*

Saturday, 6th: More than 30 hours of continuous shelling of the city. The worst so far. More than half of one of the "Unis" skyscrapers burnt down. Residential blocks on Koševsko hill on fire; "Vaso Miskin" factory, the psychiatric hospital casualty department damaged. Five patients and a nurse injured in the clinic for lung diseases at Podhrastovi. The "Marshal Tito" barracks, more than a hundred houses at Vratnik, ten flats in the "Ciglane" residential area, the Sarajevo Tobacco Factory, the Catholic Church in Novo Sarajevo, the old people's home and residential areas in western parts of the city catch fire, having been hit by shells. Seven people dead, and 52 injured.*

Sunday, 7th: Barrages exploding over the city. An infantry attack from Grbavica repulsed. More than 10,000 shells fall on Novo Sarajevo. The heaviest attacks are on the "Electrical Power Industry" building, the City Dairy building and the Railway Station.*

Monday, 8th: *The mortuary is too small for all the dead. Twenty nine dead and 418 injured. Battles going on at Vraca, Žuč, Mojmilo, Nedžarići, Butmir and Poljine. Vidikovac and the "Osmice" motel taken over. Destruction at "Oslobođenje". In the Koševo Hospital the quantity of blood used today equals fifteen days' requirements under normal circumstances.*

Tuesday, 9th: *The first issue of "Zemlja" (The Country) magazine comes out. After 30 hours of captivity, the "White Eagles" finally let fifteen professors and eight nuns leave the Franciscan Theological Faculty in Nedžarići. Shells fall onto the First Grammar School, Pofalići, Velešići, Vojničko polje...*

Wednesday, 10th: *The Yugo-Army fires twenty-two cluster bombs at the defenders on Žuč Hill. Shells fall all over the city. The Post Office relay on Trebević blocked. Telephone communications interrupted. Fourteen people killed, 129 injured. Shelled are Pofalići, Velešići, "Bristol" hotel, "Šipad". Breka residential area, Stup (infantry fights), Pero Kosorić Square, Alipašino polje, Buća potok, Buljakov potok, Butmir, Dobrinja, Sokolje, Briješće, Baščaršija, Bistrik, Kovači, the outskirts of the Stari grad municipality, the Economic Bank on Obala (on fire), Koševo, Koševsko brdo... After 10 o'clock – air-raid sirens. A successful exchange (of POW's) is carried out at Vrbanja. An exhibition of photographs by the reporter Milomir Kovačević "Wounded Sarajevo" is set up in shop windows in V. Miskin Street.*

Thursday, 11th: *Nine people killed and a hundred injured.*

"The night overwhelmed the senses. Sleep, broken and interrupted by waking up and looking at the watch. It is good, we slept for two hours, then for one hour, then for forty-five minutes. And it goes on like this the whole night.

"Morning. The day's sunshine and warmth seem to disperse all the evil of the night. If I had not got a calendar, I would believe it was June.

"It is quiet. The radio, the only voice of reason, announces that the firing has calmed down. I cannot tell whether the fighters got tired or their barrels got so hot that they had to cool them.

In my street, there have been no cars for days. A village idyll with frogs croaking by a stream, owlets and nightingales at night in tree tops in the unpopulated neighbouring suburbs on the slopes replaces car roars. Until just yesterday we could not fall asleep by the open window. The noise of the cars was continuous.

"Sunshine, green, May, quiet..."

Who would think it is wartime, that Sarajevo is bleeding, dying, in its death rattle?

There is the thud of horses' hooves on the asphalt. No, it is impossible. A horse has never walked this way. Am I dreaming? Or, might someone have bought a brown horse to bridge the shortage of petrol? Some people have ideas how to become their own grandfathers and travel. Every means is faster than just feet.

I rush to the balcony with a child's smile on my lips. The striking of the hooves resounds more sharply. Sunshine, morning, May. A horse, hitched to a cart, passes by my house. It hurries towards the city centre. Rubber wheels make the sound of the shod hooves more solemn. A coachman with a whip sits with a middle-aged man next to him. A woman sits with her back turned to the two men, facing the cart.

There is a big white coffin.

On it, there is a big cross. It is on the lid. Straw is around. The woman, with her head bowed, supports her forehead with her hand.

The horse hurries towards the city centre. The thud of the horse's hooves still resounds. The childhood images of some carts on Vukovar roads and Grandfather's wide streets of Banat fade away. The coffin with the cross enters my eyeballs, cuts into them. It is white. I cannot remember ever seeing white coffins. Are they not the colour of natural wood or brownish? This one is white. On its lid, there is a cross, a big one.

The thud of hooves fades away.

It is May. The bloody morning painfully carries on the nightmare of the Sarajevo nights.

Cato and Carthage had touched Sarajevo. The foolish Nero enjoys the nights of my city. He really does not care that this is not Rome. He rejoices at the flames which do not

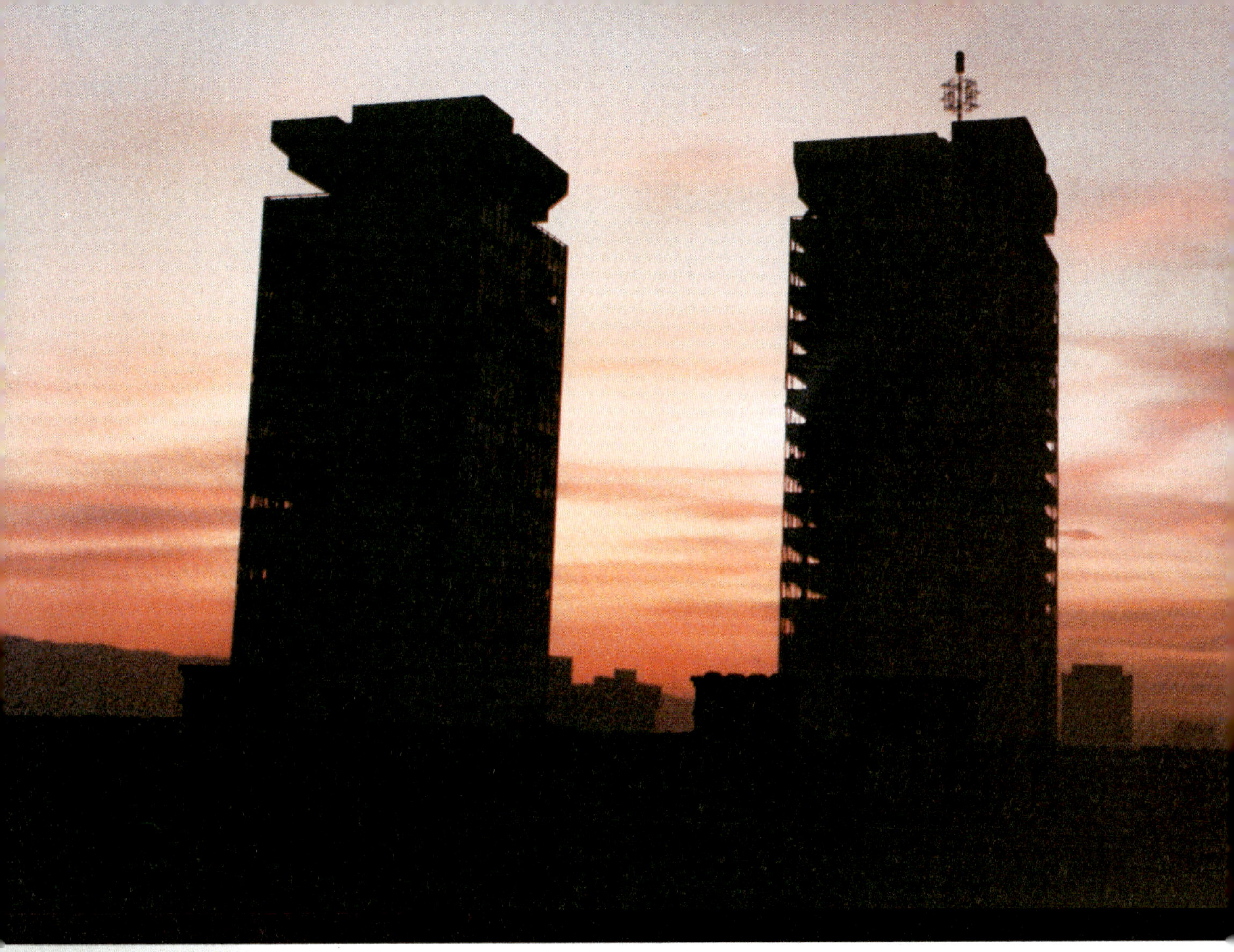

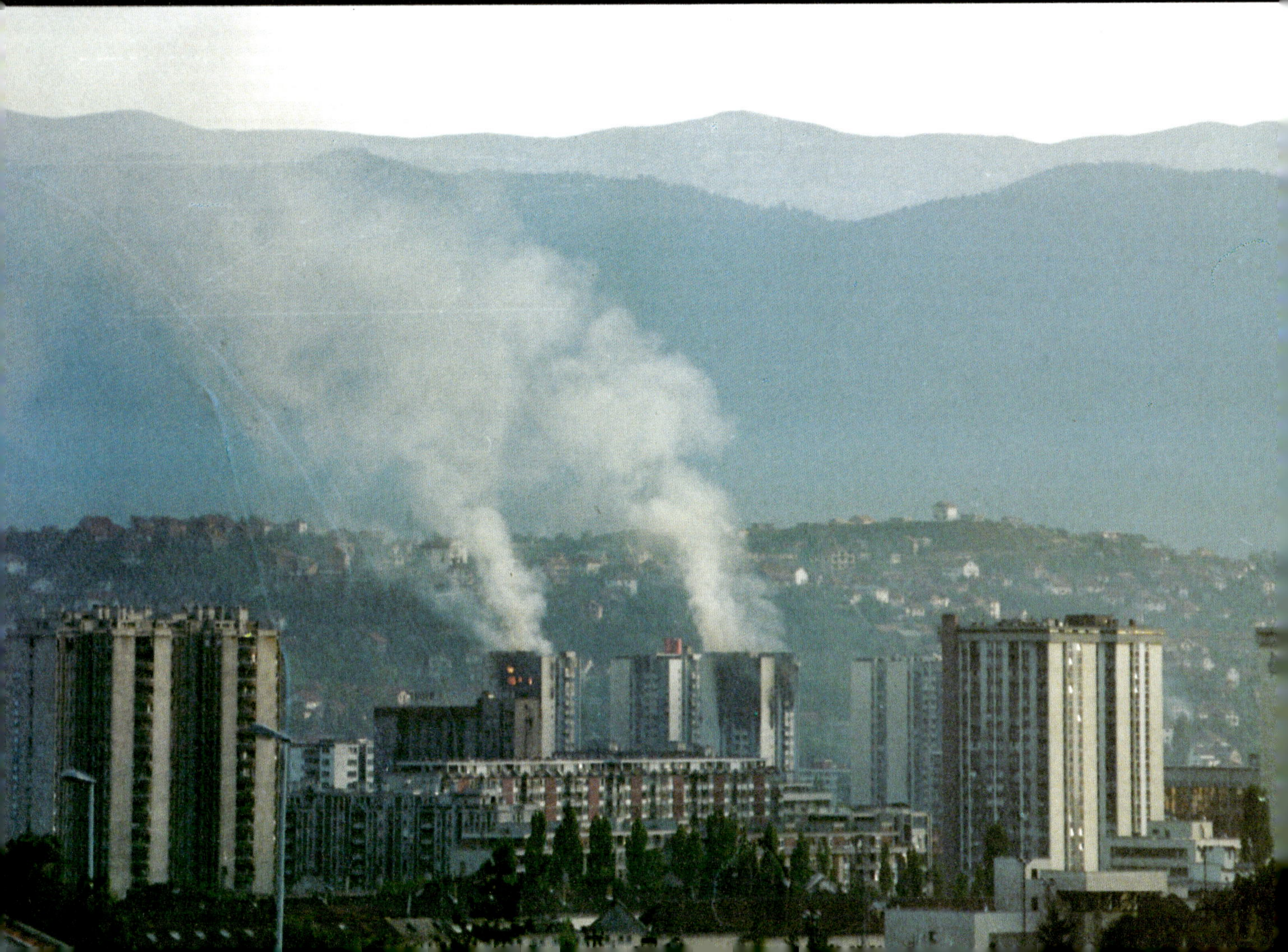

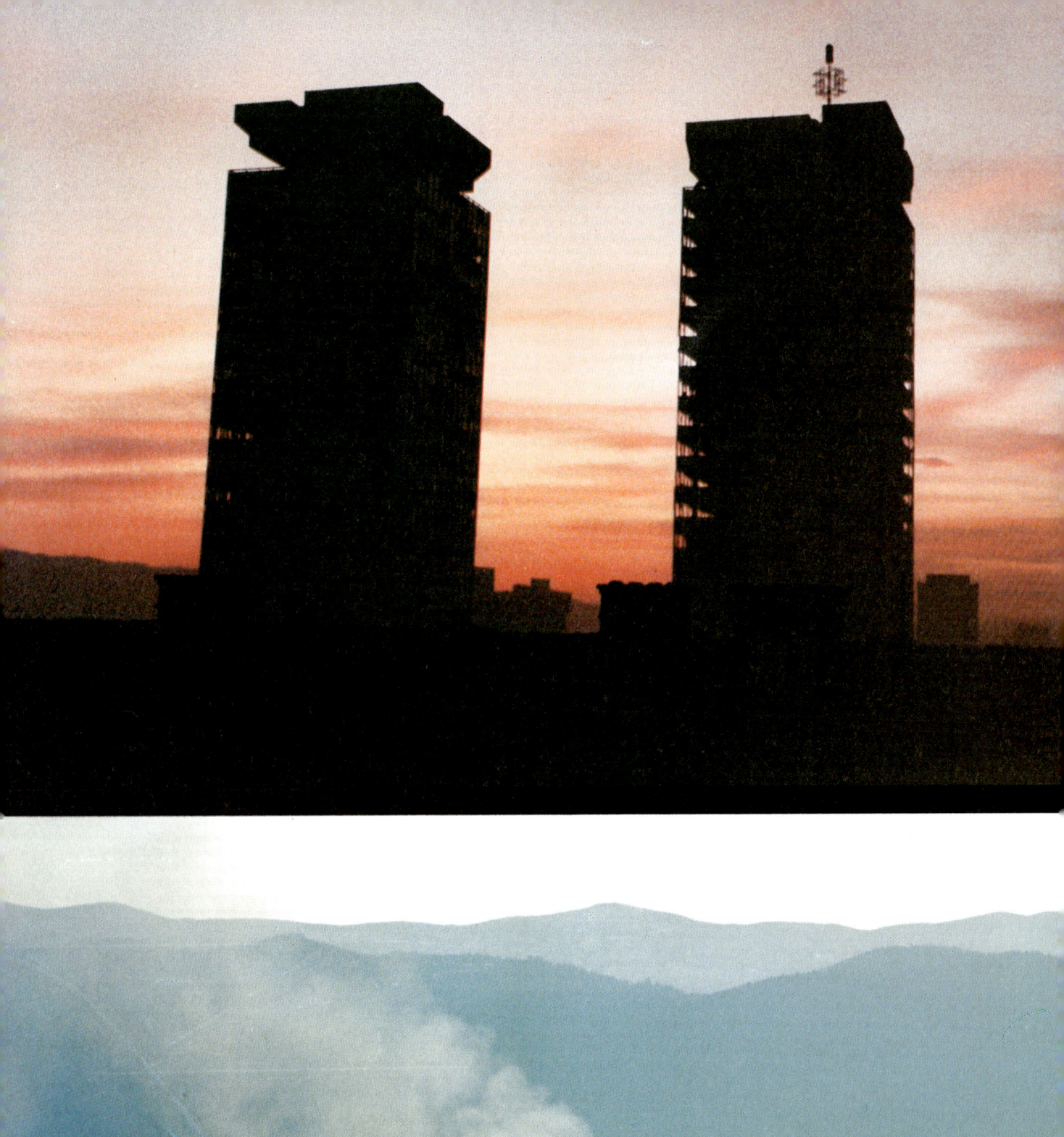

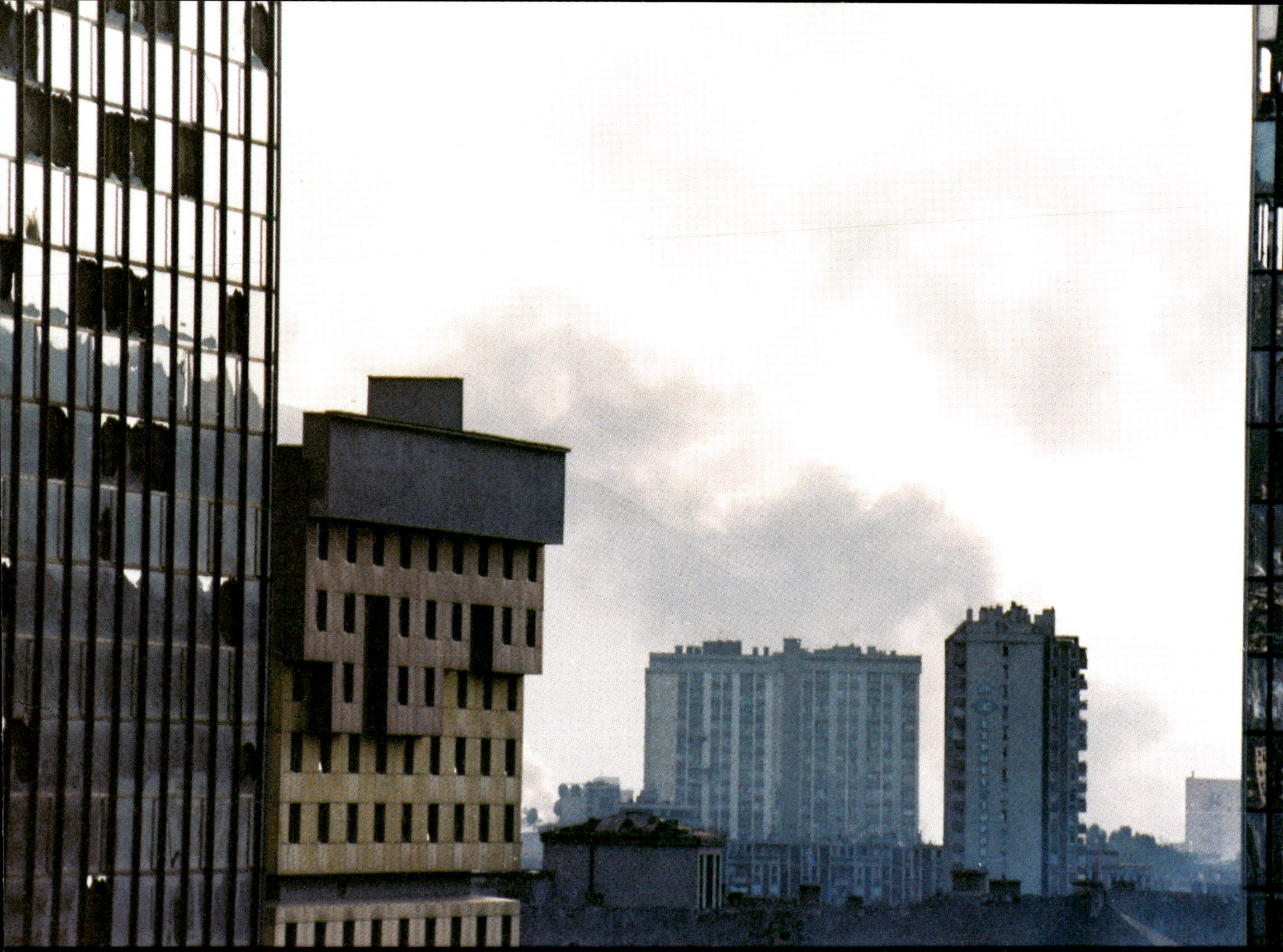

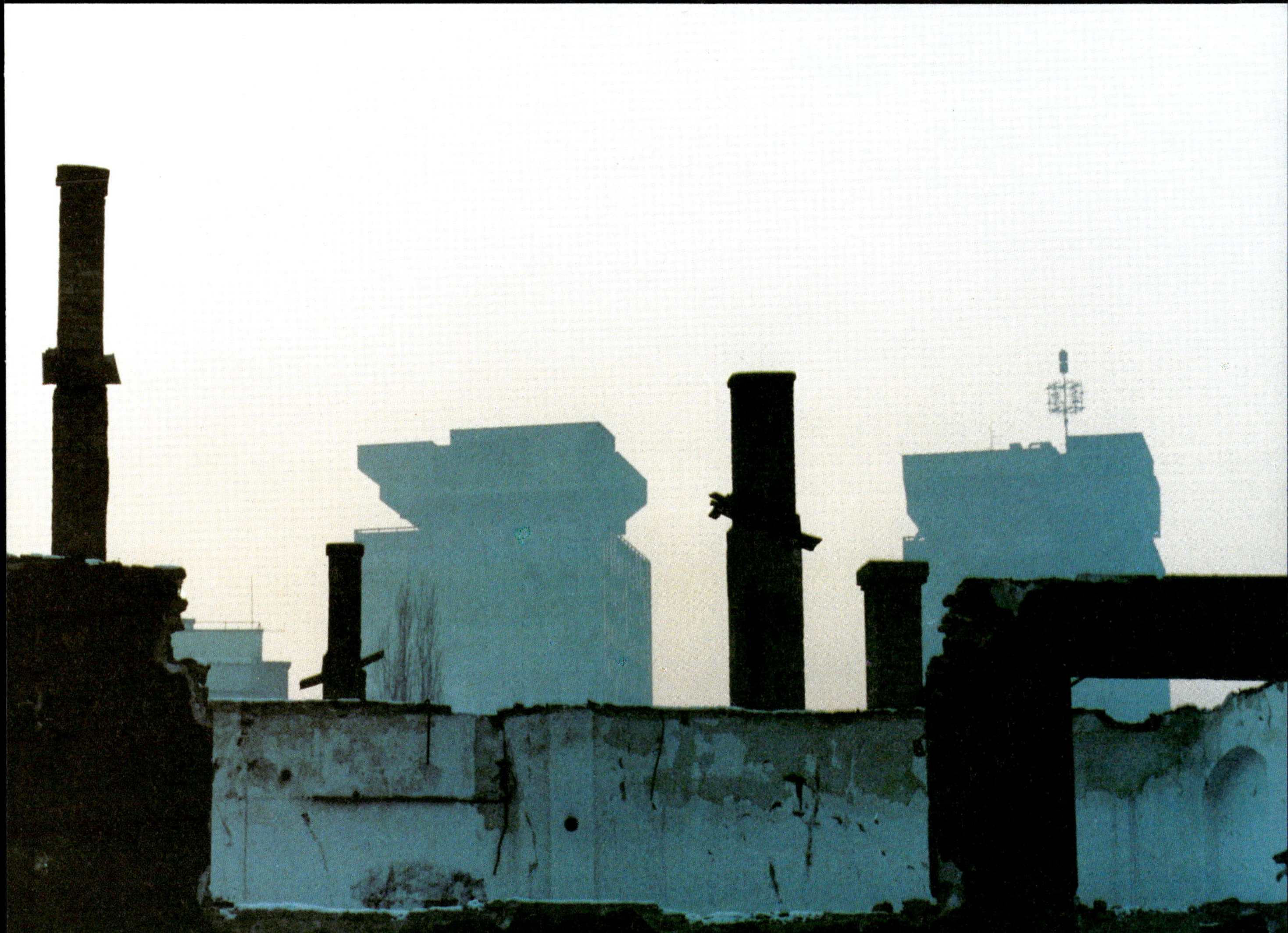

go out. The fire destroys flats, buildings, factories, institutes, places of worship, the railway station, the magnificent sports hall... The firemen are helpless, they get killed, they put out fires. There is not sufficient water and there are dozens of fires. Homes with ironed and perfumed bed linen, dusty bookshelves with books that can never and nowhere be bought again, paintings by old masters or in friends' studios, workshops where our grandmothers used to earn their living by hard work are wiped out.

It is sunny and warm in May. There are no clouds, but it pours and pours from the sky over the city. When we were small children, we used to say, happily running about, that gypsies were getting married when it rained on a sunny day. Nobody was getting married, and shells were raining down on the city. We learned about calibres of mortars, guns, tanks and multiple rocket launchers. Sarajevo became the biggest roulette game in the world. Thirty-seven numbers on its wheel changed every moment. Each shell meant an ominous loss, it hit, destroyed, killed, crippled and burned. The city was shelled without planes. The sky was clear, but deadly. We did not have to read "Dying Spring" by Zilahi. We lived and died in it. Its title became our daily routine.

The citizens saved themselves by going into shelters and basements. We crouched in the stale air and the dark. We counted the explosions. We gradually got lost in our calculations, started anew, and once again.

Circle Two of Hades never comes to an end. Some time at the end, on May 27th, blood gushed and soaked loaves of bread and ice-cream cones. Two evil roses were suddenly cut into the asphalt. They fell one after the other near the City Market, on a city mall, a spot always busy.

After roaring thunder, there was blood and screams, wailing in Vaso Miskin Crni Street. The blood suddenly coloured the pavement red, the outer walls of the buildings, stones from which bread and ice-cream were sold to long queues of men, women and children. The blood soaked into the bark of the nearby trees and the glass of the shopwindows broken long ago. "Blood everywhere... One moment, there is no blood, but the next everything is red with it... One can only wonder – where does so much blood come from?" says Neven Kazazović, a journalist who was selling newspapers that morning and who miraculously survived to be an eyewitness to the crime that took place at a kiosk some twenty metres away.

It happened before ten o'clock. The shells on the asphalt took away 17 citizens of Sarajevo, and 156 people finished up in hospital beds. Many of them in wheelchairs for ever.

And only two 82 mm shells fell.

Our colleague Muhamed Rokolj, a graphic designer, could not compose himself for days. He was pushing in the

A general danger alert going on for about ten days. Heavy shelling of Stari grad (Vasin Han, Sedrenik, Vratnik, Baščaršija), Mojmilo, Stup; the building of "Bosnaputevi" is on fire...

Friday, 12th: *Sarajevo has been without electricity and water for four days. Shelling of the city. Battles on Hrasno Hill, in Pero Kosorić Square and Mojmilo. A tank fires at "Oslobođenje". Shells fall on Kobilja glava, Velešići, Otoka, Pofalići, Koševsko brdo, Dobrinja, Alipašino polje and the narrower area of the city centre. Stari grad (the old town) is attacked from Gornja Bioska and Vasin Han, and Baščaršija from Borije and Hreša. Two foreign jurnalists injured (George Gobe, an APP Agency correspondent and Alfonso Rojo from "El Mundo" – Spain). Dr Mario Suško, a professor at the Department of English at Sarajevo University, a Dobrinja inhabitant, announces that he will commit suicide on June 15th, disappointed by the passivity of the world, which is doing nothing to deblock Sarajevo. His intention is to make the world aware of its inability to stop the war in B-H.*

Saturday, 13th: *Fourteen people killed and 125 injured in Sarajevo. Shelling of Butmir, Kotorac, Dobrinja, Stari grad (Širokača, Sedrenik, Miloš Obilić Street, Hrid), Butmir, Otoka and Mojmilo. An exchange of captured women and children. The 30th "Sarajevo Poetry Days" literary festival begins.*

Sunday, 14th: *After six days, the city gets some electricity. The remaining food thrown out of deep freezers. Bread production uncertain owing to yeast shortage. Shelling of Vasin han, Bjelave, Ciglane,*

Koševsko brdo, Hrasno. Mojmilo hill liberated from the enemy.

Monday, 15th: *The Government of B-H elected. Shells fall onto Hrid, Širokača, Vasin han, Baščaršija and Logavina Street. Antiaircraft machine guns continuously firing. Dobrinja fired at from Lukavica.*

Tuesday, 16th: *Four killed, forty-one wounded. Alija Izetbegović: "I believe that there will be intervention, but I am not sure whether it will happen in time. The events in B-H are happening very fast, while the world's organization mechanisms are slow..." Seriously injured are Ivo Štendeker, a journalist on "Mladina" and Jana Schneider (a "Sterne" and "Newsweek" correspondent). They were kidnapped by SDS terrorists. Ivo Štendeker died of haemorrhage.*

Wednesday, 17th: *Artillery and infantry battles in the locality of Osmice, Zlatište and Hrasno. Shells fall on Širokača, Dobrinja, Mojmilo, Nedžarići, Alipašino polje and Butmir. Four killed and twelve wounded in the Airport residential area. Artillery firing at Švrakino selo, Otoka and Buća potok. A sniper wounds a seven-year-old girl in Adem Buća Street. Six killed, 138 injured. The seriously wounded Jana Schneider finally released.*

same queue with a bag and wallet to buy bread. "It exploded unrealistically," he said. "Suddenly there is nobody around me. All of them are lying. I stand up. Blood, bits of human bodies, screams. They all lie. I touch myself, I rub my eyes, I touch myself again.

"And then I start to run. I run along the street. I run as fast as I can. Next to me, I notice, Neven is also running. We do not look back.

"He glances at me, he stops after two or three hundred metres. He peers at my leather jacket, at my right shoulder. He asks me if anything hurts. He looks at my shoulder.

"'No', I reply.

"I touch my shoulder where he is looking.

"'Brains', he tells me.

"'What?'

"'There are some brains on your shoulder. Human brains.'

"I touch my head, my shoulder. Only my lower leg hurts, it bleeds.

"A part of somebody's brain has been on my shoulder."

Each day we wrote another story about that massacre, the evil that befell us. I recognized Nero and Cato walking through Circle Two. The faces of others were in the dark. Bullets tirelessly buzzed at crossroads. The snipers were not inactive. The eyes and breath of gunmen were behind curtains. They shot at everything that moved. They laid their gifts onto the altar of death.

The timetable of dying was getting more condensed. We were disappearing with the city. Nero's disciples took away from a burned up crowd what we could not lay into coffins. We will drag it like a heavy Calvary cross of our times, like a tabut (lidless Muslim coffin) up a steep cliff in a funeral march without an escort that makes it easier for the bearer to carry the burden.

The Institute for Oriental Studies was irretrievably destroyed. The building itself is unimportant. Its passages in the attic are irrelevant. They do not constitute treasure. They only guard it. They sometimes do not succeed even in that. All the sorted out material and manuscripts in oriental languages were destroyed by fire. They had not been destroyed by hundreds of earlier fires that had razed Sarajevo over the centuries. They grew, being enlarged over decades by the care of dozens of scholars since 1950 and by being kept in the manuscript collection, the archives and the library. The fire unified the earlier efforts and care and scattered items. They ceased to exist in a May night, one of the richest manuscript collections in the Balkans, containing 5,263 codices. It contained manuscripts from history, politics, theology, geography, Islamic philosophy and Sufism, manuscripts of the Koran and Hadiths, divans – collections of poems by our own and Ottoman authors, encyclopaedias. Each manuscript was unique. The oldest preserved manus-

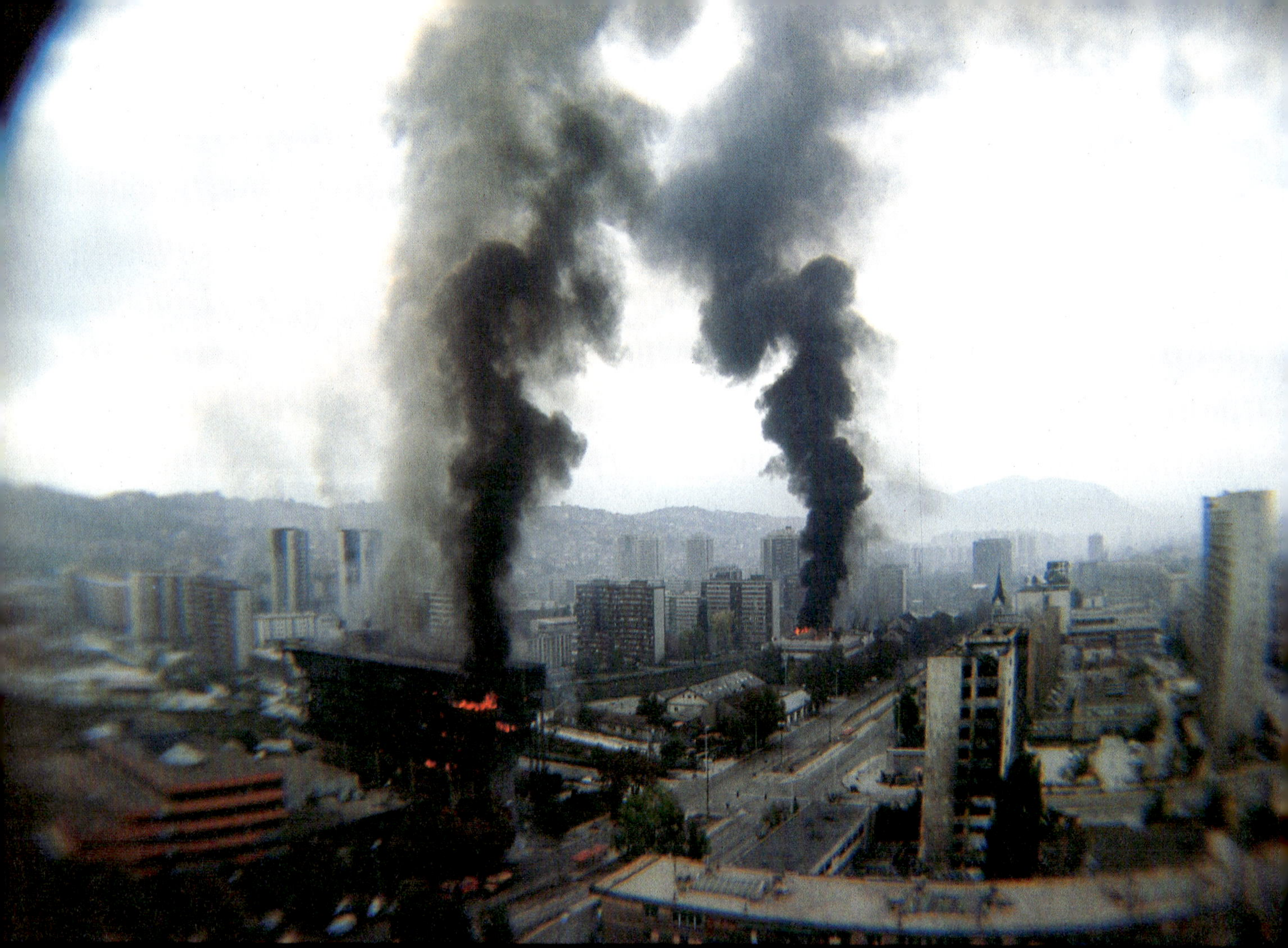

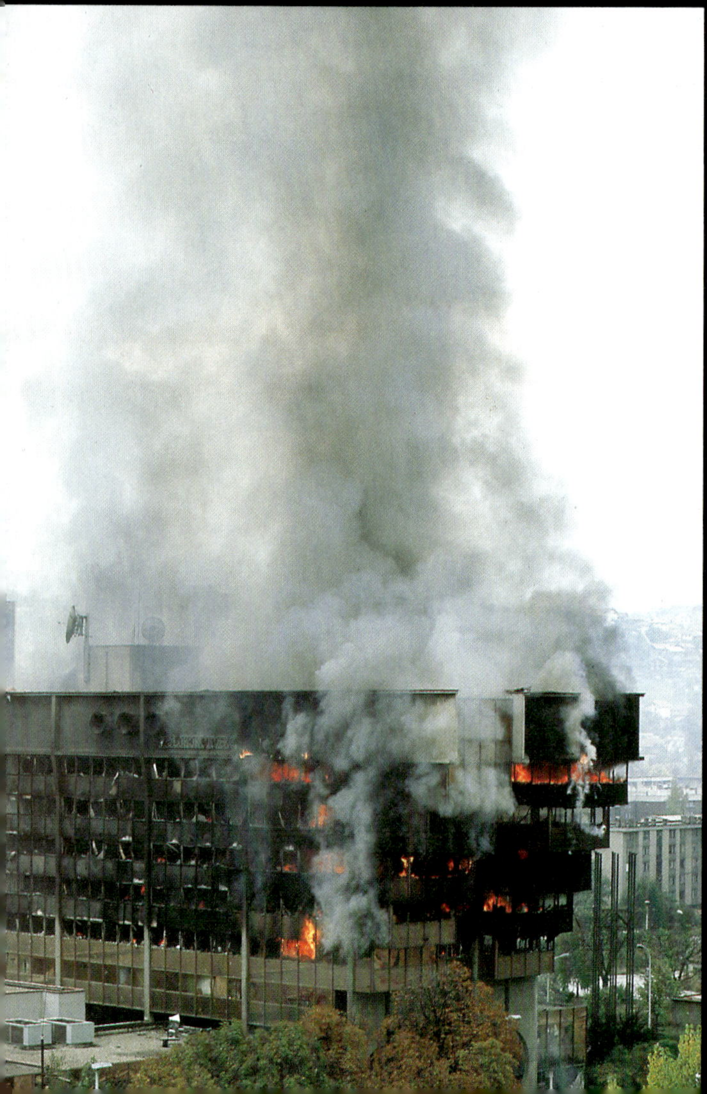

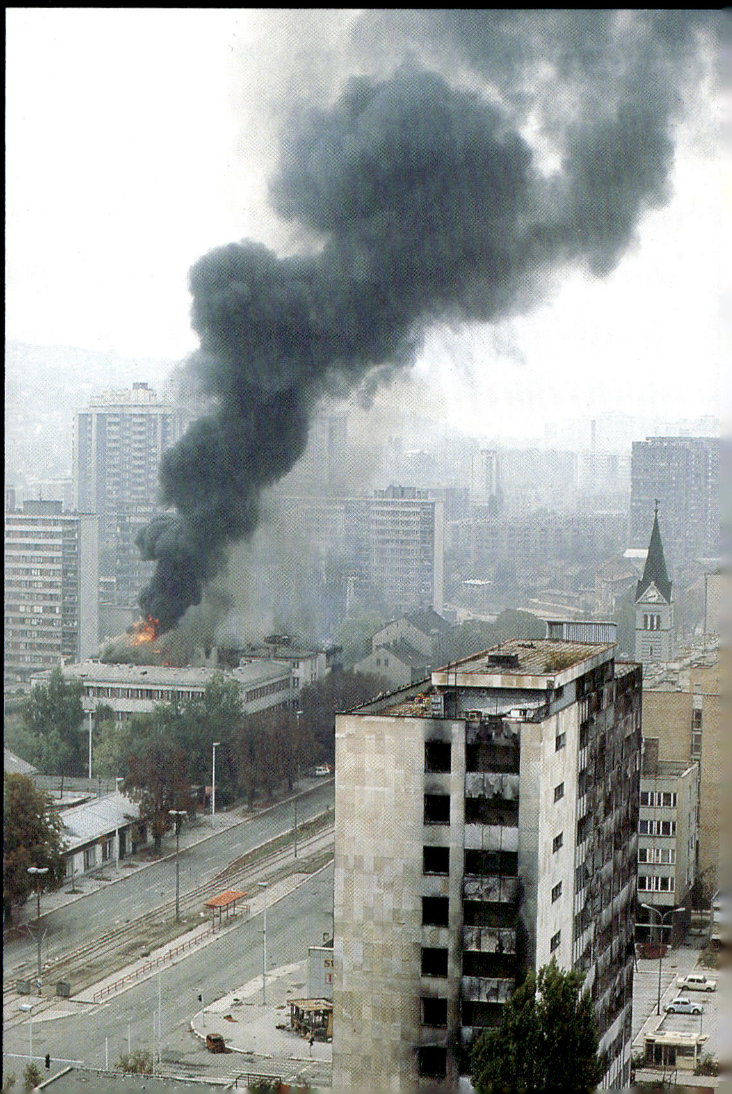

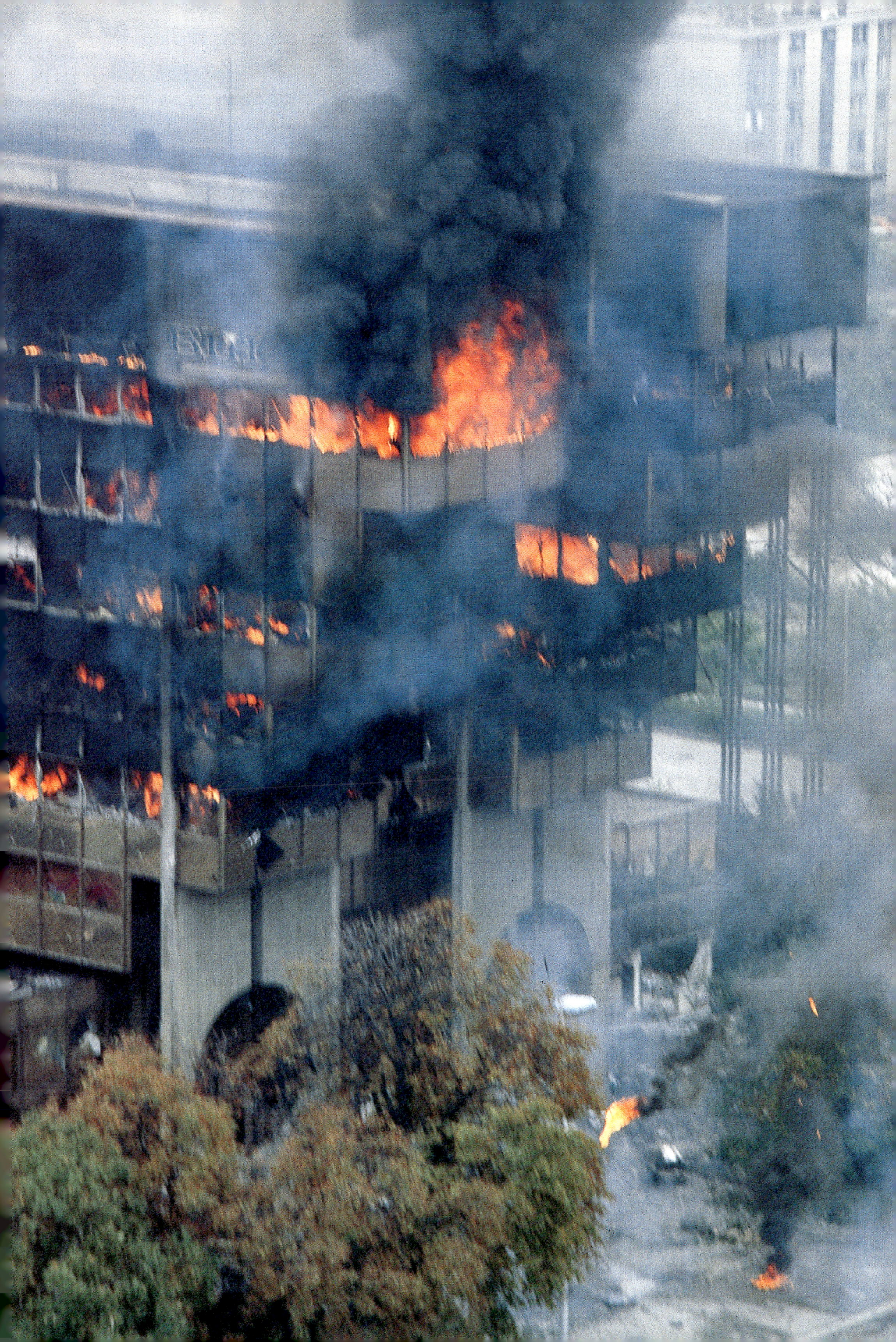

cript dated back to 1204. It contained 263 sheets written by Ahmed b. "Abdullah oa Qaíd Abu Shuga" as-Salhy copying a work of Shari'a from the second half of the tenth century. Irretrievably destroyed was also a fragment of an astrological paper illustrated with miniatures. The miniatures represented the zodiac signs. It was one of the best known. There were also the works of Hasan Kaimija, Ibrahim Munib Pruščak, Mustafa Muhlisija, Sheikh Jujo, Omer Novaljanin, Mehmed Mejlija, Muhamed Musić Allamek, Ahmed Mostarac, Muhamed Nerkesi, Salih Sidki Hadžihuseinović Muvekkit, and many others.

The archives of the Institute for Oriental Studies consisted of four collections: Manuscripta turcica, The Collection of Sigils, The Vilayet Archives and The Collection of Deeds. They were a mirror of the long Ottoman rule over these countries. Manuscripta turcica had more than 7,000 documents. Original fermans (orders or decrees) and barats (charters) from the 16th to 19th centuries of extraordinary artistic value had been preserved. Those imperial orders and charters were decorated by sultan's horses' tails (tugovi or tuzi). The barats (charters) of Muhamed IV from 1604, Mustafa III from 1757 and Selim III from 1802 excelled with their artistic value. That collection also possessed orders of Bosnian valis (governors), deeds, court verdicts, excerpts from summary records (defters), financial documents, etc.

Thursday, 18th: Bernard Henri Levy, a French philosopher, Jules Herzog, a writer and a journalist, and Filip Dustija Blazije, a member of the European Parliament, arrive in Sarajevo. Battles in the Airport residential area. Ten people die, their throats cut. The City Hospital (earlier the Military Hospital) – the target of an artillery attack (floors 4–12 damaged). Thirty marriages registered in the Centre municipality since the beginning of the war. Mehmed Husić, editor-in-chief of "Svijet", his wife and two children are captured by SDS terrorists and taken away from their flat in an unknown direction.

Friday, 19th: In the Airport residential area, the enemy kill 40 people by cutting their throats. Battles in

Dobrinja and Alipašino polje residential areas. Artillery firing at Buća potok, "Pavle Goranin" residential area, Čengić vila (from Lukavica and Nedžarići), Vojničko polje, the "Oslobođenje" building (hit by 30 shells), Hrasno hill, Pofalići, Velešići, M. Tito Street, Ciglane, King Tomislav Street, Bare, Jerčedoli, Bistrik, Vasin han, Logavina Street and Baščaršija. The Presidency and UNPROFOR (Stjepan Kljujić and Colonel Grey) sign an agreement by which Sarajevo Airport is to be taken over by UN forces (after the withdrawal of the ex-JNA units which had occupied it). Midhat Ajanović's exhibition of caricatures opens.

Saturday, 20th: *The Presidency of the Republic proclaims a state of war. Serbia, Montenegro, the JNA and the SDS terrorists are defined in a preamble as the aggressors. A general mobilization on the whole territory of B-H. Working hours from 7 a.m. to 7 p.m. compulsory for all employed in B-H. The Presidency functions as the supreme Command of the Armed Forces of the Republic of B-H. The "Oslobođenje" skyscraper burns down, having been hit for several hours by artillery shells fired from Nedžarići and the Airport. The premises of the "ŠIPAD" company and the Credit Bank were destroyed, i.e. six upper floors of the skyscraper near Stup and four floors in the direction of the centre of the town. Shells fired at Vojničko polje. A hundred and eighty tons of food, medicines and water arrive as a present from the "Équilibre", a French humanitarian organization.*

The collection of sigils contained 66 complete records of qadis (Muslim judges) from all around Bosnia and Herzegovina during the Ottoman rule and several fragmentary ones.

The Vilayet Archives made up the largest part of the Archives. They housed about 200,000 documents of the vilayet administration ranging from those forwarded to or received from lower administrative units to documents of the central government in Istanbul.

Tapijas (public documents on the ownership of land) from the last century were kept in a special collection. All the Bosnian qadiliks (areas under a qadi's authority) were registered in there with the owners' names and the quality and area of the land owned. It was a sort of a directory of owners and a map of Bosnia and Herzegovina based on the land owners from the last century.

These original documents went up in flames. The library housing more than ten thousand volumes directly or indirectly related to Oriental studies was also consumed. A wealth of photocopies and microfilm of material taken in the world's archives from the 15th and the 16th centuries was also destroyed. These documents without which we shall be permanently poorer were irretrievably gone. Unfortunately, they cannot be replaced, collected again, written, or allowed to get old. We have lost them for ever. Some consolation, in those days, were the words of Dr Srdjan Janković. He had borrowed two oriental manuscripts which had remained with him. He did not take them back although he had been warned to. The absentminded professor was fortunately late, which saved the manuscripts. Had there been more negligent readers of the originals, some more might have survived, too. The fiery door of Sarajevo had closed behind us. We withstood this round as well.

We have not memorized any of the past. Oblivion has covered the remote witnessing of the destruction of these Bosnian books as heresy by the campaigns of many different inquisitors. We do not have to believe the Benedictine abbot Orbiny's claim that Sultan Mehmed El Fatih, after the conquest of Jajce and the fall of Bosnia, killed all the Bosnian noblemen who accepted his invitation for consultations. He also burned up all their documents. This claim of Orbiny's is confirmed by the fact that the archives of the Bosnian Court Office and of the Kotromanić dynasty have never been found. Neither have any of the charters which would, by their contents, open the door to mediaeval Bosnia and the over three hundred years of the state. It was fire that was a judge at that time, too.

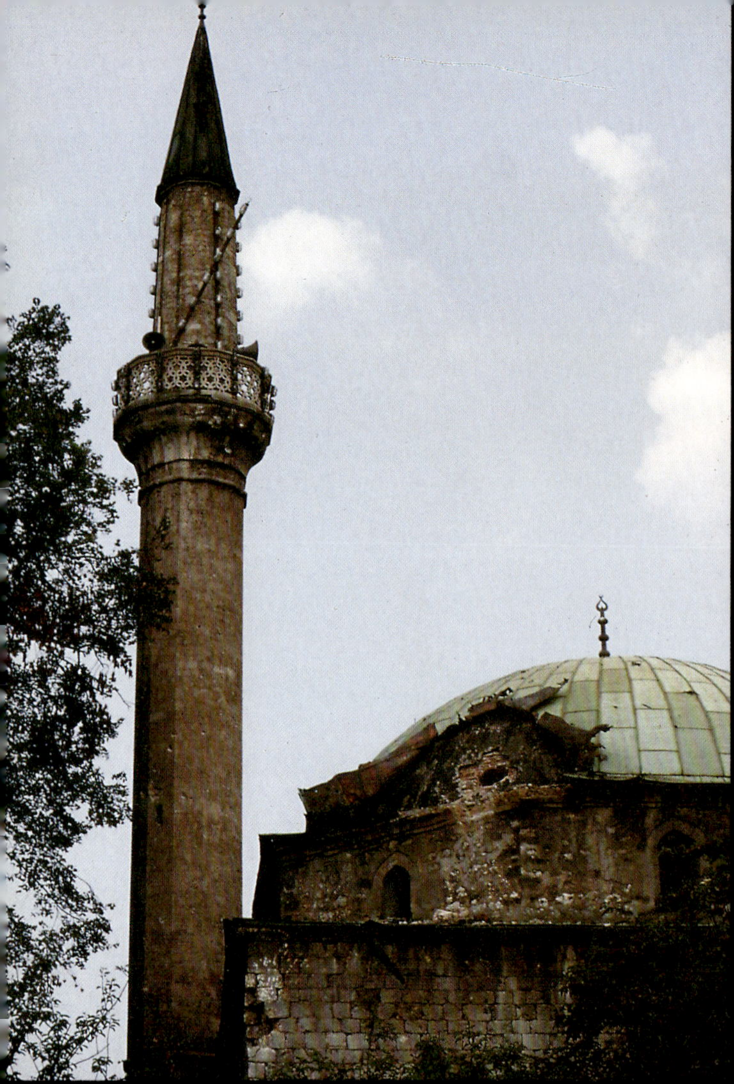
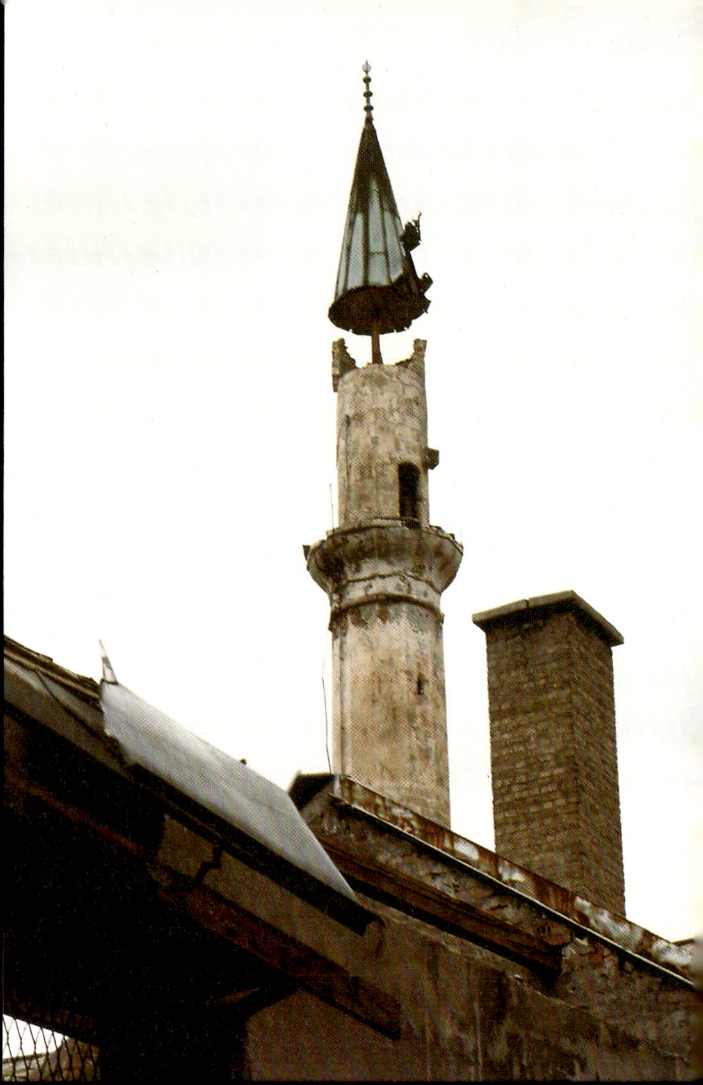
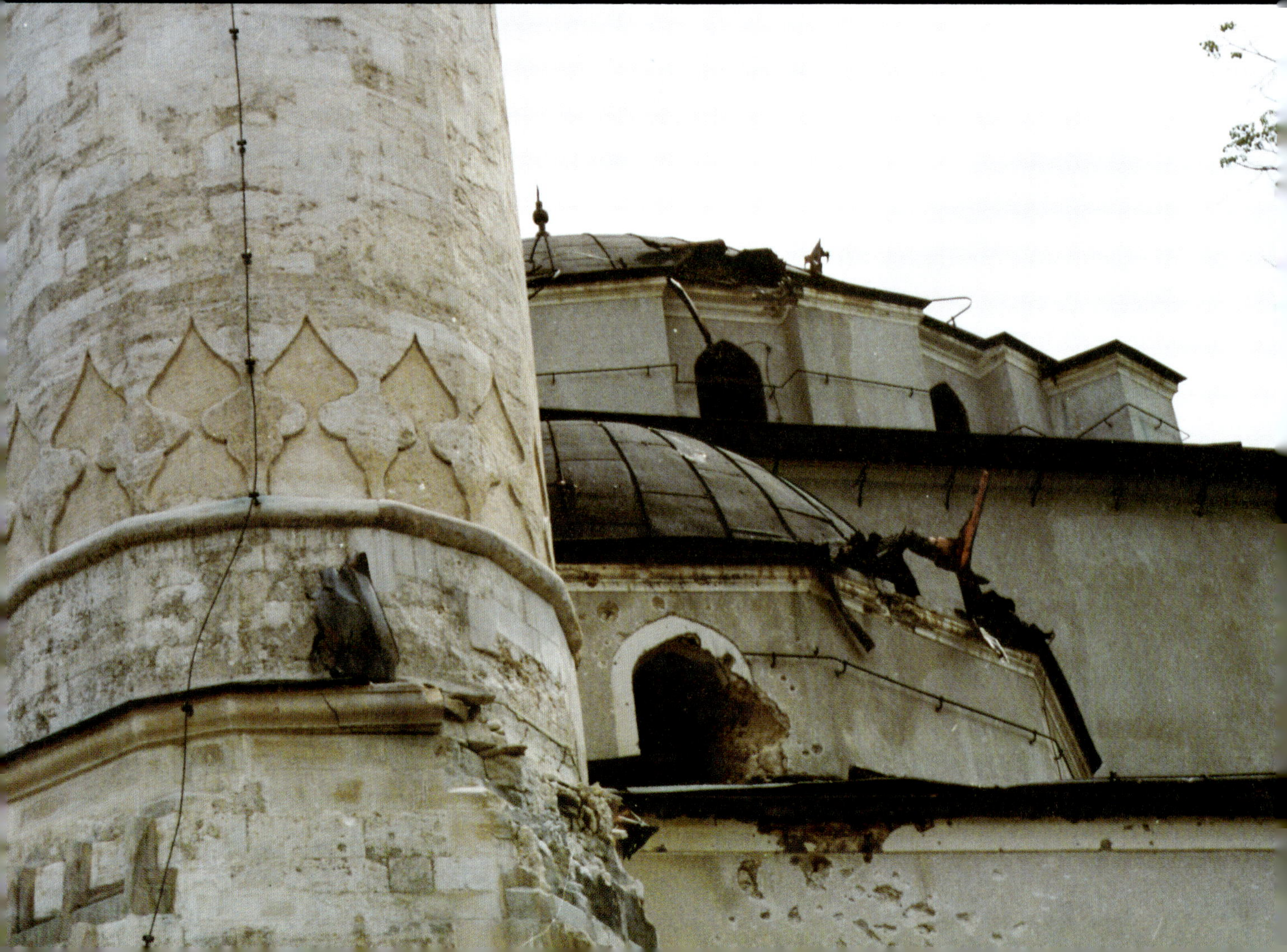

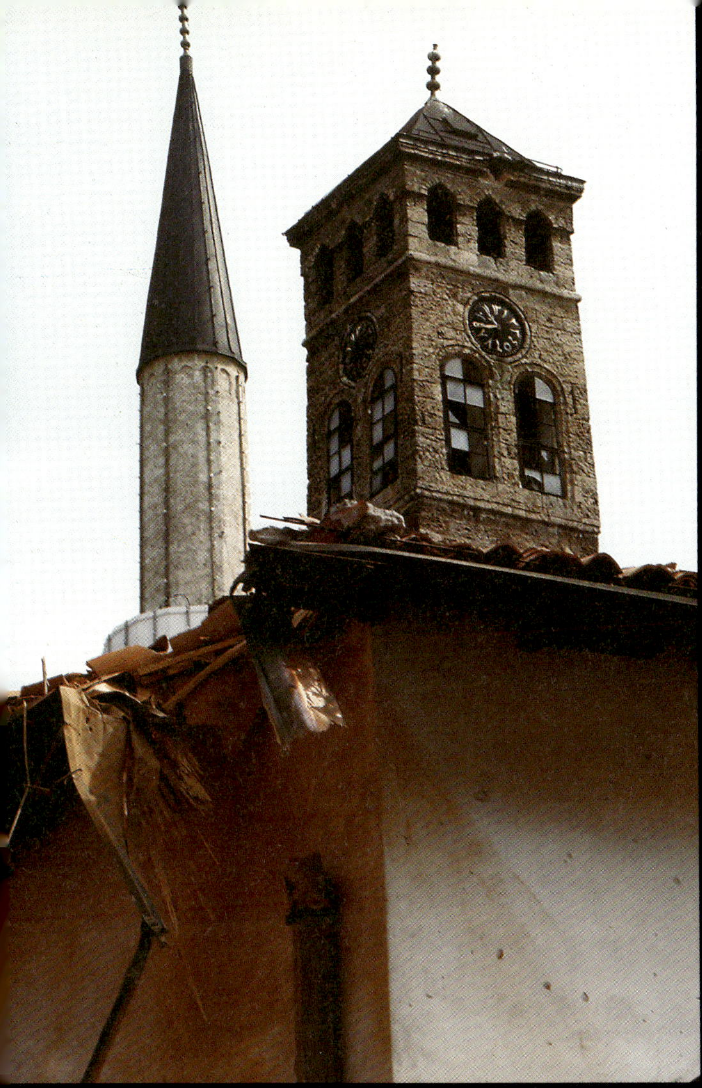

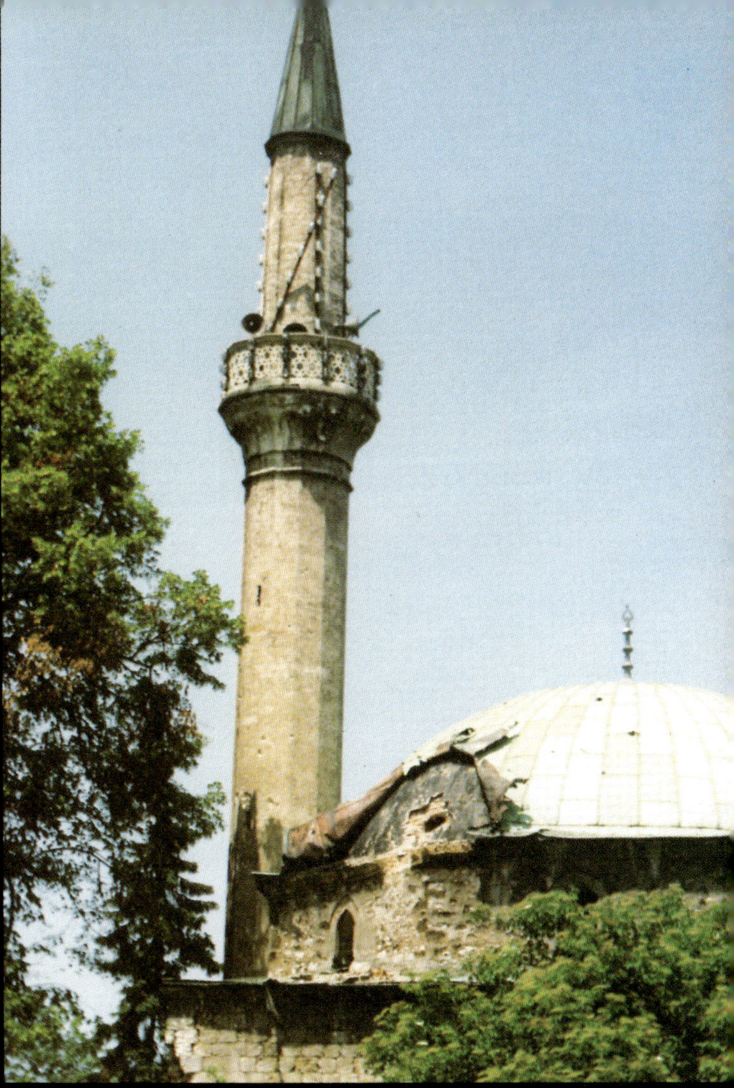

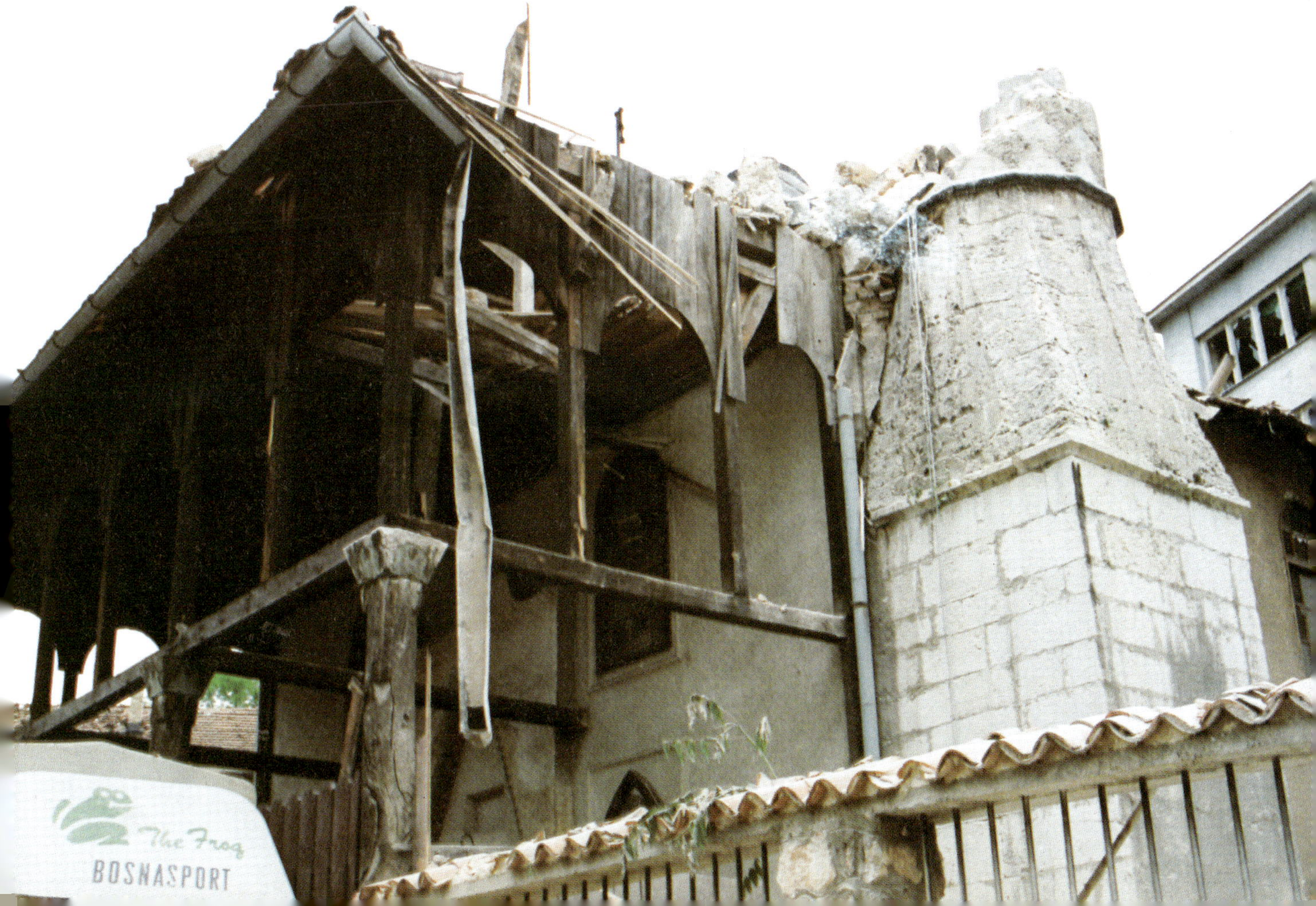
The Frog
BOSNASPORT

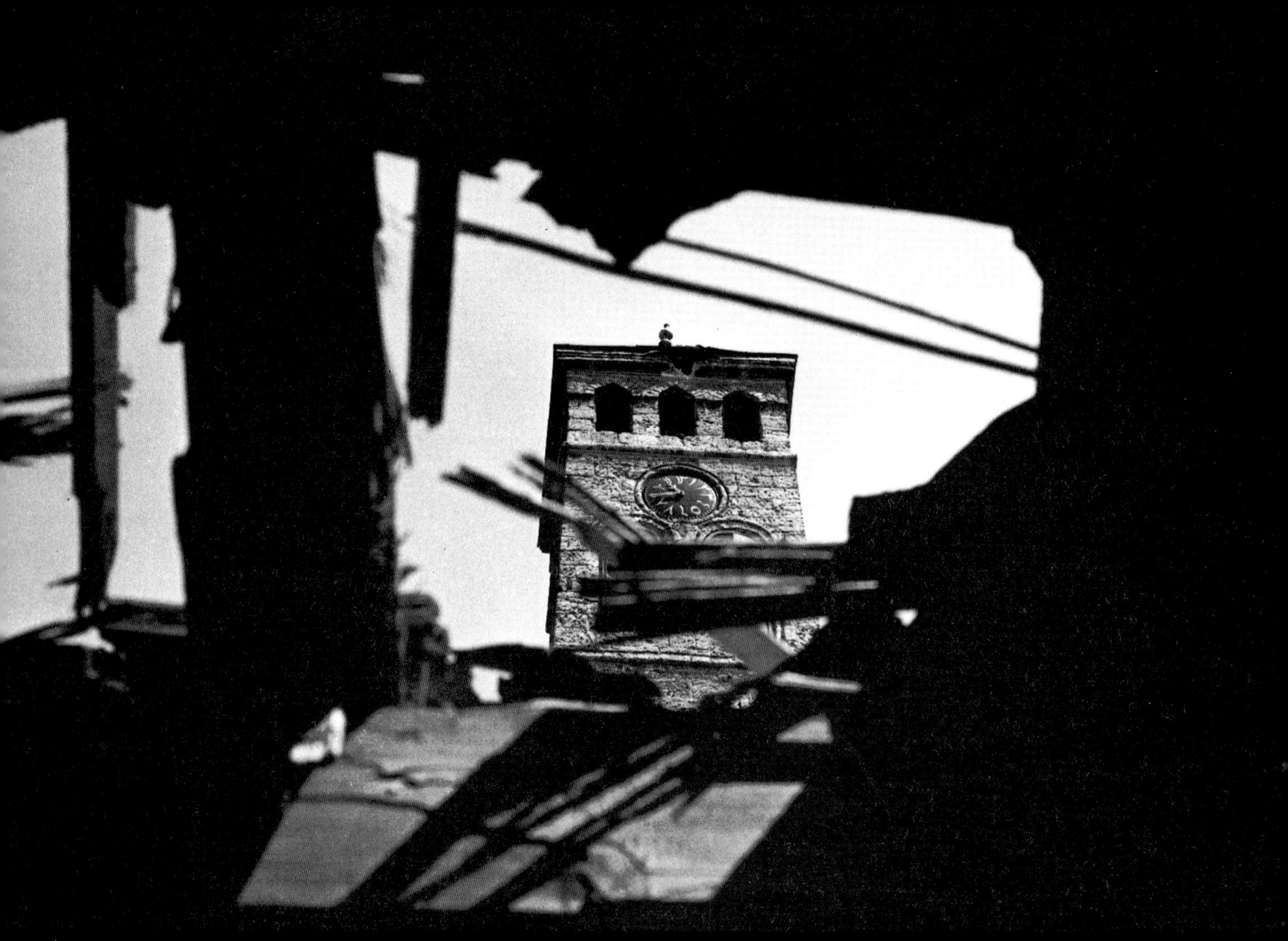

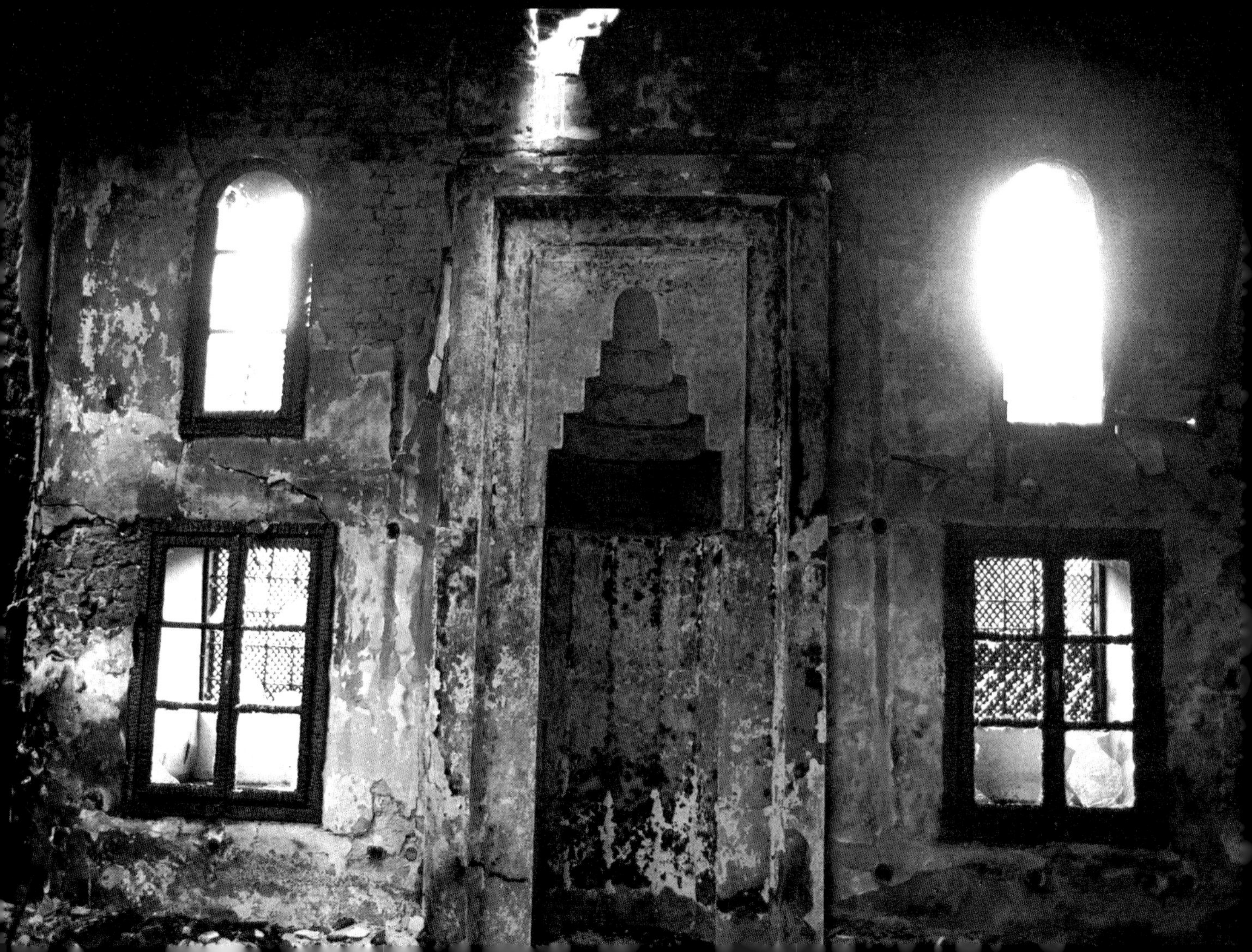

CIRCLE THREE

Sunday, 21st: Shelling of Dobrinja (together with an artillery-infantry attack), Stari grad (the "Moris Moco Salom" Elementary School), the Brewery of Sarajevo, a mosque in Logavina Street, Širokača, Hotonj, Ugorsko, Kobilja glava, Koševsko brdo, Butmir and Marijin Dvor... Killed by shell fragments was Saša Lazarević, 25, a Sarajevo TV reporter, the man who was the first to take photographs in the early morning hours of the March barricades in Sarajevo.

Monday, 22nd: The order about mobilization and the decision proclaiming the state of war printed on the front page of "Oslobođenje". Sarajevo covered with blood. Nineteen people killed and 96 injured – as a result of the shelling. Thirty-six of the injured are taken to the City Hospital, 18 to the Orthopaedic Clinic and 42 to the Traumatology Clinic. Shells fired at M. Tito, Radić and Šenoa Streets, the locality of the City Dairy, Miss Irby Street and Marijin Dvor. Alija Kućukalić, (born in 1937 in Sarajevo), a sculptor and a professor of sculpture at the Academy of

I withstood Circle Two, Dante. It abounded with fire and shelling. Statistics counted 50,000 shells fired at the city. Four thousand tons was sent by mortars, tanks, howitzers, and guns. One square kilometre of Sarajevo took 4,700 shells.

How could I, then, remember all that multitude of images and persons I faced. I shook with a fever caused by a drama of the convoy of despair. A column of children with mothers ten kilometres long was held as stakes in a political gambling house at Ilidža for three days. They served as hostages in a dirty game. They showed us that we could not leave this place either, even when we only tried to send away our children and women. Nobody close to me was among those five, seven, or ten thousand fellow citizens who were fleeing this hell. Nobody close to me, but still they were all mine. The city was leaving itself. Its youth went in search of some new sun. We were condemned to imprisonment and dying.

Shells destroyed the city's maternity hospital. The city's cradle was destroyed. At that moment, there were 70 new-born babies in it. There were 130 women; some had already had their babies, while others were waiting to become mothers. The place where the life of the city starts was destroyed. We all, with faces lit up with joy, daily left that building on a hill, with a warmth of the future citizens of Sarajevo.

I had stepped into a camp. The largest concentration camp in the world locked its gates. It had gradually become so since the beginning of April. They did not let us find our way. Suddenly, the whole place was shut off, locked and cemented. I slipped within its cold walls and barbed wire. I stayed there as a prisoner through all the other circles. I did not even try to get out. I could not see the number on my back. I did not roll up the sleeve on my left upper arm, either. I was not interested whether it had been tattooed and when, or how many figures it consisted of. I am not sure I would have withstood it had I known, at that moment, what it really bordered on. I wonder whether I would have even wanted to try. There are few of us who would have thought differently. For me, those were only barricades, some masked men, automatic rifles across their chests, cartridge belts and sand bags.

I stirred up the beliefs of others that all this would last only for a short time, only for a short time, a very short time. Others lived on in the same way. They did not accept that the time we lived in would last. The border of civilian society, travelling, the European way of life was behind us. It moved away gradually. We believed we had apparitions, we were covered in mist. It moved away faster and faster, further and further. Our city–amphitheatre has always been rimmed with hills, fog, clouds, rain and snow. Now it is chained up. We could not get out of it. We all suddenly

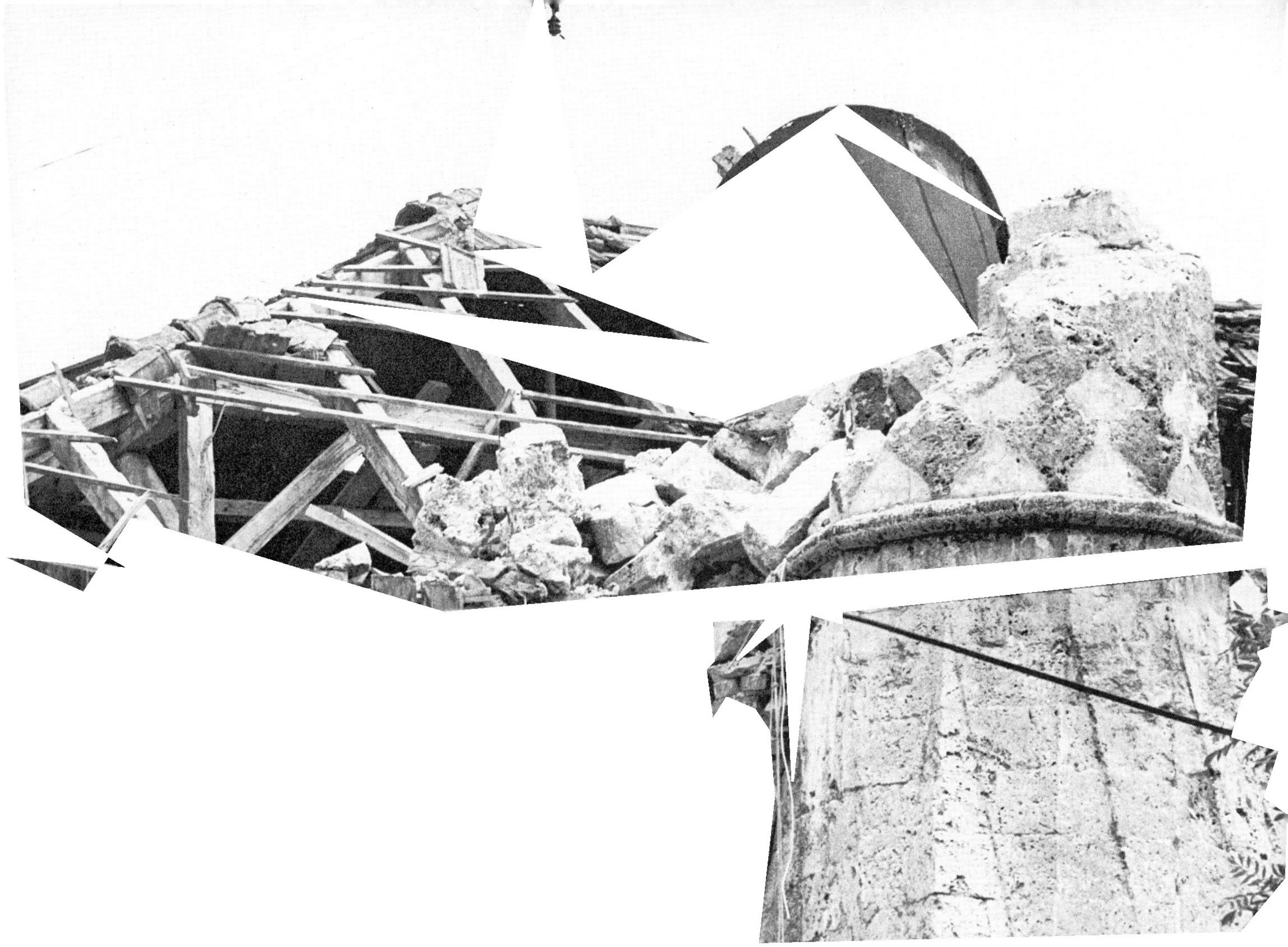

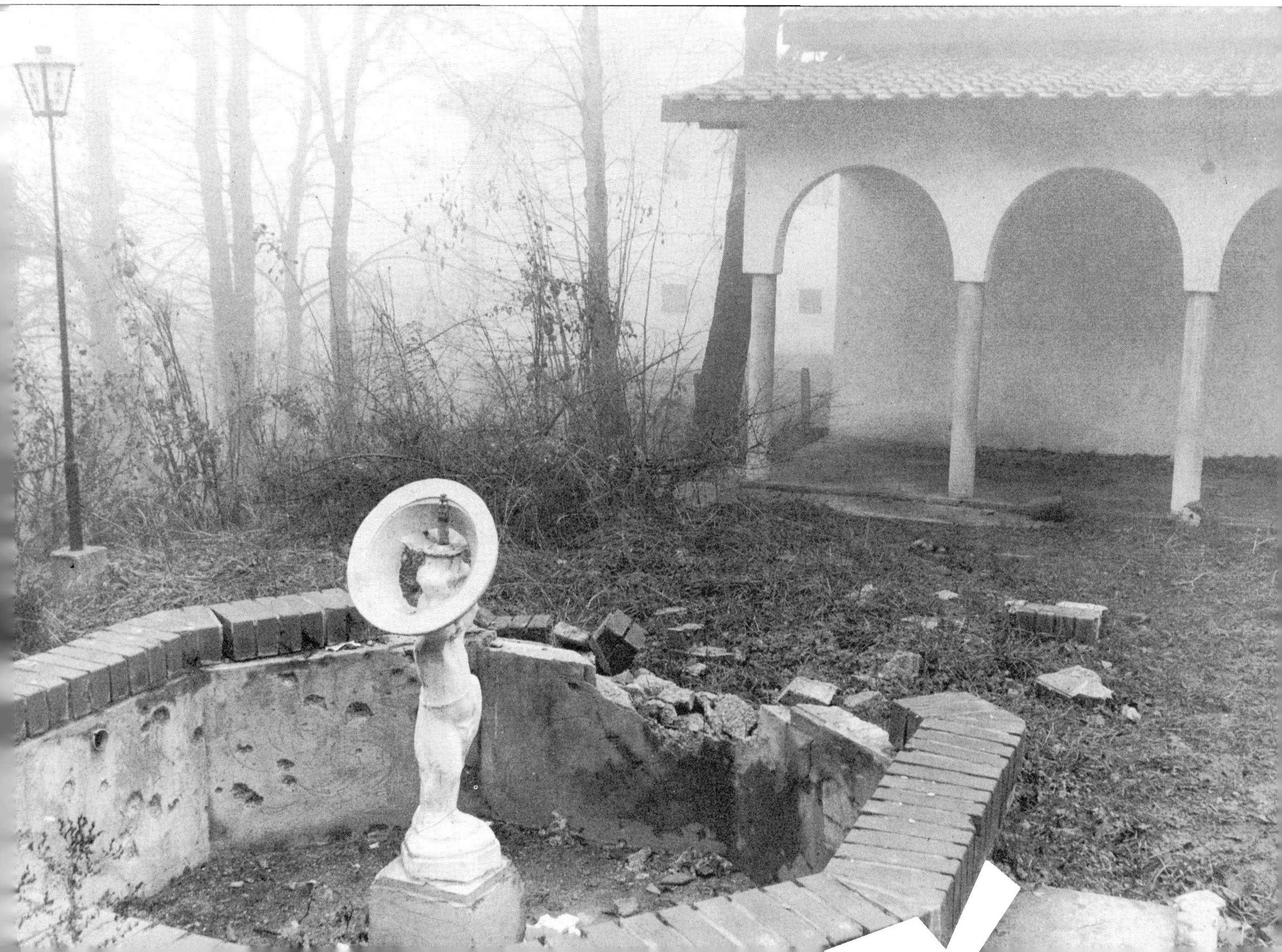

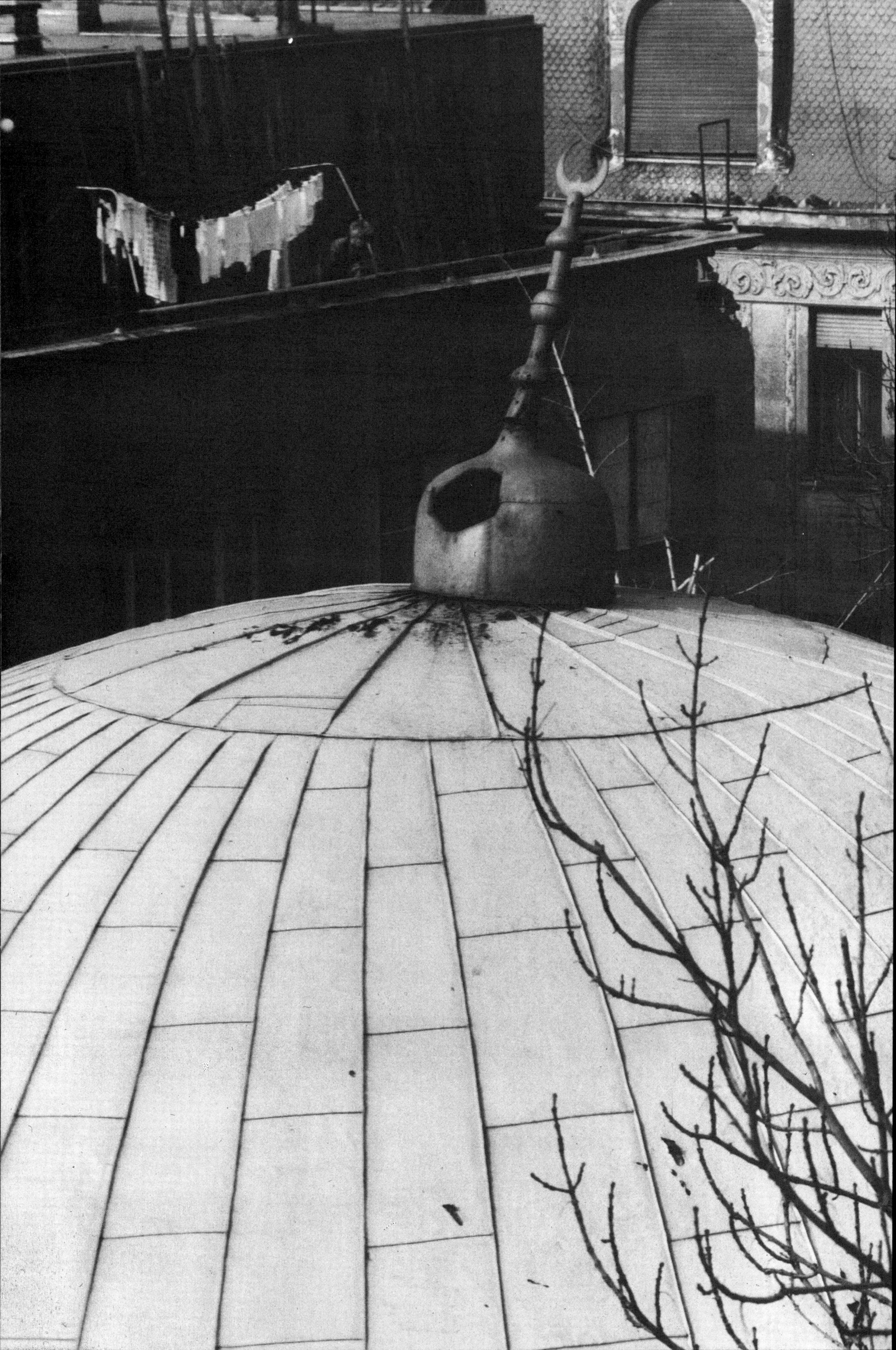

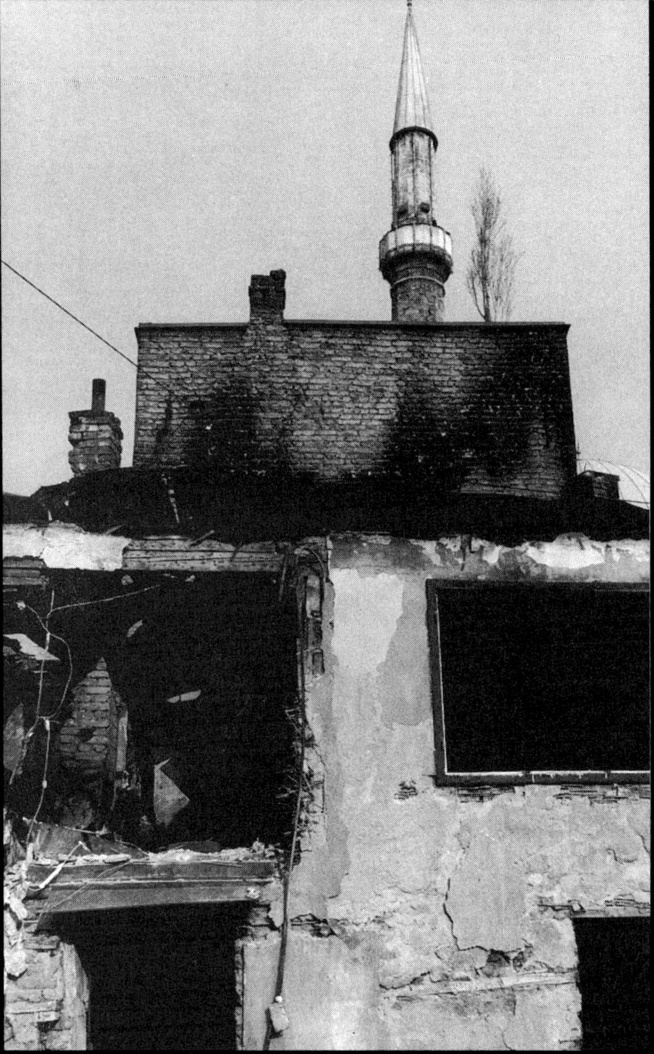

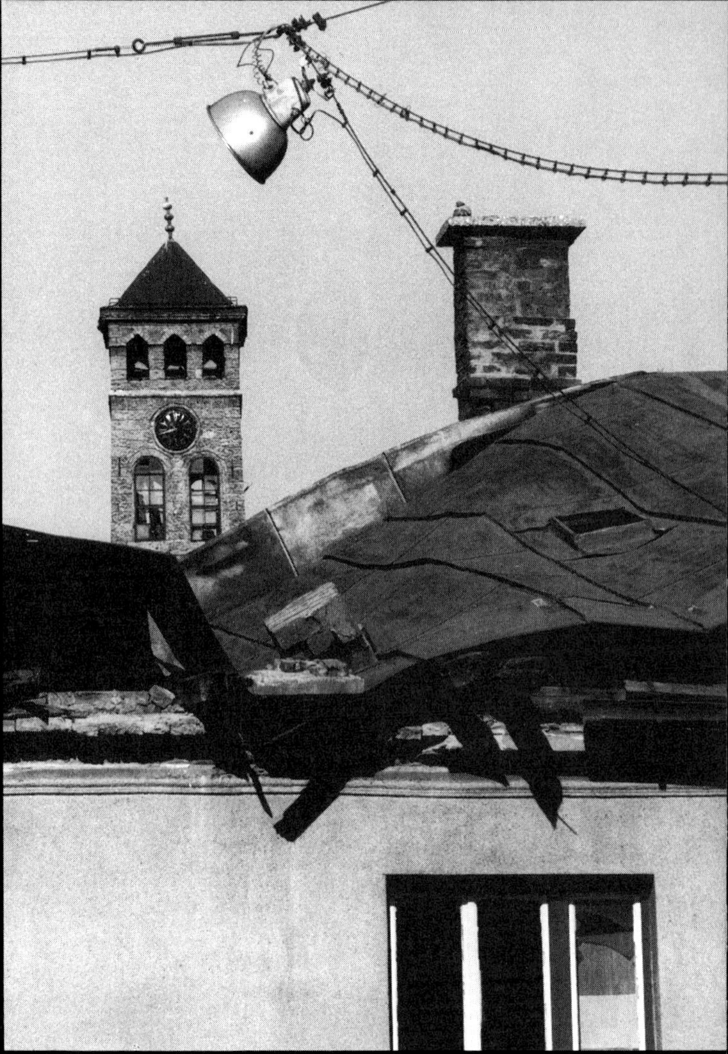

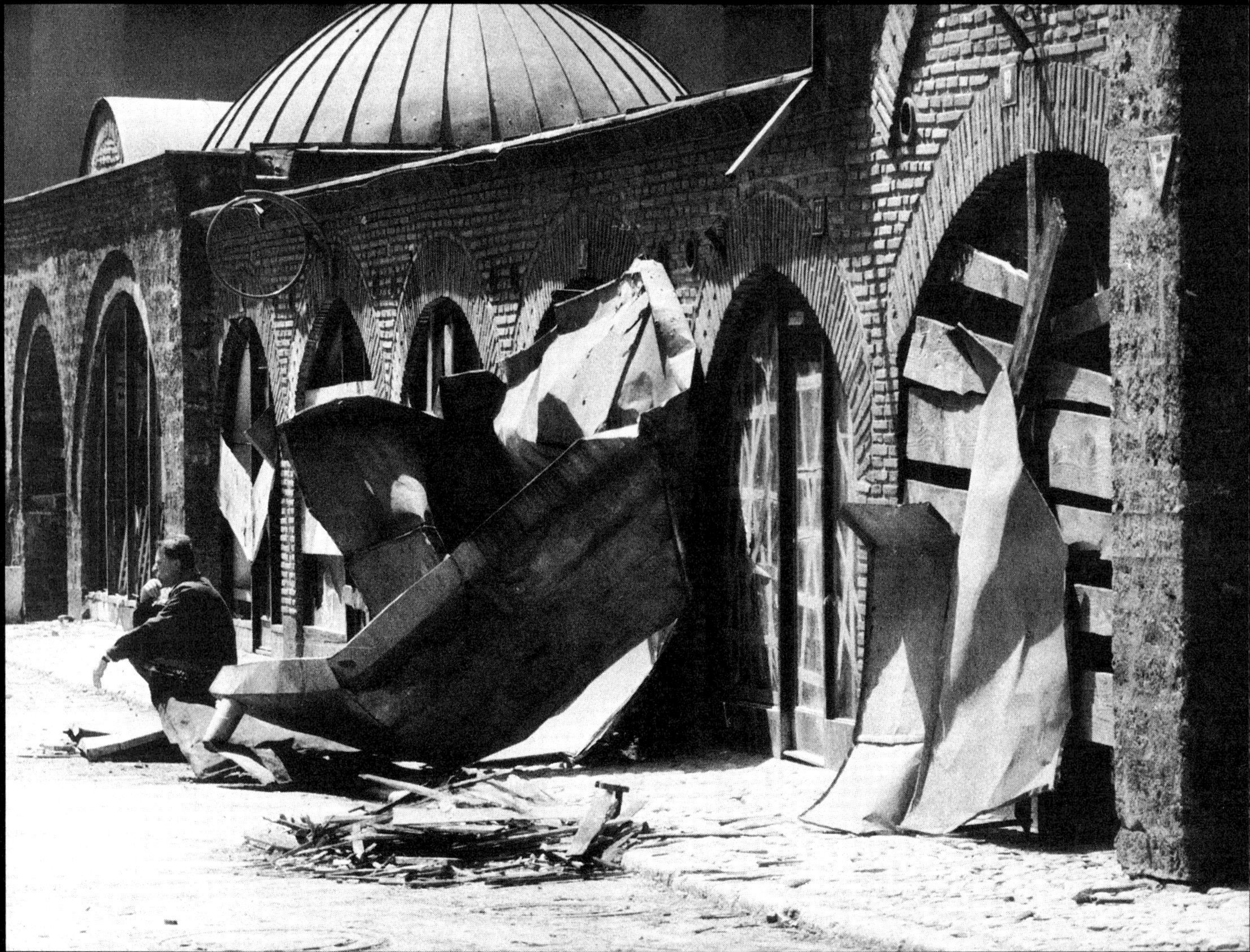

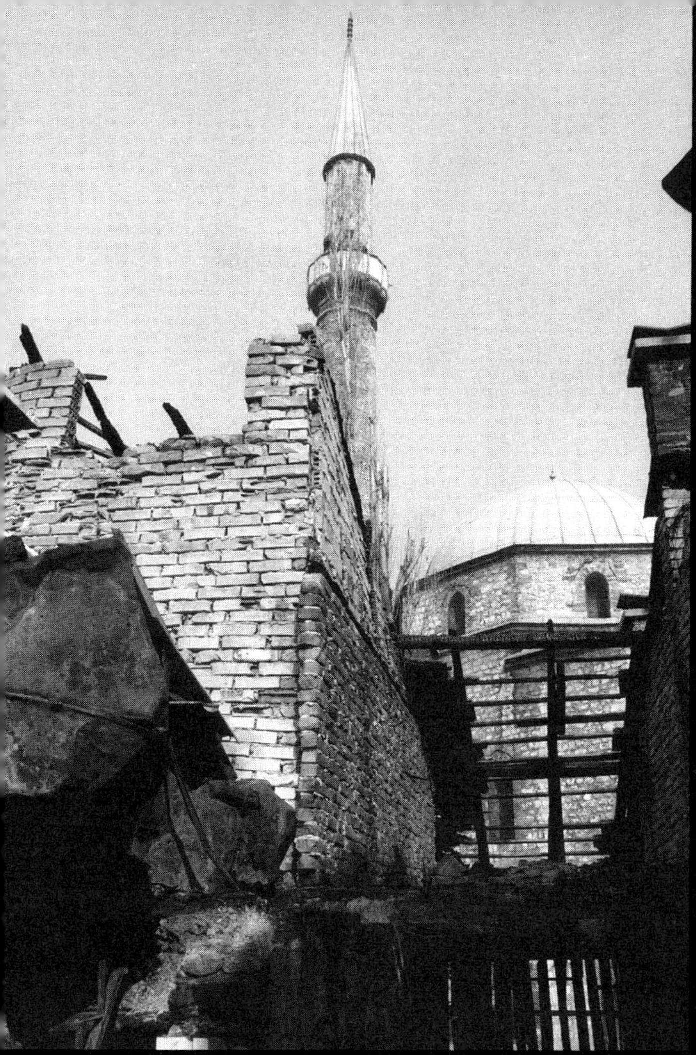
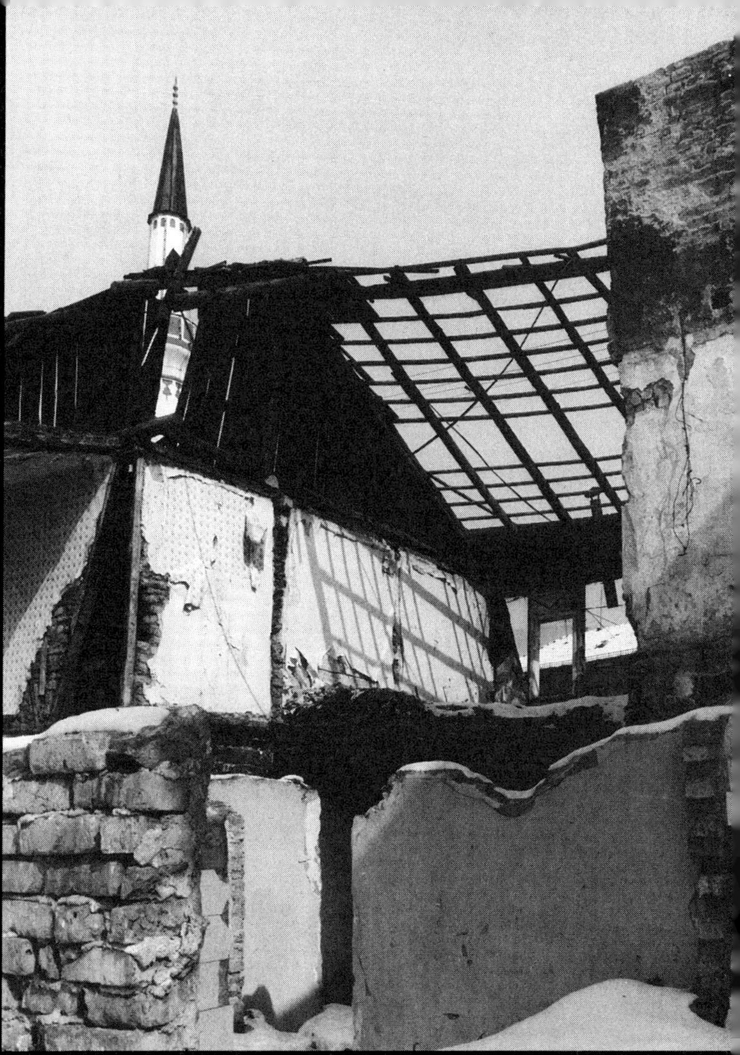
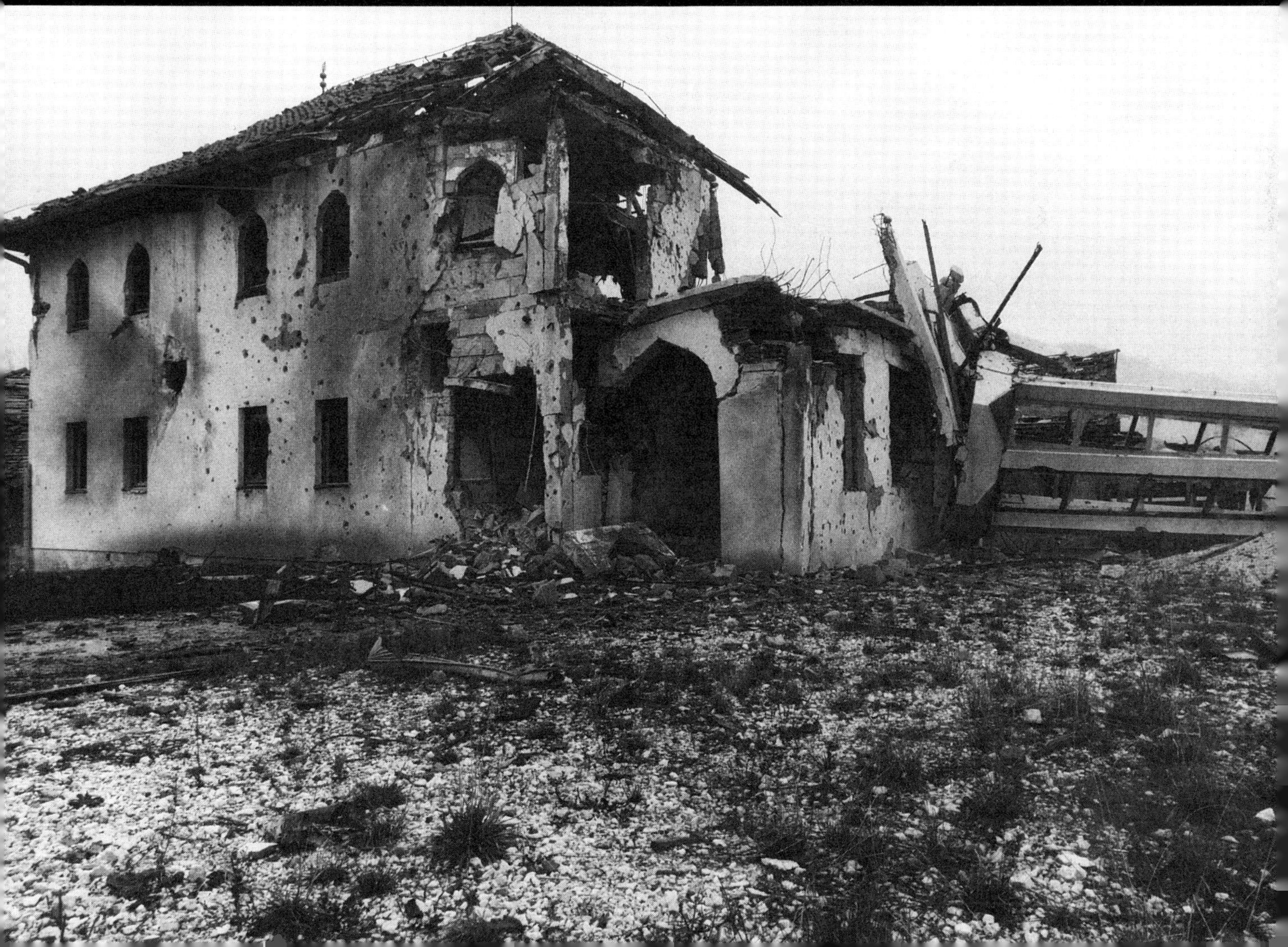

became the target. Sarajevo had been turned into a dartboard. Here the target is not missed. They shoot at random and hit the target. "At random" are the words which mean nothing in Sarajevo. Everybody is a random target here. It is irrelevant how many murderers there are. It is irrelevant whether the murderers get three hundred or three German marks per citizen of Sarajevo. The cardboard targets in a circus rifle range are perforated hourly. The gunners do not win crepe paper roses. This is not war. Here massacres follow one another. Weapons are up there, some distance away, but the lead is nearby. We are down here, digging our tombs. The siege has turned us into mice caught in a trap which it is impossible to get out of.

What are the meanings of the words camp, ghetto, prison, concentration camp, place of execution? My eyes reach where my feet cannot. I look out of the window of my room. I look out on the street where I must gladly walk. I stand outside the cafe I used to sit in. It is always the damn same. The body cannot go further than one kilometre, two, five. What I want is human, natural. I would like to reach, at least, the edge of this circle, of this field of vision. I am not even allowed that. Sarajevo has a noose around its neck.

I leaf through my diary: "Fear hangs in the air. It gets into the pores. It drizzles on us. It soaks our souls. It penetrates into the bones. It goes up and gets into the brain. Our alter ego vanishes. Fear is all around...

"All of a sudden, we are not able to explain that word. Fear, what does it mean?

"I drank up my glass of fear. I could not say if it was bitter, sweetish, pungent or sour, whether it smelt bad or not, or, perhaps it was blessed. Anyhow, how could the taste of a pear be described to a person who had never had a bite of one? And I wanted, in fact, to talk to him about a special sort of pear.

"The same is with fear.

"I swallowed it. I am not sure I felt any difference..."

Sarajevo lives the life of a mediaeval besieged town. Here some new time has started to follow the schedule of a prison. All mediaeval towns were built on hills, with moats, stone towers, massive doors and drawbridges made for the town gates. Sarajevo has no ramparts, it is in a valley, hills surround the city. Its army is its population, yesterday's carefree young men from the discotheques and cafés which did not close until very late at night: artisans, clerks, doctors, chimney sweeps and drivers. We are divided into those who will survive and those who will not. I recall Goran's story from his college days about his father and our professor, Dr Samuel Kamhi, and their war camp days. The struggle for survival was reduced in the lower bed. He was not able to stand up anyhow. He rocked the upper bed by taking his exercise. He struggled to survive. They both managed to. What are we to do in our camp?

Fine Arts in Sarajevo, killed by a shell.

Tuesday, 23rd: An artillery attack on Dobrinja. Shells fall on the Centre, Marijin Dvor, Novo Sarajevo, Stari grad and Čengić vila (three people dead, five wounded), Širokača, Buća potok, Alipašino polje, Koševsko hill and the Olympic village, Mojmilo. The attack on the water supply system in Faletići repulsed. The TV-transmitter on Bjelašnica bombed from the air. 26 killed and 223 injured in Sarajevo in two days.

Wednesday, 24th: A doctor, Gordana Vujović, is killed and three nurses injured in a hospital bus which is drilled by a SDS antiaircraft machine gun. The bus is fired on from the Jewish cemetery. Shelling of Stari grad, Dobrinja. Infantry clashes at Mojmilo, Vojničko polje and Pero Kosorić Square.

Tuesday, 25th: Air-raid sirens sound three times. Eleven dead and 74 injured. Snipers wound seven people at Skenderija. The agony of Dobrinja and the Airport residential area. Houses fall down. A terrible explosion and fire in "Strojorad".

Friday, 26th: So far the number of people killed in this war in Sarajevo is 1,320 and the number of wounded amounts to 6,448. As many as 4,000 hospital beds are not in use any longer. So far 200 doctors and medical staff have been either killed or gone missing in this whirlwind of war. Tanks fire at Dobrinja, Pero Kosorić Square, Ivan Krndelj Street, Otoka, Koševsko hill, Butmir and "Oslobođenje"... Snipers and machine guns firing at Koševsko brdo and Zlatište.

Saturday, 27th: Battles around Vrbanja Bridge and the Jewish cemetery. Shelling of Hrasno hill and Mojmilo. Snipers fire at Marijin Dvor, Skenderija, M. Tito and Đuro Đaković Streets. An antiaircraft machine gun fires at the "Electrical Power Industry" and Pero Kosorić Company. The "Velepekara" (The Town Bakery) without yeast, the city without bread.

Sunday, 28th: An unexpected one-day visit by French President François Mitterrand (he breaks the three-month long blockade). A walk around destroyed Sarajevo. A visit to the Military Hospital (hospital capacity 85% destroyed). He places a rose in Vaso Miskin Street, the place of the massacre of innocent people who were queueing for bread. At its special session, the City Assembly confers the title of a honorary citizen on Mr. Mitterrand "as a sign of gratitude for the support and solidarity of the Republic of France and the French people in the most difficult moments of the 500-year-long history of Sarajevo." After Mr. Mitterrand leaves, shells start falling on Dobrinja from the Airport. The decision of the War Presidency of B-H that work is compulsory for all the employed brings life back into the city. Many companies start working again. The first marriages in Novo Sarajevo. The first lorry with food arrives in the blocked Dobrinja. It is driven there by a Military Police unit, led by Kerim Lučarević, having first captured Mojmilo Hill.

Monday, 29th: The airport taken over by UNPROFOR. Three minutes to 7 p.m., i.e. three minutes before the Security Council session begins, General Mladić's

A ray of light pierced through the keyhole. The army, the former Yugoslav People's Army, was let out of the besieged city. The biggest barracks in the city. – "Marshal Tito" – was emptied on June 5th. Through one of the gates the heavy weaponry left; and Sarajevo got its first tank. Through other gates officers and soldiers of the army that had attacked the city, that kept it besieged, left the city. That was a relief. The city is now without military power in its bosom. A wasp's nest which, day and night, disrupted traffic between the eastern and western parts of the city, spreading death, and which was a wound in city's tissue, left its cage. In all that there was a trace of mercy with images of a military bandsman leaving in an endless column of private cars of military personnel, women and children. They were escorted by their families. The car stopped at a crossroads. It would not start again. Nobody among his fellow officers who were leaving would help him. They passed him in panic while he was helplessly waving his hand. They left and did not look back. The musician, confused, wanted to leave but he could not. The boys who were monitoring the column rushed to help him. He thanked them gratefully. He was leaving but, as he said himself, he did not know where to go. In all this there was some unusual link with the past decades. The army left the large barracks. The darkskinned, frightened musician left as well. In another barracks, the one where the Headquarters was located, there used to be a painter's studio. It was in Turkish times. The barracks was called Kršla and it was newly built. Captain Mustafa of Anatolia had his studio in it in 1868. He painted portraits of high Turkish officials of that time, and taught drawing at the Turkish military school in Sarajevo remembering his studio in Paris. He was the first Muslim painter with a European education in Sarajevo.

The city remained with itself. The links with the world had been cut. We could not reach even Kiseljak, which is only just over twenty kilometres away. It is there that visitors from the world reach and from there they go into the world. It became immeasurably distant. Everything became unreachable. The post did not work. We did not send letters or receive them. We relied on the telephone. But it also was increasingly often silent. We could not use the roads, either. The railways stopped. The sky was blue and clear, and the sunshine was warm. It was the time for going to the seaside, for getting ready for the summer holidays, for buying new sunglasses. Planes did not land. The city was becoming a black hole in space. We could not get out of our chasm. Our souls travelled to the sky, but our bodies remained less than two metres under the ground. We walked hopelessly. Around us, in other parts of Bosnia and Herzegovina, the camps multiplied. There were some with prisoners known as concentration camps. In some there were refugees and displaced persons. They multiplied like amoebae all over the unhappy country of Bosnia and Herzegovina. It was unbelievable. Was World War Two being repeated? Was it spreading beyond these areas? The circle of Sarajevo resounded with the knowledge of the fact. The news about slaughter, torture, and exodus reached us. Unseen, mediaeval massacres took place in villages surrounding the city (Anatovići, Dobroševići...), in some city suburbs (Aerodrom). All that happened and did not happen here. The city was cut up and confined. Some of its parts lived their microlives. Each part of the city seemed to be a separate camp shack. The new settlement Dobrinja, which grew up near a river with the 1984 Olympics, was a detached camp. Nobody entered it, nobody left it. Only the brave and skilful could cross the minefields on Mojmilo hill. Grbavica, a settlement built some forty years ago, was another camp in the control of an army belonging to the parastate of the Serbian Democratic Party. Vogošća and Ilidža shared the same camp authority. We knew little about their regime. Also cut off were the settlements of Otes, Sokolovići, Butmir and Hrasnica.

A part of the city around Stup lived its own life. It was an unrealistic enclave of peace and a place where we could and could not go to. People concocted a myth about prosperity, order, and armies which came there to enjoy themselves, to trade and have peace. All the microgods united and separated in that area of the city.

The camp set its rules. A new discipline of trading in people was started. There were exchanges of prisoners of war. It was mostly reduced to the exchange of captured soldiers or snipers for women, children and old people. Elsewhere this is done simply. A soldier is exchanged for a soldier, a warrior for a warrior. Here we have a novum. Novum balcanicum, bosniacum. It was not rare that corpses became goods to trade in. On a slave market, men and women were bought with money. Here corpses were exchanged for living people with a lot of bargaining. The photos of the dead disclosed the pictures of horror. More and more frequently private exchanges of people took place in secret. A mother, sister or son had to be rescued. All the qualities, people, honesty, words, norms and morality were denied. The price was too high, but there were still customers. However, the trade was quite often interrupted. The slaves were not too tame. People serving as goods did not accept the price. Those brought for exchange did not want to get out of the city. They did not accept their role. They chose the city. They were and they have remained citizens. The mischievous Đorđe Balašević read from our lips: "All this will pass. Sarajevo will exist." Thus we built a telephone message into the anthem of the city.

Fewer and fewer things were left to us. Bread and newspapers were the only signs of life. There was nothing else. People waited on pavements for hours to buy bread. It

army starts withdrawing from the airport. At about 8 p.m. the first plane with humanitarian aid lands (technical equipment for reception of food cargoes). Soldiers of a Canadian battalion are in charge of airport security. Shells fired from Mrkovići, Hreša, Ljubin izvor fall onto Podhrastovi, Grdonj, Panjina kula, Breka gornja and Sedrenik. Apart from Croatia and Slovenia, eastern Bosnia, Jajce, Bugojno, Bihać, Kalinovik and Ilijaš, telephone communications have been interrupted since yesterday with Banja Luka, Bosanska krajina, Sokolac, Han Pijesak and Pale. Lines to Belgrade are reduced by 50%, and only 15% of the capacity for Novi Sad can be used (out of 300 available lines). Communications with the world are being carried out on 120 lines only, instead of the earlier 10,000. About 1 p.m. injured by shrapnel are a French journalist, Jean Hatzfeld, a "Libération" reporter and an English journalist, Kevin Weaver of "the Observer".

Tuesday, 30th: *General Lewis Mackenzie from Canada cancels flights because of the fighting in Dobrinja after five planes land with more than 30 tons of food and medical supplies. The first quantity of medicines sent to Koševo Hospital. Shelling of Dobrinja and the Airport residential area. Four people killed and thirty-five injured in the city. Shortage of packaging prevents milk production. Haso Tajić, editor-in-chief of "Privredne Novine" (Business Gazette) injured.*

JULY

Wednesday, 1st: *Aid provided by the humanitarian agencies*

"Merhamet" and "Caritas" arrives in Dobrinja from Kiseljak, thanks to Mrs. Pava Barišić's courage. Shelling of Dobrinja. Five people killed and thirty wounded in the town.

Thursday, 2nd: *A new year, the 1413th year of the Hejira. The reis-ul-ulema, hajji Jakub Selimoski, wishes all the Muslims a Happy New Year. Taxi drivers inform the mayor that they will offer their services free of charge until the end of the war. Four killed, twenty injured in the town. Yeast arrives in the "Velepekara".*

Friday, 3rd: *Lord Carrington and Jose Cutilheiro in Sarajevo. After Carrington's departure, shells are fired at Dobrinja, Baščaršija, Faletići and Vasin han. An anti-aircraft machine gun continuously fires from Vraca. On the barricades of Nedžarići there are several injured. Shells fall around the Presidency building. Ten dead and forty injured in Sarajevo. Fifty tons of food arrive at Sarajevo airport.*

Saturday, 4th: *Skirmishes in Pero Kosorić Square. Shelling of Hrasno hill, Stari grad (Vasin han, Širokača, Jarčedoli, Faletići and Hrid), Soukbunar, Koševsko brdo and Marijin Dvor. Infantry clashes at Nahorevo, the Jewish cemetery, around Vrbanja bridge and in the "Oslobođenje" building. According to information of the Children's Embassy, there have been 750 children killed and 4,500 injured in Sarajevo. Tank missiles fired at Kobilja glava (seven dead, one injured.) Shells also kill four deer, a fawn, two chamois, a pony and a donkey. Animals in the zoo have been 9 days without food. Pionirska dolina captured together with*

was sold direct from vans. One loaf or two at the most per customer. The only newspapers were the Sarajevo dailies. Others had not managed to reach the city since the beginning of April. They were still sold by journalists who worked as newspaperboys.

The atmosphere was hurried. The shells did not pick out only buildings. They found people and places where people met. Snipers too. Fire-collectors sent signals by means of light and reflections from mirrors. The fifth column moved from Madrid to Sarajevo. The suspicious generalissimo had invisibly and destructively overwhelmed the Republic and Madrid. The fifth column in Sarajevo earned its black points. Their culmination was the cemetery. The last farewell to the dead became the favourite target for those who fired the shells. They were shot at mercilessly. On the hour every afternoon shells fell on funeral processions, on those sad reunions over dug up clay. They multiplied the numbers of burials. The schedule was changed. The time of shelling followed, too. They were reduced to morning and night burials. Obituaries more and more rarely stated the hour of funerals. The plan was to kill life in the city. We were supposed to rot away with fear in the basements. They killed our deaths, too. The parts of the city we could not reach hid their camps. Notorious became Kula, Lukavica, Pale, "Sonja's" inn at Vogošća, basements and garages at Grbavica and Ilidža. The news about crowded cells where prisoners could not even sit down, about overflowing chamber pots they were not allowed to take out, about rape and murder. Time will clear up these darkest pages of this city, its history and its dignity.

My friend, who studied in Sarajevo long ago, Saša Popov, broad-minded and attentive in the way the Lalas (residents of Vojvodina) are, offered to come over here as early as April, to be like a Spanish volunteer for us. In the long night conversations on the rare telephones we still had, he was clear: "The bench in Nuremberg will be too small." It will be small, I know. He saw this very clearly from the banks of the Danube, even better than we did ourselves, it seems.

The camp lived on. The chestnut trees in the avenues of Sarajevo blossomed white. I recognized the magnificent paintings by Safet Zec in them. I saw his paintbrush and eyes in each treetop. I had a rest from all this at the windows of the mahalas (residential quarters of the city) that inspired his oil paintings. I could still see the windows with glass and flowerpots. I returned to his stone walls, high garden fences, green rivers resting under green treetops and green bushes. Those walls are all around us, but not so beautiful and eternal. I hoped for a fast end to the confinement. I leafed through an old map of graphics by Mersad Berber, done by the craftsmanship of Alojz Heđi Bimbo (how is he getting on, sick, in Grbavica?). I read again and again the poetry of

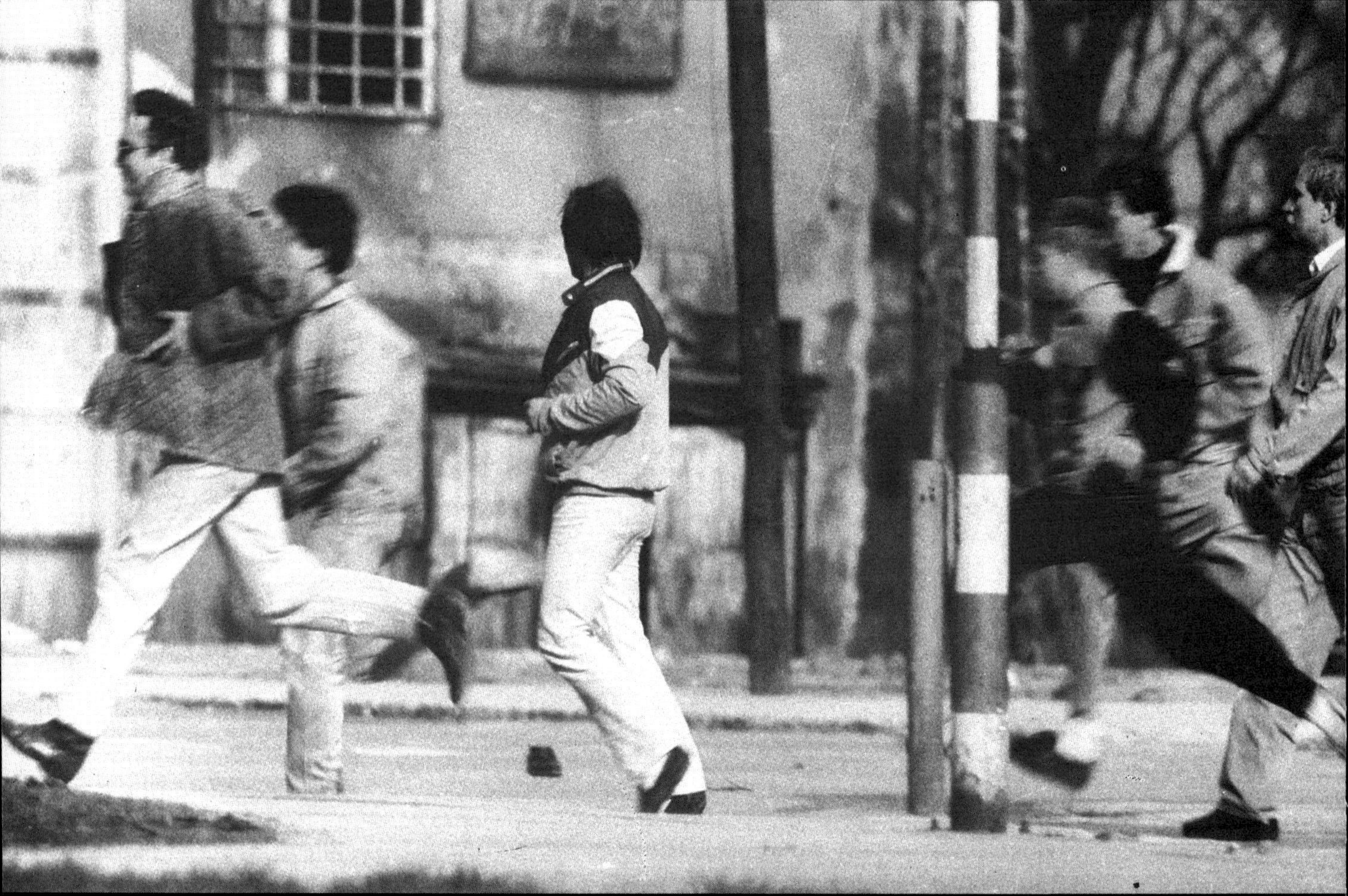

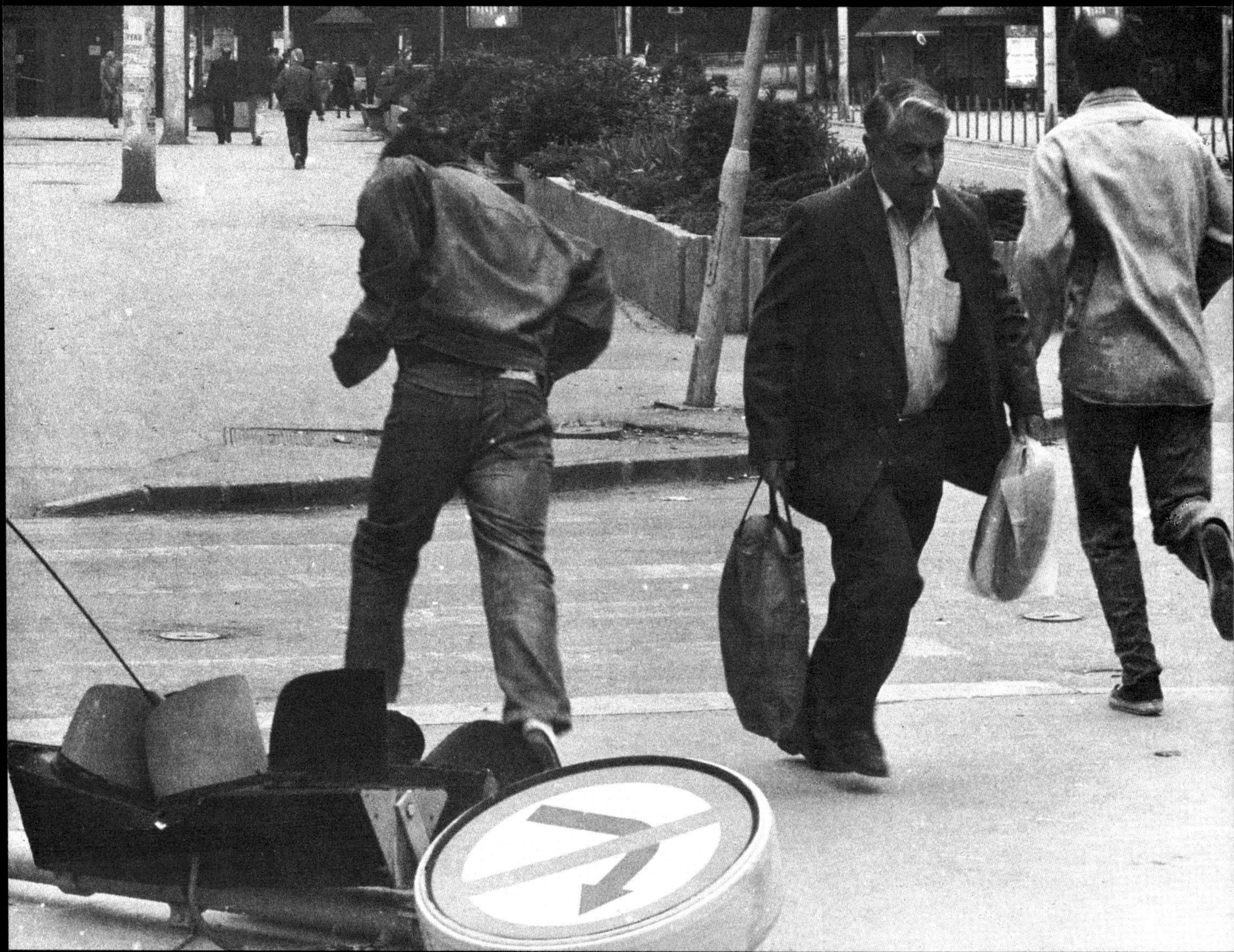

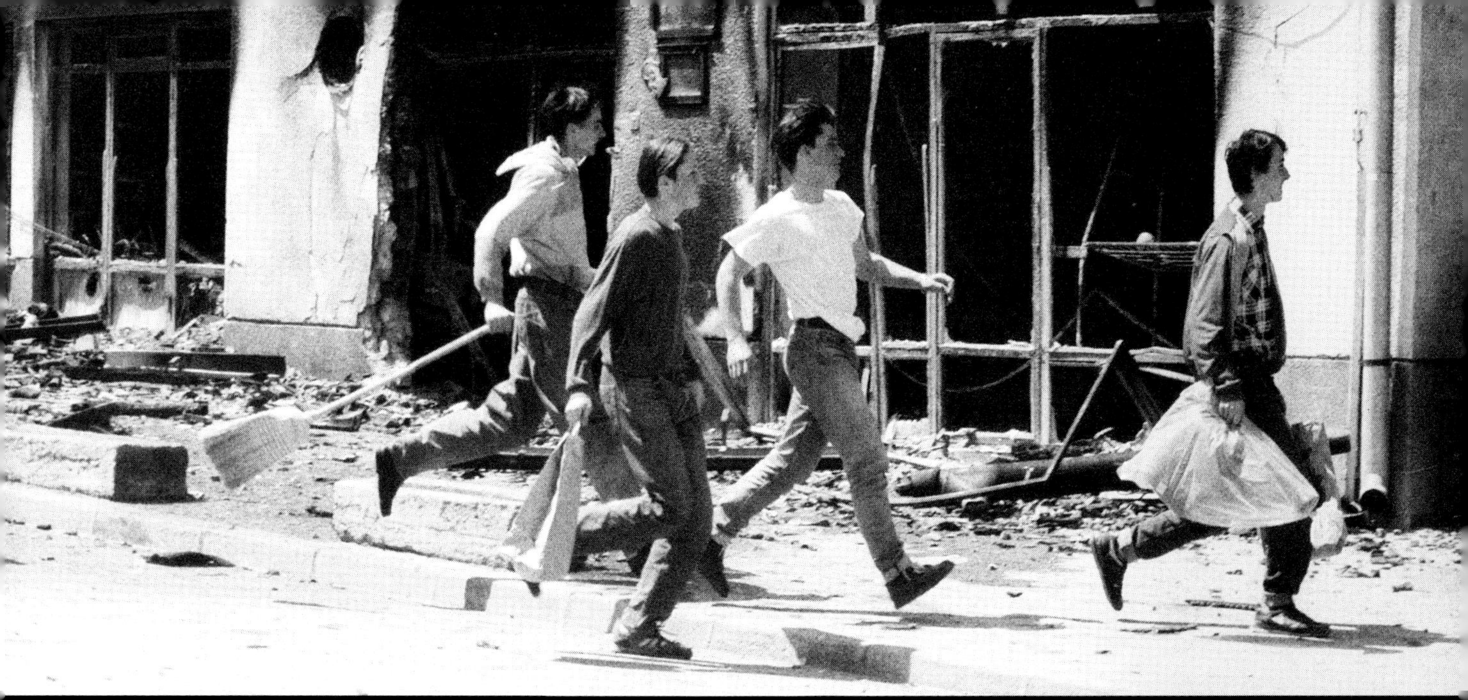

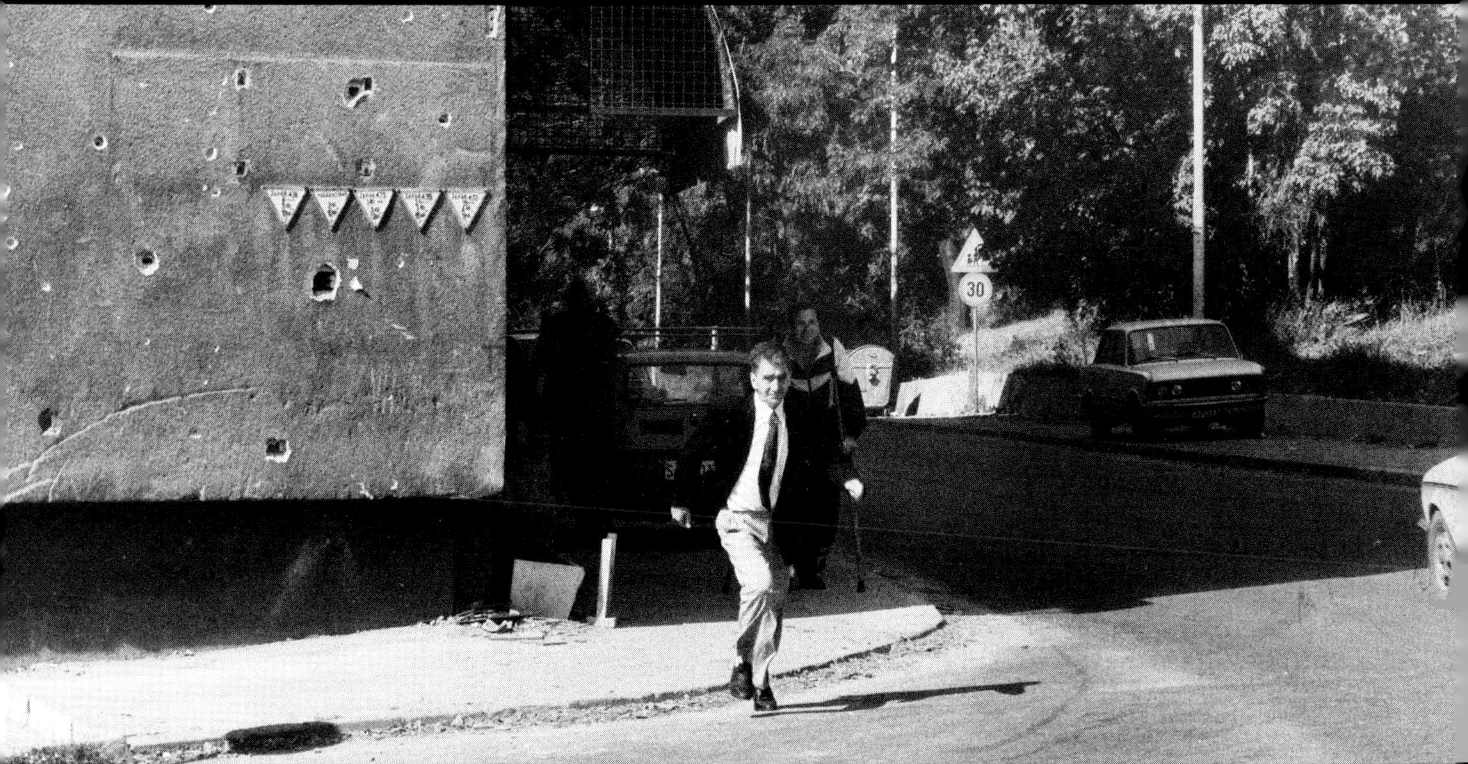
30

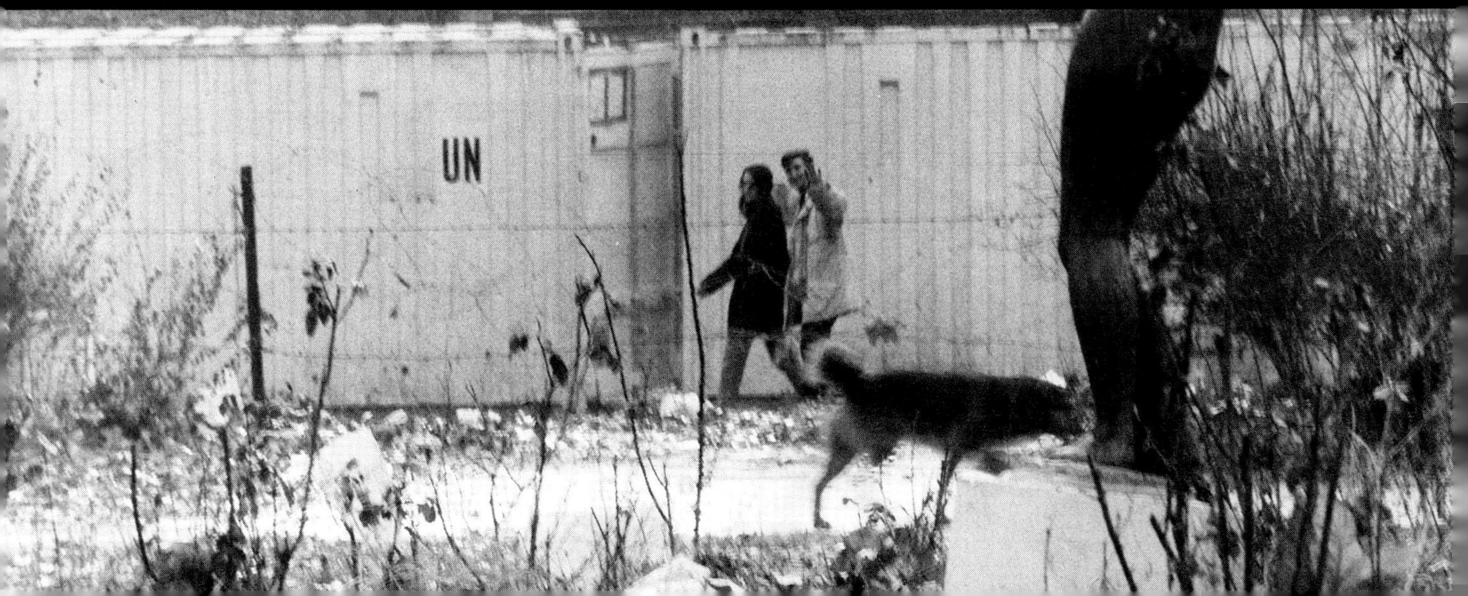
UN

Sarajevo. I cured the bites of words of the desperate painter who plunged them bloodthirstily into my soul. Rage blurred his sight. I felt sorry for him wiping the saliva away after the bite. I will get away somehow. This will heal. So I lived the life of a camp prisoner. I swallowed the remaining air. It was not too stale. Our Gulag was counting on Europe's help. I trusted in the good will of the international community. We dreamed of a power that could drive this power out. Journalists and politicians dosed us with the military intervention we hoped for. Drop by drop, sometimes in spoonfuls. We were like prisoners who daily tormented themselves thinking about amnesty. They are the ones who will get it on the next public holiday.

But nothing happened.

The airport was closed. The roads remained blocked. The railway station was no longer there. Traditional graduation anniversaries due in June were cancelled, delayed until the time of peace. We waited and walked the circle. Life was reduced to basements shelters. The more courageous went out to shops and markets. They found nothing. Only death was permanent. It made no selection. We all were candidates for death. It took us away mercilessly. We did not manage to get over one death when another came, then three more...

The experienced general of the blue berets, the Canadian McKenzie in Sarajevo comprehends: "One needn't be a genius to see that the situation is moving its way towards catastrophe." The same day the French President, on the pavements of Sarajevo, explains: "My first task is to get acquainted with the real state of affairs."

And so on, endlessly.

The French humanitarian organization "Equilibre" succeeds in getting into the city. They bring us as much as 180 tons of aid... At Dobrinja doctors perform operations by candlelight. The clinic is improvised in a basement. The patients must survive. Hospitals, those which were built for the sick and their treatment, are far away, in another camp, in the centre of the city... At Kobilja glava, a settlement three kilometres from the building of the Presidency of the Republic, children pick red cherries from a cherry tree. A shell hits them. They become corpses and cripples at the age of nine, twelve, seven...

The city has no electricity. The city has no water. For six days in a row, there is none. Shells fall all around my flat. They shoot at the building where I live. They hit the building next to ours, then the one next to it, then the following one... They shoot at everything. They do not make any selection. In the neighbourhood, some hundred metres away from my balcony, a shell hits the kitchen in a family house. Sisters Mediha and Rabija and their children were killed: two-year-old Zlata and fourteen-year-old Amela. Amela's father survived. He is disabled now. Doctors are

the zoo (a lion and a lioness, two tigers, three bears, a leopard, two bison, two wild boars, a llama, two ponies, several monkeys and a lot of birds). At night between 29th and 30th, the zoo keeper, Ešref Tahirović, is killed.

Sunday, 5th: *General Satish Nambiar, commander-in-chief of UNPROFOR, is in Sarajevo again. In 24 hours 14 planes land at the airport with humanitarian aid from Great Britain, France, Italy and Norway, a total 140 tons. So far 310 tons of food have arrived. Shelling of a soup kitchen and the Aneks residential area – four injured. Four people killed and forty wounded in Sarajevo. Shortage of electricity and water.*

Monday, 6th: *In Sarajevo, 6 people killed and 40 injured. Without electricity is 80% of the city. The shortage of electricity cuts off the water supply. Mehmed Husić, editor-in-chief of the "Svijet" magazine, is released at Vrbanja Bridge, and two professors of the Islamic Theological Faculty in Sarajevo, Ibrahim Džananović and Nijaz Šukrić, are exchanged at Kobiljača.*

Tuesday, 7th: *Four killed, thirty-six injured. Flour, pasta and sugar sold on the outskirts of the town only for ration coupons. In two days sales are to be organized in the city centre as well. Forty-four hostages from Ilidža and Kula exchanged in front of the engineering PTT Engineering, now the headquarters of UNPROFOR.*

Wednesday, 8th: *Tanks fire from Vidikovac and Trebević at Zlatište and Širokača. Artillery fires from Vučja Luka at Vasin han,*

Hladivode and Faletići, from Borije at Bistrik. Artillery attacks on Breka, Brekin potok and Kobilja glava. Snipers operate from Vraca and the Jewish cemetery in the direction of crossroads. Shelling and anti-aircraft machine-gun fire at Ciglane and Koševsko brdo. An anti-aircraft gun fires from Osmice at Gorica. Shelling of Soukbunar, Pero Kosorić Square, Hrasno, Hrasno hill, Pofalići, the "Vaso Miskin Crni" factory, Dobrinja, Mojmilo, Sokolje, Vojničko polje and the Olympic village. Slaughter in Dobrinja, next to the former UPI restaurant: three killed, thirty injured.

Thursday, 9th: *About 3.30 p.m. shells again set on fire the Olympic sports hall at Mojmilo. The fire is extinguished at about 6 p.m. but the hall is almost completely burnt down. Shells from Trebević fall upon Hladivode, Vasin han and Faletići; the city centre is fired at from Hreša. An artillery-infantry attack on Pero Kosorić Square, Hrasno, Hrasno hill, the airport residential area and Žuč hill. Alipašino polje, Kobilja glava, Hotonj, Dobrinja, Sokolje, Stup, Mojmilo and Hrasnica also fired on. Air-raid sirens. Dragica Pirnat, a trade unionist, dies at the age of 103.*

Friday, 10th: *Shelling and artillery attacks on Dobrinja. Shells fall on Hrasnica, Mahmutovac, Alipašino polje, Mojmilo, Hrasno, Hrasno hill, the "Vaso Miskin Crni" factories, the School of Economics and the "Bristol" hotel. So far, 120 aeroplanes from all over the world have landed at Sarajevo airport bringing 1,147 tons of food to the citizens of Sarajevo.*

fighting for his son's life. And the obituary with four names and surnames is stuck on a post in front of the house. All around are walls and barbed wire that tears our womb. My eighty-year-old father-in-law and mother-in-law managed to get away from Grbavica. They took with them only a white bag with food and some medicine. They left behind all they possessed. Their personal documents and glasses stayed in the high grass behind the skyscraper. They saw their friend, sixty-five-year old Meho from the block of flats next to theirs on a truck for the transport of people.

October 7th, 1912 was a date in the history of the city. Sarajevo was in the dark for the first time since 1895, since the city had been supplied with electricity. The explanation then was that "the amount of electricity in the upper town put the lights out". The overload on the power plants put it into history. Now it was shells that put out the bulbs. Dr Aleksandar Semiz shines in the darkness of Circle Three: "We embarked on war surgery with no experience whatsoever, or preparation for anything of the sort. All our experience has been acquired in these eighty days since the aggression began.

"Here, this is the experience from the Vietnam war, then from the Korean war. No, it does not help us much with what is being done here; the ammunition used in this aggression, such destruction and bestiality have never been seen before. Here are some examples. The speed of the bullets that wound our defenders is 1,000 metres per second, which is three times faster than the speed of sound. Can you imagine how powerful a shot is. The weight of the shot is 82 kgs per square centimeter, which means if the area of a wound is 4×4cms, the pressure on that small part of tissue is one ton. Injuries caused in that way are horrible and have never been recorded in literature."

The circle still lasts. It never ends. We have nowhere to go, to find shelter. Tons of pressure per centimetre of skin wait for us.

My former neighbour Azem Ademi is not here any more. He defended the city at the age of 52. He left behind four daughters, one son and his Fata, ill, in their two-bedroom flat in Alipašino polje. Two days later, Alija Kučukalič did not come for his newspaper. He had regularly bought it every morning. He stood with me without uttering a word. Then he went to Jasmina. They talked more. One can always talk more with women. They smoked the cigarettes they had just bought. They did so every morning. They remembered camping, they talked about the summer that was approaching, about Orebič and Perna, the camp and the sea breeze. The sculptor was alone. He had sent his family to a safe place. Alone was his sculpture of a woman sitting with her arms outstretched on the plateau in front of the cultural-sports centre Skenderija. You could not go there for weeks because of shells and snipers. Nobody dates at "the

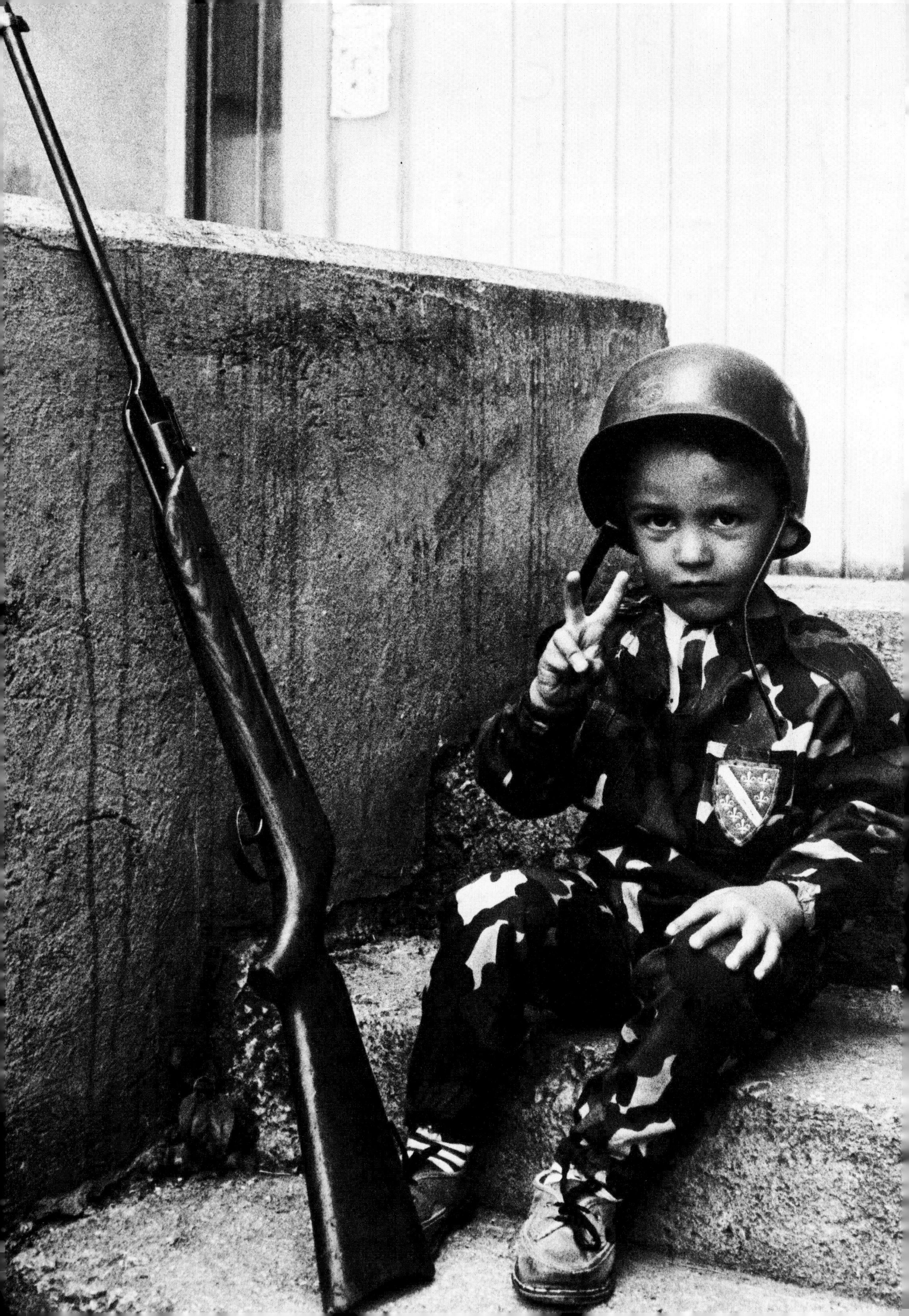

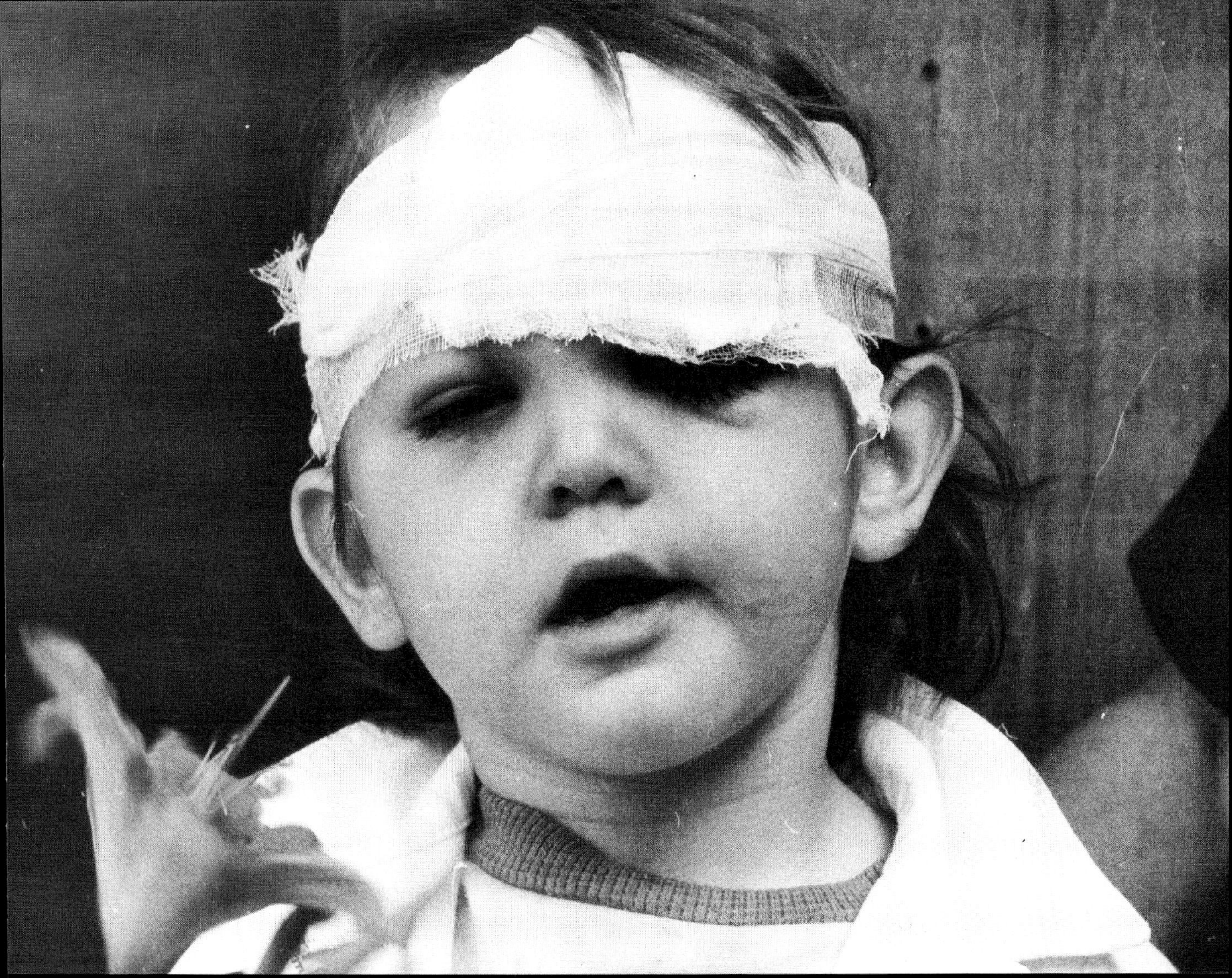

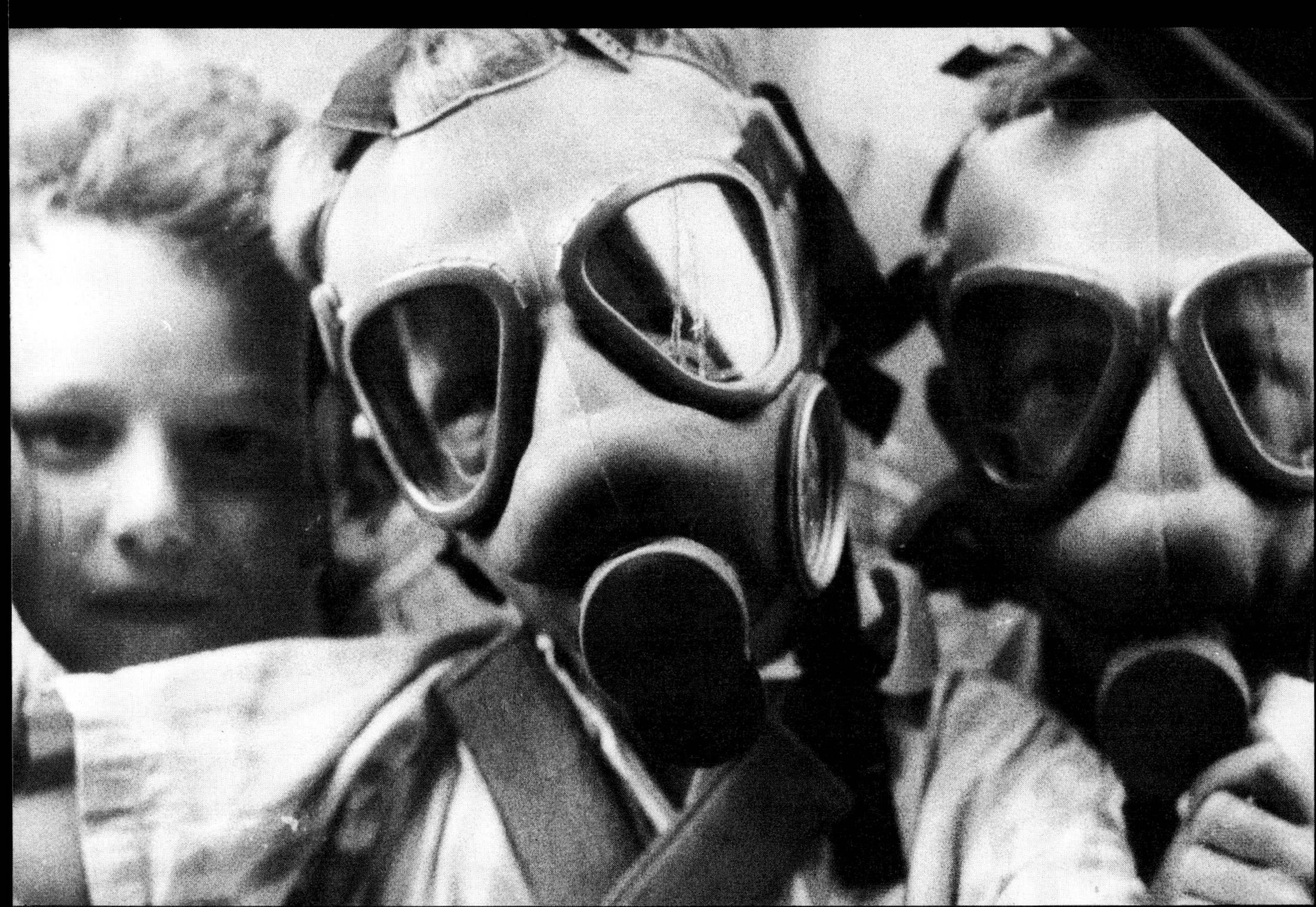

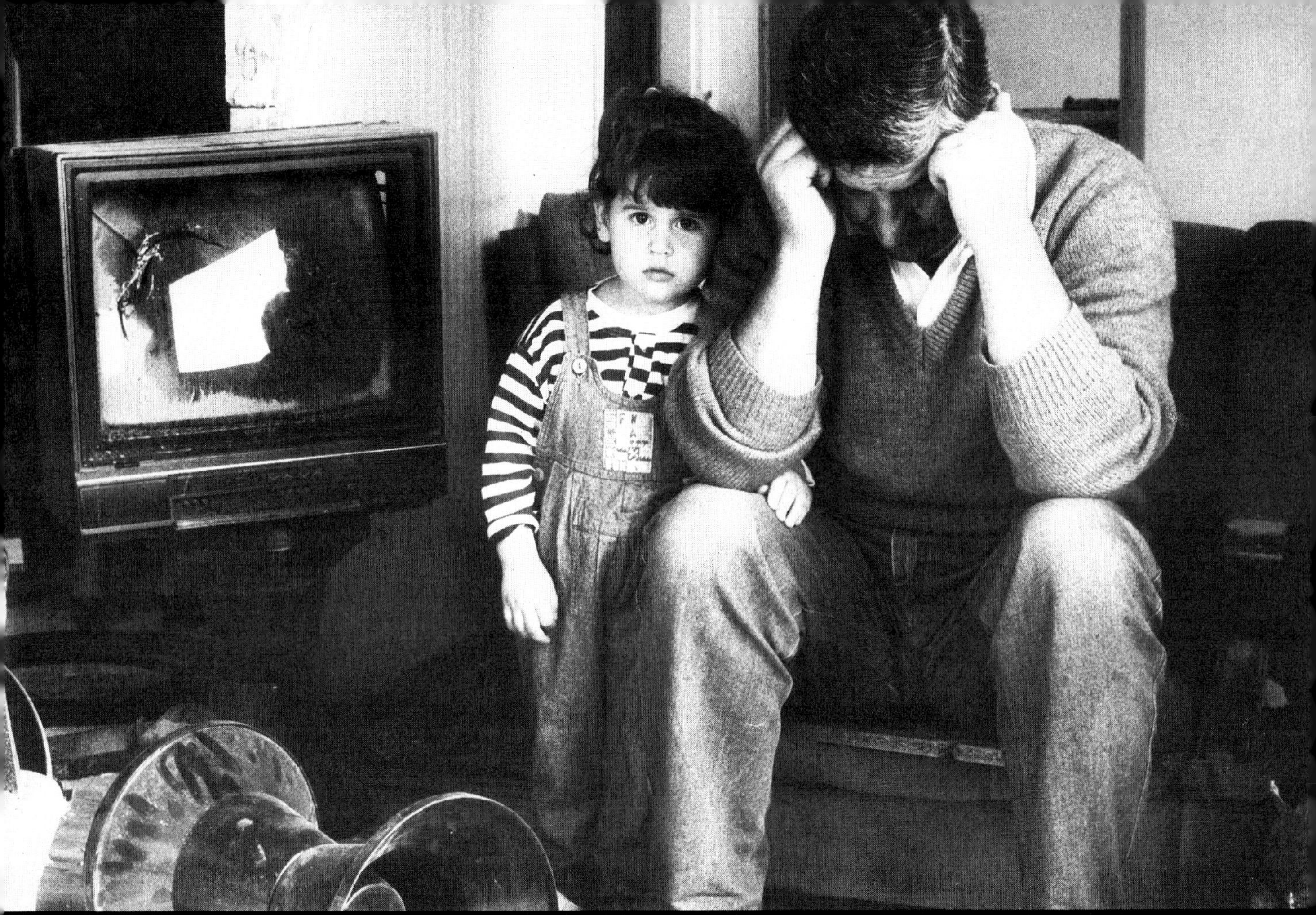

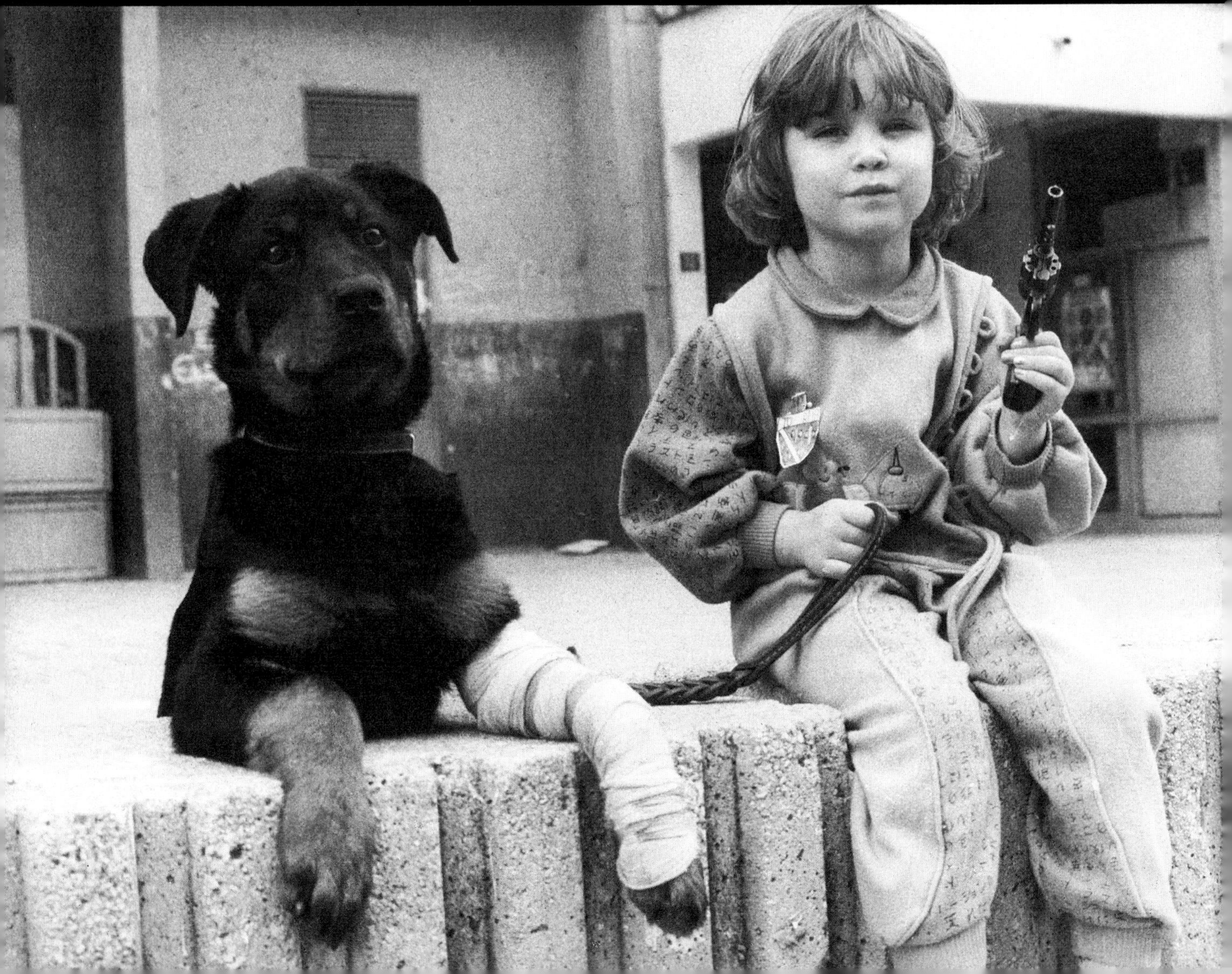

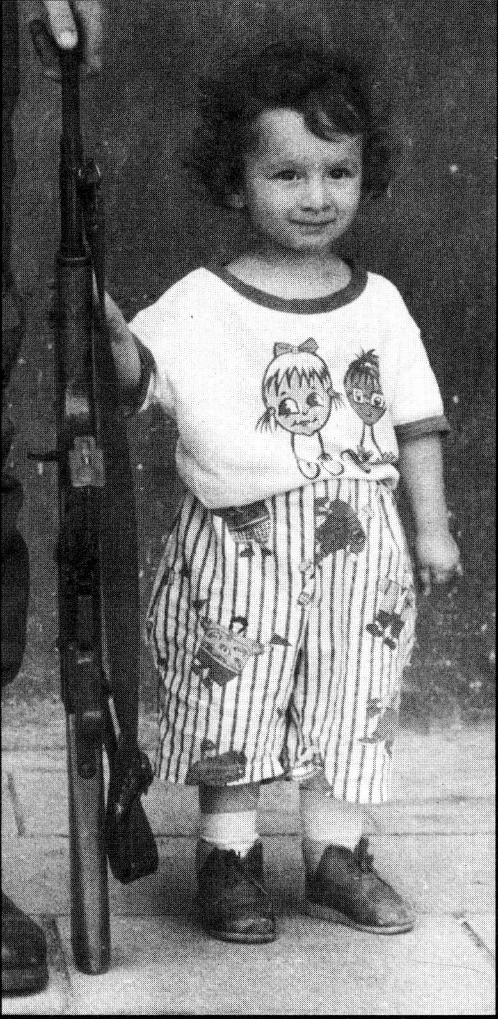

MACKEREL
FOR UNHCR SARAJEVO
FO/07303
THROUGH UNHCR ZAGREB
UNHCR

outstretched auntie." A shell hit him at the front door of his house. It took away a professor of sculpture at the Fine Arts Academy, a dear person, an artist. Next day, I did not want to sell one copy of the newspaper. Almost the same hour "Colonel Dragan" joined him in the Small Park. In the small park behind the post office, near the Court of Justice and the petrol station, there was slaughter. The first shell killed two people, and wounded several more. Dragan Medenica ran out of his entrance. It would have taken him only some thirty metres to help his friend Velid Nalić. Velid was sitting near the entrance playing with two children. He was wounded. Dragan did not manage to walk those thirty metres. The second shell caught him on his twentieth step. According to the table of Sarajevo, shell killing usually happens in pairs. Very often even three come in a series. We have learned this, but it does not manage to stop the screams of the wounded. And it is usually painful. Thirty-seven-year-old Dragan did not succeed in helping his friend Velid. He will not manage to help his four-year-old Nataša, either. He, Edin and the friends from the surrounding buildings, helped us on May 2nd when the post office burned. They protected the entrances with weapons, tried to extinguish the fire in the post office, and defended us. A few days later, auntie Ljubica Despotovič left us. Buco's mother died. Simply, as though she had wanted to die. She did not accept going through one more war. I copy from my diary: ". . . The Lav cemetery is being filled up. There is less and less green grass. There is more and more dug up clay. Plots for burials of Muslim, Catholic, Orthodox and atheists are being dug. Khojas and priests pray at the same time and relatives silently bid last tearful farewells to those killed. The lawns behind the old monument are still quiet. The sculptures from 1916 are at the base of the dying lion. It was also wartime. Soldiers were buried here as early as 1878. After four decades there were a lot of burials again. The following war brought new graves, too. Now it is also a time of war, of death and of burials.

"Up to the left, I can see my friends. Sorrow on their faces. Buco, his wife and her father are dressed in black. Others, as if they had come running for a minute. They are all in sports clothes. The whole Sarajevo is in flight, in a shelter of its own. We do not manage to look decent even at a funeral.

"All this lasts just a short time, it is hurried.

"And the coffin of plywood. Near it, a tomb marked with the name, the years of birth and death in plastic letters nailed on it. The coffin is not a coffin. It is not the coffin we know: usual, massive, carved, with handles and a lid, coated with varnish, polished. It is made of raw, unpainted plywood slapped together. I have never seen such a coffin . . ." There is nothing. Not even coffins. We remain with our pain. And our memories with it. I come across a letter on the obituary

A convoy of 11 lorries full of food also arrives for the citizens of the Butmir residential area. Eight citizens of Sarajevo killed and twenty injured. A bus of the City Transport Company full of passengers is hit by bullets on the main crossroads, near the Faculty of Natural Sciences and Mathematics. Four killed, eight injured. Snipers operate throughout the town, using illegal dumdum bullets. Hajrudin Šiba Krvavac, a film director, dies.

Saturday, 11th: *Turkish Foreign Minister, Hikmet Çetin, arrives in Sarajevo. An anti-tank shell is fired from Grbavica at a UNPROFOR personnel carrier. It misses, but three people are killed and several wounded. It happens in Vojvoda Putnik Street at about 12 o'clock. Shelling of Dobrinja, a water reservoir at Kobilja glava, Velešići, Pofalići, Ciglane and Koševo. Transmission lines damaged at Bačevo (the main source of the municipal water supply).*

Sunday, 12th: *The popular TV programme "I Want to Say" shown for the last time. A shell falls on Hrasnica (3.30 p.m.) killing four, slightly injuring two and seriously injuring two children. The Orthopedic Clinic shelled as well.*

Monday, 13th: *Killing in front of the UNPROFOR building: one child killed, about twenty injured. Sixteen 82-mm shells fall within 75m. The injured are between 13 and 17 years old. Also shelled is the city centre. St. Joseph's Church at Marijin Dvor hit. Shelling of Dobrinja and the "Podhrastovi" Clinic for Lung Diseases.*

Tuesday, 14th: *Six people killed, forty-two injured in Sarajevo. The agony of the old people's home at Nedžarići continues. The home is without electricity, water, telephone, food and medicines. So far about 40 residents have died. There are still 230 of them. Twenty-seven were taken in by families at the beginning of the war. Most of them are bedridden (and they wet their beds).*

Wednesday, 15th: *There are 5 killed and 46 injured in Sarajevo. Shelled are the "Pavle Goranin" residential area, Hrid, Vasin han and Stari grad. Snipers shoot at the "Holiday Inn" hotel – wounded are Joseph Ageto, a member of the French humanitarian mission "Équilibre", Slobodan Tasić, a journalist of "Reuter" and CNN and Miodrag Rajak, a reporter for TV B-H. Shells set fire to the garage of the "Put" public utilities at Nedžarići. The Supreme Court of B-H (a five-member council) confirmed the Higher Court decision of June 23rd to ban the SDS and its activities. Mortar shells fall from Vidikovac upon Hrid, Mahmutovac and Vasin han. Anti-aircraft machine guns and anti-aircraft guns fire from Osmice and Trebević. There is firing from Kromolj, Jagomir and Poljine, and fighting.*

Thursday, 16th: *Nine killed and fifty-nine wounded in Sarajevo. Salko Hondo, 55, a photoreporter for "Oslobođenje" killed by a shell at the market place.*

Friday, 17th: *British Foreign Minister, Douglas Hurd, visits Sarajevo. He pays a visit to Vaso Miskin Crni Street, the scene of the bread queue massacre. He does*

page. It is written by Amela Šetkić to her fiancé Ramiz Bahto, on the occasion of the fortieth day commemoration:

"Dear Ramiz,

"Forty days filled with pain and sorrow have passed since you left me forever. It is painful to think that you are not with me any more, but the pride that I had in you will be in my heart forever. The time elapsed is a weak consolation to me for you whom I boundlessly loved, and lost too early in such a cruel way.

"You were and will be my ideal and support for ever.

"My parents and my brother sympathise with me in my pain. Lovers meet and set new victories where the eyeballs dimly see them.

"Thank you for the boundless love and attention you lavished on me.

Yours 'Little One' . . ."

Ramiz was twenty-one. He left at the beginning of May when love and nature bloom.

How many letters like this one remained in the city? With time, we shall be sending, receiving, reading them and warming our hearts with more and more of them.

We are living an unwritten Greek tragedy from hour to hour. The worry for Nihad stirs my fear every day. He is in the intensive care ward. Will at least one of his legs be saved? The right one has already been written off. He, in his delirium, threatened the doctor that he would kill anyone who amputated it. He is twenty-eight. How will he run after his four-year son Ado, walk arm in arm with Indira? He did not manage to get the body of his brother-in-law from the bobsleigh track. Nor did his friends from Mahmutovac for days. He was informed that his brother had been wounded at Dobrinja. He rushed across Mojmilo and the minefield. In the Aerodrom suburb there was hell. It had lasted since midday. He learned about his father's death on a balcony in Franca Prešerna Street, about his mother being shot through her neck, about his brother who had been wounded pulling out his father's corpse, about the fire which had burned everything they had – the flat and the furniture. Only the father's corpse remained with the legs on the balcony and the body in the living room. He had lost his head. He had plunged into death. A bomb had exploded at his feet . . .

And my poet wakes me up again. He lies down in the Koševo valley, down where we are still digging new and opening already existing graves. Silvije Strahimir Kranjčević calls me. His poem "The Night of the Dead" tells me:

"While the weeping bells toll through the gloomy avenues.

"And a touching song resounds, the proud avenue shines.

"And warm tears are shed, and pale hands wipe them, on an old cap or a piece of cotton . . ."

How many stories shall we manage to survive? The theatre is somewhere far away. Here life goes out.

From the vault, they take out the banknotes which were withdrawn some time ago. They attach a seal on them. They are valid only in the Sarajevo camp. The National Bank with its seal on white revives the banknotes already withdrawn. Somebody diligent patiently cuts out the five-pointed star from the top of the decades-old coat-of-arms of Bosnia and Herzegovina. The factory chimneys and ears of grain are still there, but the five-pointed star has disappeared. Everything is history. Traces are left behind. We remember masses of small things. The coat-of-arms is not old, nor is it new, but the banknotes are in circulation.

The building of "Oslobođenje" (Liberation) is in flames. The floor with its publishing department burned out. In a burst of destruction the fire destroyed desks, computers, printing presses, archives, contracts and workers' employment booklets.

The "Oslobođenje" skyscraper is burning. My writing desk, the bookshelf with books, finished manuscripts and photographs are burning. A part of my life, memories, notes, telephone numbers and letters go away.

The "Oslobođenje" building is burning.

I cannot rush there to help with the fight against the elements. I cannot. I am ten kilometres away. My car is riddled with shrapnel. This is not a natural element, but an intention to wipe everything out, to make it disappear.

... Some thirty manuscripts ready for printing were burned up. The efforts of the writers and editors were reduced to ashes. Five books of poetry by Miroslav Antić burned up. Two of them had never been published. We did not manage to save them. Gone up in flames was also the last book of the late Oskar Davičo: "A Traitor by Profession." He did not succeed in completing volume three of his autobiography: "A Corpse by Profession"; an interesting book by doctor Nura Hubijar "How I Taught a Fish to Swim" is no longer there. It should have come out by the end of last April. I commissioned a translation from German of the book "The Bosnians are Coming" and five books of Rodoljub Čolaković's manuscripts, a travelogue by the gynaecologist Miro Kundurović for the beginning of last June and the celebration in Graz..."

Gone are the efforts we made, the examination of each sentence, the search for hidden sense in what presented itself.

So much written treasure was irretrievably destroyed by fire. It was killed before its birth.

In a camp they always murder out of their unruliness. Undesirable culture has been burnt at the stake for centuries. Its embers never warmed anyone up. The pyromaniac Nero never built a new Rome. Neither did the house painter Adolf manage to do so with Berlin. Nor will

not, however, visit the city hospital, as planned in the protocol. An agreement about a 14-day ceasefire in B-H to come into effect at 6 p.m. on July 19th, is signed in London. At noon a shell falls near the Presidency injuring fifteen citizens. Electricity and water supplies return to normal.

Saturday, 18th: *Sixty-three Nobel Prize Winners write to the British daily "The Guardian" with a request to stop the aggression against B-H (Desmond Tutu, Eli Wiesel, Linus Pauling, Milton Friedman, Vladimir Prelog and others). Two killed and 56 wounded in Sarajevo. Twenty invalid chairs, eight operating lamps, six operating tables, ten hospital beds for an intensive care unit, one anaesthesia apparatus and one auxiliary operating table come with the humanitarian aid. Sixteen aeroplanes land with 172.6 tons of food and medicine.*

Sunday, 19th: *Milan Panić, Prime Minister of the so-called Yugoslavia visits Sarajevo. He meets the President of the Presidency, Alija Izetbegović, in the UNPROFOR building. A minute after 6 p.m. 82-mm mortars fall upon Pero Kosorić Square, the "Oslobođenje" building and from Poljine shells fall on Kobilja glava. Ten children and two women are injured by shell fragments at Vojničko polje, only two hours after 6 p.m. – the time when the ceasefire in B-H, as agreed in London, is due to come into effect. Two girls are killed – the sisters Nevzeta and Ismeta Mulić, refugees from Foča.*

Monday, 20th: *Slaughter in Magribija Street at 11 a.m. Three shells hit twelve citizens – two of them die.*

Shells fired at Dobrinja, Breka, Stari grad, Butmir, Sokolović kolonija, Kobilja glava, the Catholic Church in Novo Sarajevo, Širokača, Vasin han, Soukbunar, Bistrik and Alipašino polje. Infantry breakthrough attempts at Pionirska dolina, the Breka residential area, and near Vrbanja bridge. The airport is closed. Shelling around the airport.

Tuesday, 21st: *Before Sarajevo airport is closed 2,468 tons of humanitarian aid have arrived (2,289 tons of food, 130 tons of medicine and 20 tons of medical supplies). The aid satisfies only 12.3% of twenty-day requirements of Sarajevo or 2.8% of B-H. After 24 hours the airport opens again. The Faculty of Mechanical Engineering, Dolac Malta, Čengić vila and the Catholic Church in Novo Sarajevo are shelled.*

Wednesday, 22nd: *A heavy artillery attack on the Dobrinja residential area of Sarajevo at about 5 p.m. One killed, six wounded. So far, there have been 1,467 killed and 8,355 injured people in Sarajevo, 50% of whom are seriously disabled. Yesterday, there were 23 killed and 122 injured in B-H. In Sarajevo, five people are killed and forty five wounded.*

Thursday, 23rd: *Shelling of Hrasnica, near the Hall of Culture, where people are queueing for humanitarian aid. Three people are killed, five seriously and eighteen slightly injured. About 1,000 displaced persons come daily to Sarajevo, their number being 28,000 so far. An exchange of POW's and arrestees takes place near the "Delminium" boarding house. Out of 33 people arrested 17 do not want to leave Sarajevo, so they are*

the ashes of Sarajevo obliterate letters, sentences or reason.

Our camp did not manage to receive new convicts, either. The door was closed too tight.

And then suddenly, some time towards the end, when the looks of expectation were thinning out, an olive branch landed. Noah's Ark before Sarajevo. The pigeon was Mr François Mitterrand. Without announcement or preparations he landed at the closed airport of Sarajevo. He unblocked it!? The first truck with food reached the annex called Dobrinja where 40,000 people lived in March.

History grinned at us. It was St Vitus's Day, June 28. The year 1992. The guest was the top official of powerful France. In 1914 it was also St Vitus's Day in Sarajevo. It was also warm as it is now. We had a guest, also a top political personality. His name was Franz Ferdinand, archduke and heir to the throne of the powerful and enormous Austro-Hungarian monarchy.

I leaf through my diary:

"It is St Vitus's Day in Sarajevo. It is the summer of 1992.

"The day is sad like the months preceeding it.

"The war, bloody and perfidious, has become our daily routine. Shells roar. Every morning there are new wounds in the asphalt, in the walls of our rooms, ridges of roofs, in the bodies of the city and the citizens whom luck abandoned just on that day.

"There are no red carnations at the charnel house of the Chapel of St Vitus's Day heroes. The roof of the stone chapel gapes. The shell did not spare it. The assassins of Sarajevo fell into disfavour. The footprints of Gavrilo Princip were removed from the asphalt pavement. The plate commemorating the scene of the assassination was smashed to smithereens. The nose was cut off from the museum replica of the head near which the words 'We loved this people' were chiselled. The members of Young Bosnia are not alive any more. They wanted freedom, love and happiness. Grey-haired old men passed into eternity. I used to meet them at the café of the Central Hotel every month on the first Thursday after the twentieth, at 6.00 p.m. in the summer and at 5.00 p.m. in the winter.

"Today I still meet only the grandson of Cvjetko Popović. He sells 'Večernje novine' (The Evening News), he remembers his grandfather, some photographs and letters.

"History turns its massive wheel..."

Mr Mitterrand took a walk round Sarajevo. He wondered at our camp. The wrinkles on his face did not move. He did not receive revolver bullets. Gavrilo Princip died long, too long ago in the humidity of the Terezien Tower. Mr Mitterrand elegantly laid a red rose on the bloodstained pavement in the street where a month earlier the citizens of Sarajevo had been massacred. They had been queueing up to buy bread. He also visited the former military hospital,

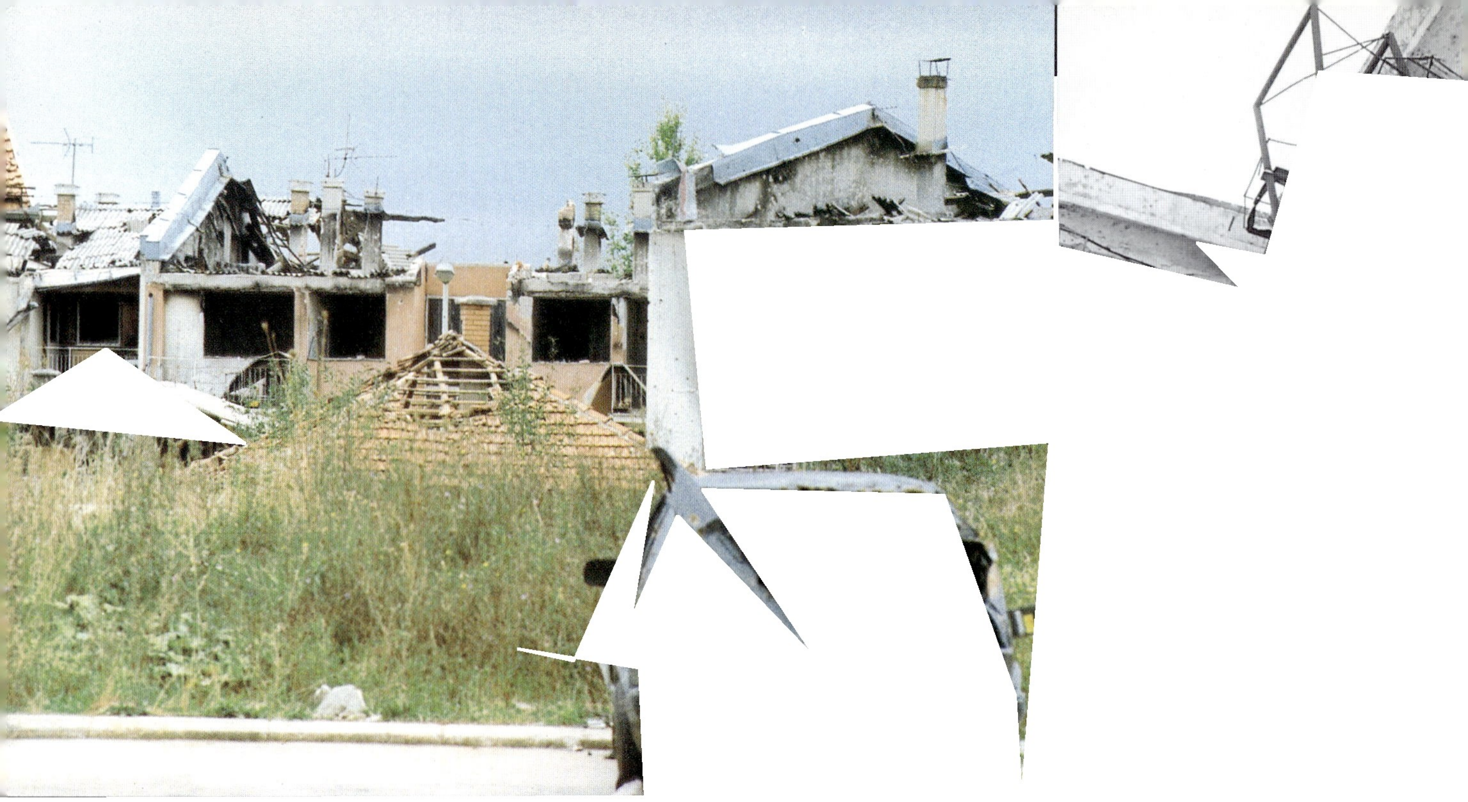

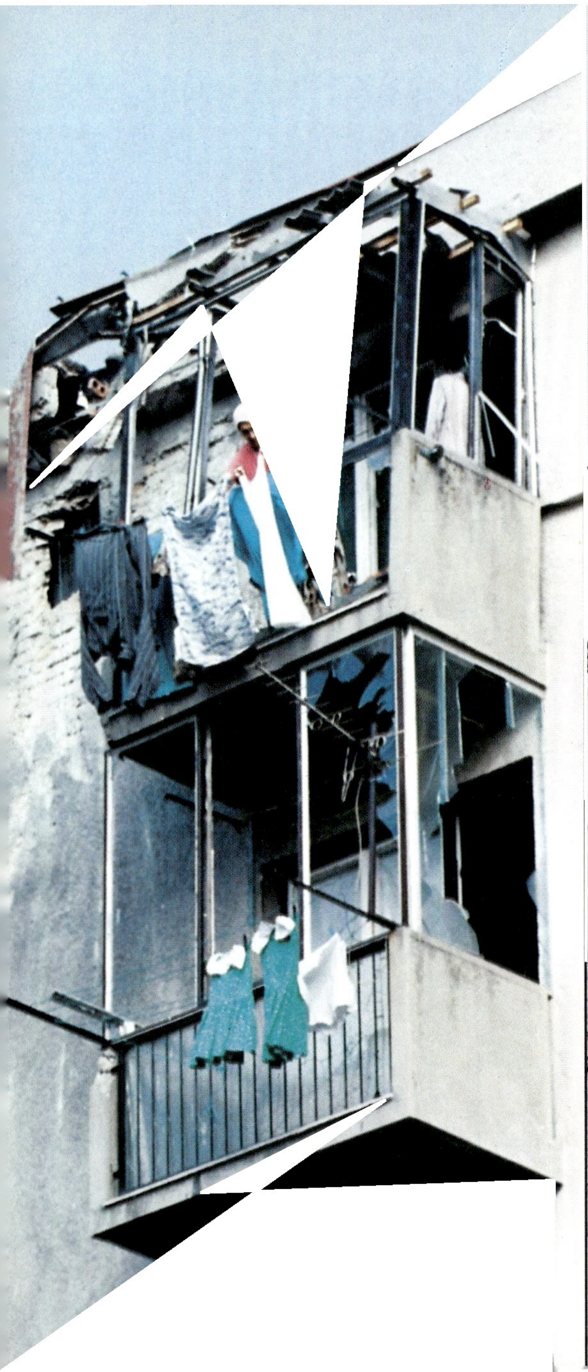

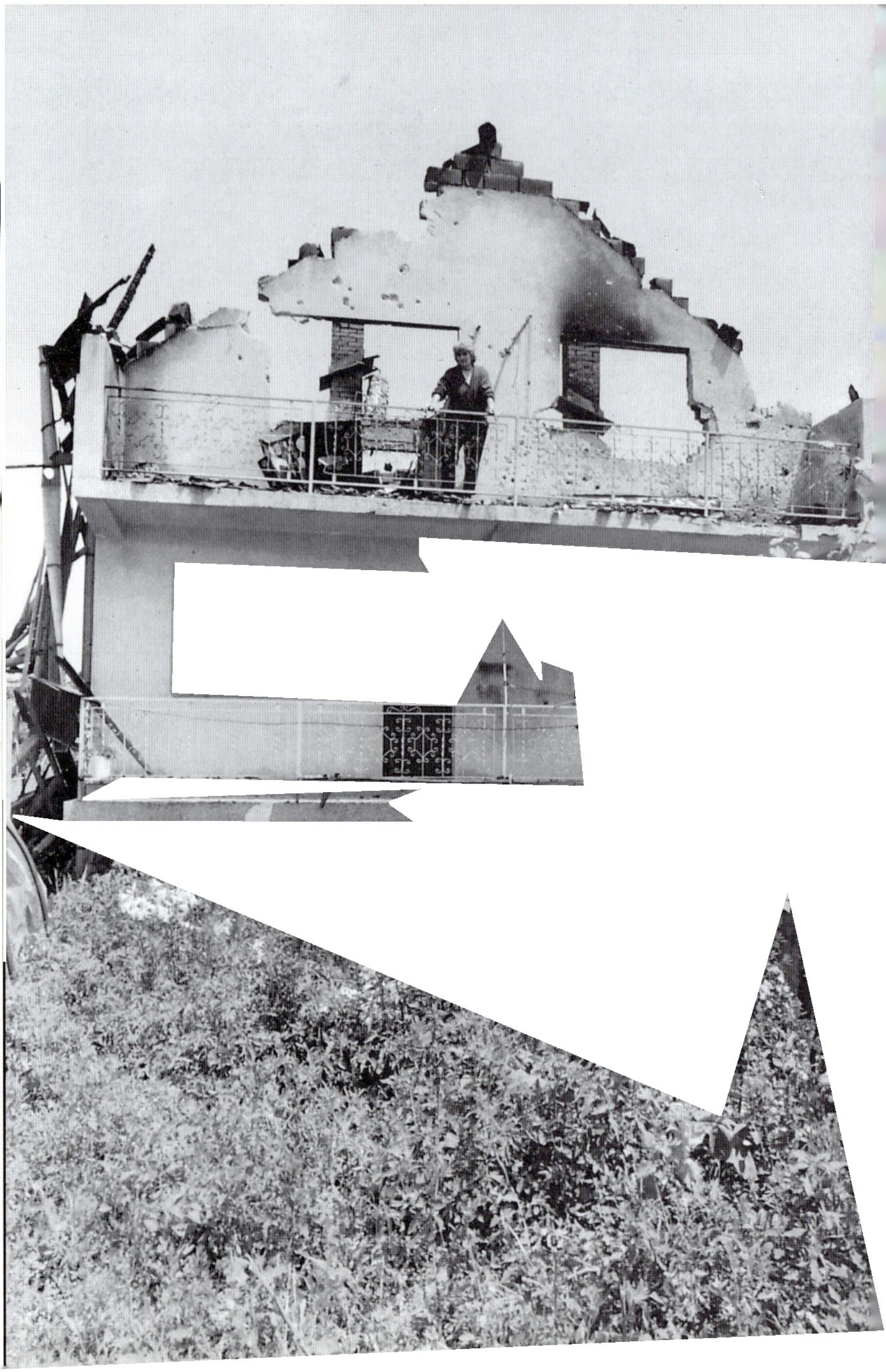

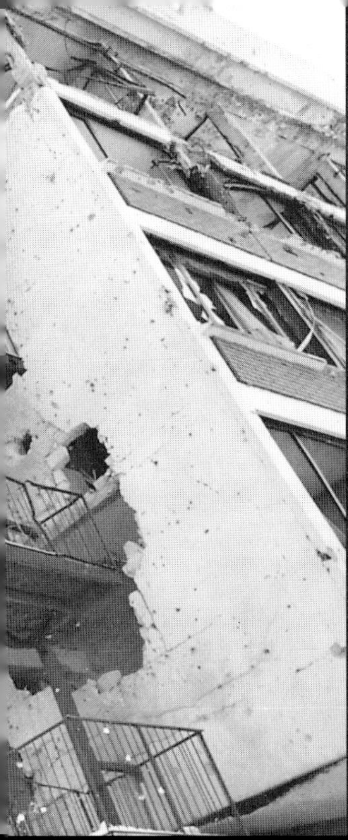
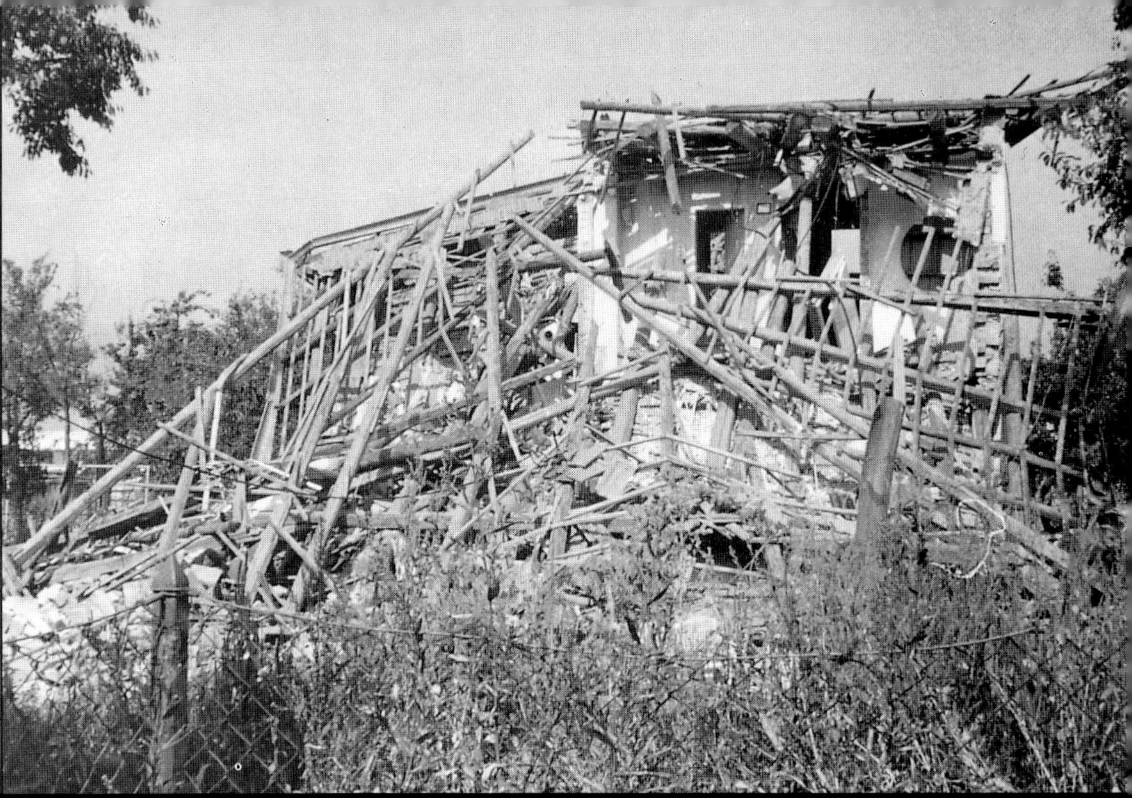
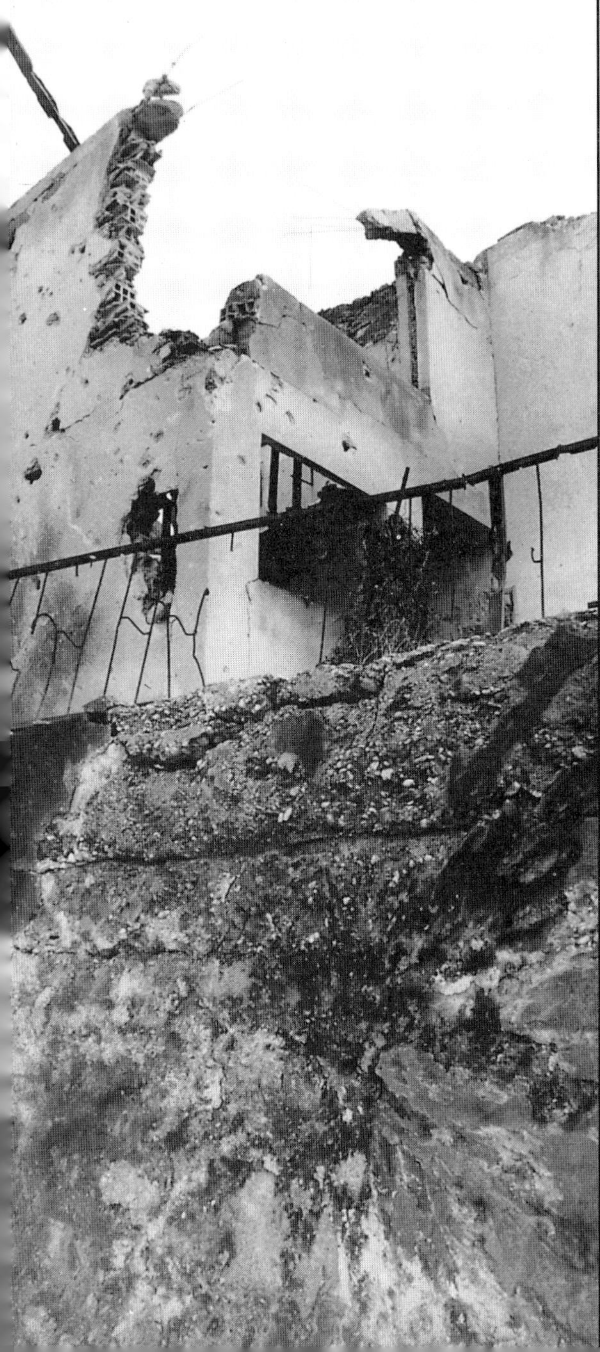
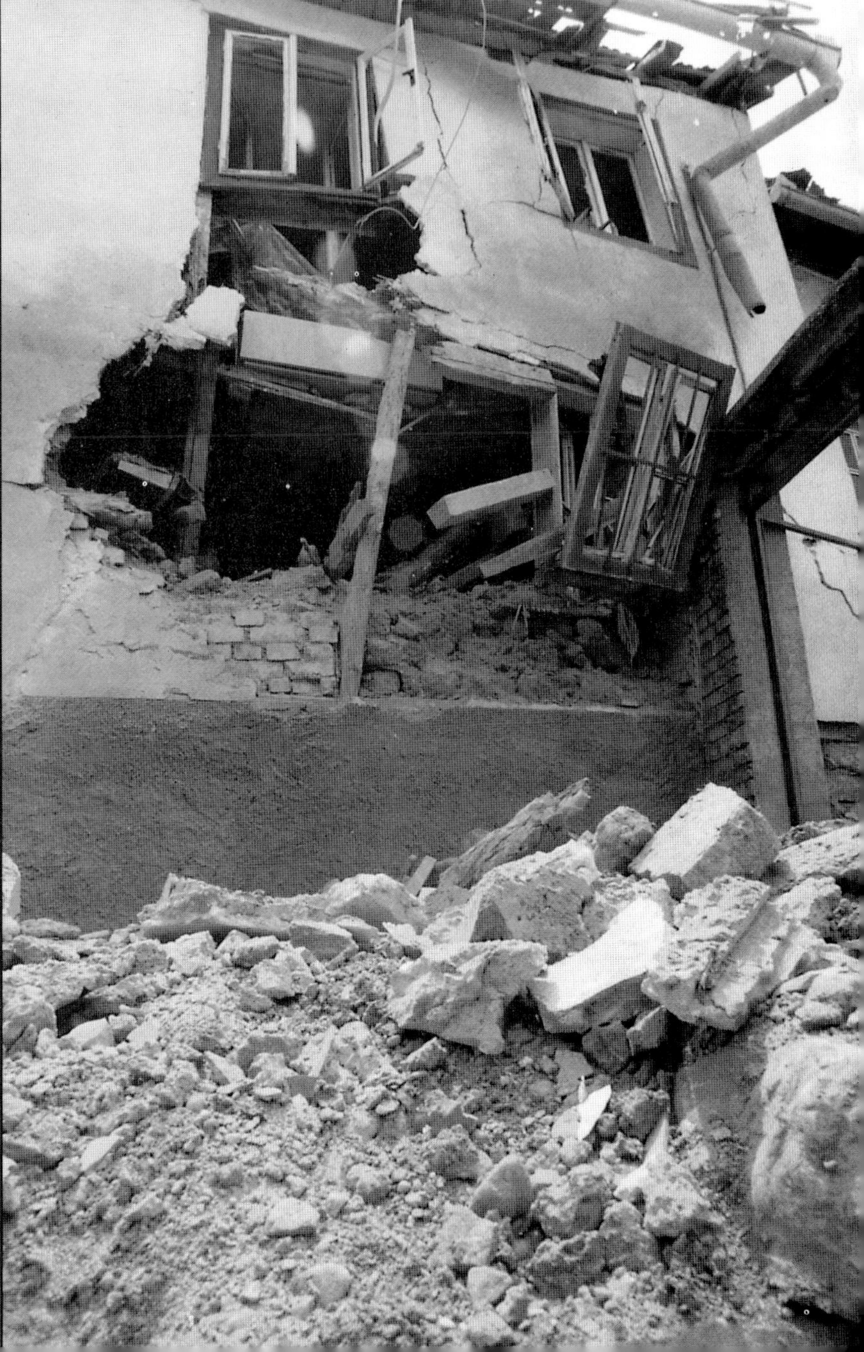

now the city hospital, and perhaps the French Hospital. He looked with dignity at its broken windows and the hoisted white flag with a red cross riddled with bullets. The mayor of the city, as a sign of our wonder and gratitude for the knowledge that aircraft could land at our airport, awarded him honorary citizenship. The Frenchman became a Sarajevan. He expressed his thanks and, touched, flew away after a few hours' stay here.

I do not know what happened to the olive branch. Perhaps we could have made some salad out of it. There must be some vitamins in olive leaves.

I walked further. I was finishing my circle. The camp was quiet again. Only shots, death and darkness all around.

The number tattooed on my lower arm did not itch. The mirror did not reflect convict's clothes on me, the number on the left side of my chest, or those large figures on my back.

released. Margaret Roth, a news photographer for American CNN is seriously injured by shell fragments. Branko Tešanović, one of our best TV cameramen, dies of injuries caused by a sniper. Mark Dalmage, an American TV reporter is wounded. John Ashton, an American free-lance reporter, is wounded in Otes.

CIRCLE FOUR

Friday, 24th: The Olympic team of B-H (23 members) goes to Barcelona for the Olympiad. In Sarajevo 10 are killed and 65 injured. Shells explode all over the city: the centre, Hrasno, Pero Kosorić Square, Dobrinja, Vojničko polje, Mojmilo and Sokolović kolonija. Infantry attempts at breakthroughs at Zlatište, the Jewish cemetery and Soukbunar. No water in most parts of the city.

Saturday, 25th: A shell injures about ten people in front of the Presidency. The "Pavle Goranin" residential area and Čolina kapa shelled. The State Commission for exchange of POW's publishes a list of 57 prison camps with more than 95,000 prisoners.

Sunday, 26th: Shelling of Stari grad (Kovači, Tito Street), Pero Kosorić Square, Hrasno hill, Alipašino polje, Otes, Hrasnica, Sokolović kolonija and Vratnik. Sniping from Grbavica and the Jewish cemetery. From June 29th to July 24th 2,149 tons of various food is delivered. Of this 2,082 tons is delivered to and distributed in Sarajevo. There are also 169 tons of medicine and medical supplies. Also 109.7 tons of

It is pitch dark at the entrance I am leaving. It is dark all around. I grope about. Humid walls are all around us, some sticky stuff flows down them. Blood, screams, explosions. Is it the same music, which is only being repeated? What on earth do the dwellers of hell eat? Their shacks are roofless. The slates and singed beams are broken. Holes in the walls gape. Bricks and mortar are littered over the beds and on the floor. There are some bits of a broken dinner service and crystal glasses. Pieces of broken glass remind me of the former window-panes of Sarajevo. The creaking of the door closing behind me rouses me. Pieces of paper are stuck on it. Something is written on them. There are several of them. It seems that they were left there by those who believed they would be able to come back. They will serve as signs in a maze. There were some of them also in the circles I had left. I had not paid any attention to them before.

I read. Above the signature of Jana Schneider, a war reporter for "Newsweek" and "Stern", it says: "... What is happening in Bosnia and Herzegovina is something that the world has never seen. I have often said that the Holywood war films are something that only the imagination of screen-play writers can conjure up. What is happening in Sarajevo, I can responsibly say, is exactly what one can see only in Holywood's best spectacle. Without exaggeration, without imagination. Crude and cruel reality.

"All this is madness. So are my wounds. Rumours are spreading that I always run risks. I am always on the front lines. That morning the sun was shining, I was away from the front lines and as I threaded my way through high grass, I laughed. And there was a truce! Then one shell fell, then another, a third ... The seventh one. As if they had been shooting only at Ivo and me..."

Up in the corner I can hardly make out the letterhead of the Traumatology Clinic in Sarajevo. It does not say where and how Ivo Stendeker was buried.

"... Today I saw and survived a great human tragedy... Bleeding cannot be stopped by announcements, declarations, embargoes... The world is forced to take some measures which will stop the bleeding." Signed Hikmet Cetin, the minister of foreign affairs of Turkey.

"I remember how I watched the Olympics in Sarajevo on TV and thought what a beautiful city Sarajevo was. At that moment I did not think that I would be an eyewitness to its destruction," wrote the Russian major Jevgeny Tepljakov.

"... What I know is that Europe cannot be built on the ashes of Sarajevo; I know we cannot speak about 'peace' in Europe if we accept the erasing from the map of one city – the symbol of the continent; what I am convinced of is that we cannot endlessly repeat 'Maastricht is making progress, Maastricht is making progress' if we, at the same time,

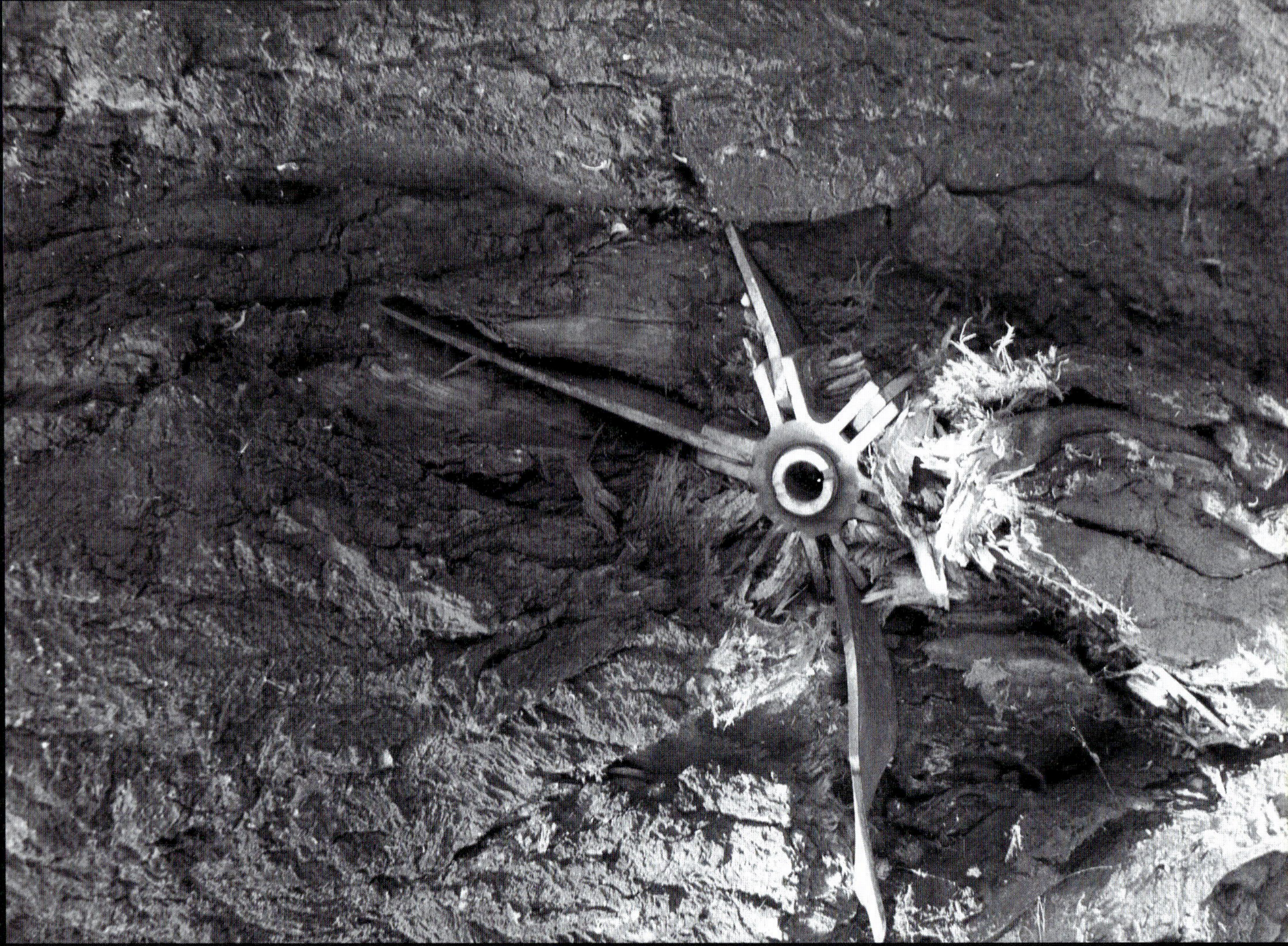

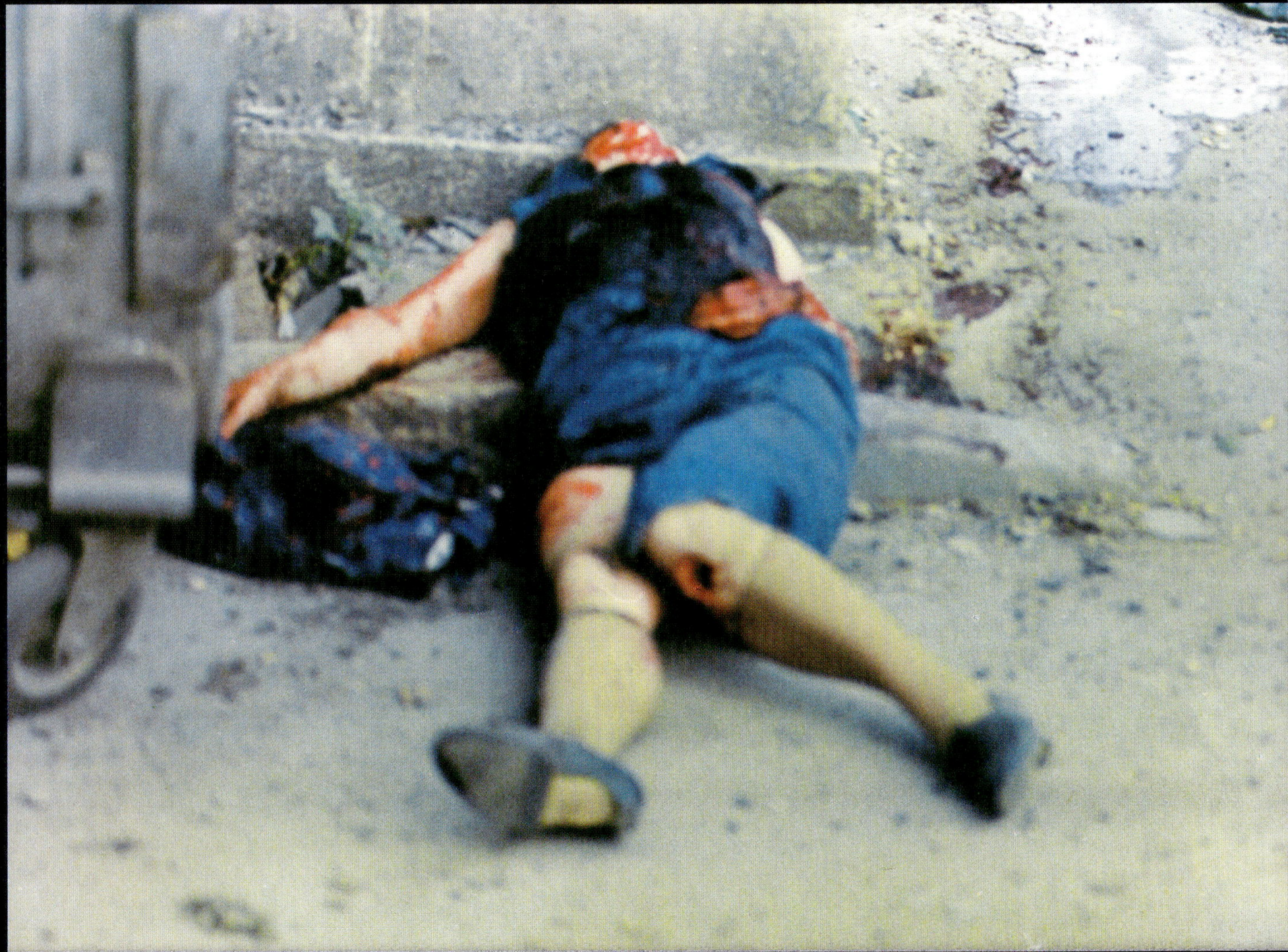

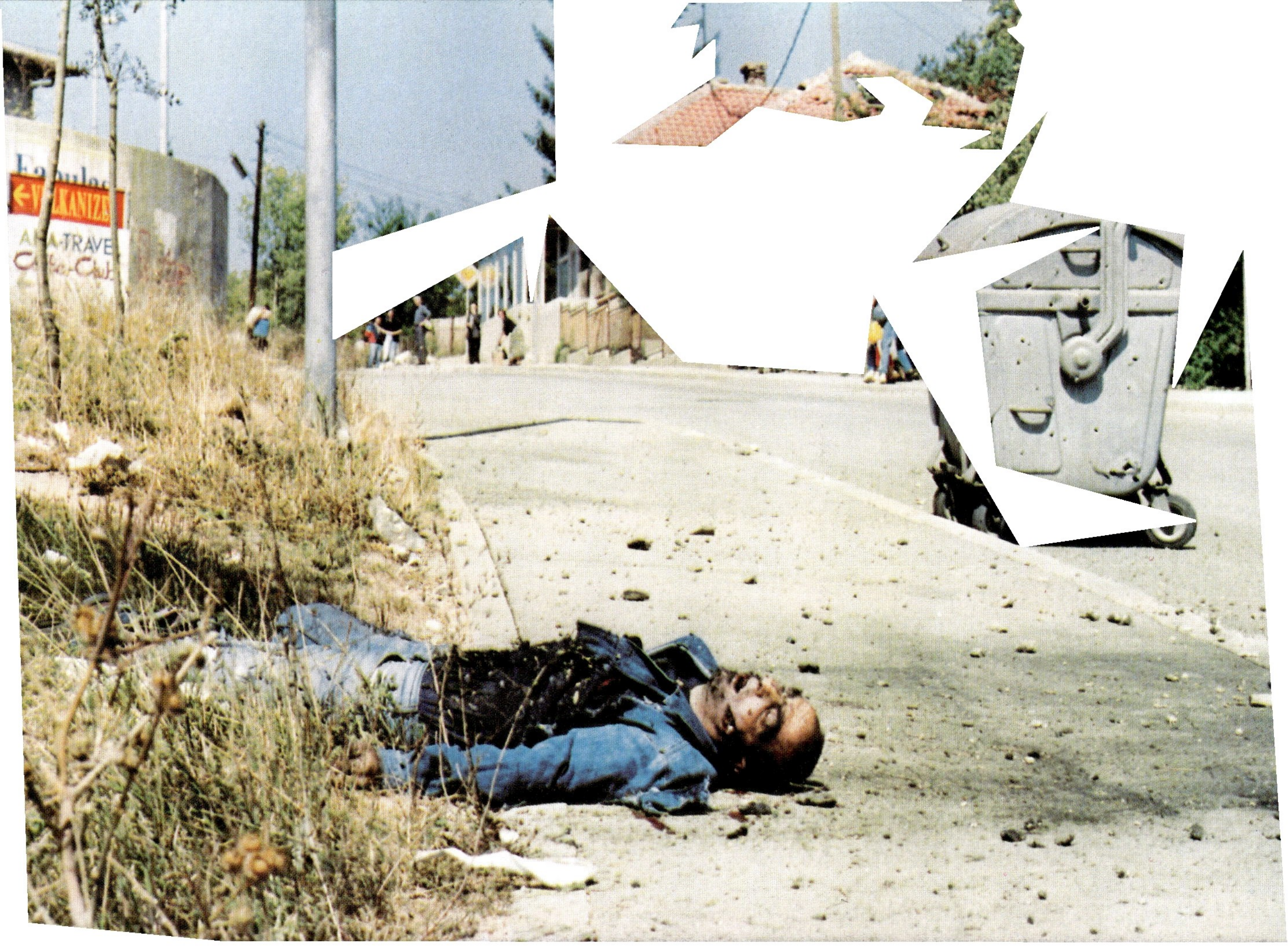

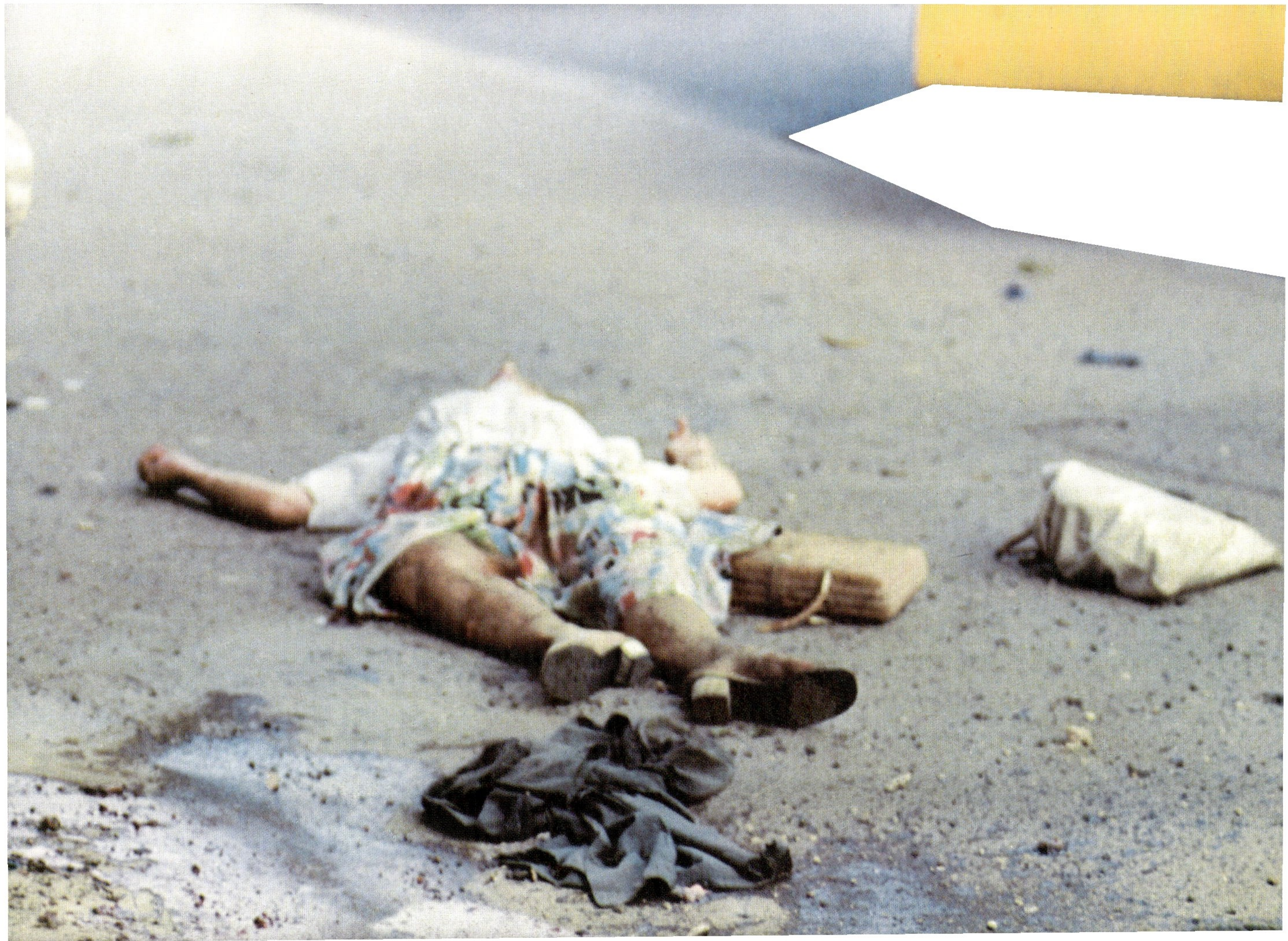

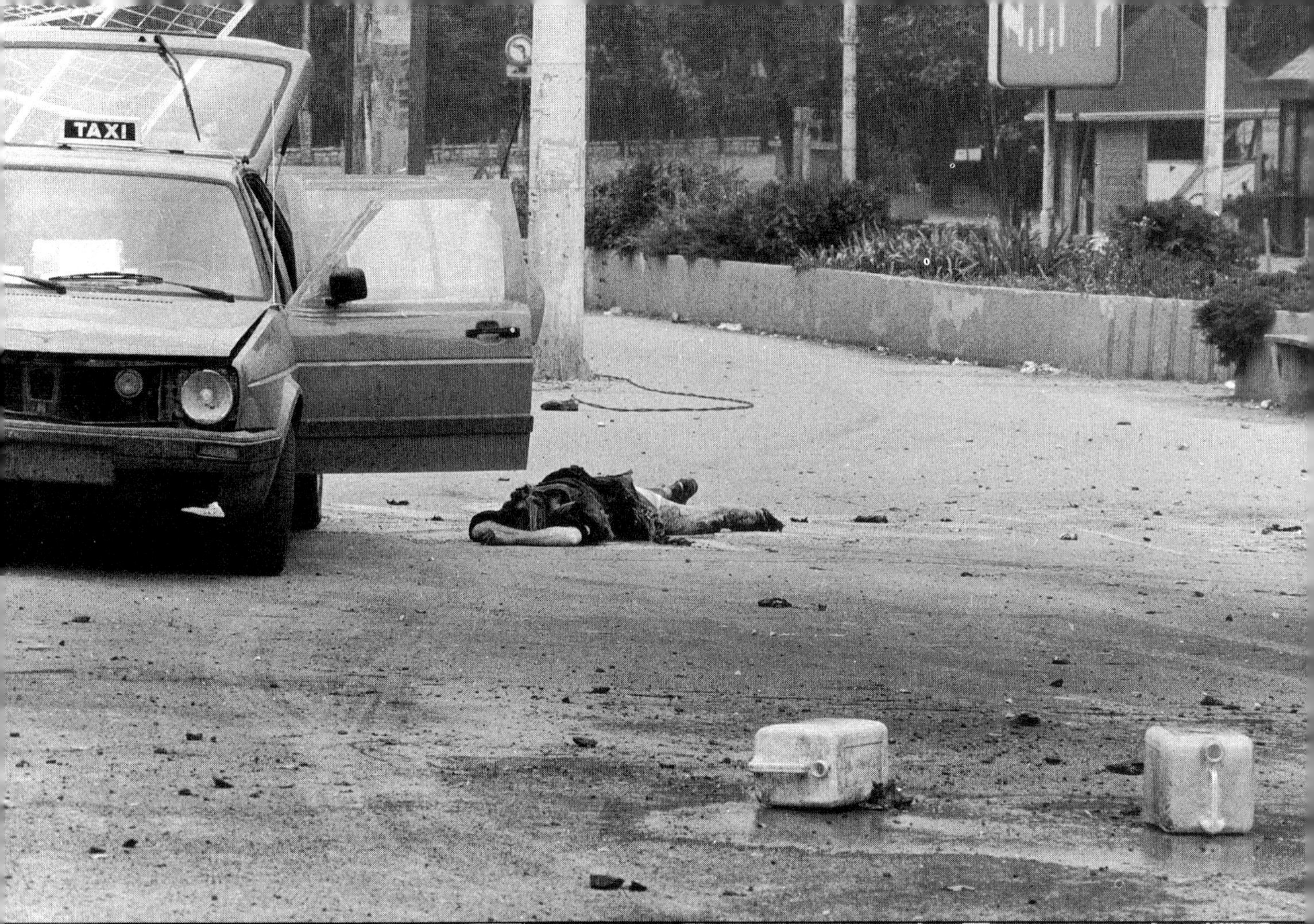
TAXI
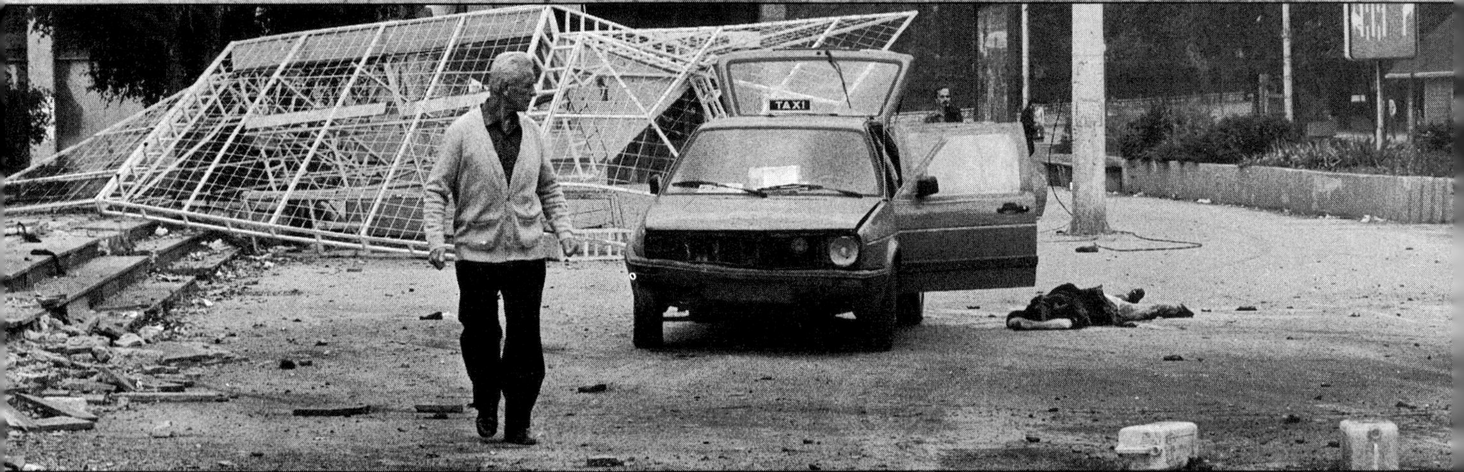
TAXI
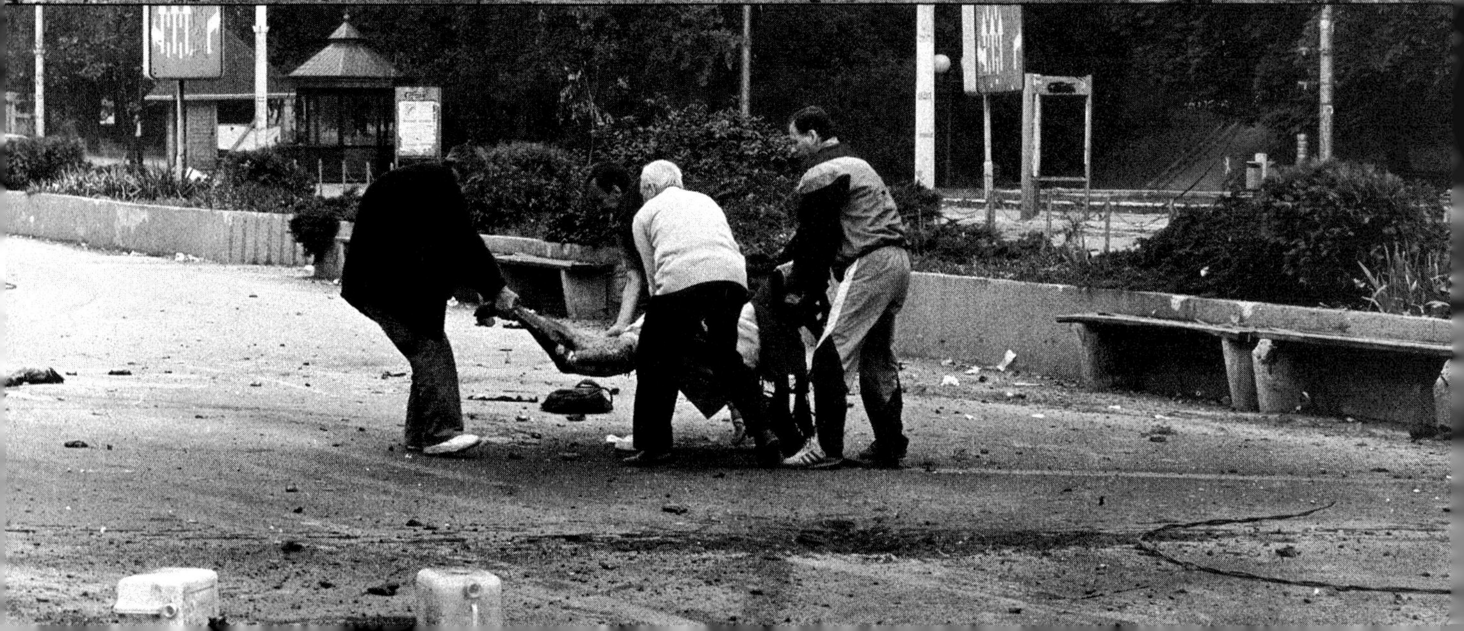

SARAJEVO – THE WOUNDED CITY

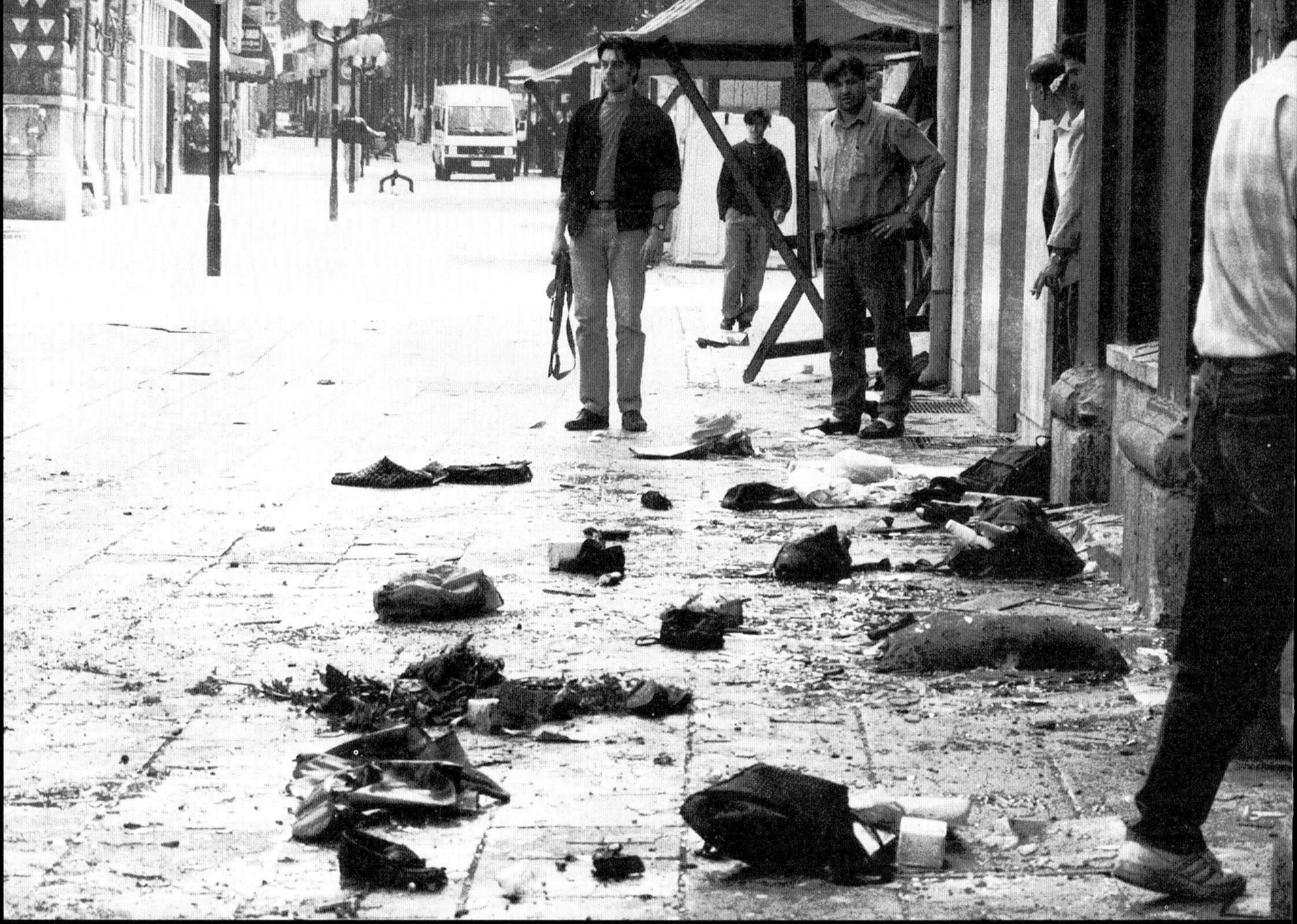

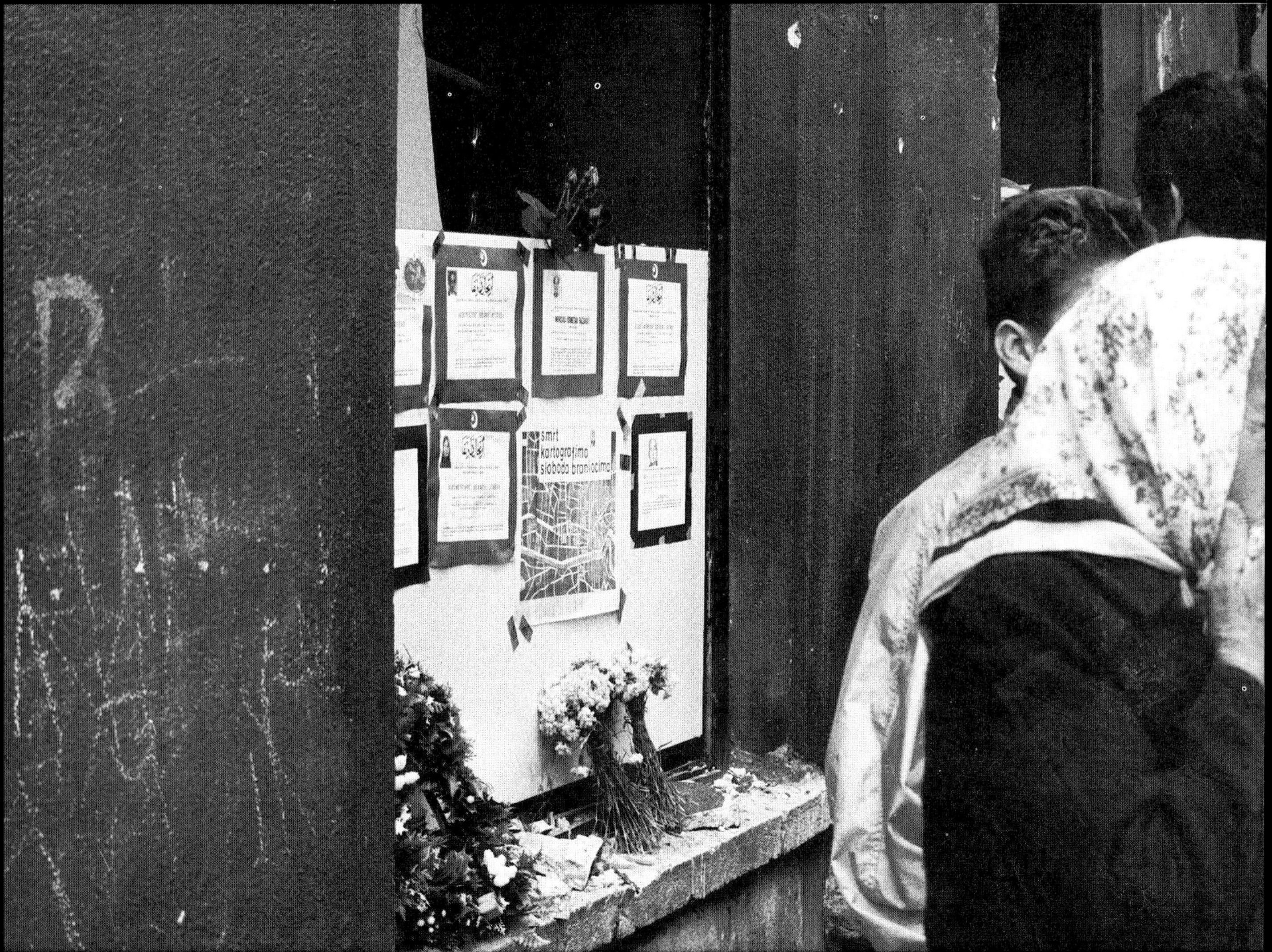
smrt
kartografima
sloboda braniocima

POMEN
GRAĐANIMA SARAJEVA
ŽRTVAMA FAŠISTIČKOG
TERORA 27·V·1992

accept a step backwards which would be caused by the fall of this Bosnian-Herzegovinan city..." Bernard Henri Levi leaves his, I do not know in which in order, message.

He adds the oral message of the first personality of the Bosnian-Herzegovinan state. He will report it, when he goes back, to the leaders of his country: "We are at the end, we have no more food, weapons, or hope! We are the Warsaw ghetto – do you understand? Will it be allowed once more that the ghetto in Warsaw dies? We shall die, too, all of us. I do not think we shall have any choice."

On one side, there is a note of the leader of the Liberal-Democratic Party of Great Britain: "It is easy to go in for politics from a distance of a thousand miles... It is very important to understand that Sarajevo and Bosnia and Herzegovina, if nothing is done, will become a horrible war precedent for the whole of Eastern Europe. Western Europe must know that the winter here will kill more people than the war." Signed Paddy Ashdown.

I wonder whether the journalists Lila Perišić and Husein Taslidžak will manage to come back for their pieces of paper. Will they manage to find other papers of theirs? I remember a small part of Lila's letter: "Together with the four apocalyptic riders, you foolish authors of the idea of ethnically clean areas whose peoples have lived together for centuries, mixed like kneaded dough, you have introduced, as an advance guard, the fifth rider – HATRED – in these parts of cultivated spirit but of cruel and savage living. Awesome, monstrous, destructive and irrational. Into the country of Bosnia and Herzegovina, which did not, if anybody else did, deserve it in any way..."

At the bottom of Huso's lines I find: "...They killed eleven friends and acquaintances of mine, imagine that, from only one street, named after a great writer, a street only a few hundred metres long.

"J'accuse! says the great writer. I probably have the right to accuse, too."

I walk over many messages that have fallen off. The glue did not hold to see those who hope to come back, for salvation. I can hardly make out the excerpt: "...And my life has stopped. I am dead. The only thing that remains for me is to go to a monastery..."

I do not know myself where I got my piece of paper from: "The nocturne of Sarajevo..."

A pitch-dark night. You can see nothing. How dark must pitch be?

Krleža roams through the province of my memory. His Arabic proverb, so appropriate for everywhere else, is absurd here, this bestial anno domini. There are neither dogs barking at night nor caravans passing by. Or, they, perhaps, bypass us in a big arc. We believed we are on a road one must go in order to live. Europe could not reach Asia without us. Asia, without us, would be deprived of

baby food and 10.8 tons of baby milk (which is 53% of the monthly requirements) are delivered. These supplies satisfy 6.2% of the total requirements of the citizens of Sarajevo. According to UNHCR data, 1,897,000 people in B-H have left their homes by July 22nd. The Presidency of the City Assembly confers honorary citizenship on Vladimir Prelog, the Noble Prize Winner and humanist. The "Ideja" Publishing House promotes the first book written and published in war-torn Sarajevo – "Letters from War" by Kemal Kurspahić.

Monday, 27th: *The Military Hospital has its name changed into the French Hospital. Shells fall on Marshal Tito Street near the Institute of Hygiene.*

Tuesday, 28th: *There are 35 wounded at Dobrinja. More than half are injured by snipers. Two people lose their lives. Shells are fired at Dobrinja, Vratnik (one dead and five wounded), Zetra (a warehouse clerk dies), the city centre, the "Holiday Inn", the Assembly of B-H, Sarajevo Liberators' Street (one killed, two injured), Hrasnica, Sokolović kolonija, Breka potok and Koševsko brdo. An infantry breakthrough is attemped from Vojkovići on Hrasnica.*

Wednesday, 29th: *There are still problems with the electricity and water supplies. An average salary in B-H is about 30,000 dinars, while the monthly requirements of a four-member family for basic foods, just to survive in this war, are 400,000 dinars according to data provided by the Association of Independent Trade Unions of B-H. Two shells fall on Ciglane at about 10 a.m. – killing one and injuring* *eight. Snipers fire at Stari grad, Skenderija and Novo Sarajevo. There is shelling of Pero Kosorić Square, Alipašino polje, Dobrinja, Kobilja glava, Ugorska, Menjak, Hotonj, Barice, the outskirts of the Stari grad (old town) suburb and the centre of Baščaršija, Hrasno hill, Mojmilo and the "Oslobođenje" building. Rocket launchers are also used.*

Thursday, 30th: *At a children's playground in Blagoja Parović Street a shell kills a boy and a girl and injures 19 people. Shells are fired at Širokača, Sedrenik, Vasin han, Kobilja glava, Vratnik, Ciglane, Đure Đaković Street, Alipašino polje, Švrakino selo, Dobrinja, the "Oslobođenje" building and the Faculty of Civil Engineering. An infantry attack on Brekin potok. All telephone communications are cut. Two months ago communications were stopped with West Europe, and now with Serbia, Montenegro and Macedonia. A complete communications blockade of the town.*

Friday, 31st: *After midnight a new, heavy attack on the city. The whole city is shelled. There is shooting at Osmice, Poljine and Nedžarići. About fifty shells fall on Dobrinja. Also shelled are the Presidency of the Republic of B-H, Koševsko brdo, Breka, Ciglane, Boljakov and Buća potok, Stari grad (Širokača, Vratnik and Sedrenik), Hrasno hill, Pero Kosorić Square, Pofalići, the "Lav" cemetery, Stara Breka, Brekin potok, Mahmutovac, Čolina kapa, Kobilja glava and Stup... Attacks come from Poljine, Blagovac, Trebević, Brus, Zlatište plateau, Lukavica, Rajlovac*

Europe. Today they are where they are, and we are not a road any longer...

Look, today my Krleža would be 99! What a coincidence. I was proud of that nocturne. I was convinced that he had written it in Požega. Slavonian woods, vineyards and barking dogs. Far in the north, they must be still barking. Here, even dogs' barks are less and less frequent. The dark is denser and denser..."

I wonder what I can do. There is no choice. There is no sound either. There is no television or radio news. Relays and TV repeaters were occupied or damaged. Newspapers come out only in the printing house "Oko". Only "Oslobođenje" and "Večernje novine" come out every day. They are read only in the area of Sarajevo with asphalted streets that can be covered in one or two hours' time. One cannot go farther. Blocks of some other truths roll around us. They rush into the besieged valley. In the "Oslobođenje" building some tough people sleep, eat and work in a stuffy shelter. They do not know about pyjamas and slippers. They carry them uselessly in their bags. Explosions shake the printing presses, overturn the desks, stop the rotation, burn and destroy printing presses, archives, the photolaboratory, the printed and blank sheets. They are still in there. They are working. They may be finishing their last newspaper. They have not left their corridors for a week, but the newspaper is on the city streets every morning. Fresh printing ink on smaller and smaller white of the dwindling paper stocks is a sign of remaining life. It is now that I feel the scope of the words of the esteemed writer Marijan Matković. He said them to me leaving after a visit while we were preparing Krleža's polemics for printing: "This is a fortress. This is the last built fortress." It seemed to me that he exaggerated. One builds neither a castle nor a tower from glass and aluminium strips. However, "Oslobođenje" persevered. The voice of those sentenced to destruction was heard beyond the selling points where the journalists stood instead of newspaperboys. They wrote and sold what they had written. Their fellow journalists from the world spread their cries and their truth for them. They were wounded, killed and captured in this way. They could not reach where their professional curiosity led them. The world learned that, in the dark of Sarajevo, there was still some light, there were those who wanted to survive, who moved, stood up, wanted to go somewhere, wanted something.

I read from my diary: "I leaf through the Bible. I search, I feverishly look for my lesson. Is it 'Jeremiah's Lamentations'? How remote, centuries remote, those carefree grammar school days seem to me, that boringly deserted square in Požega in the afternoon and the sloping roofs of houses, church towers and that glazed niche in the wall. Underneath – a white plate with engraved letters coated with gilt. And Jeremiah's words: '.... all ye that pass

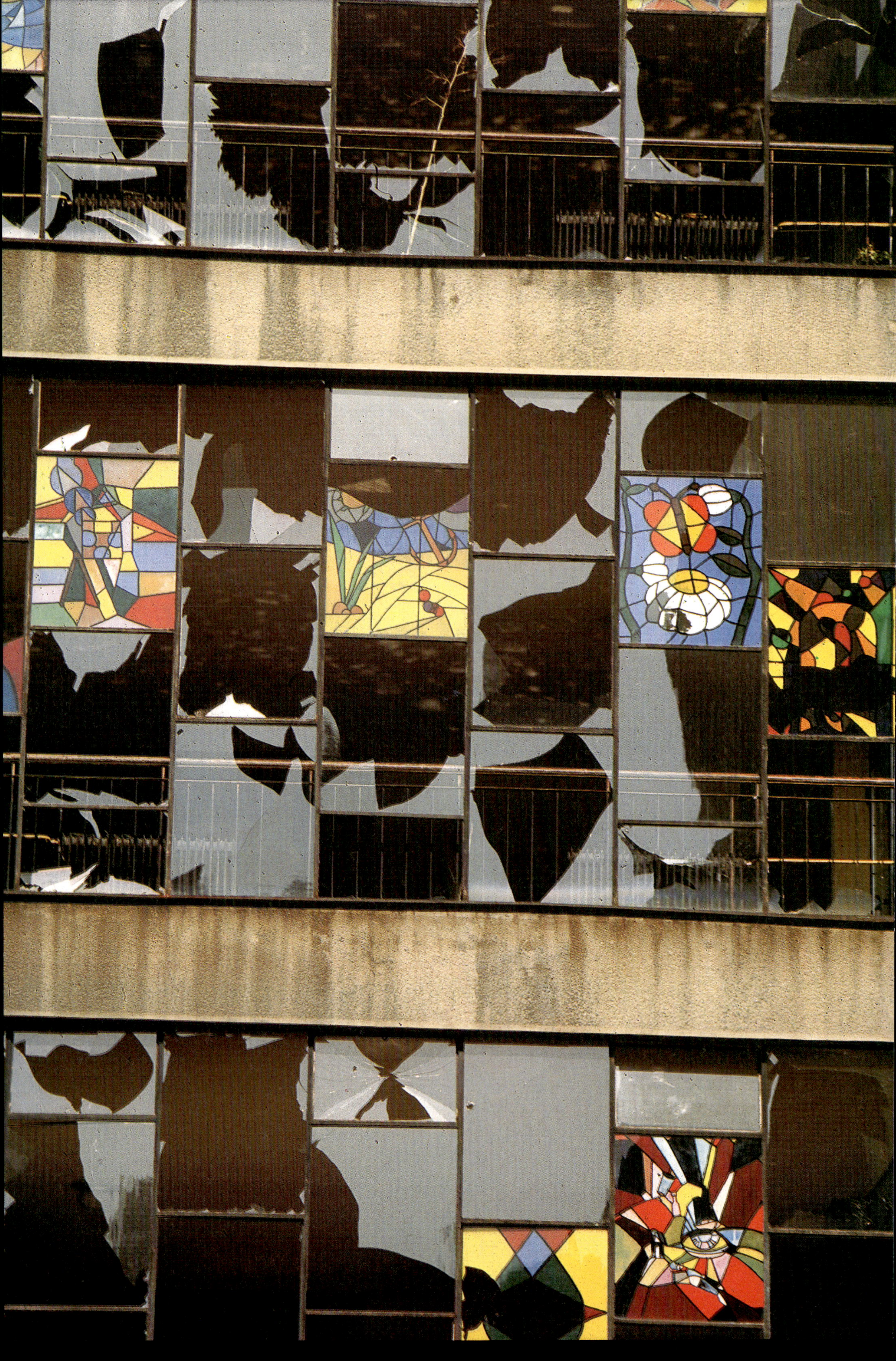

and Butilo using artillery, rocket launchers, mortars, and anti-aircraft machine guns. The French Hospital by 4 p.m. has received eleven dead and 151 wounded, and the Traumatology Clinic has received eight dead and 57 injured by 2 p.m.

AUGUST

Saturday, 1st: *Anti-aircraft machine guns, anti-aircraft guns, rocket launchers and other weapons are firing at the city. The targets are: Vasin han, Širokača, Sedrenik, Vratnik, Ciglane. Kobilja glava, Breka, Koševsko brdo, Alipašino and Vojničko polje, the "Oslobođenje" building, Stupsko brdo, Sokolović kolonija, Briješće and Hrasnica. Snipers fire at Pero Kosorić Square, Bratstvo-jedinstvo Street and Trščanska Street. Paddy Ashdown, the leader of the British Liberal Democratic Party, is in Sarajevo. In a bus taking 47 children from the "Ljubica Ivezić" orphanage to Saxony in Germany two babies are killed. The bus is fired at with an anti-aircraft machine gun near Nedžarići.*

Sunday, 2nd: *Artillery shells fall from Zabrđe onto Sokolje, and the School of Economics; mortar shells are fired at the "Bristol" hotel and howitzer shells from Rudine at Panjina kula, Grdonj and Breka; artillery fires from Vraca at Zlatište. An artillery breakthrough attempt at Pero Kosorić Square. Eighteen killed and fifty-five injured in Sarajevo.*

Monday, 3rd: *A hell of a night! The city comes under heavy artillery attack from rocket launchers, tanks and mortars. Hit are Vratnik, Vasin han, Babića bašta, the Presidency of B-H, Pofalići, Vojničko polje,*

by behold and see if there be any sorrow like unto my sorrow, which is done to me...' It was left out, I learned later. It still torments me: 'Hasn't it stopped?' And I went so many times to the market with my mother, read the memorised message by heart or climbed the quiet of nearby vineyards. Yes. Unfortunately, up on the hill, Calvary with three warning crosses steeply raised..."

On some other pages it was written: "There is no peace in the valleys of Bosnia. The hills moan. Artillery shells echo. Multistorey buildings fall to pieces. Shells over Sarajevo furrow the asphalted streets and grey pavements like a plough. They will plant bitter seeds in its pores. Hatred already tastes bitter on the lips..."

How unrealistic are the letters on the paper that slipped from an old memo pad. It says: Tibor Sekelj I–VI. In order: "1. Caravan of Friendship (Africa); 2. Tempest over Akongawa; 3. Along the Silk Trails; 4. Nepal; 5. Oceania; 6. Tierra del Fuego – Alaska. Twenty quires all together plus two sheets of illustrations (slides). A joint editorial with two editors from each. Joža Horvat – the review. Zagreb. Format B. These are top masters to do the editing."

Below: "Laszlo Toth."

I cannot find my way. I crawl. I meet hunger at the table. It sits. It does not feel like leaving. It does not only pass by. It does not stand. It takes a rest on the table at which people have their meals. It rests its head upon its arm. It grins at me when I pass it by. We still have some food in our freezers. The freezer has been an inevitable piece of furniture in very home for years. The freezer beat inflation with its contents. It was full of meat, vegetables and cheese. And it was refilled. We were hamsters which were safe. Now in our pantries there are a few kilos of flour, sugar and salt. We brought there, in recent months, some food supplies. One never knows what will come tomorrow. There is and there is not electricity. We get along with nettles and dandelions and some other supplies that are running out. These are the only vegetables we can buy. Everything is falling apart. The accepted standards disintegrate, the system, earnings and consumption. People are jobless. Everything has stopped. It does not move. Some firms were ruined, others have no work, have nothing to do the work with. There are no roads, no communications. Firms are dying. We are all jobless. It is wartime. War brings hunger, disease and misery. We sink deeper and deeper. We spend our last money. Everything is priced in German marks. I stood in the city's centre for days – at the market at Ciglane, the former wholesale market for agricultural produce and other foods. There was nothing. The whole selection of foods offered by middlemen and blackmarketeers could fit in two smallish plastic bags.

There is nothing.

Hunger grins repulsively. It sits triumphantly on the dining room table. It does not move.

The first aeroplanes carrying humanitarian aid land. Food reaches Sarajevo. We start getting aid. We live on charity. The world shows mercy. Charity has become our fate. We wait for it to come from the sky. It cannot come into our hell any other way. The first tons of medicine, food and blankets arrive. July's quantities are both beneficial and comic. We feel them more and more. They do not supply even a tenth of the city's needs.

We are not yet aware of the meaning of the words: "Only in deeply unfortunate countries do they establish offices for refugees and displaced persons and ministries of reconstruction." They were uttered by thirty-four-year-old Martin Raguž. He is the minister of employment and social policy, and the country is Bosnia and Herzegovina.

Dr. Ante Marketić is no false optimist, either. "Over only three months everything that can happen at all, only here and in no other place in the world, happened in Bosnia and Herzegovina. An omnidestructive war, with human victims, suffering and destruction of all the bases of life unseen so far, led Bosnia and Herzegovina to the edge of its survival as a state."

There is no ray of light anywhere.

Soup kitchens are being opened. Instead of an outstretched, empty hat for a help, people come with empty plates. Patiently and miserably they queue up for their ladle of soup, boiled rice or beans. There are more and more underprivileged people. The infection of poverty attacks all of us. The news of the month for the city is: "The yeast for 'Velepekara' (Town Bakery) has arrived."

"Give alms to the poor. Give alms to the poor. God bless you, oh, you are merciful. May God bestow fortune and health and everything good on you. May you never be like this. May you always have and give to others. Give alms, give alms to the poor..." I mutter the prayer of the city. Never before has the city knelt down. Never in its history has it been so miserable and humiliated. The ears of the world did not manage to hear the tune from our beggar's street organ. We concealed it with tears. Our empty hat collected the charity from the world. Hunger would have finished us off. The hat on the ground became bigger and bigger and we organized ourselves less and less. There was no counter service by which we could alleviate what was given. We waited for our morsel to be thrown in to the old, empty hat. Hunger entered the zoo in Pionirska dolina (Pioneers' Valley). For nine days the pets of the youngest ones in the favourite walk of the Sarajevans were without any food. Shrapnels and snipers killed the roe deer, the chamois, the llama... Doing his job, Ešref Tahirović, the keeper of the animals was killed. The zoo was on the new borderline of the city. We could not go further. They would have killed us had we approached. I wonder if a city rumour

*Dobrinja (14 injured), Švrakino selo, the heart of Baščaršija (the Bey's Mosque, Bezistan), Širokača, Koševsko brdo, Pionirska Street, Ciglane, Breka, Soukbunar, Hrasno hill, Pero Kosorić Square, Omer Maslić Street, the area around the City Dairy, the tobacco factory and the orphanage in Humska Street. Stup hill is also shelled. So far 3,411 tons of food has come to Sarajevo airport, which satisfies 12.2% of the monthly requirements of Sarajevo's citizens, or 2.62% of all the citizens in B-H. As for medicine, the quantity amounts to 191.9 tons, or 7.6% of the requirements for Sarajevo. Up to now, the war has claimed 1,569 lives in Sarajevo, 830 of them children. Seriously injured are 9,333 people, 70% civilians, 20% children. Electricity and water supplies inadequate owing to breakdowns at Bačevo and Mojmilo and damage to the low-voltage system.
A convoy of 22 lorries carrying humanitarian aid as part of the "Wounded Zadar to Wounded Sarajevo" campaign, which started at the beginning of July, finally arrives.*

Tuesday, 4th: *Infantry attempts to break through at Hrasnica, Mojmilo, Dobrinja and Sokolović kolonija. Shelling of the "Lav" cemetery. The airport is shelled. Destruction at "Oslobođenje". The airport is closed.*

Wednesday, 5th: *Shelling of Stari grad (hundreds of shells fall on Hrid, Sedrenik and Širokača – five citizens killed, forty injured), Čolina kapa, Pero Kosorić Square, Hrasno, Alipašino polje and Mojmilo. Four killed in the centre. Fighting at the Jewish cemetery. An infantry attack*

from Vraca and Grbavica on Hrasno hill and Pero Kosorić Square. Fourteen people are killed and 130 injured in Sarajevo. The airport is closed.

Thursday, 6th: *An infantry attempt to break through at Dobrinja. Fighting at Čolina kapa. The centre of the city is shelled. A shell falls on the Presidency of B-H injuring several people. The Sarajevo War Theatre (SARTR) is founded. The airport is closed. Thirty killed, ninety–six injured.*

Friday, 7th: *Shells fall on the crossroads of Ivan Krndelj and Braća Ribar Streets killing 6 and injuring 8 people. Shells fall at about 2.30 p.m. around the "Sarajka" department store and Marijin Dvor killing 6 and injuring 10. Shelling of Baščaršija, Sedrenik, Vasin han, Otoka and Dobrinja.*

Saturday, 8th: *After 2 p.m. shells start falling on the Sarači, Kazandžiluk, Vaso Miskin, Defenders of Sarajevo Streets, on the Orthodox church, Hrid, Vratnik, Širokača, Jarčedoli, Sedrenik (poisonous gas is used on Čolina kapa), Vojničko polje, Dobrinja, Alipašino polje, Kobilja glava, Donji Hotonj, Koševsko brdo, Bare and the "Viktor Bubanj" prison complex. The public bathhouse is set on fire. Twenty-three people are killed, 114 wounded in the city. After three days, the airport opens again. The repaired transmission line is hit again.*

Sunday, 9th: *A rather peaceful day. Five people are injured in Dragica Pravica Street by shell fragments. Shell fragments also injure some people at Jarčedole, Hladivode and Hrid.*

about a slaughtered antelope, which was not tasty even after roasting, is a joke.

Deaths kept surprising us with no answer. Dragica Pirnat, a legend of the trade union movement, left silently. She remembered the last century as a twelve-year-old girl. She survived many rulers and states, good and bad. She took away with her many stories and traditions from the asphalt of Sarajevo and her own part in the general strike of 1906. The heart in the chest of the warm Hajrudin Šiba Krvavac did not hold out. The film director did not live to see the end of this war. He left behind an action film trilogy about the antifascist struggle, about Valter and Sarajevo. Into all that film shooting he incorporated a scene with unarmed parents, a scene so familiar today, going to Baščaršija to collect the bodies of their dearest ones in front of the fascists with their rifles pointing at them. Salko Hondo, a newspaper photographer on "Oslobođenje", did not come back from work. He photographed what he was asked to. At Ciglane, he photographed a long queue for water at Boro "Carnation's". A chronicler will write down in journalistic style: "The film will somehow reach the editorial office to show in this tragic way as well that, in journalism, there are still people whose deeds outlive them." A shell killed him some twenty metres from the place where I stand every day. I had left the place some ten minutes before that. He might have wanted to greet me, to joke, to see what remained of the market near a luxurious city quarter that used to be overcrowded... The shell came in suddenly. The murderers always choose the places where people meet. Their favourite targets are: funerals, hospitals, crossroads and markets. One shell can claim more victims. Shrapnel tore into the people who had come to buy something at the market, as they were used to doing. They found nothing. The shell hit a pillar. The woman who sold rolls every day ran between the counters. She hid herself behind a concrete pillar. She got her breath back and went back to sell rolls to her customers. She reached for her bag. The scream came: "Where is my hand?... Hand... Hand..."

All this is a game of evil. We cannot get out of it. In it, it is unbearable. We stamp our feet. We grope. There is cold and misery all around. It is summertime, but our blood freezes in our veins. It is warm and sunny, but one cannot see anything.

I go back to a page in my diary: "I do not know myself why, these war weeks and months, my thoughts take me to Miloš Vidaković. He was a Sarajevo scholar, a child of this city. He spent his early days all over Bosnia following the teacher's suitcases of his father. He got to know Vienna, Geneva and Florence by studying there. He ended his life as a refugee in Wales. Tuberculosis prevented him from surviving the autumn of 1915. I keep thinking of the verses of 'A Crazy Poem' by that twenty-four-year-old, one of the best

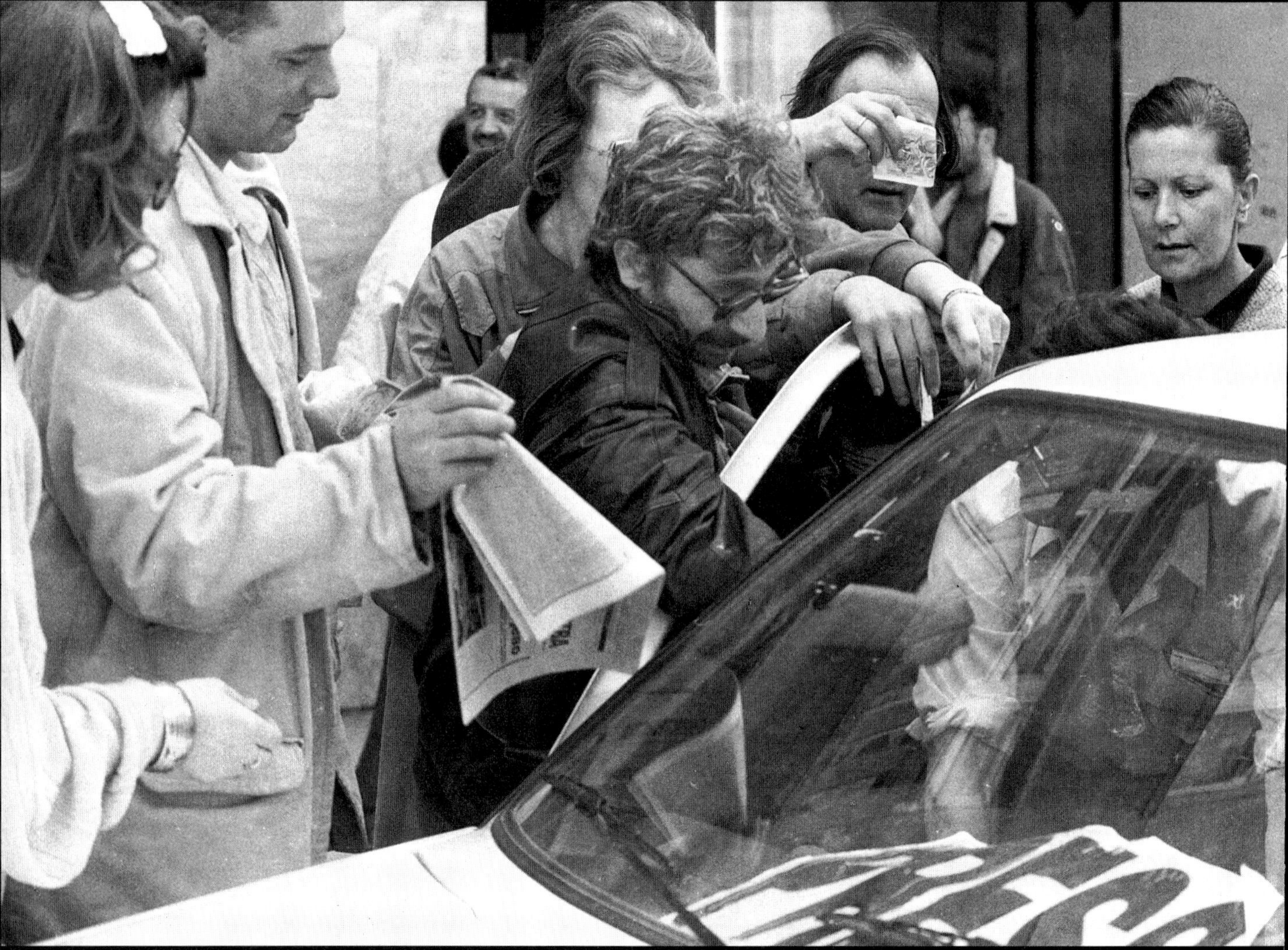

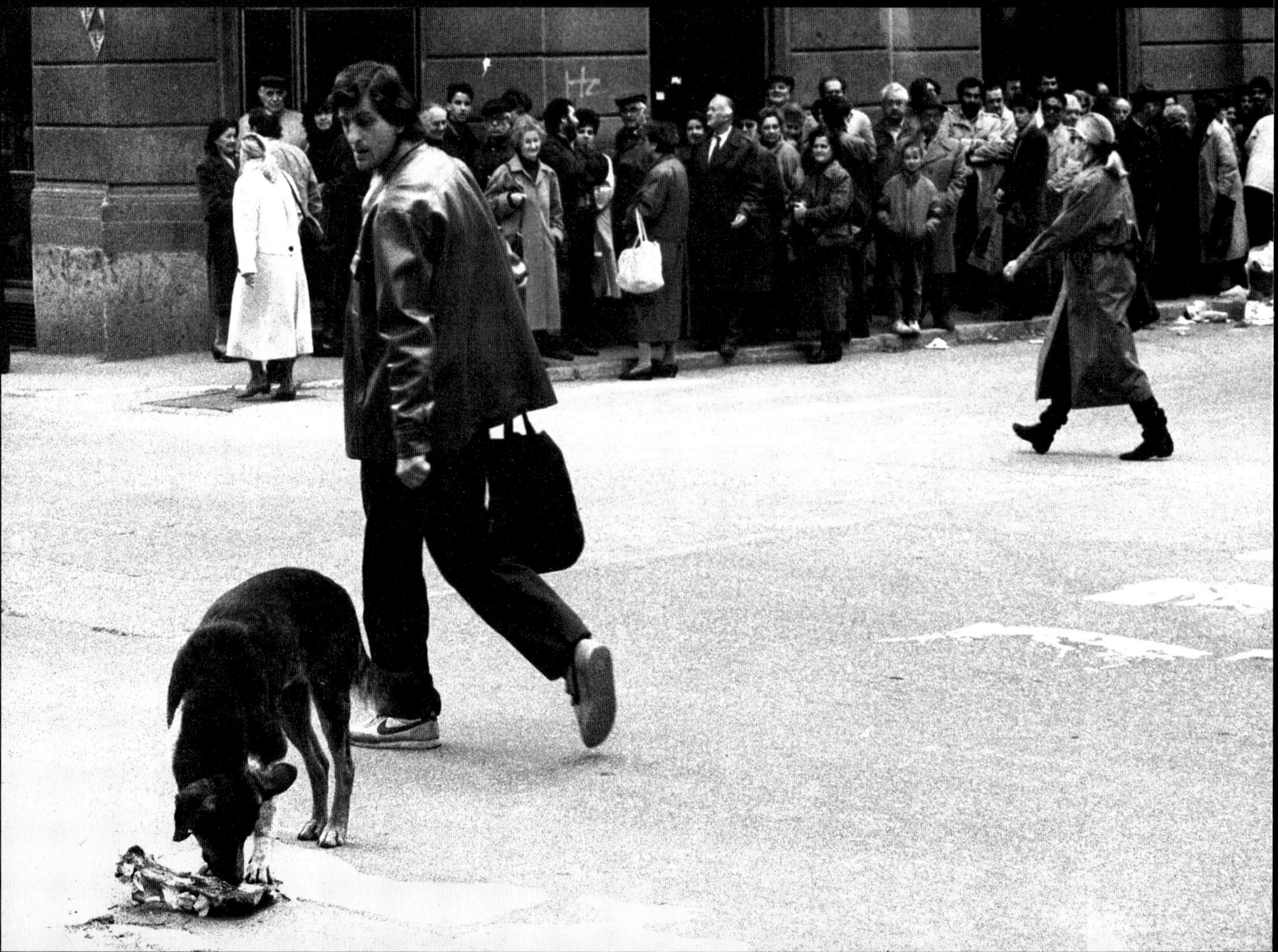

Following a decision by the Serb authorities at Ilidža the Bačevo springs are closed.

Monday, 10th: *In the 130 days of the war in Sarajevo 1,682 people have been killed. According to hospital records, 9,446 have been seriously wounded – 25% of these are children – and 85,000 slightly injured. In more than a hundred prison camps more than 100,000 people have been interned. In a period of ten days, humanitarian aid is distributed to 304,096 citizens of Sarajevo. The total weight of that aid amounts to 4,407,196 kg. The units of the B-H Armed Forces (OSBiH) from Hrasnica and Sokolović kolonija exchange prisoners for their dead soldiers.*

Tuesday, 11th: *The parish office at Stup is hit by a 105-mm howitzer shell. The centre and Stari grad are shelled in the afternoon. Shells fired by a tank at Nahorevo hits the Maternity Hospital and Ciglane. Projectiles from a rocket launcher fall onto Pofalići and in the vicinity of the tobacco factory. The city centre is targeted from Borije and Trebević. Širokača, Hrid and Vaso Miskin Street are fired at by a mortar and an anti-aircraft gun. Several shells fall on Dobrinja after the arrival of a humanitarian aid convoy. An infantry attack from Donja Bioska on Hladivode.*

educated of Young Bosnia's members. He did not have time to establish himself as a poet and critic: 'This is a poem without rhythm and rhyme, this is a poem written in simple words, since the music of its verses will not lend it the beauty it does not ask for. This poem is not good and it is broken off like a grey stone from our hearts, deep and silent like a cave...'

"Oh, who among us can boast that none of their grandfathers hung from the rope at the church door, that nobody's skull grinned on a stake at imperial bullwarks, and all that because of lofty wishes for the sunshine."

Then I recall again my February conversations in Vienna. How far is my usual melange coffee, newspapers and the "Central" cafe! There a sculpture of a dear guest with his coffee still in the corner by the entrance. All that is so inconceivably far. Too distant are also those neat shopwindows, the Graben and Kärtner Strasse, a tram ride and meetings with Mr Pavao Urban. A "J" is interpolated between his name and surname. It could stand for Joseph, but he says himself that it stands for Jusuf. He, a born Sarajevan, keeps his part of Sarajevo. He is the founder of the twenty-five-year-old society of Bosnian-Herzegovinan-Austrian friendship. I leaf through a complete set of journals from 1915 in his home. I look at the almost new dark blue captain's uniform of his father from World War One. He shows me Aichelburg's book on the Sarajevo assassination, too. We talk about the book "Die Bosnakien kommen". The tune of the march with the same title still echoes in my ears. I have not had electricity for days so I have not been able to see and listen again to the cassette I received as a gift." "The Bosnians are coming" was one of the military operations at the time when Miloš Vidaković on his deathbed coughed up blood on the banks of the Vardar River. At the other end, somewhere near Graz, his peers rest in peace. The Bosnian-Herzegovinian youth of that time rests in the peace of birch woods. A military cemetery, designed as is appropriate for the powerful Austria-Hungary, every June tells, with that march and commemoration, of the elite Austro-Hungarian troops made up of Bosnians. The military march reminds us of the battles in which, over four decades until 1918, our grandfathers and great-grandfathers took part wearing the uniforms of the first, second, third, fourth, and many other regiments. The commemoration is common, as are the plots with the graves of Orthodox, Muslim, Catholic and Jew. The only thing different is the numbers on the uniform buttons. The numbers stood for regiments. Everything else is common. So they lived, travelled and died all over the world, not only on the Bosnian hills...

"Die Bosnakien kommen", Meleta, Graz, regiments and those melancholy memories over coffee. The breath of Bosnia is felt in Vienna, too. On the Graben there is that

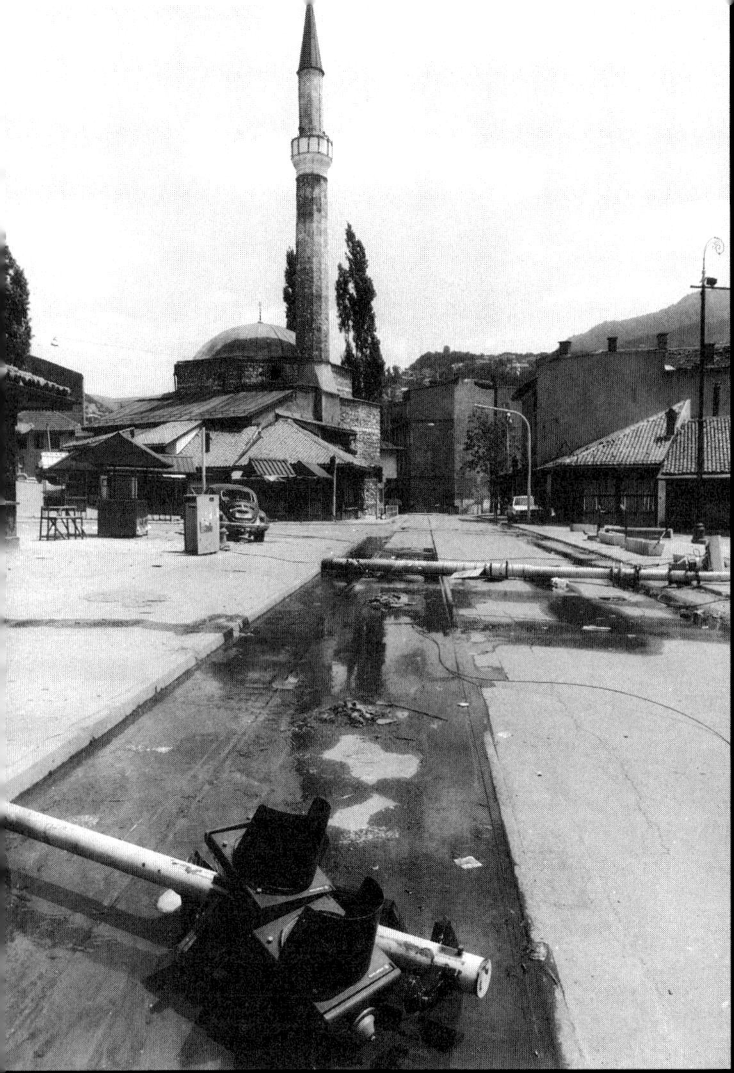

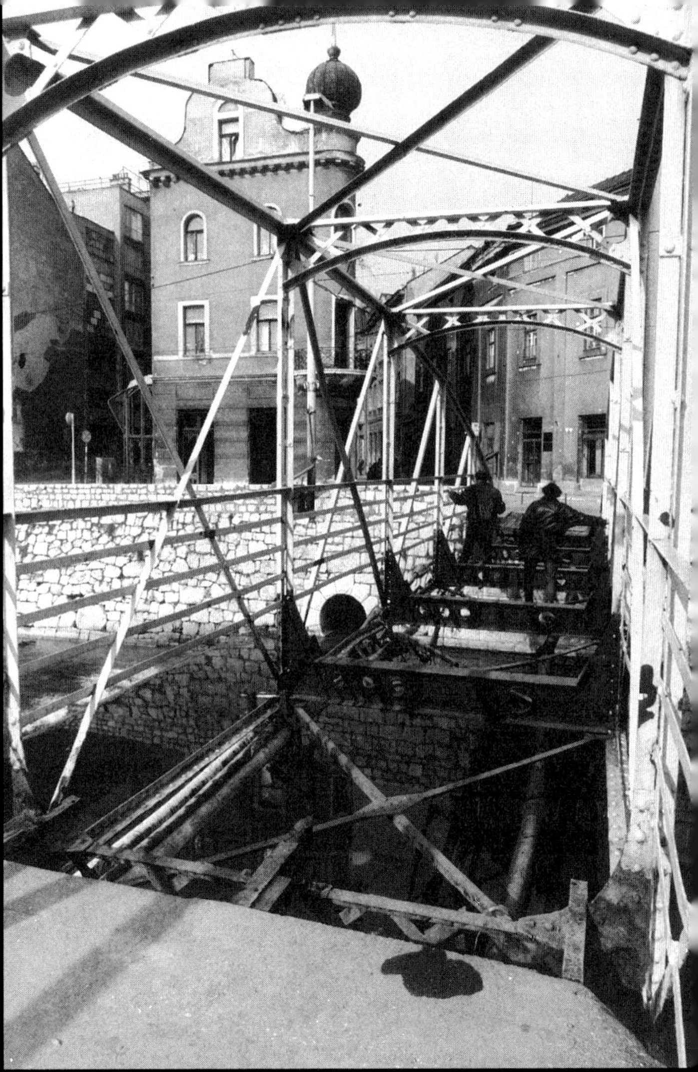

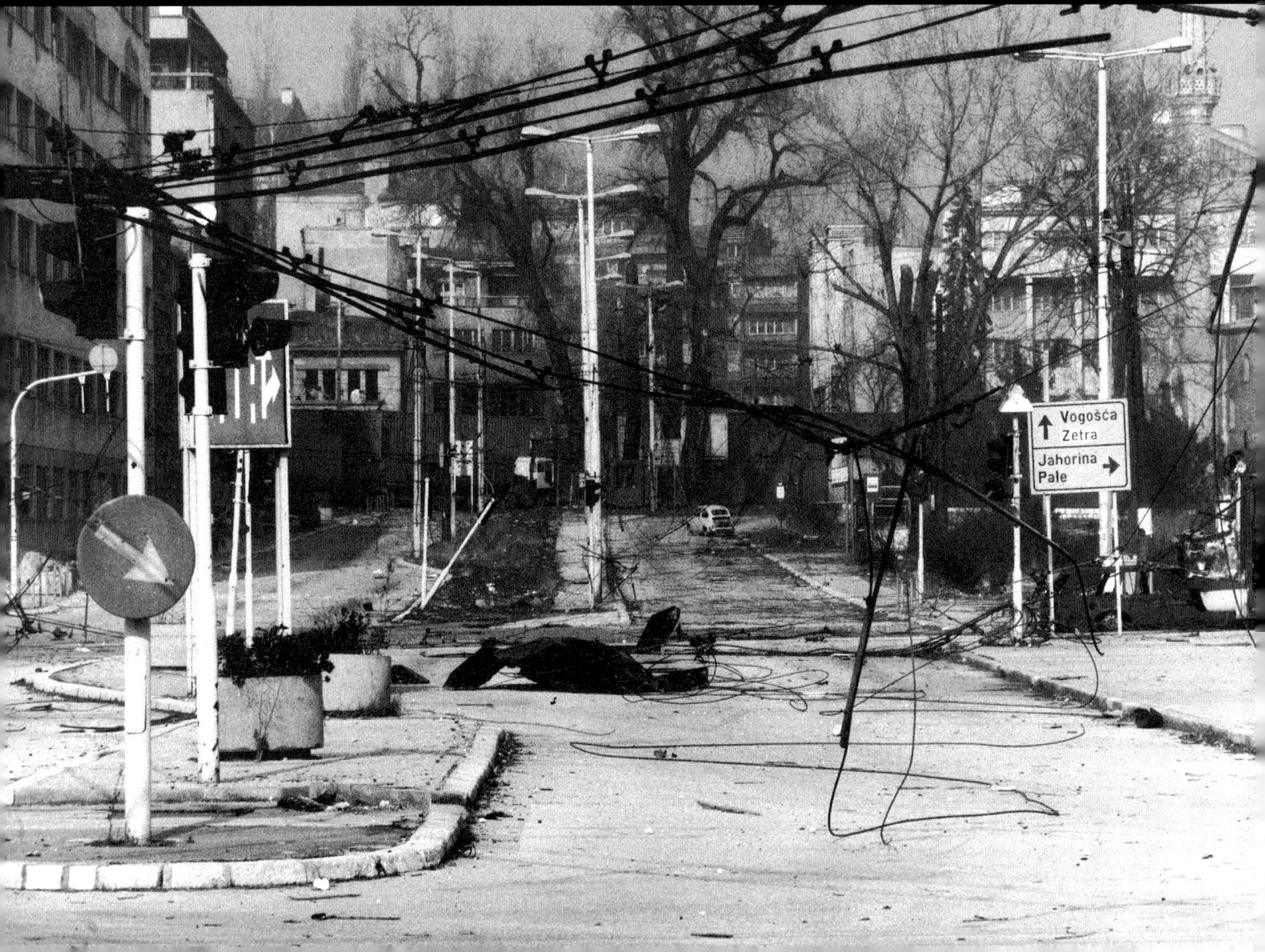
Vogošća
Zetra
Jahorina
Pale

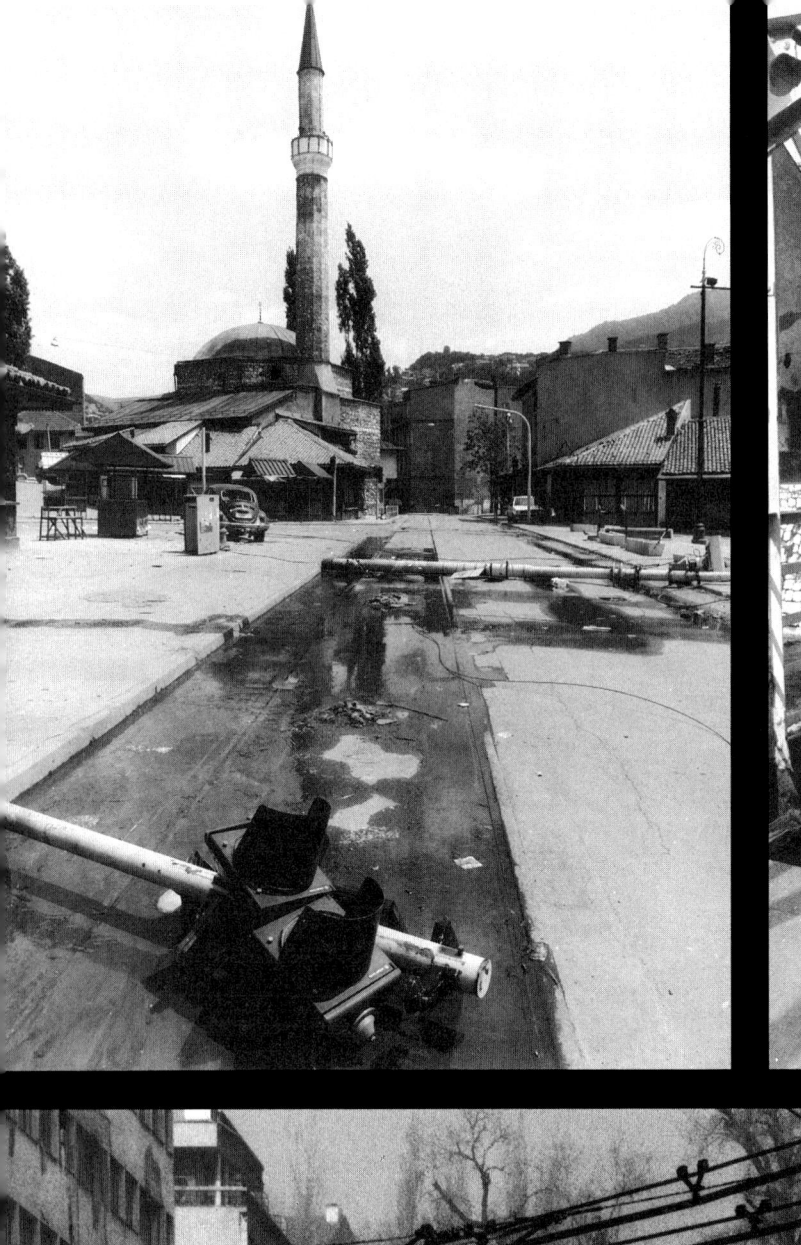

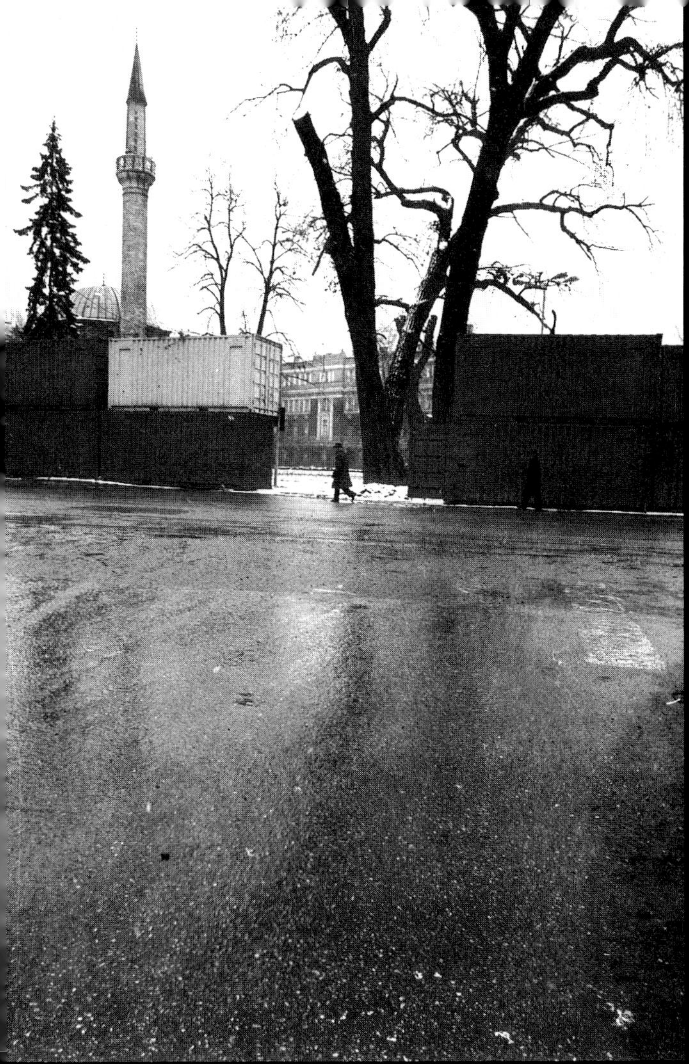

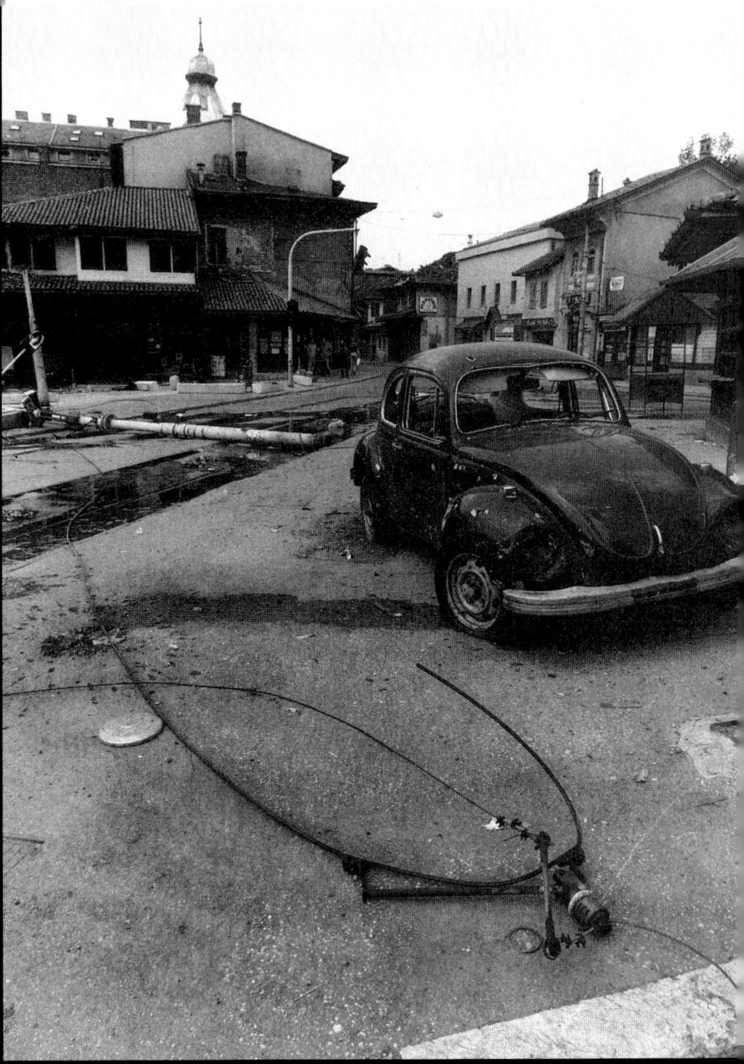

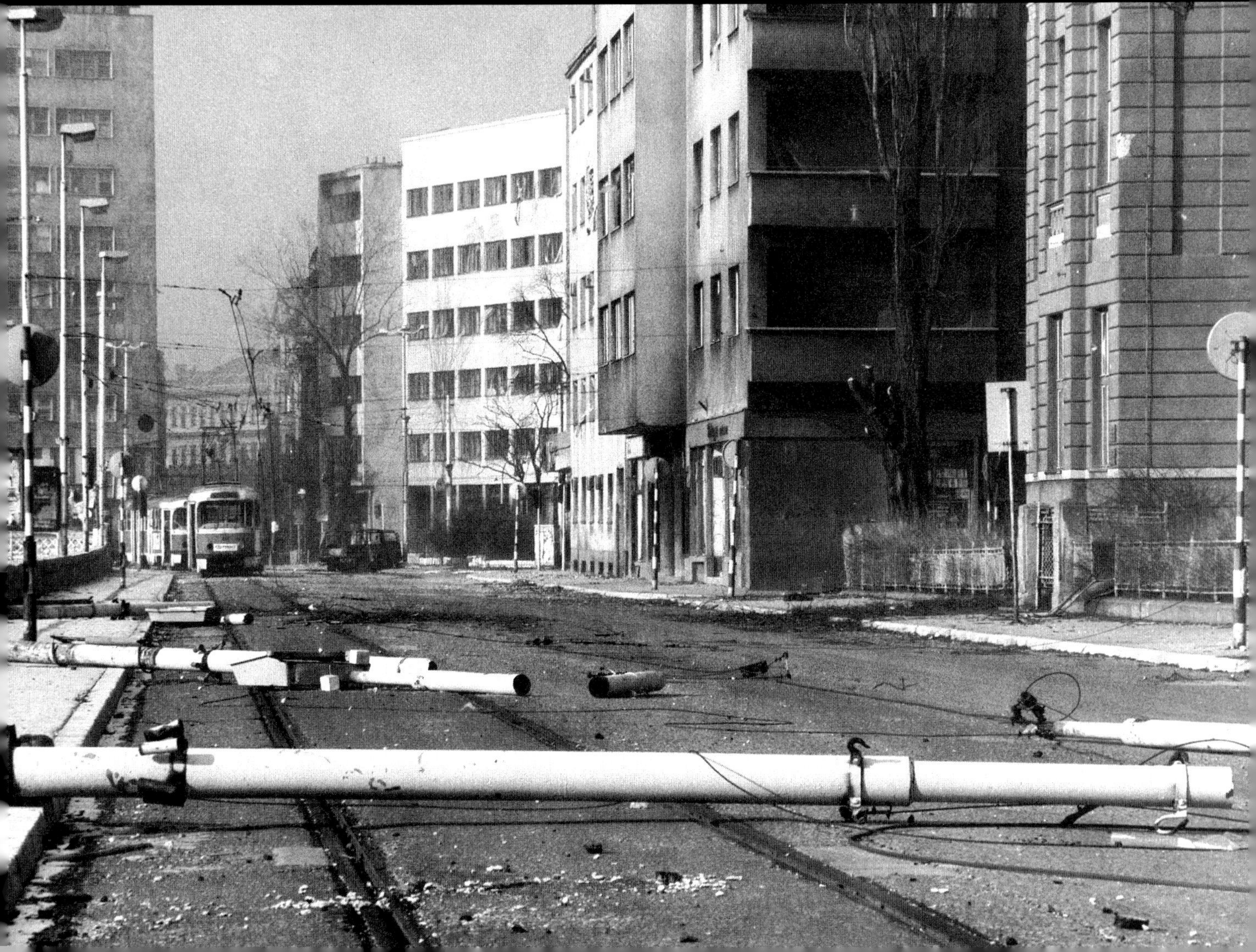

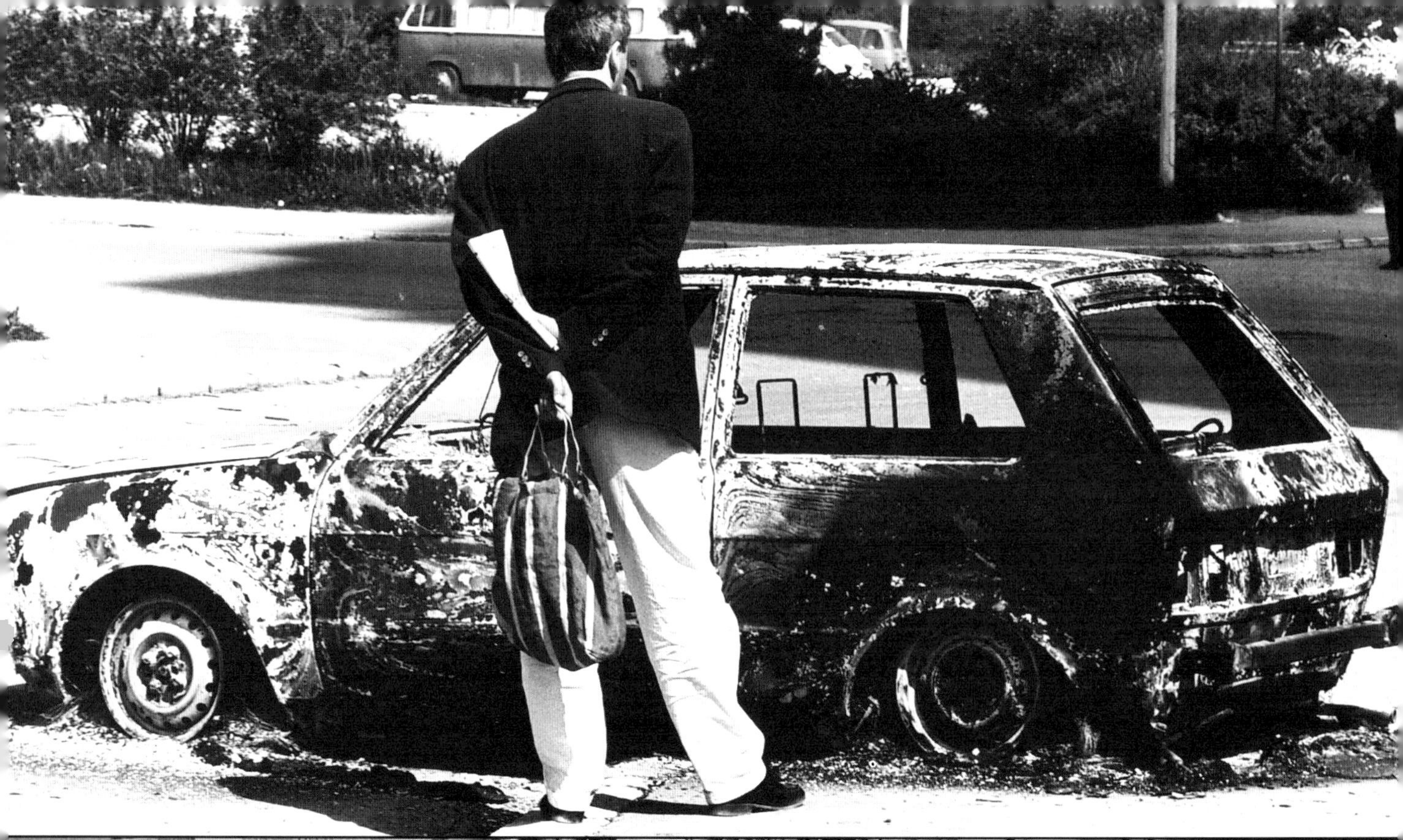
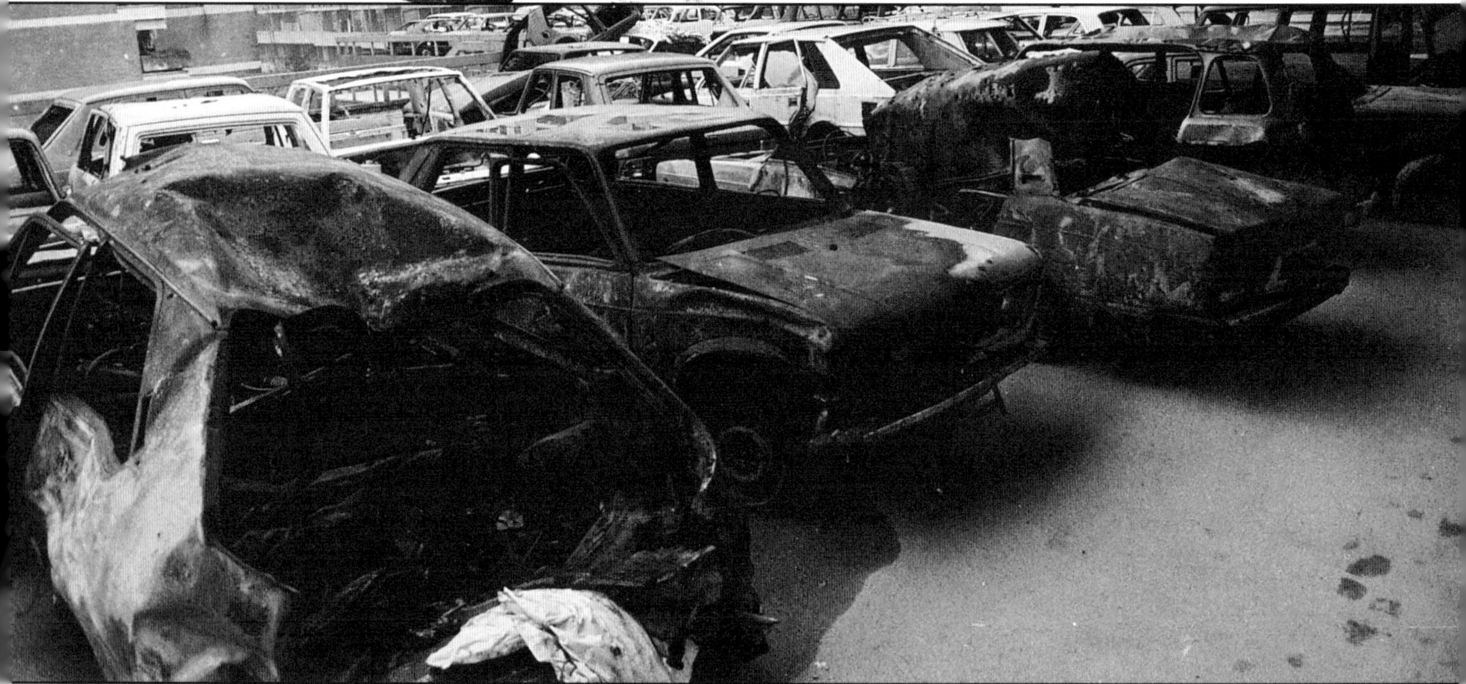
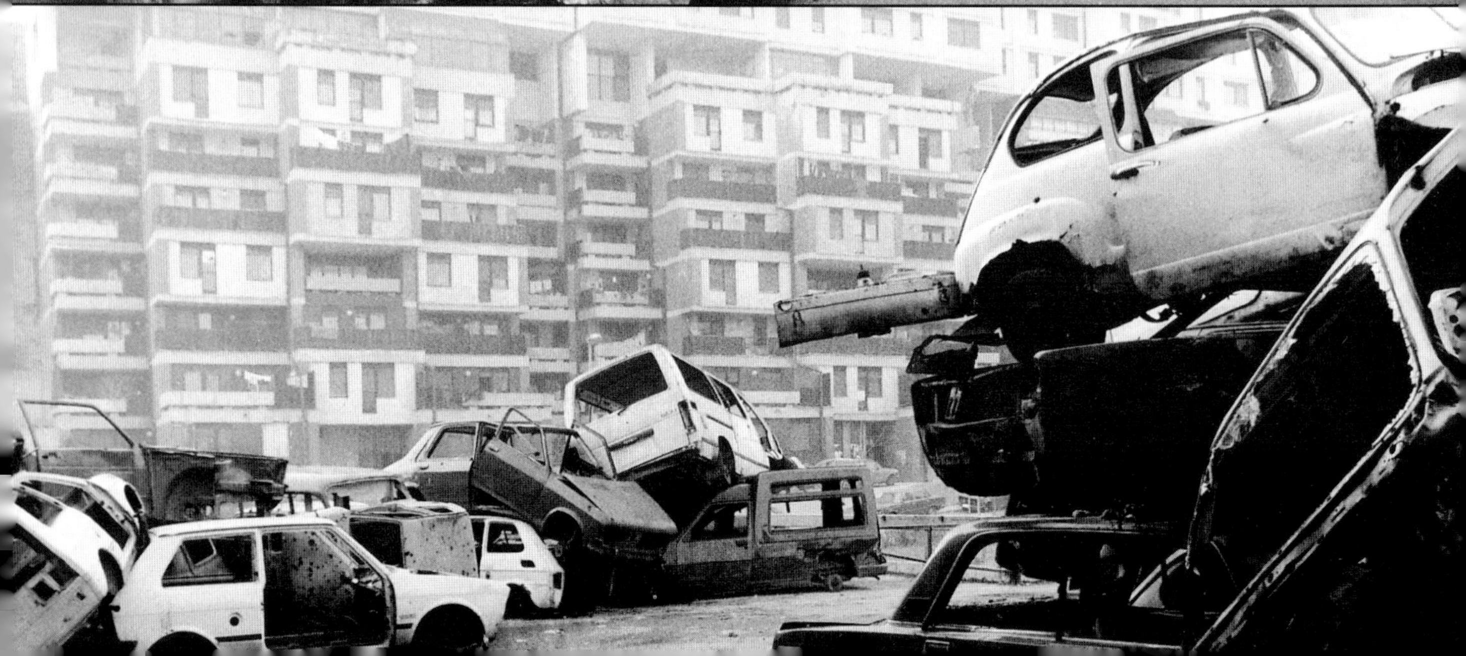

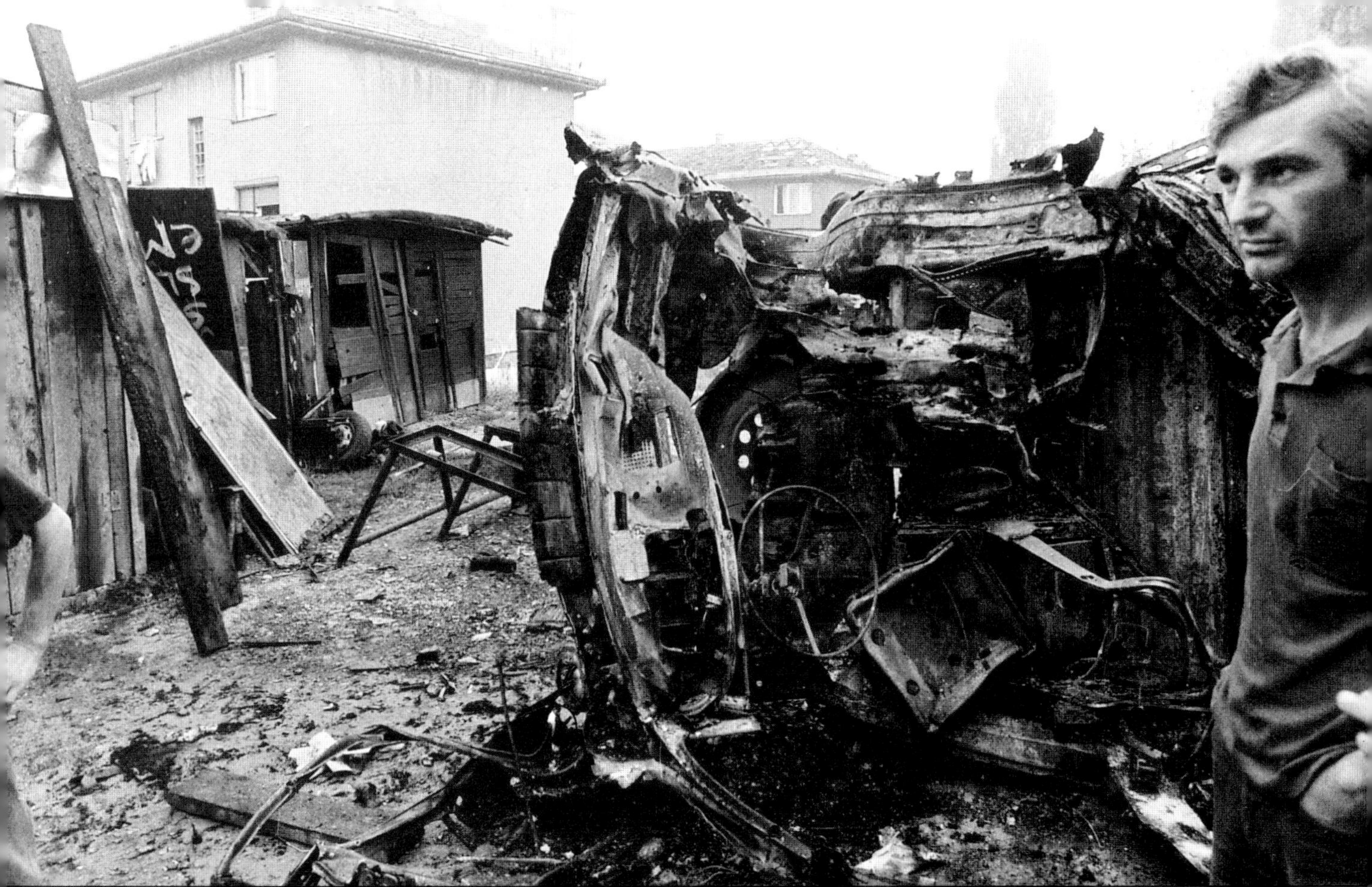
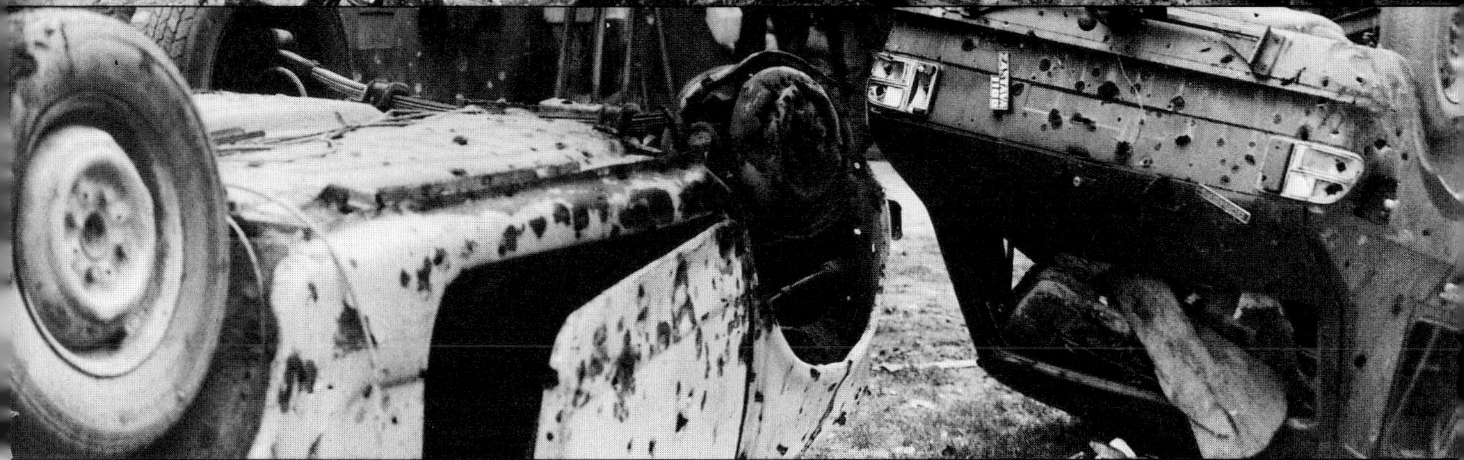
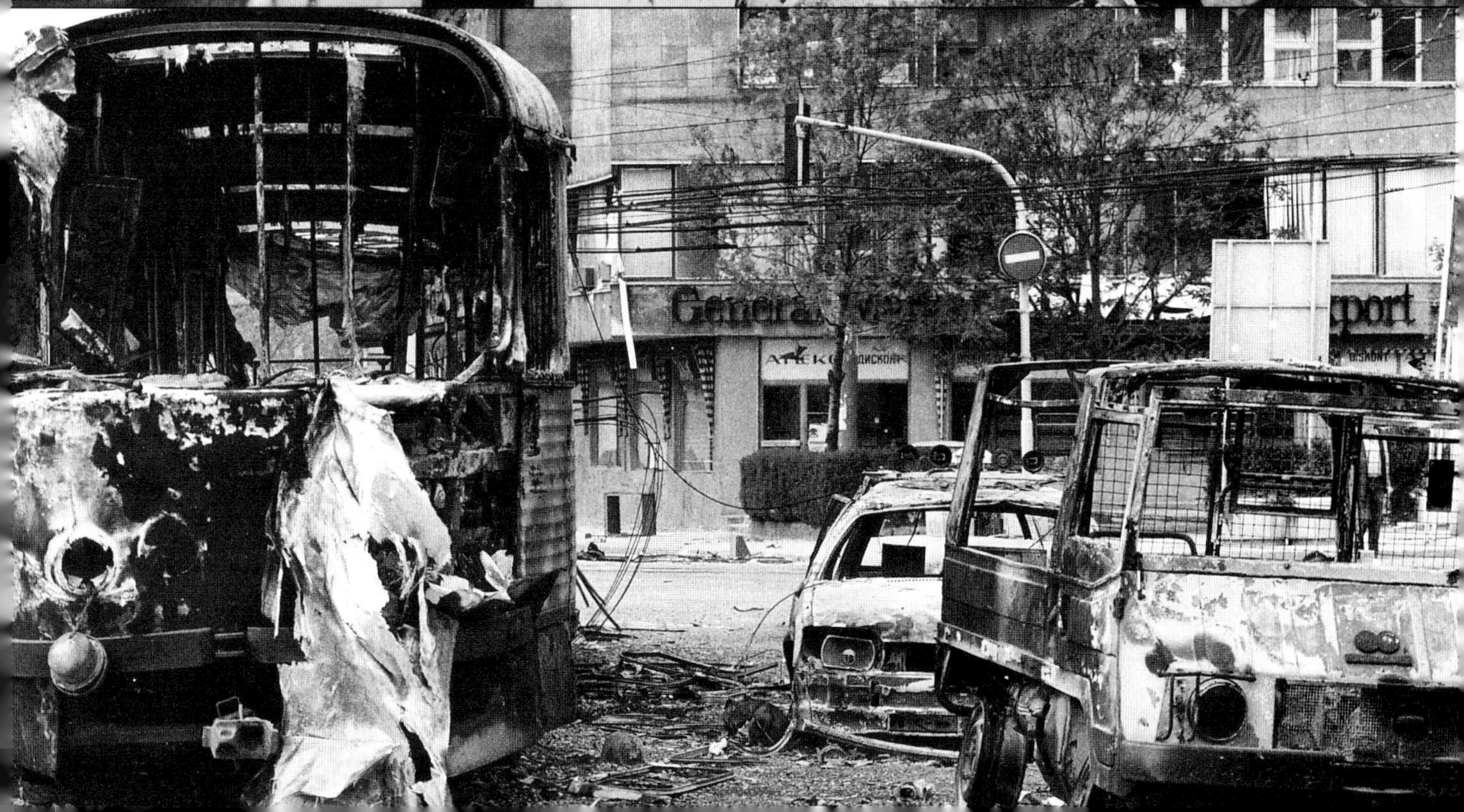

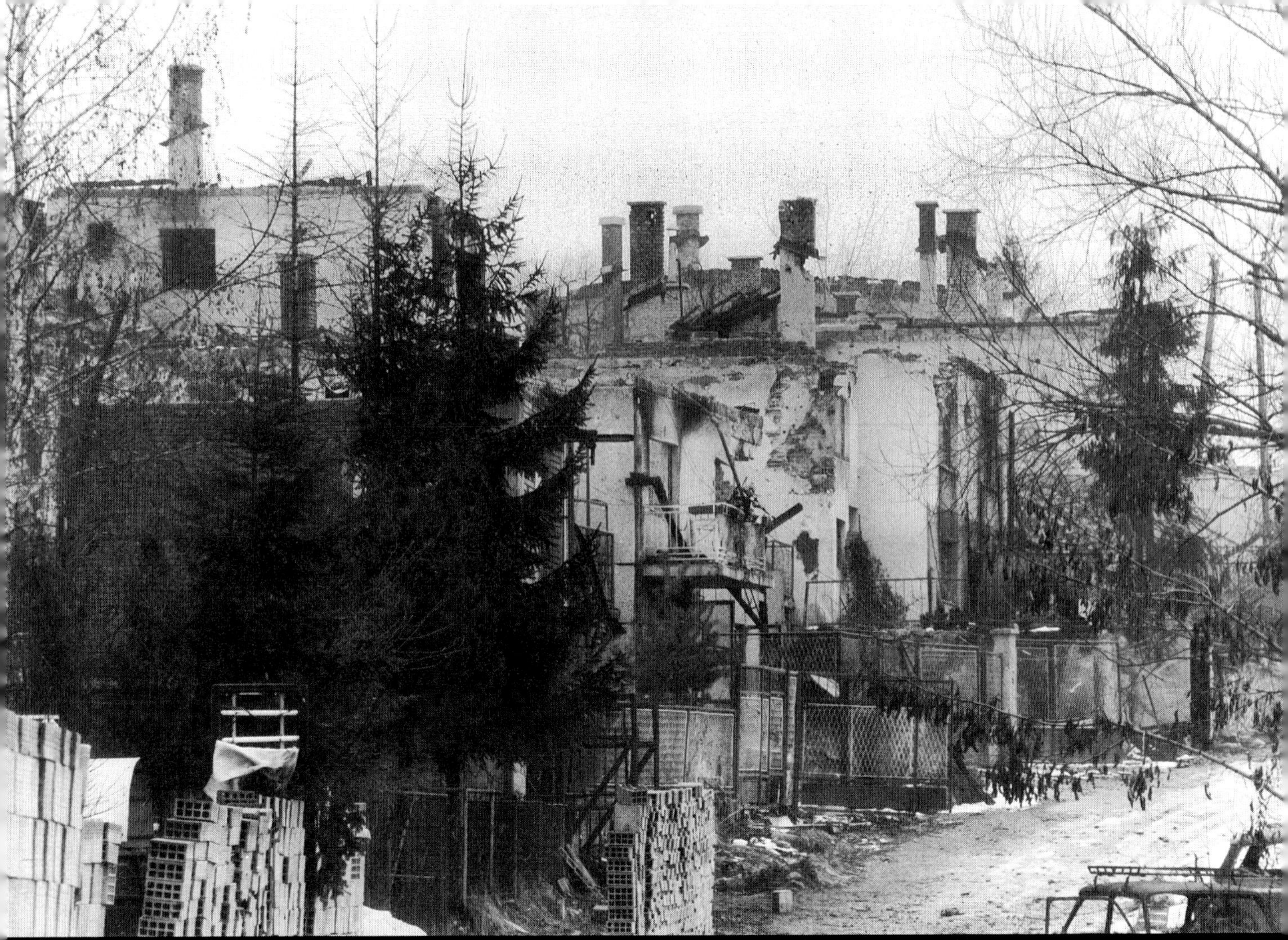

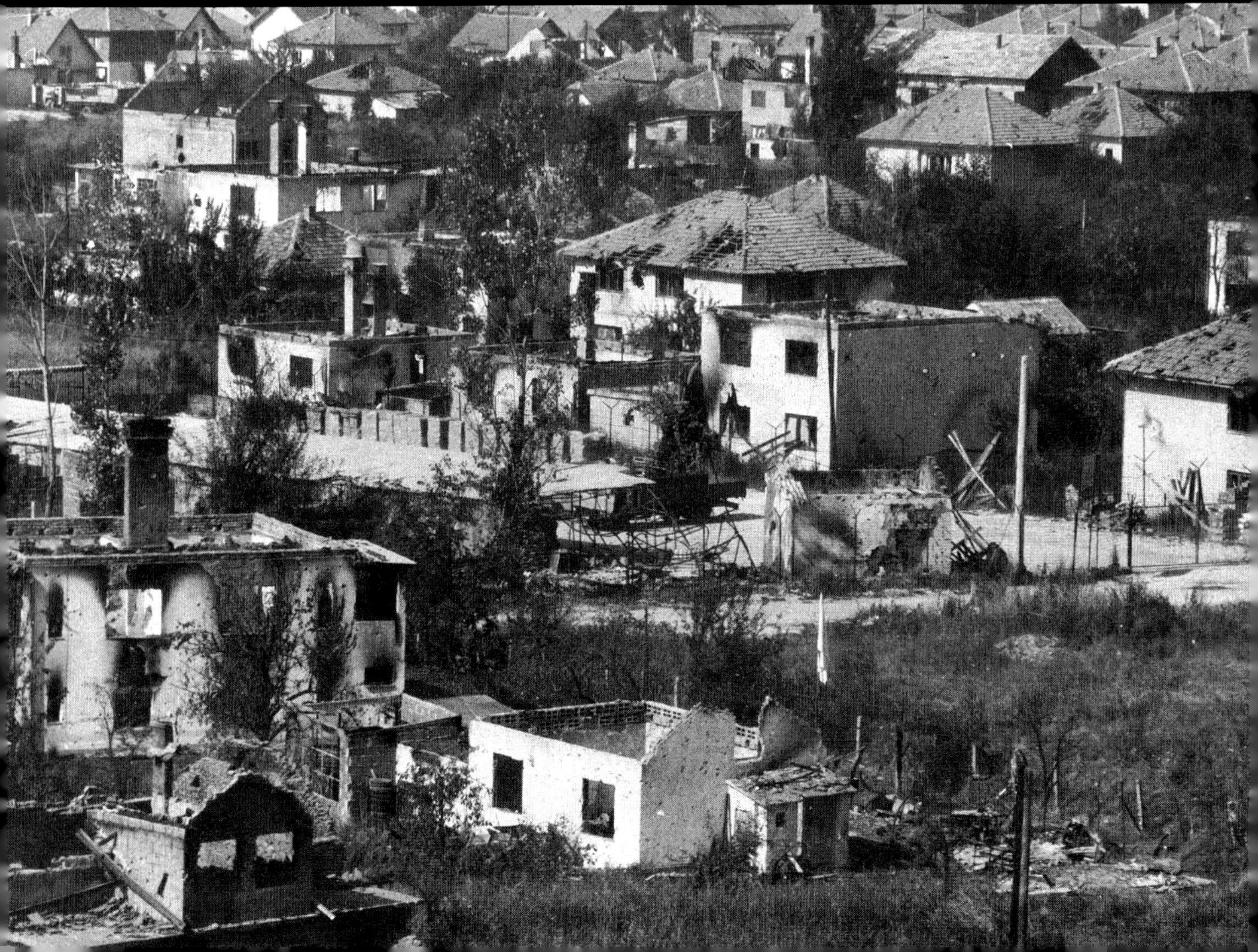

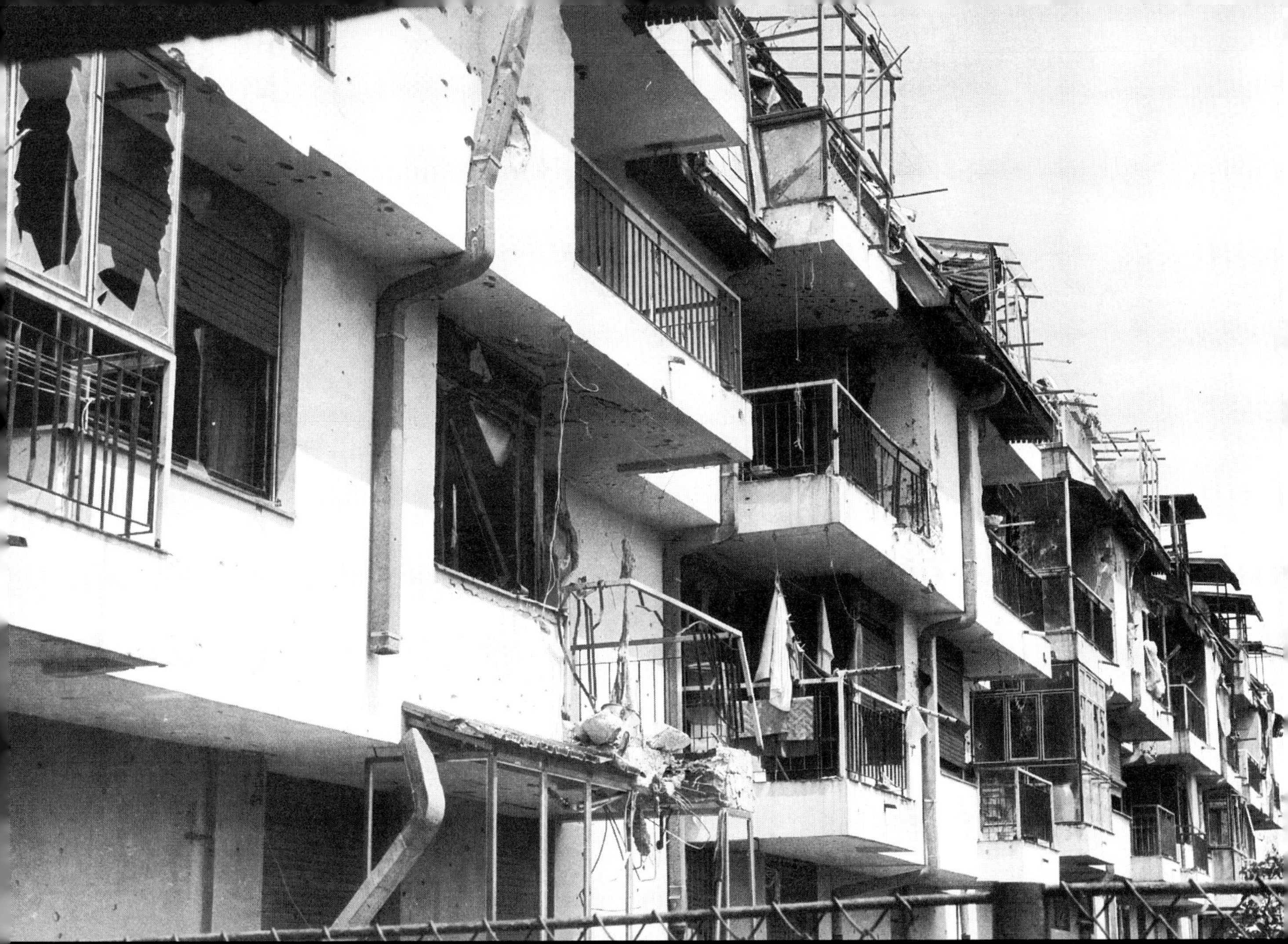

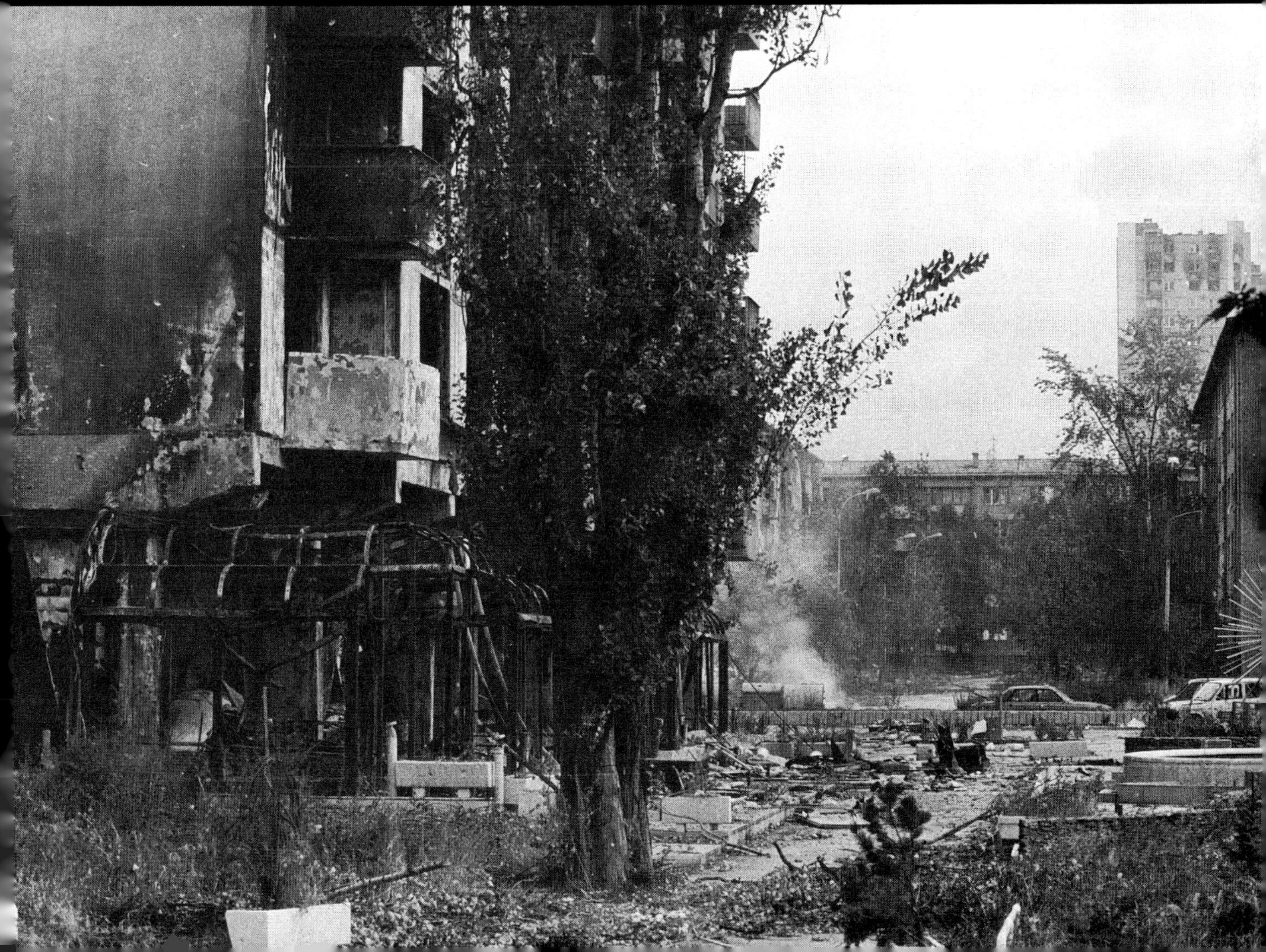

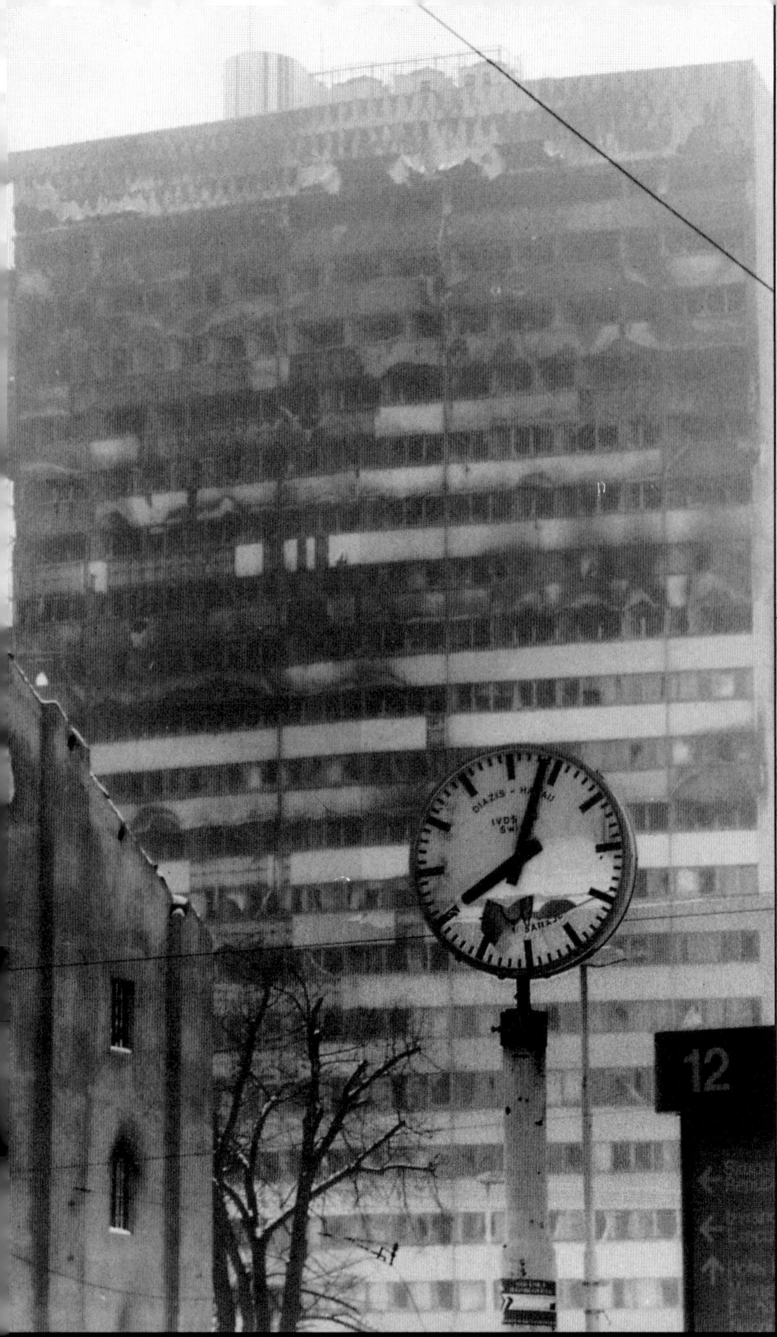
12

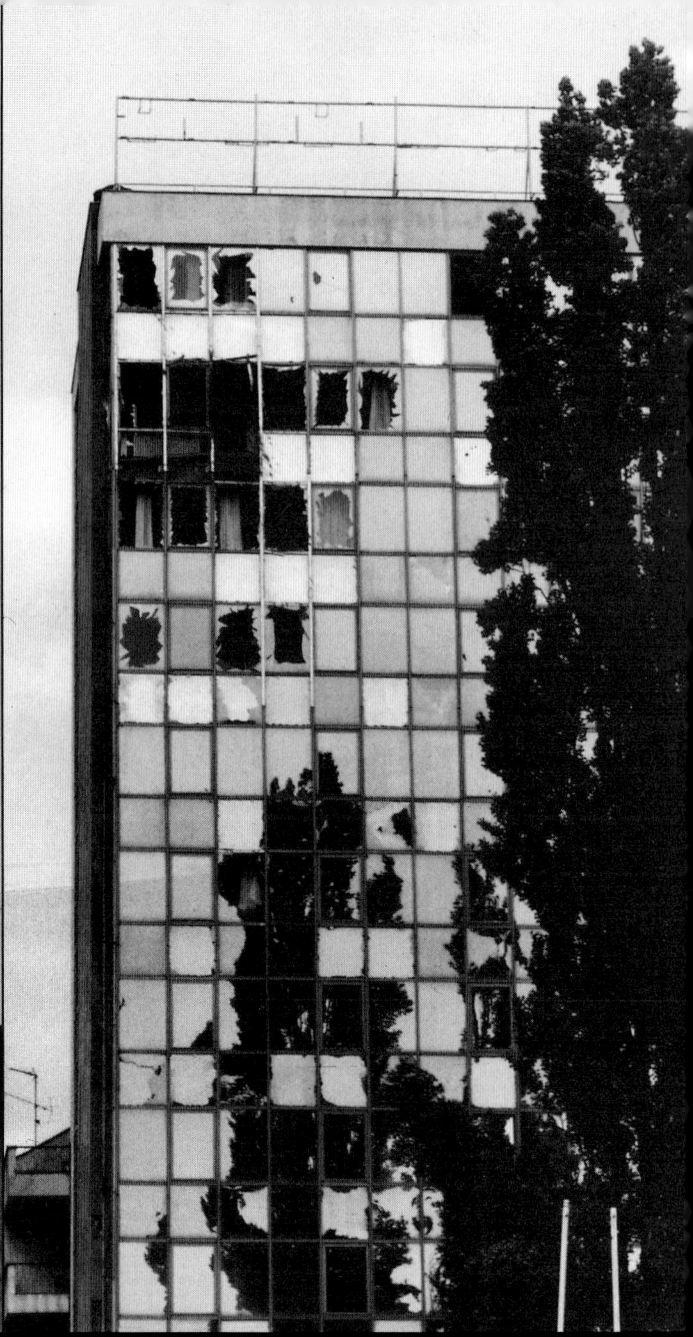

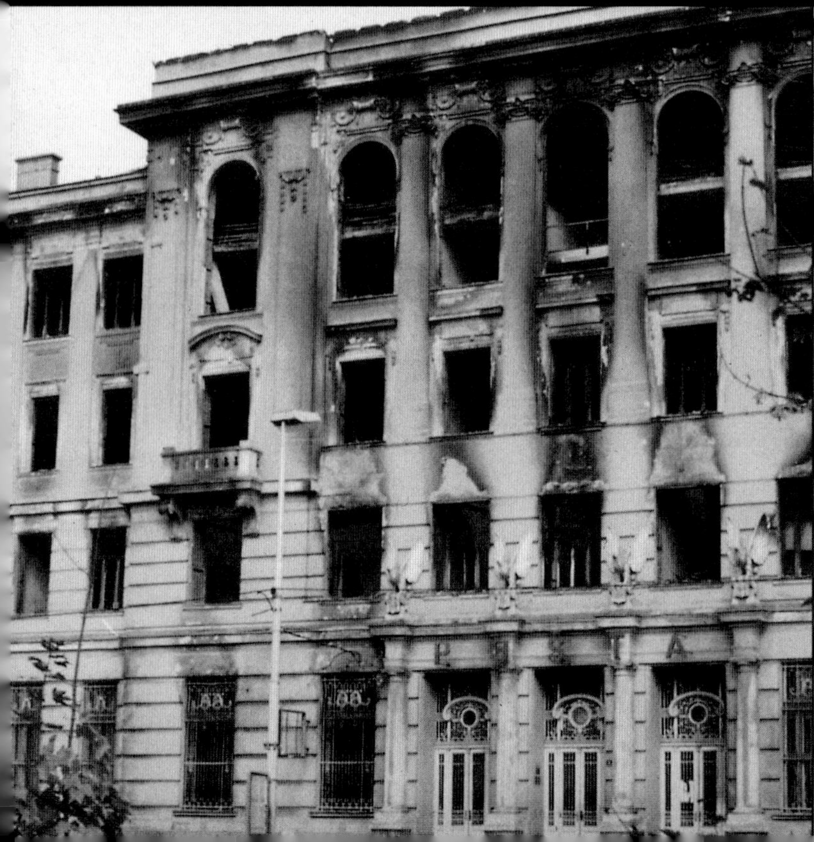

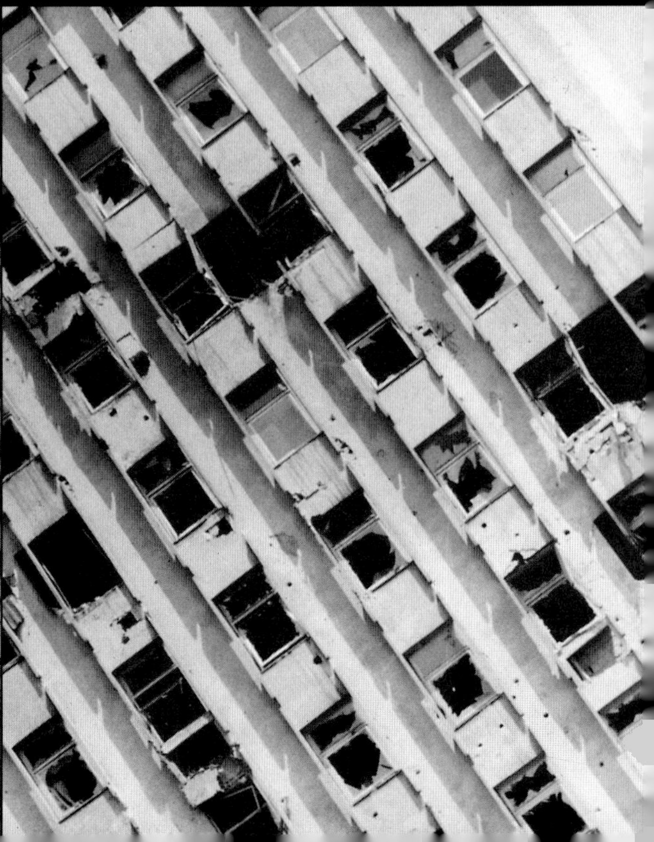

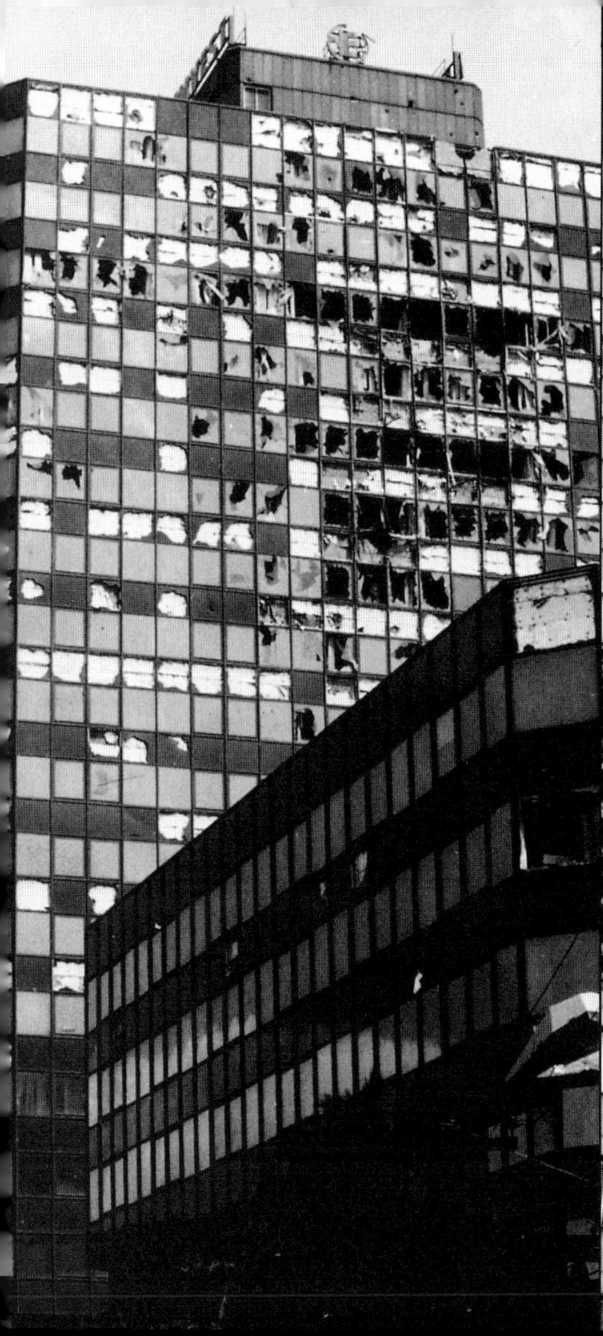

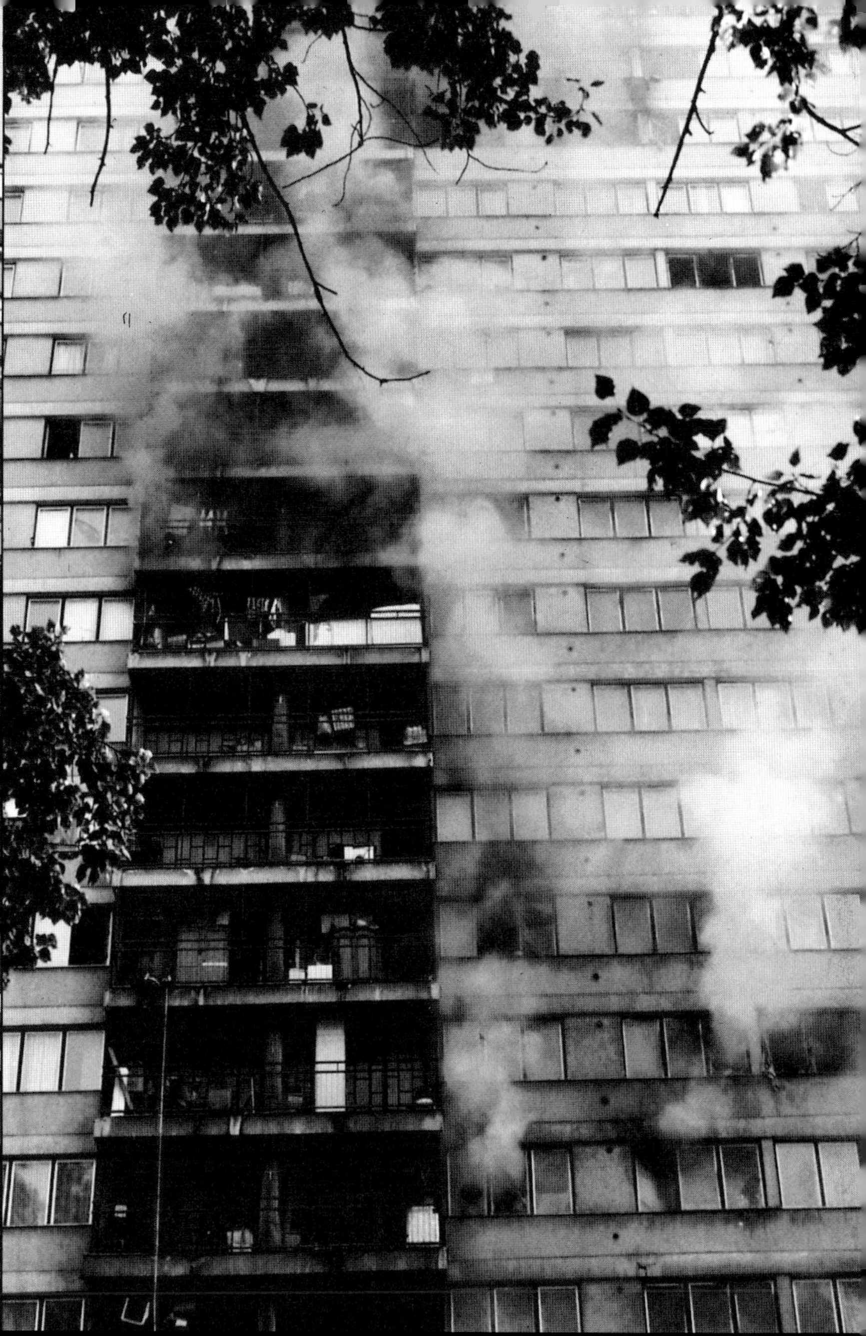

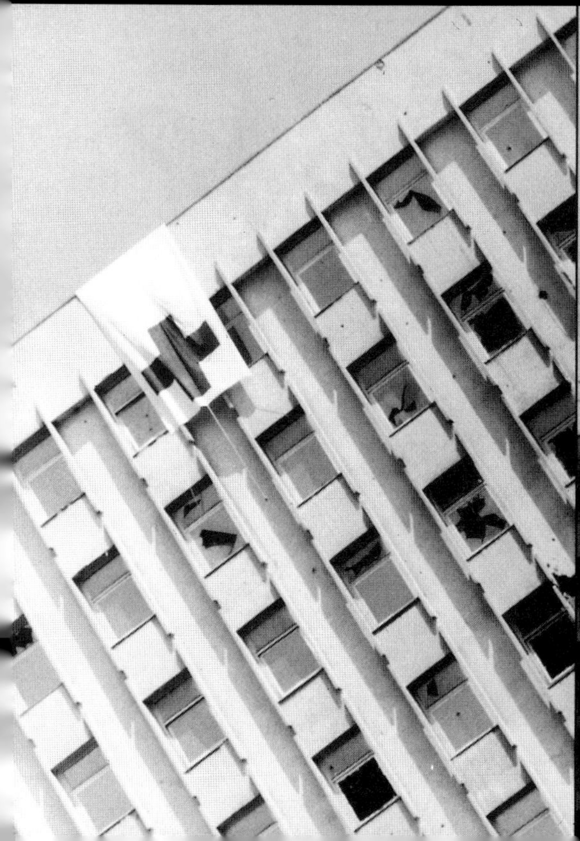

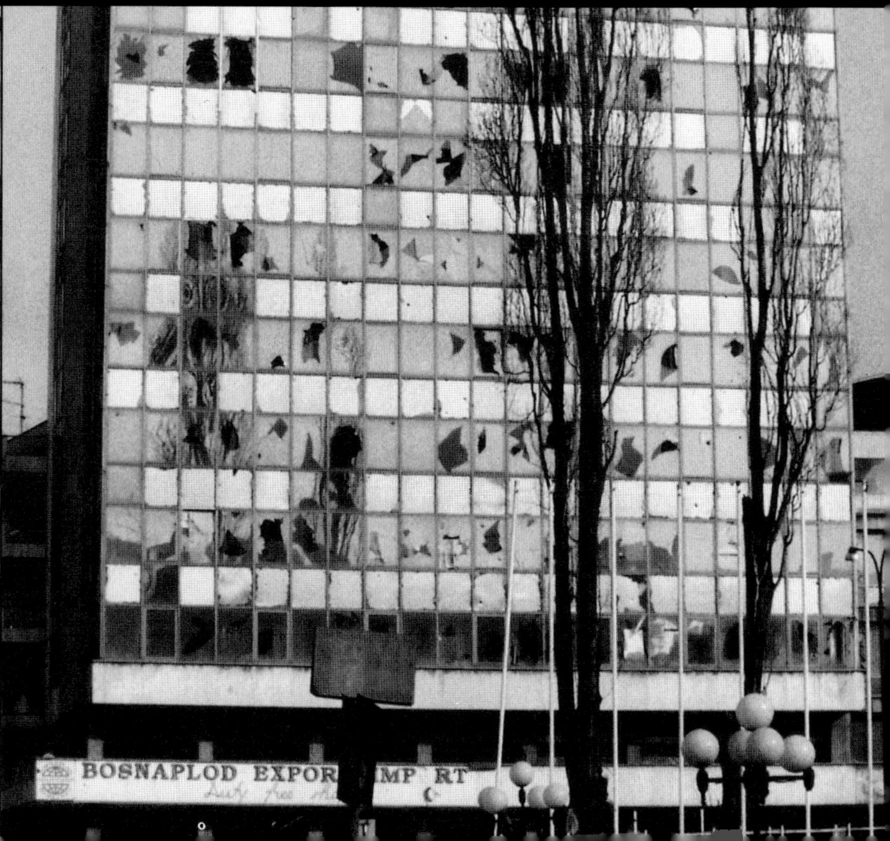
BOSNAPLOD EXPOR IMP RT

coat-of-arms of ours with a hand and sabre in a series of symbols of the Austro-Hungarian provinces... And that "Crazy Poem", some dates in June and memories of the past...

What is all this for? Where can one go past the graves we dig up with bulldozers? Will birches here be able to cover with their shades the names and dates of births and deaths of those leaving forever? Well, whom can I tell that in Sarajevo 15,000 tombstones have been destroyed? How and to whom can I explain when I cannot believe myself that, on the side where we cannot reach, the new cemetery at Vlakovo was levelled to the ground with bulldozers? At the same time, however, we bury the dead in our gardens, under the windows of our rooms. And how could anyone understand that every third inhabitant of this poor land does not live at his prewar address? Well, none of my family lives where he used to live. We all have some new addresses, some new destinations of refugees. Will the words of Ivan's mother mark us for decades? She learned about the death of her neighbour in Mrkonjić Grad, her Varcar: "Lucky him, he died in his home and was buried in his graveyard."

How many grains of happiness remain in every circle we walked. It was not long ago that I said, in one of my newspaper articles, that they could not deprive us of our cemeteries, they could not destroy them. The dead and the memories of them are only ours. But they destroy tombstones, too. Will the earth throw their bones out as well?

Explosions, screams, blood again.

I do not know whether I am finishing or beginning the circle. It is impossible to tell the months from one another. Circles, sheets, dates merge. There is no light from anywhere. Some dear people, acquantances' children, women leave through steep, impenetrable walls...

Wednesday, 12th: Shells set the "Oslobođenje" building on fire. After many troubles, the B-H Olympic team returns home. A convoy of more than 300 mothers and children goes to Split organised by the 1st Children's Embassy. The electricity and water supplies are critical owing to the aggressor's blackmail.

Thursday, 13th: David Conkrite, a journalist of the American ABC TV is killed by a sniper's bullet. Shelling of Baščaršija, Vasin han, Vaso Miskin Street, Dobrinja, Sokolović kolonija, Sokolje, Briješće, Vojvoda Putnik and Živko Jošilo Streets, Breka, Kobilja glava, Breka potok and Ugorsko. The aggressor does not allow repairs to high-voltage transmission lines. The Bačevo, Mošćanica and Jahorina water supply systems are out of use. The city is without enough electricity and almost completely without water.

Friday, 14th: Eight killed and 53 injured in Sarajevo. The city has been without electricity for seven days. Evening shelling of Ugarsko and Barice from Poljine. Shells fall on Sokolović kolonija.

CIRCLE FIVE

Saturday, 15th: *The introduction of B-H money is announced. The National Bank issues banknotes of 10, 20, 50, 100, 500 and 1,000 B-H dinars. They are to be in circulation from August 17th. Exchange rates of the dinar: 1 BH dinar equals 10 YU dinars; 1 DM = 350 BH dinars; 1 Croatian dinar = 2 BH dinars. Roger Echegerai, the Pope's personal envoy, visits Sarajevo and celebrates mass in the Cathedral commemorating the Assumption of the Virgin Mary. Shells fall on the Presidency (one dead, five wounded), the Third Internal Medicine Clinic of Koševo Hospital, Dobrinja, Sokolović kolonija, Ugorsko, Barice, Kobilja glava and Koševsko brdo.*

Sunday, 16th: *Water supply still critical. No electricity because transmission lines have been demolished. Five people killed and 85 wounded in the city.*

Monday, 17th: *Shelling of the old part of Baščaršija. Fire in the "Europe" hotel is caused by incendiary shells. Some shops at Baščaršija also catch fire.*

The heat struck me. I had felt it unheadingly before, too. I did not pay any attention to the flame I could not see and whose heat I had unpleasantly put up with all this time. I became aware of it with time. It became less and less bearable as I went deeper down. It burst with all its force. It gushed all of a sudden. It melted those who approached it incautiously. They rushed towards it like moths towards the light. It bewitched them. They could not resist it. They became more and more helpless. I saw those who until then had been firm and vital become doughy wax candles.

They melted gradually. They vanished faster and faster. It heated irresistibly. Hatred was the stake. It attracted with the first step from Circle One like a magnet. Only the rare ones, but with difficulty, succeeded in avoiding it. It spread over the face and into the eyes; it penetrated into the skull, chest and womb.

I was on the edge of a volcano crater. I could not step off. I dragged my feet. I hardly walked a few centimetres of the way. Curses, insults, names and words which are hard to repeat hummed around me. The heat merges with everything, it radiates and impregnates the whole circle. I hardly manage to open my eyes. I must squint if I want to see anything at all. Those who have given up looking sweat around me. They close their eyelids. I do not know whether they enjoy the warmth or are tortured by the heat that seizes them. Is that Cato or Marcus Portius the Elder covered with his toga constantly repeating: "After all, Carthage must be destroyed... After all, Carthage must be destroyed..." Next to him, an old goggle-eyed woman mentions the Huguenots. She grins. The name of St. Bartholomew is on her lips. She mutters: "Night will fall. It will be a holiday..." And an icy smile. Look, Catherine de Medici warms herself up here over 25,000 slaughtered Parisians. A chubby woman with a crown opened her eyes wide. The heat must have blinded her. I cannot tell the colour of her eyes. The white swallowed the iris of her eyes. She slowly melts. "Out! Out of my kingdom. Out, Judas..." A valuable rosary is in her hands. Behind her, there are some disguised men under hoods; they have pulled their hands into the sleeves. Well, it must be Isabella I the Catholic. She goes on expelling the Jews from Spain, she impoverishes the country. I can see Caligula personally. The Roman emperor blasphemes against his people. He cannot get over the fact that they all have not got only one head. He grins, mutters and rubs his hands. The blood on his palms has dried. He draws back his hand to strike: "One blow and the head is off. There are no more Romans." He waves his hands in the air. He adjusts an imaginary head. He rubs his hands, he mutters. Many women push in the crowd. I have never met so many on this way. Frowning, Mary Tudor plays with gold coins in her lap. She says something about Catholics, Protestants, and a war that must be waged. Down there is a thin saint-like Turk. An enormous turban covers him. It makes him look calm like a saint. I can almost hear him say something. He speaks. It is quiet. I push my way close to him. I can hear some insults about Vienna, infidels, the army. He complains of Belgrade. He smells of stale prison air. A crooked sabre hangs down his thigh. The military leader Kara Mustafa confesses before his execution. Down, in a river of olive-green uniforms, there is a dark, smallish man with a parting on the right side. His hair falls down to his left eyebrow. His moustache does not go wider than his nostrils. He moves his right, stiff hand up and down. In his left hand he squeezes a piece of cloth with the Star of David on it. I only understand: "Mein Kampf... Mein Kampf, also..."

The heat disturbs me. The whole history of civilization seems to have gathered here. This is a living museum exhibition at Madame Tussaud's all in one place. I cannot see well enough. They push around me. How many similar faces from the pages of books, encyclopaedias and museum exhibitions there are! Why have they flocked here? I recognize some contemporaries, too. They have also come here. How did they manage to come so early? Don't I meet them every day!? Why did they hurry? They hide their eyes. They, surprised, turn their heads to the side. They notice I am only passing. I do not manage to leave. All around me there are TV personalities. They look at me, they smile...

I close my eyes. I shake my head. I am quiet. I slowly open them again. Everything is the same. I still see the same picture as a while ago. I am exhausted.

Somebody suddenly takes hold of my arm. A blue-eyed man cheers me with his smile. His eyes tell me to rely on him. He whispers in my ear:

"...It is unfortunate that nobody wants to or knows how to do it. For a fatal feature of that hatred is exactly the fact that the Bosnian man is not aware of the hatred in himself, that he shrinks from analysing it, and hates anyone who would try to do so. However, the fact is that in Bosnia and Herzegovina there are more people who are ready, in fits of unconscious hatred, for different reasons and under different pretexts, to kill or to be killed than in other Slavic and non-Slavic countries which are much bigger in terms of population and area... Hatred rouses man against man and then brings them to poverty and misfortune or buries both of them; hatred which is like cancer in the body, consuming and eating up everything around itself and dying in the end, as such hatred, like the flame, has neither permanent form nor personal life; it is simply an instrument of instinct for destruction or selfdestruction, it only exists such as it is and only until it has completely carried out its task of total destruction.

"Yes, Bosnia is a country of hatred. That is Bosnia. On

Tuesday, 18th: Sarajevo airport closed at 11.30 a.m. A British C 130 Hercules is fired at by an anti-aircraft gun. Shells fall on the centre and Baščaršija (5 people dead, 30 injured), Bare, Betanija, and the slopes of Trebević. The building of the former Institute of Agriculture is on fire. The citizens of Sarajevo start getting some water. Following the decision of the War Presidency of the so-called Serb municipality of Ilidža, made on July 22, the Bačevo springs are not to be used to supply the city with water but now it is being used again. In order to use the available space as rationally as possible, the daily "Oslobođenje" is forced to make uniform and reduce size of obituaries, letters of thanks and commemoration notices.

Wednesday, 19th: Instead of BH Dinars, Sarajevo gets war coupons. They are valid just like dinars, which could not be delivered to besieged Sarajevo. UNPROFOR is not willing to take responsibility for the BH dinars' delivery. The substitution of YU dinars by BH coupons will last until the 24th of the month. Ten people are killed and 67 injured in Sarajevo. There are increasing cases of stomach diseases, enterocolitis and hepatitis A. Not a single aircraft lands in the city.

Thursday, 20th: A hellish night! Stari grad, (The old town), the centre, Novo Sarajevo (New Sarajevo) and Novi grad (the new town) are fired on from Trebević, Hreša and Poljine. A forest above Bistrik catches fire. Artillery shells hit the building of the "Electrical Power Industry", and the Faculty of Mechanical

Engineering; some floors of the government building are on fire. Also shelled are Dobrinja, Stup, Stup Hill, Butmir, Kobilja glava, Ugorsko, Donji Hotonj, Šip, Bare and Barice. A soldier of the Ukrainian unit of UNPROFOR is killed in the courtyard of the "Marshal Tito" barracks. Eleven dead and 55 injured in Sarajevo.

Friday, 21st: At about 8.30 a.m. shells fall near the "Markale" market place, the "Sarajka" department store, in Skerlić Street, in front of the Presidency. Four people are killed near the "Casino". Eight vehicles of the UNPROFOR destroyed in the "Marshal Tito" barracks. The Traumatology Clinic receives 12 people injured near the market place; one dies. Thirteen people are injured in front of the Presidency; in Skerlić Street one man is killed. The problems of water supplies get worse. Husein Taslidžak, a journalist, is killed at Dobrinja.

Saturday, 22nd: At least ten people die from pieces of shrapnel. Five people are killed at Butmir, three at Sokolović kolonija and one at Hrasnica. There are people killed at Otes too. Shells fall on Stari grad, Hrasno hill, Pero Kosorić Square, the area around the casualty department, Alipašino polje, Mojmilo, Dobrinja, Ciglane and Breka. The students' hostel at Nedžarići is on fire. The headquarters of UNPROFOR is shelled at 12.30 a.m. Shells fall on the "Marshal Tito" barracks and the Ukrainian unit. There are 30 people killed in B-H, 19 of these in Sarajevo, and 104 injured.

Sunday, 23rd: At least 27 citizens are killed. Stari grad has 14 killed, 23 injured;

the basis of an unusual contrast, which in fact is not so unusual and could be explained by a meticulous analysis, one may as well say that only a few countries have such a strong, firm character, so much tenderness and passion, such deep feelings, loyalty and steady devotion and so much thirst for justice. However, tempests of hatred, hurricanes of controlled, strong hatred which matures and waits for the right time are hidden underneath all that in opaque depths. The relation between your love and your hatred is the same as between high mountains and a thousand times bigger and heavier geological strata on which they repose. So you are destined to live on thick layers of explosive which is, from time to time, lit just by the sparks of your love and your ardent and cruel sensitivity... Most of you are accustomed to keeping that hatred in all its strength for what is nearer to you. The sacred things you love are always behind three hundred rivers and mountains, and the things you despise and hate are there, on the other side of the courtyard wall. Thus you love your own country, ardently love it, but in three or four different ways which exclude one another, deadly hate and often clash...

"Perhaps Bosnian man should be warned to beware of hatred, congenital, unconscious, endemic hatred at every step, in every thought, in every, even the most sublime, feeling...

"That specific Bosnian hatred should be studied and prevented as a dangerous and deeply rooted disease. And I believe that foreign scholars would come to Bosnia to study hatred as they study leprosy only if hatred were an equally recognised, selected and classified subject of study as leprosy is...

"I would be asked, like all others, to take sides, to be hated or to hate. But I did not want it nor did I know how to. I might, if it must be so, accept being a victim of hatred, but to live in and with hatred, to take part in it – I cannot do that. And in a country like Bosnia, he who does not know how to or, which is worse and harder, he who does not want knowingly to hate, he is always an alien and traitor, but often a martyr, too..."

Well, that is "A Letter of 1920". Isn't it a story by Ivo Andrić? A doctor and doctor's son Maks Levenfeld support me. I again think about the reasons why he left Bosnia. I cannot resist it. It takes me further. One sentence occurs to me: "May God save me from laying guilt on the whole nation for the crimes and guilt of its individuals and betrayers." I recognize Professor Muhsin Rizvić's voice. He has lost weight during this war. He looks a little older than before. We have all grown older. We have all lost even those kilograms that were not a burden to us.

I walk and cannot find the appropriate words. I become aware of the poverty of the language. I cannot remember the word for the thing that has befallen us. How can

I scream when I lack the word? It is weak, too pale if I say: fascism, massacre, murders, urbicide, sadism, devastation, apartheid... All this cannot be expressed by one word, by one notion that grows here and which comprises all the darkness of past centuries and Lucifer's imagination of our contemporaries. They are talented, I must admit. Repulsively talented.

An enormous burning cloud of hatred hovers over my city. The city, where four of the five world's biggest religions have coexisted for centuries, is melting in a burst of heat. I can see how gradually and hopelessly flats, places of worship, streets, museums, monuments and people are being destroyed. Civilizational values are being wiped out. There are fewer and fewer people. On the track of Circle Five there are corpses of two babies from the city orphanage, five passers-by who were killed in the centre of Baščaršija, a five-member family with a neighbour who burned, eight people outside a supermarket at Alipašino polje who were killed, five people killed at the seat of the Supreme Authorities of the Islamic Community, two at Dobrinja... There is continuous shelling of the Lav cemetery. The living who came to bury the dead join them. The column of the disabled is getting longer and longer. In the diary for the sixth is written:

"Rain washed away blood from the pavement near the Second Grammar School. Only a stain on the asphalt remained. Next to it, on the lawn, a shallow hole. You can see clay and pebbles. Green grass is around.

"A black, asymmetrical, greasy stain is there. It is a landmark. At that spot one man was killed. One more Sarajevan left. For ever. Only the bloodstain is on the asphalt diluted by last night's shower. There is no obituary on the tree. There are no flowers on the stain. There are no leaves on the tree. There are no flowers on the stain. There are no tears on the cheeks of the rare passers-by. They do not even stop at the stain. Only a few flies are stuck on the pavement...

"We are poorer for sorrow. I do not feel any pain. We are deadened. No cries are heard. Only fifty metres away, the man lived for years just off the park and the café 'Šetalište'. He was a friend, father, son and husband... He did not come back after a walk with his dog.

"Sarajevo, we are choking?"

On the 25th, the same:

"One more infernal day. It has been roaring through the whole city since nine o'clock. They have been shooting from all sides.

"People, bewildered, run in the street. They find refuge somewhere. Others peep through their entrance doors. Then they run again..."

It is a summer day, an August day. "Twenty people have been killed and 128 wounded during the last twenty-

Stup and Pero Kosorić Square – 4 killed at each; Širokača and Bjelave – 3 killed at each; Cicin han – a two-month-old baby killed; the students' hostel at Bjelave – two students and a woman killed. Shells fall on the "Europe" hotel, Bjelave, Breka, Koševo Hospital, Dolac Malta and the PTT Engineering building in which UNPROFOR is stationed. Projectiles with poison gases are fired at several parts of the city. The aggressor's attack prevents the repair of a transmission line that is being carried out under UNPROFOR supervision. Nenad Kecmanović, a member of the Presidency of B-H, informs "Tanjug" that he is not a member of the Presidency any longer.

Monday, 24th: *All the residential areas of the city are shelled. Targeted are Koševo Hospital, the French Hospital and the casualty department. Sixty-five shells fall in Logavina Street alone. Other parts are also shelled: Širokača, Vasin han, Baščaršija and Medresa. Rocket launchers fire at Alipašino polje, Švrakino selo, Sokolje, Briješće, Boljakov potok and Dobrinja. The "Oslobođenje" building, the "Zora" factory, "Centrotrans", "Feroelektro", the tobacco factory, some flats at Mojmilo, the Faculty of Civil Engineering, "Vranica", the old people's home, the post office in Novo Sarajevo and Koševo Hospital are on fire. The war in Sarajevo has so far claimed 1,829 lives; 10,887 people have been seriously injured, 13,500 slightly injured, 6,550 missing or dead. "Wounded Pictures – Sarajevo '92" is the name of an exhibition displaying paintings and* objects d'art by well-known artists which have been either damaged or destroyed in the attacks on the town. A symposium on "Genocide in B-H in 1992" is held.

Tuesday, 25th: The town hall is burnt down on the night of the 25th/26th. Shelled is the General Consulate of the Libyan Arab jamahiriya. At Pero Kosorić Square 93 flats burn down, and on the 17th floor of the "Dvojka" skyscraper, the five-member family of Abid Rondić die in fire. The "Alhos" factory is on fire. Martin Bell, a BBC journalist, is wounded.

Wednesday, 26th: The old Yugoslavian dinars are not valid any longer. The exchange of old money for new is extended in the Sarajevo region until Saturday, August 28th. Electricity and water supplies still critical.

Thursday, 27th: A massacre at Čengić vila (Danilo Đokić Street): several people killed and injured. Twelve killed and 80 wounded in Sarajevo. As many as 218 cases of enterocolitis are recorded in Stari grad alone.

Friday, 28th: One of the "Oslobođenje" skyscrapers demolished (at about noon). After two fires and continuous shelling the reinforcements simply gave up. Ronald Niser, the Lord Mayor of Innsbruck, comes to Sarajevo. Fourteen killed, 145 wounded. For the last seven days there have been 146 people killed and 813 injured. Enterocolitis is spreading.

Saturday, 29th: The 96-hour countdown for placing heavy weaponry under UN control has not started yet. Reis-ul-ulema Jakub Selimoski, the head of the Muslim community in former Yugoslavia, is wounded by

four hours," announces Radio Sarajevo. There are injured and dead all over the city. We are all candidates for death. Every foot of the city is a target..."

I stop at August 28th:

"For many, there is nobody to write a newspaper obituary. Neighbours, acquaintances, unknown people get killed. They are buried by those who were close to them. Everybody rushes, takes to foolish flight...

"Yesterday my colleague Divna told me about Vesna Bugarski, a neighbour of hers. She was killed in her presence. She saw her in the courtyard through the bathroom window. That was the usual path of the residents of a house in Obala Street. They have not been able to walk on the street side for months. She set off for the city market. She was sitting on the ground dressed in pink trousers, she says, after the explosion. A dark red blood stain spread over her thigh. All that happened in a fraction of a second. Two cars arrived from somewhere. They took her to hospital. All that was accompanied with piercing screams from The First Grammar School building. In Bosnia and Herzegovina's oldest grammar school building refugees had found a shelter. The screams pierced to the bone. They resounded through the womb. However, it was, it seems, only because of what they had seen. Apart from fear, the eyewitness from the Grammar School building had no other consequences.

"At noon we received the news of her death. A young man brought it, a Local Defense driver whom she had taught English... That same day, while she was cooling off in the mortuary, some people tried to break into and occupy her flat. They were in a hurry. Divna hardly managed to stop them. She sent, through radio hams, a message of sympathy to her brother in Belgrade.

"There was no mention of it in the newspapers. The radio reports on the number of the wounded and killed. Sarajevo had, during the last twenty-four hours, as the announcement says, twelve dead. No names are given. The reports do not give professions, addresses, marital status, qualifications, either. Numbers are given statistically. It is done neatly. You cannot discern the destinies behind the numbers.

"Today the same again. The numbers go up, they multiply... It was reported that near the 'Tvin' shop in Džemala Bijedića Street a shell had wounded over twenty citizens. The news first said there were two dead. Later the number doubled.

"Behind each number there is a man. Behind him, like a shadow, there is wife, family, friends and a past.

"The number of the killed near the 'Tvin' included Željka, the wife of the journalist Fahro Memić. Željka Vrdoljak, I think she was also a cousin of Gordana's, was a quiet librarian at the Institute for History. She was, I say...

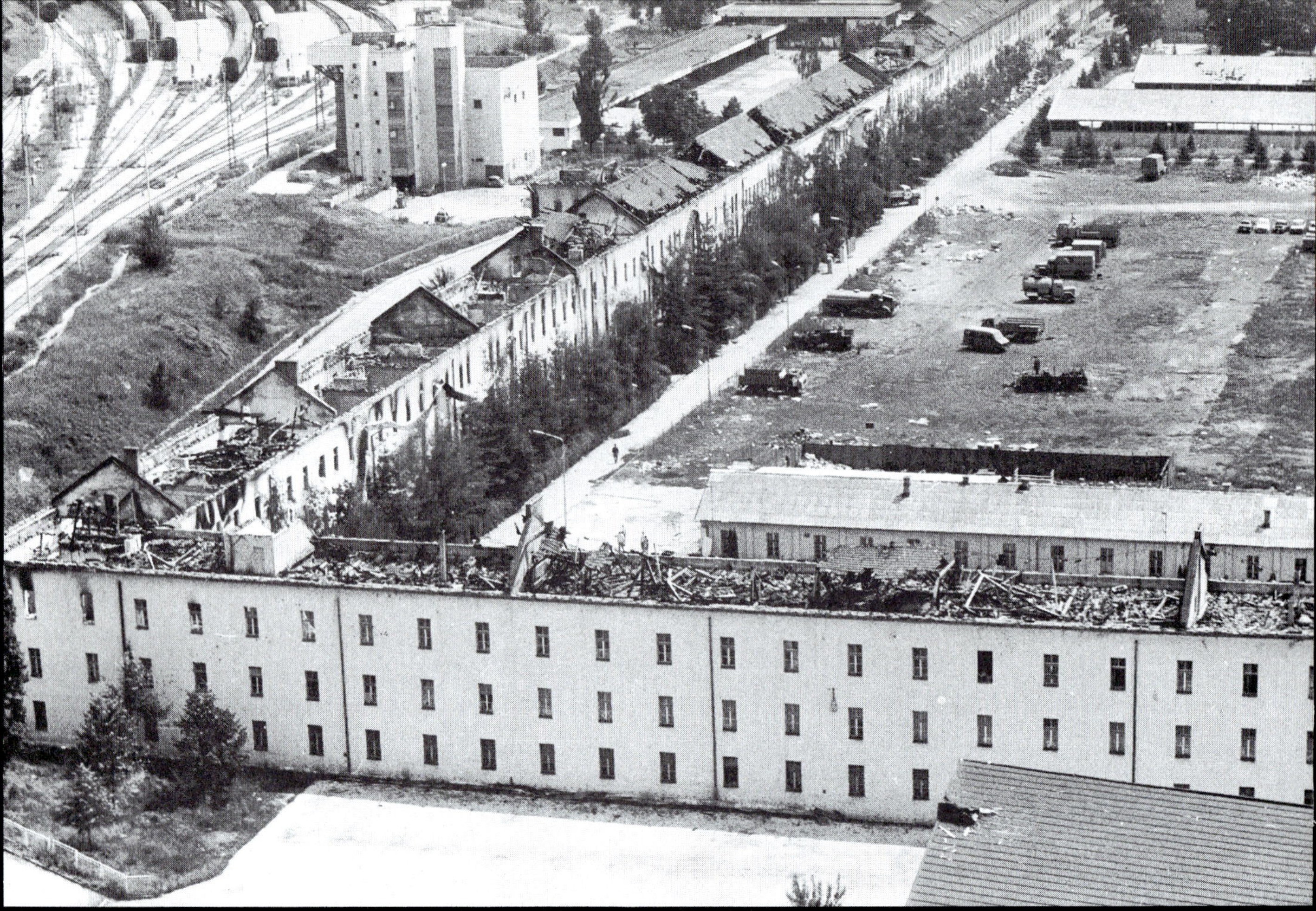

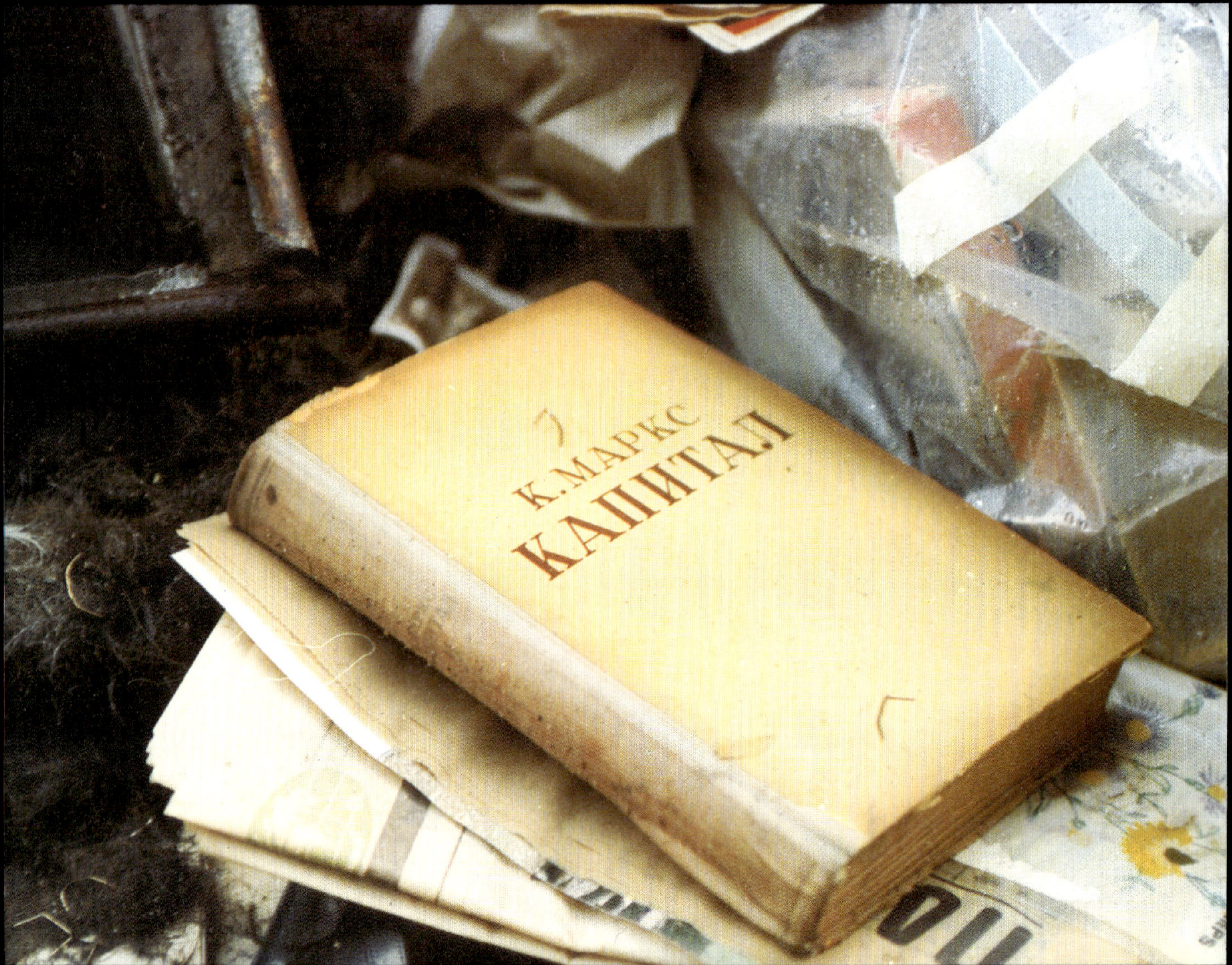
К. МАРКС
КАПИТАЛ

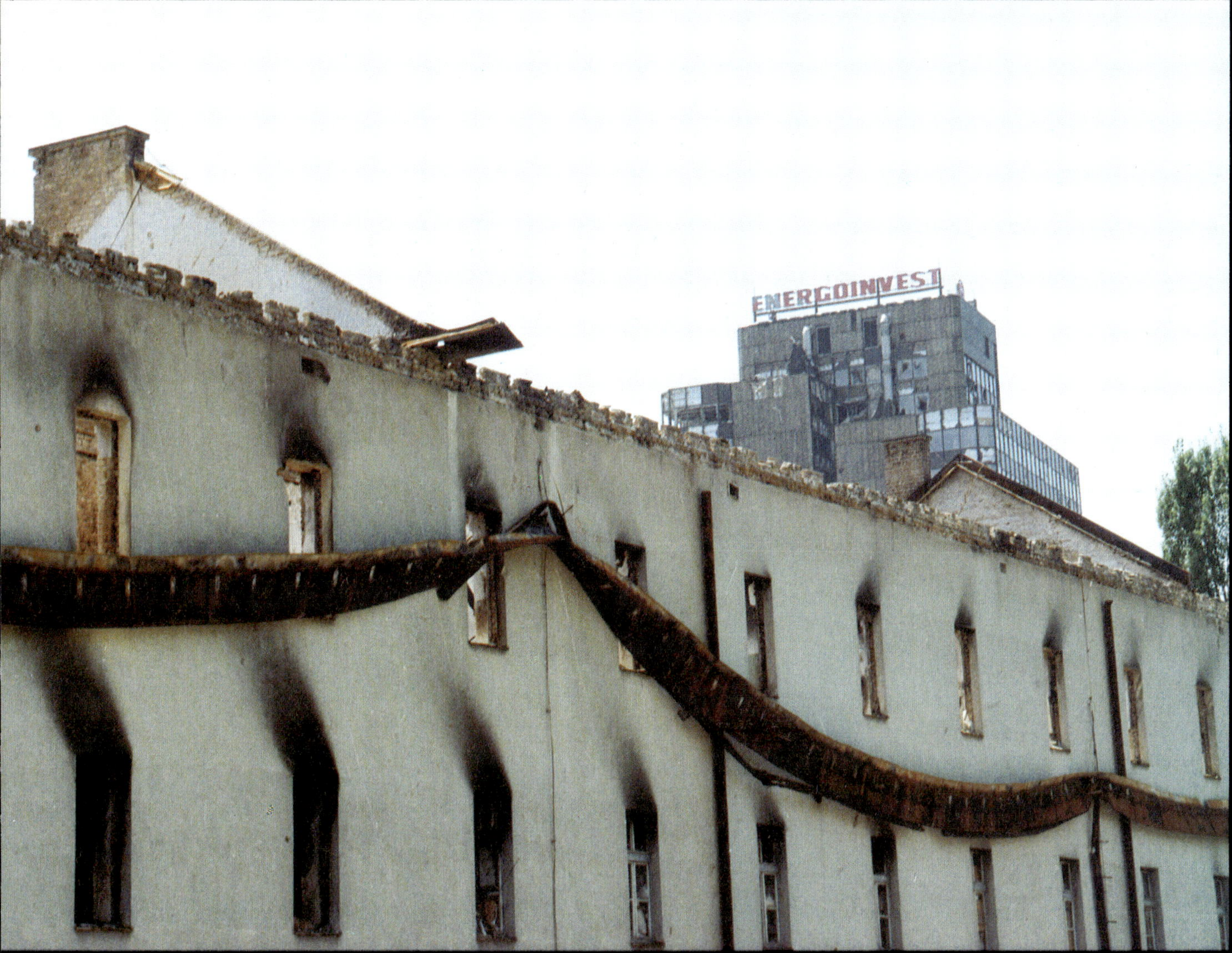
ENERGOINVEST

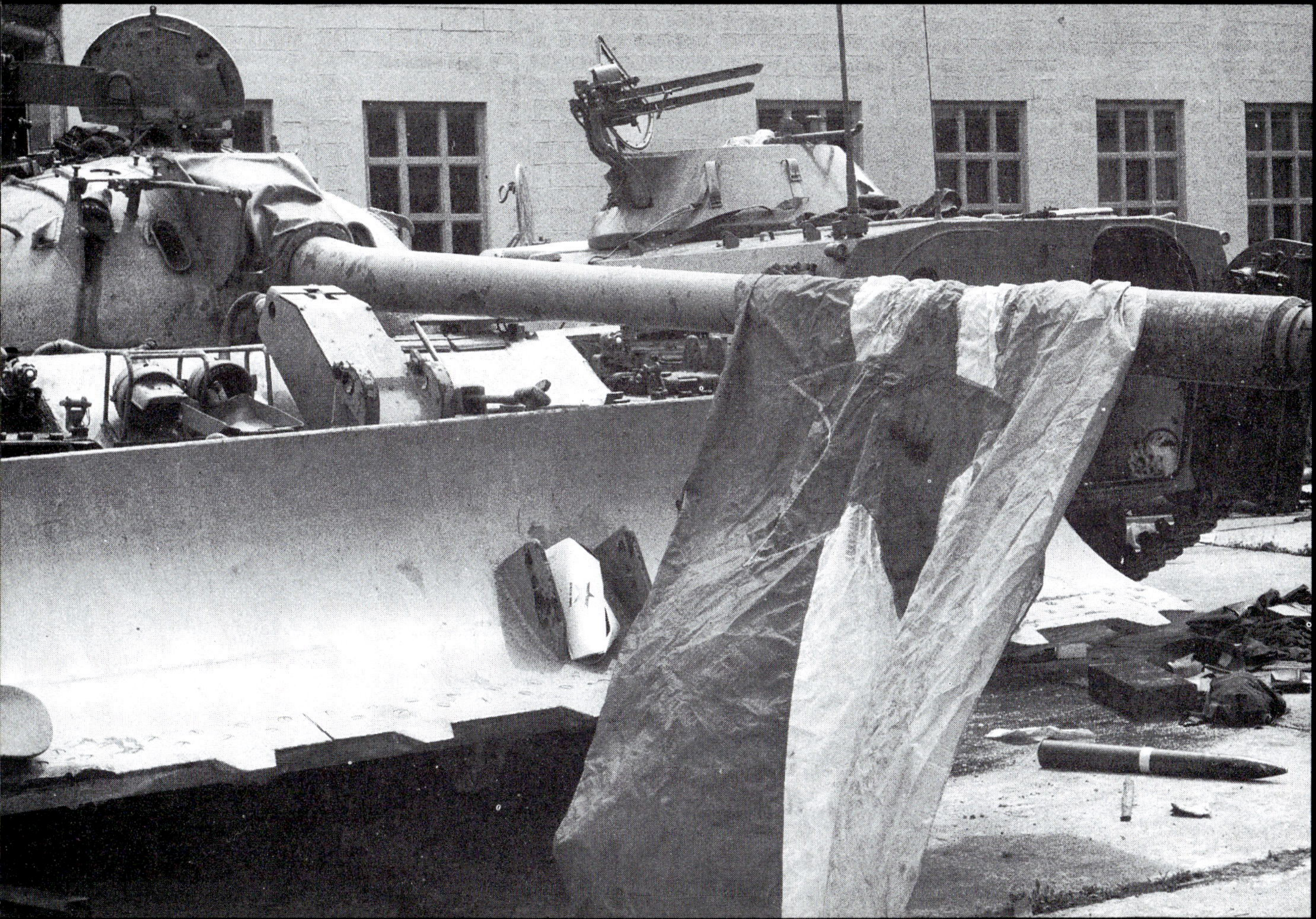

"Fahro started off for work at "Oslobođenje". She went to buy bread. And... she was killed in a second.

"An eyewitness to it talked yesterday, in a radio report, about that massacre, parts of human bodies that were thrown as far as the roofs of neighbouring houses..."

Everything is done in haste. Burials are usually painful peace. They are done slowly. They take time. In Sarajevo, this summer, nothing is as it used to be. You can hardly catch up with the speed with which everything passes.

An obituary with a photograph in the newspaper. It was placed at the top of the page. It is a small privilege that typographers give their colleague and friend, when our closest ones leave. The hour of burial is not given. The destination is, of course, the cemetery Lav (The Lion). The bereaved are: son Damir, mother, father and husband...

At the same time this morning the driver who takes the newspapers to selling points brings the news. He hands me my stack of newspapers for sale, tells me about Željka's death, and about the death of Svjetlana's husband as well. He was, he says, wounded at the same time as Fahro's Željka, but he died before reaching the hospital. In the newspaper obituary the bereaved are three daughters, wife, parents and sister. Dragan recently worked as our newspaperboy at Čengić vila, not far from his flat. He also went out to buy some bread.

The funeral. It is eleven o'clock a.m. We arrive a few minutes before. Fahro stands by the tomb which is being filled in, covered. They are shovelling the last lumps of earth onto it.

Everything is done hastily. Even faster than the announced schedules.

Down, behind us, a funeral, three-four tabuts (boards on which Muslims are buried). Some distance farther, up to the left, one more grave is being covered with earth. I cannot see Svjetlana. People are scattered among pyramids, crosses, gravestones, tombstones. It is a hot August day. There is some shade under the trees. There is less and less green grass in the old cemetery...

A shell goes off. Then another. Some bullets whizz above our heads. We turn our eyes to Poljine. We cannot see anything. Death comes from there. Those who sow the shells are somewhere up there.

We hurriedly hide behind a few metres high sculpture of the lying lion. Our eyes inexorably turn to the Olympic sports hall "Zetra". It has been burned up. The remainders of warped sheet metal have become big scabs on the metal framework. It also looks like an unrealistic coffin. The beauty of the city has been turned into a sad death chest by those from Poljine.

Sarajevo looks mortal today, only dying all around. And the lion we are is dying. It was erected in 1916 at a military cemetery that was being filled at that time.

shell fragments. Five people are killed and several wounded in the Seat of the Muslim Community. Three UNPROFOR soldiers are also injured by shell fragments.

Sunday, 30th: *A massacre in front of a self-service shop near the market place at Alipašino polje. A 120mm shell fired from Grbavica kills 8 and seriously injures more than 50 citizens. The wounded and the dead are taken away from the scene in two vans and six private cars. Up to now, four firemen have been killed and 28 injured in extinguishing hundreds of fires. No electricity, no water. Twelve dead and 70 injured in Sarajevo.*

Monday, 31st: *By August 30th, there have been 10,358 people killed (1,954 in Sarajevo), 43,635 seriously wounded (11,649 in Sarajevo), 75,000 slightly injured (14,500 in Sarajevo). The number of those missing assumed dead is 53,100 (6,600 in Sarajevo). There are 630 people in Sarajevo suffering from enterocolitis and 24 from hepatitis A; a few cases of typhoid fever have been recorded as well.*

SEPTEMBER

Tuesday, 1st: *Four high calibre shells fall on Solidarity Square at Alipašino polje, near the market place. Four people are killed and eight injured. Shells kill two and injure 28 at Dobrinja. The enterocolitis and dysentery epidemic is spreading. Thirteen people are killed and 119 injured in Sarajevo. There has been no electricity since August 29th. At 2.30 p.m. a sniper hits an "Oslobođenje" van which was taking people home from work. Seriously injured* was Almira Šehić, a technical editor.

Wednesday, 2nd: *25 people are killed and 144 injured. Enterocolitis is spreading. Pensions increase by 118.46% in relation to March. An average pension in B-H is 44,495 dinars. The lowest is 10,941 dinars. Foreign currencies go down on the black market. A kilogram of meat costs 10 DM (down from 17 or 20 DM). Bread on the black market costs 1 DM per kilo.*

Thursday, 3rd: *Shells fall all over the city. Four children are killed and three seriously injured in Alija Hodžić Street. Mark Goulding visits Sarajevo. A plane of the Italian Air Forces UN 2117 "AY-22" on a flight from Split to Sarajevo is shot down near Fojnica. Four members of the crew die. There is neither water nor electricity. More than 1,000 citizens of Sarajevo are suffering from enterocolitis. Shortage of food in the hospitals. The first verdict is pronounced by the District Military Court. The Economic Chamber of B-H states: "Damage to economic structures caused by the war amounts to several billion dollars." 750,000 people are without work (including farmers). The monthly income of those employed is 10 DM on average.*

Friday, 4th: *By a Presidency decree having the force of law the Institute for Investigation of Crimes against Humanity and International Law is established. There is neither electricity nor water. There are 300 new cases of enterocolitis. A BBC reporter, Kate Adie, is wounded. 3,783 tons of food arrives in the period between July 29th and August 31st. Every citizen should*

Shells fall very close. Explosions resound through a massive Austro-Hungarian building. In the meantime we run for the bus. It is not there. We hide with others in the entrance to a house in Danijela Ozme Street. On the door there is a death notice. In its black frame, and in pen, a ball-point pen, they wrote the customary death notice on Željka's death. Why is it here? Oh, yes. She was born Vrdoljak. I look at the doorbells. Up on the left it says: VRDOLJAK. She lived here. Yes, her parents are here. They are old. They are in their eighties. How do they feel? They were not at the funeral. Fahro probably did not let them go. The cemetery is shelled on the hour and on the half hour too. If not, snipers fire bursts at the cemetery. They sent their shower of death today as well.

How do they feel? Well, the building on the left of theirs burned to the ground. The building in the courtyard also burned to the ground, the one looking onto the park and Tito Street. Two floors above, the bohemian bar "San" burned, too. Hit and destroyed were also two flats on the upper floor of the building that theirs looks on to. All this here is a crater of evil. And now the loss of their daughter. What else will happen to them? How desperate it must be to be helpless. Add the burden of age as well.

"Oslobođenje" fills three of its eight pages with obituaries. On the 24th it says that at the cemetery "Lav" there are burial places for only a fortnight more. At the same time Tadeusz Mazowiecki sinks into Bosnia and Herzegovina's pain: "Europe should feel pangs of conscience."

We hurry towards the exit. I cannot see Svjetlana anywhere. I look back. I look for her to express my condolences.

An acquaintance of mine tells me in a low voice so that others cannot hear: She is in Igalo.

I think that she was still here in July.

The news keeps spreading around the city. Who will explain to the children and Svjetlana that Dragan Kadijević, a father, son, brother and godfather is not alive any more. He is not alive any more.

The coffin left. There was a notice on it in the newspapers. None of his dearest ones was escorting the coffin. I wonder by who, when and how they will be informed that on August 27th a newspaperboy's job, buying bread, looking at family photographs, were interrupted...

Today the radio resounds with the news from Stari Grad (The Old Town). Last night five citizens were killed. I cannot get any information from other municipalities. There are five people fewer in just one night. What is in store for us today? And the day after tomorrow?...

Shells fell on the centre at midday. We went to see Ilija and Filip at the Presidency. They have no news about uncle Sudo. It has been like that for days. He is not on their list. They do not know, they say, where he is.

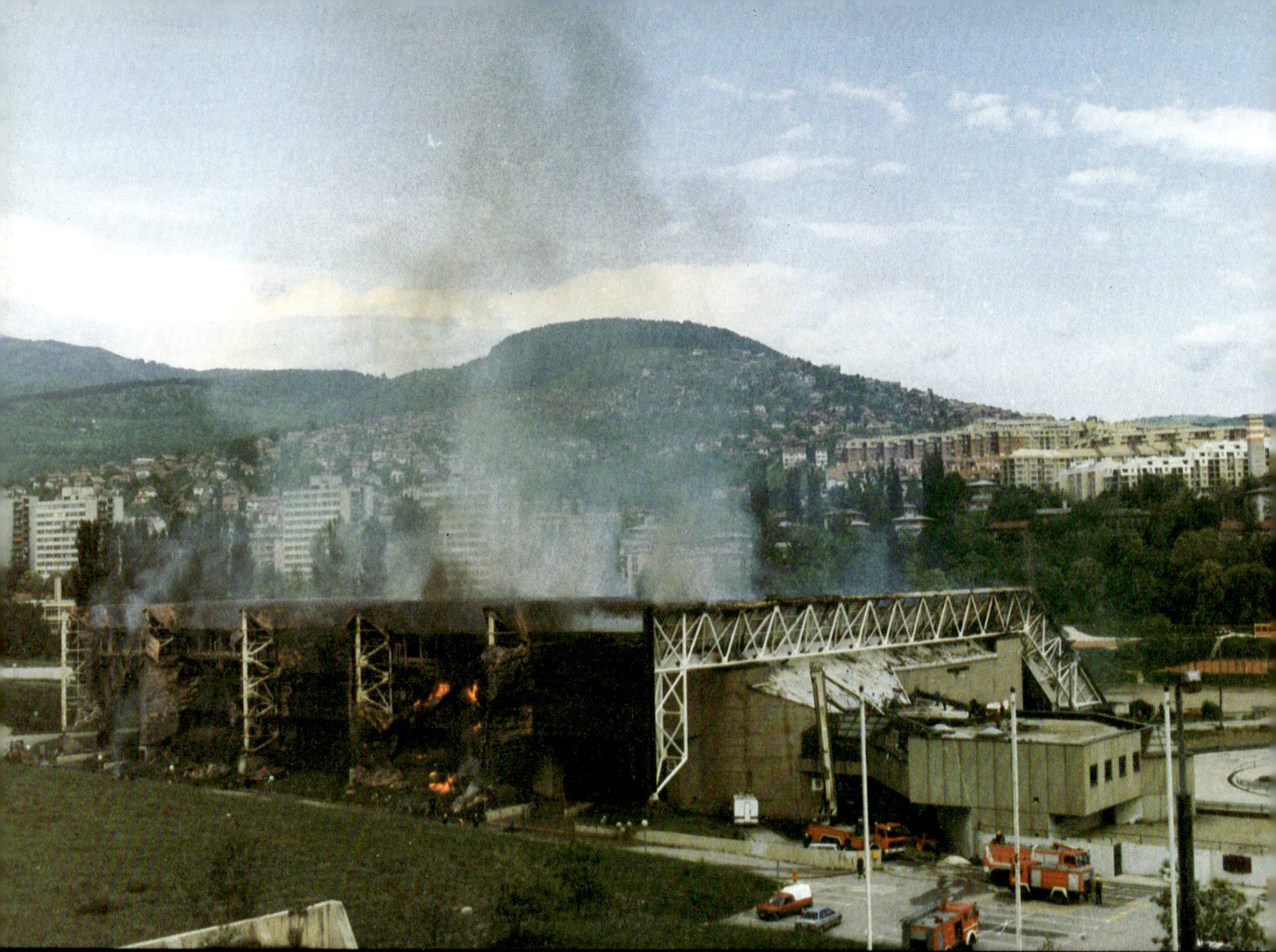

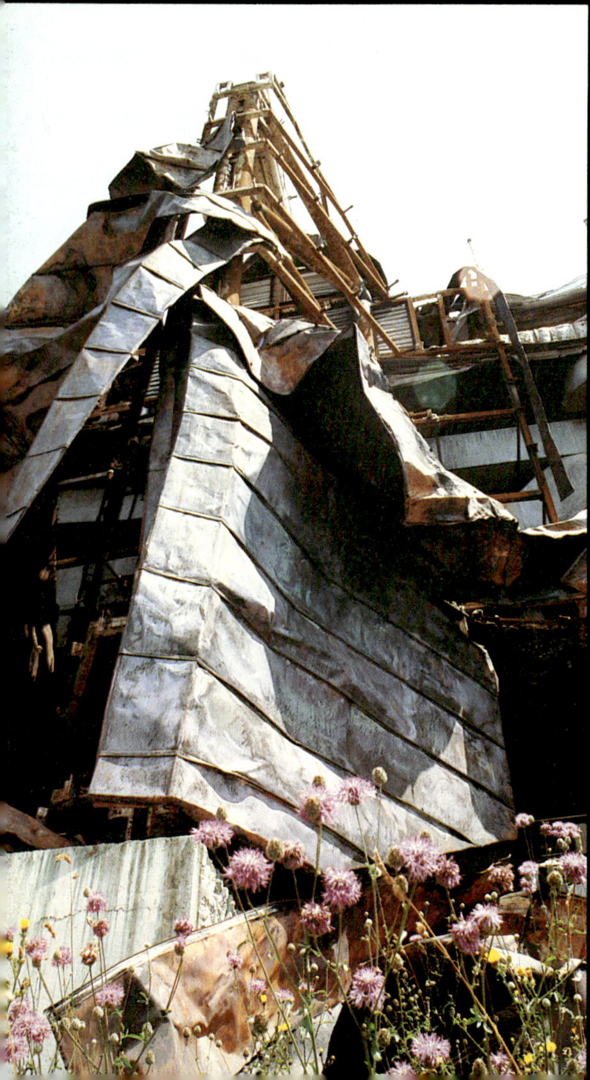

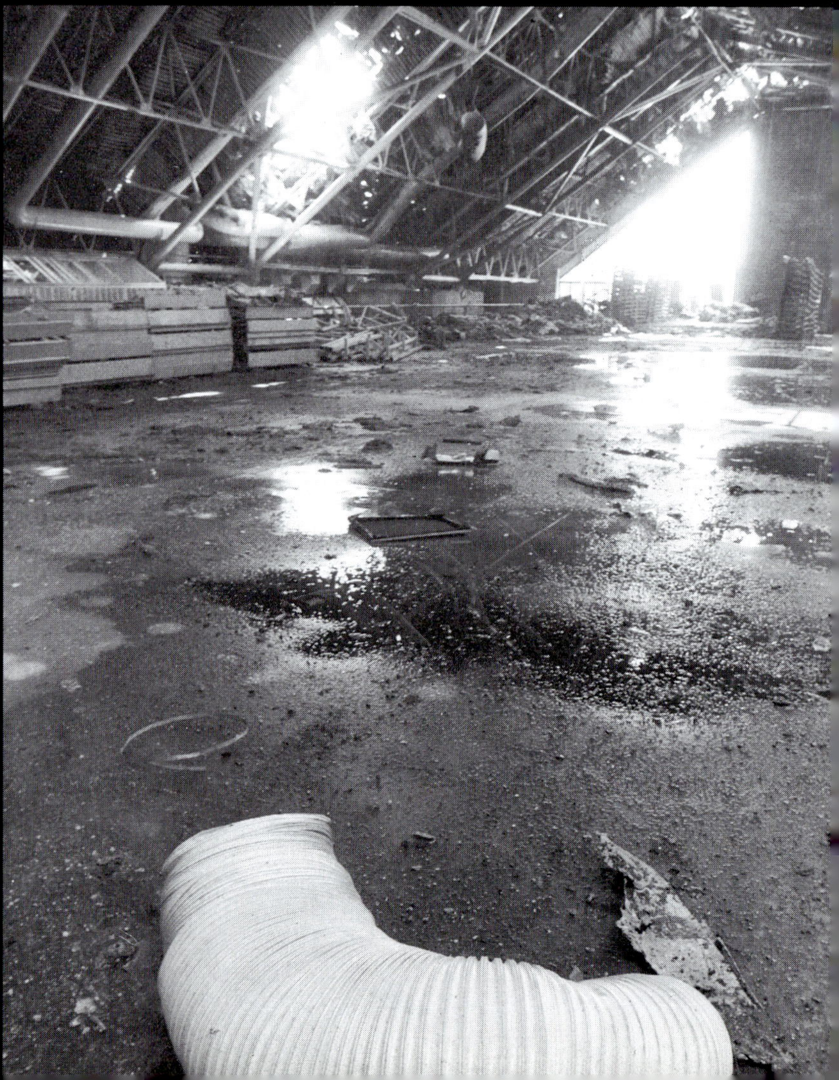

ZETRA

OLIMPIJSKI CENTAR

over what is going on here. It is evident that they have not done enough. Here horrible things are happening...

We sink deeper and deeper. Dimitrije Pfamfilov's words still echo in my ears. I heard them at a poets' meeting in June 1991. I did not want to accept them. He spoke about his Vukovar and that he was getting ready to flee. A doctor who sat up till dawn at an inn on the bank of the Danube with our best-known poets was fleeing without knowing where: "Hatred has been sown. It is worse than radiation. It won't disappear for the next fifty years. It has settled in people. They will take it with them far from their towns."

In the heat of Circle Five, Catholic Queen Isabella is again in my vicinity. She holds the arm of her Don Ferdinand II. They are celebrating five centuries. They see off three sailing boats. The names written on the masts are: "Santa Maria", "Nina" and "Pinta". The Genoan Christopher Columbus leaves for India to come back from America with two redskinned men that he will give to the royal couple as a gift. Jewish ships with exiles simultaneously sail in one direction only. Behind them, a centuries –old thought lingers on: there are human dramas that come from afar. Commemoration of five centuries does not refer to the discovery of the continent. They are charmed, no, not with the unification of Aragon and Castille by a marriage, but by royal edict. They are in the splendid Alhambra, in Granada filled with music, castanets and love. They all recite simultaneously: "After thorough consideration, we order the expulsion of all Jews from our kingdoms so that they never come back... We order all Jewish men and Jewish women, regardless of age... to leave..., themselves, their sons and their daughters, male servants and female servants and Jewish relatives – children and adults... They will not be allowed to return to the land of our states by their own choice, or in transit or in any other way..." A small man next to them smiles. For a second, he is a dignified rabbi. Then he is an arrogant and powerful archbishop. I cannot tell whether the Jew plays a Catholic canon or I am seeing apparitions caused by heat. He melts in the heat. Rabbi's and archbishop's vestments replace one another. The Torah and the Talmud are in his hands, but next moment he tramples on them. Images of modesty and anger replace one another. Oh, yes, Salomon Levi of Burgos becomes Pablo de Santa Maria. In his neophytic zeal he looks for Jews here as well to push them into the baptistry.

Behind Catholic Isabella a Spanish Dominican, the great inquisitor, Tomas de Torquemada. In his hands dark grey, couleur isabeau, the Queen's robes. She did not take them off before the last Muslim authority was overthrown on the Iberian Peninsula, before Granada was taken. Mediaeval Spain with the stake moves into my home.

Those expelled travel with their property thrown into the disposable plastic bags one uses when going to the

consume 1.5 kg of food a day, but at the moment can get about 400 grams. The humanitarian aid consists mostly of rice, flour and ready-to-eat meals (combat rations).

Saturday, 5th: *Sarajevo airport still closed. A convoy of 10 lorries arrives from Split with about 100 tons of food and blankets. There are 6 people killed and 79 wounded in Sarajevo. The beginning of the new school year is still uncertain. As the Bačevo springs have been out of use since yesterday, water is distributed to the citizens by water tankers.*

Sunday, 6th: *The whole town is without a single drop of water. Cyrus Vance and David Owen require Radovan Karadžić, president of the usurping Serb republic of B-H, place all heavy weapons under UN control by noon on September 12th. No humanitarian aid lands at Sarajevo airport. A convoy from Split arrives with 63 tons of food. A mortar shell destroys a lorry with blankets in the UN warehouse for humanitarian aid.*

Monday, 7th: *13 people killed, 77 wounded. The number of people suffering from enterocolitis in Stari grad and Centre municipalities is 1,765. Artillery and mortar shells fall on the outskirts of the Stari grad municipality – Širokača, Hrid, Mahmutovac and Vasin han. Skenderija and Soukbunar are fired at from Hreša. Anti-aircraft machine guns and anti-aircraft guns fire at Baščaršija, Grdonj and Brekin potok. Also shelled are the residential areas Pavle Goranin, Alipašino polje, Vojničko polje and Dobrinja. Continuous heavy fire from Nedžarići and*

Kasindo Street at Stup hill (more than a hundred shells fall in less than an hour). A shortage of medicine in hospitals. The dress rehearsal and the first night of the play "Shelter" by Safet Plakalo and Dubravko Bibanović are held. This performance is being staged by the Sarajevo War Theatre (The SARTR). The Bačevo springs get electricity, so water gradually reaches the consumers. Izet Sarajlić, a poet, is wounded in his flat. The flat is destroyed.

Saturday, 12th: *Tanks fire at Pero Kosorić Square. Two killed, six wounded. The outskirts of Stari grad are shelled. Also shelled are Blekin potok, Stara Breka, Panjina kula, Grdonj and Koševo hill. Tanks fire at Sokolje. Artillery at Kula, Lukavica and Nedžarići targets Kotorac and Butmir. Artillery attacks on Stup, Stup hill and Otes lasts for an hour. Shells fall on Kobilja glava, Hotonj and Barice. The epidemic of enterocolitis improves.*

Sunday, 13th: *Artillery fires at the sloped parts of the town and the residential areas Otes, Azići, Sokolje and Stup. Flights with humanitarian aid from Zagreb to Sarajevo are renewed. A heavy artillery attack on Doglode and unprecedented atrocities against civilians. Foreign students protest in front of the UNPROFOR headquarters. They request to be allowed to go home. So far six of them have been killed.*

Monday, 14th: *The other "Oslobođenje" skyscraper is demolished. Rocket launchers fire at Stup. The heart of Baščaršija is subject to destruction once again. Artillery fires at the outskirts*

market. They do not manage to get their mementos in them. Bewildered, they flee their homes where they were born. Behind them, their patrimony vanishes in flames. All they had is destroyed. Places of worship and graveyards are wiped out by hatred. Black sites of fire spread throughout the land of Bosnia. The Romanies also go on leaving for Split from their settlement at Butmir. Here there are no more roads and journeys. The Romany tents also vanish in the blaze of war. The whole city lives on alms. It cannot give alms. It hopes for them every day. The gypsies must move their tents in order to live.

Caravans bereft of children's joy leave the city. Only occasional buses with exchanged prisoners with ghostly looks come here. A convoy of sympathy and assistance "The wounded Zadar to the wounded Sarajevo" arrives. For the first time, in a received parcel, a friend gets a packet of candles, cheese and a few metres of plastic foil to replace the broken glass of his windows. They torment us with water and electricity. We have not had them for weeks. We lower our level of civilizational living. We hurry with plastic canisters for water to distant springs. We can still find some water there. We come across our acquaintances in parks where they tear the wooden bench seats off. They use them as fuel. They can cook a meal over them. Gradually, in my neighbourhood, crosses and pyramids vanish from graveyards. They cut them, first secretly and then without feeling any shame. Passing by, I read silently and surprised the names of those buried. Over them the neighbours, having no electricity, cook their scanty lunches, dinners, and heat water for washing. It is still summertime. A sentence of the United Nations High Commissioner for Refugees, Mrs Ogata Sadako, still hovers over us: "The severe climate in Bosnia and Herzegovina could cause more deaths than the fighting has done so far."

Another wave of heat strikes me. The night shells set fire to the pseudo-Arabesque Town Hall building. Some thirty of them hit the roof, shot through the glass dome and stopped in the bookcases and desks in the reading rooms. Flames swallowed up the National and University Library. Precious written material was ablaze, a hundred-year-old building with chairs decorated with engravings, its arabesques and stained glass windows gradually disappeared. In flames were over a million books, magazines, newspapers, manuscripts and maps... One of the city's landmarks vanished. The staircase collapsed. The fire ate up the slender pillars. One of the most valuable examples of all the South Slavic peoples' heritage vanished. The source of Bosnia and Herzegovina's identity was destroyed. Lucifer's laughter resounded through the ashes of the libraries of cultural societies "Prosvjeta" (Enlightenment) and "Napredak" (Progress), through the destroyed Austrian reading room, ashes of the collections of periodicals, special collec-

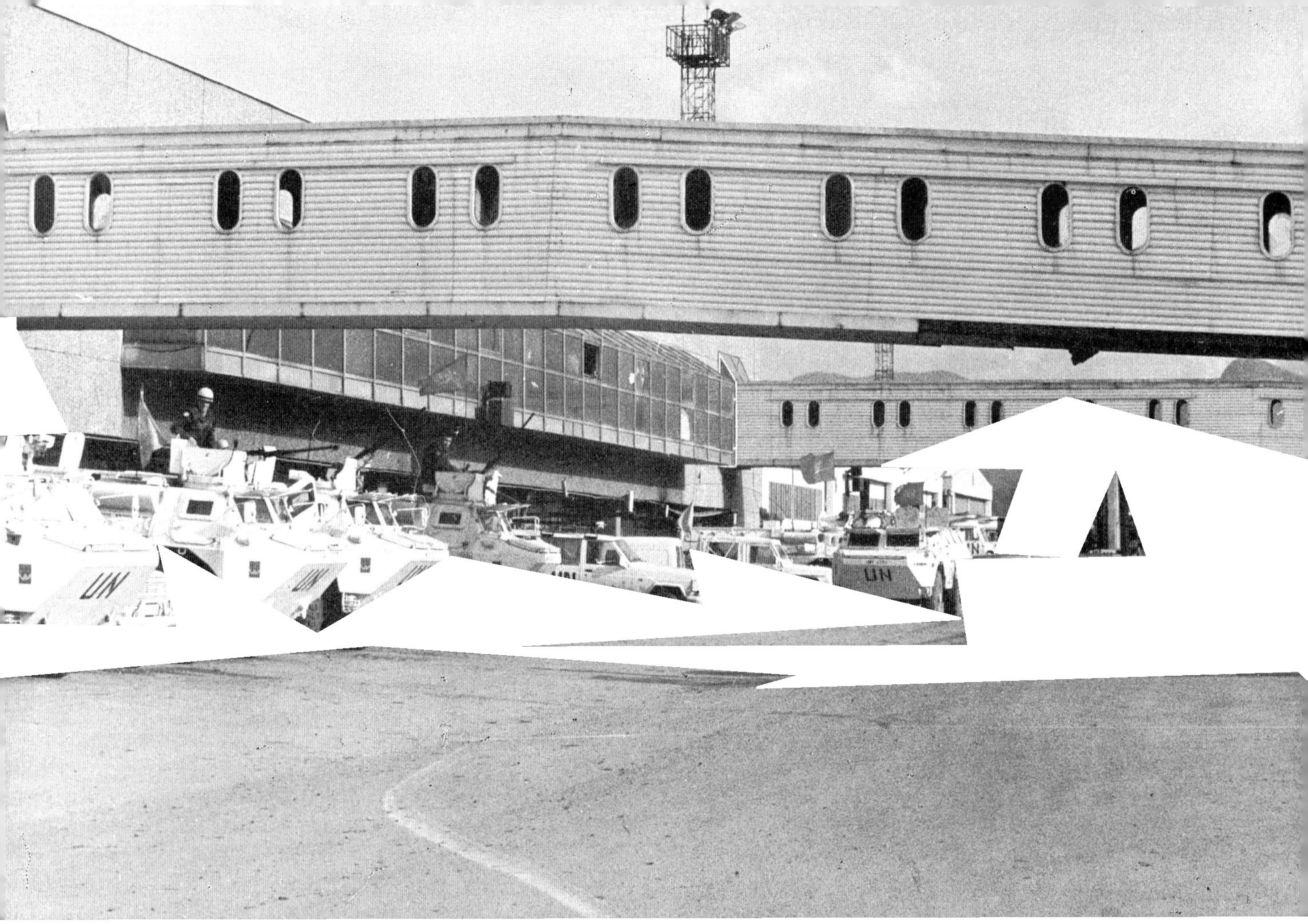
UN

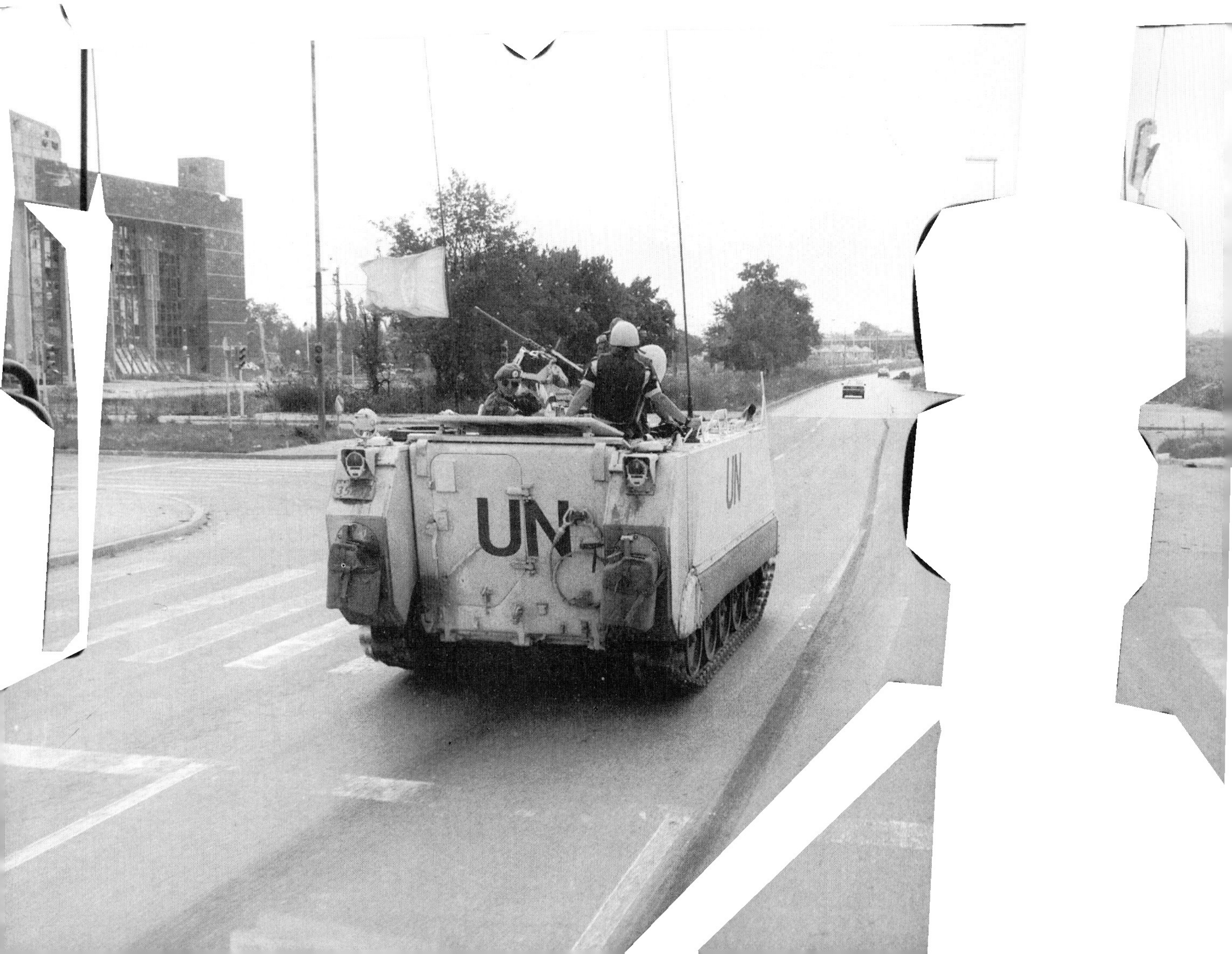
UN

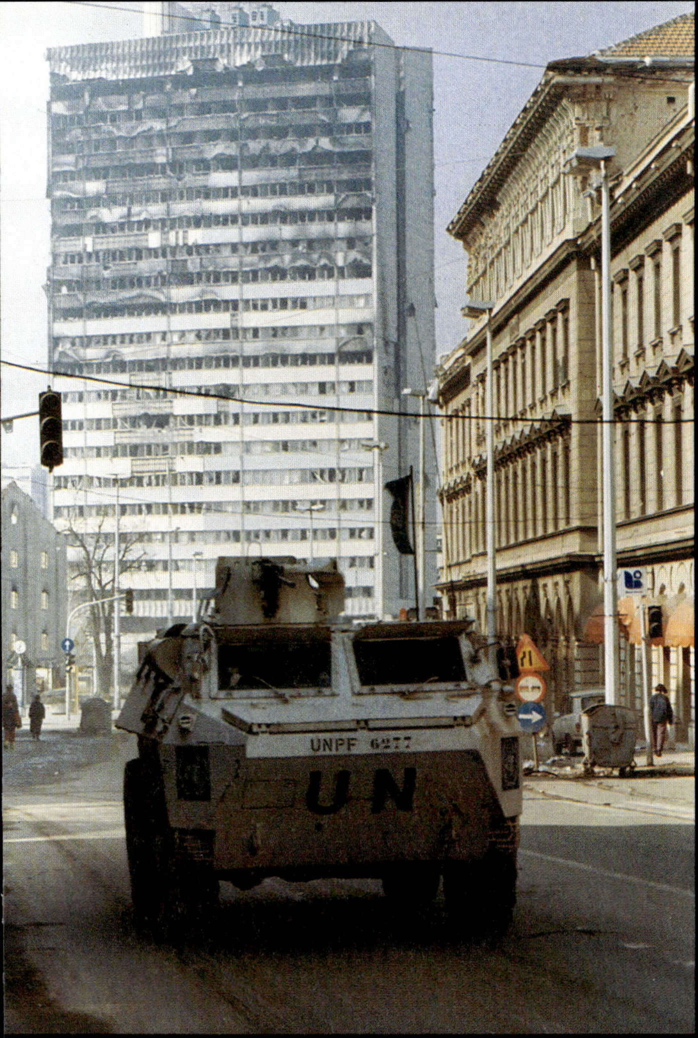
UNPF 6277
UN

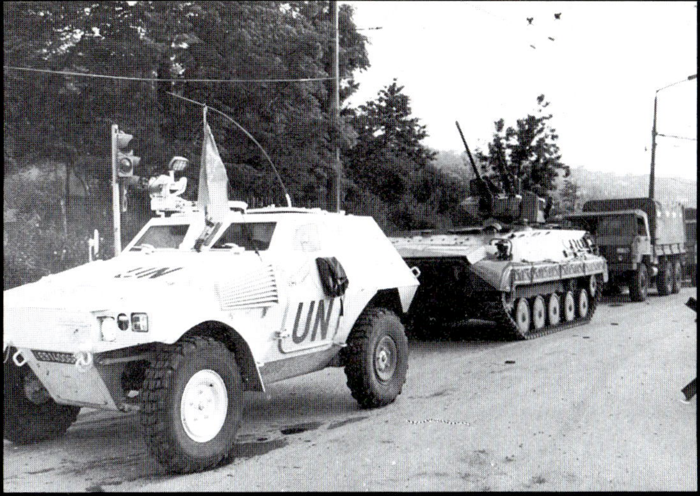
UN

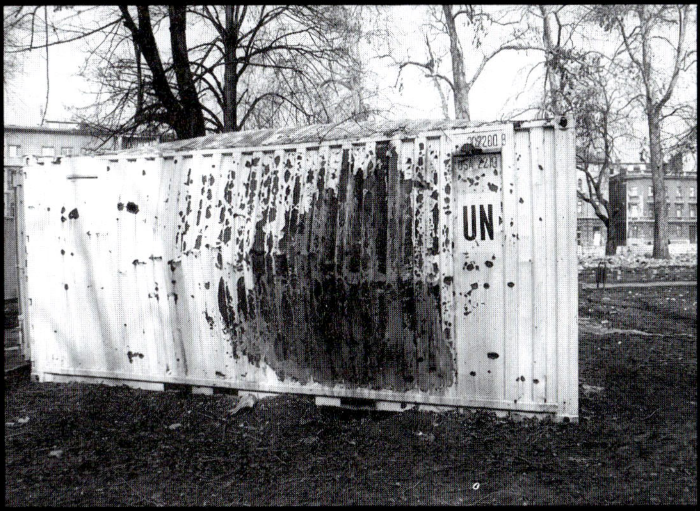
UN

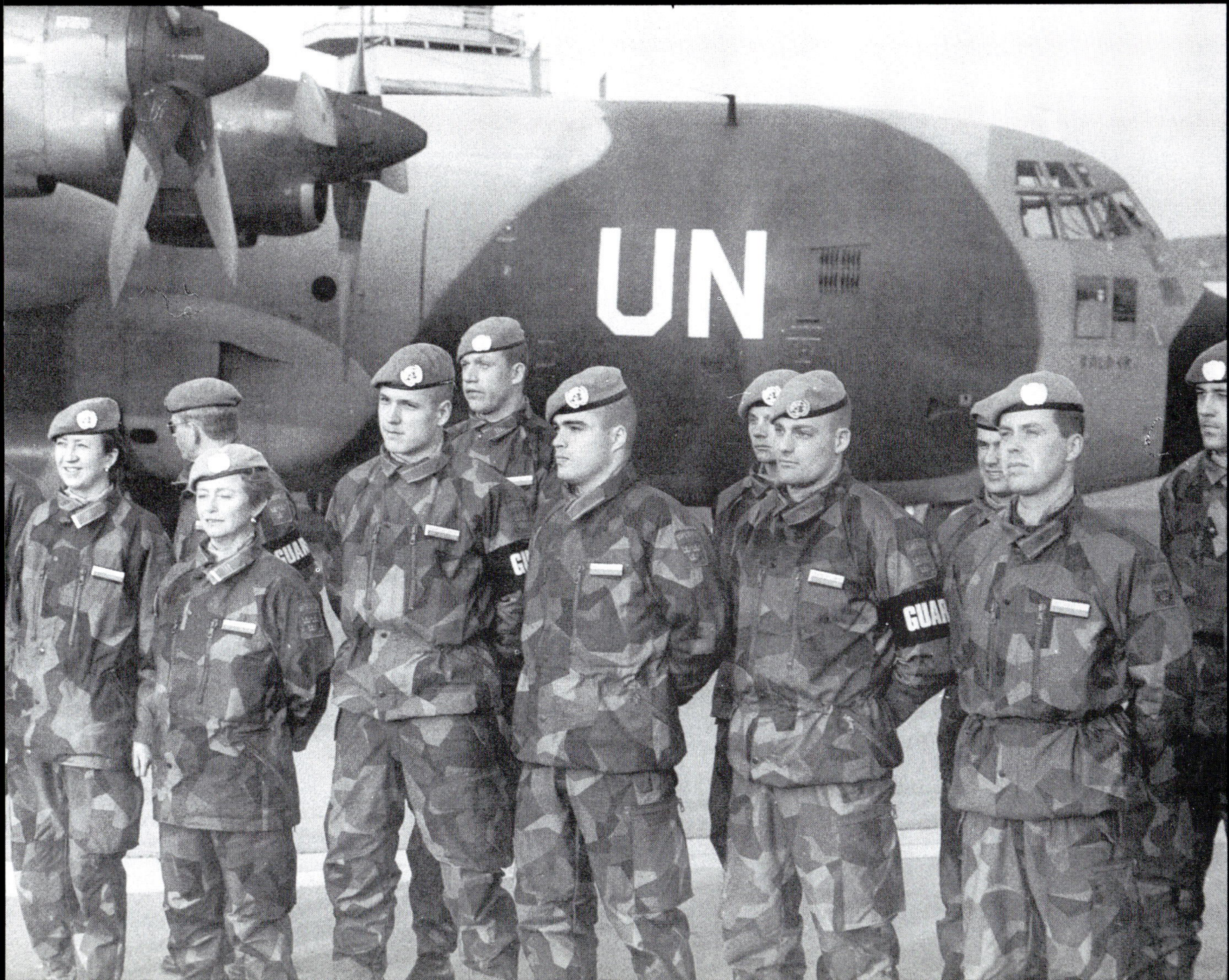
UN

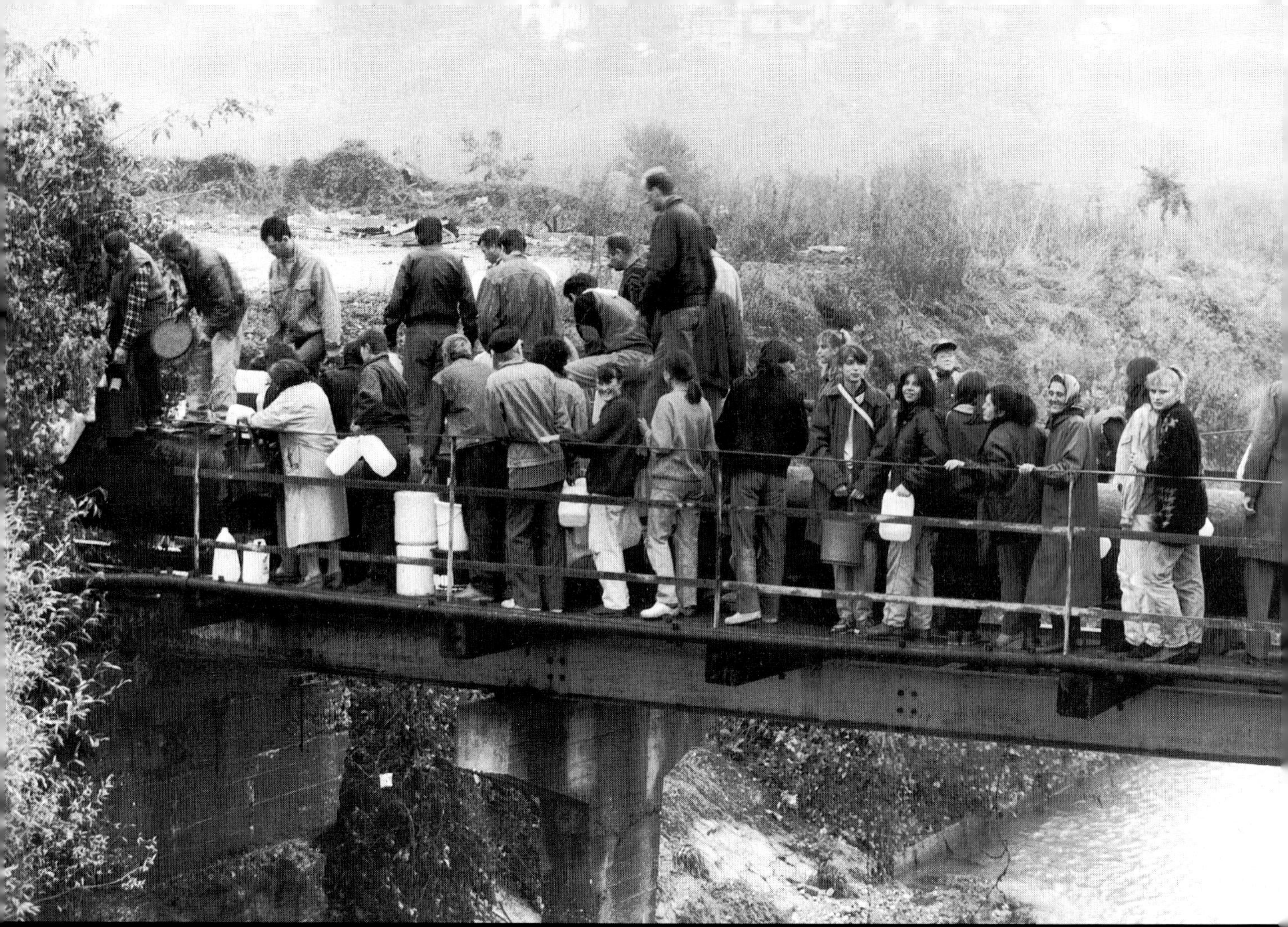

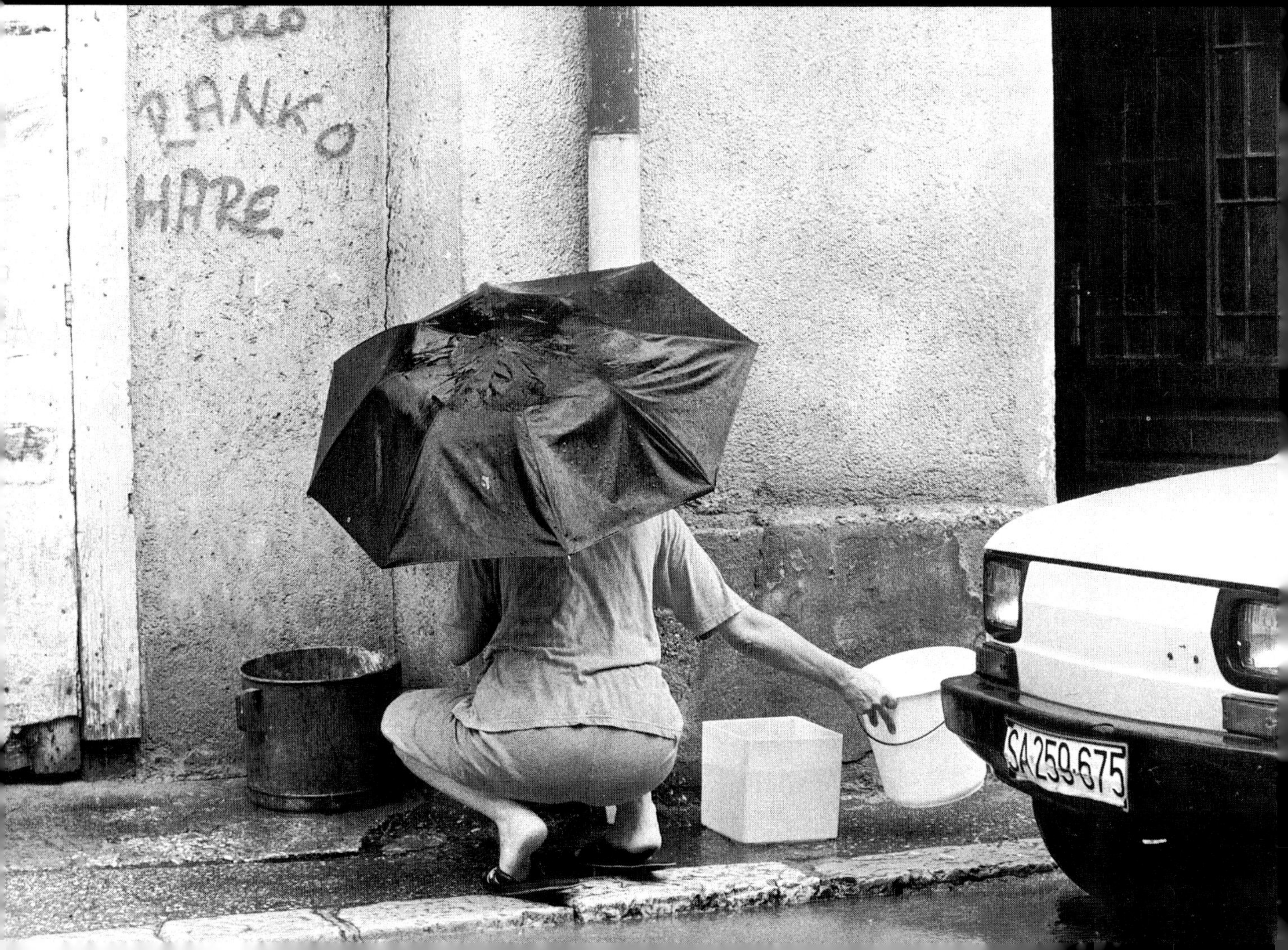
SA 259-675

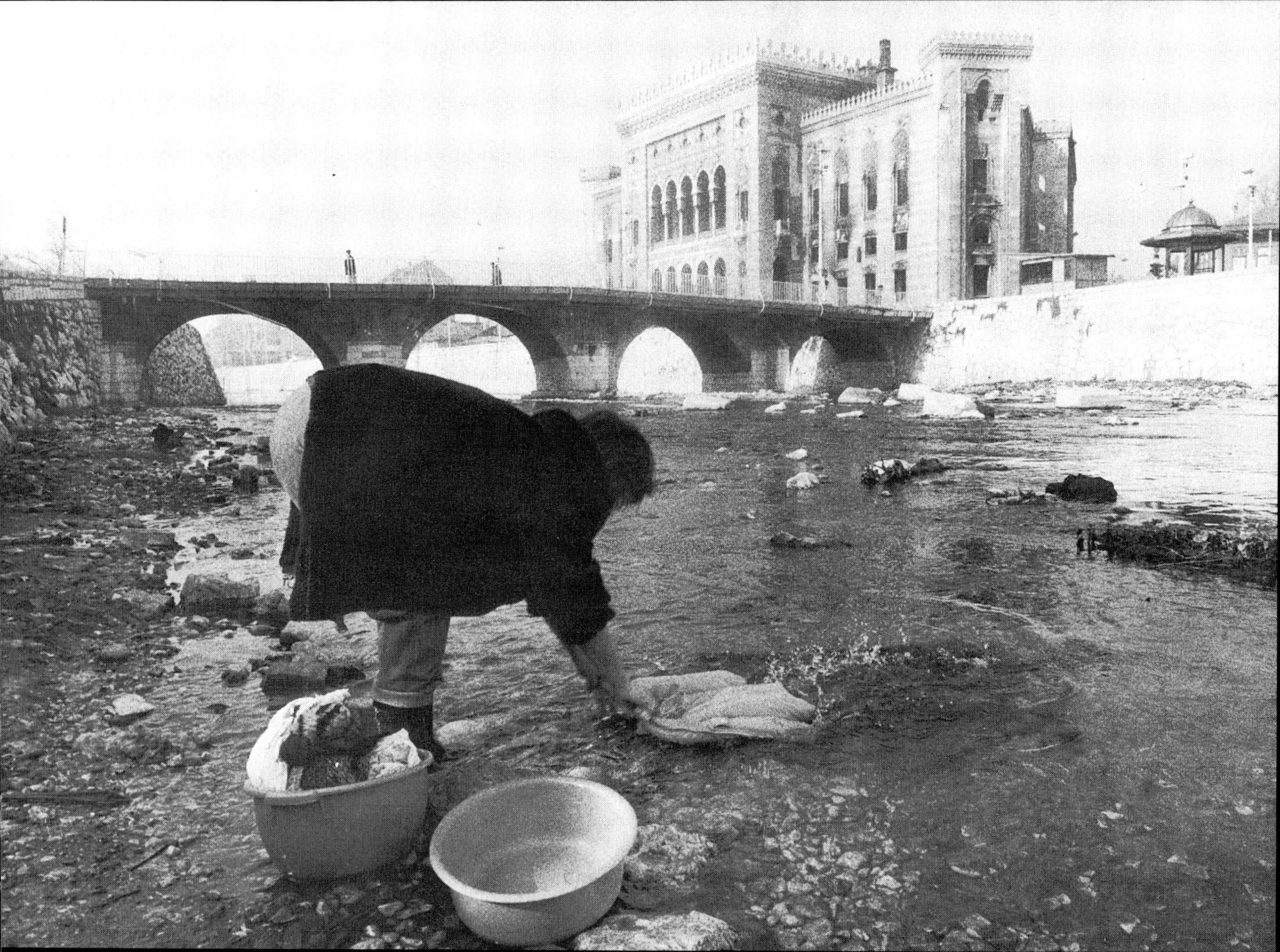

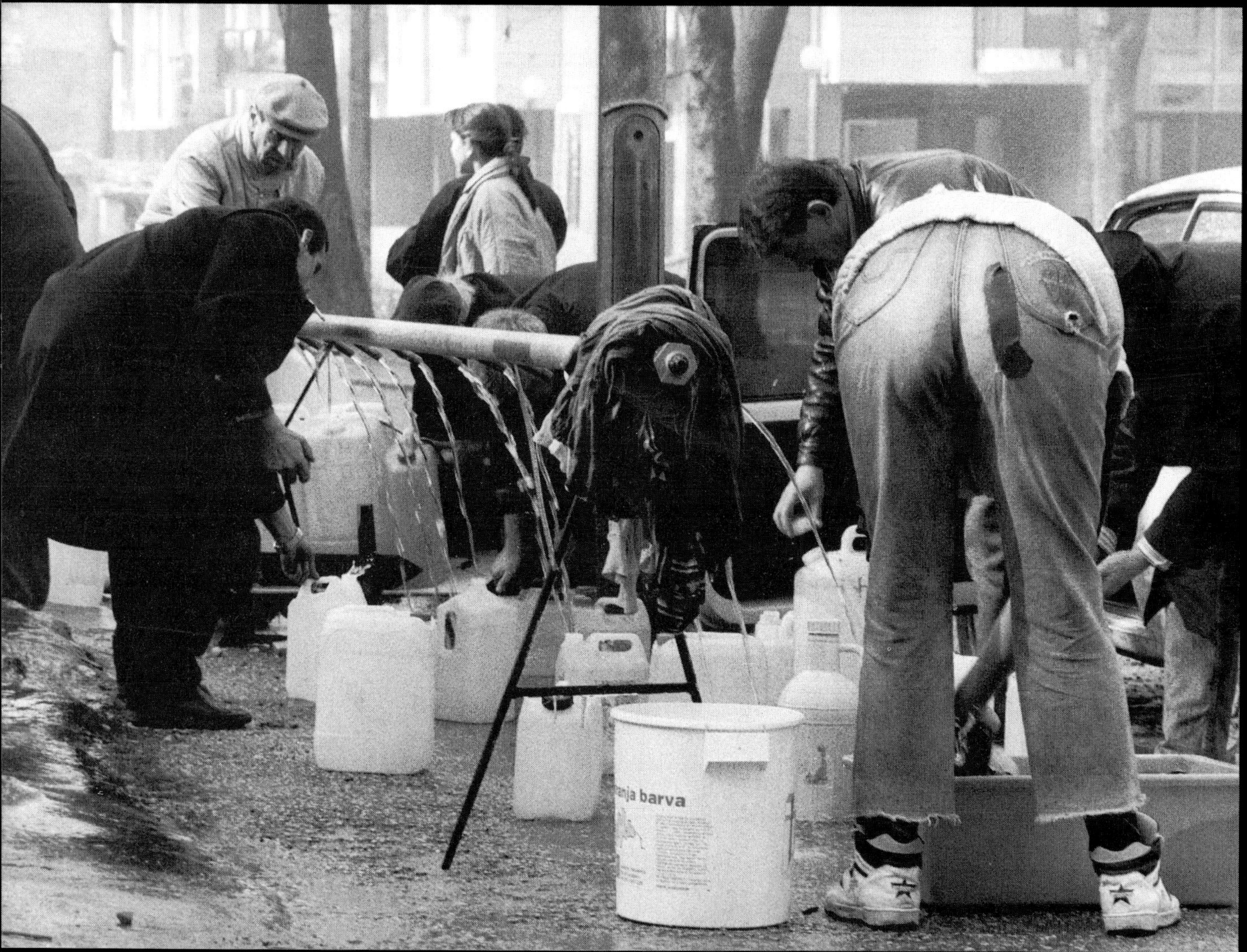
barva

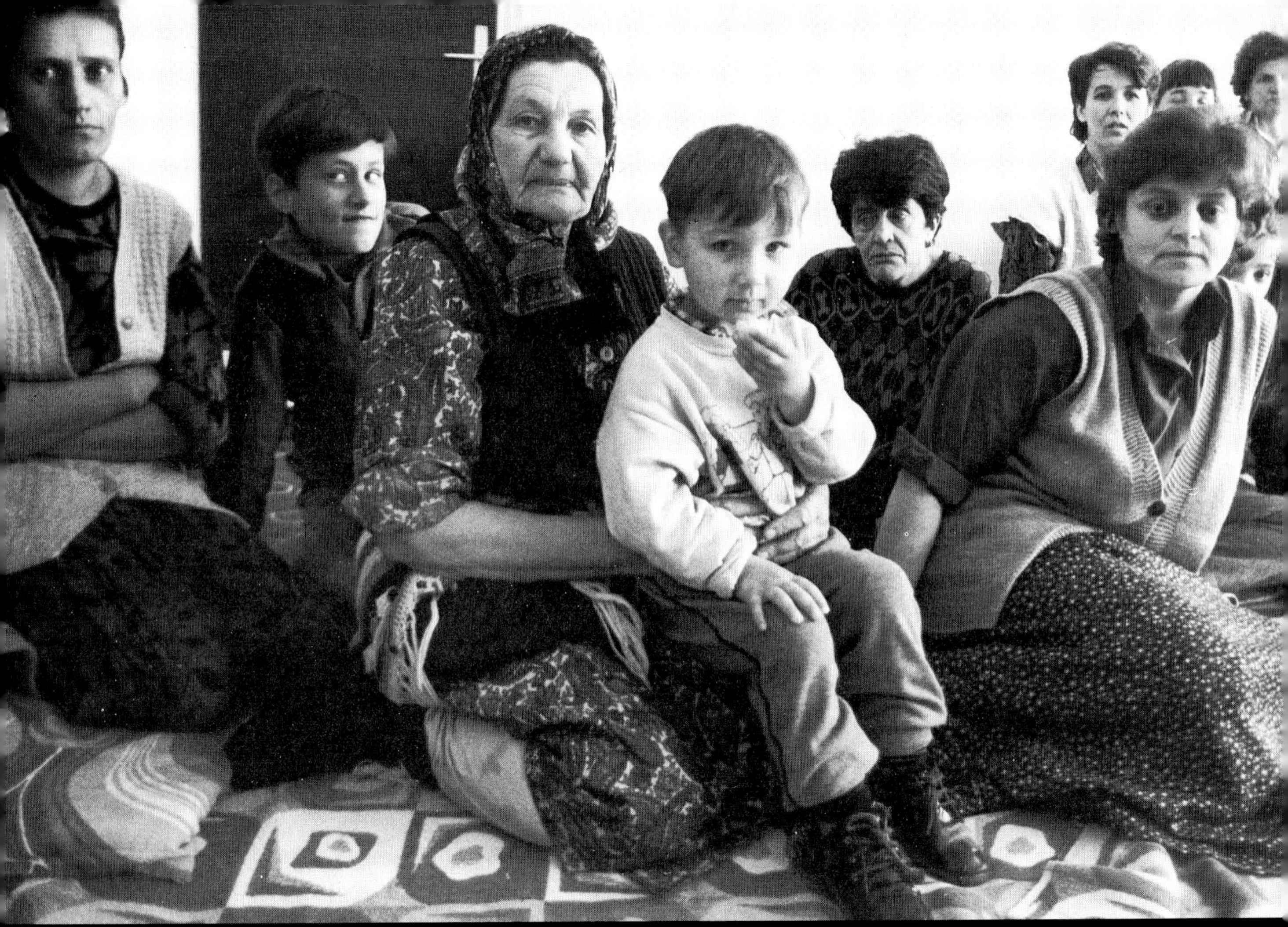

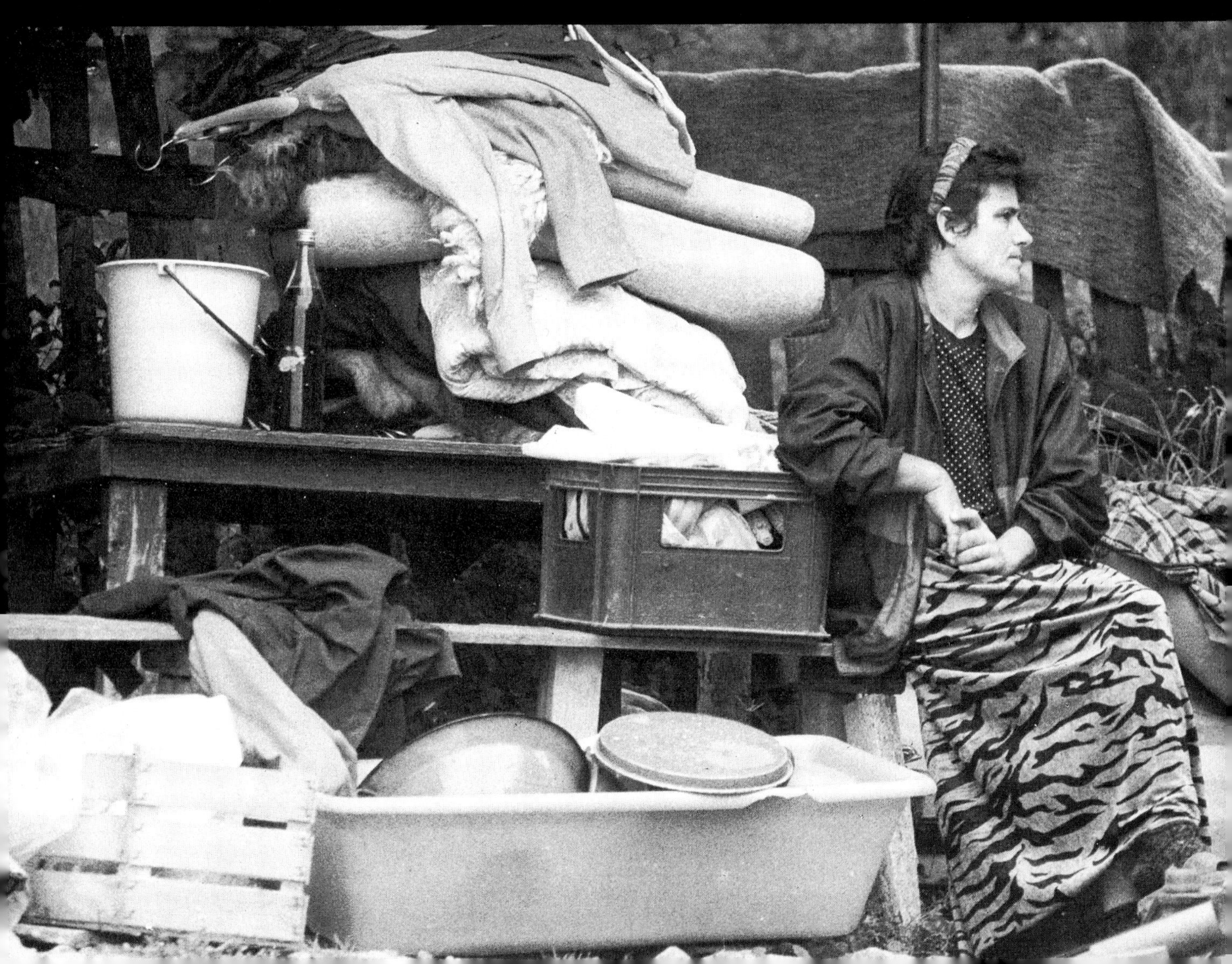

SARAJEVO – THE WOUNDED CITY

tions and well kept rare items... Singed book leaves from the library which the city wept for floated over the city. Many rushed to help with rescuing. It was too late. Science and treasures impressed on paper sheets were helpless faced with fire disaster. Saddened professors, men of letters, students and citizens silently stared at the fire that took away a part of us. A doctor's telephonic sentence, uttered up on the hills, hums in my ears: "We are going to level everything to the ground... Then we are going to build again..." That same lean humanist read those volumes, studied in the shady rooms of the town hall, grew up in our shaded city, and then in May left heated by the fire of hatred. I wonder when he will manage to rewrite and print all those burnt books. How will he manage, once he has destroyed us, to learn all those languages and writings in order to restore what has vanished? How will he fit his new creation into those singed book leaves that fell, seized by the flames and wind, onto the streets, courtyards and cul-de-sacs of Vratnik, Bistrik and Baščaršija... They were collected up by boys, and by an old acquaintance of mine as well. The sober scientist came helpless with a bundle of what he collected and long, long stared at the ghostly black window holes still smoking. From a heap of ashes and bricks on the pavement a brass window handle stuck out. It was still warm when I squeezed it in a hopeless spasm. The inquisition stake took away all my yellowed, dear souvenirs, the years I spent in the temple of science where one used to enter on tiptoe and speak in a low voice.

Fortunately, they saved "Bosnica", the books relating to Bosnia and Herzegovina, the ones written here or by authors from Bosnia and Herzegovina. Saved from ruin was also the majority of rare books and numerous famous manuscripts. Could this cataclysm have been reduced, or delayed for later if there had been more water to put out the fire with, if there had been more fire engines? The words of the town hall security chief torment me: "First, two fire engines arrived. Had we had only half a cistern of water more, we would have extinguished the fire..."

The heat would have started it the next day or some other day. Hatred choked us, assaulted us. "We'll plough Sarajevo", was the message from those behind the guns, those watching us from the hills. Plough! Not only plough it, but plough it under. Did the destroyers of the neolithic Butmir, the Romanies' settlement at Ilidža, the mediaeval St. Peter's Cathedral and Vrhbosna, Hodiđed and Bosnian charters also have the same aim?

Three days later, on August 28th, the ominous shells and flames defeated one of the two "Oslobođenje" skyscrapers. A greeting card for its 49th anniversary came too early. Its metal and concrete framework collapsed like a pack of cards. Even the ash of the manuscripts and books we were planning to publish was gone. A part of myself was

of Stari grad: Hrid, Širokača and Gazin han. Infantry clashes around Marijin Dvor and Vrbanja Bridge. Shells fall on Pero Kosorić Square and Hrasno hill. Three blocks in Ivan Krndelj Street catch fire. Artillery shells fall on Dobrinja, Alipašino polje, and the residential areas Pavle Goranin and Vojničko polje. Also shelled are the "Holiday Inn" and the TV Centre. Thirteen people are killed, 82 injured.

Tuesday, 15th: The number of those suffering from enterocolitis is decreasing. A little more peaceful. Shells fall on city areas in the afternoon.

Wednesday, 16th: A rather peaceful day. Artillery targets the outskirts of Stari grad, Breka, Alipašino polje, Vojničko polje and Mojmilo. in the afternoon and evening. Infantry fires from the direction of Vraca and Grbavica. Infantry clashes occur on the line Doglodi-Stup. Eighteen people are killed and 163 wounded in Sarajevo. The town has electricity again in the afternoon. Sefer Halilović, chief of staff of the Supreme Command of the Armed Forces of B-H, offers to exchange captured aggressor's soldiers for the writer Vladimir Srebrov. The Children's Embassy staff write a letter to Mr. Alija Izetbegović, asking permission for a convoy of 1,500 mothers and children to leave the city.

Thursday, 17th: All day and night hundreds of shells fall onto almost all the city's areas. The aggressors' infantry tries to break through Pero Kosorić Square and the free territory of Vogošća, on the line Doglode-Stup, using 20 tanks in the assault. Also shelled is the PTT

Engineering building, now the seat of UNPROFOR. The departure of the Children's Embassy convoy is delayed. Owing to a two-month delay 60 children lose the opportunity of being accommodated in Belgium.

Friday, 18th: Not a gram of food arrives. The Children's Embassy stops evacuating children from Sarajevo. Shells knock down a 110-kilowatt transmission-line in Vogošća. Sarajevo is in the dark. Salaries are 3–10 DM, while the monthly consumer goods basket for a four-member family costs about 150–200 DM. Owing to the destruction of many companies three quarters of those employed are without salaries. Victor Jackovich is appointed U.S. ambassador in B-H.

Saturday, 19th: Severe fighting occurs on the Doglodi-Stup line. Hundreds of destructive shells are fired at the city, mostly Novi grad. The building of the B-H Government is set on fire. Hit once again is the blue helmets' headquarters in the PTT Engineering building. According to a decision of the UN Security Council the so-called FRY cannot represent the former SFRY at the UN. There is no electricity. The damage to the transmission lines is worse than was assumed. There is no water in the sloped parts of the city.

Sunday, 20th: Compared with the relatively peaceful morning the afternoon was a real hell. Still no electricity. James Grant, executive director of UNICEF, is in Sarajevo. He visits the Clinic of Paediatric Surgery at Koševo. No humanitarian aid arrives in Sarajevo either by air or land. Sixteen dead and 66 injured.

wiped out. My publishing activity was killed by the shells and fire. We had a Cato and Carthage lesson of destruction and killing in Sarajevo.

Europe was amazed. It was selfish. It watched television pictures of our reality, leafed through the newspaper front pages with the photographs of horror and sipped its cool drinks on the beaches. Well-earned holidays should not be disturbed. On my table it was written:

"The smell of the sea has permeated my room. It is dusk. August. We have lived in the children's room since the beginning of July. Shells visited our house. They entered the flats of my neighbours. The old woman on the sixth floor did not manage to finish her afternoon coffee yesterday. Nor did her fifty-year-old daughter and her one-armed lady neighbour. The shell prevented them. They finished up in hospital, bleeding. There is the smell of the sea in the children's room. Here are some more valuable things from the living room: my books, family photo albums and necessary documents. Some people may be swimming somewhere. Does it exist at all? Is the sea warm this summer? Who is sunbathing in that recess 'of mine' between the rocks? It is all the fault of a can of shrimps. We kept it for months. Tonight we eat it slowly, with lots of bread. The images of Thailand, of the long sandy beaches of Puket, a smile on the face of each Thai came back. The sea smell permeated my soul. This is my first summer in the last thirty years that I have not gone to the seaside, have not swum, bathed and sat on the beach..."

Under the window, pieces of glass break under the shoes of my neighbour who is on guard.

I cannot hide my bitterness. Mr Levenfeld, I must confide in you. Look at August 23rd in my diary:

"Nothing new at Beki's."

I do not dare to look into his eyes. We joke. We reduce everything to joking. We are not able to talk seriously. We try to revive all our childhood joys hidden in the depths of our souls.

Twenty-nine days have passed since we learned that his father had been taken away from his flat. A lady from the neighbourhood, from a block of flats at Grbavica, rang up. She got through to Belgrade. She called a cousin of Beki's. She asked him whether the name Šemsudin Gavranka Kapetanović meant anything to him. To the confirmation that they were related, she introduced herself. She left her Belgrade telephone number. She said that Anja and her mother were at home and they were well. Sudo was not there. He had been taken away ten days earlier. She managed to leave for Belgrade with her son, to find refuge.

He was taken away. He is not here.

His name has not been on the list for days. It was not on Friday, Thursday, Wednesday... We regularly go to the State Commission for the Exchange of Prisoners and

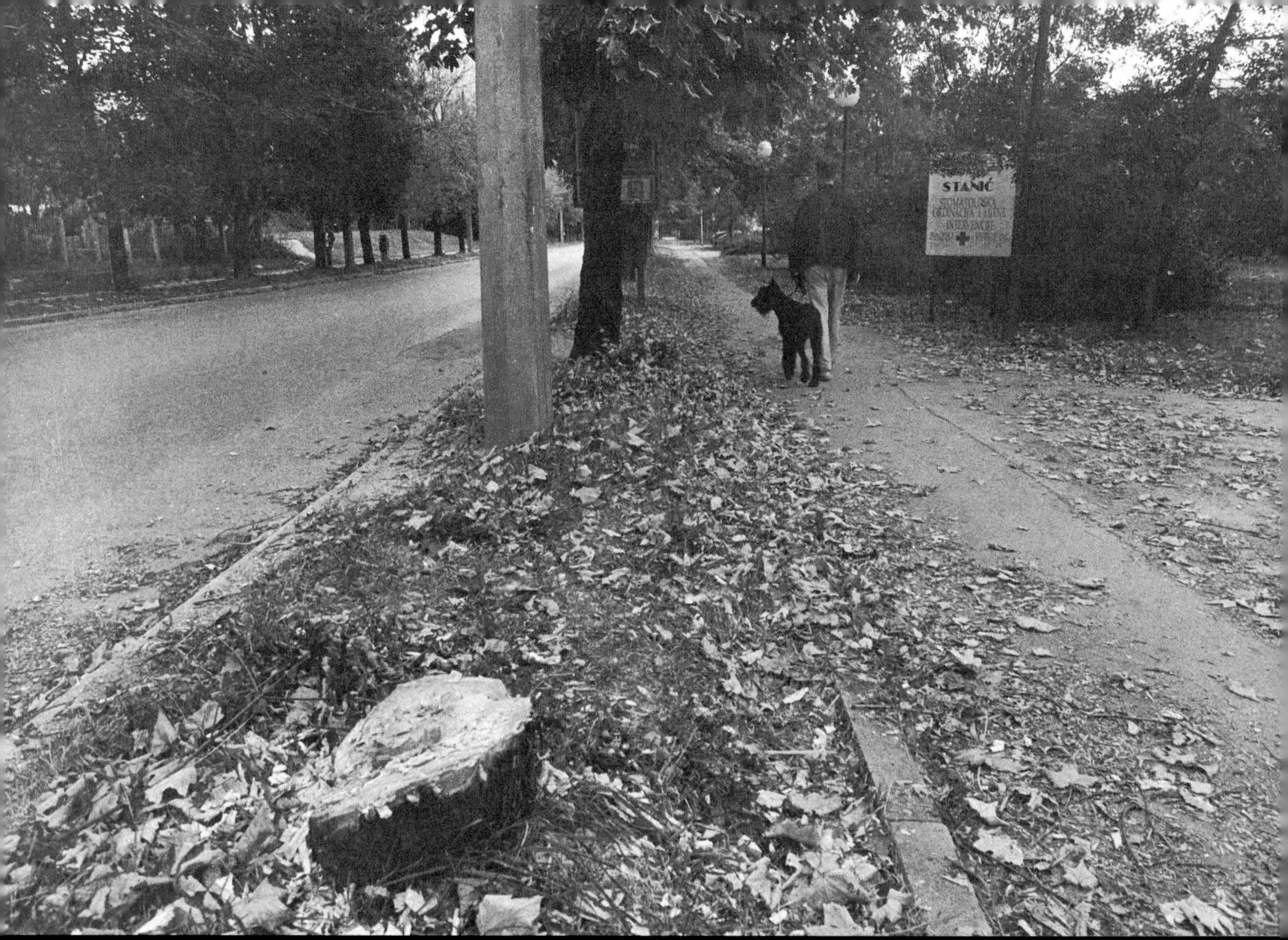
STANIĆ

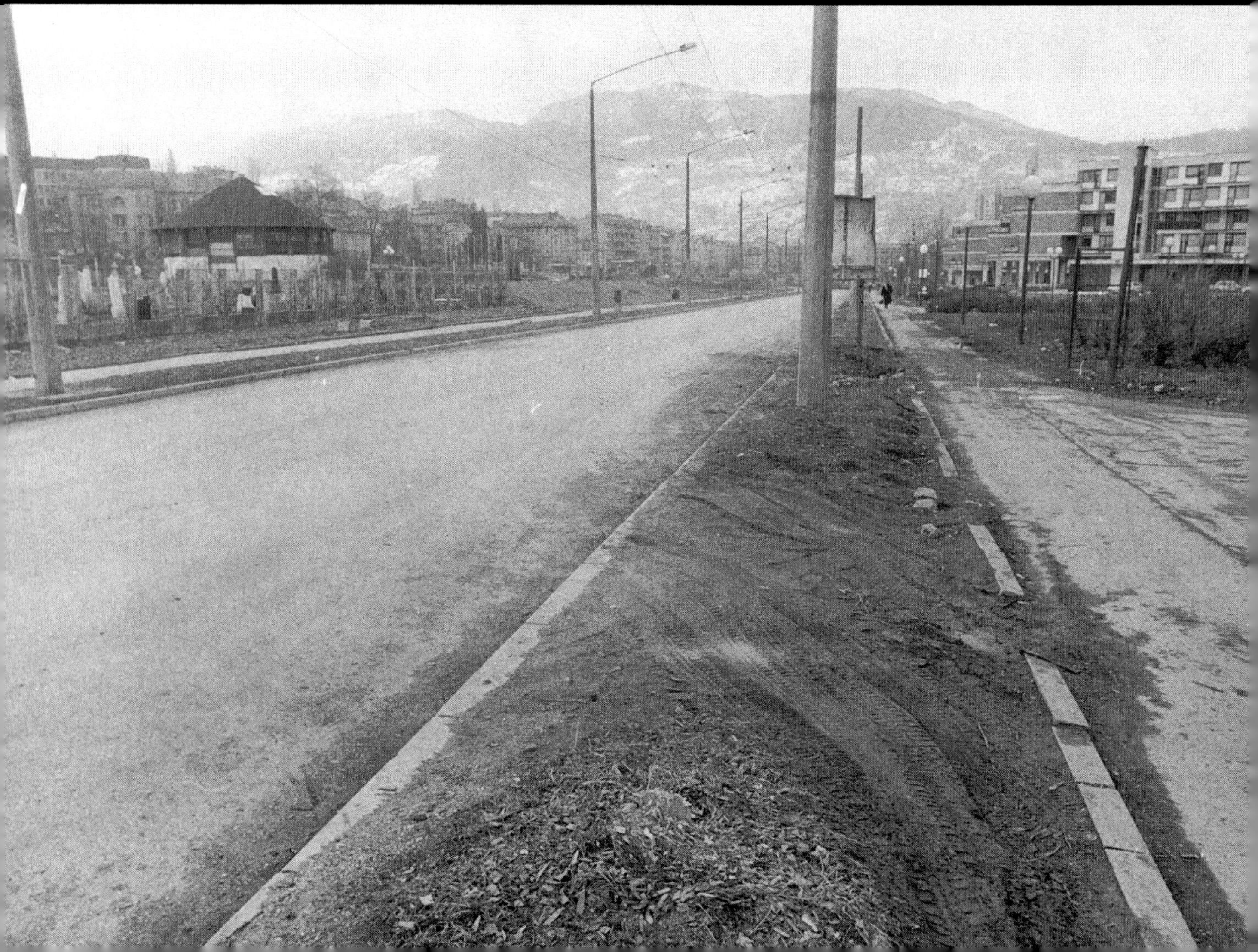

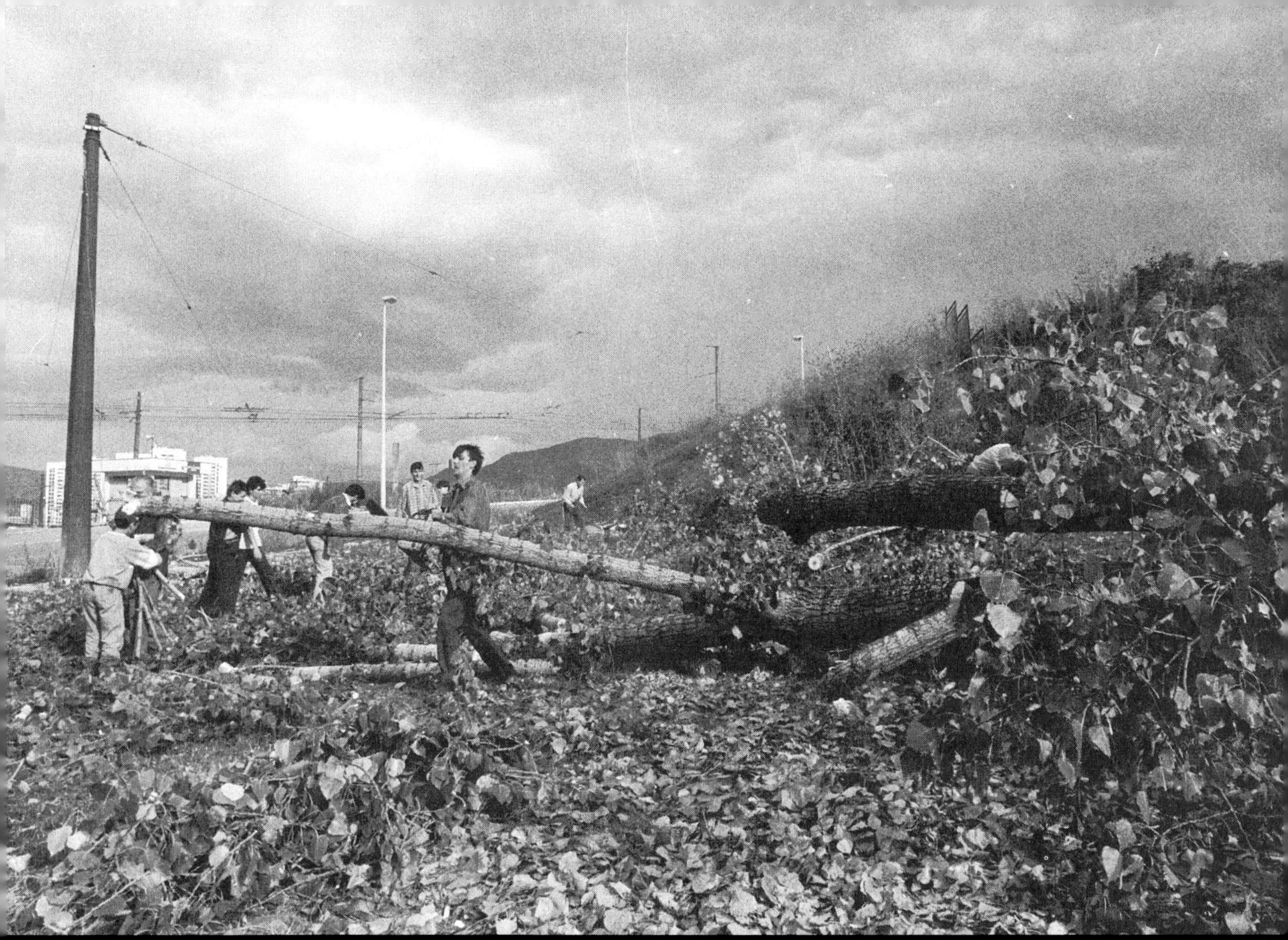

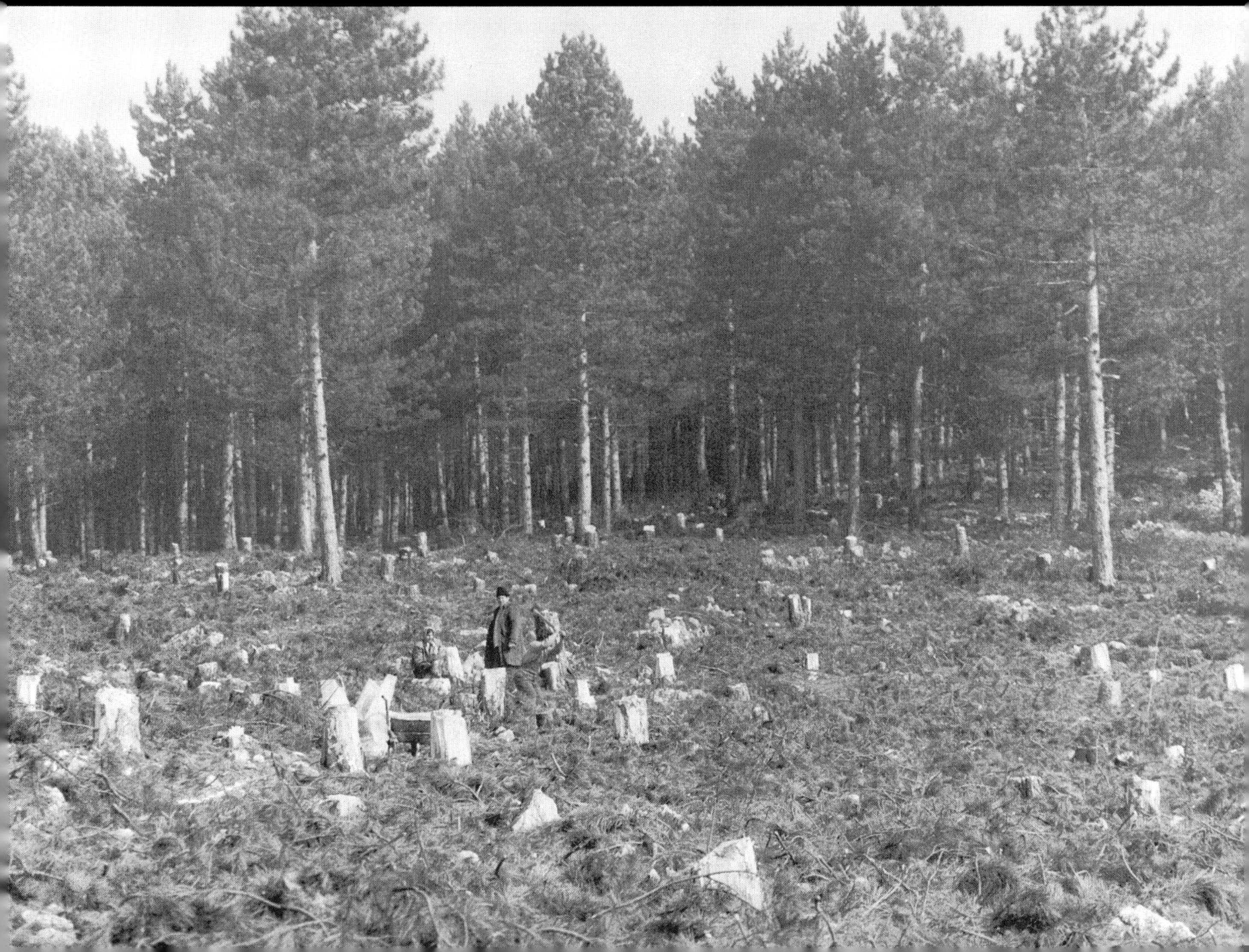

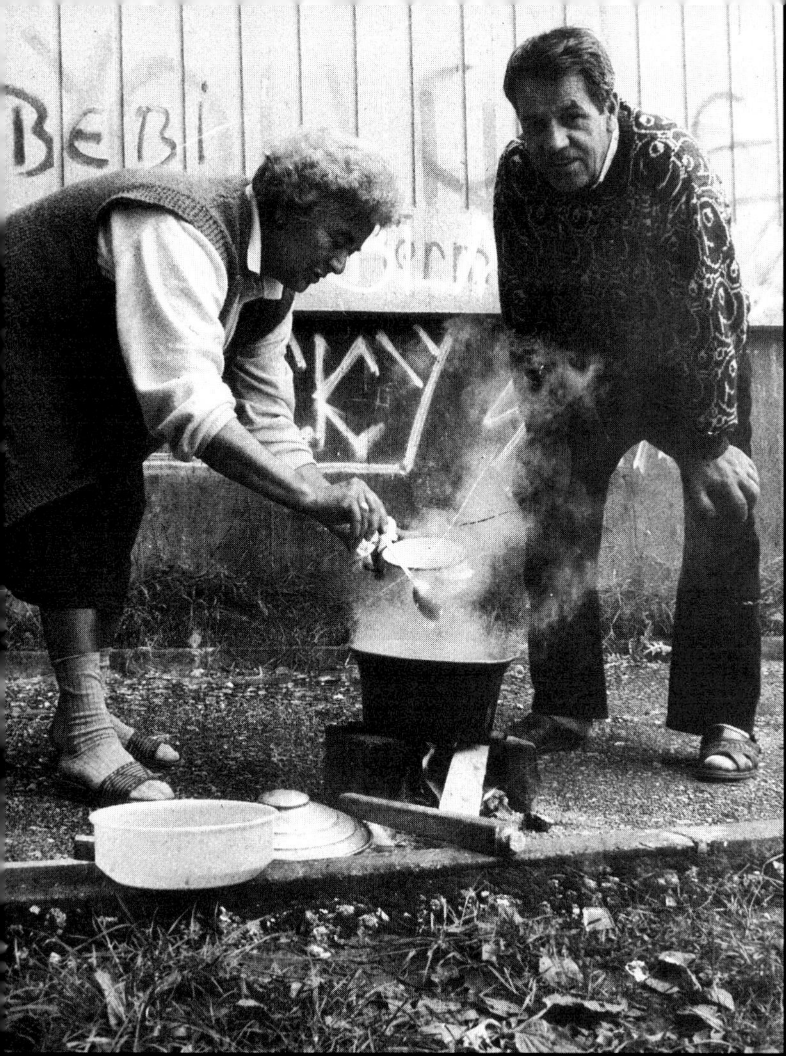
BEBI

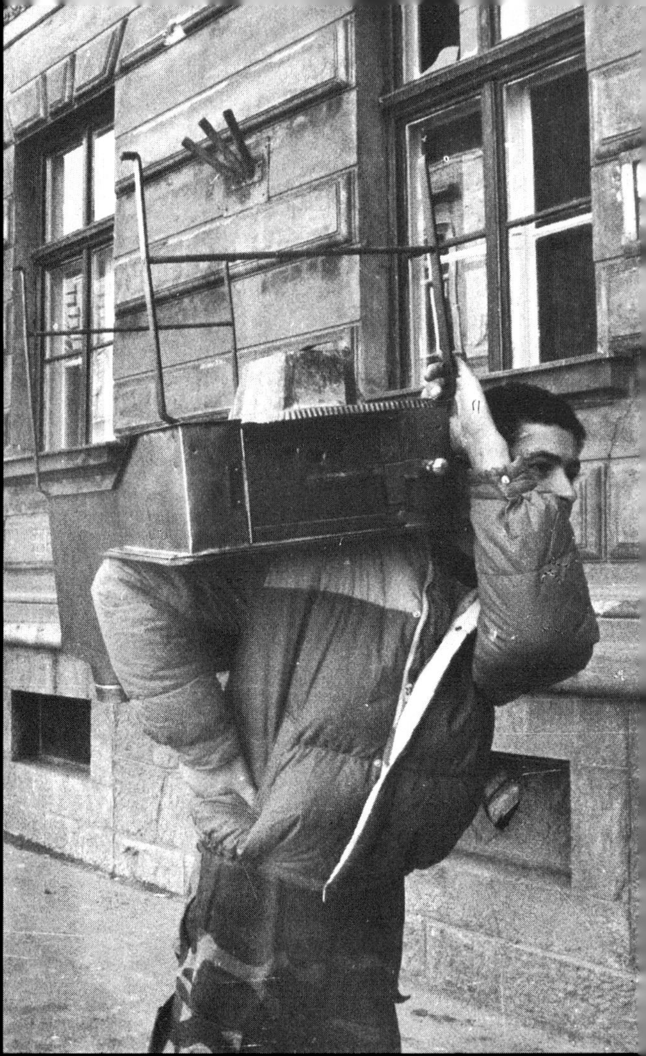

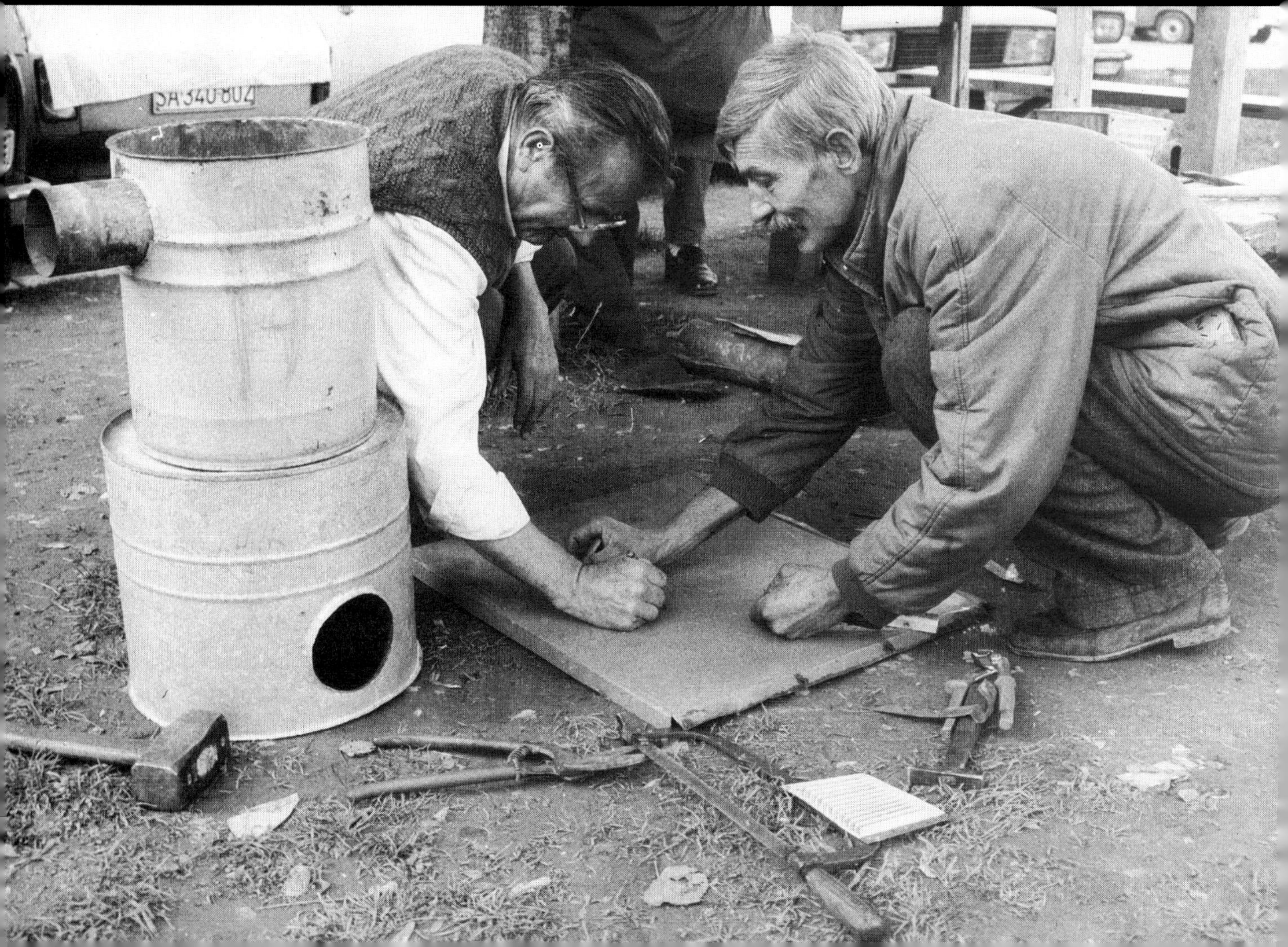
SA 340-804

151 SARAJEVO – THE WOUNDED CITY

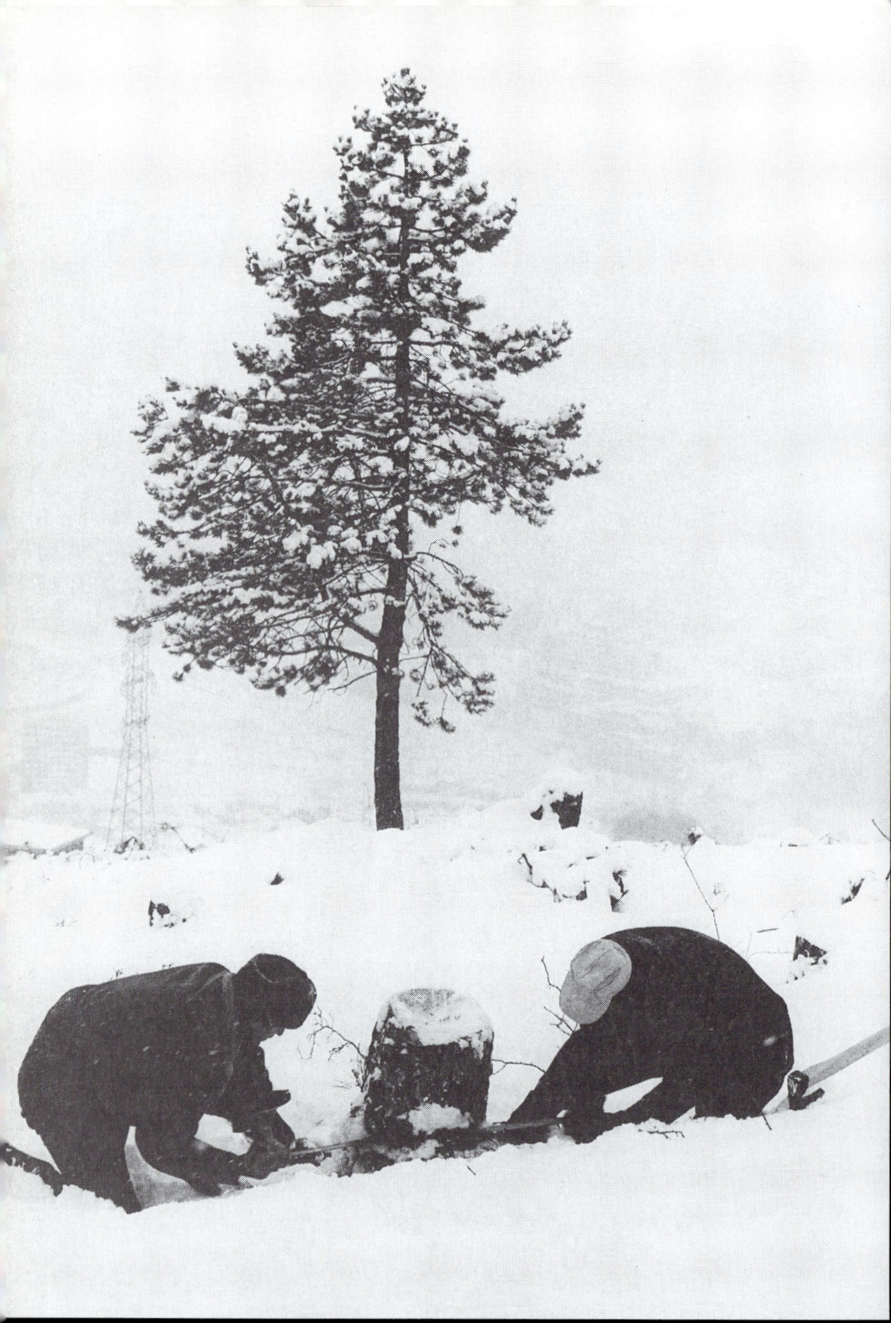
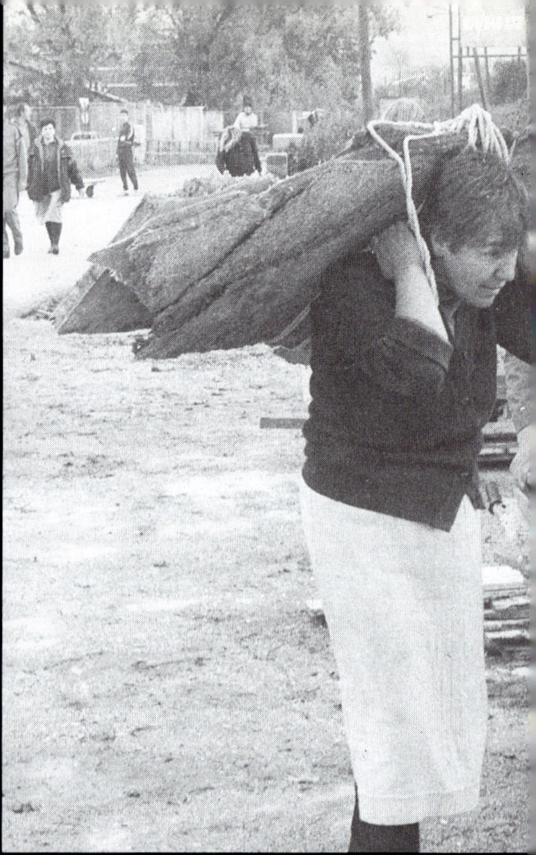
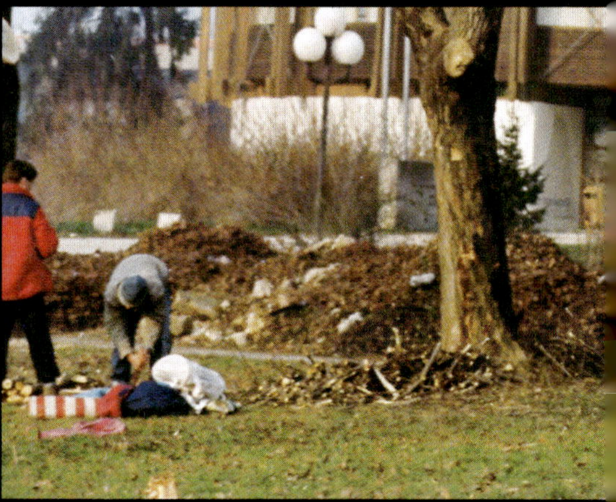
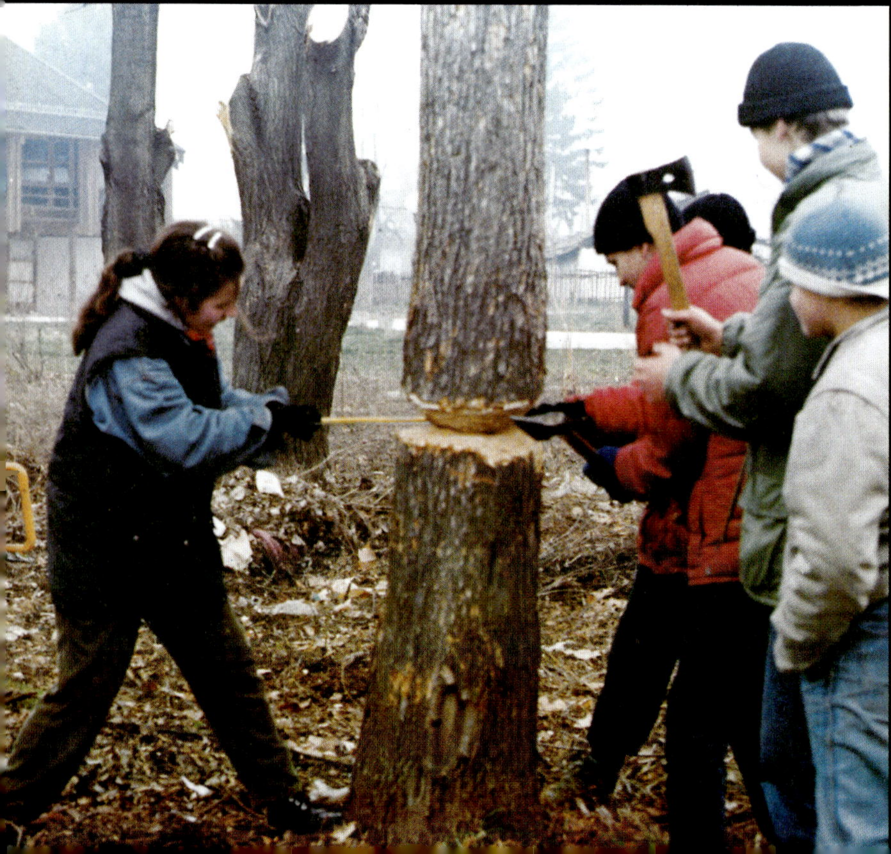
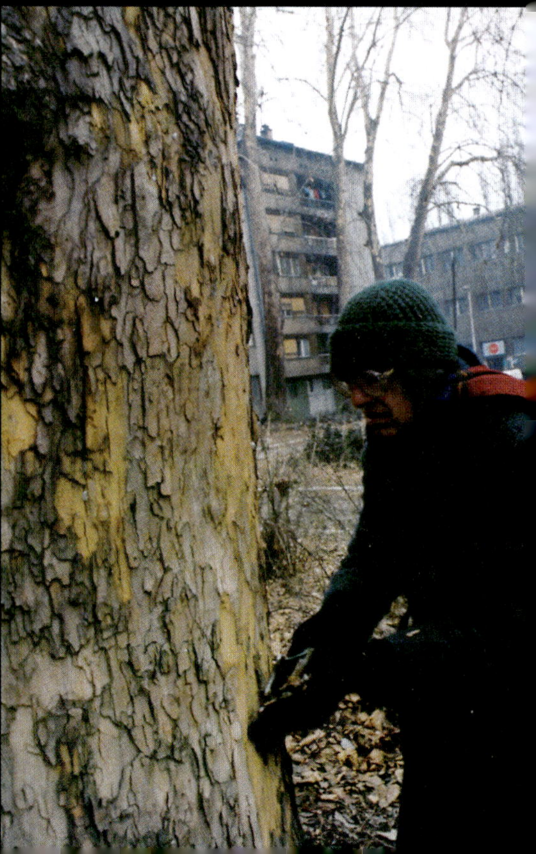

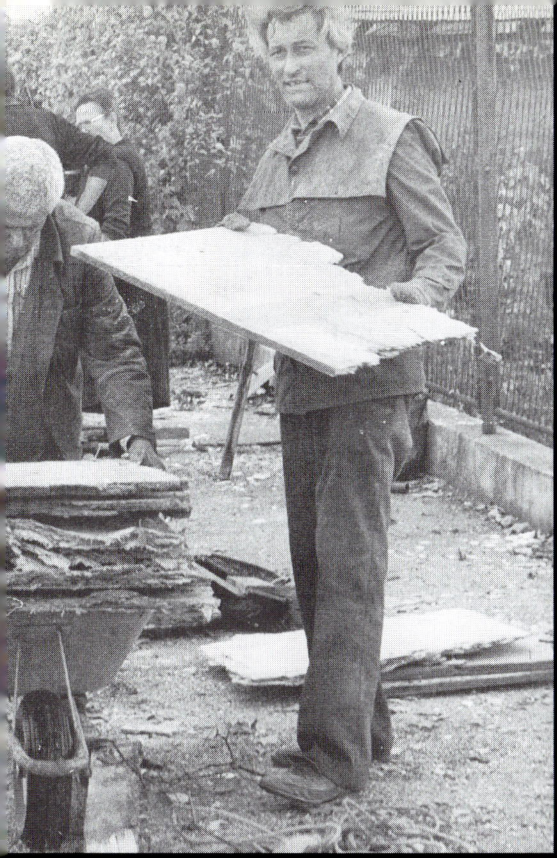

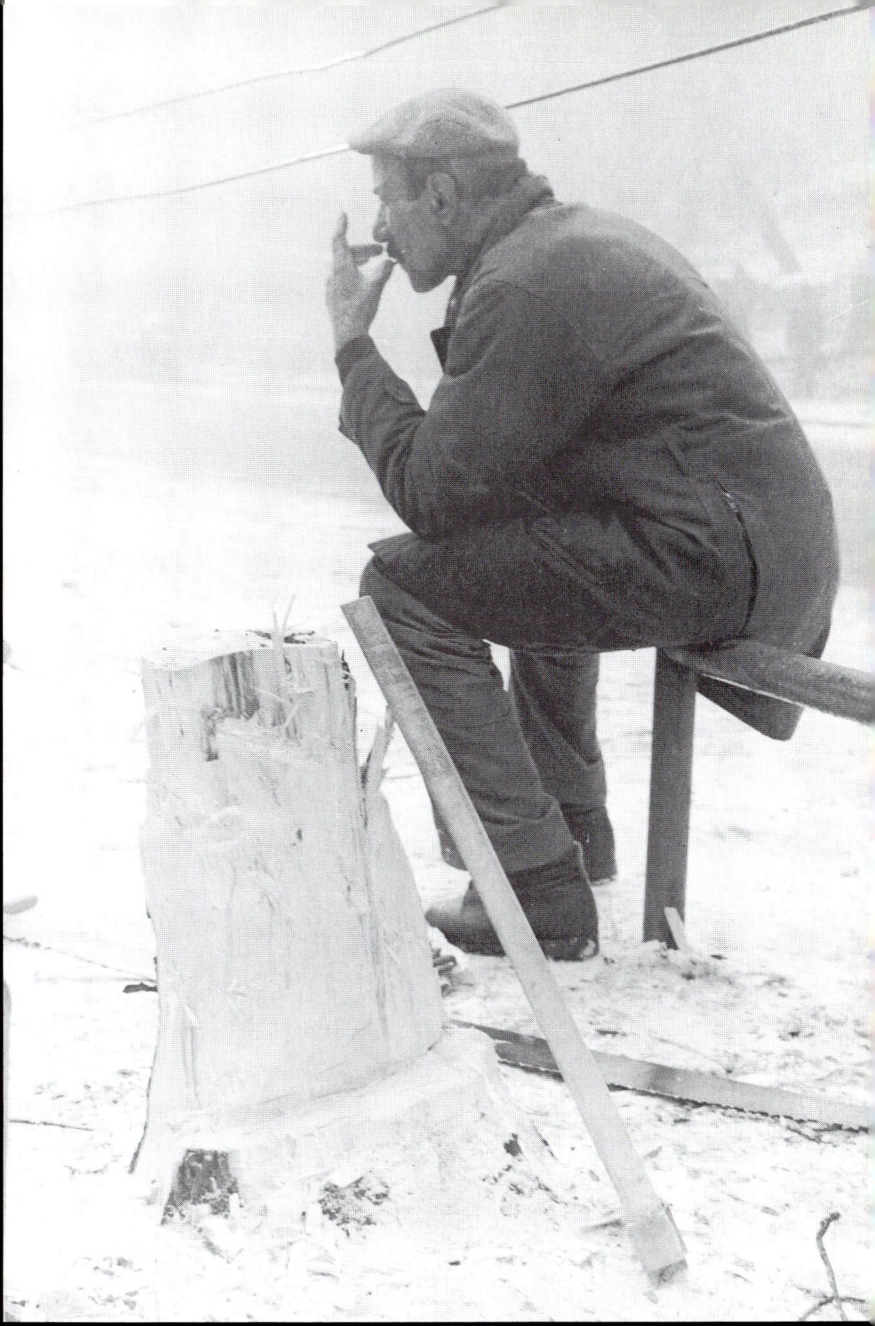

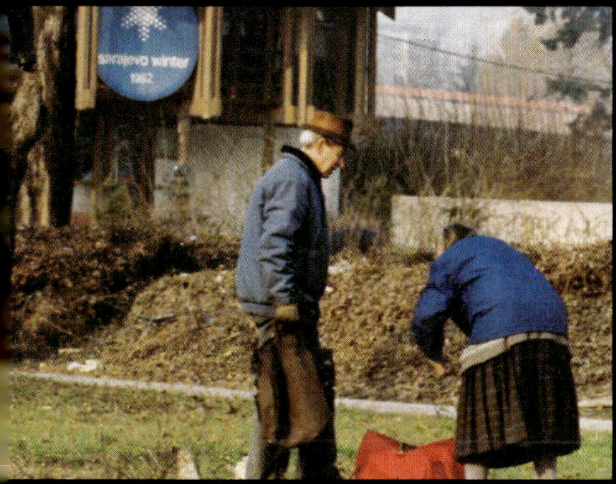

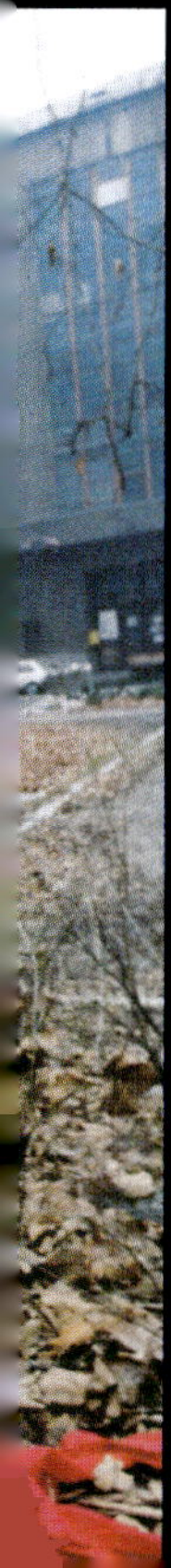

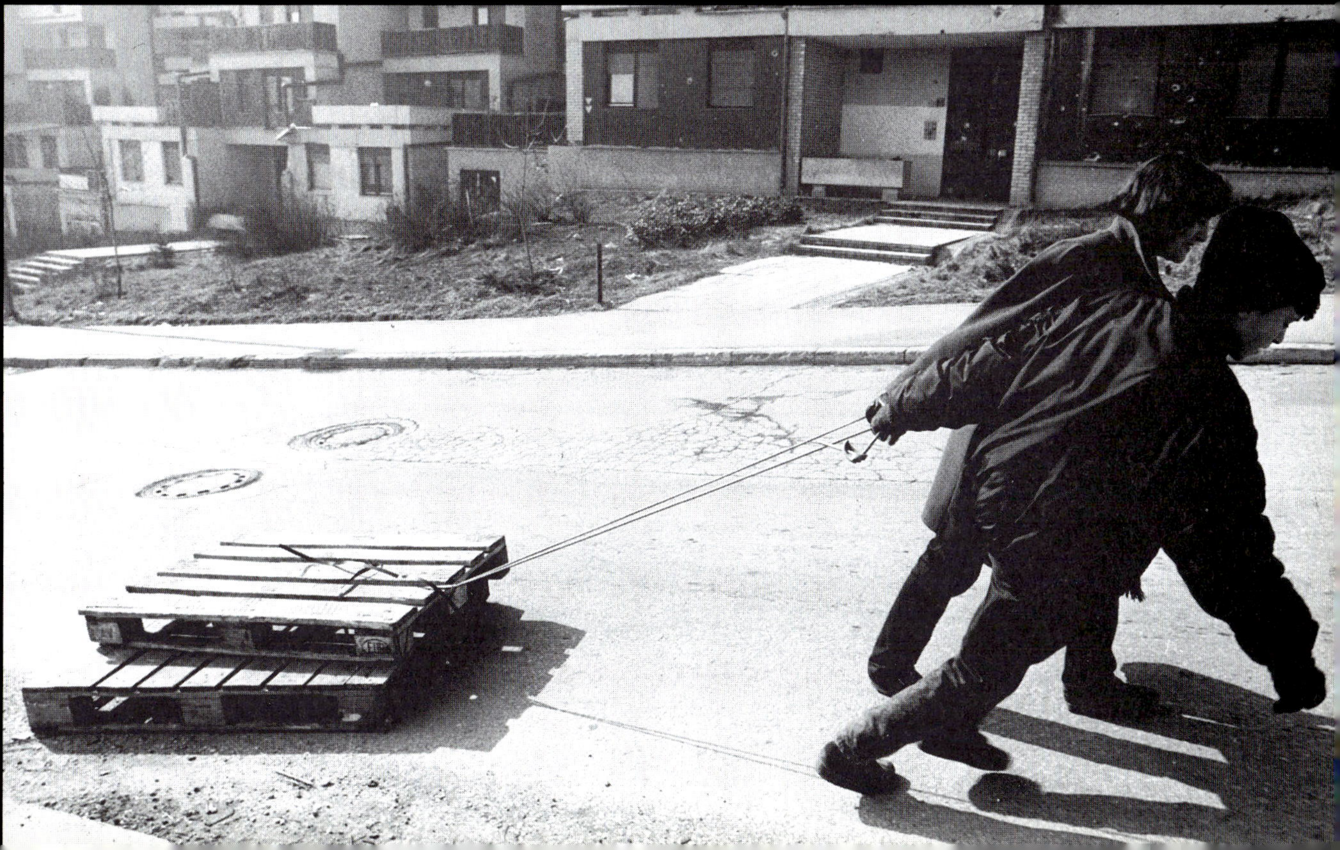

Corpses. Our friends work there. They do their best to find out as much as possible, to find him.

Oh Lord, he is probably not alive any more.

We all think about this. We do not even accept such a train of thought.

We learned that on leaving, he took out his ready insulin. He had a quantity sufficient for ten days. He had to take it twice a day. He gave it to a young lady neighbour, also a diabetic. He just said: "Take this, please, I will not be needing it any longer." A calm eighty-year-old retired lawyer took his war load on his back. He left the insulin and syringes that he badly needed. He was taken away! He is not here. We are silent. From time to time our eyes fill with tears.

"Don't, Miki!" Beki interrupts the fateful tear. He changes the conversation to another topic.

How did he die? I only hope he did not suffer.

How painful it is to think about a dear person, a friend's father, as one deceased. All our thoughts are hopes that he had not been tortured or humiliated, that he had not suffered...

Help me get out. I feel this heat softening my bones. It slowly spreads through me. My limbs go limp. We must move on. We must, even though we do not know where to, but as far as possible, as far as possible, Mr Levenfeld. You know, you will not, as Andrić wrote, succeed in getting further than 1938, the Spanish Civil War and a little Aragon town of a forgotten name. Your hospital and the wounded were bombed from the air. Vain was the common motto: "Non est salus nisi in fuga." I do not know whether salvation lies only in fleeing. How could I find and take with me Bekir's father? Uncle Sudo, where are you? Where can I look for you? We live in the same city, but too far away, somewhere in Grbavica. What is going on with the sickly sixty-year-old Alojz Heđi Bimbo? He stayed at 95, Rave Janković Street. Zlatko Topčić too is at 7a, Lenjinova Street. He is with his mother. The young writer follows in his father's footsteps as a camp inmate. Topčić Senior was the only writer who survived the Ustasha concentration camp at Jasenovac. I published his book of prose so many years later, entitled "Ljudolovka Jasenovac" ("Peopletrap Jasenovac"). The word ljudolovka is untranslatable. Basically, it is a cage for only one man. It is made of barbed wire and the prisoner carries it with him. He cannot leave it. He sleeps in it, relieves himself and walks about the camp. Will Zlatko manage to witness the camp he lives in?

What has happened to my friend Hrvoje Malić?

Monday, 21st: The area in and around Sarajevo is shelled. Žuč and Kobilja glava are most heavily attacked by the aggressor's artillery. Most people injured in Sarajevo are from Stari grad. A shell falls on Albanska Street killing one and injuring several others. Shells fall onto the following streets: Vojvoda Putnik, Omer Maslić and Blagoje Parović, also on Pero Kosorić Square, Stup, Otes, Azići and Sokolje. There are 22 killed and 64 injured citizens. At 10.15 the remaining 110-kilowatt transmission line is destroyed. The city is without electricity, which means without water as well.

Tuesday, 22nd: "The autumn starts at 8 o'clock and 42.8 minutes" says the Astronomic Observatory of Sarajevo. The sun rises at 6.35 a.m. and sets at 6.47 p.m. A relatively peaceful day. And yet there are some dead and injured people. The building of the Mechanical Engineering Faculty and some cars in Blagoje Parović Street are on fire. The "Bitumenka" factories are also fire. The establishing of an air-corridor for humanitarian aid delivery is delayed until October 1st. Three GRAS (city transport) bus-drivers working for UNPROFOR driving out foreign students who happened to have stayed in war-torn Sarajevo are arrested at Ilidža.

CIRCLE SIX

Wednesday, 23rd: Several shells fall on Novi grad. Also shelled are Stari grad, Dobrinja and Vogošća. 14 killed and 11 wounded. Two convoys come from Split through a land corridor with 111 tons of flour and rice. Two French soldiers and a man from "Valter Perić" are injured while trying to repair a transmission line under UNPROFOR's control. Chemist's shops have got some medicine but prices are exorbitant.

Thursday, 24th: The format of "Oslobođenje" is reduced, once again, to a quarter of its standard size in peacetime. The shells claim many lives. Two killed and 10 wounded in Omer Maslić Street. A shell hits a bus killing one passenger and injuring several. Two more citizens are killed in a car. A sniper kills two and injures four people at Dolac Malta. We are still in the dark. "Oslobođenje" gets a new subtitle printed in large letters: BOSANSKO-HERCEGOVAČKI NEZAVISNI DNEVNIK (The Bosnian-Herzegovinian Independent Daily Newspaper). A Waquf (a Muslim endowed bank) is established in Sarajevo.

I come across Gaspar de Guzman, the Duke of Olivares. He repeats, as he did at the beginning of the 17th century: "Cabezas, seńor, cabezas que asto es lo que non hay! Donde no hay cabezas no hay nada" (It is people, sir, people that are lacking! Where there are no people, there is nothing). He helps me pass unhurt through the hot Roman triumphal arch and descend into the next circle. The unhappy omnipotent minister of King Philip IV did not manage to bring the Sephardim back to Spain. The inquisition was more powerful. He hardly managed to refute the accusation that he was a Jew himself, or at least a cristiano nuovo.

I look back. Well, that is the triumphal arch from the Roman Forum. It was built by Titus Flavius, the son of Vespasian, later emperor, in order to crown his victory and the taking of Jerusalem.

I am hungrier and hungrier. I am hungry for the first time. I have never been so hungry. The food in our pantries has run out. We cannot buy any in Sarajevo.

The heat of the triumphal arch still gets warmer. Some women curse Don Fernando and his Isabella. They talk about a house they sell for an ass, about a vineyard they offer for a dress. I cannot tell the present day from past centuries. People, those expelled, and the stake get mixed up for me. An American woman sings her ancestors' song:

Onde esta la jave que estava in kason
Mis nonus la truserun con grande dolor
De la casa de España, de España..."

She notices that I do not understand her. She introduces herself to me: "Flory Jagode, born Altarac from the Bosnian village of Vlasenica." Would you mind translating for me:

"Where is the key that was in a case
My ancestors took with them painfully shaken
From home in Spain, in Spain..."

I cannot remember if Titus's triumphal arch was carved from the stones of the destroyed Jerusalem temple. He built it a few years after the book of St. John's Revelation. The apostle may have simultaneously written the Apocalypse of the world and its destruction, of an ominous destiny for mankind. They were contemporaries of the first century. It might have been hard for Titus Flavius Vespasian to drag all those massive rocks as far as Rome. He destroyed the whole city. He vented his power and anger on a two years' siege. He spared only the western wall. Accidentally, I believe. "The Wailing Wall" has remained until the present day as a holy spot in Jerusalem. And a warning. Powerful Rome and the defeated Jews made up history simultaneously. What will remain of Sarajevo after the siege of 1992 and 1993. Do we have to have one more descendant of Vespasian and the year 70 A.D.? Must Doctor Moritz Levy, a learned Sarajevo rabbi, have written just in my city the

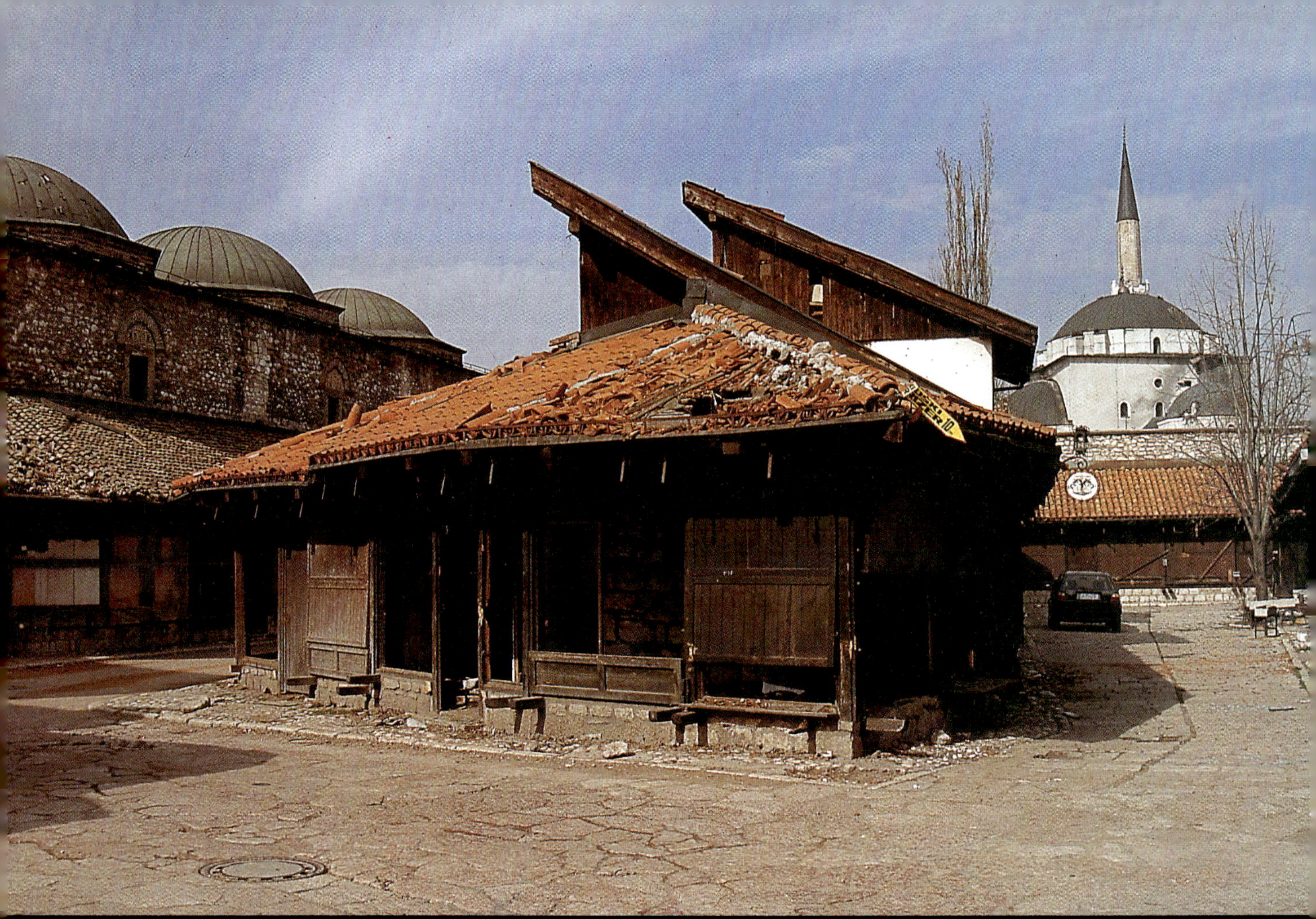

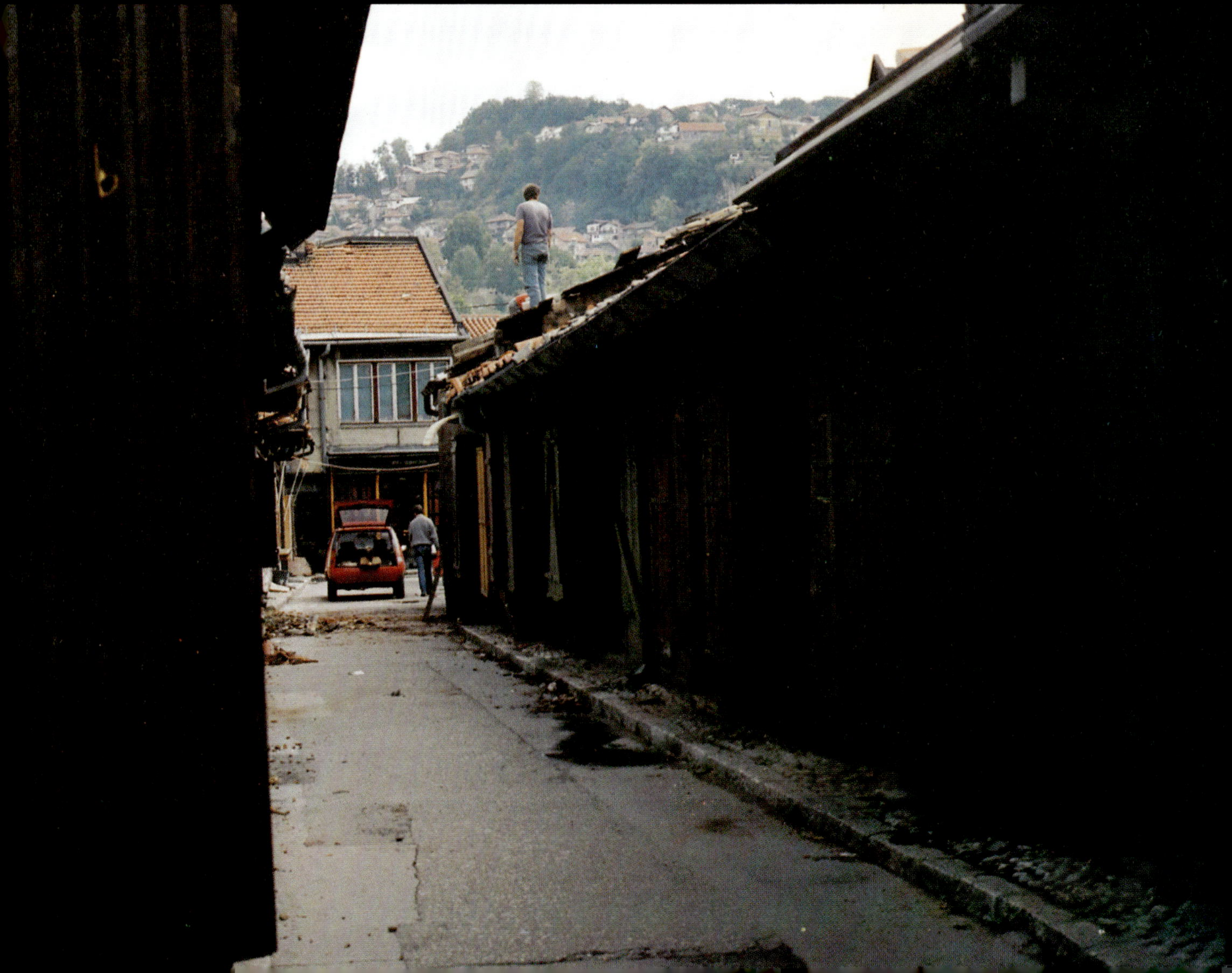

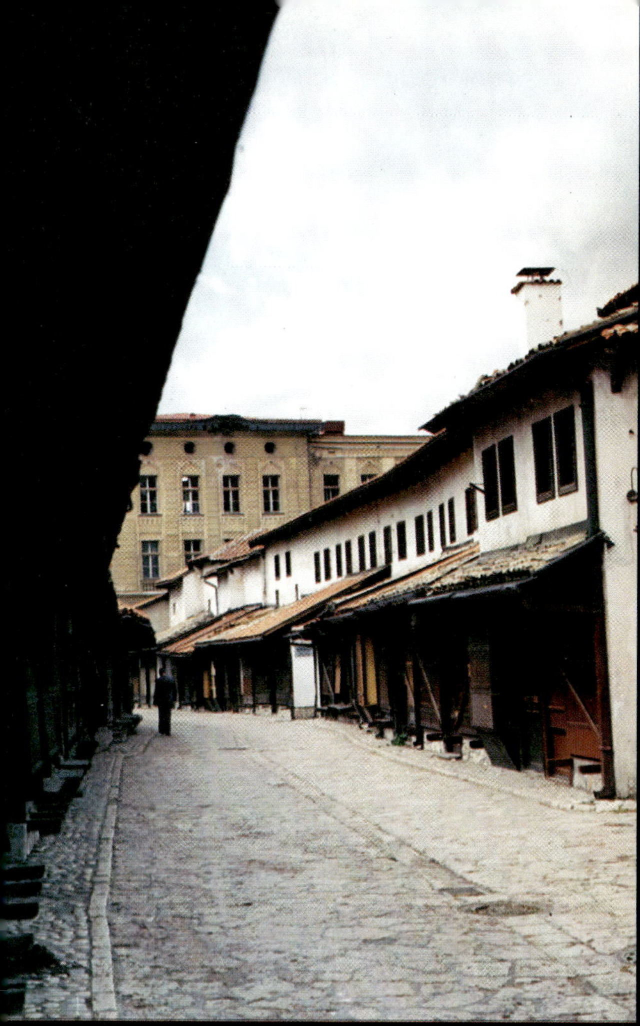

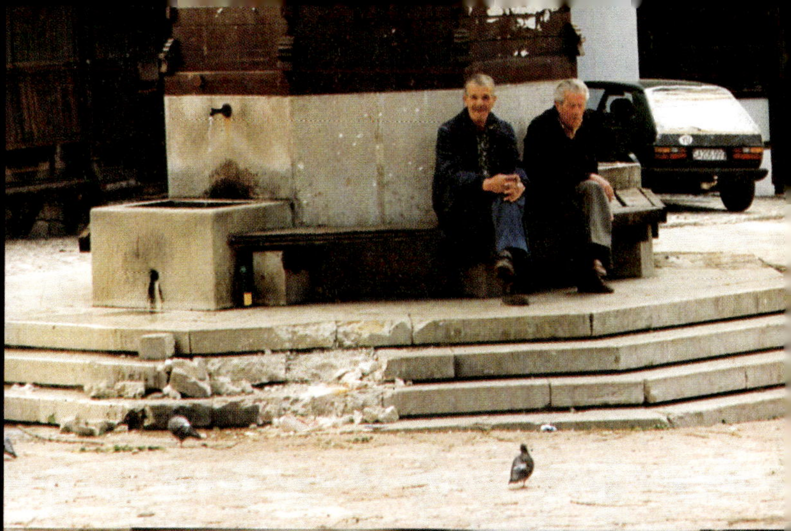

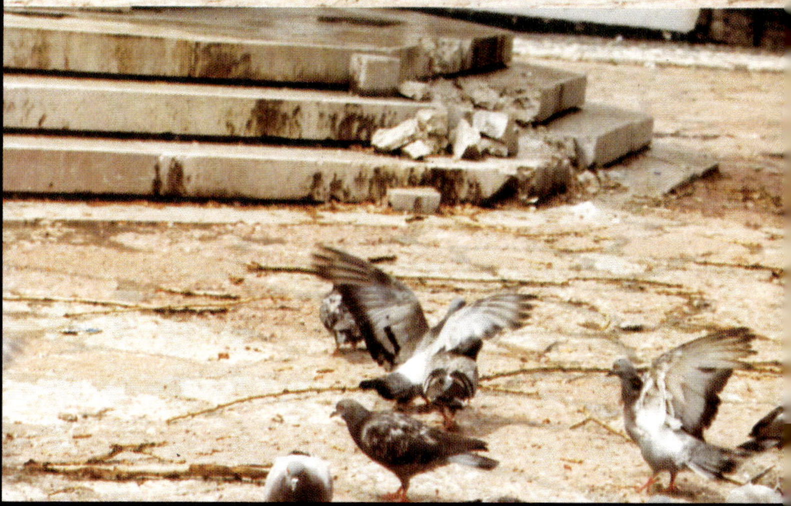

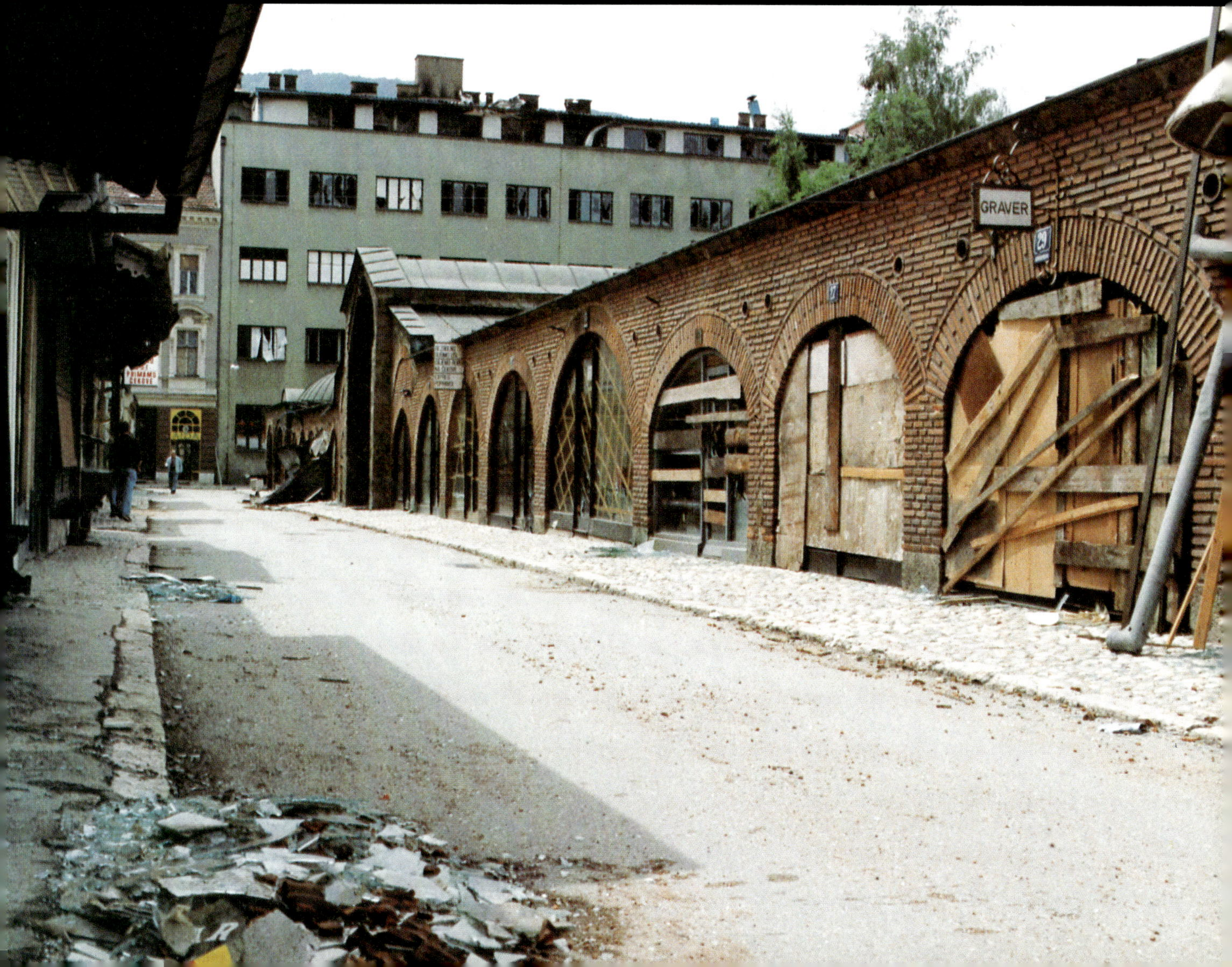
GRAVER

romance "El sitio de Jerusalem" (The Siege of Jerusalem) in 1911? Did he, for our sake, preserve for the world one of the rarest romances from the Judeo-Spanish poetic tradition? Horrible are the scenes of a desperate mother who, tortured by starvation, kills her child and becomes a cannibal. The preserved verses of cruel beauty pierce to the bone.

> *Vesinas, las mis vesinas*
> *las de abajo y las de arriba*
> *hagamos una merenda*
> *y degollemos a los hijas.*
> *Que ha de venir el enemiqo*
> *y muriremos a la hambre. –*
>
> *(Lady neighbours, lady neighbours of mine*
> *you from below and you from above*
> *lunch let us prepare*
> *let us our sons slaughter.*
> *The enemy is due to come*
> *And of hunger we shall die.)*

And the son's reply to his mother:

> *"Y quardadvos una manica*
> *por podervos conortare..."*
>
> *(... And save one little hand*
> *to console yourself with...)*

Do I have to go once again through all the tragedy of a city condemned to vanish. Destruction, killing, starvation and oblivion... Will a piece of stone remain here from which some future people will carve a tombstone and stop at it to shed a tear. I do not know who the capo in this camp is. I do not see a path to salvation. I sink deeper and deeper. I am in Circle Six.

I do not know whether the pictures of the city or Lucifer's circles torture me more. The dates merge, interweave. I live my diary:

"I get up early. I hurry for the market under the flyover at Ciglane. On its fringes is the former 'élite city suburb'. The stomach of the city – the market – is like the city itself – empty, dirty and devastated. Dealers in foreign exchange are persistent. They buy and sell German marks, some dollars, pounds and Swiss francs. They scorn lire. They do not accept Canadian dollars. Citizens, excuse me, some rare women citizens too, go around the empty counters. They wait for Godot who might come, who knows, with a basket of potatoes or onions... Tomatoes did not show up even on television. There is no paprika this summer, either.

"Only newspapers and a seller of paper – ecological

Friday, 25th: Artillery attacks on the Centre and Stari grad municipalities. The most severe ones are in the city centre and Stup hill. Two shells fall at about 1.30 p.m. injuring 14 at Dobrinja III. Ten people are injured by shells that fall on Đuro Đaković Street. Directly hit is the former Military Hospital. There are 17 killed and 93 injured in Sarajevo. The situation in terms of medical supplies, electricity and water is extremely difficult. Sarajevo's daily requirements for coal are 400 tons and for wood 120 cubic metres. Dr. Željko Puratić, a professor of classical philosophy at the Faculty of Philosophy in Sarajevo, is killed by a sniper.

Saturday, 26th: A peaceful morning. Parts of Stari grad and Stup hill are heavily shelled at about 2 p.m. There are 21 killed and 104 injured in the city. The GRAS drivers – Fair Madžur, Mehmed Popović and Sulejman Dizdar–are still captives at Ilidža.

Sunday, 27th: Areas of Novi grad, Stari grad and Vogošća. Infantry attacks on Novo Sarajevo. Chemicals are used in an attack on Žuč and Kobilja glava. Another artillery attack on "Oslobođenje". The "Zora" chocolate factory is burnt down as a result of shelling. Fighting prevents all traffic of the UN forces between the airport and the PTT Engineering building. Promotion of Misha Glenny's book "The Fall of Yugoslavia".

Monday, 28th: More peaceful than usual. The whole town is without water. Only the Jahorina springs are in operation. No electricity. Telephones do not work owing to a shortage of fuel. The epidemic of enterocolitis *is becoming less severe. The International peace Foundation awards Kemal Kurspahić and Gordana Knežević, editors of "Oslobođenje", a prize for war journalism.*

Tuesday, 29th: *Still without electricity, water and oil. Flour supplies come to an end. Today begins the 5753rd year according to the Jewish calendar – Rosh Hoshanah. Clashes at Stup and on Žuč Hill. Artillery barrages at Žuč, Hotonj and Barice. The most competent people of the OS BiH (Armed Forces of B-H) declare: "Sarajevo will be unblocked before winter!" The "Energoinvest" administrative building is on fire. Six floors are burnt out. The operating theatre of the State Hospital will close tomorrow between 9 and 10 a.m. owing to a lack of fuel for the power generating unit. A convoy with 38 tons of flour, rice, detergent and blankets arrives from Split. The B-H Home Office issues a statement that nobody is allowed to cut down trees in the town. Criminal charges will be brought against those caught in the act.*

Wednesday, 30th: *No electricity, no water. 550 citizens are expelled from Grbavica as a result of the ethnic cleansing policy. The City Hospital (the earlier Military Hospital) is without any source of energy. The State Hospital is supplied with water by water tankers.*

OCTOBER

Thursday, 1st: *Two killed, 39 injured. No water. Not a single aircraft with humanitarian aid lands at Sarajevo airport. Two convoys come from Zagreb and Split overland with 182.9 tons of food and detergents. Some oil is*

bags are constant here. The only vegetables here are one or two bunches of some green leaves from the neighbouring gardens, a kilo or two of unripe fruit. They are a kind of tiny apples, a few pears and white plums. There is nothing else to buy. Fruit and vegetables do not come over here. They do not visit us, either. We still keep in our memories of last summer and autumn, crowded counters and overloaded lorries waiting at the market gates. Only futile memories...

"The two of us work. A lawyer and a publisher now sell newspapers. During the whole morning we manage to earn DM 1.5. It must be the equivalent of 10 Austrian schillings. Bravo.

"One cannot buy a box of matches with it. Until only yesterday we earned three or four thousand German marks a month. Today less than fifty..." (September 30th)

The September days go on:

"Literally each Sarajevan constantly carries a death notice in his pocket, his own death notice. No, they are not death sentences. Some other people signed them much earlier. They carry them out from hour to hour. There are no fewer than ten executions a day. It is not infrequent that we have close to forty of them...

"We are all death candidates.

"Here, it is not a philosopical option.

"The reality, vulgar and ominous, is the death notice sticking out of your jeans back pocket. We hope they will not pull it out..." (September 9th)

"Even misfortunes get tired." (September 14th)

"People's faces reflect misery.

"The market has been without anything for days. It lights up the faces of the Sarajevans like the most powerful searchlight. It reveals them. Our attention goes from man to man. They pass by, stop, walk on.

"Everything is the same.

"There is nothing..." (September 15th)

"A musician, a clarinetist, a man from my grammar school days, my first café nights, has been at the market for two or three days. He stands, greyish and wrinkled, at a counter with two packets of cigarettes and a pair of women's yellow, high boots. They seem to be new, Italian.

"He waits. A bag hangs over his shoulder. He does not take it off. He does not want to stand there. He would rather leave. As if he were passing by.

"He recognises me. He feels uneasy. He says he spent three months in the barracks. He did not want to leave with the former Yugoslav Army. He stayed here. They left. 'Why should I be with them?' Now he does not get any pay. He needs money for bread, to buy something if he finds anything at all." (September 19th)

"There is no electricity. There is no water. Is this the seventeenth or the eighteenth day we have been without electricity...?

KARAMEHMEDOVIĆ
HIKMETA

LIPOVAČA
MIRZA
1952 1992
HASANOVIĆ
TEUFIK
METILJEVIĆ
MIRSAD
1945 1992

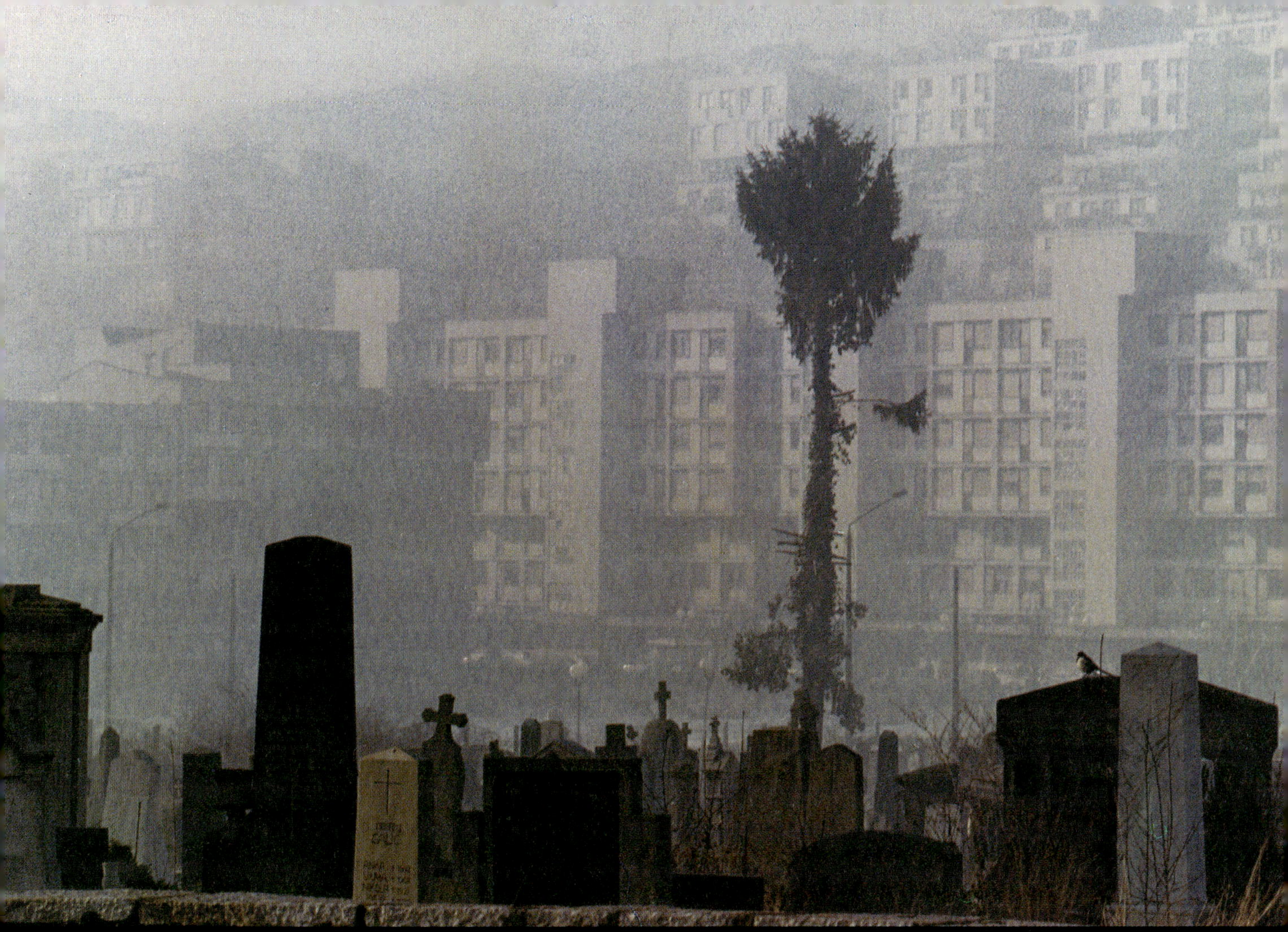

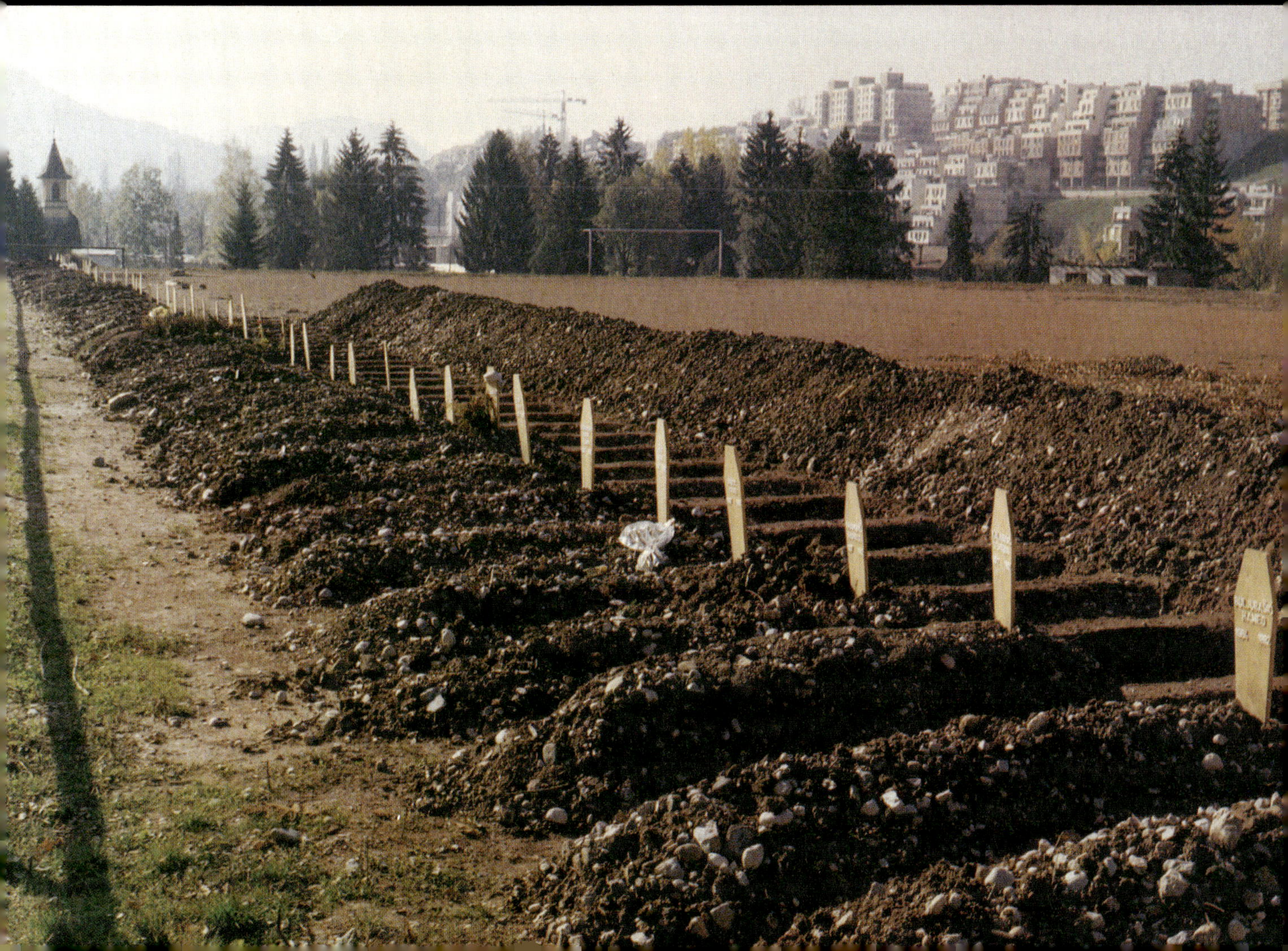

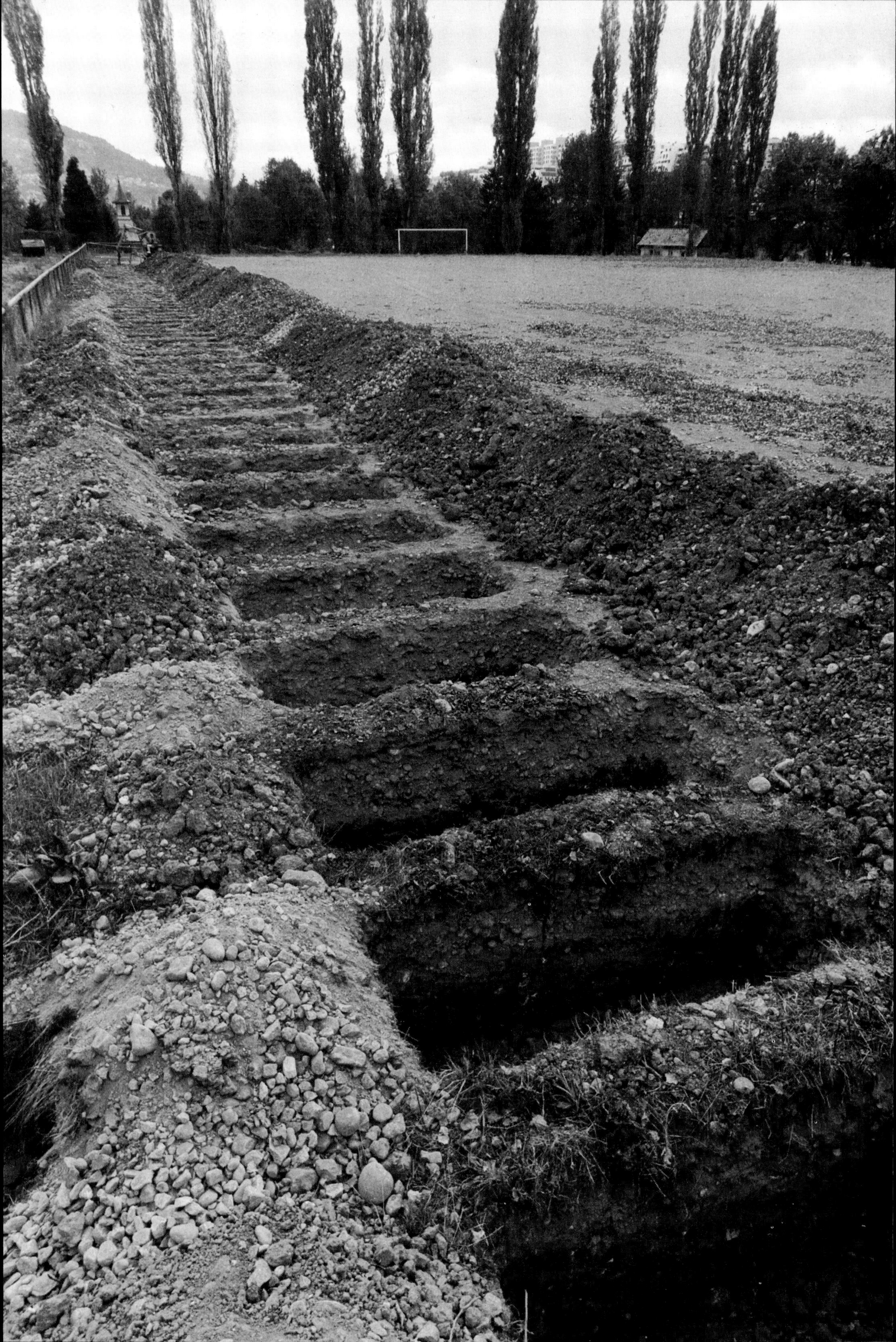

163 SARAJEVO – THE WOUNDED CITY

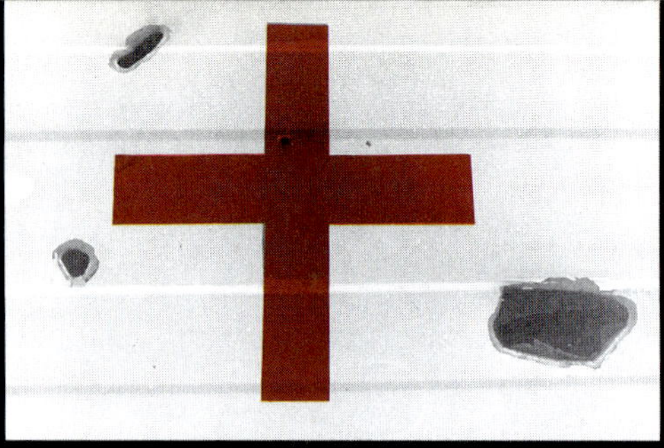

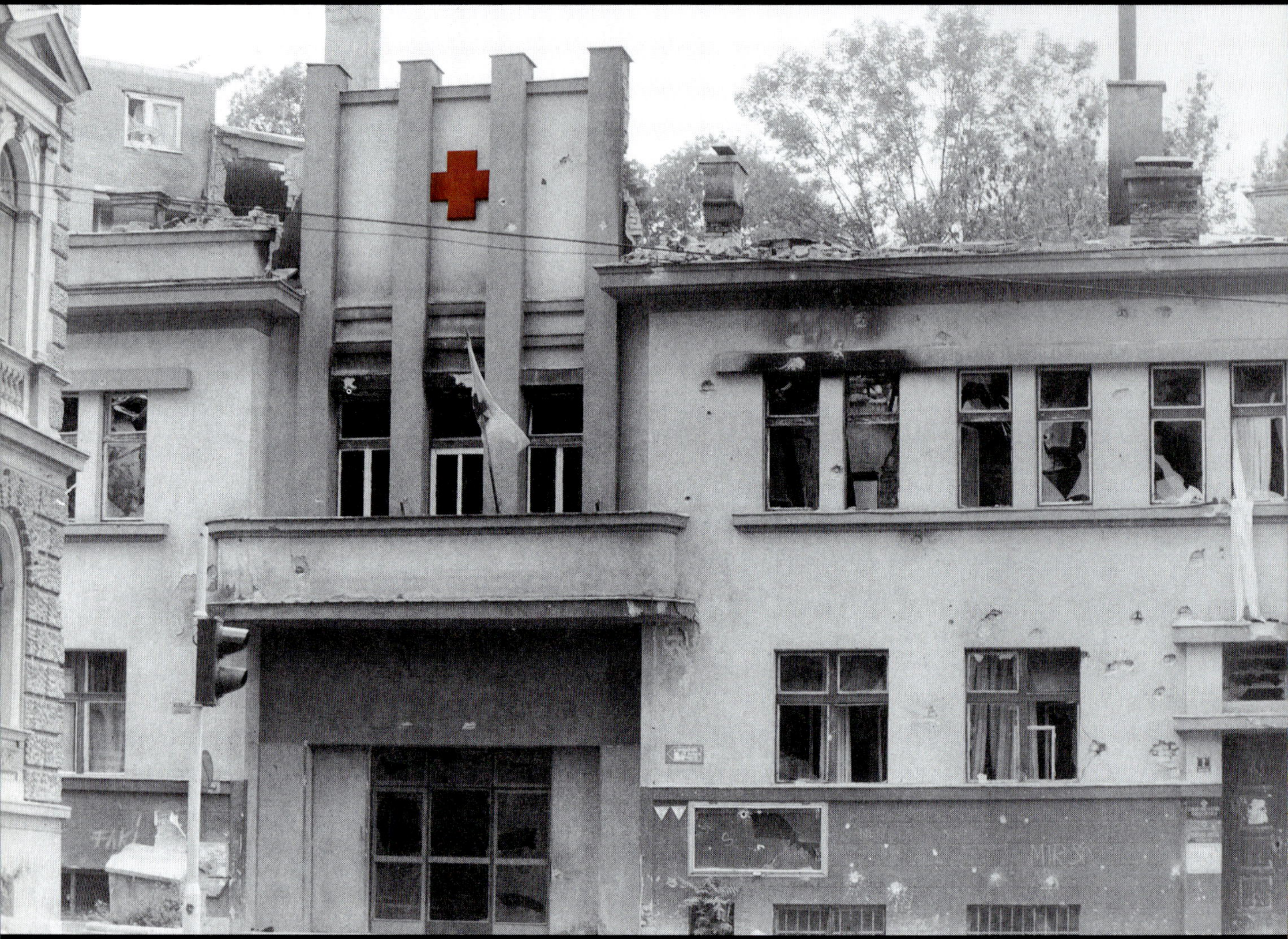

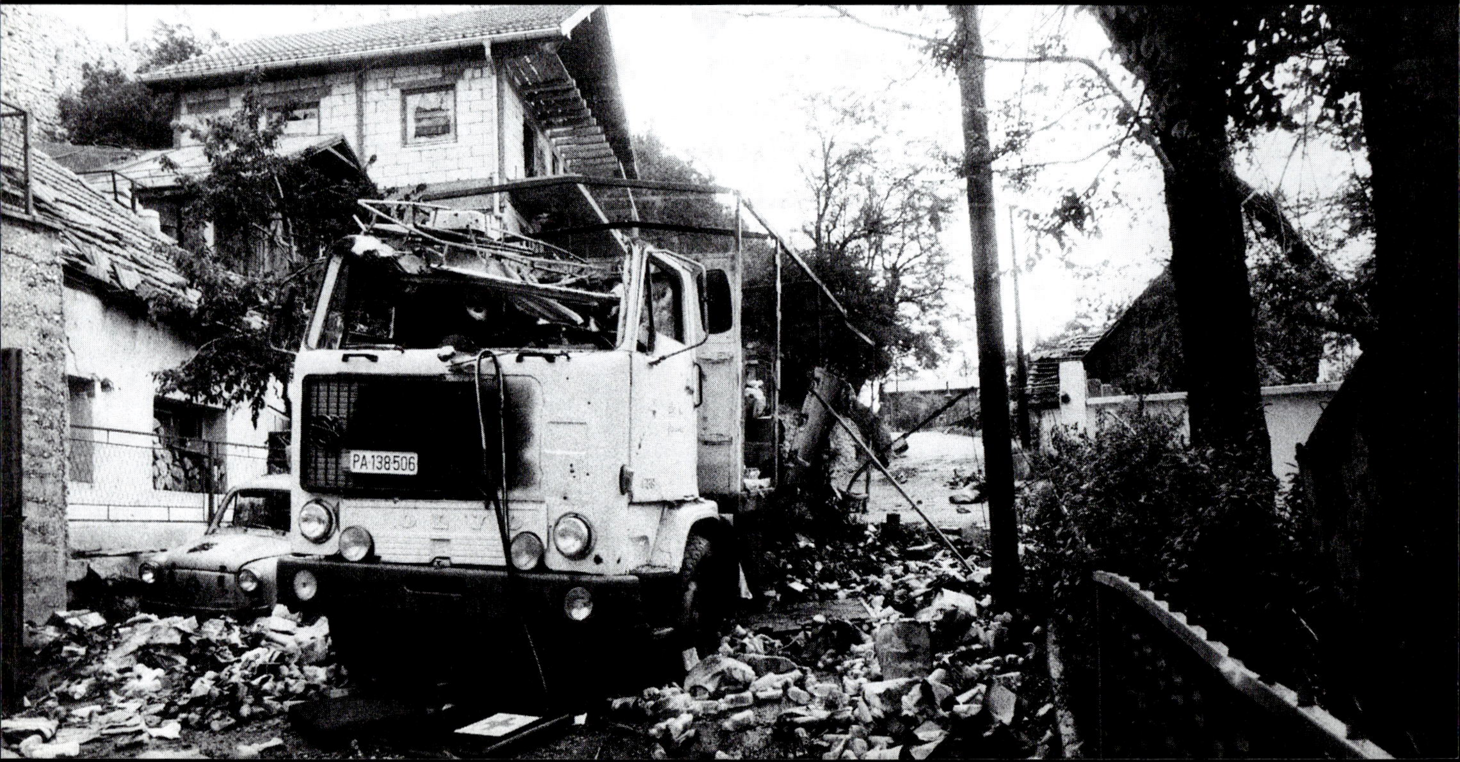
PA 138506

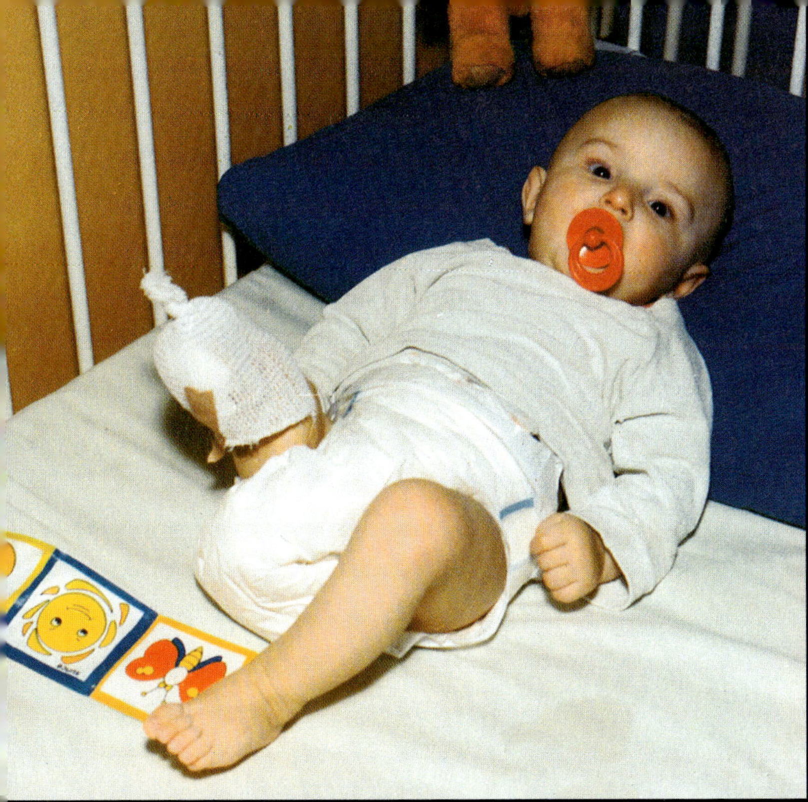

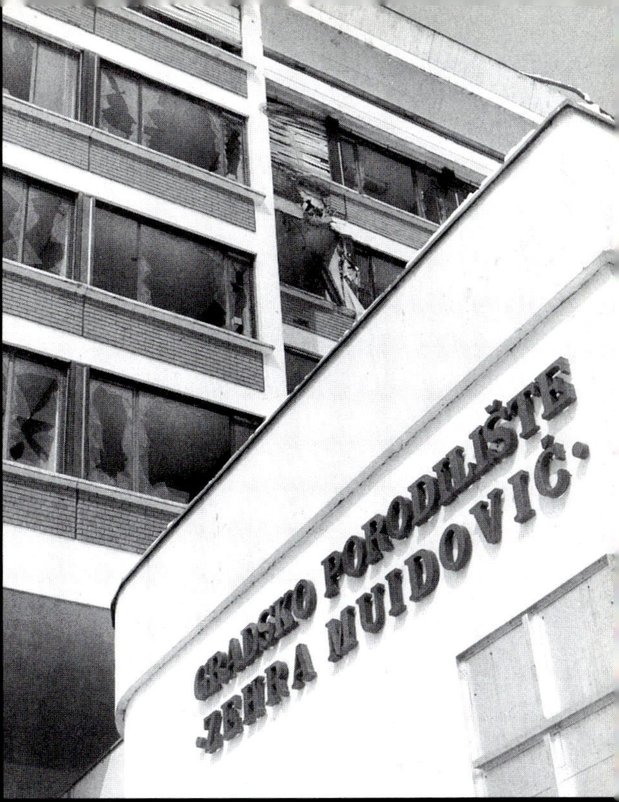
GRADSKO PORODILIŠTE
„ZEHRA MUIDOVIĆ"

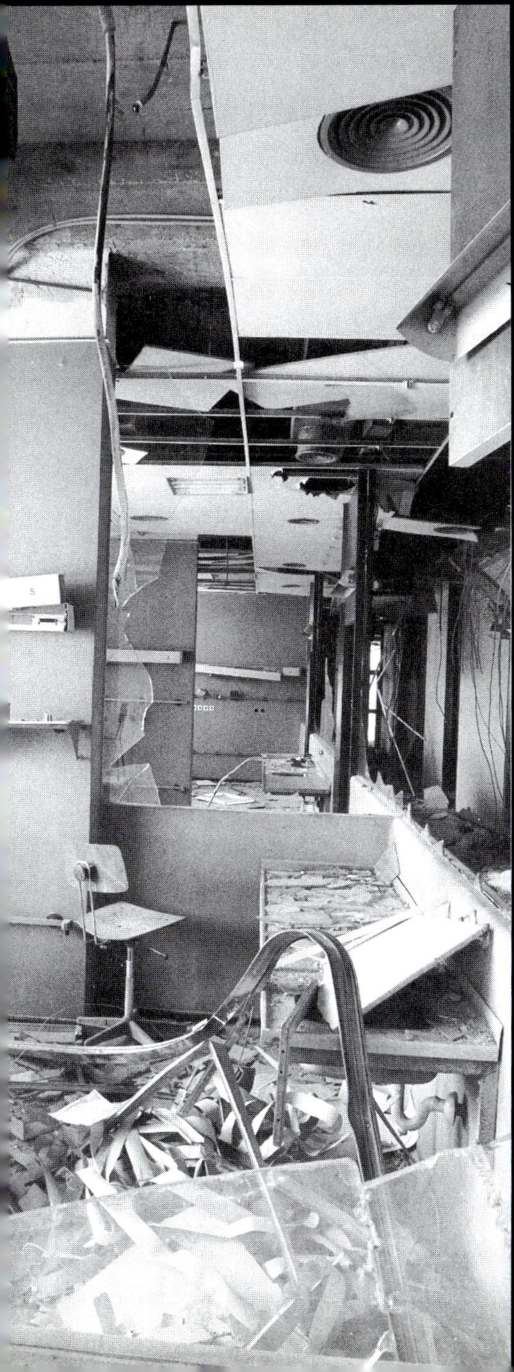

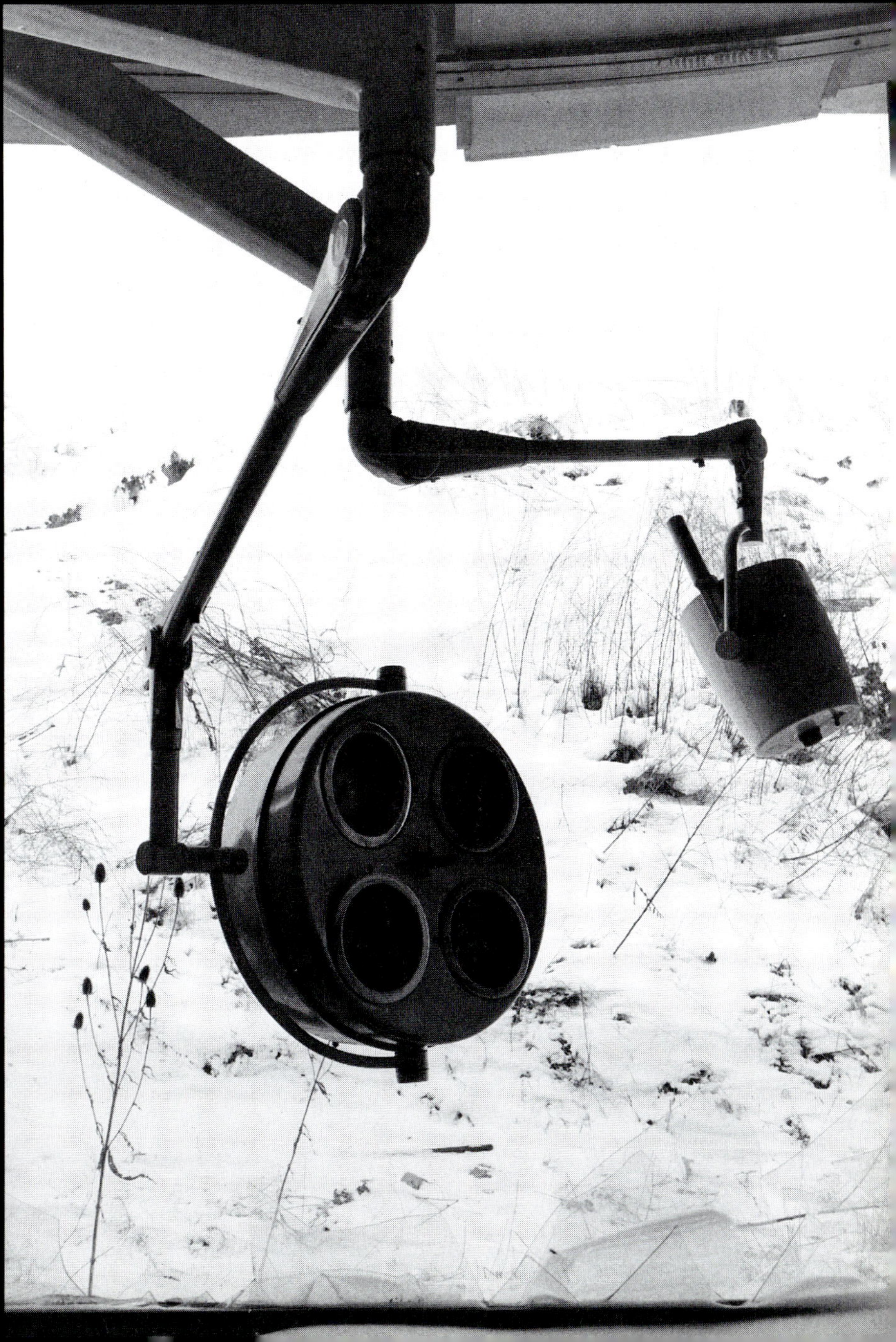

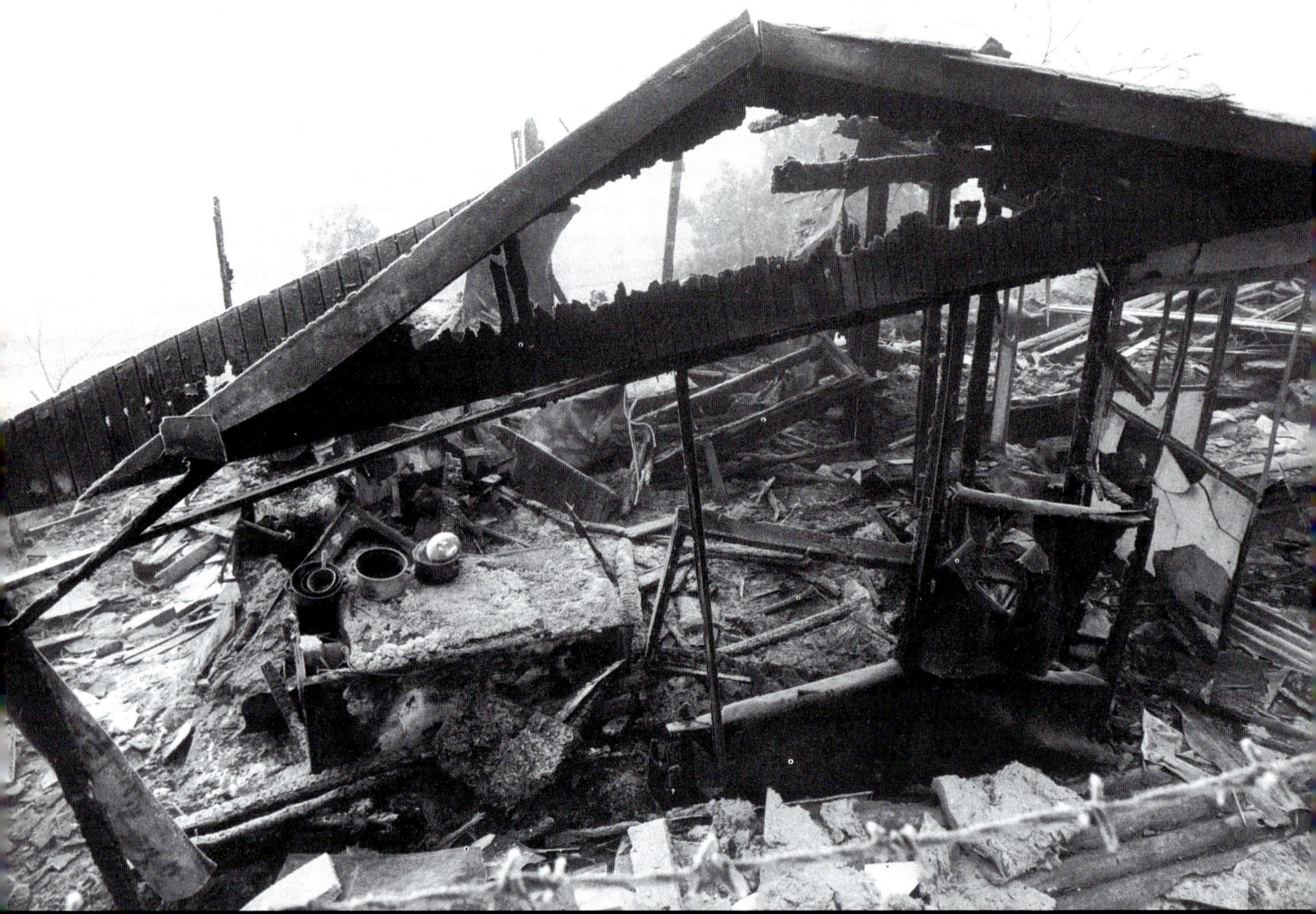

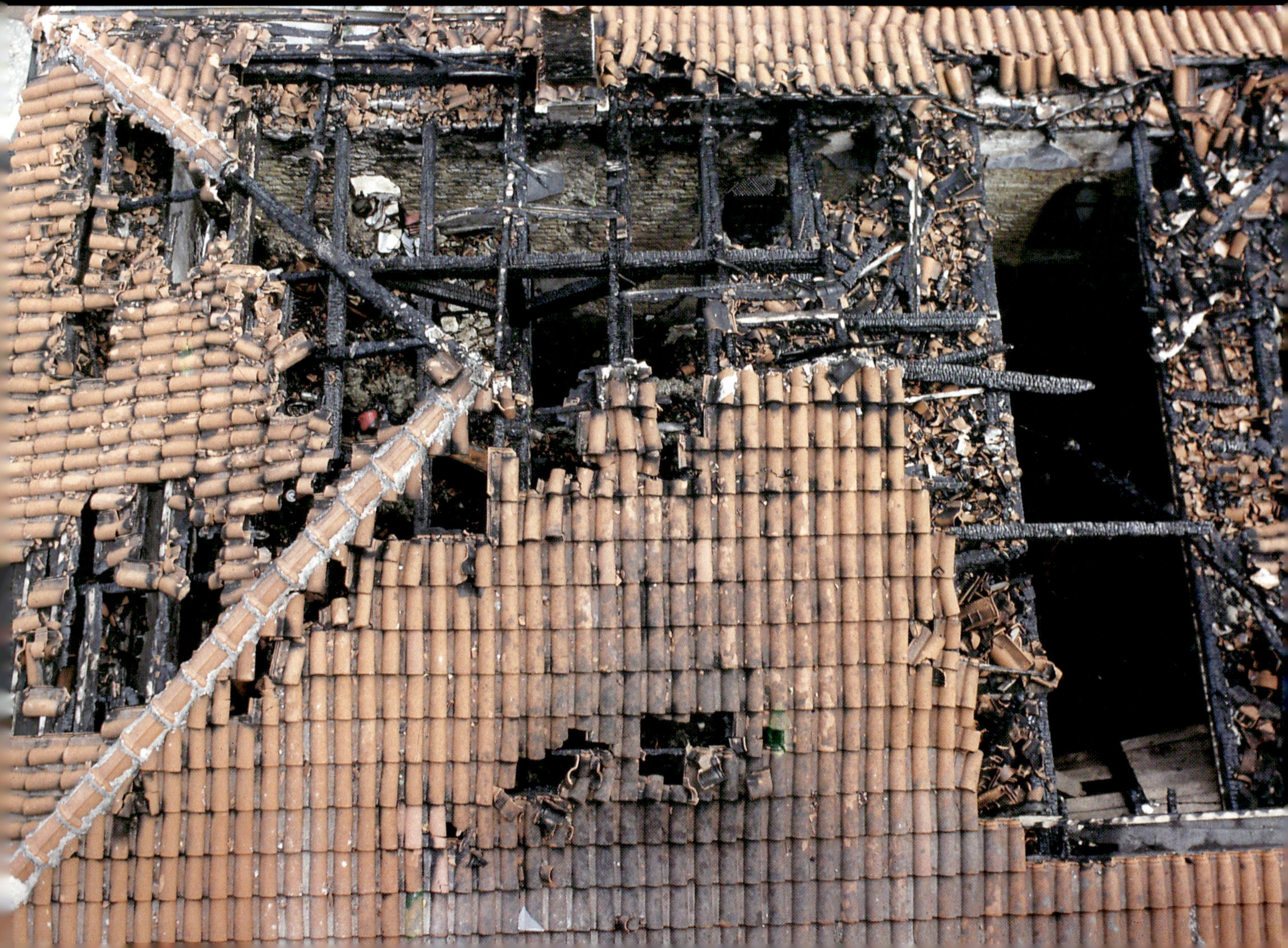

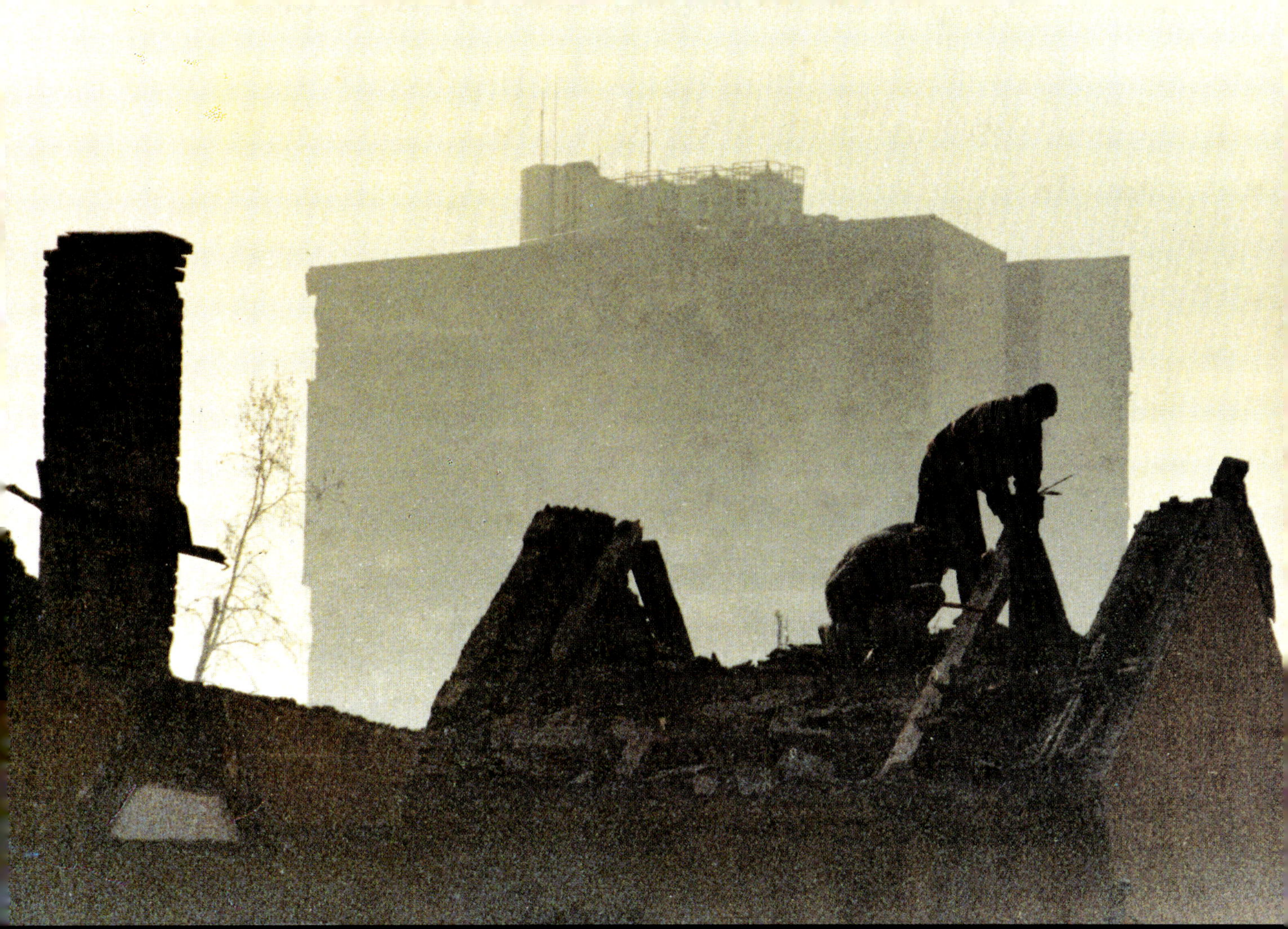

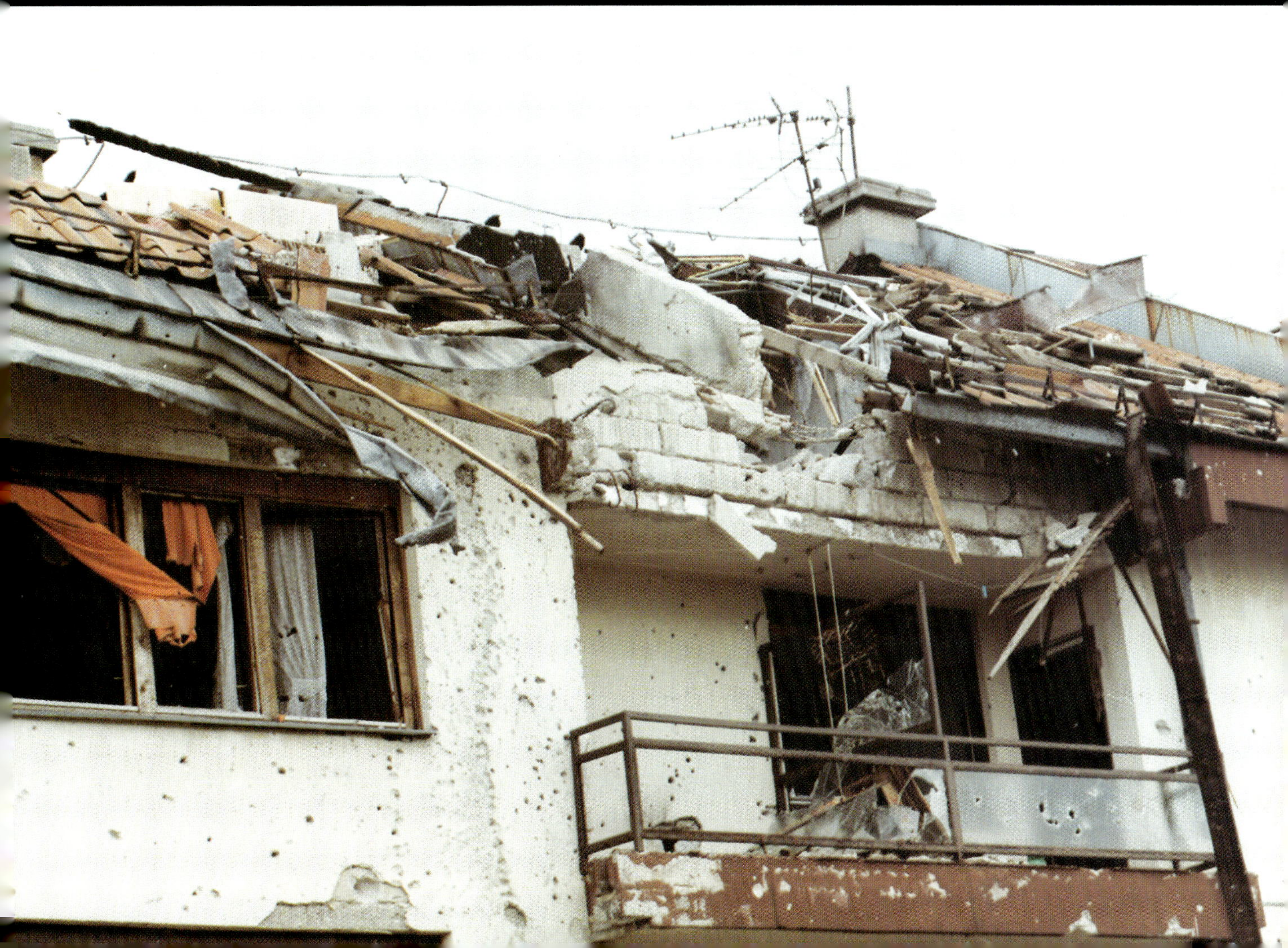

ČASOVNIČAR

ADVOKAT

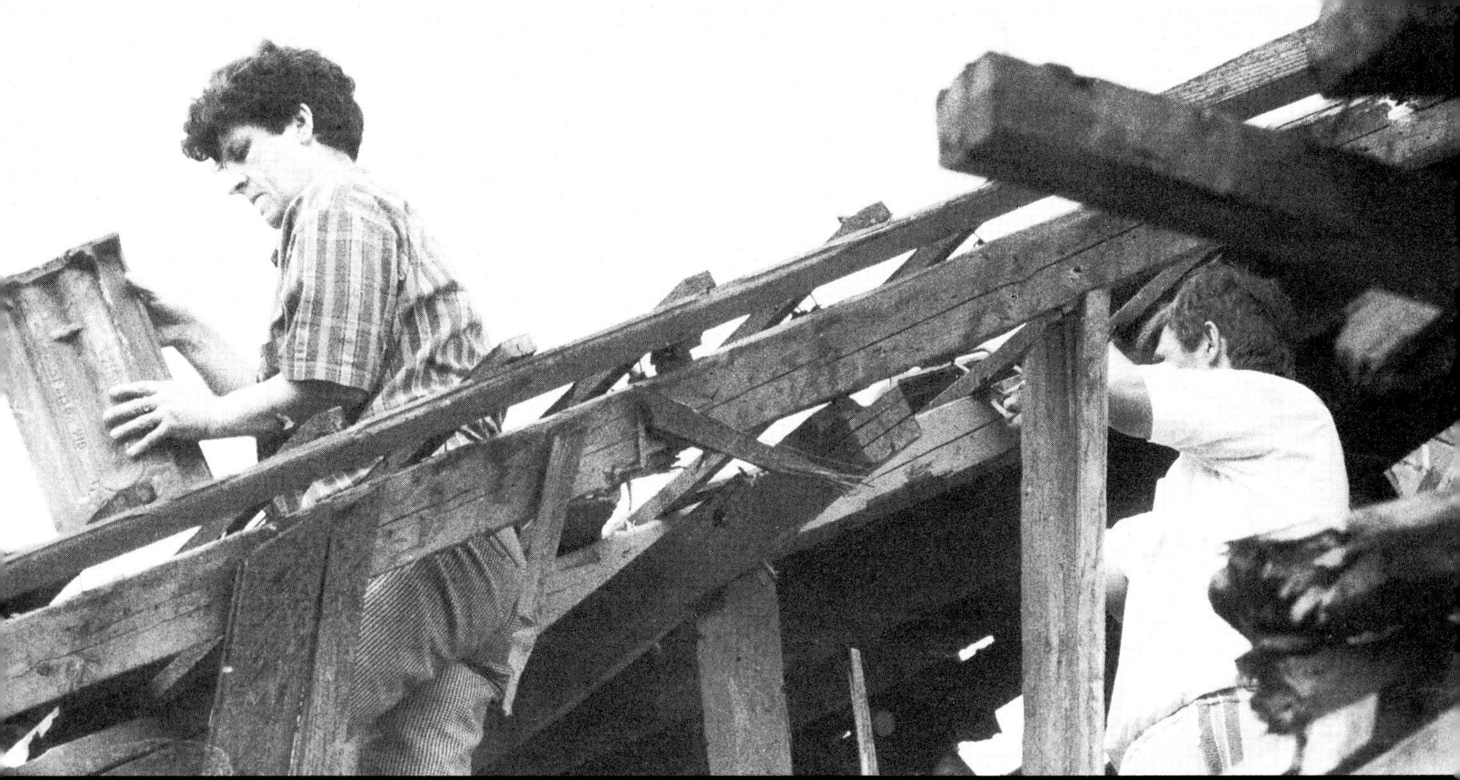

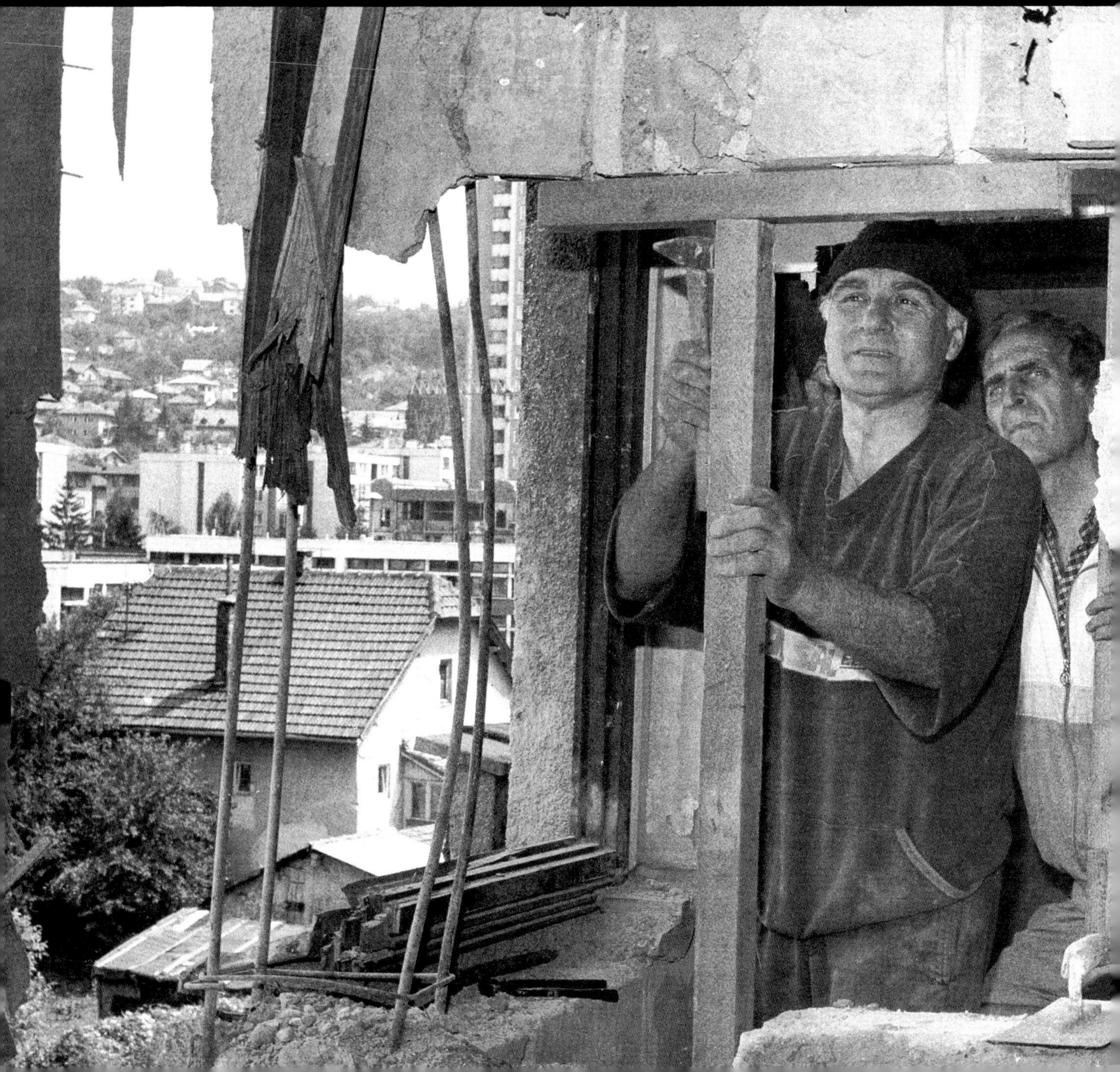

"Nobody bends to pick up coins. They do not mean luck here. They do not bring it. Nobody expects them to. They are discarded. In the streets, at every step, you come across them. I pick up some of them. I also step on telephone tokens. They are useless. There are no telephone booths. There are no telephone lines. Also useless are billiards chips or ones marked: Knutssen Casino Sweden. In the pocket of my grey summer jacket I find a metal token. There is a hole in the middle of it. I turn it in my hands. No, it is not a parking token. What is it for? Then, amazed, I recognize it as a platform token for the bus station."

The bus station? Platform? Buses? Seeing off or meeting someone? How much, in such a short time, we forget so quickly and inexorably. I cannot even imagine a bus ride.

"I wander about the city. I am filled with satisfaction. I received an unusual letter. It was waiting for me at Marko Kovačević's. I collected it today. The date on it is September 16th. It is from Kemo Bakaršić. He warmly, kindly thanks me for the mention of his speech at the Sephardim '92 commemoration. All that was written on an Austro-Hungarian picture postcard with Bey's mosque and ruins of the Tashlihan in it. I did not have that one in my postcard collection.

"The city is sunlit, washed by last night's shower. It is peaceful. They presented us with an abundance of shells.

"In Tito Street, near the department store which gapes with a hole made by a shell, there are some human brains. Even the summer shower did not wash them away. I avoid stopping and taking a look at them. There are also some bits of bone on the dark bloodstain on the pavement. It is a human joint with some flesh on it. I avoid any anatomical comparison with myself. I force myself to forget immediately what I saw. A torn women's sandal warns as if it were stopping us. We hurry along with Duško Stajić. He carries an armful of some fifty unsold copies of 'Oslobođenje'. He says: 'It hit a man directly here yesterday.'

"We walk on. Others hurry, too.
"And nothing.
"It was yesterday.
"Yesterday a man was killed near the 'Svjetlost' bookshop, too.
"I wonder if there is a place where nobody has been killed.
"And the city is sunlit..." (September 30th)
"– Would you like to buy two small knives?"
"– Pardon?"
"– Would you like to buy two small knives, two small knives?"
"– No, thanks. I only sell newspapers.

---

provided the hospital for generating units for 15 hours. The area of Stup and Žuč are shelled. Anti-aircraft guns and anti-aircraft machine guns fire at the western parts of the city. Hrasno hill, Pofalići and Pero Kosorić Square. Snipers are active at the city's crossroads.

Friday, 2nd: Artillery attacks on Stup and Breka residential areas. The forcible eviction of Muslim and Croatian citizens from Grbavica continues. Repairs on a transmission line are being carried out under UNPROFOR protection. Enterocolitis is raging again. A hundred-day diary of the taxi-driver Miomir Plakalović by Aleksej Nejman is published under the title "A Taxi Named Desire". Appeal from the City Assembly: "Citizens, please do not cut down trees". A truck with medicine and medical supplies arrives at Dobrinja from the little town of

Vannes in Bretagne upon the initiative of the French battalion of UNPROFOR.

Saturday, 3rd: After a month, the humanitarian air-bridge is reestablished. Shelling of the edges of the old city, and in the afternoon the whole city. At the *moment there is not a piece of gauze in Sarajevo, and the daily requirements for it are 10,000 metres. The epidemic of enterocolitis goes on. There are 24 killed and 198 injured in B-H (10 killed and 80 injured in Sarajevo).*

Sunday, 4th: *Four aircraft with humanitarian aid land at the airport. The departure of convoys with mothers, children, the sick and the exhausted for Split, Belgrade, Prague and Lisbon is uncertain. Residential areas and industrial plants are shelled. The targets are, as usual, the edges of the old city, the heart of the city, Darovaoci Krvi Street, Pero Kosorić Square, Stup, Dobrinja, Otoka and Sokolje. No electricity, no water. Transmission lines are being repaired. UNPROFOR gives 5 tons of oil from their own supplies for hospitals and the post office.*

Monday, 5th: *Sarajevo is burning. No water. No electricity. No gas either. The city is without bread. An overall attack on the town. The most severe attacks are on the line Vrbanja Bridge– Pero Kosorić Square–Alipašino polje. Many houses and buildings catch fire after being hit by fire from tanks, howitzers and rocket launchers situated on the surrounding hills. Schools, kindergartens and health centres are burning. Fires in the "Holiday Inn" hotel, the "Electrical Power Industry of B-H", skyscrapers in Živko Jošilo and Bratstvo and Jedinstvo Streets and skyscrapers at Pero Kosorić Square. In the evening the municipality of Stari grad, Alipašino polje, Dobrinja, Marijin Dvor, Ciglane, Stup and Sokolje are shelled. The Assembly of the Novo Sarajevo municipality is on fire. On*

"– I have them here in my bag. You know, I must buy some bread.

"I shrug my shoulders. I am confused. The woman hurriedly vanishes in a crowd of market shoppers.

"In my mind's eye I can see a black imitation leather bag in the woman's clenched hand. I do not remember her face. She slowly lifted her bag and pointed to it, repeating her sentence for me. I did not understand her. I was surprised.

"I perhaps did not want to understand her. What could I do with those two knives of hers? It is wartime. But I did not manage to offer her some money. I could have hurt her feelings. However, I did not.

"The woman offered me her two knives. She needed some bread. Yesterday, or perhaps a day or two ago, a man, dressed in a faded brown spring overcoat, came up to me. Others were in shirts, light pullovers or perhaps linen jackets. It is summertime. He offered me a table lamp. It was handmade, red and white plastic, trash in a plastic bag. In fact, he was showing me his offer. This tells me he knows me. I do not remember him, but he started the conversation like an intimate... What can I do? A person selling newspapers must reckon on being addressed in the confidential form. Did he sell it? I still see him in a brown spring overcoat, bent. He nods his head to greet me. He has not bought any newspapers for some time. I have not seen his plastic bag, either." (September 26th)

I sink back in the dark. I am about to explode but I cannot. A cry does not come out of my throat. I crawl farther. I still hear the story about a stolen and slaughtered cow. The day's news is still the news about the thieves who stole a cow. A man was minding it after he brought it from a village in the city's vicinity when he fled his home. It gave milk to feed his children and some twenty other children from the neighbourhood. They stole it from him. They took it to another part of the city and slaughtered it. They wanted to eat meat, fresh meat. They planned to sell some as well. They fixed the price: DM 35 a kilo. The police caught them. Journalists and photographers fulfilled their writing quotas. The city was disgusted about it. It fed on the story. A cow was killed. The city is hungry. Nobody wonders how and from where the cow reached the city.

The Horsemen of the Apocalypse caught me up, then overtook me. War, death, plague and starvation are no longer just Dürer's historical engravings. They rode along my roads. I got accustomed to them. They looked at me. They passed on. Disease entered the city. Enterocolitis attacked children. It spread to adults. Mediaeval hygienic conditions struck us. We were waterless. No electricity for months. We had it on the 8th and on the 21st it was cut off again. A barrel of water was sold at the market for ten German marks. The Ministry of Health wrote to the world: "In this land of terrorism, starvation, epidemic, genocide,

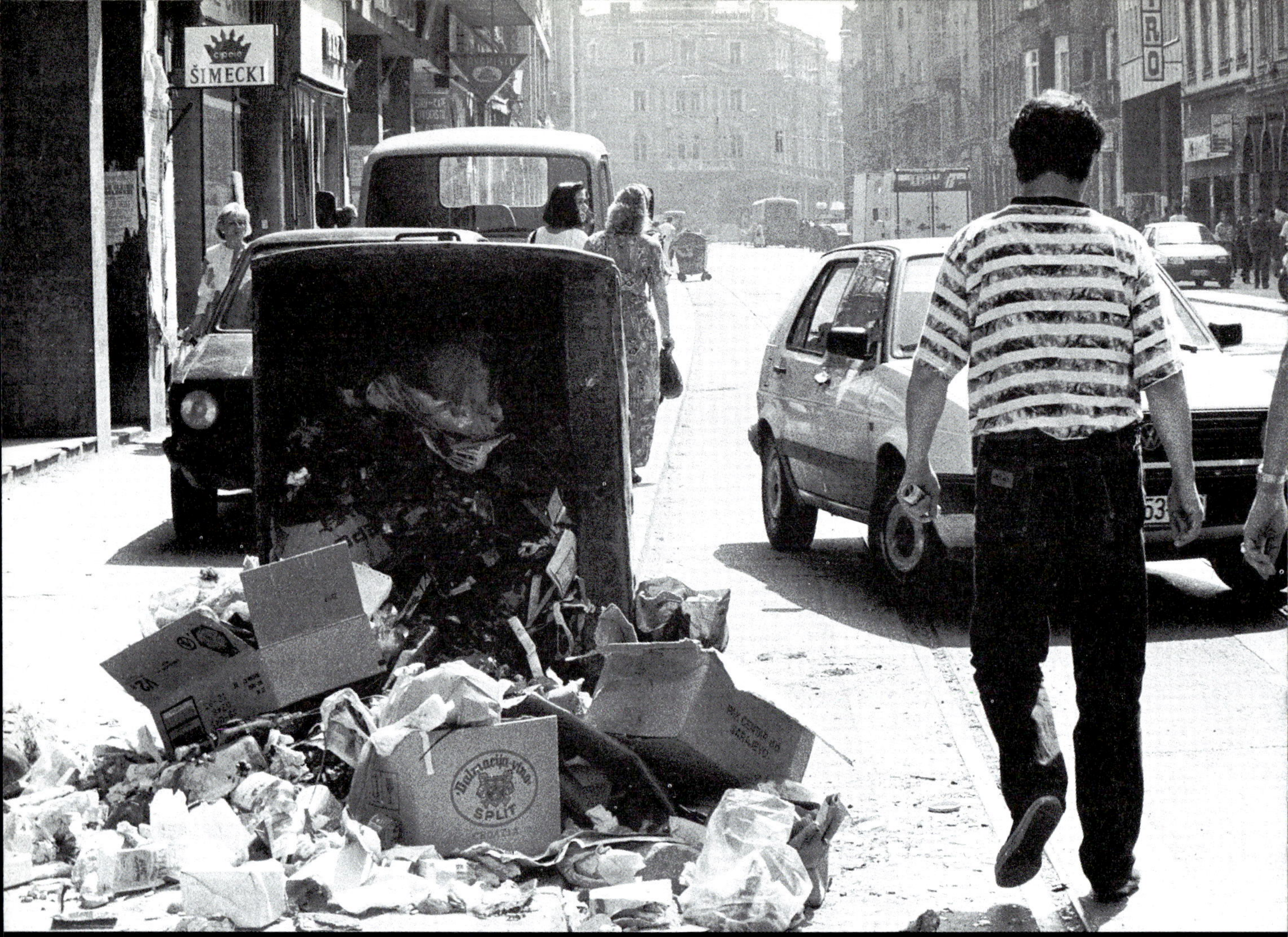
ŠIMECKI
SPLIT

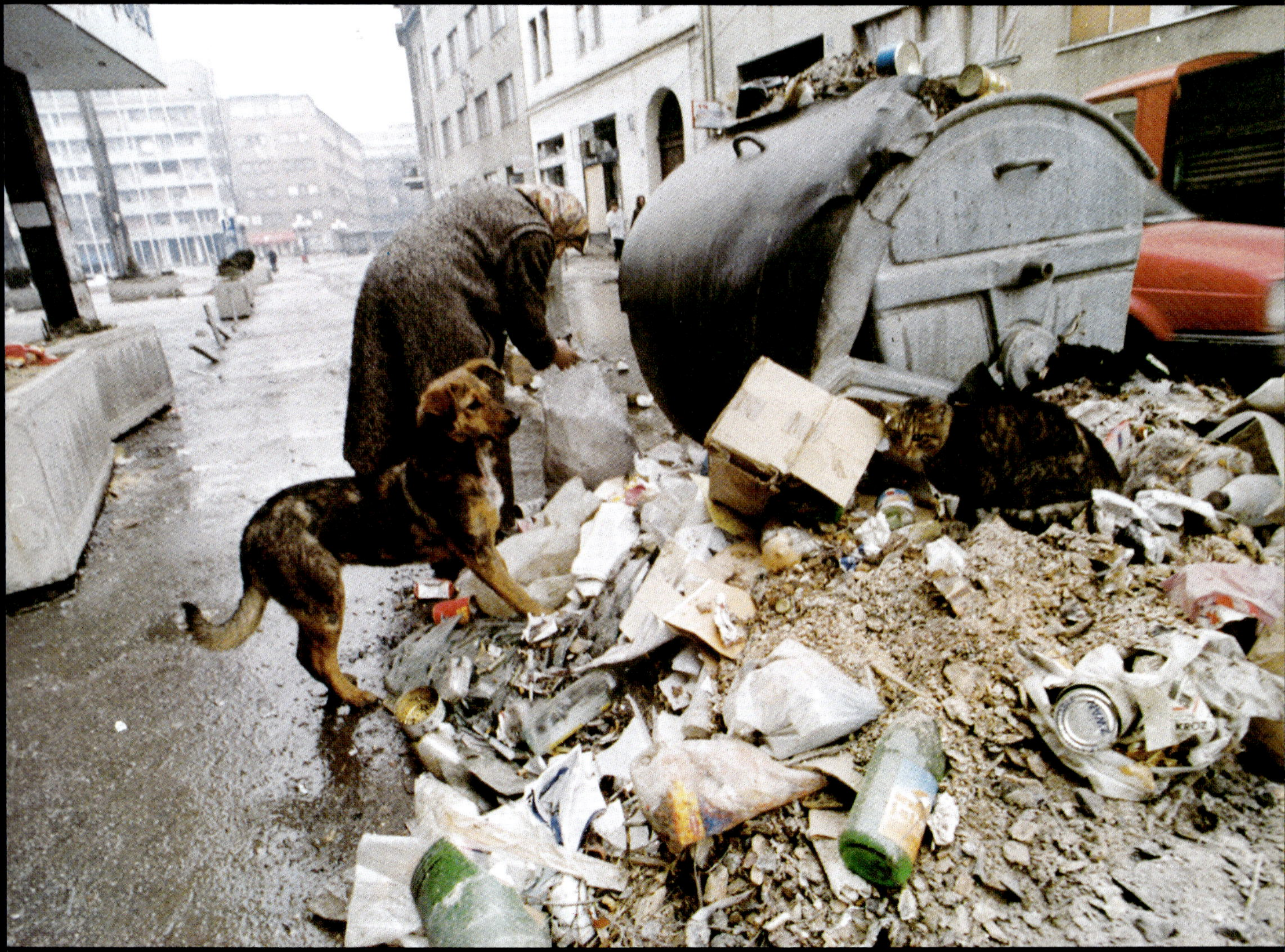

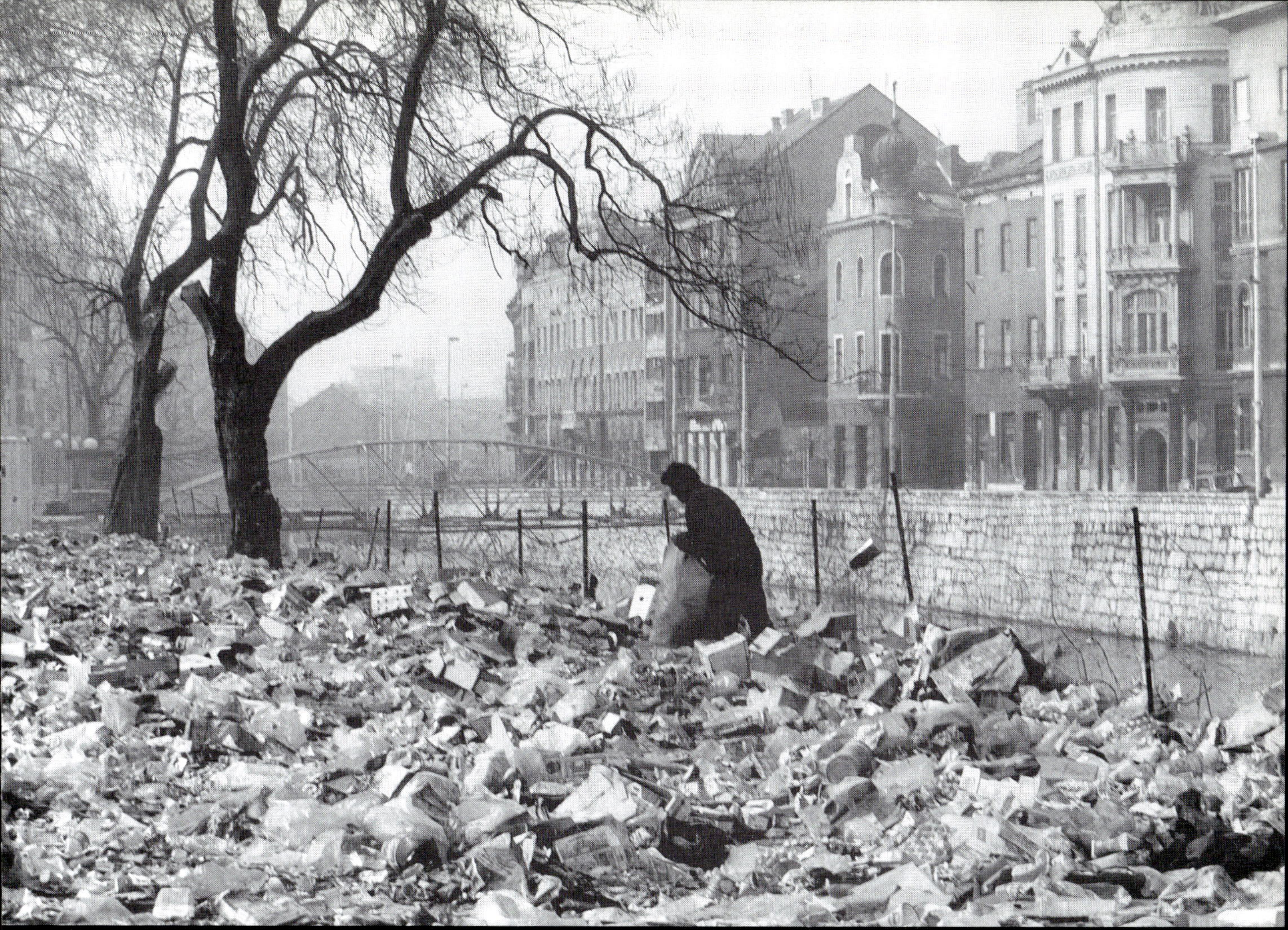

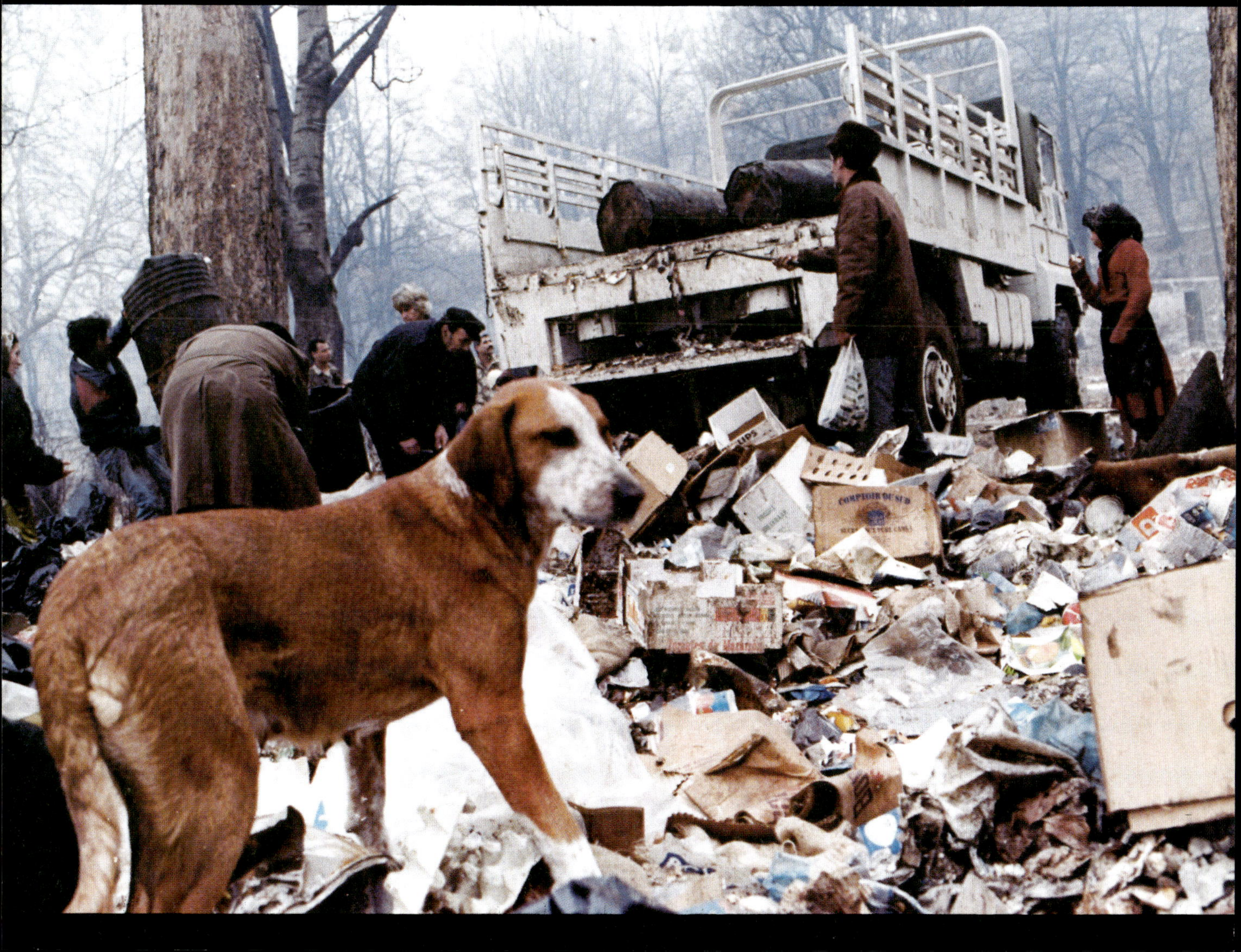

poisoning and mass slaughter there are still living people you can help if you want to." At the same time 1,700 patients were starving in the hospitals. Over a thousand medical workers were entitled to a meal only after a continuous shift of twenty-four hours. They say briefly: "We have nothing to make soup out of. We have no spices. We cannot even make tea. In Geneva, the vice-president of the government of this wretched country explains to the world that this winter over 100,000 people could die in Bosnia and Herzegovina. Hunger and cold shake the ground I am on.

At Dobrinja, a residental quarter built on the eve of the Winter Olympics in Sarajevo, nettles have been the only food for months. It is no better in other parts of the city. Nettles, bitter old chicory and tough cabbage leaves are sold at market counters. Nobody offers a whole head of cabbage. I have not seen one during these summer and autumn months. The leaves we used to throw away when preparing cabbage for meals are now sold. And they find customers. People are happy when they manage to get a bunch of seven or eight leaves for themselves. The one who, however, succeeded in coming across a head of cabbage said it was being offered for twenty German marks. And it was sold immediately. It was no heavier than 3/4 of a kilo.

fire is also the well-known 20-floor building named "the box of matches". Prices on the market: 1 kg of pumpkins 10 DM, 1 kg of tomatoes 20 DM, five onions 25 DM, 1 kg of beef 30 DM, 1 kg of coffee 40 DM.

Tuesday, 6th: Novo Sarajevo is targeted by the shelling. Blocks of flats are on fire. A building in Ivan Krndelj Street, another in Ivan Ribar Street and a tall apartment block in Pero Kosorić Square catch fire. Infantry attempts to break through into the city at Hrasno, Dobrinja, near the Jewish cemetery and Zlatište. 25 killed and 133 injured in the city.

Wednesday, 7th: The city is without electricity, water and gas. Artillery attacks from Marijin Dvor to Otoka, Hotonj, Žuč and Kobilja glava. Infantry clashes in Pero Kosorić Square. Bread is baked in "Velepekara" only for the hospitals.

Thursday, 8th: Infantry clashes in the area of Doglode. Occasional shelling of Stari grad and Butmir. Telephone lines which start with the number four are out owing to a lack of fuel. The State (French) Hospital has continued its work thanks to fuel received from UNPROFOR and special units of the B-H Army.

Friday, 9th: The town is still without electricity. A relatively quiet day. Shells fall on Stari grad. Tank attacks on Doglode. 12 killed, 62 wounded. The *epidemic of enterocolitis slackening. UNPROFOR takes the necessary measures to provide unhindered delivery of humanitarian aid in winter time.*

Saturday, 10th: *A shell falls onto the "Ljubica Ivezić" Orphanage. Three children killed and 13 seriously injured. Artillery shells are fired at Baščaršija, the sloped parts of Stari grad, Alipašino polje, Dobrinja and the State French Hospital... Infantry attacks along the Stup-Doglode line. The Presidency of the Republic of B-H defines a five-day time limit for the return of all officials to the capital (those appointed by the Assembly and the Presidency). There are 11 killed and 53 injured. One UNPROFOR soldier is killed and three wounded near Stup, on the way to the airport. Stjepan Šiber lodged a protest with UNPROFOR over the cancelling of the humanitarian aid deliveries to Butmir and Dobrinja. No electricity. A transmission line is damaged. The 100th anniversary of the birth of the Nobel Prize Winner Ivo Andrić is not commemorated in any way.*

Sunday, 11th: *Explosions are occasionally heard in the outskirts of the Stari grad, Dobrinja and Vogošća residential areas on the free (unoccupied) territory. Hospitals have neither electricity nor water and they are also running out of oil. The situation with medical supplies is getting better. There are 16 killed and 118 injured in Sarajevo.*

Monday, 12th: *Heavily shelled are Stup, Stup hill and the Otes residential areas. The patients in Koševo Hospital are given only a sandwich for lunch.*

We are all equal in our poverty. We all suddenly have nothing. We stand, we squat, we kneel in front of the world with outstretched hands and stomachs stuck to our spines. Our empty bowels growl. We cannot calm them. "Give alms to us! Give alms, may God repay and help you and your children..."

The whole city becomes a ragged, poor beggar. Mr Tadeusz Mazowiecki, appointed by the world as our tutor, sympathizes with us: "There are no human rights in Bosnia and Herzegovina."

How would I show him around the city? I would have to introduce him to the people I usually greet. We would meet a woman acquaintance of mine who, after a vain visit to the market, tells me about food and meat. With a glow in her eyes she talks about her son and a neighbour who prepare pigeon stew. Her son patiently catches city pigeons on the balcony. He sticks bits of bread on fishhooks tied on a line and catches seven or eight pigeons. It is enough for three of them to have a meal.

What would Noah have done if his dove had not returned with an olive branch? We may be envious of this preacher – a righteous man this year. He survived a general flood, tempests, an abundance of water. At Dobrinja, after cobwebs covered the taps, they took a plumb line and a dowsing rod. And as during World War I, when some armies, afraid of poisoned wells, had companies of dowsers to find water for new wells, so Anto and his daughter Antonia Leko dowse for water for the whole suburb. Field water pumps at the wells found by dowsers brought salutary drops.

Thirst, hunger and misery.

Does anyone hear us at all?

The planes with humanitarian aid started flying over here with this war. We admired the size of the American Hercules aircraft. Some ten, fifteen, nineteen planes landed daily. They brought food, medicine, blankets and medical supplies. They were hit by bullets and rockets. The world wondered who was shooting. Would the beggar who humbly sits with his head bent on the pavement near an empty hat kick his own hat? Does anyone listen to me at all?

I meet my neighbour Zvonko. He vacillates. He makes excuses: "I'm going to 'Caritas'. What can I do? I hesitated for two hours, I didn't know what to do for days. I'm ashamed. I have to. I don't know what to eat. It's for the children's sake. I managed to find and buy some buns this morning. They have got more expensive. The only important thing is that we can get them. It was this morning. What shall I do tomorrow? What about the day after? I still have some savings, but there's nothing to buy. There's no food...

"What shall I do? I'm going to register with them. I've got nothing more to eat..."

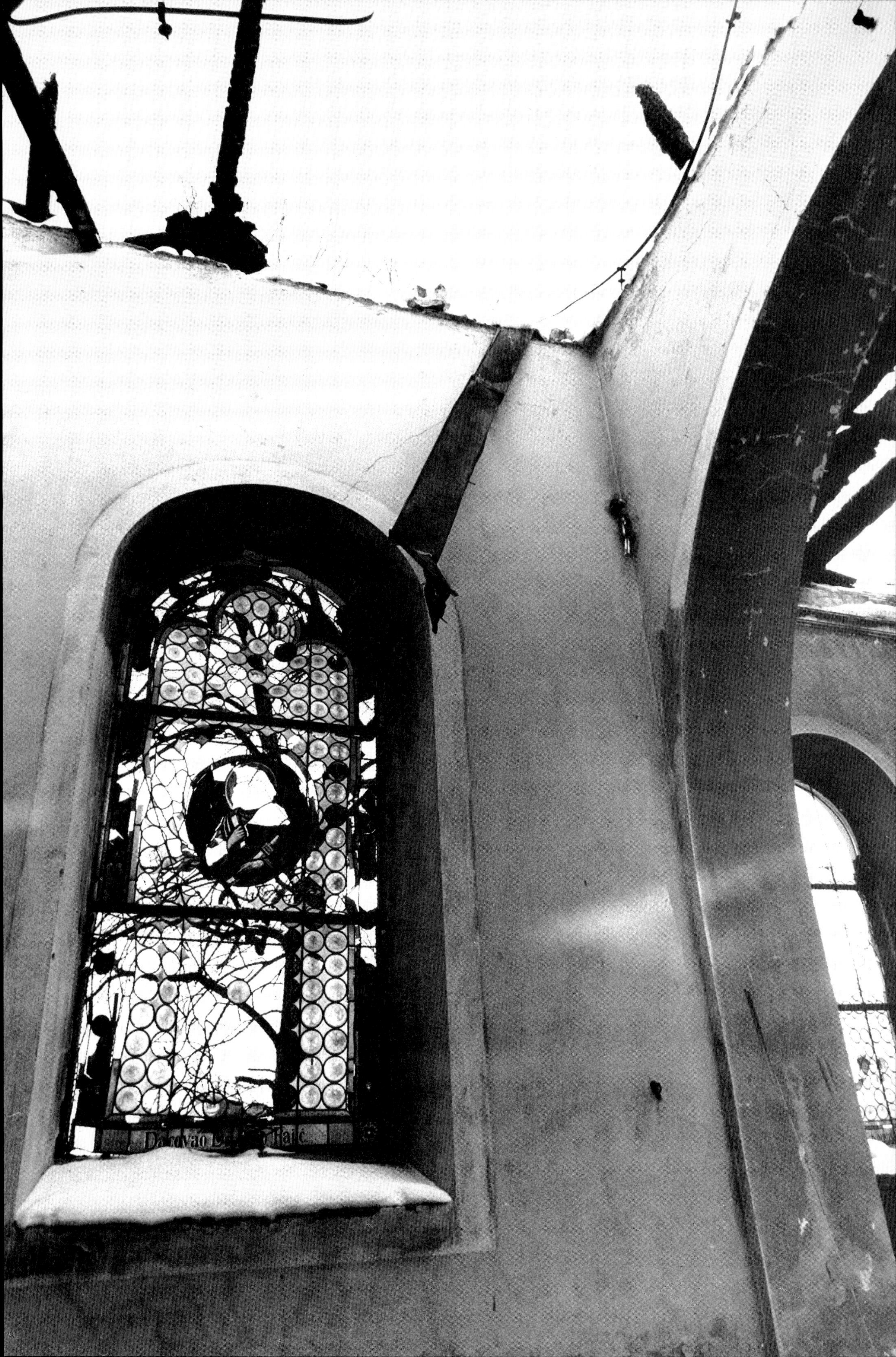

177 SARAJEVO – THE WOUNDED CITY

The whole city goes round empty shops, walks about aimlessly, but they return home empty-handed. Salvation comes from the sky. It is brought by the planes with humanitarian aid, UNHCR convoys, UNPROFOR soldiers. All these come slowly, too slowly. Hunger has moved in to our homes. It grins victoriously at the dining tables of the Sarajevans.

Nobody cares whether the sell-by date is past for the food they find shoved somewhere. What matters is to eat. All the refrigerators and freezers were disconnected long ago. Electricity turned them into useless cupboards. There has been no electricity for days or weeks. We had to eat up the frozen food quickly or throw it away. There was not too much of it left anyhow. We have new cooking arts. We all create our own tips for survival. A war cookery book is being written. In it, no meat, no vegetables, fats, eggs, cheese or fruits are used. We gradually introduce the food we get in the humanitarian aid sent by the world. At the beginning we looked for support from the charitable societies "Caritas" and "Merhamet". The first disappointments followed. Selection for help is made according to religious criteria. The first rejections arrive, but so does bitter realisation as well. Atheists do not know whom to turn to. The whole city hurries to "La Benevolencia", to the Adventist Church, whose existence many did not know about at all. There are more and more hungry people. Soup kitchens are being opened for the most underprivileged citizens and refugees. The column of the underprivileged gets longer and longer. A friend of my father's, a retired judge and his wife, also a pensioner, are in it. Roses are pulled out of balcony flowerpots. Lawns around houses are turned into vegetable gardens. Tomatoes and green peppers grow in flowerpots. The quick-witted ones pick their own onions, lettuce and mangel. They vigilantly guard them from thieves. Other people search parks and green areas of the city for chicory and nettles. We eat everything, but there is nothing.

There has been no water for days, weeks. Taps are dry. We walk miles to fetch water. There is not enough of it even for drinking. Hygiene is at the lowest level. It includes only the essential washing. I am envious of the French kings; they did not long for bathrooms and had servants who fetched water for their rare baths.

In the zoo, the remaining animals die of hunger. They do not manage to survive. The streets are full of dogs abandoned by their owners. Man betrayed dog. He fled the city leaving behind his pedigree dog. The latter did not have any food. The oldest domestic animal, Canis familiaris, has been abandoned. Man's truest friend from the Neolithic to the space age was left to itself. Dobermans, poodles, terriers, Dalmatians, Irish setters, Pekingese, sheepdogs of Shara, and other quadruped inhabitants of pedigree search

No water, no electricity. The work in the operating theatres is limited by a lack of oil for the generators. The enterocolitis epidemic is spreading again. Six people are killed and 20 wounded. A Red Cross convoy with 6,500 people bound for Split and Belgrade is stopped. After an eight-day break the city receives gas again. The salary of a Presidency member amounts to the equivalent of 20 DM, calculated according to black market exchange rates.

Tuesday, 13th: *No electricity. No water. A relatively quiet day. In the afternoon and in the evening the areas of Stari grad, Centre and parts of Vogošća are shelled. There are new cases of enterocolitis. 11 killed and 42 wounded.*

Wednesday, 14th: *Still without electricity. Telephones beginning with the numbers 4 and 5 are cut off and now with 6 as well. A peaceful day. Five killed and 55 injured in the city.*

Thursday, 15th: *No electricity, no water, no telephone communications. A relatively quiet day. Michael Meyers, a special envoy of the American senator Ted Kennedy, visits Sarajevo. A convoy with 180 Jews and members of the Jewish community leaves Sarajevo organised by "La Benevolencia" Society. There are 16 killed and 106 injured in B-H; in Sarajevo 6 dead and 36 wounded. The heating period of Sarajevo, which used to start on this date, will not start today. A large number of structures and plants of the "Toplane" (The Town Heating Plants) are either damaged or destroyed. There is a shortage of B-H dinars in*

Sarajevo. Money will be provided by additional printing. For that purpose it is necessary to provide the printing shop with 800 litres of oil. 50,000 letters have been sent from Sarajevo on Red Cross forms and 11,000 letters have come to Sarajevo in the same way.

Friday, 16th: *There is electricity in Sarajevo. After 8 hours the aggressors destroy the only 110 kilowatt transmission line which supplied the town with electric current. Since the beginning of this war 127,448 citizens in B-H have died. The number of those killed registered in health institutions is 15,546. Also registered are 129,000 injured people. On average, there are 84 killed, 580 dead or missing, 648 injured and 5,403 expelled every day. So far 9,867 tons of humanitarian aid have reached the republic via Sarajevo, satisfying 2.2% of the total food requirements. 6 people are killed and 35 wounded in Sarajevo. A protest is lodged by the Main Board of the HDZ (Croatian Democratic Community) against the desecration of cemeteries.*

Saturday, 17th: *No electricity again. The aggressor does not allow the transmission lines to be repaired. A relatively peaceful day. Sporadic skirmishes at Stup. The epidemic of enterocolitis is still going on.*

Sunday, 18th: *The town is heavily shelled. The barrage lasts from 10–12 a.m. with shells falling on almost every square metre of the town. The mills of "Žitopromet" are hit. All the factories for bread production are in flames. The surrounding*

for food in piles of rubbish around dustbins. They do not find any food. In Kralja Tomislava Street, some hundred metres away from the Republic's Presidency building, I watched a magpie that struggled with a tin of paste. On the stone wall, it persistently and skillfully tried to open the tin lid with its bill and claws. Then it pecked, pecked the empty inside of the tin... Struggle for survival sharpened selection.

We looked for a better aspect of resisting the misery that had struck us. We began to look at hunger in a different way. We realized we were microbiotic. Our menu consisted of bread, pastry and cereals. We ate quantities of fats and albumen below any minimum. We became camp inmates with scanty and uniform food. The city lost weight. The citizens grew thinner and thinner. This looked nice and charming at the beginning. Later it was not so. Good-looking women had more and more wrinkles. Men suddenly grew old. We wasted away. Docent Dr Svetlana Zec was explaining to us professionally: "All lunch packets for American soldiers, tins of meat and other things, contain lots of preservatives. These attack a completely "cleansed" organism that during these six months has weaned itself off the artificial additives, preservatives, colouring and antibiotics that we used to consume in juice, cheese and smoked meat products. They attack the liver, kidneys and gall bladder. Simply, our cleansed organism treats them as poison and they can produce carcerogenic effects.

What can we do? A lunch packet for one American soldier became a meal for at least a four–member family with a lot of rice and bread. Dr Zec advised us at the end of September: "First of all, we must keep what we have attained: a cleansed organism. Therefore, each new food, except rice, pastry and few vegetables, must be taken gradually to enable the organism to adapt. You ought to divide a tin or a lunch packet into a few meals or days rather than 'surprise' your body suddenly by its contents.

"Another golden rule of nutrition under these circumstances is: eat five or six times a day, never once or twice. You should also have a sip of liquid after each swallow: boiled water or tea. In this way the food will stay longer in the stomach. It will be absorbed gradually. The feeling of satisfaction lasts longer."

Who cared about all this? We were happy when we got an extra spoonful of food. Our bowels growled. Bread, macaroni or rice could not satisfy us. Nor did Liza, a female Scottish sheepdog belonging to a friend of mine, accept such food. He had to open the last tin of meat for her. After months of hunger we tasted our first mouthfuls of cheese. Humanitarian aid arrived in the city, but intermittently. The radio often announced: "Not a gram of food has arrived in the city." The sky was not kind to us. In September, when

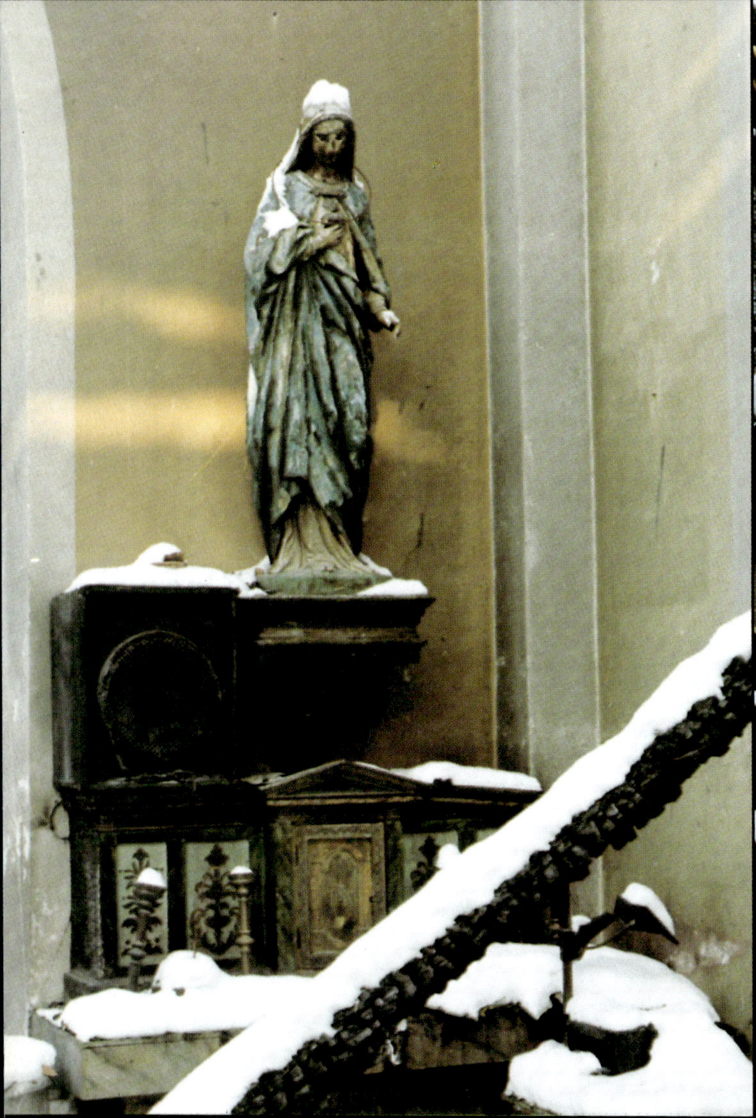

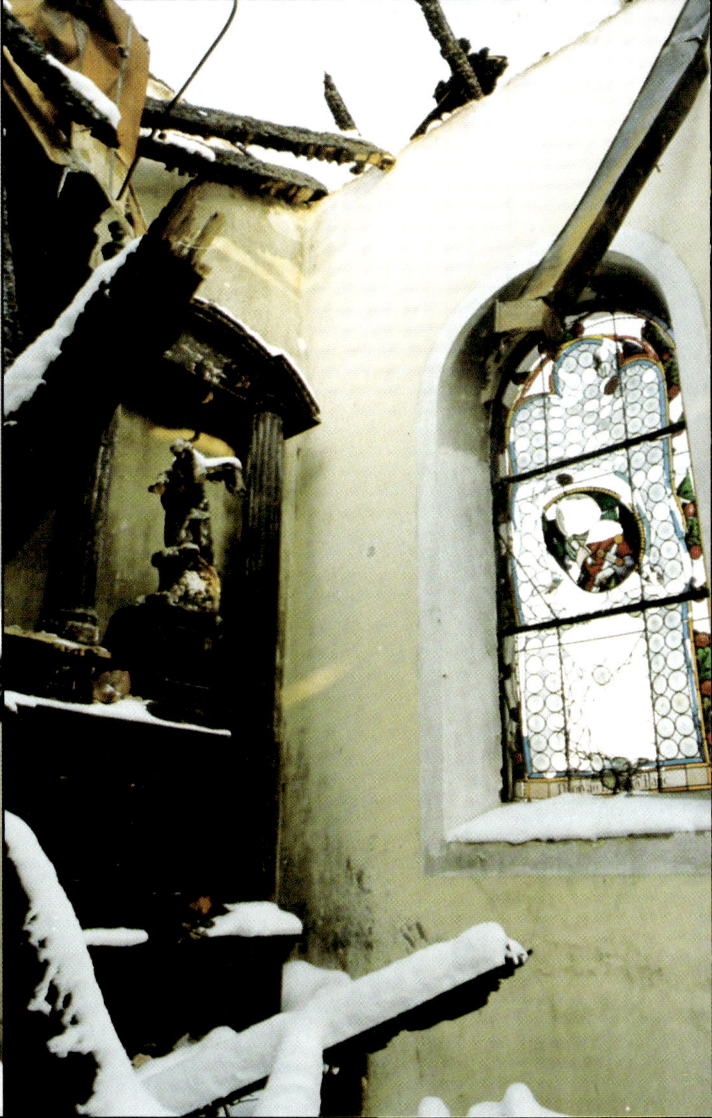

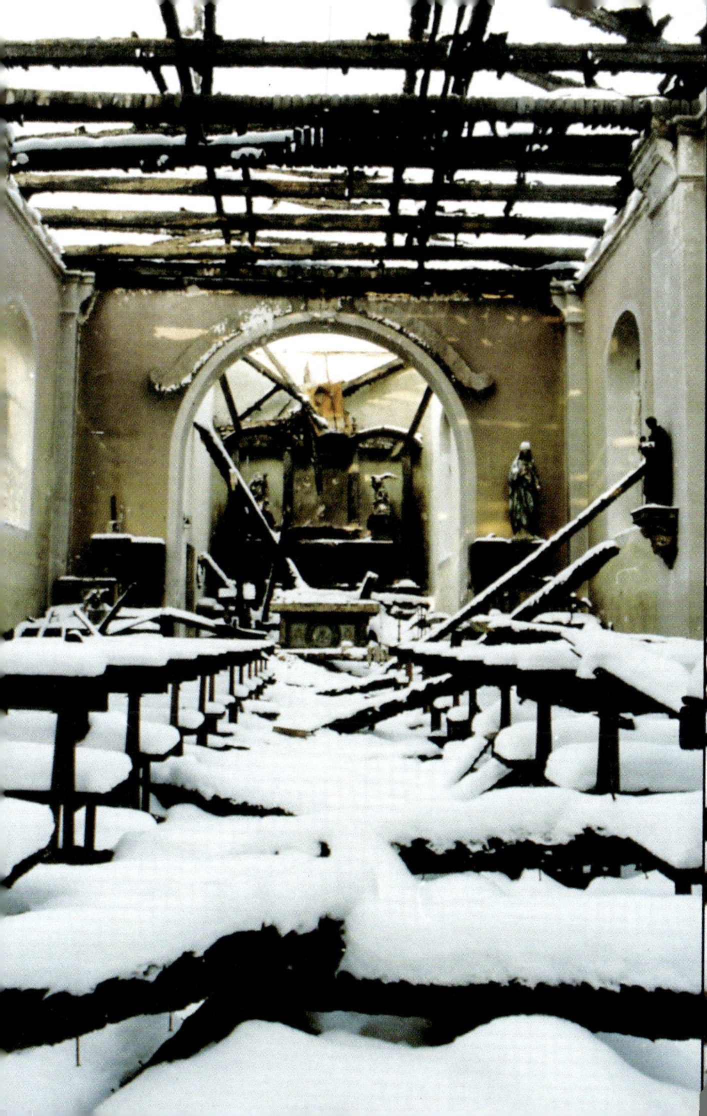

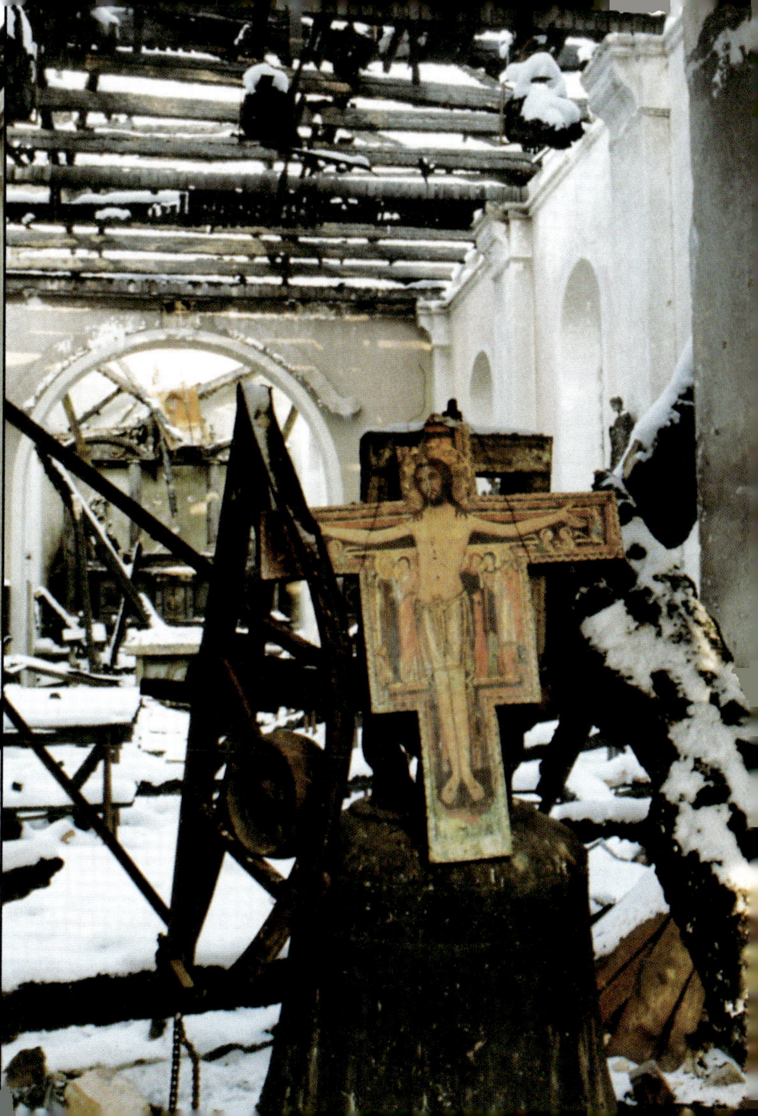

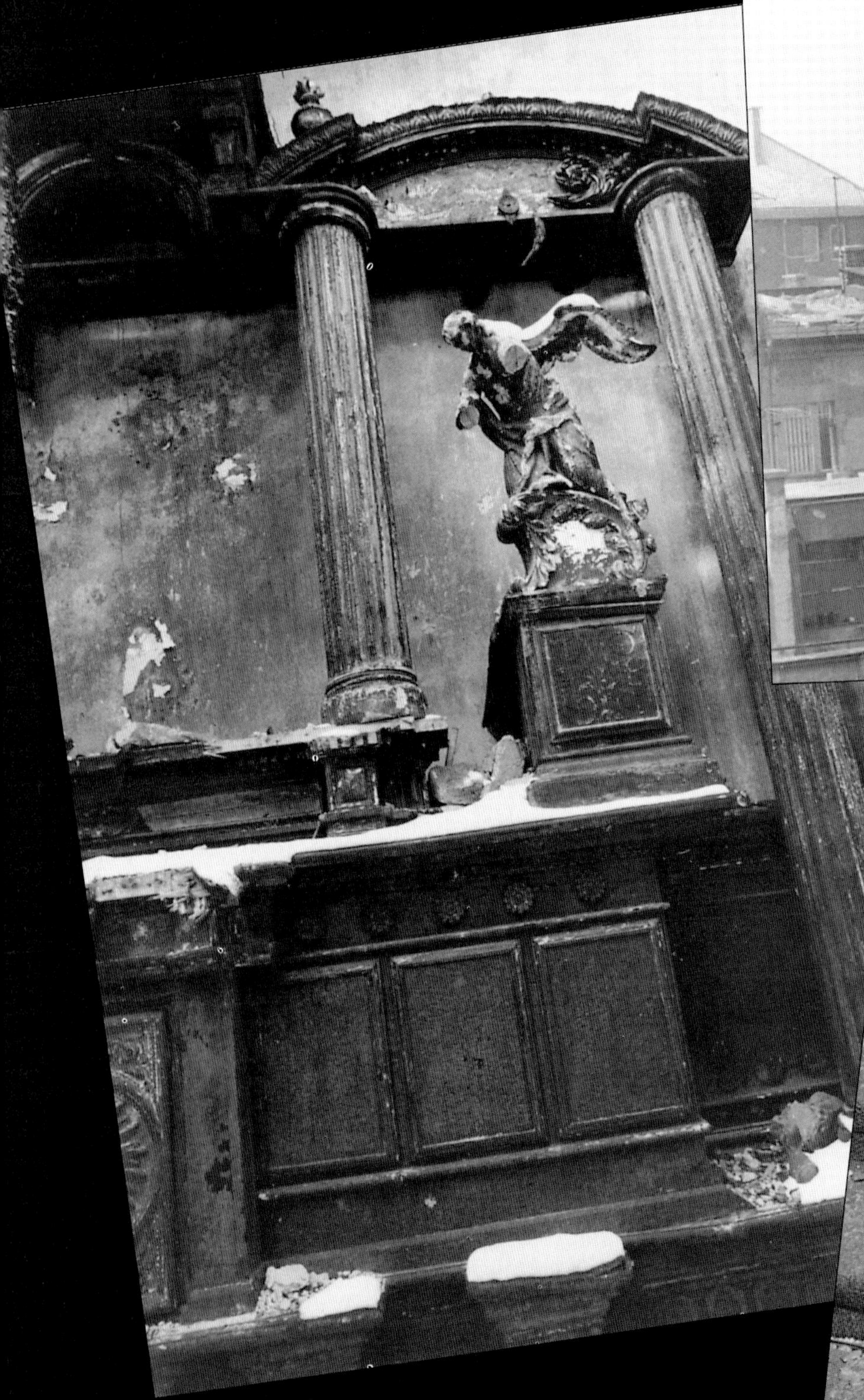

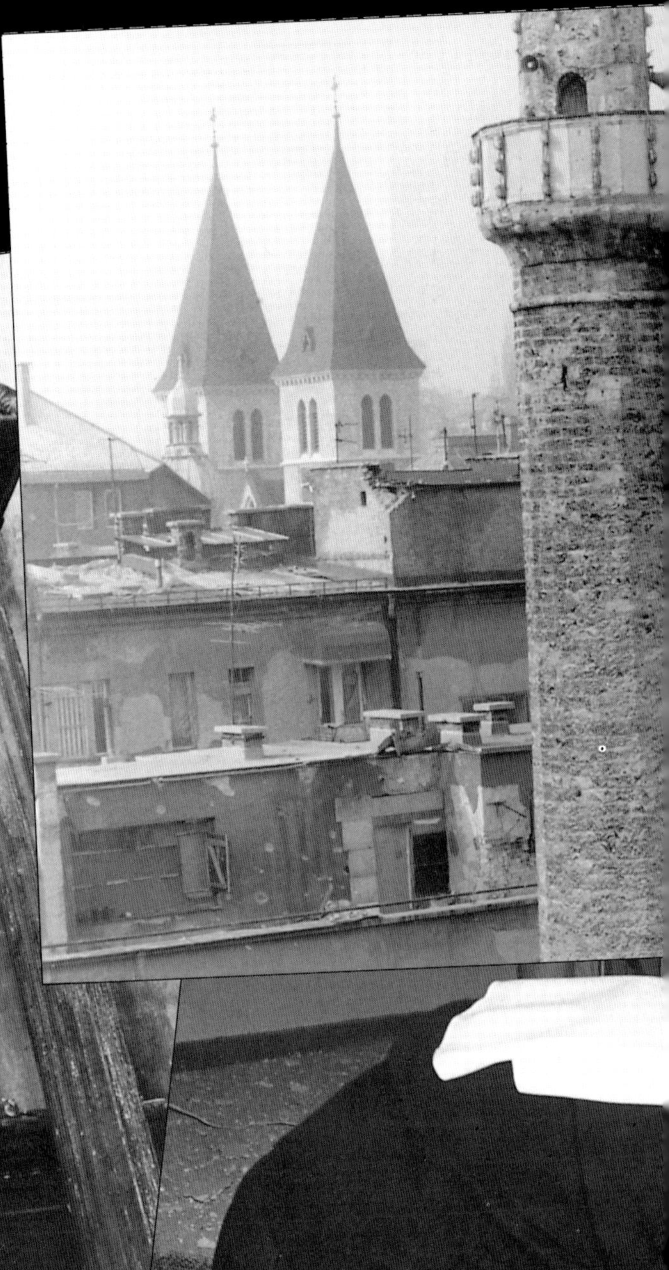

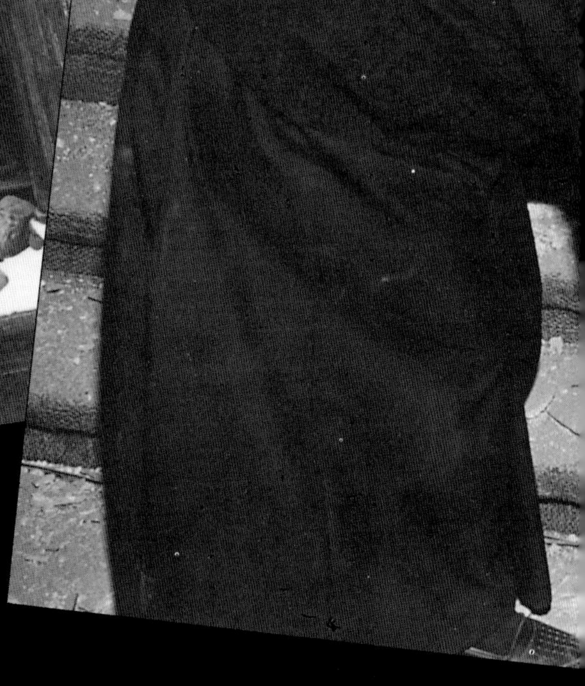

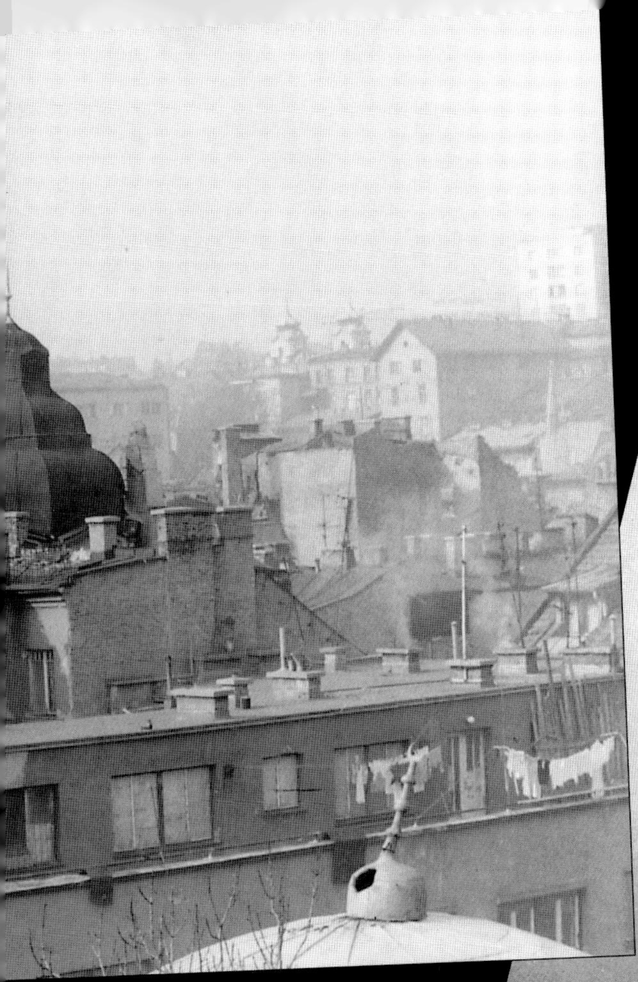

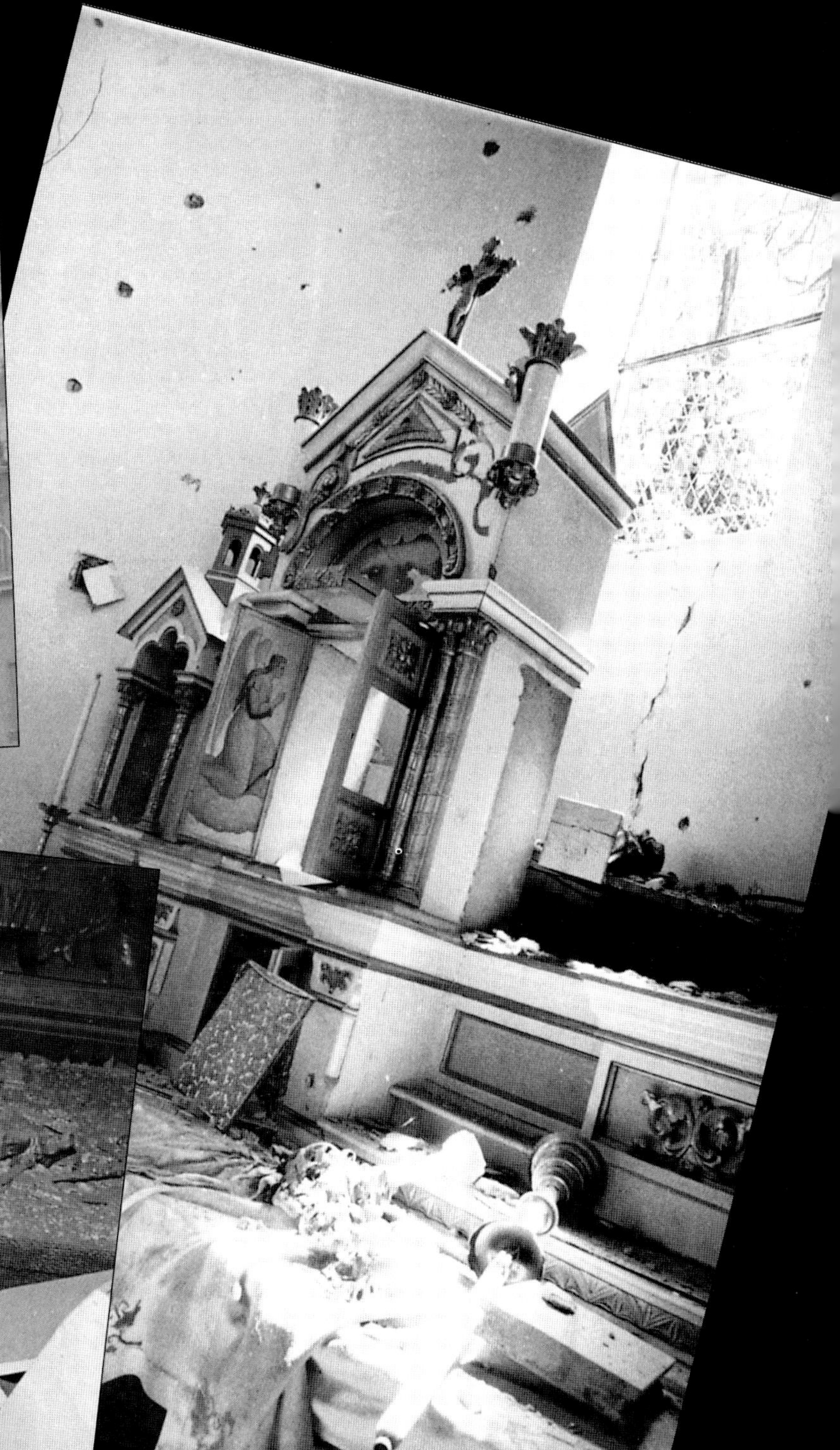

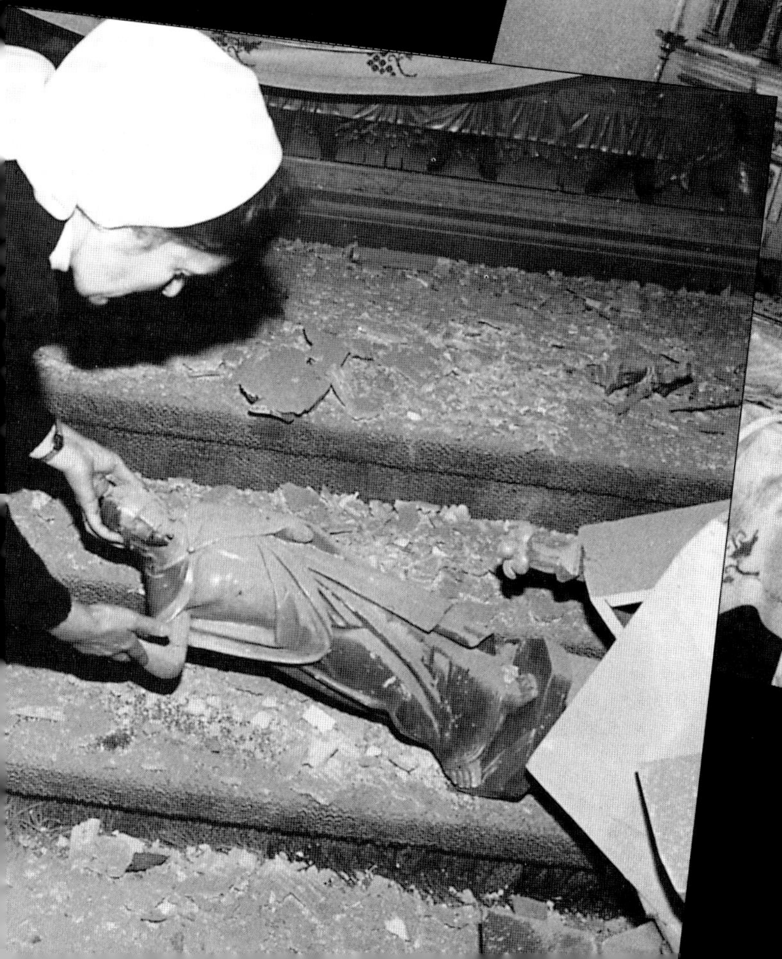

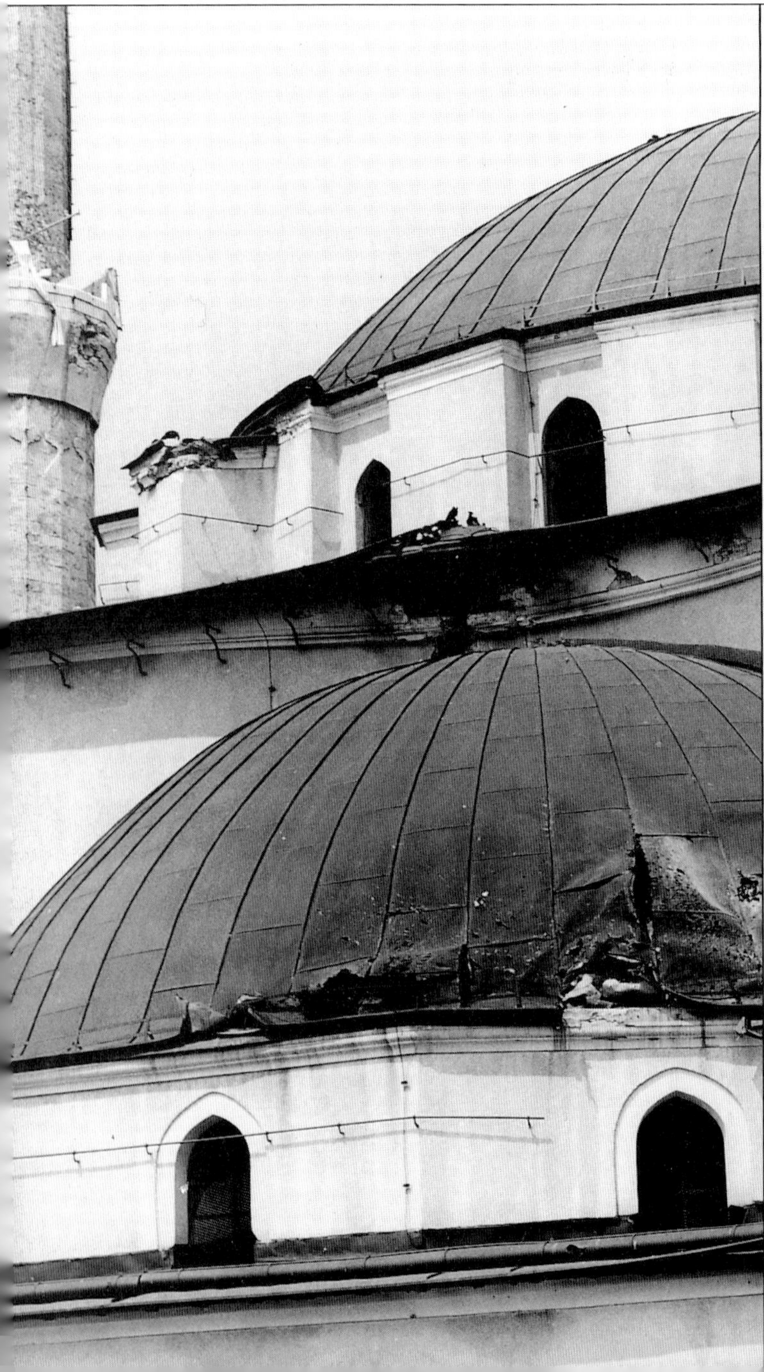
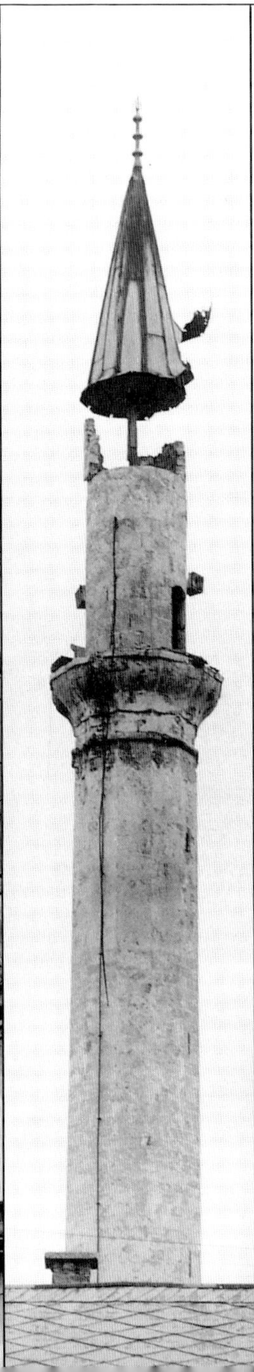
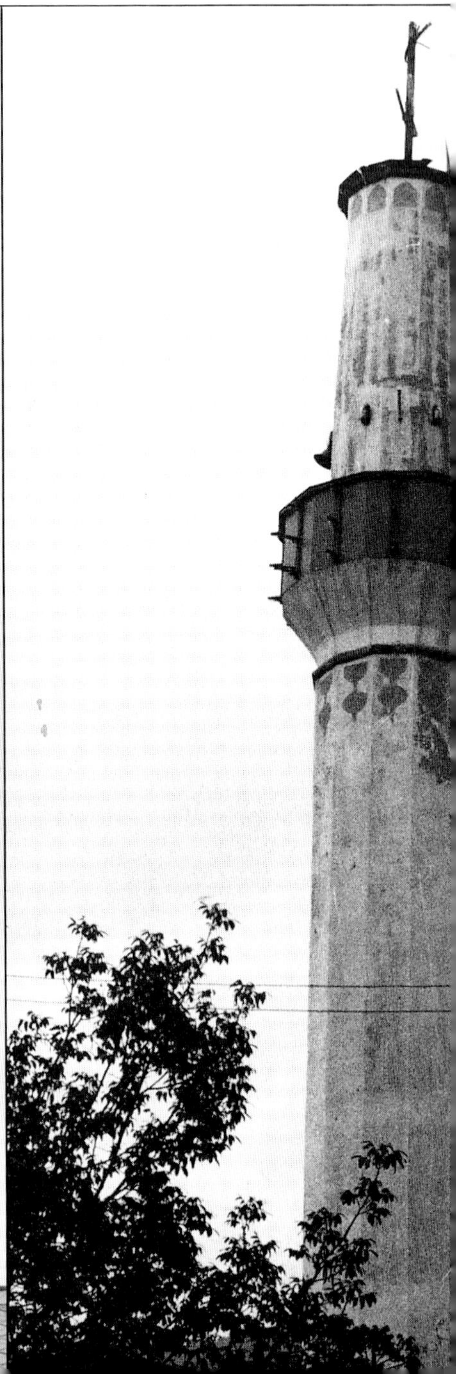

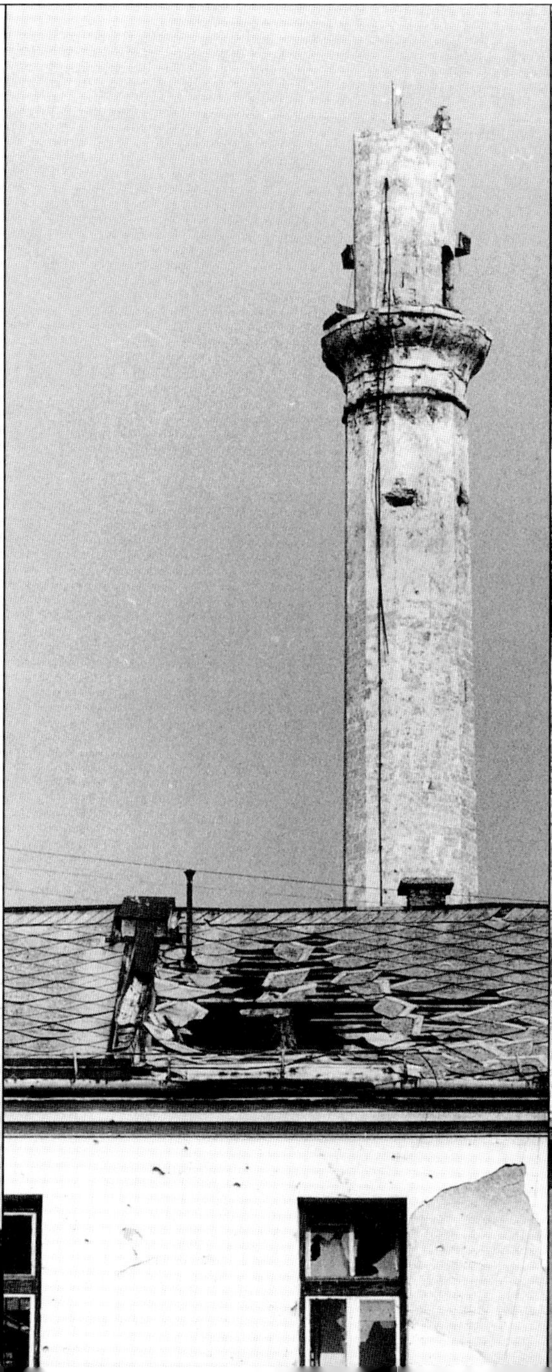
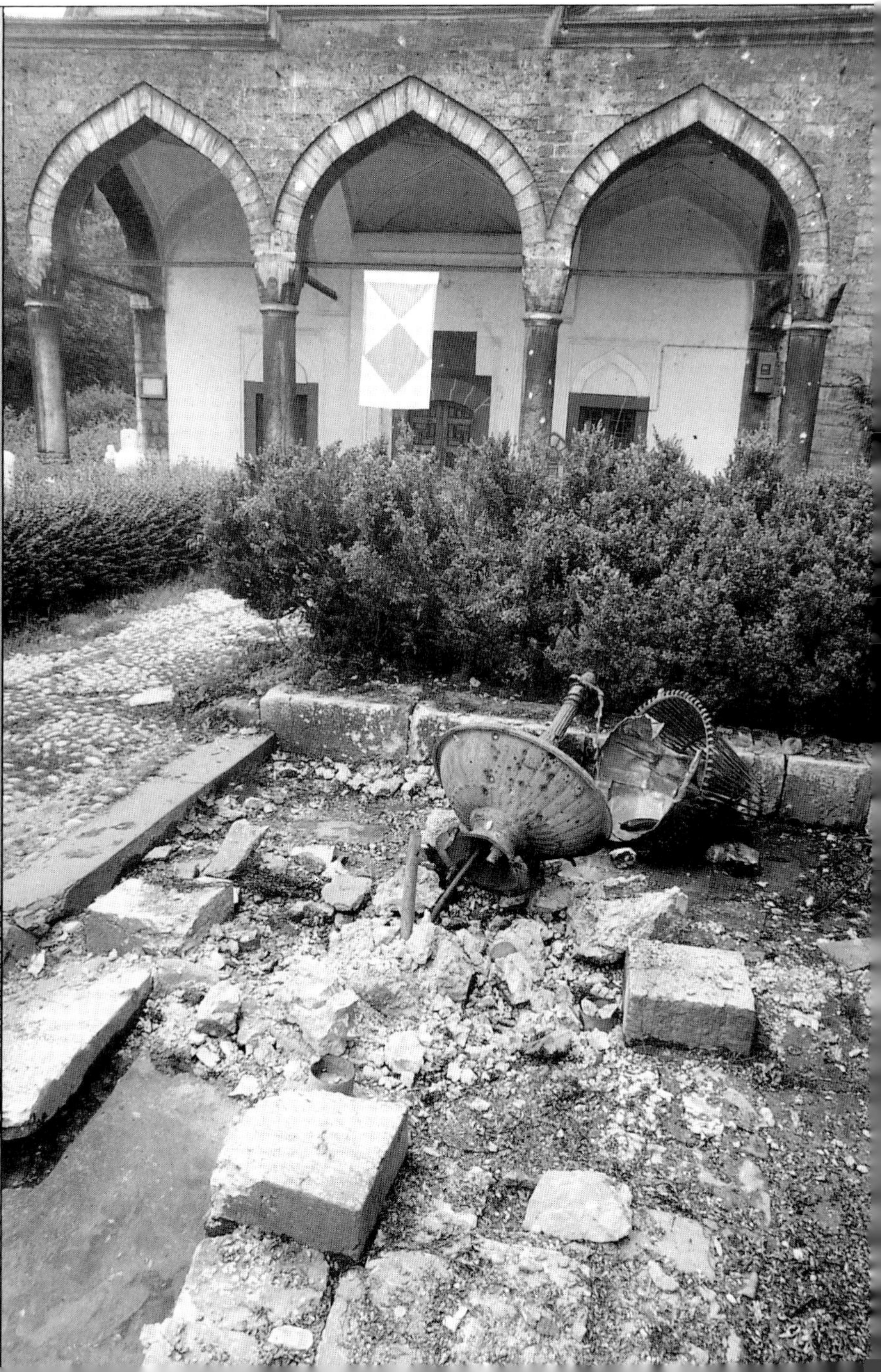

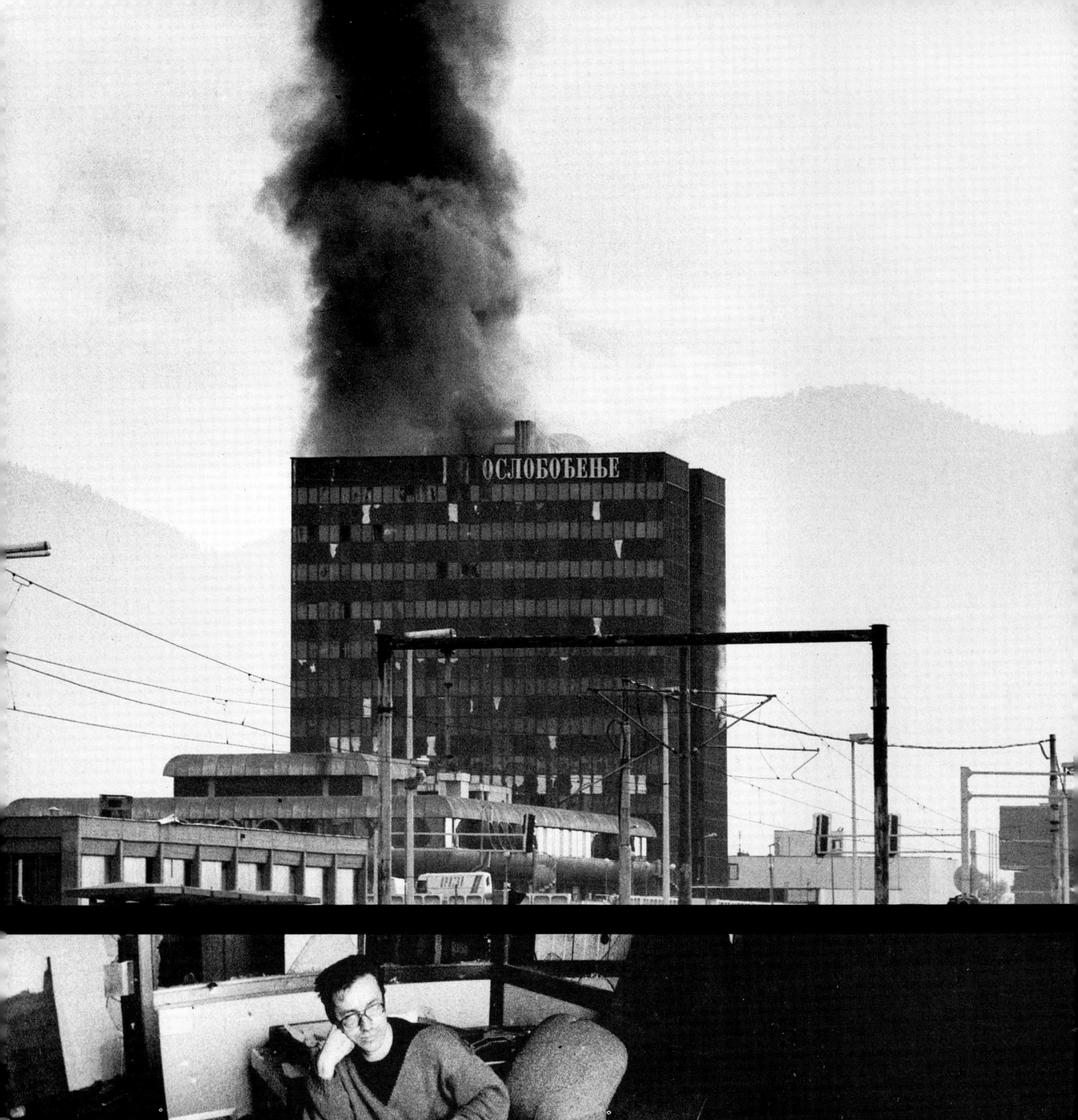
ОСЛОБОЂЕЊЕ

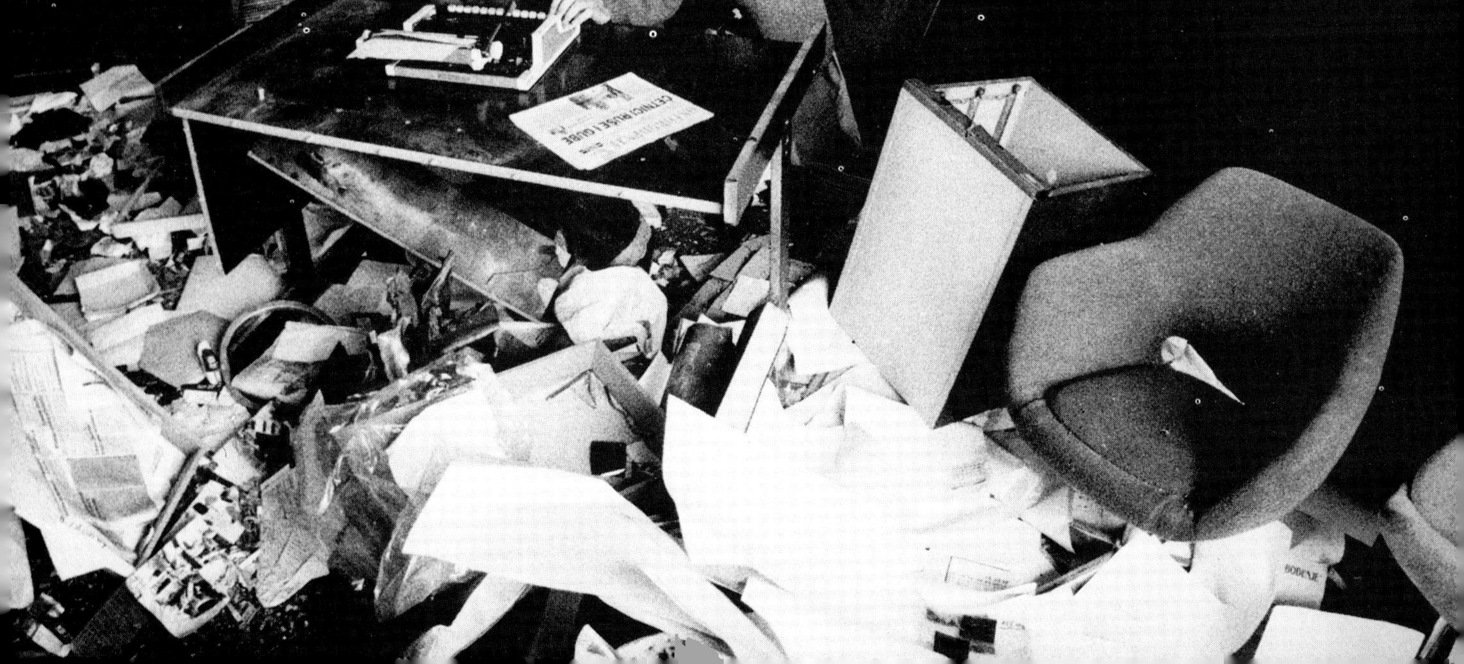

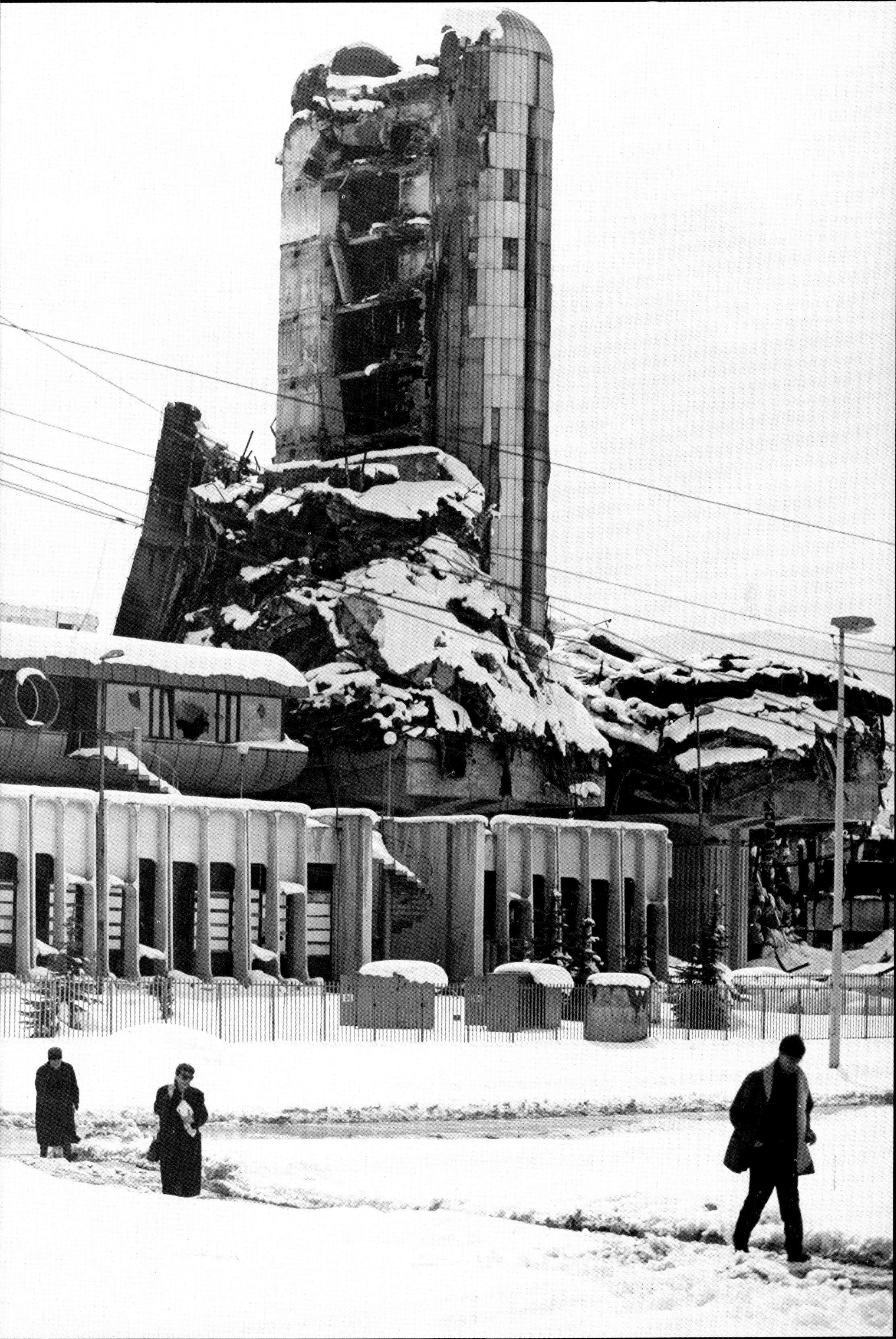

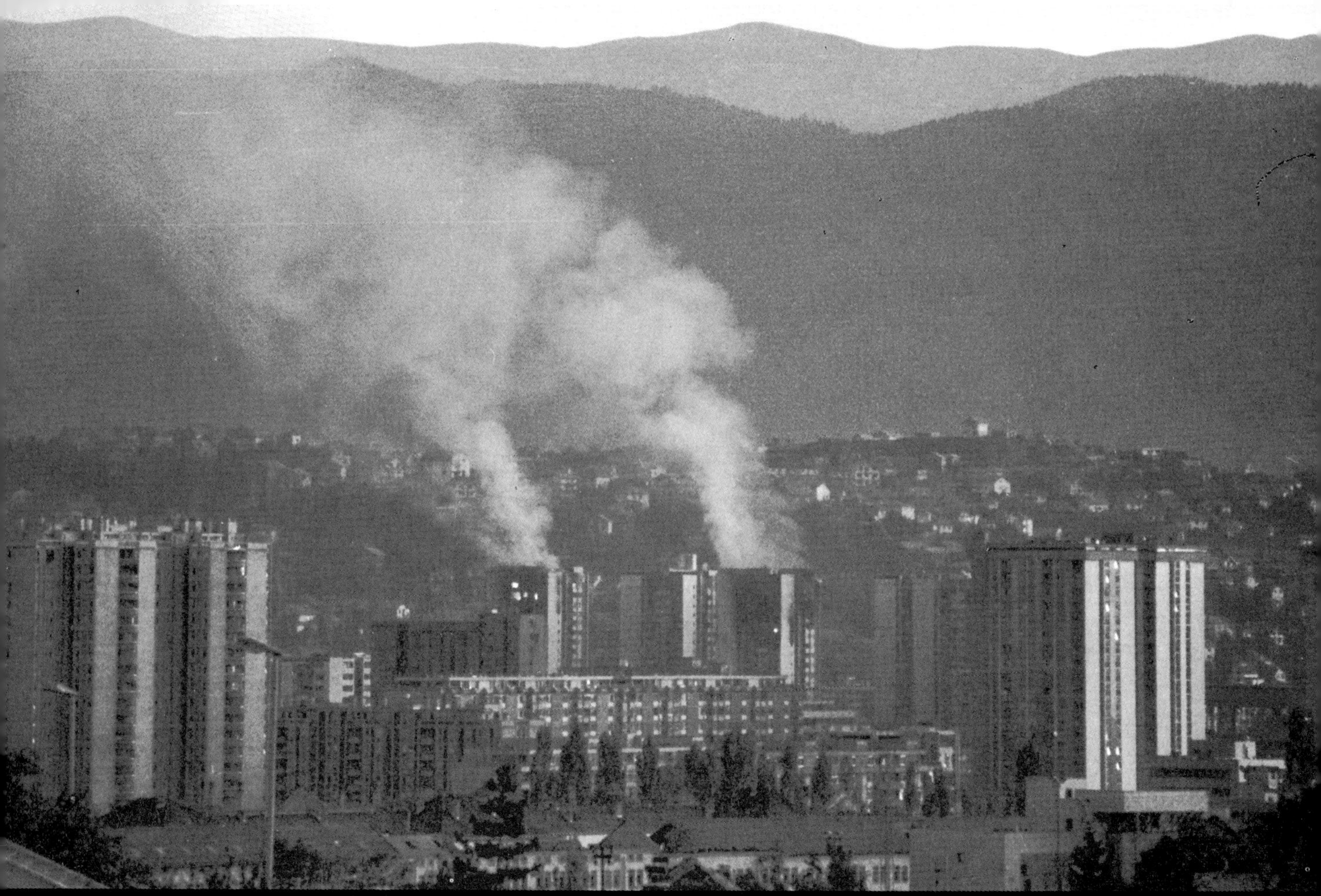

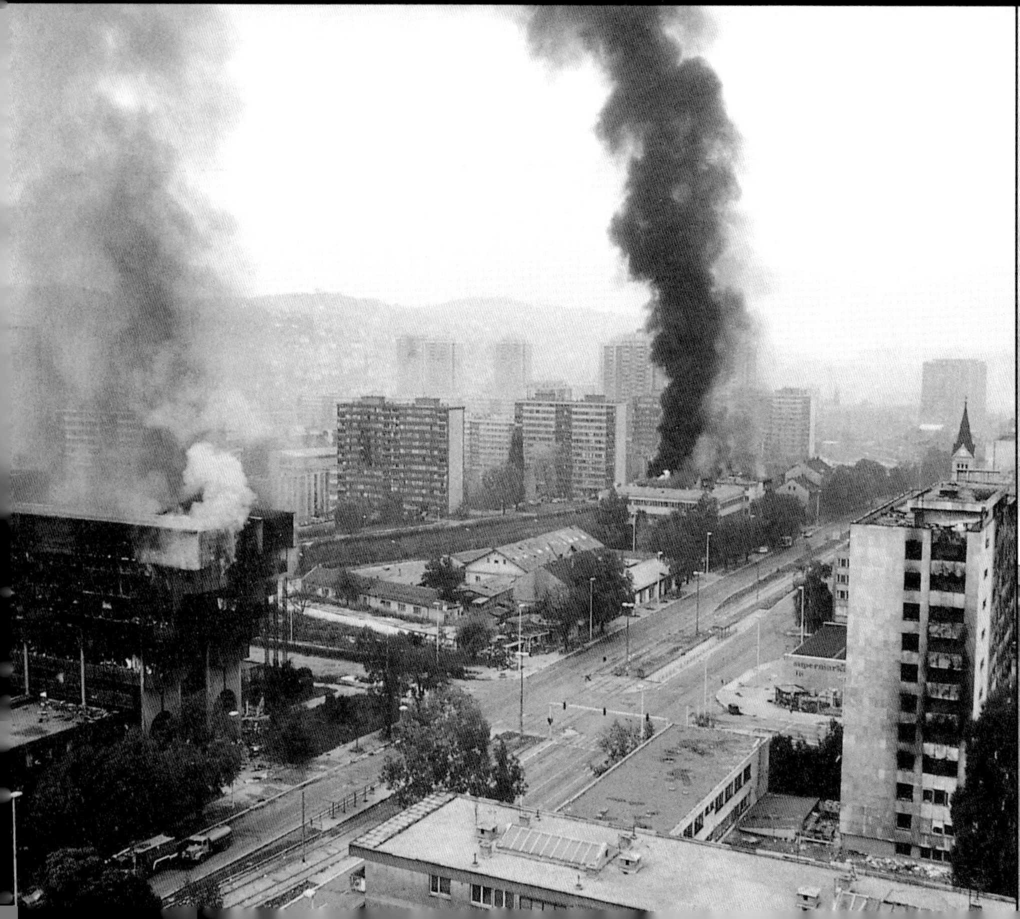

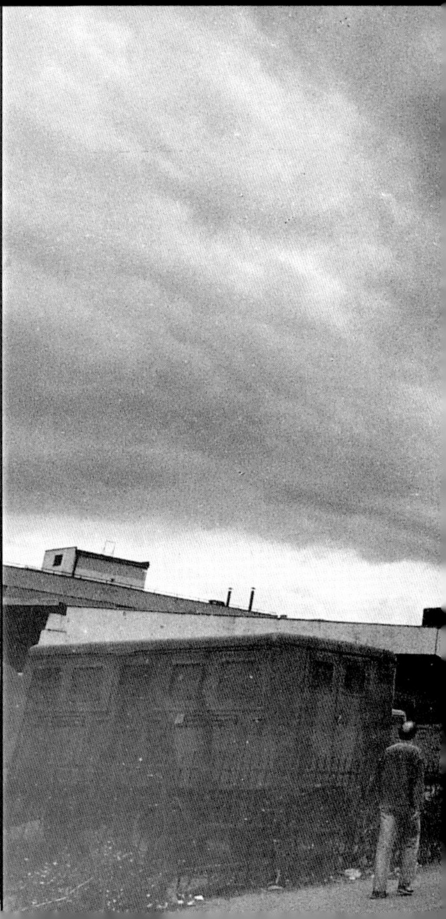

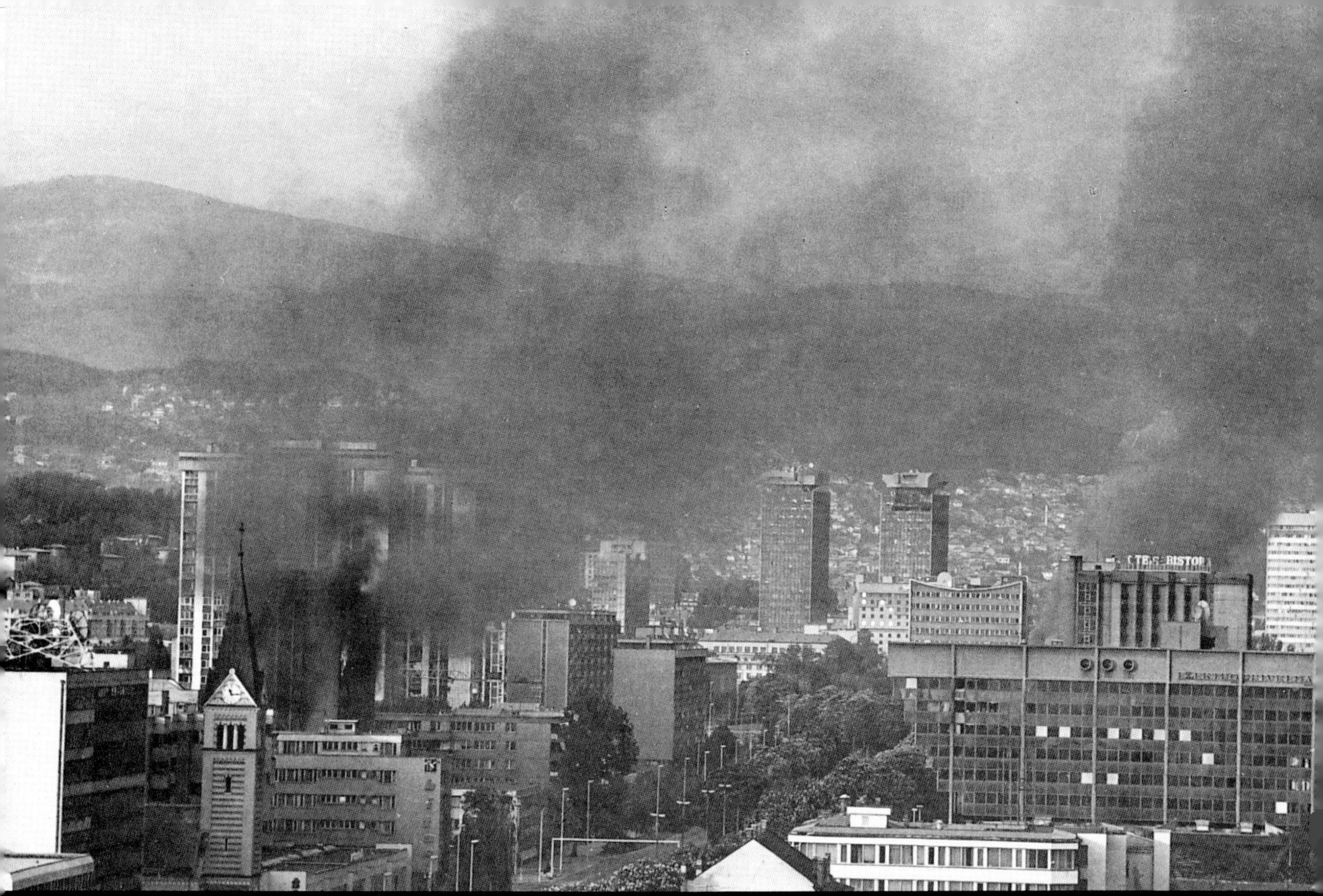

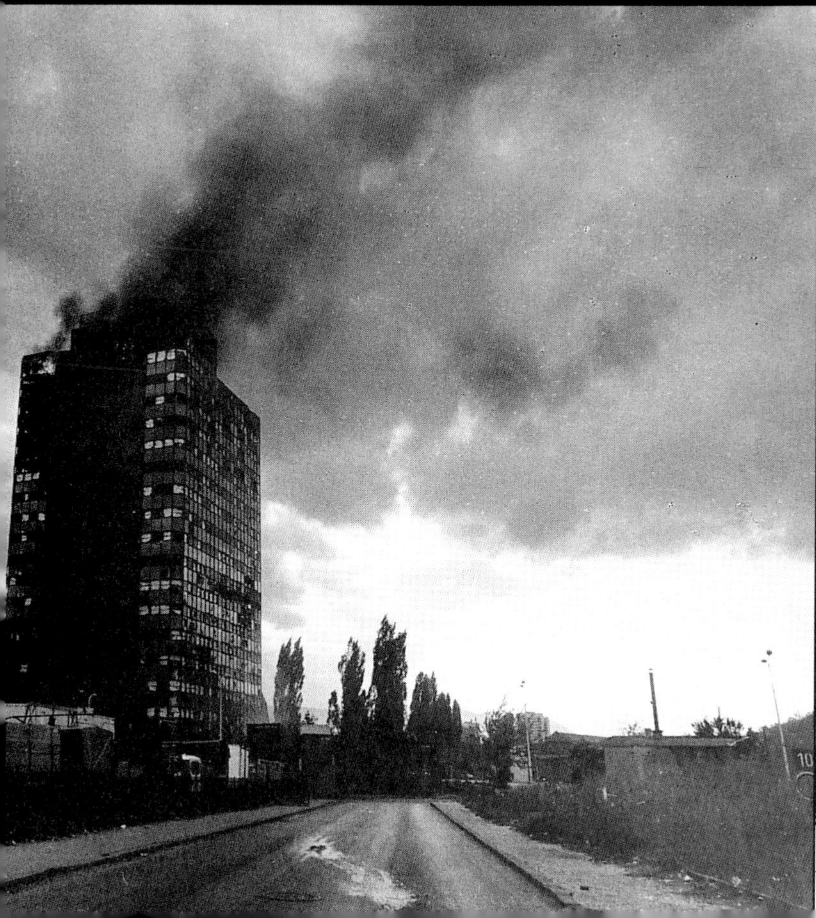

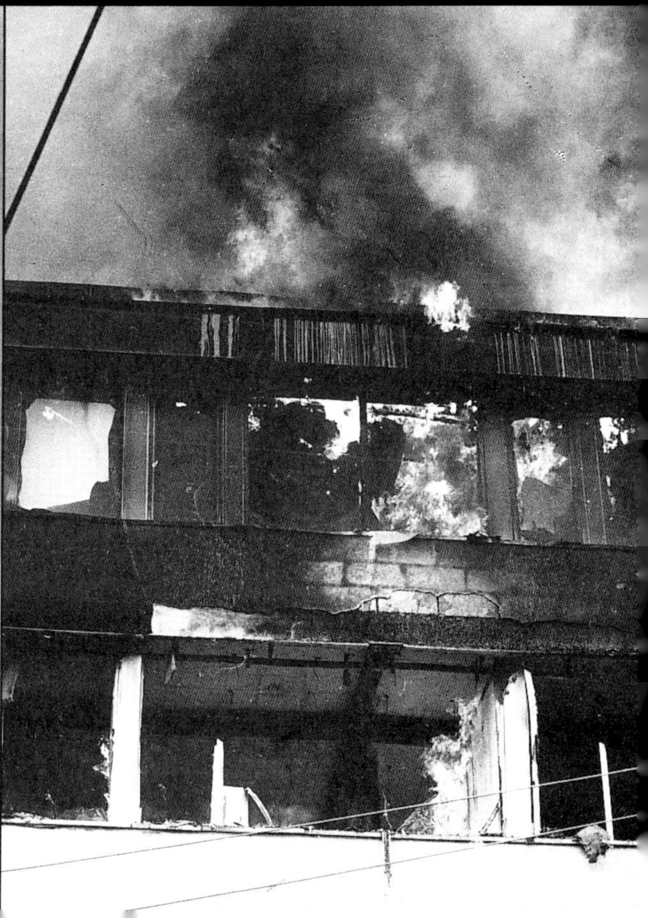

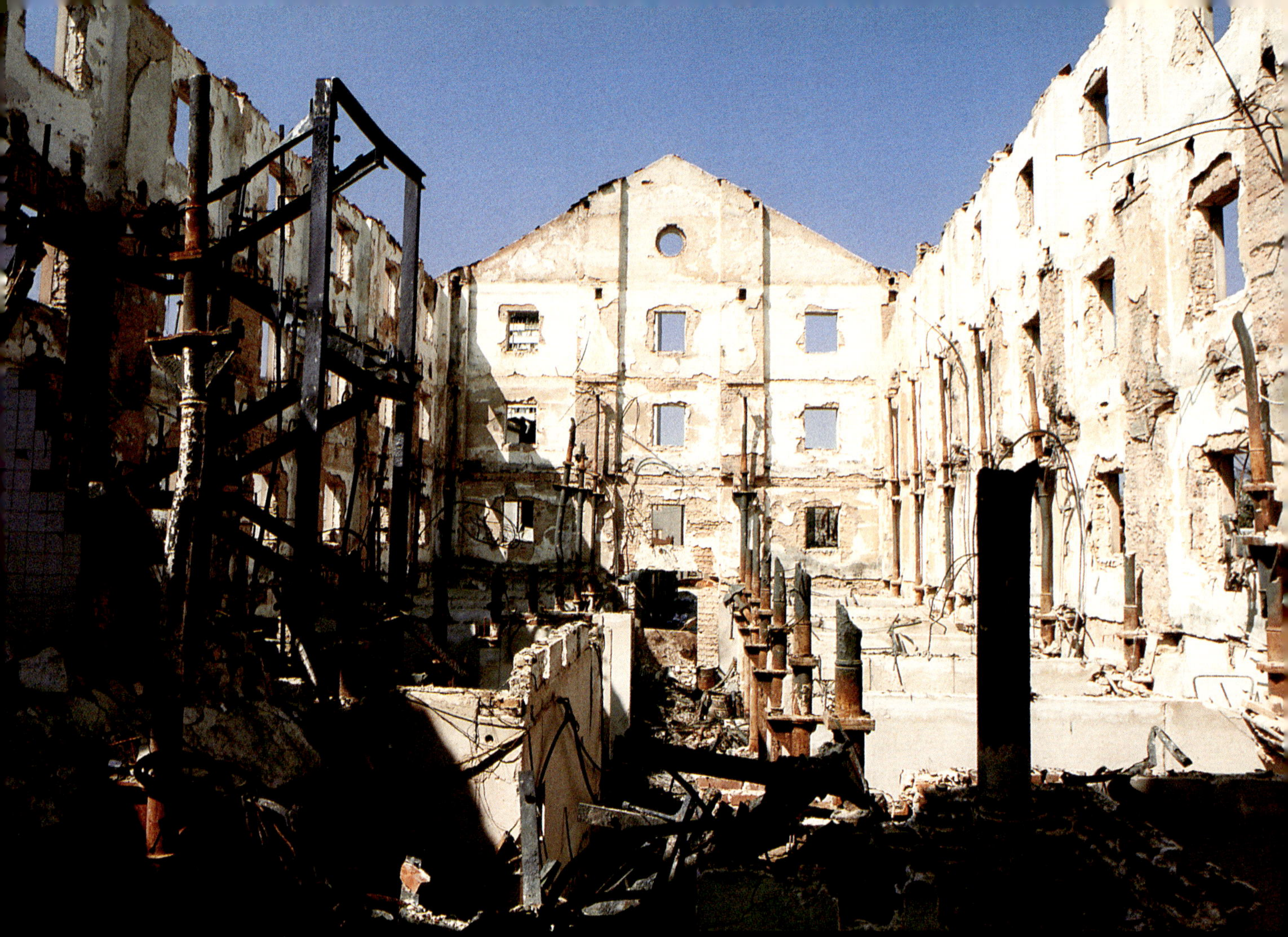

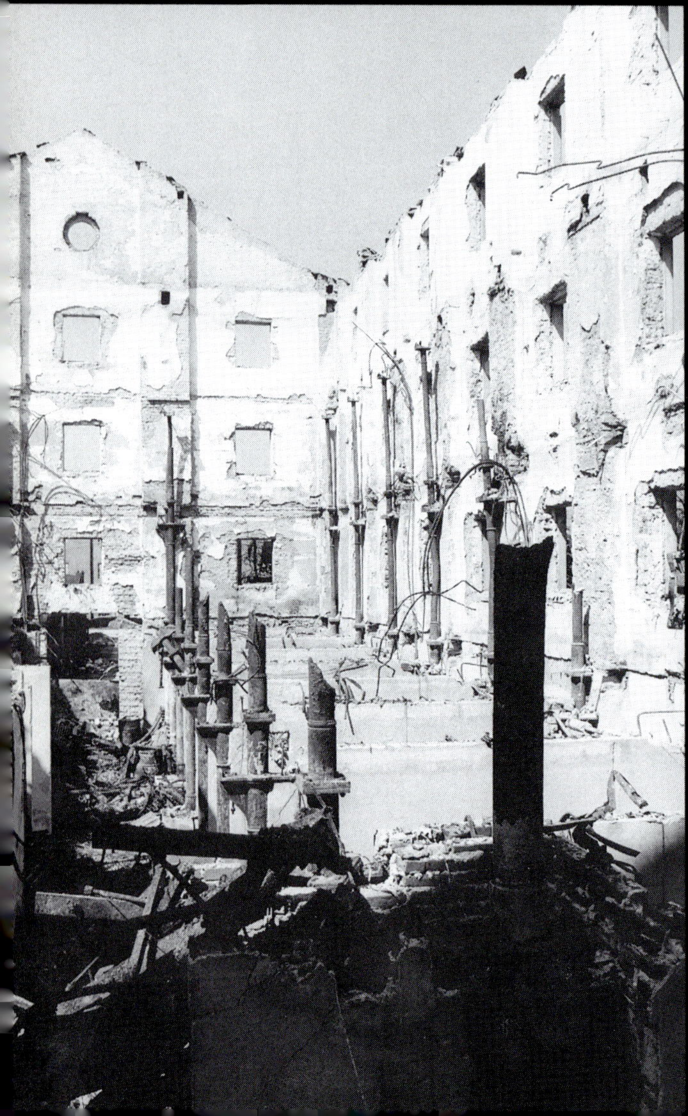

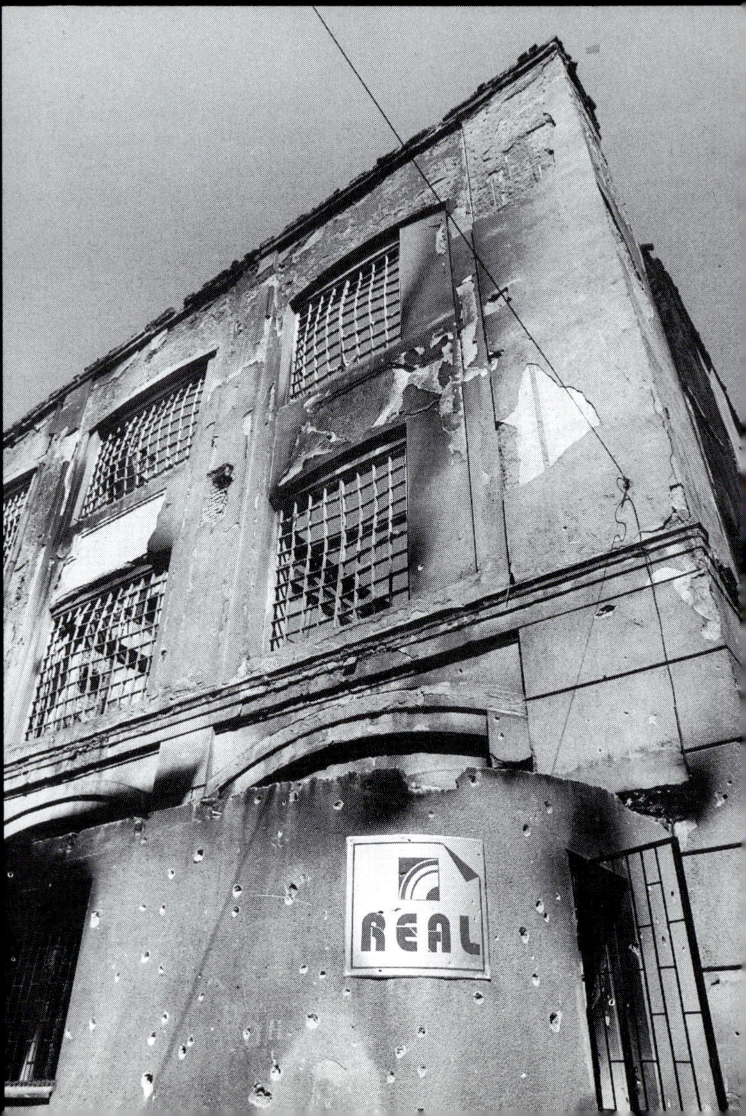
REAL

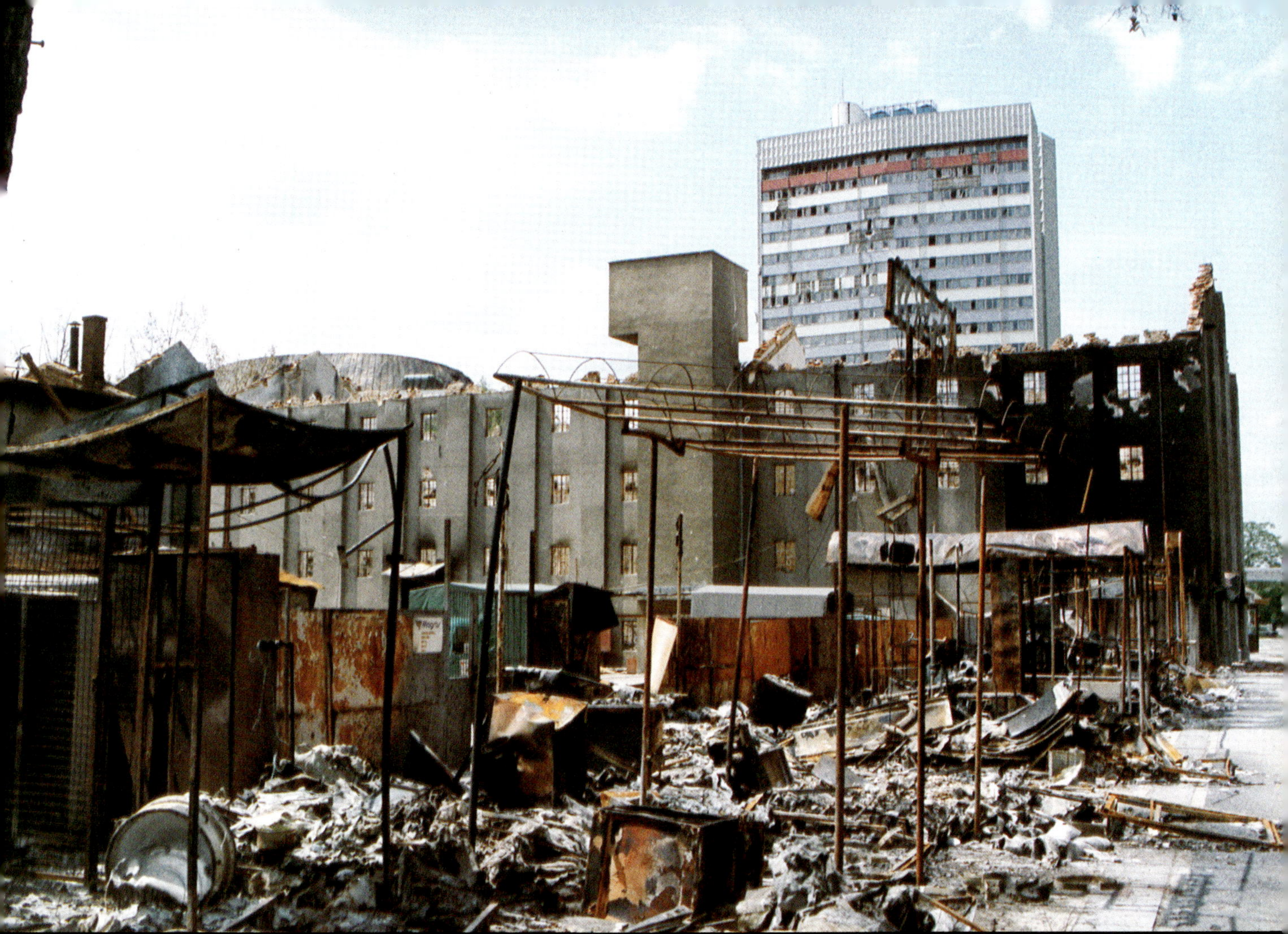
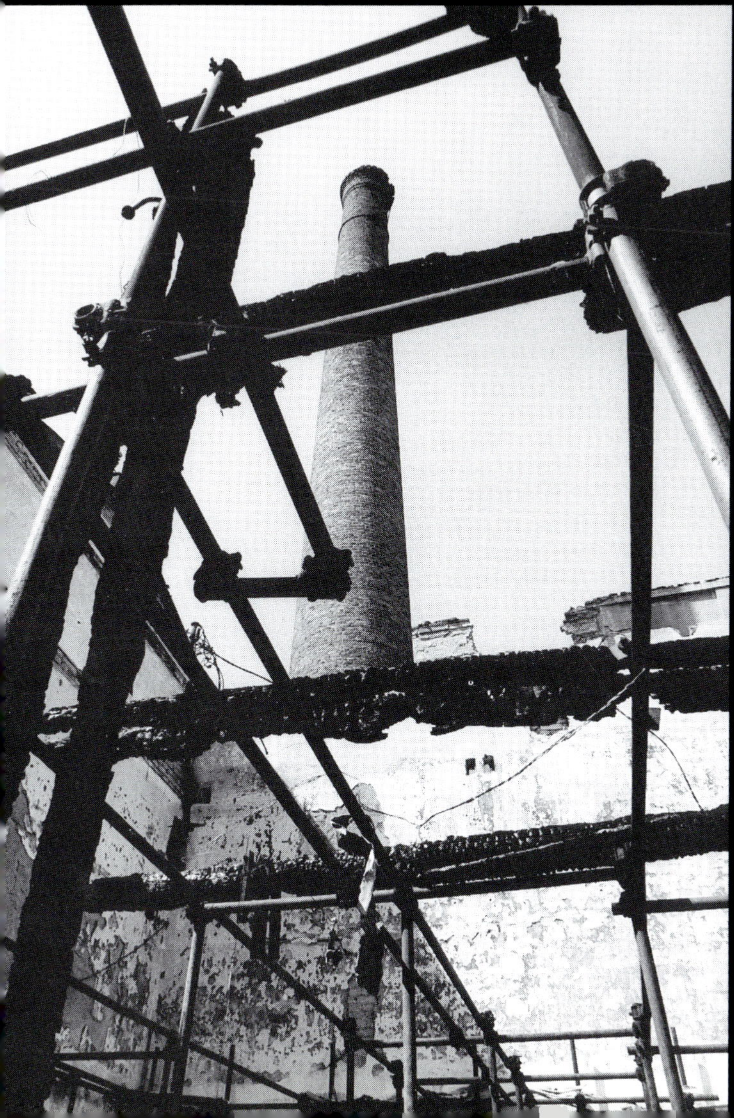
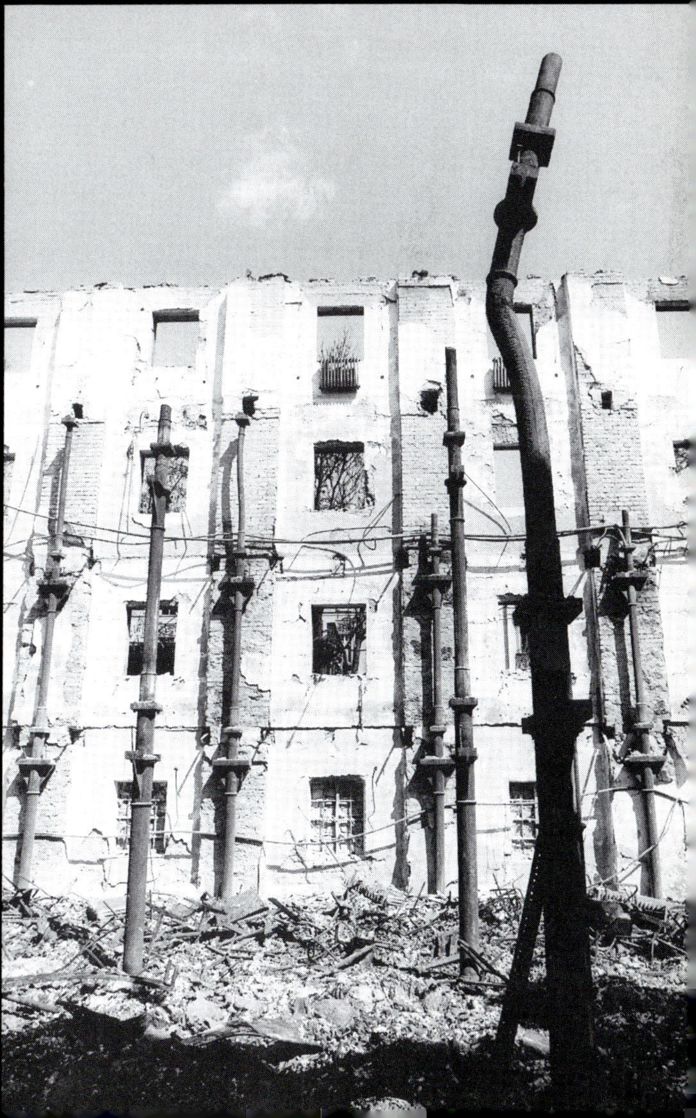

market counters are traditionally overloaded with vegetables, the city had nothing to eat. We spent the time preparing fruit and vegetables for winter and waiting for the alms from the world. A Jewish saying could not apply to this city: Ken in trapo krepi toda buenu li paresi. (To the one who grew up in rags everything looks fine.) We were closer to that one: The stomach does not have a window.

How can I explain to the soldiers with blue helmets that we were knocked down into the mud of misery, that we never used to be as we are now, that such a misfortune has befallen Sarajevo for the first time in more than five centuries of its existence. In the darkness of Hades the archaeologist Robert Munro consoles me. He was at the Congress of Archaeologists and Anthropologists in Sarajevo in 1894. He repeats a sentence from his book for me: "The most hurried atmosphere is at the food market. Here, in the morning you can see offered on the counters along the streets: poultry, meat, fish, vegetables, fruits, etc." Captain Edmund Spencer speaks over his shoulder. In 1850 he wrote: "A rich person's meal usually consists of ten to twenty dishes, and even more: among sweets there is cream-pie, a mixture of eggs, milk and honey, and this is always served."

How far away all this is! I read to them a June letter from the Dobrinja children. They sent it to George Bush and François Mitterrand. "Hunger has already walked in through the doors of our dark and humid cellars. We are not sure whether we shall have enough strength to resist it.

"As much as we crave chocolate and bananas, which we are entitled to after all, so much we crave bread and freedom.

"We know you are the president of a country where all the children are fed, free and happy. Do not allow us to forget what the smell of bread is like, how the sun shines and what it is like to be free." Confused, Munro and Spencer look at me. I explain to them that they are the current presidents of two most powerful countries, the USA and France. They cannot understand why the Sarajevans walk the path of hunger.

The only certain thing we got was portions of death. They did not get any smaller. I am not sure if the news of the 19th that the undertaker's stopped working could have touched us. There is no more timber for the coffins and tabuts, for pyramids and crosses. Shortage of oil had stopped the hearses. In order to bury our dear ones we had to get five litres of petrol or oil. Where from? I do not know, but we had to.

Everything was being pulled down. On September 14th the second skyscraper of the "Oslobođenje" newspaper publishing house collapsed. Tank shells and fires pulled down the mast of a ship that did not want to stop. It did not

structures and silos have hundreds of holes in them made by armour-piercing shells, projectiles from rocket launchers and incendiary shells. In no more than 2 hours 42 people are taken to the Traumatology Clinic with shrapnel wounds. The State Hospital is hit by five artillery shells. 72,000 square metres of hospital space has been either destroyed or captured and 2,400 hospital beds are out of service. UNICEF enables the evacuation of 3 wounded children to Germany for further treatment and rehabilitation.

Monday, 19th: *The city's telephone lines do not operate. Local buses do not run because of a lack of fuel. A relatively quiet day. Occasional shelling. The transmission line near Vogošća is demolished again. Still without electricity. Owing to a shortage of gauze in hospitals operations are in danger of being completely stopped. 9 killed and 108 injured in Sarajevo.*

Tuesday, 20th: *The outskirts of Stari grad municipality, Hotonj and Kobilja glava are shelled. The UNHCR cancels the road convoys of humanitarian aid after last week's incident on the Mostar-Sarajevo route. On the black market 1 kg of coffee is 40 DM, 1 litre of cooking oil 20 DM, a jar (800 gr) of lard 15 DM, 1 kg of pumpkins 20 DM, 1 kg of beetroot 6,000 BH dinars (an average pension is 3,000 dinars) and a second-hand kitchen stove 200 DM.*

Wennesday, 21st: *Some parts of the town have electricity. The town gets water as well. A relatively quiet day. Vasin han and Novo Sarajevo are shelled.*

A special UN envoy, Tadeusz Mazowiecki, is in Sarajevo. Satish Nambiar, commander in chief of UNPROFOR is in Sarajevo. The B-H dinar is devalued. The official exchange rate is 550 BH dinars to a German mark.

Thursday, 22nd: *21 killed and 38 injured. Artillery targets Stup and Otes II, Nova Breka and Sedrenik. Local buses have not been running for seven days now owing to the lack of fuel. Sarajevo airport opens after a one-day break.*

Friday, 23rd: *Negotiations start among the spokesmen of the Commands of the B-H Armed Forces, the HVO (the Croatian Defence Council) and the aggressor's army under the auspices of UNPROFOR. In the 200 days of the war 127,751 citizens are either missing or killed.*

Saturday, 24th: *Hospitals are without medicine and food for the patients, even for new-born babies. 6 killed and 42 injured in Sarajevo. So far 19 UNPROFOR people have been killed and 250 injured in B-H.*

Sunday, 25th: *Artillery fires sporadically and not so intensively from Borije and Mirkovići at the autskirts of the town. Local transport is blocked – no fuel for the buses.*

Monday, 26th: *Shelling of the town and suffering of innocent citizens. In the "Hall of the Lilies", the union of the resistance movement, veterans of the district of Sarajevo hold their inaugural meeting. Nineteen foreign aeroplanes with humanitarian aid land at the*

consent to sink. The staircase with its lifts is ghostly, while on the lower deck a newspaper is being created and printed. It comes out every day. On its pages Bajram Danoš speaks desperately in the name of the Sarajevo Romanies: "I know we're all underprivileged. We receive humanitarian assistance. In my family we are twelve and when I get twelve tins what does one tin a day mean for the twelve of us? We need at least twelve loaves of bread. I could buy them somehow before this. I used to bring them home, the children ate them and were still hungry. Now I give them a tin I get as humanitarian aid, the children eat it up and they are still hungry. Today I can't boil bran for them either, because I have no fuel. We have no food, either. We have nothing, and there's nobody to beg from. They're all underprivileged and have nothing." With hopes and promises that they could leave, they sold their cookers and got ready for the trip last summer. They stayed until the winter.

The city was packing its bags. Many were getting ready to flee. Farther from Hell. To go as far as possible. Convoys were announced and then cancelled. They were leaving but they did not go out. Children, the sick, the old and the frightened wanted to leave. They could not. We are destined to be here and together. It is here that we met, wondering, the first parcels for the city. They arrived on September 24th. Their contents were strictly controlled. They must not contain smoked meat products, coffee or vegetables. Cerberus kept Sarajevo under control. Cerberus created the circumstances in which parcel crumbs fall into our outstretched palms.

There is a ray of light.

For three days, starting from September 11th, the city resisted the imposed lethargy, hunger and death. "SEFARD '92" was taking place. Sarajevo commemorated five centuries of the Jews' expulsion from Spain and Portugal, from the western lands (S'fard), with a cultural event. The city and the remaining small Jewish community reaffirmed an old sentence of a Belgrade Sephardic Jew: "Lus di Saraj ne aj i sjeti partis de el mundo." (There are not such people as these in Sarajevo on seven sides of the world.) Sarajevo, here, in the most difficult year of its existence lamented one of the most tragic and painful episodes of European and world history. The city that had eight synagogues and which was called Jerušalajin ketan, or Little Jerusalem, was proud of its fellow citizens. The most frequently quoted sigil of a Sarajevo qadi of 1557 was brought to temptation. It witnessed to the presence of Jews in the city, which was taken as the date of the Sephardim's arrival in the city. According to Moise Franz, the year of arrival of some thirty families of Portugese Jews was 1539. Others claim that the Jews have been present in these parts since ancient times. Evidence of this is the discovery of an

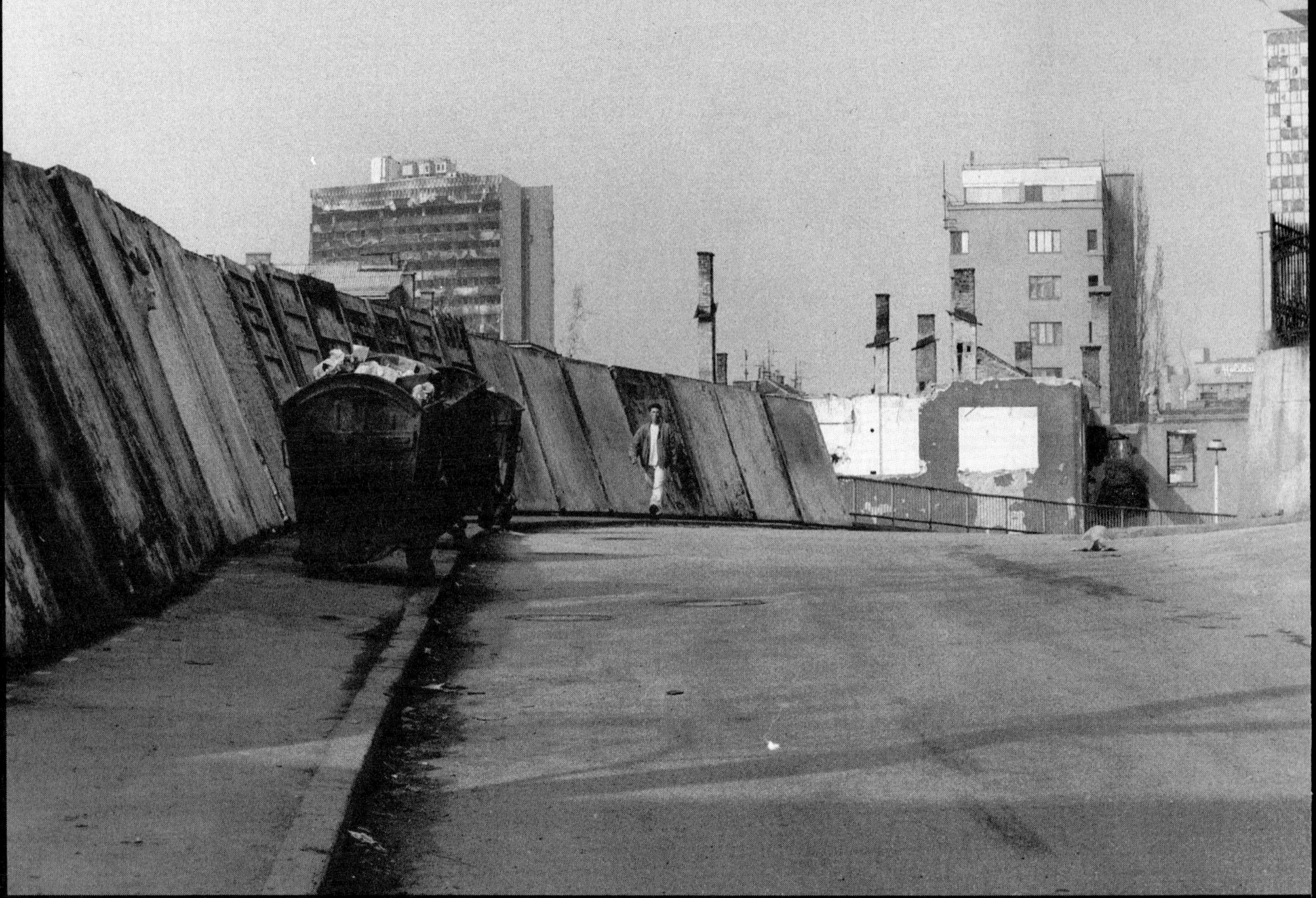

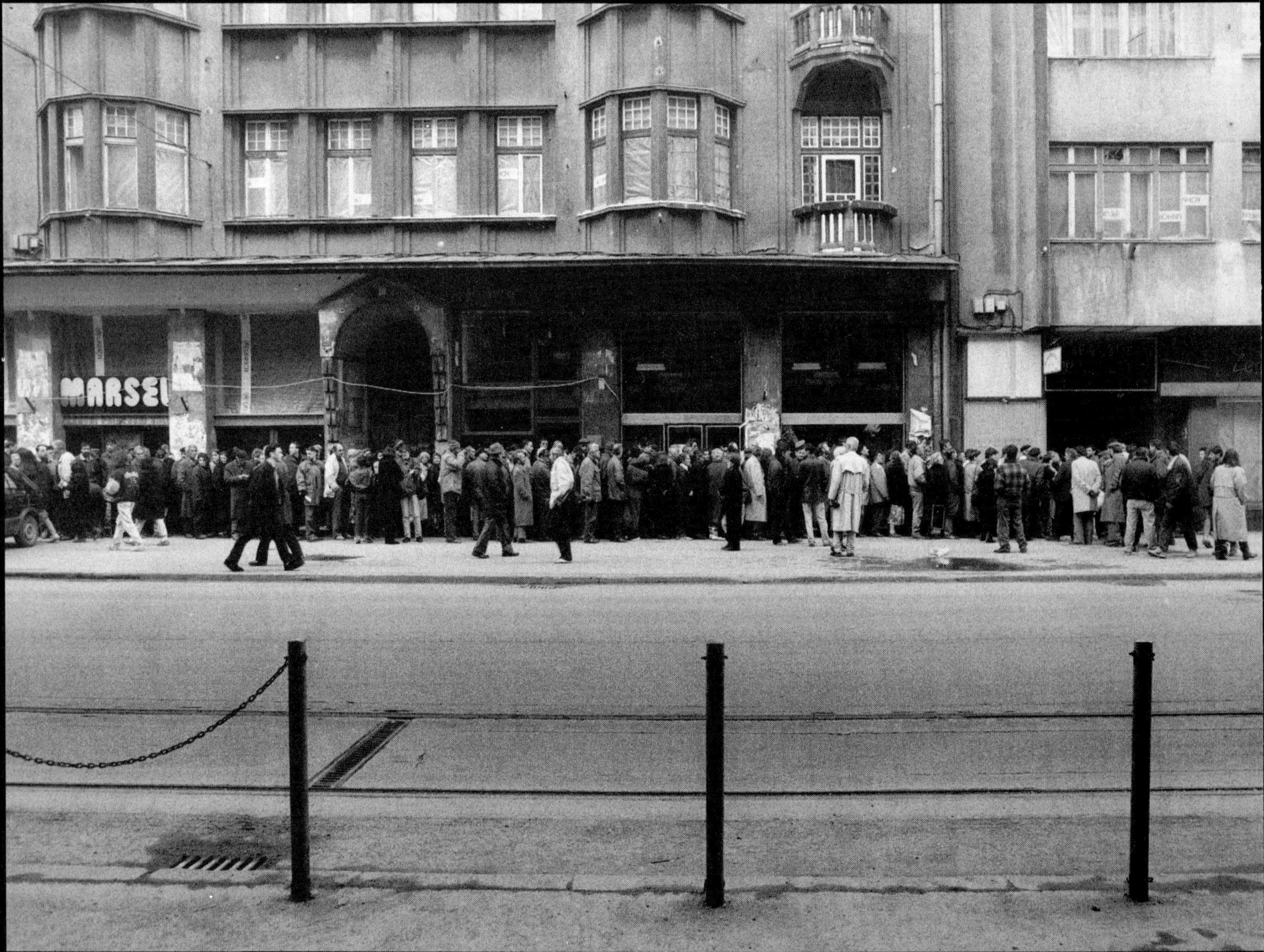

airport. This is the 1,214th humanitarian flight since UNPROFOR took control of Sarajevo airport.

Tuesday, 27th: An ordinary war day. Shells fall on almost all parts of the city. Snipers fire at citizens. Most frequently shelled is Stari grad. Also shelled are Marijin Dvor, Breka, Šip, Alipašino polje, Dobrinja and Mojmilo. The B-H trade unions demand that the city and republican authorities do everything they can to provide the necessary quantities of fuel, especially coal, wood and gas to protect the citizens against the oncoming winter. The city's buses are running. August pensions are expected to be paid out on Friday. There is a shortage of gauze, bandages and medicines in almost all hospitals in B-H.

Wednesday, 28th: A draft of the Constitution of Bosnia and Herzegovina is revealed in Geneva. 30 tons of flour are brought from the airport to the "Velepekara". Strictly forbidden is the illegal felling of trees in the city and its suburbs according to an order issued by the chief of staff of the Supreme Command of the B-H Armed Forces, Sefer Halilović, the deputy minister of defence, Munib Bisić, the minister of the interior, Jusuf Pušina, and the minister of forestry and wood processing industry, Dr. Hasan Muratović.

abraksas stone excavated in Logavina Street with a cock's head and snake's legs. And then, as the highest spiritual satisfaction, there is the new knowledge of the Sarajevo Haggadah. Its guardian, the librarian Kemal Bakaršić, M. A., published his study on its preservation during World War II. He refuted an enrooted story about keeping the Haggadah in a mountainous village near Sarajevo. He revived once more an old Latin saying that books also had their destinies. To the well-known resourcefulness of the National Museum's director, Dr Jozo Petrović, at the meeting with a German general who came to take the Haggadah away, he added the names of other curators of that time. Hiding the Haggadah in the basements of the Museum is linked with the name of Derviš, the son of Munib, Korkut, as well as storing it in a safe building in the wall of the National Bank. In the general gloom and darkness it was as if we saw anew that jewel of the world, the illuminated mediaeval Sephardic codex. We hold it in our hands, as is appropriate, during Passover. We remember the legends of the release of the Israelites from slavery in Egypt.

We follow the story about the misfortunes and expulsion, about hopes and salvation, murmuring in a melancholy way:

> *"This is the bread of misery and misfortune that our fathers ate in the land of Egypt*
> *Let those in need enter and celebrate Passover*
> *...*
> *This year slaves, next year sons of freedom."*

The centuries get mixed up for me. How much symbolism and melancholy there is in these verses! How many people and peoples have written about their sufferings in just this way for millenia! And with constant endeavours to forget the pains and sufferings and to glorify freedom. Did the Jews do just that in Babylon, Egypt and in the civilisations I admire?

I stagger, I groan, I fall down, I stand up. I would like to leave as soon as possible. Hunger torments me. I live my diary:

"Morning shooting wakes me up. A curse overpowers the crushing of the glass under feet, under my window. This means that some of boys have set off again, before dawn, to Kromolj and Poljine.

"Late last night it roared around Vogošća. From Poljine tracer bullets flew towards Kobilja Glava. Others flew in from Žuč. Detonations, shots and roaring were heard. Some shells ploughed through the sky over our blocks of flats. One seems to have fallen in the neighbourhood. It may have hit our roof too. Shrapnel, like hail, tapped on the neighbour's roof, on the parked cars drilled with bullets and on the asphalt.

Obavještavamo poslovne prijatelje i radne ljude Radio-televizije Bosne i Hercegovine da je naš radnik

SRĐAN (MLADENA) MUMOVIĆ

poginuo kao borac braneći Sarajevo 1. avgusta 1992. godine.

Sahrana će se obaviti u nedjelju 2. avgusta 1992. godine u 10.30 sati na groblju »Lav« u Koševu.

Radni ljudi Televizije Bosne i Hercegovine

Duboko ožalošćeni obavještavamo rodbinu, prijatelje i komšije da je naš dragi i voljeni

SRĐAN (MLADENA) MUMOVIĆ

preminuo 1. avgusta 1992. godine u 32. godini kao branilac svoga Sarajeva.

Sahrana će se obaviti u nedjelju, 2. avgusta 1992. godine u 10.30 sati na groblju »LAV« u Koševu

OŽALOŠĆENI: majka Dušanka, otac Mladen, brat Dragan, snaha Suzana i ostala rodbina, prijatelji i saborci iz specijalne jedinice Armije BiH.

Duboko ožalošćeni obavještavamo rodbinu, prijatelje i komšije da je naš dragi

NEDŽAD (SALIHA) PECIKOZA

preselio na ahiret 31. 7. 1992. godine u 21. godini kao šehit braneći svoj grad.

Dženaza će se obaviti u nedjelju 2. 8. 1992. godine u 11.00 sati na groblju »Lav«.

OŽALOŠĆENI: otac Salih, majka Sajma, braća Senad i Alen, snaha Sajma, bratična Aldijana, te porodice Pecikoza, Zulić, Šutrović, Ćosović, Husamanović, Huskić, te ostala rodbina, prijatelji, poznanici, komšije i njegovi saborci, posluga artiljeraca Mehe Košarića.

Obavještavamo rodbinu, prijatelje, saborce i poznanike da je naš dragi

MIRSAD (MUHAMEDA) OMEROVIĆ

preselio na ahiret 31. jula 1992. godine u 34. godini.

Dženaza će se obaviti 2. avgusta 1992. godine u 11 sati na groblju Lav.

Ožalošćeni: otac Muhamed, majka Razija, braća Avdo i Adem, sestre Mina, Hanifa, Zumra i Nafa, supruga Sabaheta, kćerka Dženita, porodice Omerović, Gušo, šure, svastike, badže i mnogobrojna rodbina. BB

Sa neizmjernim bolom javljamo rodbini, prijateljima i komšijama da je naš voljeni sin, suprug, otac i saborac

SENAD (RAŠIDA) BAJRIĆ

poginuo kao šehit 31. 7. 1992. godine braneći Sarajevo od četničkih hordi.

Sa ljubavlju i poštovanjem trajno ćemo čuvati uspomenu na tvoj plemeniti lik. Dženaza će se obaviti 2. 8. 1992. godine na groblju »Lav« u 11.00 časova.

DUBOKO OŽALOŠĆENI: otac Rašid, majka Fata, djeca Hamza i Alena, braća Elmir i Admir, sestre Mersima i Mirsada, supruga Jasna, tetić Sead, punac Esko, punica Sena, šurak Emir, Munira, te porodice Bajrić, Delija, Ahmetagić, Mujkić, saborci iz I Podrinjske brigade kao i ostale mnogobrojne komšije i prijatelji. BB

Tužnim srcem javljamo rodbini i prijateljima da je naš dragi

SENAD (RAŠIDA) BAJRIĆ

braneći svoju domovinu BiH poginuo kao šehit dana 31. 7. 1992. godine u 25. godini.

Dženaza će se obaviti 2. 8. 1992. godine u 11 sati na groblju »Lav«.

VJEČNO OŽALOŠĆENI: supruga Jasna, majka Fata, sin i kćerka

Duboko ožalošćeni obavještavamo rodbinu, prijatelje i komšije da je naš dragi i voljeni

RISTO (MILADINA) JOŠILO

preminuo 1. avgusta 1992. godine u 27. godini kao branilac svoga Sarajeva.

Sahrana će se obaviti u ponedjeljak 3. avgusta 1992. godine u 10.00 sati na groblju »LAV« u Koševu.

OŽALOŠĆENI: otac Miladin, majka Nada, sestra Milosava, sestrična Maja, zet Dane, baba, stričevi, ujaci, tetke te porodice Jošilo, Popović, Malešić, Đokić, Kokot, Brajić, Huremović i ostala mnogobrojna rodbina, prijatelji i komšije. BB

Sa dubokim bolom javljamo rodbini, prijateljima, komšijama i poznanicima da je naša draga

VASVIJA (HASANA) ARNAUTOVIĆ rođ. PAŠIĆ

preselila na ahiret 31. jula 1992. godine u 90. godini.

Dženaza će se obaviti 2. avgusta 1992. godine u 12 sati na groblju LAV.

OŽALOŠĆENI: sinovi Nusret i Hajrudin, kćeri Mersija i Hasija, zet Rahmo, snahe Šerifa, Ema i Nermina, unuci Senad, Kemal, Edin, Almir, Jasmin, Armin i Elvir, unuka Indira te porodice Joldaš, Hamamdžić, Šaćiragić, Zec, Voloder, Ahatović, Pašić, Hakulija i ostala rodbina i prijatelji. 8501

Tužnim srcem javljamo da je naša draga majka, baka i sestra

MARIJA JURIĆ

preminula 28. jula 1992. godine.

Sahrana je obavljena 30. jula 1992. godine na groblju LAV.

OŽALOŠĆENI: kćerka Željka i Ljerka, sin Petar, sestra Sofija, braća Luka i Franjo, zetovi Klaudije Šober i Ivan Baković, snaha Marija, unučad Danijel, Željko, Vida i Tanja kao i ostala rodbina, prijatelji i komšije. 8479

Duboko ožalošćeni obavještavamo rodbinu, prijatelje i komšije da je naš dragi i voljeni

DAVOR ZENGA (ANTE) GUTIĆ

preminuo 1. avgusta 1992. godine u 27. godini kao branilac svoga Sarajeva.

Sahrana će se obaviti u nedjelju, 2. avgusta 1992. godine u 10.30 sati na groblju »LAV« u Koševu.

OŽALOŠĆENI: majka Zrinka, sestra Sanda, brat Darko, porodica Milošević i ostala rodbina, prijatelji i saborci iz specijalne jedinice Armije BiH.

Tužnim srcem javljamo rodbini i prijateljima da je naš dragi

KEMAL (DŽEMAILA) ČOLAK

braneći svoju domovinu BiH poginuo kao šehit dana 31. 7. 1992. godine u 20. godini.

Dženaza će se obaviti 2. avgusta u 11 sati na groblju »Lav«.

VJEČNO OŽALOŠĆENI: majka Naza, sestre Hamida, Šefika i Mevlida, brat Šefik, porodice Čolak, Crnčević, Herić, Čehović i ostala rodbina i prijatelji.

Obavještavamo sve naše prijatelje da su od zločinačke ruke četnika Vojislava Maksimovića na kućnom pragu ubijeni naši dragi

ZAJKO SOFRADŽIJA 1931 – 1992.	**OMER SOFRADŽIJA** 1935 – 1992.
SALKIJA BERBERKIĆ 1936 – 1992.	**HABIBA EKMEČIĆ** 1916 – 1992.

PORODICA SOFRADŽIJA 8475

Obavještavamo rodbinu, prijatelje, poznanike i saborce da je naš dragi

MERSAL (ESADA) PLAKALO

poginuo kao šehit braneći Sarajevo 31. jula 1992. godine.

Dženaza će se obaviti 2. avgusta 1992. godine u 11 sati na groblju LAV.

OŽALOŠĆENI: otac Esad, majka Hajra, sestra Sanela, brat Kemal, snaha Dina, bratić Tarik, dedo Hašim, nana Mujesira, Malkija, amidže Šavko, Eso i Fiko, daidže Husko, tetke Samija, Iza i Azra, porodice Plakalo, Hajdarević, Pandžić, Žiga, Ćatović, Vranj, te mnogobrojni prijatelji i komšije. BB

Javljamo tužnu vijest da je naš dragi tata, djed i brat

NEDŽIB MULABDIĆ

preminuo 1. avgusta 1992. godine u 88. godini.

Sahrana će se obaviti u nedjelju, 2. avgusta 1992. godine u 10.45 sati na groblju LAV, u Sarajevu.

OŽALOŠĆENI: sin Siniša, kćerka Jasmina, unuci Feđa, Ras, Sonja i Nina, sestre Nedžiba i Ferida, snaha Tanja, zet Ismet i ostala familija. 8502

Tužnim srcem javljamo rodbini da je naš dragi

STANISLAV (NIKE) VIDOVIĆ

tragično preminuo 31. 7. 1992. godine u 57. godini života.

Sahrana će se obaviti 3. 8. 1992. godine u 10.15 sati na groblju Lav.

OŽALOŠĆENI: supruga Mira, sinovi Igor i Zoran, snaha Svjetlana, sestre Slavica, Ivana i Vera, te obitelji Grizelj, Semrad, Gavran, Bušić i mnogobrojna rodbina, prijatelji i komšije 8504

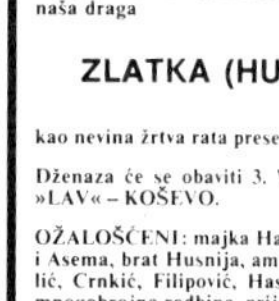

Duboko ožalošćeni obavještavamo rodbinu, prijatelje i komšije da je

FAHRUDIN (RAMIZA) KULAŠEVIĆ

preselio na ahiret kao šehit u 32. godini braneći Sarajevo.

Dženaza će se obaviti u nedjelju 2. 8. 1992. godine u 11,00 sati na groblju Lav, gdje će se i pokopati

OŽALOŠĆENI: otac Ramiz, majka Fatima, braća Fehim, Ferid i Mirsad, bratići Vahid, Sead, Enisa te porodice Kulašević, Redžović, Isaković, Neziri, Beriša te ostala mnogobrojna rodbina, prijatelji i komšije

Javljamo tužnu vijest rodbini, prijateljima i komšijama da je naša draga

ZLATKA (HUSE) SALČINOVIĆ

kao nevina žrtva rata preselila na ahiret 1. VIII 1992. godine.

Dženaza će se obaviti 3. VIII 1992. u 11.00 sati na groblju »LAV« – KOŠEVO.

OŽALOŠĆENI: majka Hatka, sestre Džemila, Fadila, Nafija i Asema, brat Husnija, amidža Hašim, porodice Dijab, Sarajlić, Crnkić, Filipović, Hasanbegović, Arnautović, Bilbija, te mnogobrojna rodbina, prijatelji i komšije. 8603

Tužnim srcem javljamo rodbini i prijateljima da je naš dragi

ZAJKO (BEĆIRA) ŠALAKA

braneći svoju domovinu BiH poginuo kao šehit dana 31. 7. 1992. godine u 37. godini.

Dženaza će se obaviti 2. 8. 1992. godine u 11 sati na groblju »Lav«.

VJEČNO OŽALOŠĆENI: supruga Refija, djeca Amir, Azra, i Amra, majka Fatima, sestre Hamkija, Begija, Nura, amidža Mujo i ostala rodbina kao i porodice Šalaka, Halilović, Bjedić i Fehratović.

Tužnim srcem javljamo rodbini i prijateljima da je naš dragi i nikad prežaljeni

ENVER (JUSA) ŠUKALO

rođen 1960. godine u Foči

braneći svoju domovinu BiH poginuo kao šehit dana 31. 7. 1992. godine u 32. godini.

Dženaza će se obaviti 2. 8. 1992. godine u 11 sati na groblju »Lav«.

VJEČNO OŽALOŠĆENI: majka Ema, sestra Enisa i drugi te porodice Jaganjac i Šukalo

Duboko ožalošćeni obavještavamo rodbinu, prijatelje i komšije da je naš dragi i voljeni

DANILO (STANKA) STANKOV

iznenada preminuo 1. avgusta 1992. godine u 67. godini.

Sahrana će se obaviti u nedjelju, 2. avgusta 1992. godine u 10.15 sati u Sarajevu na Groblju »Lav«. Kuća žalosti Ul. Dž. Bijedića 92/II

OŽALOŠĆENI: supruga Mira, sinovi Borislav i Ranko, sestra Dobrila sa porodicom, snahe Emina i Snježana i unučad Goran, Gorana, Ivana i Igor, šura Duško sa porodicom. Bliža i dalja rodbina, te porodice Milošević, Šinik, Šašić, Šehović, Lendić, Erlbek, Tarabar, Trtak i ostala mnogobrojna rodbina, prijatelji i komšije. PL

Sa dubokim bolom i tugom obavještavamo rodbinu i prijatelje da je naša draga i plemenita majka, sestra i nana

ZARFIJA (ALIJE) BAJRAKTAREVIĆ rođ. SERDAREVIĆ

preselila na ahiret kao šehit, 31. jula 1992. godine u 78. godini od gelera zločinačke granate.

TEŠKO OŽALOŠĆENI: sin Fadil, kćerka Fahrija, snaha Arifa, unuk Nermin, unuka Nermina, braća Emin, Fehim i Edhem, sestre Atija Letić, Zekija Žmiro te familije Serdarević, Bajraktarević, Mujanović, Daut, Babić, Musić, Sarajkić i ostala mnogobrojna rodbina, prijatelji i komšije.

Obavještavamo rodbinu, prijatelje i komšije da je naš dragi

ZAJKO (OMERA) UZUNOVIĆ

preselio na ahiret kao šehit 31. 7. 1992. godine u 39. godini. Dženaza će se obaviti na groblju »Lav«.

OŽALOŠĆENI: supruga Mirsada, sin Amel, kćerka Amela, sestre Tifa i Zahida, zet Alija, punica Hafiza, šuraci Nedžad i Alija sa porodicama, svastika Niska te porodice Uzunović, Mehović, Trle i ostala familija, prijatelji i komšije

Sa dubokim bolom i tugom javljamo rodbini, prijateljima, komšijama i saborcima da je naš dragi

SULJO (ŠABANA) HAJDAREVIĆ

preselio na ahiret kao šehit, 31. 7. 1992. godine u 53. godini, braneći svoj grad, svoju zemlju i pravo svih nas da živimo slobodni i na svome. Dženaza će se obaviti 2. 8. 1992. godine u 11 sati na groblju »Lav«.

OŽALOŠĆENI: supruga Marica, majka Hamida, braća Ibro i Sulejman, sestra Hana, sinovi Remzija i Šaban, kćerka Zumra, unučad Dženita, Emrita, Almir i Emdžad, sestrići Halil i Mirsad, bratići Fikret i Arnel, bratične Indira i Ajla, snahe Iza, Fikreta, Mediha, Sena, Halima i Sabina, porodice Hajdarević, Barlov, Sejdin, Logušić, Balić, Odobašić, Karić, Papaj i druge te ostala mnogobrojna rodbina i prijatelji.

Sa bolom i tugom obavještavamo sve prijatelje i slobodare da je naš saborac

SULJO (ŠABANA) HAJDAREVIĆ

preselio na ahiret kao šehit 31. 7. 1992. godine u 53. godini boreći se za pravo na život i sreću svoga grada, svoje zemlje i svih ljudi dobre volje.

Dragi Suljo,
tvoji saborci nikada neće zaboraviti tvoj lik i tvoje djelo.

Drugi bataljon XV brigade i Komanda XV brigade

S tugom i bolom u srcu javljamo rodbini, prijateljima i komšijama da je naš dragi sin, brat i prijatelj

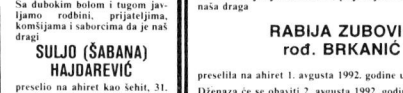

TARIK (MIRSADA) HADŽALIĆ

kao šehit preselio na ahiret 1. avgusta 1992. godine u 21. godini, braneći voljeno Sarajevo.

Dženaza će se obaviti u nedjelju, 2. avgusta u 11 sati na groblju »Lav« u Sarajevu.

OŽALOŠĆENI: otac Mirsad, majka Maida, brat Namik i ostala rodbina, prijatelji i komšije.

Sa neizmjernim bolom javljamo saradnicima, rodbini i prijateljima da je naš dragi kolega

HUSO (ADEMA) MIROPIJA

tragično poginuo 31. jula 1992. godine u 53. godini života kao žrtva agresije.

Dženaza će se obaviti u nedjelju 2. avgusta 1992. godine, u 12 sati na groblju Lav – Koševo.

RADNICI SEKRETARIJATA ZA NARODNU ODBRANU GRADA SARAJEVA

Naš dragi i dobri otac, djed i brat

LADISLAV (LADO) MOMČILOVIĆ

(učitelj u penziji)

preminuo je u 87. godini. Sahranjen je 26. 7. 1992. godine na groblju »Lav«.

OŽALOŠĆENI: djeca Zrinka, Darko, unučad Vedrana i Slaven, sestre Greta, Anđelka, Pavla, Ela sa porodicama, snaha Nađa i zet Željko.

Obavještavamo rodbinu, prijatelje, saborce i poznanike da je naš dragi

TEUFIK BRACO (NEZIRA) ŠOŠIĆ

preselio na ahiret 31. jula 1992. godine u 23. godini kao šehit braneći svoj grad i domovinu.

Dženaza će se obaviti 2. avgusta 1992. godine u 11 sati na groblju Lav.

OŽALOŠĆENI: otac Nezir, majka Fata, braća Nesib i Muhamed, dedo Asim, snaha Ismeta, bratić Tarik, amidže Alija, Sejdalija, Himzo i Ramiz, daidža Alija, strine Ismija, Zejna, Seka, Fatima i Zarfija, strine Merkija, Senija i Bisera, daidžinica Seida, tetci Murat, Huso, Osman i Mujo, te porodice Šošić, Hodžić, Džebo, Šabanović, Vatreš, Imamović, Zimić, Feriz te ostala rodbina, komšije, prijatelji i poznanici BB

Duboko ožalošćeni obavještavamo rodbinu, prijatelje i komšije da je naša draga

RUBINA (DŽEVADA) ČAUŠEVIĆ

tragično preselila na ahiret 31. jula 1992. godine u 17. godini

Dženaza je obavljena u subotu 1. avgusta 1992. godine u 12 sati u haremu Bijele džamije.

OŽALOŠĆENI: otac Dževad, majka Advija, brat Sead, sestra Selima, amidža Hazbija, strina Nisveta, amidže Remzo, Džemal i Dželko, dedo Sadik, nana Esma, daidže Ešref i Muhamed, tetke Zija Kalagdžija sa porodicom, Kija, Remza, Fatima, Samija i Sabiha, te porodice Čaušević, Mehmedagić, Porobić, Hasanović, Babić, Hrustanović, Sarvan, Hadžibajrić, Klino, Šivšić, Jažić, Rizvanović, Kobiljak, Hodžić i Konaković, komšije Alija, Habiba i Šefika, kao i ostala mnogobrojna rodbina, prijatelji i komšije.

Na ovaj tužni i neuobičajeni način opraštamo se od našeg dragog

IRFANA (FAHRIJE) FILIPOVIĆA

koji je tragično izgubio život 19. juna 1992. godine u 72. godini.

OŽALOŠĆENI: supruga Danica, kćerke Minka i Buba, sestra Šefika, Suljo, Igor i Domo, unučad Bojan, Ogi, Vanja i Gogo te porodice Filipović, Kraljevski, Rašidkadić, Muminagić, Pašić, Lončarević, Kulenović, Kaznokov, Baroš, Halilović i ostala mnogobrojna rodbina.

Duboko ožalošćeni javljamo rodbini, prijateljima i poznanicima da je naš dragi

ANTO RORA (MATE) JOVANOVIĆ

preminuo 31. jula 1992. godine u 26. godini kao branilac Sarajeva na Kromolju.

Sahrana će se obaviti u ponedjeljak 3 augusta 1992. godine u 11,00 sati na gradskom groblju u »Koševu« kod Lava – Sarajevo.

OŽALOŠENI: majka Zdravka, brat Zdenko, snaha Edina, tetke Zdenka, Marica i Mira, tetak Alija i Jovo, te porodice Jovanović, Kutlovac, Putica, Svoboda i ostala mnogobrojna rodbina, prijatelji i komšije. BB

Sa žalošću javljamo rodbini, prijateljima i komšijama da je naša draga

RABIJA ZUBOVIĆ rođ. BRKANIĆ

preselila na ahiret 1. avgusta 1992. godine u 94. godini.

Dženaza će se obaviti 2. avgusta 1992. godine u 12 časova na Hridu.

OŽALOŠĆENI: sinovi Alija, Muharem i Meho, kćeri Habiba, Šefika i Safija, zet Hamo Nikšić, snahe Raza, Hatidža i Mubera, zetovi Zaim, Haso, Šemsa, Nedim Hiko, Hamo, Dževad i Zoran, unučad Almedina, Ever, Ahmed, Mahir, Nedim, Salko, Enver, Irfan, Alma, Meho i ostala unučad i praunučad te porodice Zubović, Brković, Janjoš, Milaosmanović, Nikšić, Jažić, Hadžimujić, Šukalić, Poturić, Mlinarević, Agić, Muhić, Sokolović, Ićindić, Delalić i ostala rodbina, prijatelji i komšije. 8476

Sa žalošću javljamo rodbini i prijateljima da je naš dragi suprug, otac, deda, brat

ENVER (HASIBA) ALIĆ

preselio na ahiret 29. jula. 1992. godine u 53. godini

Dženaza će se obaviti u nedjelju 2. avgusta 1992. god. u 12 sati u groblju »LAV«

OŽALOŠĆENI: supruga Adila, sin Nezim, kćerka Munevera, zet Meša, sestra Almasa, brat Munib, unučad Jasmin i Lejla te porodice Alić, Kriještorac, Husić, Ramić, Čamđić, Kurtić, Ferizović, Šljivo, Prutina, Bečirović i ostala mnogobrojna rodbina, prijatelji i komšije.

Duboko ožalošćeni obavještavamo rodbinu, prijatelje i komšije da je naš plemeniti i voljeni

IZET (HAZIMA) MUFTIĆ

preselio na ahiret kao šehit 31. jula 1992. godine u 35. godini braneći šeher Sarajevo.

Dženaza će se obaviti u nedelju 2. avgusta 1992. godine u 11.00 sati na groblju »LAV« u Koševu.

OŽALOŠĆENI: otac Hazim, majka Vahida, supruga Kimeta, kćerke Amela i Naida, brat Zaim, sestre Emina, Almedina i Lejla, šure Ismet, Reuf i Smajo, sestrići Aida, Alija i Saša, te porodice Šehbajraktarević, Karahasanović, Vukajlović, Osmani i ostala mnogobrojna rodbina, prijatelji i komšije. BB

Duboko ožalošćeni obavještavamo rodbinu, prijatelje i komšije da je naš dragi i voljeni sin, suprug, brat i otac

DINARKO (ZLATKA) BORAS

preminuo 31. jula 1992. godine u 46. godini od agresorske granate.

Sahrana će se obaviti u nedjelju 2. avgusta 1992. godine u 10.45 sati na groblju »LAV« u Koševu. Kuća žalosti, Kralja Tomislava br. 19.

OŽALOŠĆENI: majka Radmila, supruga Nevenka, kćerka Lada, brat Predrag, punica Ana, snaha Branka, bratić Ognjen, Seka, te porodice Boras, Solar, Solaković, Ovčina, Marković, Hrenek i ostala mnogobrojna rodbina, prijatelji i komšije. 8496

Obavještavamo rodbinu, prijatelje, saborce i poznanike da je naš dragi

SEMEDIN (SULEJMENA) ETEMOVIĆ

preselio na ahiret 31. jula 1992. godine u 33. godini, kao šehit braneći svoj grad i domovinu.

Dženaza će se obaviti 2. avgusta 1992. godine u 11 sati na groblju Lav.

Ožalošćeni: supruga Ajka, kćerke Selma, Dženita i Dženana, otac Sulejmen, majka Naza, braća Džemo i Smajo, badže i svastike te ostala mnogobrojna rodbina i prijatelji, porodice Memović, Balićevac i Gojak. BB

Sa žalošću javljamo rodbini, prijateljima i poznanicima da je naša draga

SELMA (ENVERA) MUJAK

preselila na ahiret kao žrtva rata u 11. godini 31. jula 1992. godine.

Dženaza će se obaviti 2. avgusta 1992. godine u 12 časova u Jarčedolima.

Ožalošćeni: otac Enver, majka Fadila, brat Esnef, dede Ibro i Zahid, nane Behija i Sabina, amidže Sejo, Meho i Miralem, amidžince Mira, Šafija i Senija, daidža Fadil, tetka Merima i tetak Faruk, amidžići Muzafer i Muamer, amidžične Senita, Emina, Irena, tetične Amela i Amina, i ostala rodbina, prijatelji i komšije 8483

SARAJEVO – THE WOUNDED CITY

"There are few people at the market or in the streets.

"The misery of empty and dusty counters and broken shops remains. It does not go anywhere. We sink deeper into it."

We still have no news about Bekir's father. No trace. The man was taken away on July 17th. He is eighty. He is a diabetic. Can he stand the camp for thirty, fifty, seventy days? Should we give up hope just today? What will they ask in exchange for him? Will it take place... Ah, you Sir, with a Sephardic cap. Thank you for your help. You wave to me and shut the door I hardly managed to reach.

> *"Agora kale bevir per fuersa,*
> *Astas ke mes echaran a la fuesa."*
>
> *(Now we must live forced to it,*
> *Until they lay us down into the cold clay.)*

I would gladly, Your Highness, my good count Guzman of Olivares, talk about the heavy mediaeval keys that the Spanish Jews took with them in their bundles. A few decades ago a descendent of those Sephardim took with him such a key from Sarajevo. He described the house he was looking for to the guide, that one that almost five hundred years ago his ancestors had to leave in Toledo. He did not tell me that. He found it in the old square. He took out the heavy key and fearfully approached the door. The key fitted the big, plated lock. He turned it in the keyhole. And he unlocked the door. Do you remember me telling this story before, too? I liked it. The Jews retell it in Jerusalem, Sarajevo, Vienna and in American cities.

I am hungry, my dear Count. I do not know whether the key to my home is still in my trouser pocket. Shall I be able to find my door one day? Why did I have to remember Albrecht Dürer at all, search his engraving in encyclopaedias and wondering whether hunger is the second or the fourth Apocalyptic rider, if it is the big bareheaded one who waves the empty scales or, perhaps, the one hardly seen who draws his bow ready to shoot an arrow? Well, they kept galloping past me. I staggered, I stepped aside. I did not manage to see their faces. Is it important at all whether they look beautiful or awful, this or that? They are here. That is too much.

Thursday, 29th: *According to UNPROFOR, 56 shells are fired at the city. The city centre, Hrid, Vasin han, Ciglane, the area around the hotel "Bristol", the "Lav" cemetery, the area around the Cathedral and Koševo hill are all shelled. An appeal by the "Sarajevo" State Hospital for help.*

Friday, 30th: *All parts of the town are occasionally shelled. The city's streets and buildings are mercilessly targeted by anti-aircraft machine guns. 8 killed and 54 injured.*

CIRCLE SEVEN

I stumble. I fall. I cannot stand up. There is some ice under my feet. I cannot manage to stand on both feet. I slide somewhere. I can make out some light. Polished rocks surround me. I go down without straightening up. The flames of the oil lamp flicker stronger and stronger. There are more and more of them. There is an immense sea of small lamps. Around each there are a few people. They stare at the light murmuring.

No, this is not a funeral feast. It is not a requiem, either. Without knowing what it is, I silently repeat:

> "When a man dies, a part of the world dies
> And the earth becomes heavier
> more experienced
> and more human
> and bigger by a wound
> and deeper by a cave."

A familiar whisper interrupts me. Somebody I cannot see whispers into my ear:

> "I threaded through blood deep up to my knees
> and I have no more dreams."

Some other sentences mingle. A Yankee utters them: "We are lost and there is no place for us in natural space, but we are not sorry for being human because of all this. It is better to die like man than to live like animal." Oh yes, that is Mr Krutch. I cannot see him, either.

All around us only the wicks smoulder and contours of masks push and warm up their eyes over the faint light. Are the faces I can barely discern smiling? I cannot make them out. I can only see the lamps lighting faintly and the eyes they reflect in. Like a vast lake whose shores I cannot see, lamps spread flickering in the dark without dispersing it. Each of them attracts my eyes. I try anew to see the serious faces with smiles in the corners of their lips that stare and devour their flame.

I trip over something hard and round. I fall on a half-naked muscular unknown man. You can see leather thongs fastened around his wrists. Leather sandals tied on his feet, a sword down his thigh, a helmet under his arm... Around him, men dressed uniformly, but without arms. They look at him piously. Iron jingles. Now I can see, I have tripped over a chain ending in an iron ball. I make it out – I am among a crowd of slaves. I am back in the first century, but B.C. A Thracian slave, a Spartan, a gladiator, gathers around himself those whose only hope he is. The battle at Lucania is being prepared. He speaks about Rome, the arena, justice and love. A breath of death surrounds him. I can make it out. It surrounds me all the time. It grins under its hood waving its scythe. I can discern its skull with empty orbs in the dark. Who knows where, but Jan Žiška, Ulich Zwingli, Emiliano Zapata, Lajos Kossuth, Matija Gubec, Husein

---

Saturday, 31st: Hell in the city centre. The Clinical Centre and the State Hospital are shelled. The whole city is shelled. 26 bodies are taken to the Koševo Hospital mortuary. The State Hospital receives 34 injured (by 7 p.m.) and the Traumatology Clinic registers 84 injured and 10 dead. The city receives both electricity and water. Shortage of bandages, oxygen bottles, infusion solutions, analgaesics and antibiotics. Alf Hansjürgen, the former ambassador of the Federal Republic of Germany in Belgrade, now the German ambassador in the government in charge of humanitarian activities, pays a visit to Sarajevo. Fourteen aeroplanes arrived at the airport with 136 tons of food and sleeping bags. The first delivery of plastic foil to be used for window glazing also arrives. A conference is held to establish the Pen-centre of the Republic of Bosnia and Herzegovina. Tvrtko Kulenović is appointed president. The Art Gallery of B-H presents a map of graphics – SARAJEVO '92 – with 18 sheets made by the professors and postgraduate students of the Academy of

ČETVRTAK
2. APRIL
U 19.30 SATI
Dževad
Karabasan
Čudo
u latinluku
drama
DAMA
ERFLY
SUBOTA
4. APRIL
U 19.30 SATI
DAMA
ERFLY

SARAJEVO

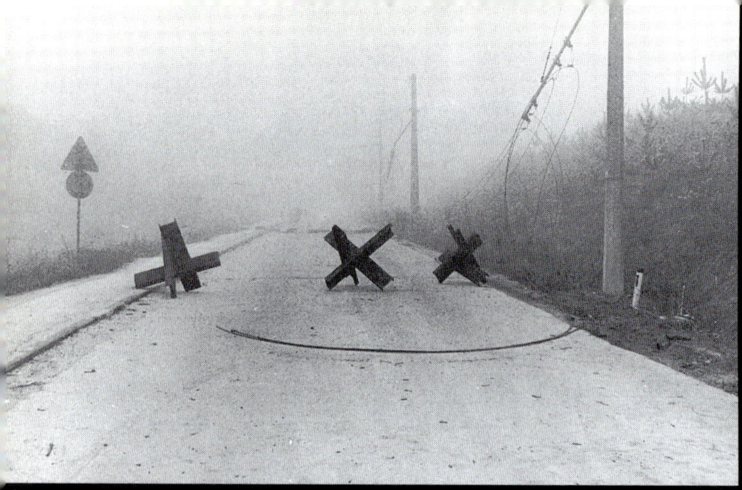

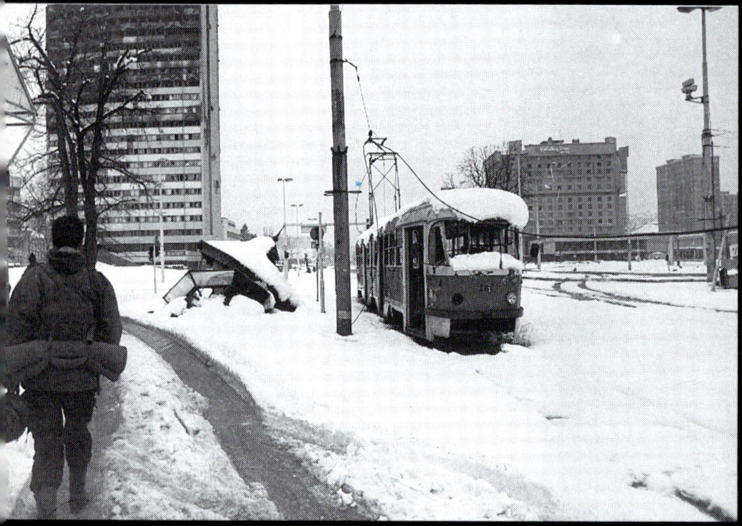

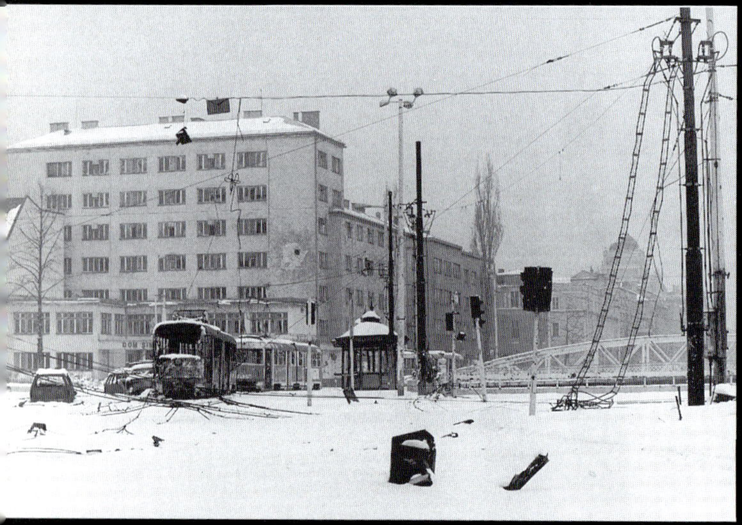

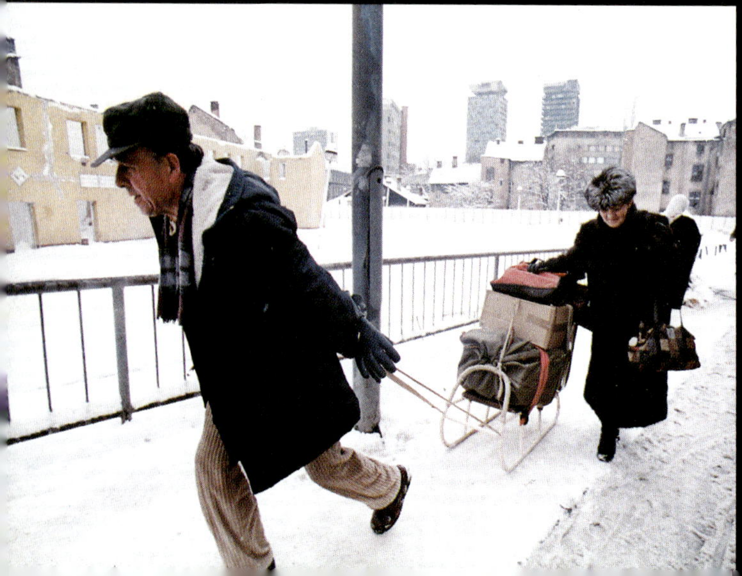

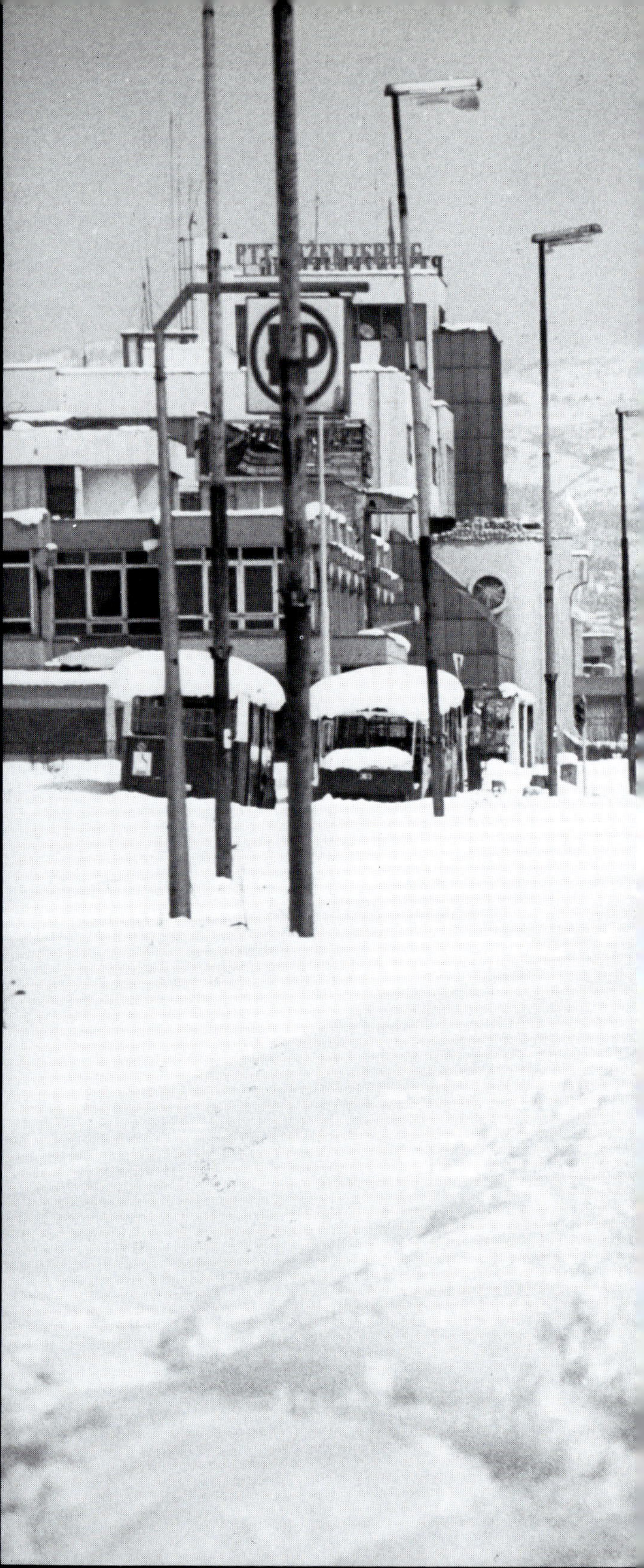

№ 395497
1
H
karta za
AUTOBUS
50
din. 60
BUS
2
KARTU ČUVATI RADI KONTROLE
1
JAVNO PREDUZEĆE
J
100
70
2

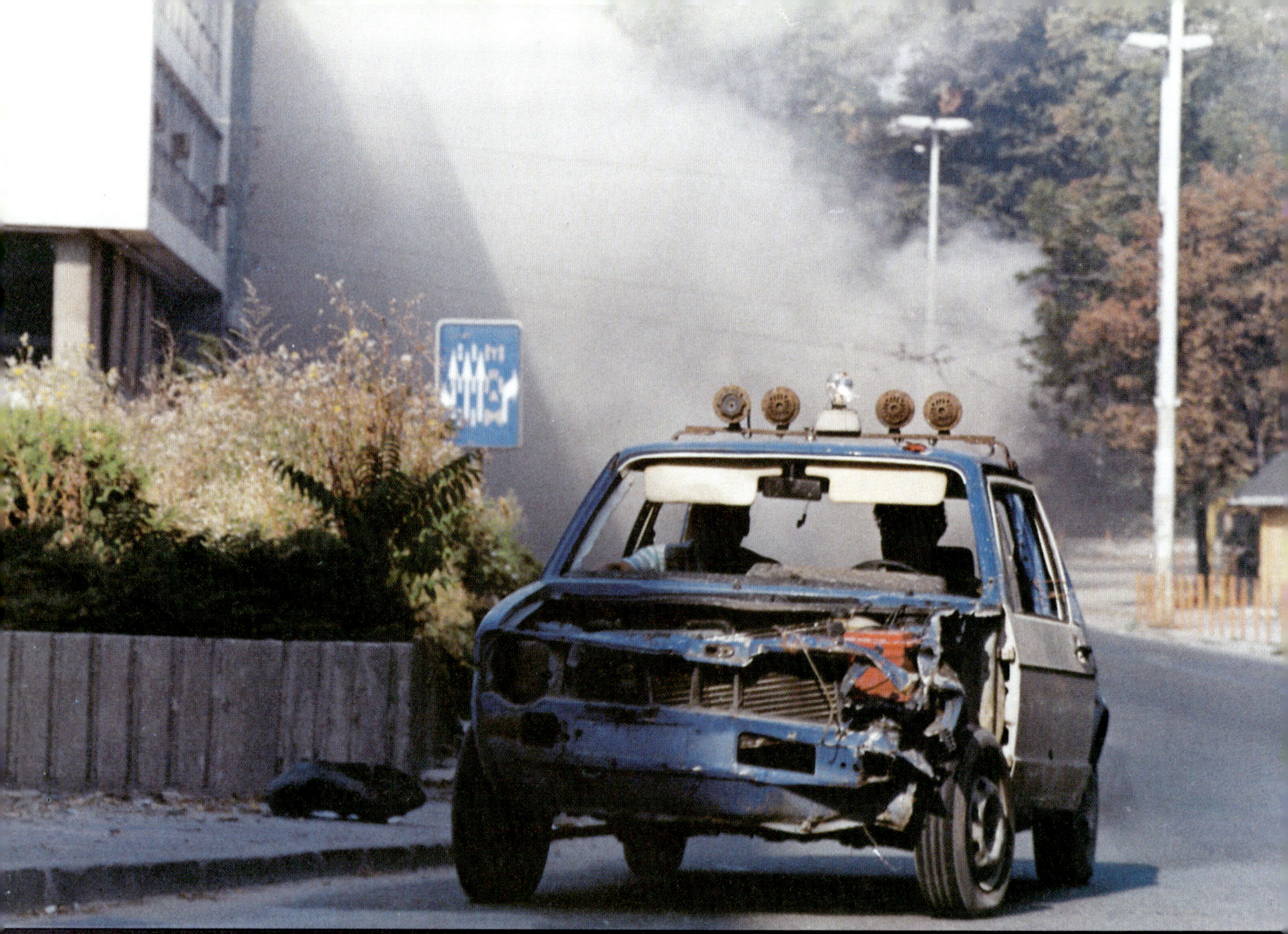

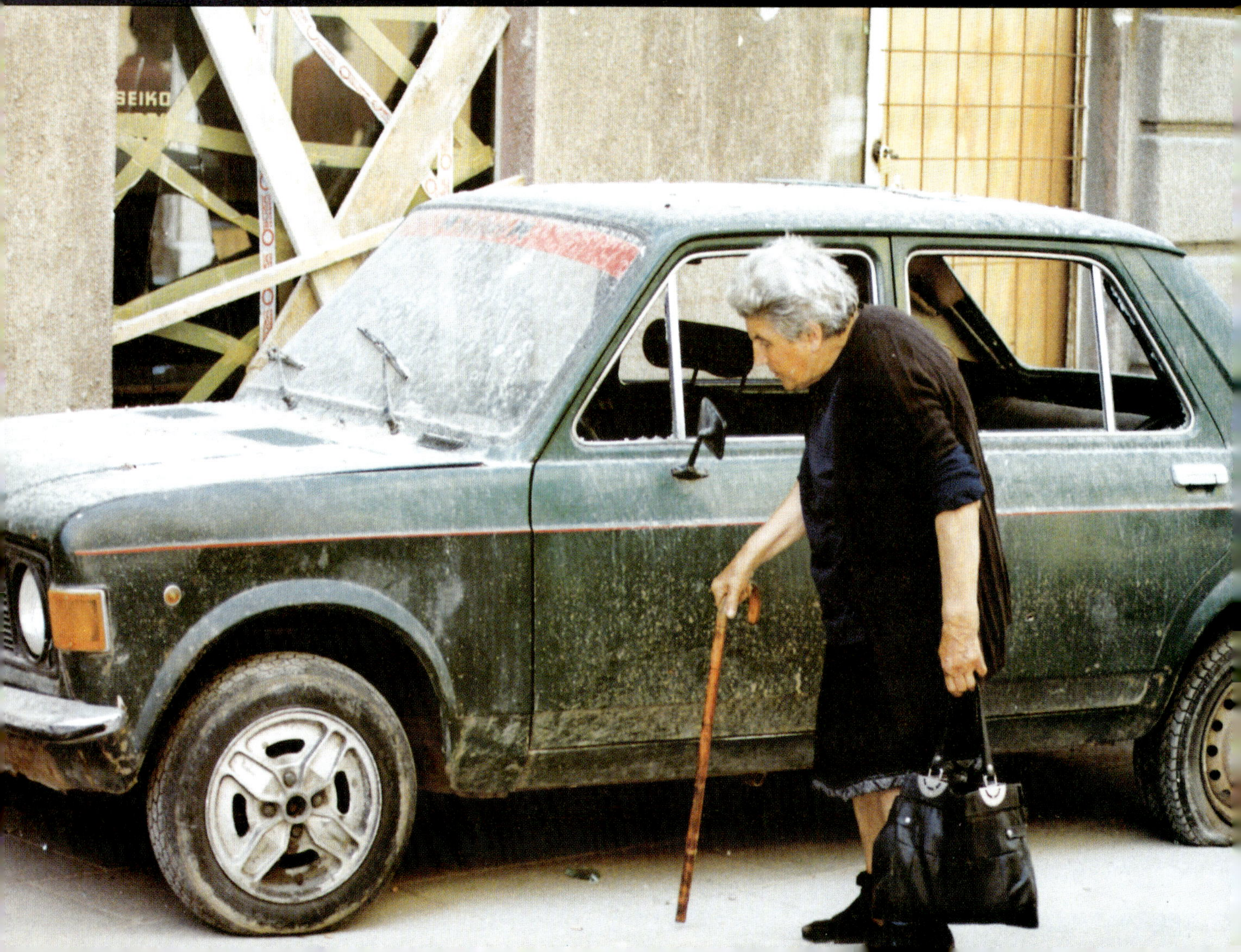
SEIKO

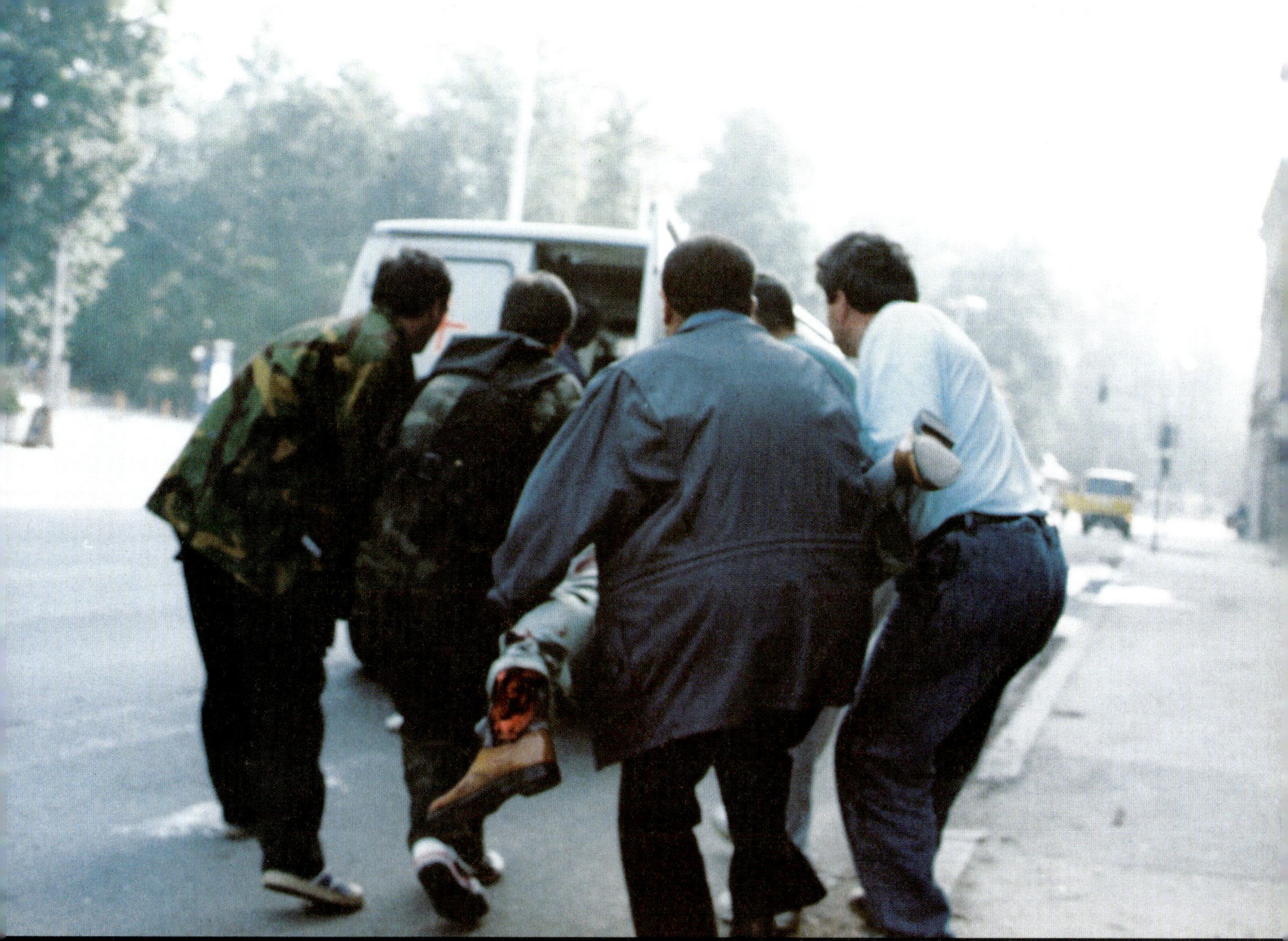

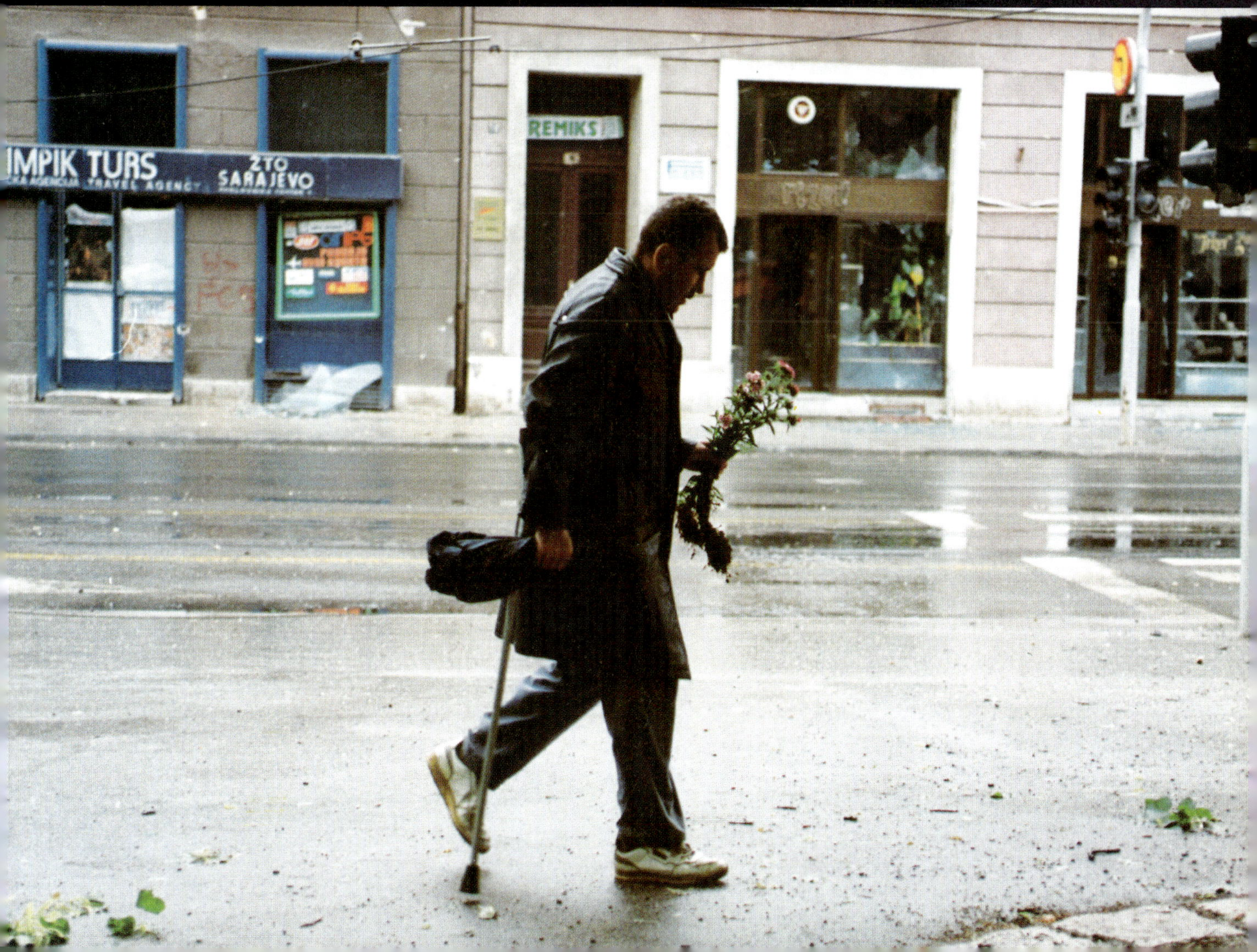
IMPIK TURS
ŽTO
SARAJEVO
TRAVEL AGENCY
REMIKS

Gradaščević, Robespierre and Pugachov are somewhere here.

Each of them had to repeat, at least silently, the sentence uttered by a Sarajevo woman journalist expelled from the Grbavica bank of the Miljacka: "My misfortune has already been forgotten." My experience that every moment is an encounter with death goes for them, too. Step by step, it is the same. On this road there are no torches. Houses and candles. They burn in the streets of Sarajevo, on the outskirts, on the horizon. I am not able to sort out the October dates of my Circle Seven. The ninth, tenth and eleventh days follow:

"Everybody who survives this war will regret it." The words of an old man echo in me. Too difficult are these war days. It is the second war for him. The days are also too difficult for us who for the first time are experiencing killing, fire, plunder and destruction.

A carpenter's on the second floor of Solomon's Palace? The very centre of the city and in the most attractive city palace they are sawing wood in the entrance!? On the balcony, window and door frames are being made. Whole doors, wardrobe parts and writing desk legs, too. On the windowsills there are a few brass handles with pieces of wood and some white oil paint."

Cemeteries are the parks of peace. And those messages spoken at funerals say the same as the ones carved into the sombre large stones:

"Rest in peace."

Mr Vancaš, excuse me. Sarajevo, my noble Josip, staggers this autumn. It must survive. That is the only thing it wants. It tries hard. The city leaders and state politicians are helpless and deaf to the messages of the dead. They do not know anything about you or about the park of peace in the Koševo valley. Is it at all important now that you, in 1884, designed and built these cemeteries, planned the paths and the plots for burials? You had the dead moved from near the tobacco factory at Marijin Dvor, from the cemetery mentioned in Isa-bey-Ishakovič's wakfname (Endowment regulations) of 1462 as a non-Muslim cemetery. By that you confirmed in your own way the verdict of 1728. At that time the Catholics were engaged in a lawsuit with the Orthodox community. They wanted to separate their part of the cemetery. It was proved in court that the cemetery had never been divided so that the esteemed court ruled for the cemetery to remain undivided.

In this long series is the 16th, too:

"We come back home. It is almost three p.m. We pass by the bare Koševo cemetery and the Chapel of St Vitus's Day heroes with a hole in its roof made by a May shell. A chainsaw makes a noise. Five or six men gather around a thicker lime tree. Its branches have been freshly cut off. The chainsaw yells loud enough. It attracts attention to itself

Fine Arts. The money of the SFR Yugoslavia becomes officially invalid on the territory of Bosnia and Herzegovina. Bihać is the last place where it is replaced by Bosnian-Herzegovinian dinars.

NOVEMBER

Sunday, 1st: *All Saints' Day or the day of all the blessed in heaven takes place without candles, without flowers, without a possibility of visiting the Vlakovo or Bare graveyards. A week of Peace for Children starts. On the initiative of the International Centre for Peace an exhibition of children's works is set up under the name "Drawings from Cellars", the topic being war atrocities. James Grant, director of the World Fund for Children's Protection, and Alain Court, a special UNICEF envoy, visit Sarajevo. A UNICEF convoy with humanitarian aid for children in which 70% of goods were from factories in Serbia, the country of the aggression on B-H, causes an international scandal. The delivery provokes amazement and revulsion among the citizens of Sarajevo. Shells fall all over the city. There are 443 mortar shells, 211 artillery and 8 tank shells fired at the localities where the blue helmets are stationed. Commemorating All Saints' Day, Monsignor Vinko Puljić celebrates a mass of peace at Dobrinja. 29 killed and 119 wounded in the city. The State Hospital sends a letter to General Morillon with an appeal for protection of this health institution.*

Monday, 2nd: *A relatively quiet day. Occasional provocations with artillery weapons. Snipers continuously fire at crossroads. Shelling of the*

outskirts of the municipality of Stari grad and Marijin Dvor. Hospitals without dressings and gauze.

Tuesday, 3rd: *More peaceful than usual. There are some shells fired at Stari grad. 12 killed, 35 injured.*

Wednesday, 4th: *A relatively quiet day. The aggressors' attacks are somewhat more severe in the afternoon in the area of the Stari grad municipality. The only surviving animal at the zoo, a brown bear, dies of hunger. After a break of almost two months bread appears in the shops. The problem of rubbish disposal from the city's streets is still unsolved. The city is covered with rubbish.*

Thursday, 5th: *Sarajevo is in the dark again. The transmission lines between Reljevo and Vogošća are damaged. The B-H Government decides to start enrolment of new university students from 9th to 28th November.*

Friday, 6th: *No electricity in the town. Water supplies critical. A complete breakdown of telephone communications. An appeal by doctors to health institutions all over the world for urgent supplies of gauze, bandages, analgaesics and antibiotics. A member of the B-H Presidency, Stjepan Kljujić, resigns from the Presidency. According to his statement, he is resigning in favour of Miro Lasić upon a HDZ request. The convoys bound for Split and Belgrade are stopped until all men from 16–60 years of age have military-medical examinations. A special issue of the Paris "Libération" dedicated to Sarajevo comes out with the diary of Zlatko Dizdarević, a journalist on "Oslobođenje". The first*

without wanting to. Then it stops. The trunk, perhaps sixty or seventy years old, falls towards the suburb of Ciglane. The hands of the men who steal cemetery trees cannot stop it. The tree, with its inertia, falls with a bang. Falling, it breaks two stone crosses. One of them has a piece broken off and the other falls, in splinters, two or three metres further.

"A few minutes later we climb Koševo hill. Up at the end of my street, on the way to our flat, I look towards the cemetery. It is bare of trees, too. As if somebody had torn off its mantle which we had got used to. There is nothing except tombstones, crosses, nishans (Muslim gravestones) and pyramids. There are no more birches. The willows do not caress former Sarajevans. Wood is necessary for survival.

"The dead will forgive the living. They forgive them even when they disturb their peace. Even the dead probably know of survival and life. Well, they are our ancestors, and ancestors, whether they want to or not, forgive their descendents. It has always been like that. It will probably be so now.

"Death continues its walk around the city.

"Even those who left are not spared war terror. Work is man's overall civilizational achievement. What has, for centuries and millenia, meant everything for Sarajevo is running out at the moment: food, patience, ...hope."

Hope?

Is it the flames in the dark the unlucky wretches from Circle Seven stare at? I am with them. I do not understand how hope has entered Hell. Is Hell with hope ever possible? We are all in the same position. Only oil lamp wicks glimmer. They do not give off heat. They do not light the way. They only attract eyes. Did I understand in Circle One where I was and where all this was leading? How did I escape the stake at which buildings, institutions and factories burned in the explosions of Circle Two? What happened to my fear, the prisoner's number on my back, Carthage, dark, and hunger? The journey gets longer and longer. We could not go back. I did not have any choice. I wished for a spark, a firefly I could hurry after. Now there is a lake of flames, the hope I try to warm myself with, knowing that it cannot warm me up. They tried to convince me this was not a war. Since May I have constantly listened to: military intervention; aircraft carriers; marine corps; desert rats; the killing must be stopped; heavy artillery withdrawals; demilitarization of Sarajevo; demilitarization of Bosnia and Herzegovina; military intervention; help with weaponry; the world; ashamed of our sufferings; the dead; exodus; refugees; dignity; military intervention; military intervention...

Mr Mohandas Karamchand, alias Mahatma Gandhi, practised nonviolence, in "The Gospels" and Leo Tolstoy

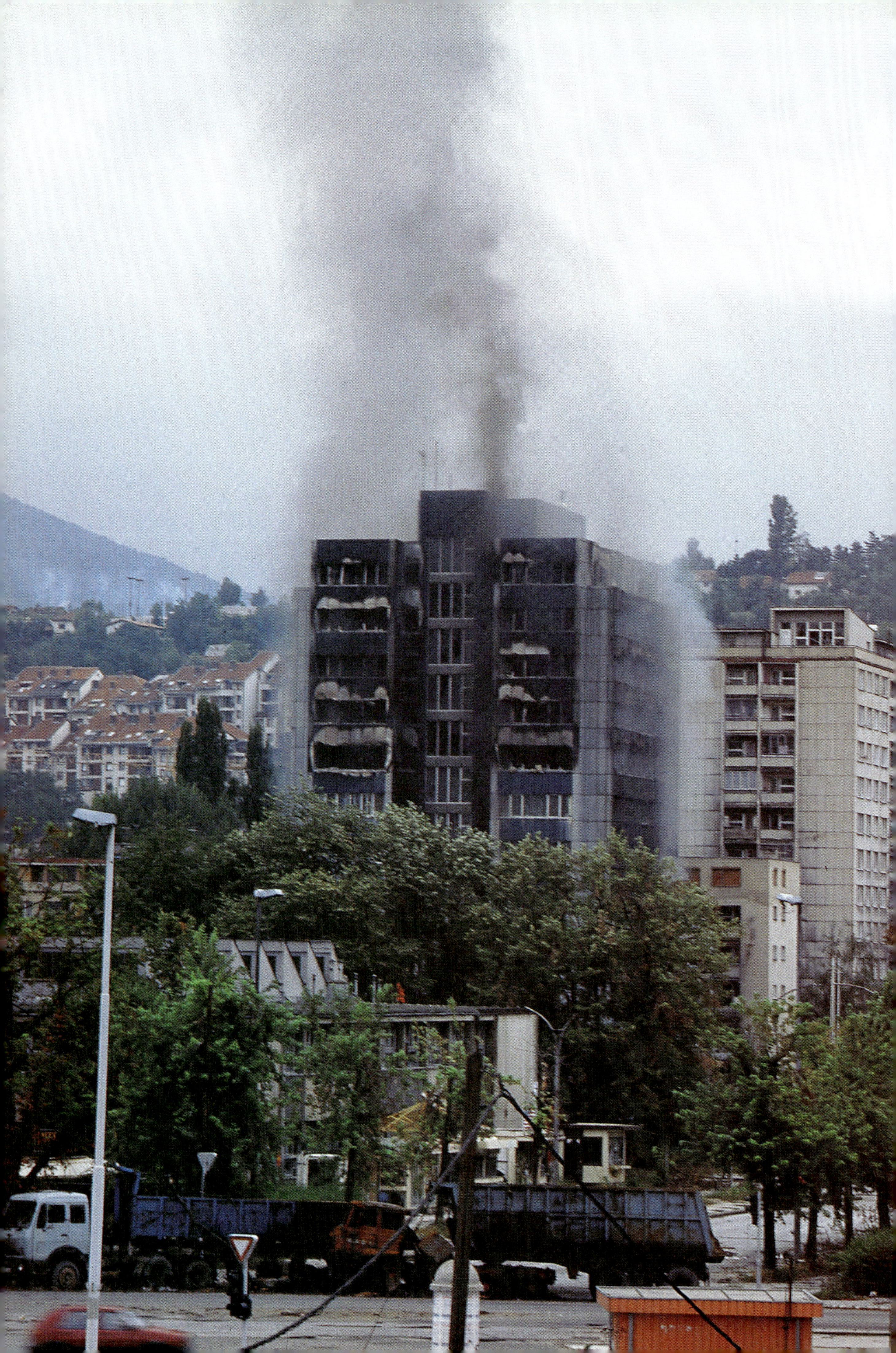

issue of the Bulletin of War Atrocities in B-H also comes out.

Saturday, 7th: *A relatively peaceful day. 5 dead and 18 injured. Hospitals without electricity, water and oil. The B-H Army Orchestra is founded. An exhibition of oil paintings and photography by Sead Čizmić and Kemal Hadžić is set up.*

Sunday, 8th: *Shells fall all over the city. Most heavily shelled are Alipašino and Vojničko polje, Dobrinja and the Mojmilo Olympic Village. In Sarajevo 8 dead and 47 injured.*

Monday, 9th: *The town gets some electricity. No water. The UNCHR stops all the exits from B-H both of citizens and the representatives of the government, except for those engaged in peace negotiations. The Clinical Centre of Sarajevo is promoted. The first Bulletin of the State Hospital "Sarajevo" is published.*

Tuesday, 10th: *Electricity provided only for priority users. No water. The main municipal spring is closed. Military negotiations of delegations of the B-H Army, the HVO and the aggressors at Sarajevo airport. An unconditional cease-fire on the whole territory of B-H is agreed, to come into effect at midnight between November 11th and 12th. 14 sick children with their escorts are evacuated to Paris by UNICEF. A dress rehearsal of the musical "Hair" is held in "The Chamber Theatre 55". A Red Cross convoy of displaced persons reaches Kiseljak. The convoy bound for Belgrade does not leave owing to a lack of buses. The Presidency of the*

you reached for a mean victory in the tradition of Indian peoples and in your own mind? How can I go to meet violence with your resistence, unarmed? You Maha Atma, Great Soul, were shot dead with a revolver bullet. You sit calm, exhausted by strikes, hunger and prison. You encourage me and show me that you enter the Hindu-Muslim conflict without killing, force or hatred. How radiant in this dark, so tiny and frail you are! I must tell you about Sarajevo, about the country where I live. How can I point out to you the destinies of the raped women and little girls who, after being raped, were kept as the objects of the tyrants' lust until pregnancy was so advanced that abortion would endanger the mother's life. I know you are going to tell me about Christianity, love and ban on abortion. Can you understand all this? I cannot. These women and little girls were not only violently raped. It was not done to them by just one or two men. They were slaves in brothels. They were kept there until their stomachs grew heavy with embryos they did not want. What to do against it? Oh, Great Soul, the man who became holy while satisfying himself on a handful of rice and honour for weeks, here only shells have been flying in the sky for weeks and for months. There are no birds. They have left, they hid somewhere, I do not know how they would sing, who would be able to listen to them. Here, it is the time of reflection with the questions: "How long will this last? Is there an end at all?"

Shall I show you what I wrote on October 5th? Before that date I used to be in a rush about deadlines for the books I published to be ready for the Belgrade International Book Fair. At that time for years I used to visit the immense halls of the Frankfurt Book Fair. I was there and walked there. Now it is the same date, but the year 1992. I wrote:

"The city is ablaze. Buildings, flats, souvenirs, jobs, everything that means something to you, disappear in the blaze. The building of Elektroprivreda BiH (B-H's Electrical Power Industry), the skyscrapers at Hrasno, the sombre building of Novo Sarajevo municipality... They destroy the "Holiday Inn", the only hotel still open in the city. The city thunders."

The gas has been switched off. There has been no water or electricity for days, for weeks. We still have only the air. They are going to turn that off as well.

At the City Institute for the Protection of Cultural Monuments I meet Vesna. She left Grbavica three days ago. She lived in the block of flats of Bekir's parents. She cut their hair in July. She says: "Their hair grew too long." That day she cut the hair of twenty-five of her neighbours, and she only used to cut her children's hair before that.

Her husband had forgotten how to walk! He could not run when he had to. A friend of his, a painter, had been hiding him for months. The painter's spirit did not surrender. He cheered and encouraged the whole block. He was

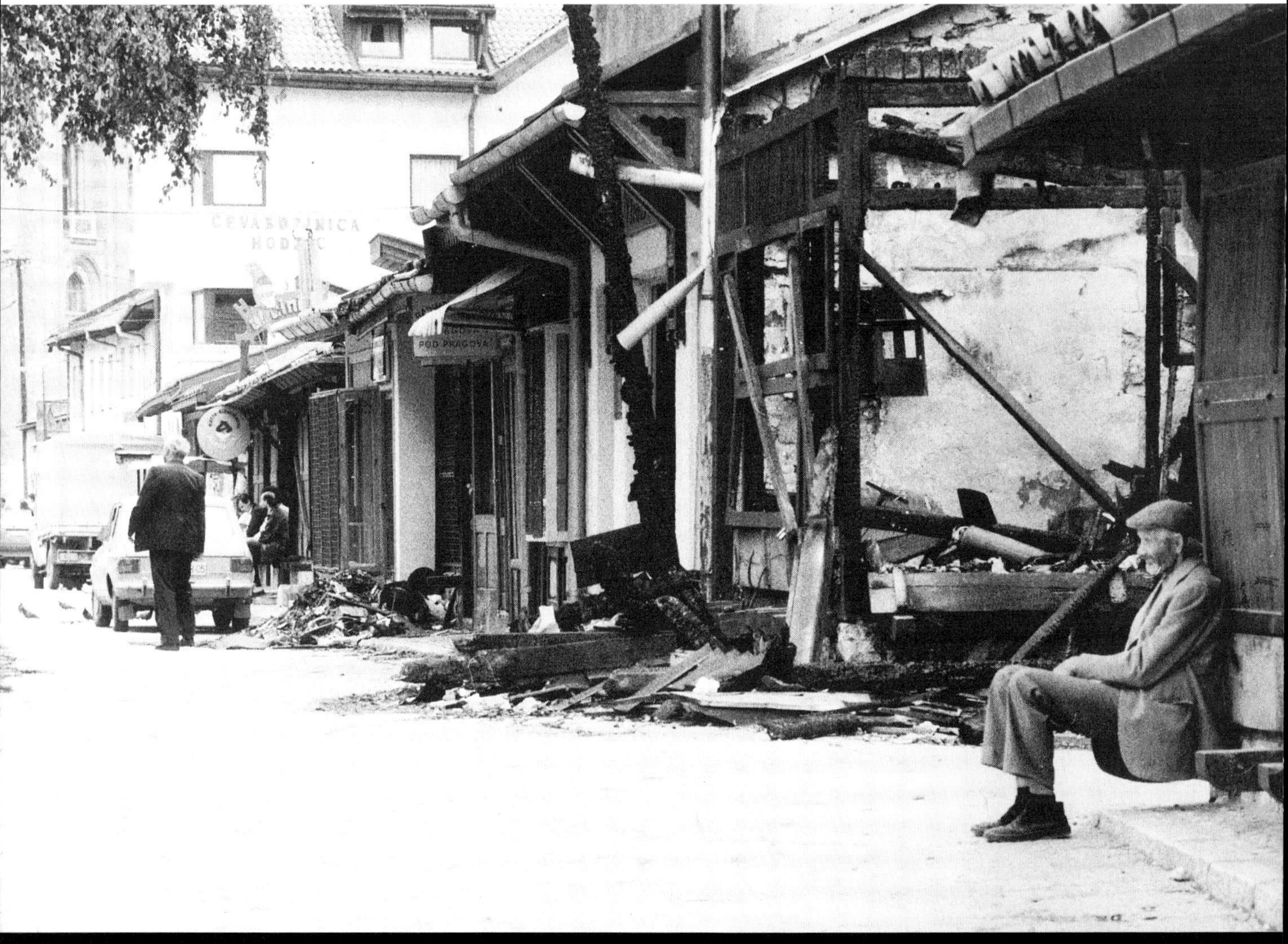
POD PRAGOVA

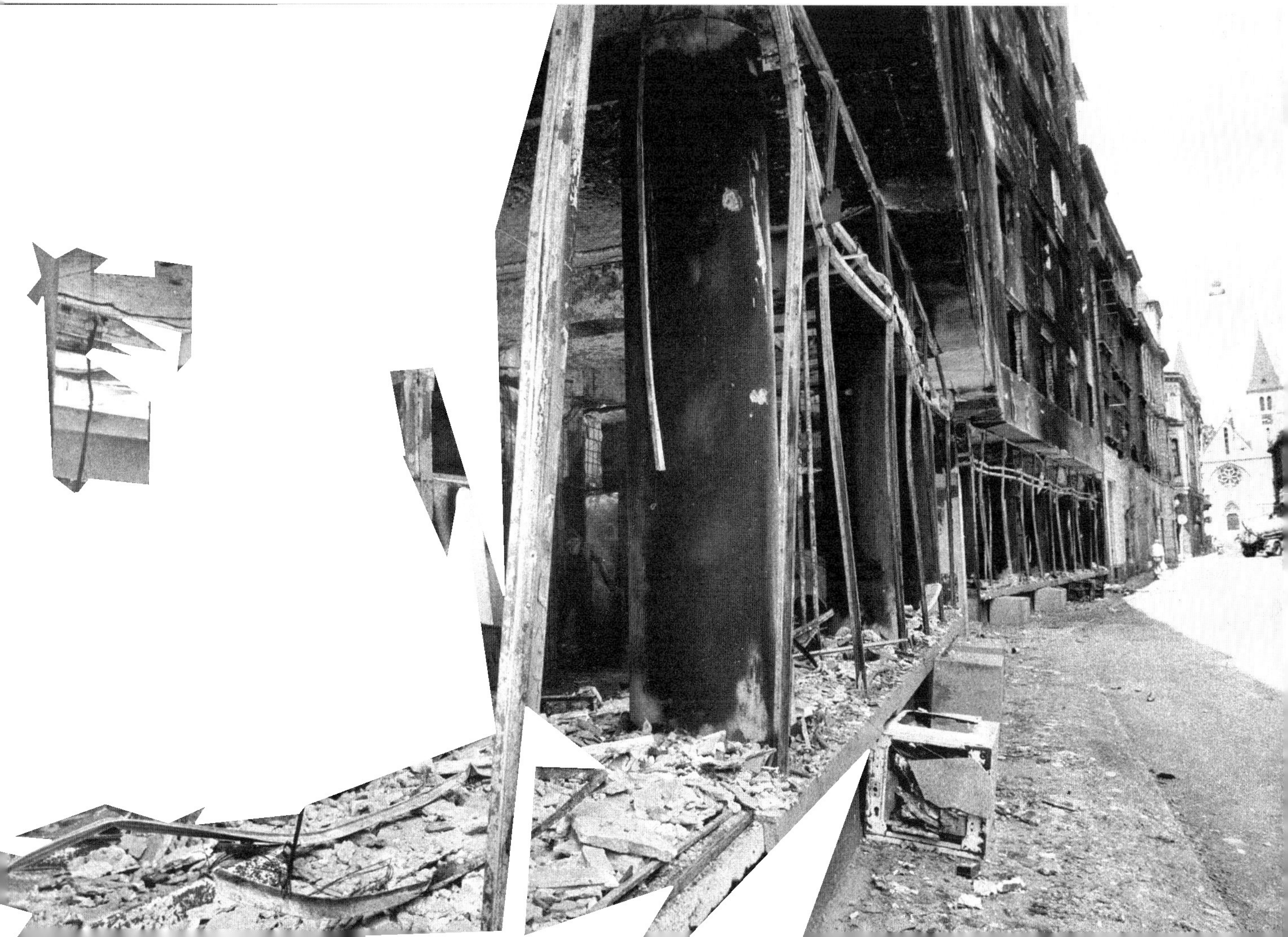

not disturbed. He was protected by his wife, so he thought. Other Muslims and Croats were expelled. She succeeded in getting out. She is cheerful.

Bekir's mother and Anja stayed there. But they also had to leave. Anja is down with apoplexy. She has been in bed for months. Even now she could not leave without a stretcher or a car. They allowed them to stay. Friends also brought their neighbours back home from the first floor. They did not allow him and his wife to leave. They interceded for them.

She shrugs her shoulders when asked how Bekir's parents are.

She confirms that uncle Sudo was taken away on July 17th. They know nothing about him.

She is silent.

I am silent, too. I dare not think the worst. It was July 17th. August has elapsed. September has elapsed... Long, too long for an eighty-year-old, an old man, a diabetic. The camp is not for a young man, either... July, August, September, we are in October. Vesna rouses me. She asks me about my book "Forgotten Sarajevo". She looks into my eyes and tells me that she must start from the beginning. All she had remained at Grbavica. Her children, husband, herself and a few plastic bags are everything that makes her home now. They have a lot. They are alive. "I'll have to start collecting books anew. I can't do without them. I am counting on your book, too."

She confirms the news about Dr Miro Kundurovič. He was taken away with no trace. She confirms our fears that he is not there, that he was probably killed. They shot the doctor in the back. They killed him as early as May. His smile, charm and spirit were gone. He left, and the manuscript of his book "I Travel, Therefore I Exist" burned up in the blaze of my office. At the Aerodrom suburb, a diskette with his book saved on it burned up. The unpublished book also burned up with Muris's computer... And the doctor, I am afraid, has gone for ever.

A day or two later nothing has changed:

We play rummy by candlelight. We bought candles queueing up, of course, in the Old Orthodox Church. The queue stopped. But we were patient. They sell two larger candles and six smaller ones for 980 dinars. Behind us two young women were joking about granny Vasilija's candlestick... Across the street, in the shopwindow of "Tapetar" which is closed, there are lists of parcels that have arrived at the charitable societies "Dobrotvor" (The Philantropist) and "Caritas" (Charity). People push. They look for their names. I do not know whether they are happy about the parcels or about the care, the knowledge that they are not forgotten, written off. The parcels satiate the hungry eyes and stomach, and the names on the list feed the soul.

Republic of B-H, functioning as the Assembly of the Republic of B-H, accepts the resignations of Stjepan Kljujić and Jure Pelivan. Mile Akmadžić is appointed as prime minister. The Presidency of the City Assembly makes a decision to provide the citizens of Sarajevo with bread with coupons. The Presidency declares the following institutions as public: Collegium Artisticum, the Youth Theatre, the City Museum, the City Institute for Cultural Heritage Protection, the History Archives, the Chamber Theatre 55, the Library of the City of Sarajevo, the Olympic Games Museum and the "Ljubica Ivezić" orphanage, renamed "Bjelave". The first part of the convoy bound for Split with children, the old and the sick leaves in 26 buses.

Wednedsay, 11th: *Not a single citizen of Sarajevo has been killed for the first time in this war. Fourteen injured are registered in health centres. The second part of the convoy for Split with 26 buses reaches Kiseljak. A driver from the convoy for Belgrade, Miroslav Biočić, is injured near the airport.*

Thursday, 12th: *The American Centre Library opens at Dobrinja. A war release of the casette "Top list of surrealists" is promoted. In B-H 15 people are killed and 125 injured; of these number 5 are killed and 24 injured in Sarajevo. According to the findings of the State Commission for Gathering Data on War Crimes 14,000 women in B-H have been raped. Among these 2,000 are aged between 7 and 18. Diplomatic relations are established with Germany.*

Friday, 13th: The "Lav" cemetery is heavily shelled during funerals. So far, the number of those killed or missing in Sarajevo is 7,468. The health institutions have only registered 2,782 deaths. In Sarajevo 44,677 people have been wounded and 12,000 of these have serious injuries. Pero Kosorić Square has its name changed to Trg Heroja (Square of Heroes) by a decision of the City Assembly.

Saturday, 14th: Electricity supplies critical. A transmission line is damaged. A failure in the gas supply to Sarajevo. One person killed and 10 injured in the city. Two buses with people from Sarajevo of Slovenian origin reaches Ljubljana. Dimitrij Rupel, the Slovenian foreign Minister, Igor Bavčar, Minister of the Interior and Petar Toš, Deputy Minister of the Interior, visit Sarajevo. Alija Izetbegović sends a letter to Dobrica Ćosić in which he inquires about and expresses his concern for the fate of the writer Vladimir Srebrov.

Sunday, 15th: The situation regarding the electricity supply of Sarajevo gets worse. Only a few shells fall on the Centre municipality on this day. Mojmilo and Alipašino polje are shelled in the evening. Buses of the Red Cross convoy carrying about 1,000 citizens of Sarajevo leave for Belgrade. There is an alarming shortage of medicine, medical supplies and electricity at the University Clinical Centre of Sarajevo. Alija Izetbegović requests Cyrus Vance in a letter to lift the arms embargo against the Bosnians.

Monday, 16th: The city is supplied with electricity. The transmission line is repaired

Passers by, with revolvers on their belts, comment loudly: "They sent parcels to the Chetniks."

People are silent. They look for their names, they push. Others cross the street, stand in the queue, wait for their two candles. They do not light them in the church, under the icon lamp or at the cemetery. We take the light home. We call on Prometheus with all his pains, while great eagles peck at his liver. I love him chained to a rock even move than the gods; he gave us fire. It is not in vain that Aeschylus, Goethe, Byron, Titian, Rubens, Liszt and Beethoven showed interest in him.

Never before have I admired the light of a wax candle so much. Oil lamps, with all the skill of making them, cannot give off such light. I had to forget Edison and Tesla. We read until dark. After that we do not know what to do. Nights are long, too long. I had did not noticed it before. Now they last, they follow one another.

I would have come back from the book fair in Frankfurt after five or six days with the knowledge that the written word lived, that it had got richer, but also sad because I would never be able to read all those hundreds of volumes, dictionaries, fairy tales and manuals and monographs. I would have been inspired with strength, refined with the world's treasure. It is different this October. Yellow and red leaves rustle under the feet. It is autumn. These leaves are not bound into books. There are no books, no fairs, no trips for me. My October 16th hovers:

"I give change for 500 dinars for a newspaper. I count out 350. A young man with a bandage over his left eye, supporting his left arm with a crutch, gives me 50 dinars back.

"'That's for you. You're the only one who sells for dinars. All others want marks.'

"'No, thank you!'

"'Do take it, please,' he insists with his gentle look. 'You're the only one who doesn't deal in marks... I also believed. I fought. I lost my eye and the toes on my right foot. I got 9,000 dinars for them.'

"Confused, I look at his beautiful, pale face with its sunken cheeks. I give up at his resoluteness. I take the 50 dinars he offered me as a tip. I would not like to hurt him. 'Thank you,' I murmur.

"He goes away limping with a ski cap pulled over his ears, in tennis shoes and a MONT windjacket filled with feathers and with an empty paper bag which a newspaper sticks out of. He leans on an aluminium crutch. He goes away. I squeeze the 50 dinar note in my hand.

"Next to me, a man shouts: 'Pie! Pie!' He almost howls in his shrill voice. It annoys me, suddenly, though I have not paid any attention to him before.

"He sells it for 1,400 dinars. Near him, there are a few bottles of 'Zvečevo' brandy. The price is written on a piece

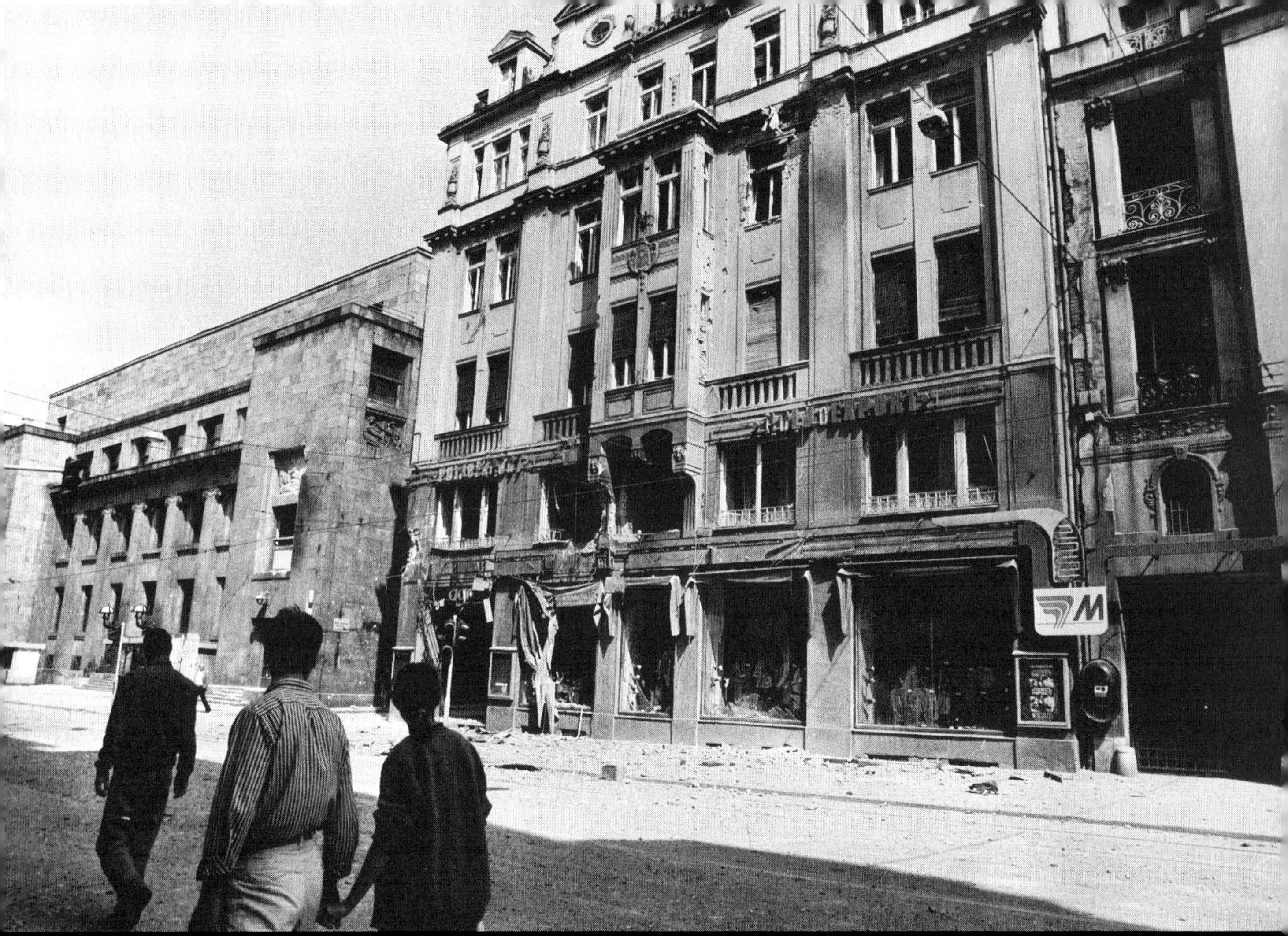
M

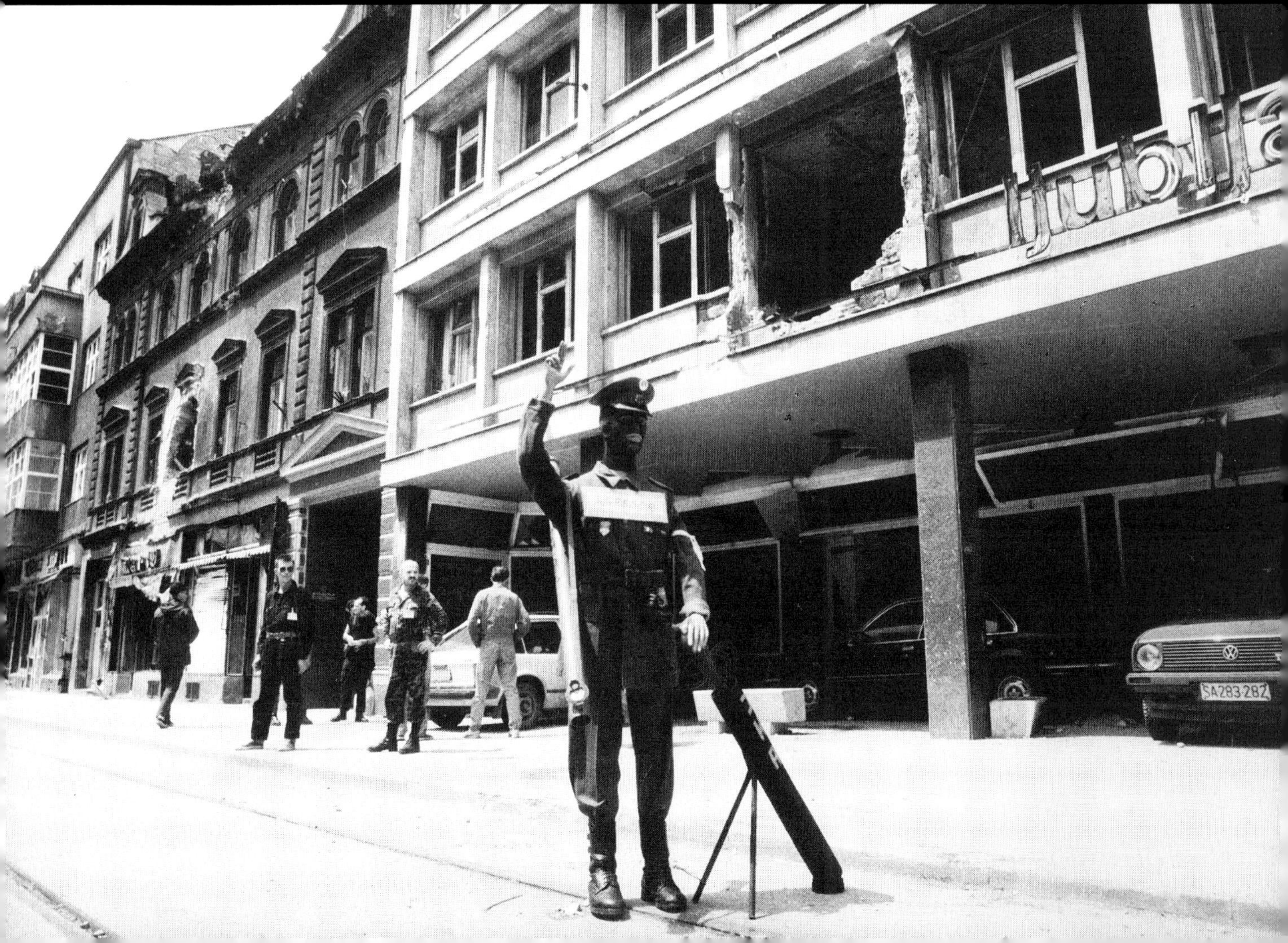
SA 283-282

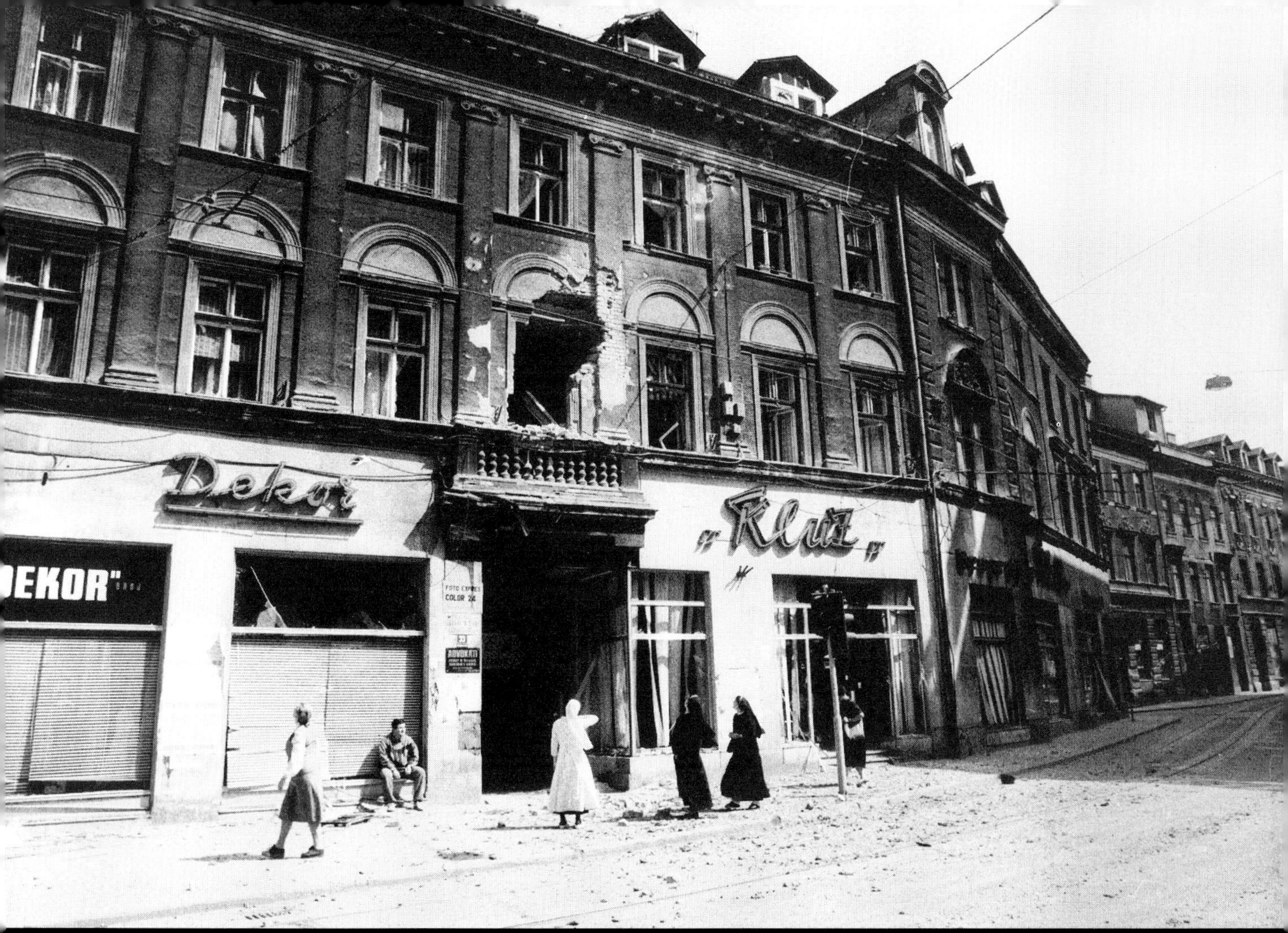
Dekor
DEKOR"

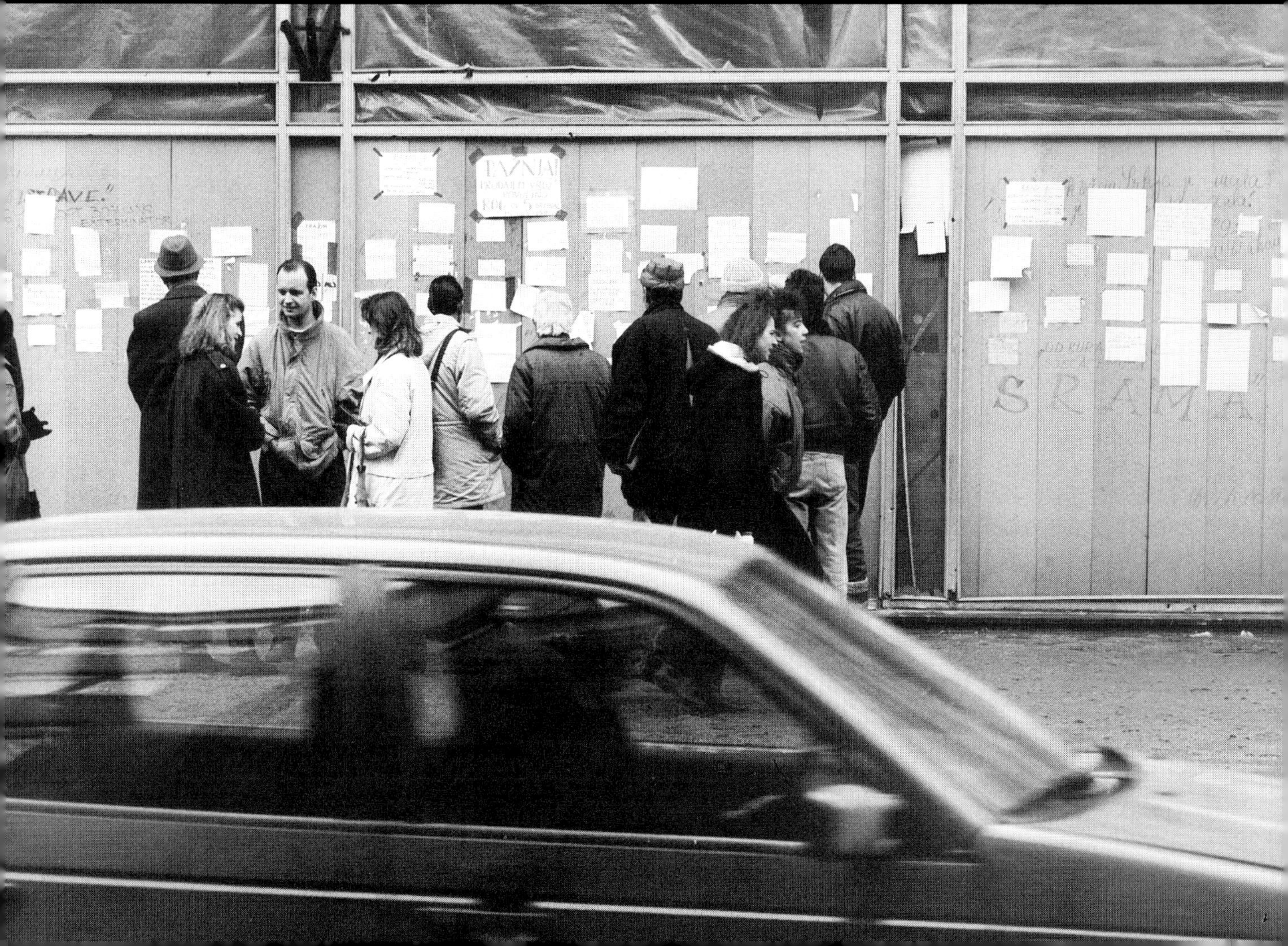
SRAMA

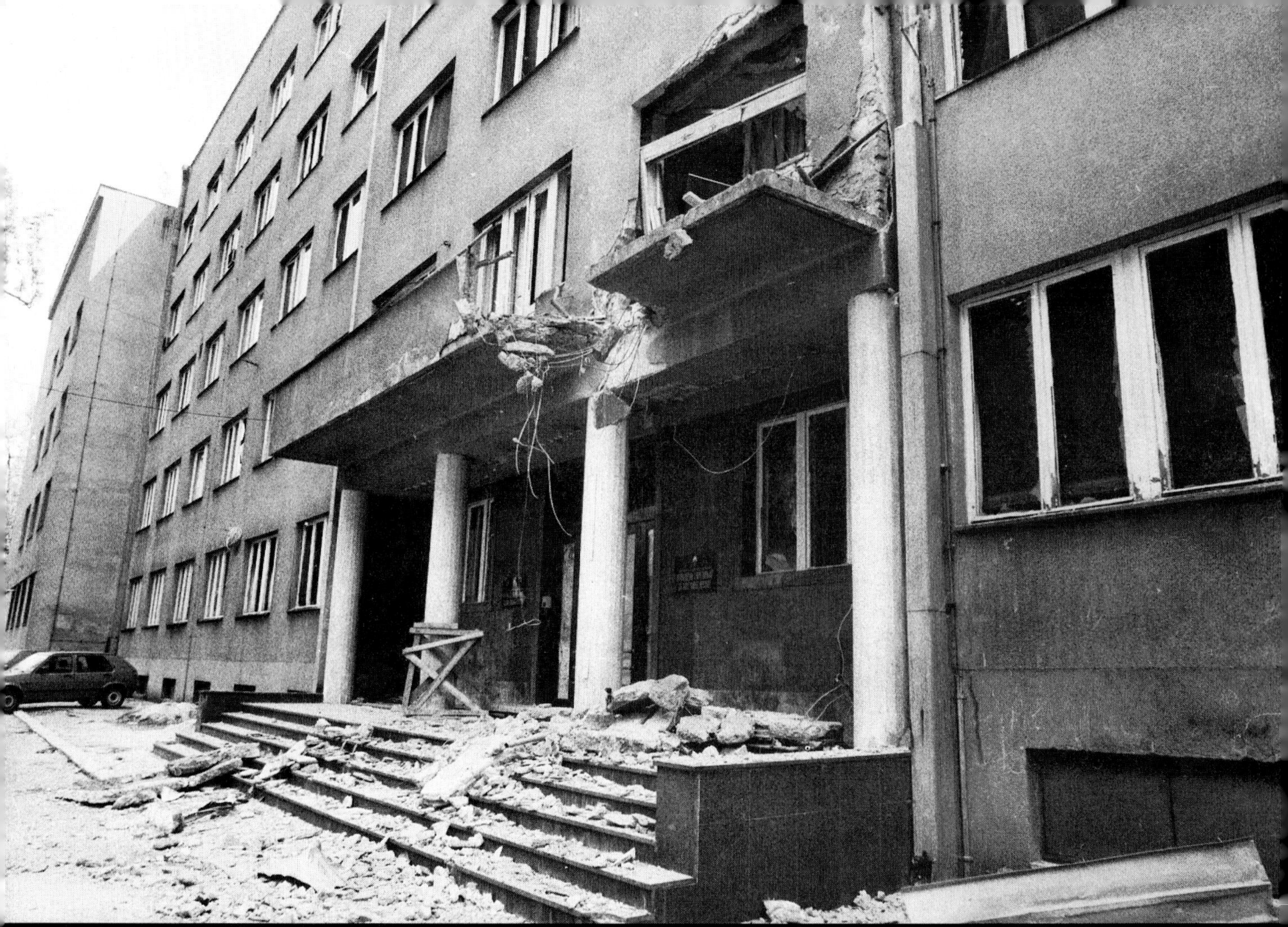

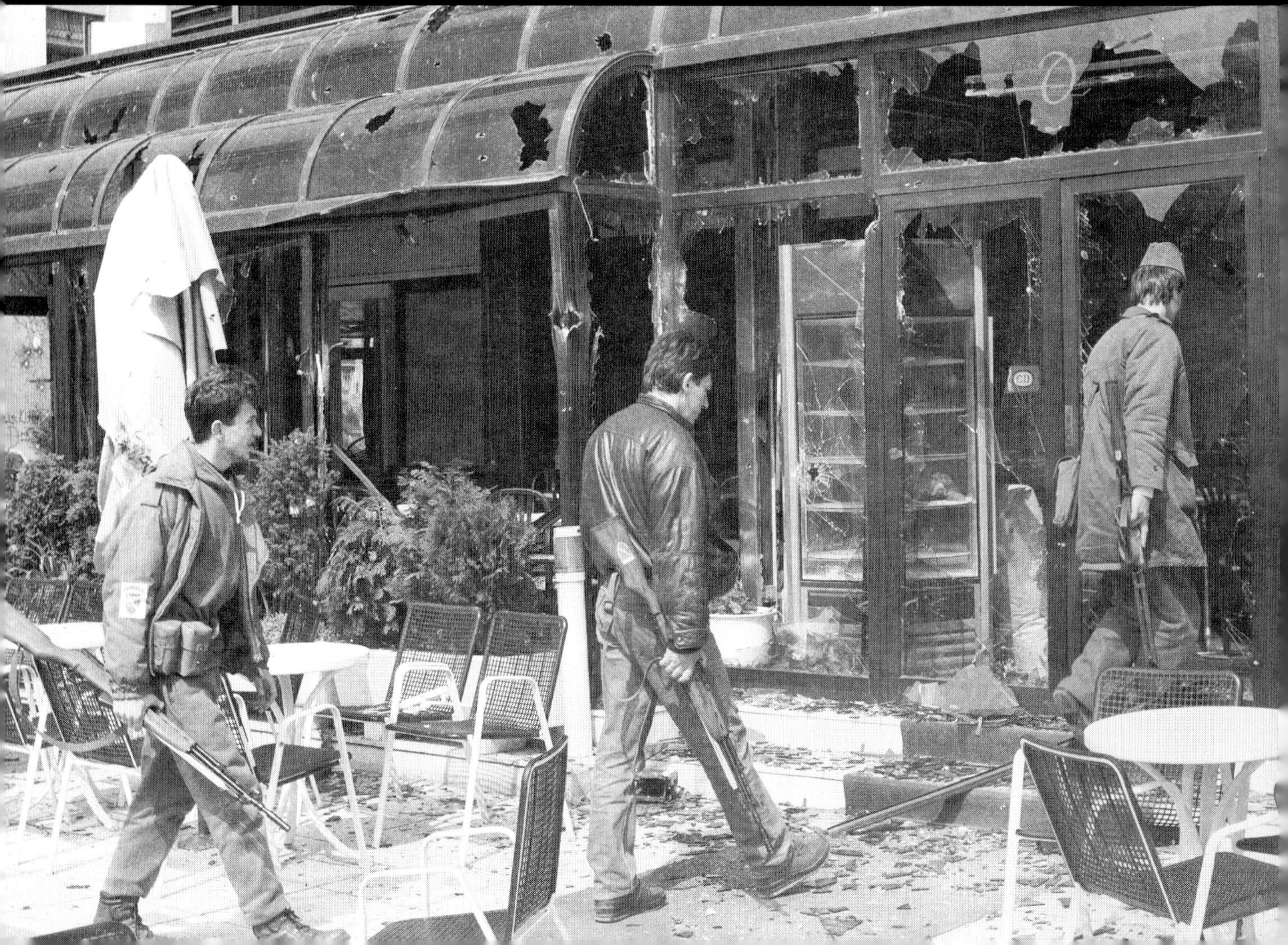

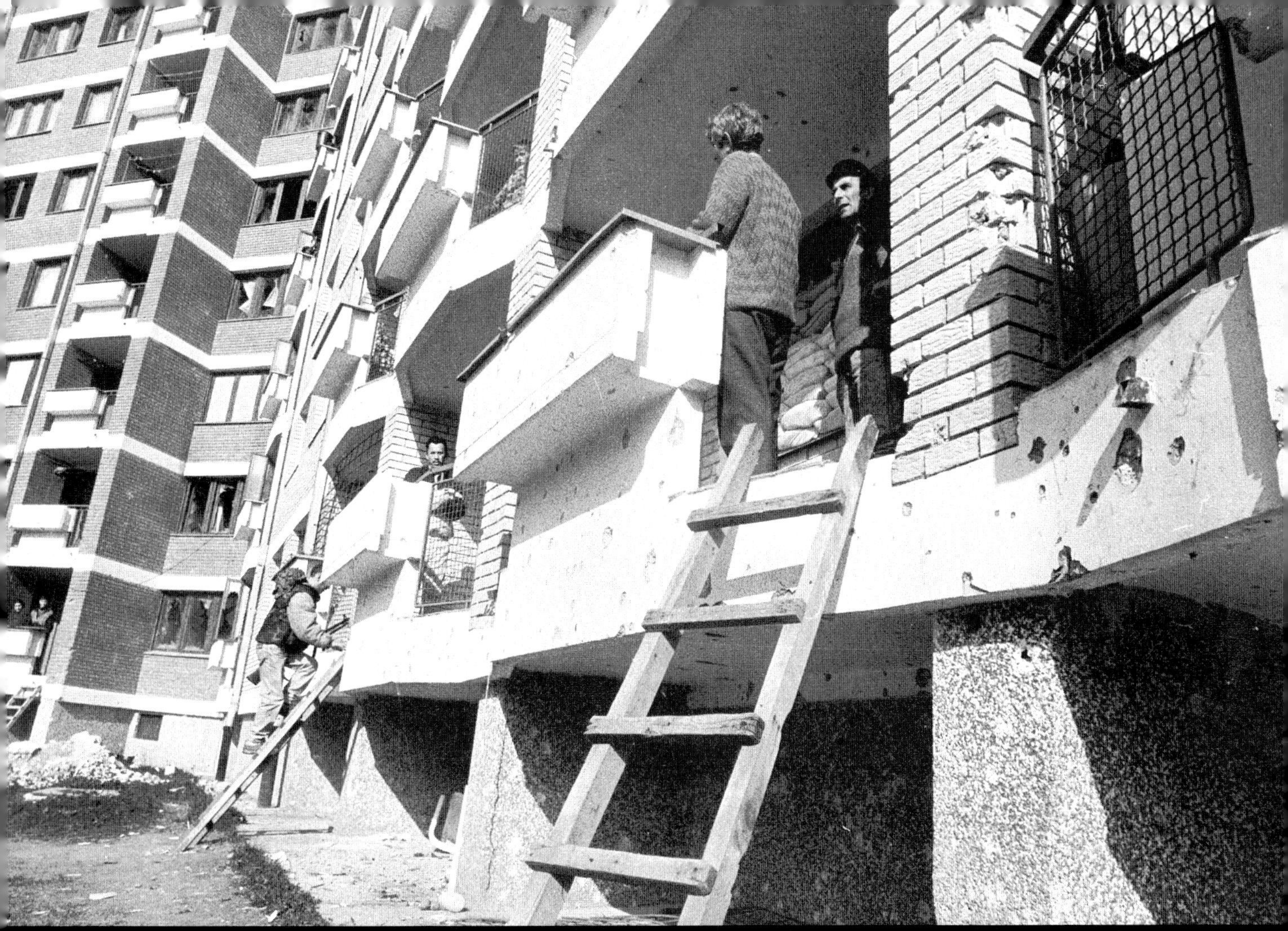

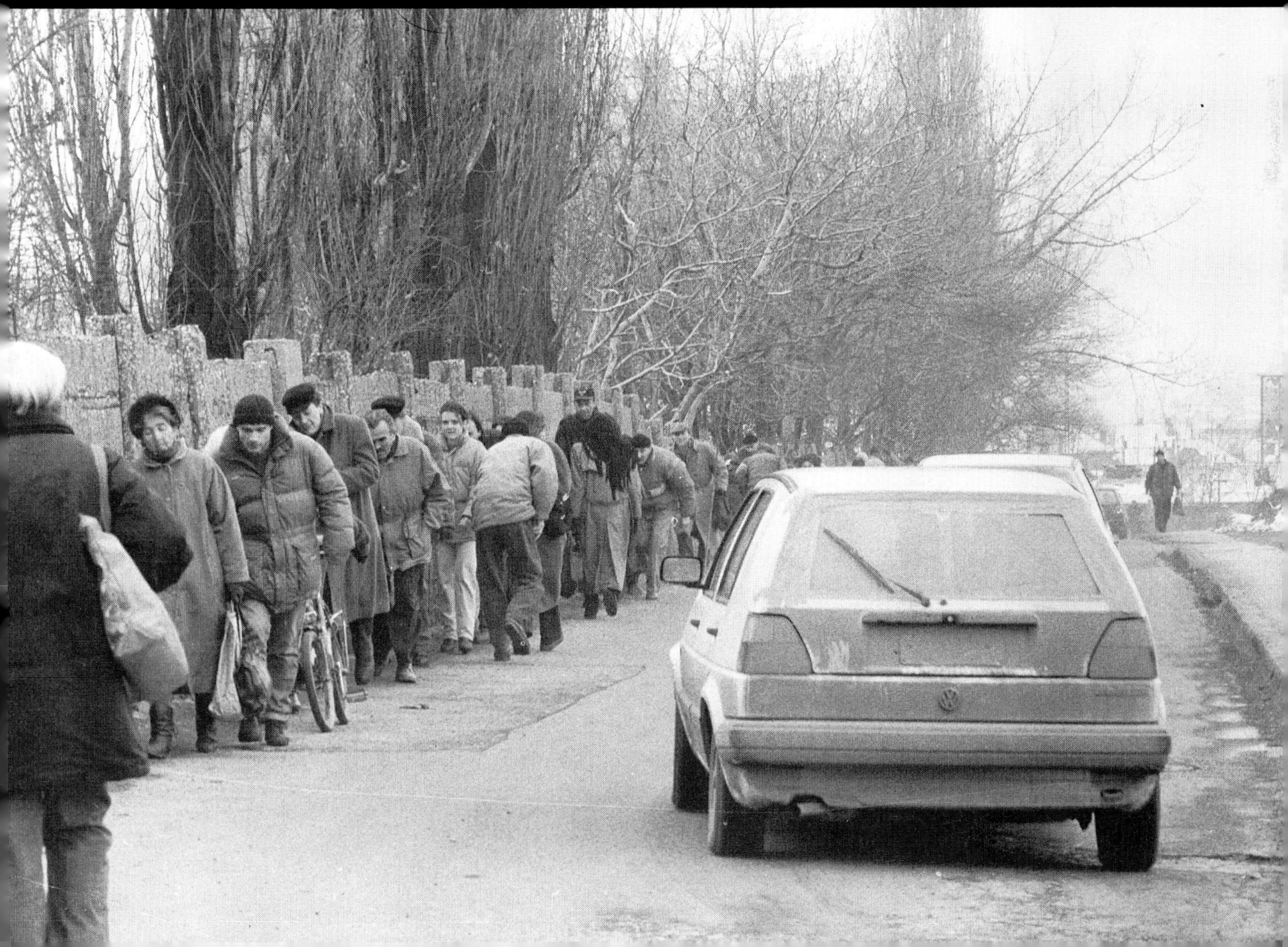

of paper: DM 25. Everything is priced in marks. A packet of cigarettes costs DM 2.5 or 3,200 dinars. The exchange rate today is 1,200–1,400 dinars to the mark.

"It is cold."

How could I warm myself up over these rays of light, Mr Mahatma? You are silent. I wonder whether you do not understand it or, simply, you do not want to. The calendar in Sarajevo is lightless. On the 3rd I wrote:

"... Pain and tears remain. Hatred grows. Revenge cures wounds. Nobody is fine.

"Will curses come down on those they are called upon?

"Will tears touch the souls and affect the destinies of those who caused them?

"How much pain will linger on even when all this is over?

"Mothers spin black wool, but there are no sheep. And death carries black flags in the streets. And tabuts. And crosses. And sermons over graves. But we used to live, live happily.

"It used to be so."

On the 6th:

"The hospital gradually stops working.

"The hospital dies.

"There is no oil for power units. We have recently had no electricity. The radio announces that incubators for babies have been switched off.

"The reporter adds in his report that worms have started to nest in the hospital's laundry. Worms in the laundry!? The hospital has enough food only for tomorrow's breakfast. It has none for other meals. On the 10th, Ivo Andrić's centenary commemoration would be held, like everywhere in normal circumstances. He is the only Nobel Prize winner from the former Yugoslavia. In Travnik, his birthplace, the daily 'Oslobođenje' would award its traditional prizes for a newspaper short story. This time nobody mentioned him. The following day the same newspaper interviewed the man who, with a sledgehammer, broke his white memorial in Višegrad, on the bank of the river from his famous novel "The Bridge on the Drina". That day a shell hit the orphanage in Sarajevo killing three and seriously wounding thirteen children in the wards of the orphanage. A month ago, a boy all in bandages on a hospital bed kept repeating: 'Is it my fault that I'm alive and they're not?' He survived a shell in a courtyard. His game with three friends was over. Nobody remembered an early speech of Andrić's: 'You know, if our people knew more about the past, I believe that many of the current misunderstandings would disappear... We would become sober and wise people if we directed the existing differences towards that water which drives our mutual mill. In fact, history has proved that nobody can live alone and we must live in a community. Not even together are we clever enough to deal with today's

under UNPROFOR supervision. A peaceful day. Occasional shelling of Mojmilo and Alipašino polje, areas in the Centre, Novo Sarajevo and Stari grad. Anti-aircraft machine guns, anti-aircraft guns and snipers fire from Vraca and Osmice at the city's main arteries. With the help of the UNHCR the "Rad" public utilities company organizes a six-day compaign to clean the city and dispose of the rubbish. After the departure of convoys for Split and Belgrade with two thousand sick children, mothers and old people, the Red Cross stops organizing further convoys. Sarajevo is visited by a delegation of the Islamic Conference Organization, headed by Hamid el Gabid, Secretary General.

Tuesday, 17th: A storm causes a power failure in the city. Owing to difficulties in providing adequate bread supplies, the City Presidency decides that each citizen, from December 1st, should get 233 grams of bread a day, according to the lists of and coupons for rations. There are 20 killed and 102 injured in B-H, and for the second day since the beginning of the war, no one is killed in Sarajevo but 17 are wounded. Dimitrij Rupel, the Slovenian Foreign Minister, writes to Dobrica Ćosić, as a writer to a writer. He requests that Dobrica Ćosić stop the continuation of the war in Sarajevo and to open the gates of Sarajevo.

Wednesday, 18th: The residential areas of Dobrinja, Vojničko polje, Mojmilo and Stup are shelled.
A colloquium entitled "The War in Bosnia and Herzegovina" is organized by the Board for Historical Science of the Academy of

Science of the Academy of Science and Arts of B-H. Two convoys with humanitarian aid arrive by way of land corridors.

Thursday, 19th: *The "SOS Lily" humanitarian agency initiates the activities to organize the return of displaced persons to Sarajevo. More than 200 tons of coal are stolen from the boiler plant storehouse at Čengić Vila. The "Pokop" undertakers need petrol for hearses and machines for digging graves. 21 killed and 149 injured in the town.*

Friday, 20th: *A transmission line collapses. Electricity is provided only for priority users. A five-month long telephone communications blockade is broken through. Some telephone lines communicate with the West. One minute of telephone conversation costs $10–15. The singer Michael Jackson sends Sarajevo a plane with food, clothes and medical supplies the value of to $2 million (reports the "Oslobođenje" correspondent from New York).*

Saturday, 21st: *Heavy shelling of Otes, Stup, Butmir, Sokolović kolonija and Kobilja glava. Anti-aircraft weapons fire at the municipalities of Stari grad, Centre, Novo Sarajevo and Dobrinja. Ten Muslims expelled from Grbavica manage to come to the part of the city near the hotel "Bristol". The Croatian Culture Society "Napredak" celebrates its 90th anniversary. Zlatko Dizdarević, a journalist on "Oslobođenje" is the first laureate of a newly established honour "The Award of Reporters without Frontiers" of a French foundation. The inaugural conference of the Association of B-H doctors of medicine*

world full of contradictions, let alone each of us individually. Belfast might be the best lesson for us. Whatever political solution is reached in Ireland, the Catholics and Protestants must live together because it is inevitable. Nobody will be so generous to present them with a new, promised land. There is not such a thing and probably never has been.'"

In the newspaper of the 14th there was an obituary with a photograph saying that on September 7th Alojz Heđi Bimbo had died at the age of 63 at Grbavica and had been buried either at Vraca or Lukavica. Forty days had elapsed before we learned about his death, and we were only some hundred metres away from each other. The river banks separated us. A few days later, his name was on the list of those who had parcels to collect.

Too late. Everything here is too late. Each fingerprint is the same. Misfortune is recognized in our pores.

On the same day, October 14th, there was a newspaper story of the woman journalist Edina Kamenica who was expelled from Grbavica. Everything that she possessed, all her life, is in two bags: "...I've taken with me nothing I loved best. Nothing. I froze, my movements became slow, my hands were not mine any more, nor my legs. Mother ran around the rooms. Mother cried, but I didn't shed a tear. I was an automatic machine before I reached this bank. Now? Now I also cry.

"...I'm unhappy about my books, my papers, the small stones and dead leaves I've been collecting all my life. All these will be thrown onto the floor, they will be trodden on, set on fire. It is the same as if all my life were under feet. All my life. I had two hours to put it into bags. (Therefore, I was a lucky one.)..."

And the same dilemma for days, weeks, months: do the convoys leave or not, do they or do they not...? Who among the helpless, the old, children, the wounded, pregnant women can leave? The number of those who would like to leave rises and falls, it is checked.

On the 18th I read a letter from Split from Zora V. to my dear Nada Salom: "...Somebody wrote somewhere that refugees wore invisible yellow ribbons that everyone could see. That's right. It is all the same if you're a refugee or have the plague. I've never been more lonely than during these four months I've been in exile. If one hadn't got a soul, one might somehow accept it. Although I know that all this is easier than living in a basement under constant barrages, it seems that it would be much easier for me to be in my basement than like this...

"You know, we live here with a guilty conscience about leaving the city and the people. This is the impression after each encounter with everyone that got out of Sarajevo. On the other hand, I know I had to do so because of the children, but it does not spare me a label... Some shells tear off arms, legs, heads, others break hearts and souls. Who can judge which is worse..."

On the 19th, the writer Sead Fetahagič writes that "our city and we in it are a world of a fantasy unknown so far." Mazowiecki on the 22nd sees us as Warsaw on the second day after the end of the war. Some others compare us to the Berlin debris across which old people carried water, wood or half a loaf of bread.

On the 27th General Philippe Morillon announces the demilitarization of Sarajevo. We immediately forget the shortage of water and electricity, everything we went through.

On the 29th I wrote:

"Three metres away from death. The distance between life and death is measured here in feet. Here seconds are another measure of hits and misses.

"And this goes on day after day. We measure survival by hours, weeks, months.

"Today a shell exploded on the handrail on the edge of the flyover under which I was selling my newspapers. It exploded just above my head.

"A piece of shrapnel I picked up from the dust was still hot. It was aimed at me, at you, it is unimportant at which one of us..."

Everything is centered around icon lamps. In a hanging silver-plated dish a wick burns in oil. New life makes the icon, and the church wall on which they are both hung is where we stand. Everything is the wall, the icon lamp, the saint's picture on singed wood or the canvas peppered with bullets.

What does the news from the beginning of July mean that trains are to start again on the Bosnian-Herzegovinian railways in ten days? Telephone lines with the world are about to be established? Sarajevo will be unblocked. Only 700 metres divide us from breaking out of the deadly encirclement of the city. Et cetera. Et cetera. Et cetera. Etc.

Wick after wick burns in oil lamps. The flashing plankton becomes visible with the stroke of a night swimmer. It flashes, but at the same time it creates unease. The dark is thick. Sparks are deceptive.

We waited for the world's help. We believed salvation would come from the West. We trusted the East. But we were alone. Helpless, we swallowed our oaths. Neither the Cross nor the Crescent carried the torch of salvation. The war I am in did not know the red cross or the red crescent. It did not know about white flags, either. It was deaf to the word, given and promised. In this war, the signatures of leaders were worthless. We crossed the crossroads of death running. We trusted God and love, we dreamed of happiness. One of the basic religious assumptions, that it is necessary to love your neighbour like yourself, was chal-

is held. Dr Faruk Konjhodžić is appointed president. The writer Sait Orahovac dies at the age of 84.

Sunday, 22nd: *No one is killed in Sarajevo. 14 people wounded.*

Monday, 23rd: *Difficulties with electricity and water supplies. The eighth round of military negotiations at Sarajevo Airport fails. At a colloquium on the roots of the genocide in B-H the professors and students of the Faculty of Political Science "Veljko Vlahović" symbolically mark the beginning of the first period of war. The thieves who stole Suad Alić's cow from Koševo hill are captured. The cow was slaughtered at Hrid by Mustafa and Elvedin Brekalović. Seven days before that they had stolen a calf from the same owner. General Philippe Morillon: "Our task and aim is to demilitarize Sarajevo before Christmas". The date for September pensions to be paid out is still unknown.*

Tuesday, 24th: *A relatively quiet day. Occasional sudden shellings of the outskirts of Stari grad and the Centre. A shell falls in Olympic Street at Mojmilo killing five and injuring nine people. Alipašino polje and Dobrinja are occasionally shelled. An American envoy Patrick Moynihan visits Sarajevo. Jacques Malik, French Deputy Minister of Defence, is also in Sarajevo. The Trade Unions of B-H* *appeal to the UNHCR to provide wood and coal for Sarajevans as humanitarian aid and to request UNPROFOR to enable their safe transport into the town. A convoy of mothers and children, organised by the Children's Embassy, leaves in the direction of Belgrade. Measures are taken to remove all damaged vehicles from public places in the city. Shortage of electricity even in hospitals. Postmen start delivering letters, which come either through the "Intersped" company or UNPROFOR.*

Wednesday, 25th: A rather quiet day. Some parts of the town are shelled in the evening. The airport is closed owing to clashes around it. The humanitarian aid in food received in four months satisfies only 6% of the B-H population's requirements, or 20% of Sarajevo's requirements. 6 people dead, 50 injured in Sarajevo. The District Military Attorney lodges a claim to begin an investigation against the Canadian General Lewis Mackenzie, who is under suspicion of having commited a war crime against civilians.

Thursday, 26th: A relatively peaceful day. Shells fall on the city centre. A convoy of 7 buses carrying 500 mothers and children leaves for Split and Czechoslovakia. In Rinaitingen in Switzerland, Reis-ul-ulema, **hajji Jakuf Effendi Selmoski, the Sarajevo Archbishop,** *Monsignor Vinko Puljić and Patriarch Pavle hold a meeting with a request that the bloodshed in B-H be stopped. Sarajevo airport hosts a meeting between General Janko Bobetko and General Ratko Mladić, the representatives of the HVO and the aggressor's army.*

lenged. We all were fleeing. Our whole families were fugitives. Few were the peaceful havens, shelters where we could rest. They were far away, out of our reach.

In the calm of the dark, near the oil lamps, I looked for Baton. I wanted to check if he was repeating slavishly: "The Romans did not send dogs and herdsmen to mind the cattle, but wolves." They took him far from Bosnia and the Daesitates to die in Ravenna. Today it is different.

It is the 24th. The month is not important anyway:

"Everybody is leaving. They go leaving no trace behind. Some do not even say goodbye. They go silently.

"The Poles and Czechs left on April 13th. Havel's plane, they say, came to pick them. All those who had some or any Polish, Czech or Slovak origins got on board and left.

"The Serbs, those under the remote control of the SDS (Serbian Democratic Party), with messages or in silence, had left earlier, much earlier. All the frightened and farsighted had left in April, March or earlier. They were Muslims, Croats, Serbs... In March or thereabouts, the Yanks carefully pulled out their citizens.

The Jews left on several occasions. In the beginning they left on their own with their families. I remember Đoko told me last summer, while we were among the August bathers on the beaches of the Pelješac peninsula, he and his brother were invited to the Jewish Community office, or some such place. They told them their mother was a Jew, they were Jews, and to let the Community know if they decided to leave. Tickets and accommodation were provided for them and their families.

Later the Jews took their friends, too, in their convoys. They had no problems at the barricades. Nobody stopped them. They took out buses and buses of people. Being a Jew was a safe exit visa.

Out went the Croats, too, via Stup and Doglode, to Kiseljak. Without problems.

People are leaving, leaving, leaving!

Two Slovenian ministers took the Slovenes out of Sarajevo. All those who brushed against a Slovene woman, Slovenia or the Slovenes, leave. By telephone they check in Slovenia whether their grandmother's grandmother was a Slovene's godmother's sister-in-law, etc.

The Romanies would like to leave. They leave the city. They have sold their cookers and there is nobody to beg from. Here everybody is given alms. They feel like leaving. Somebody promised to take them out later. They do not want to wait, they want to go now.

Foreign students had to demonstrate in order to get out. They left with the help of UNPROFOR. The bus drivers were stopped, put in prison, killed, but nobody knows exactly why and how.

The Albanians want to leave. It is not their war, they say, and they do not want to steal. They cannot work so why should they stay? There are no more pastry shops. No bakers. No shops that are open. They do not let them, but they feel like leaving. They leave, too.

Swallows have left. Storks have left. Children have left. Old people have left. The sick have left. The wounded are leaving. Politicians are leaving. Artists are leaving. Business people are leaving. The avenues and parks are leaving.

Everybody is leaving. Everybody would like to go somewhere. They all want to go for a short time or for good.

Here, the winter remains. Cold creeps into our beds, bones and souls. Cemeteries remain. The hope remains that it will be better, that all this will stop, that we shall live, that all this will pass, that tomorrow will come.

Tomorrow remains. The mornings that will brighten us up, that will come, that we wait for remain.

Some eyes, too, remain in wait. And some palms wet from waiting. You and I remain.

When will the next convoy leave! Where to!

Will there be anyone to wave goodbye from the platform...

You are here, too, Master William, with your starched collar. Do not speak to me as an actor. Do you read your text, dear Shakespeare, about young men driven by the wind around the world to look for happiness far away from home where so little can be seen?

You cannot understand me. There are no air tickets here. No train or bus tickets. No oil or petrol. There is no road they can leave along. There remain only bare feet, worn out soles and a look towards the sky. You cannot go anywhere. The Sarajevan still travels only to death.

My noble Pločar, the good Jure Franičević. I return to the first stanza of your poem that I must repeat:

"*When a man dies*
the earth becomes heavier
and deeper
by a wound
blacker by a cave
and by one nail knocked into the coffin..."

I must because I have no other choice. What am I do with a sentence from a grammar school student's letter to his parents:

"...Sadness is for all of you who remained."

Hope for a new beginning is only flight."

One can live everywhere, but only die in Sarajevo and Bosnia. This is going to last a long time.

Flee anywhere as soon as you have a chance. My struggle will be a struggle for as good a position in society as possible. If it were normal, we'd all struggle only for this...

I am choking. A multitude of sparks burning out flicker in my sight. I am pushing my way, I am sliding on ice, I am stumbling, I am fainting.

I am sinking into the dark.

Alija Izetbegović refuses Dobrica Ćosić's proposal that the two of them meet the Nobel Prize Winner Eli Wiesel and Radovan Karadžić.

Friday, 27th: *Inadequate electricity supply of the town. A relatively quiet day. Alipašino polje, Vojničko polje and Dobrinja are shelled. 3 people are killed and 23 injured in Sarajevo. A special Jordanian plane comes to Sarajevo with humanitarian aid and 90 foreign citizens from Arabic countries with their families. Sarajevo is visited by the representatives of the Helsinki Committee from Prague: Radha Kumar, director of the International Secretariate of the Helsinki Committee from Prague, Toni Benetoli, president and secretary-general of the ARCI and representative of all the European peace organizations and Aleksandar Slavevski, president of the European Cities' Conference.*

Saturday, 28th: *A transmission line feeding the Buća potok substation collapses following shelling. Most of the town is without electricity. One person is killed, 24 injured. A promotion of the "B-H Days" periodical. The Croatian Chamber of Commerce is established.*

Sunday 29th: *Eli Wiesel, a Nobel Peace Prize Winner, visits Sarajevo for a couple of hours. Sarajevo is also visited by Monsignor Gabriel Montalno, a papal nuncio in Belgrade, who comes to Sarajevo as a special papal envoy. Muslim intellectuals appeal to the Islamic Countries' Conference for help in stopping the aggression and genocide.*

CIRCLE EIGHT

Monday, 30th: The town is without electricity. On behalf of the organization "Journalists without Frontiers", Rauling Chantreau from Brest brings two lorries of humanitarian aid in food, medicine and clothes to the State Hospital "Sarajevo". An offer from le Centre Hospitalier Laënnec from Bretagne, governed by Louis Rolland, to cooperate with the State Hospital in Sarajevo is accepted with great pleasure. In the "Ramiz Salčin" Barracks (formerly "Viktor Bubanj") three POW's are killed by a 82-mm shell fired from Nedžarići. Five others are wounded. A member of the Presidency of the Republic of B-H, Ejup Ganić, declares: "A limited military intervention is possible."

DECEMBER

Tuesday, 1st: According to a decision by the Presidency of the City of Sarajevo Assembly, bread can be bought from today only with ration coupons. Every citizen can buy only 233 grams a day (a third of a 700-gram loaf). For the production of the 112,000 loaves of 700 grams required by the town it is necessary to provide 70

Where am I? The darkness has gone. I am still sliding somewhere. The whiteness hurts me. I feel it painfully in my eyes. Is someone, perhaps, silently driving me somewhere? Did I hear bells? I shut my eyes again. I try to orientate myself. Crystals of whiteness thrust themselves into my pupils. I close my eyelids tight. I hurry. I rub my eyes with my palms. I have the chills. What is it now? Peace and bells around me. When I plunge into the darkness behind my eyelids I see a luxuriant fig tree, its ripe fruits burst open. Thick juice pours out. Behind is a pomegranate with its fruits still green. Their peel is still red with the sunshine. Whiteness, dark, figs, a silent ride and the cold. Nightmare. I cannot orientate myself to what I see and what I have memorized from the past.

I look back. I look for Vergil through my half-opened eyelids. I see only big black eyes in an endless whiteness. I like their warmth. Their colour refreshes me. I have become accustomed to the dark. These black grains are something completely different. These eyes are familiar to me. Are they mine? Are they?

"The black Sarajevo eyes cast glances at me in ambush as I pass by."

Is someone drawing my attention to the warmth I let myself feel?

"How could the heart resist them, for God's sake . . ."

My toes freeze. I do not feel my hands. Look, the joints of my fingers are red. They swell. They ache. I have never had this before. I am cold. I shiver more and more. Whiteness is all around.

A spark in the dark eyes of a woman calms me down. It encourages me.

". . . I do not know what hours, Paradise beauties, look like – we should see them – but in this world the young Sarajevo girls are taken as beauties."

The good Nerkezi whispers. The Bard of Sarajevo takes me through the whiteness. Now he sends me verses to look for my angel whose wings will not get entangled:

"We shall present the pious with Paradise,

"Aren't the beauties of Sarajevo enough for those in love . . .

"Beauties like the Moon sometimes cheer up the soul of a sad man, and the mistresses of Sarajevo sometimes make one weep."

The verse I skipped returns to me:

"How could the heart resist them for God's sake,

When the black Sarajevo eyes cast glances at me in ambush . . ."

How?

A woman's gentle hands and a smile below her black eyes hold me so I do not fall down. Vergil is not here. I rely on the warmth of the black eyes. "My dear and my only little Zlaty," wrote the sick Kranjčević. He was writing to his

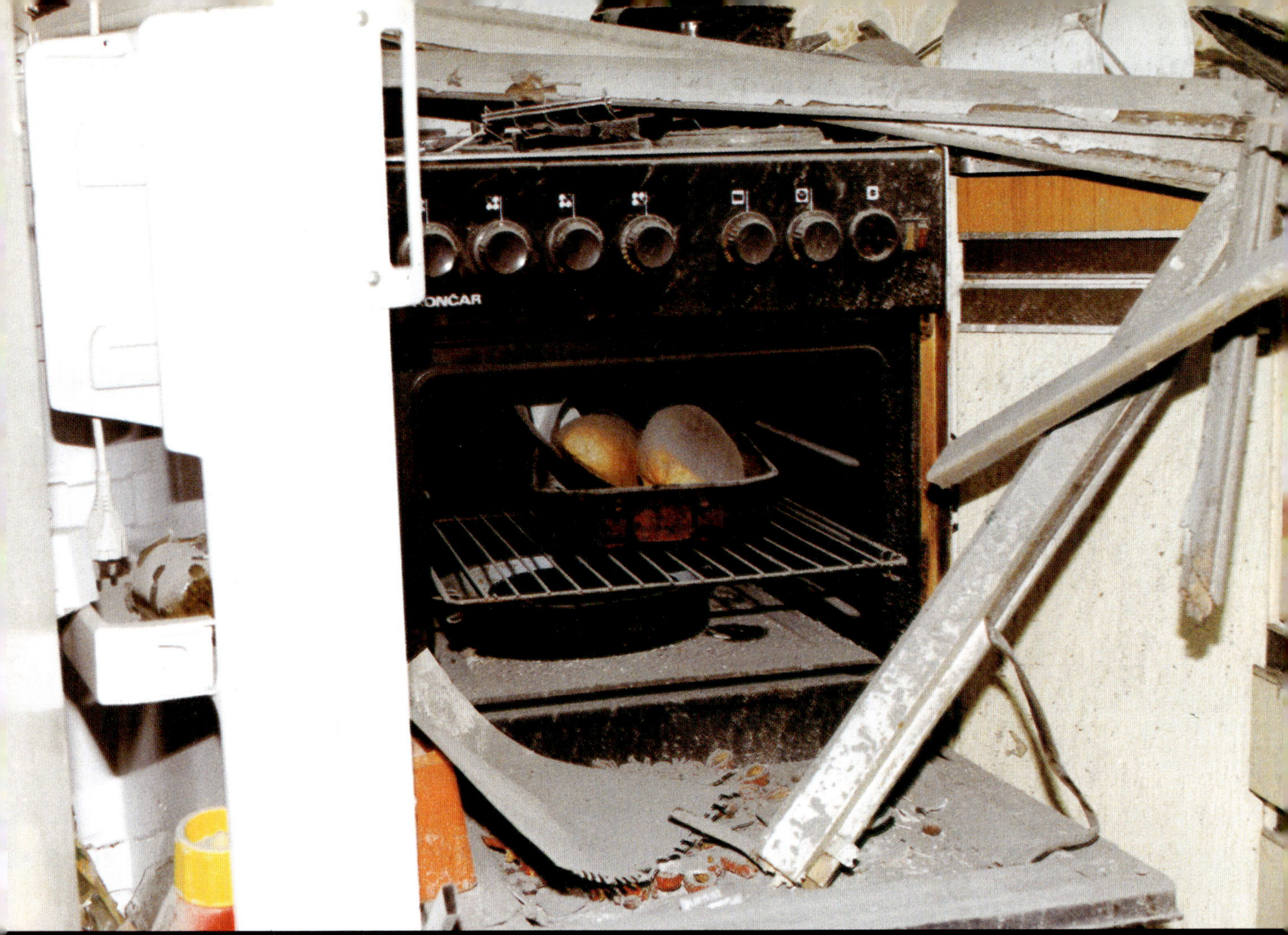

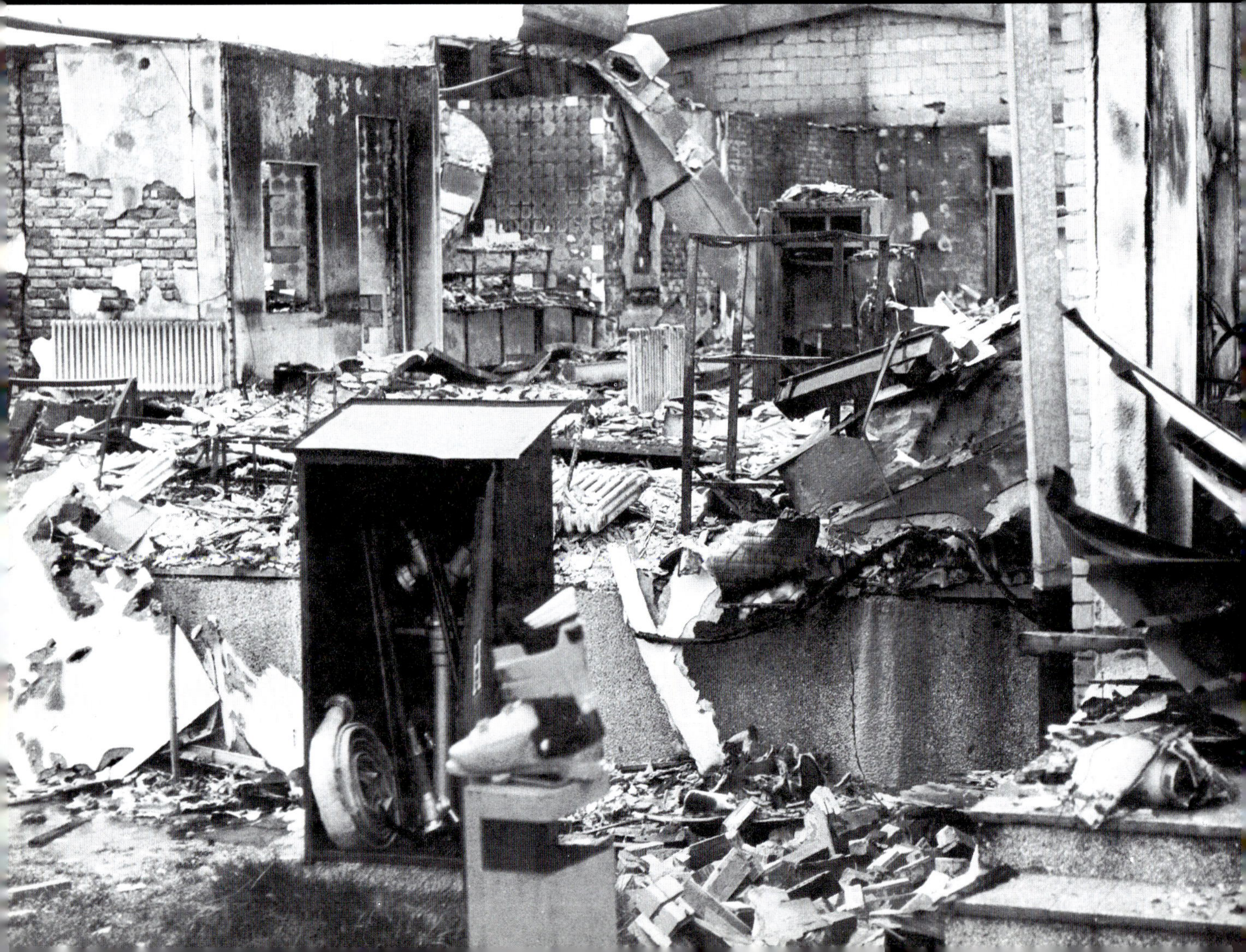

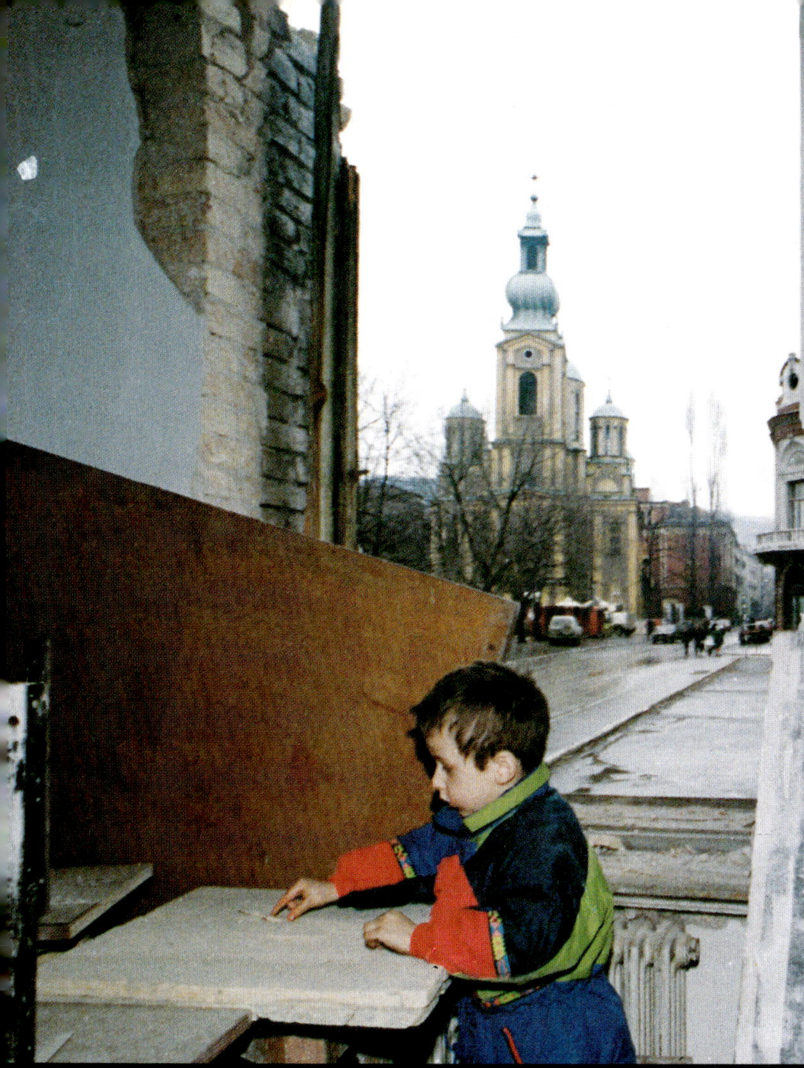

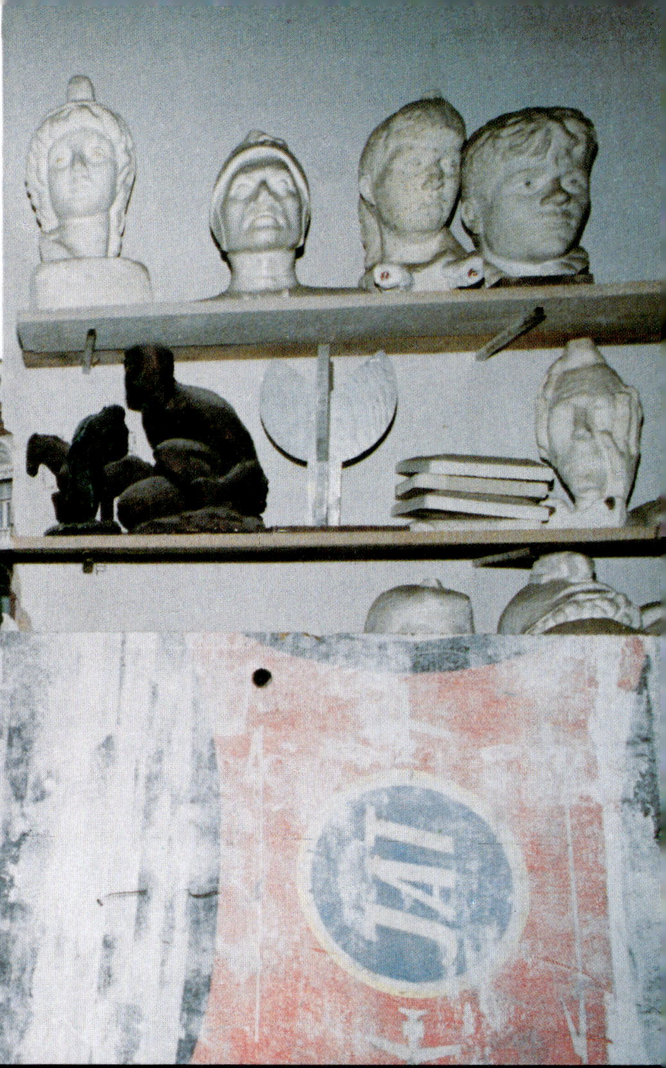

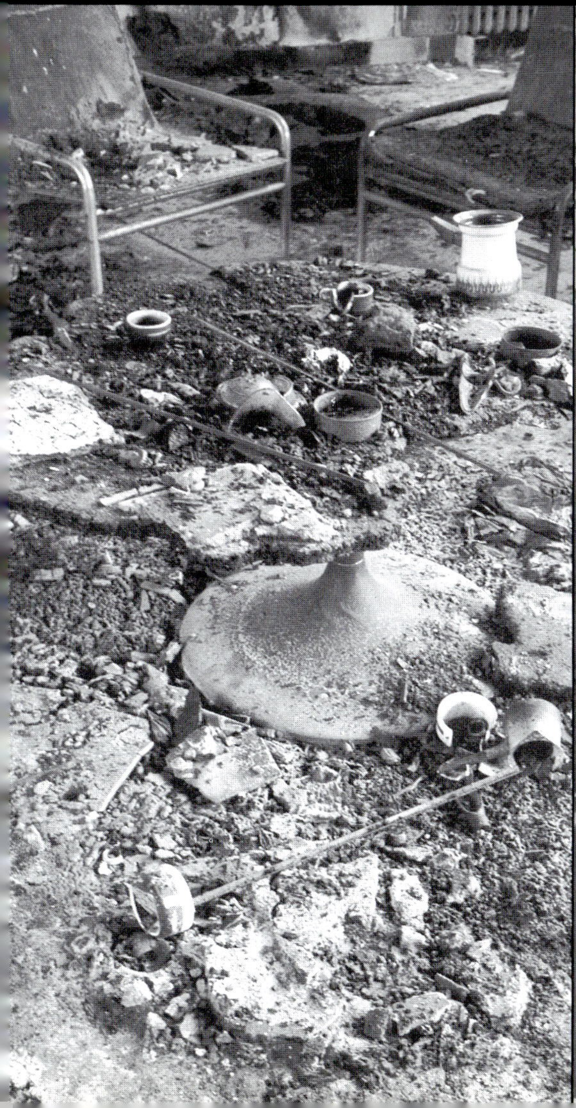

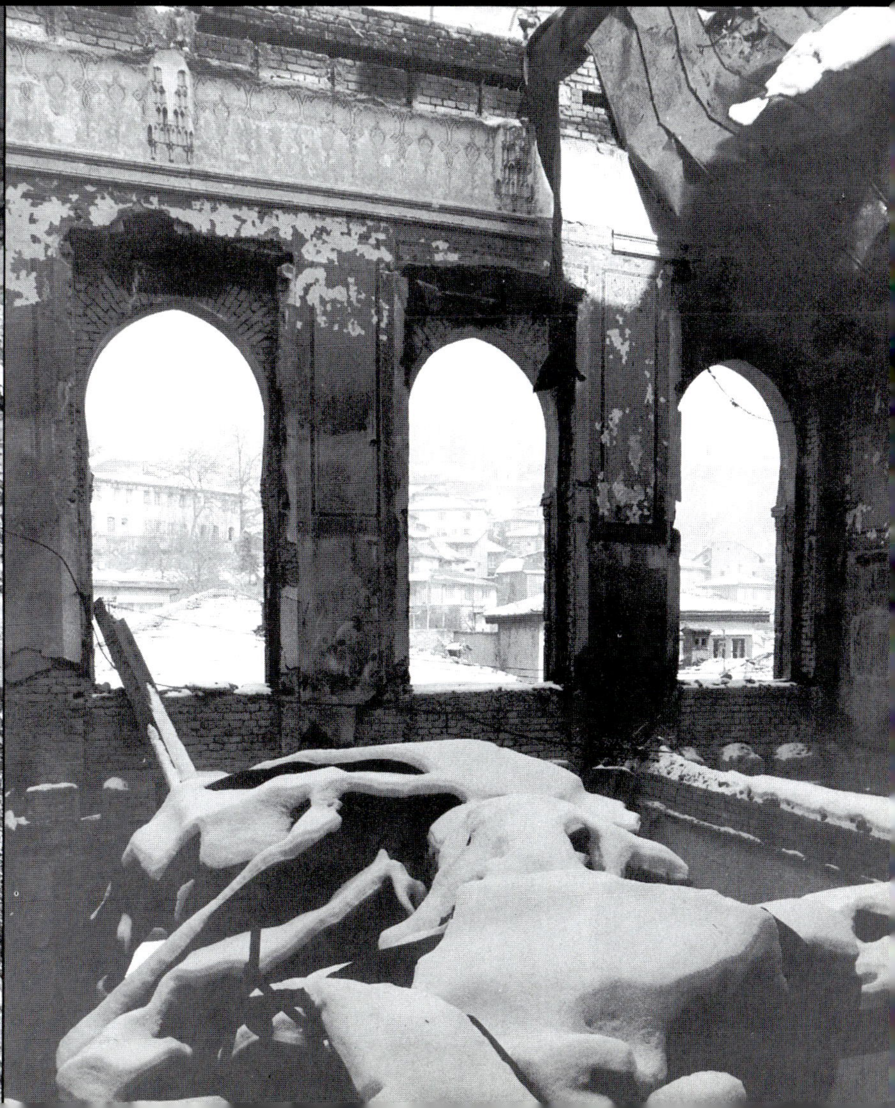

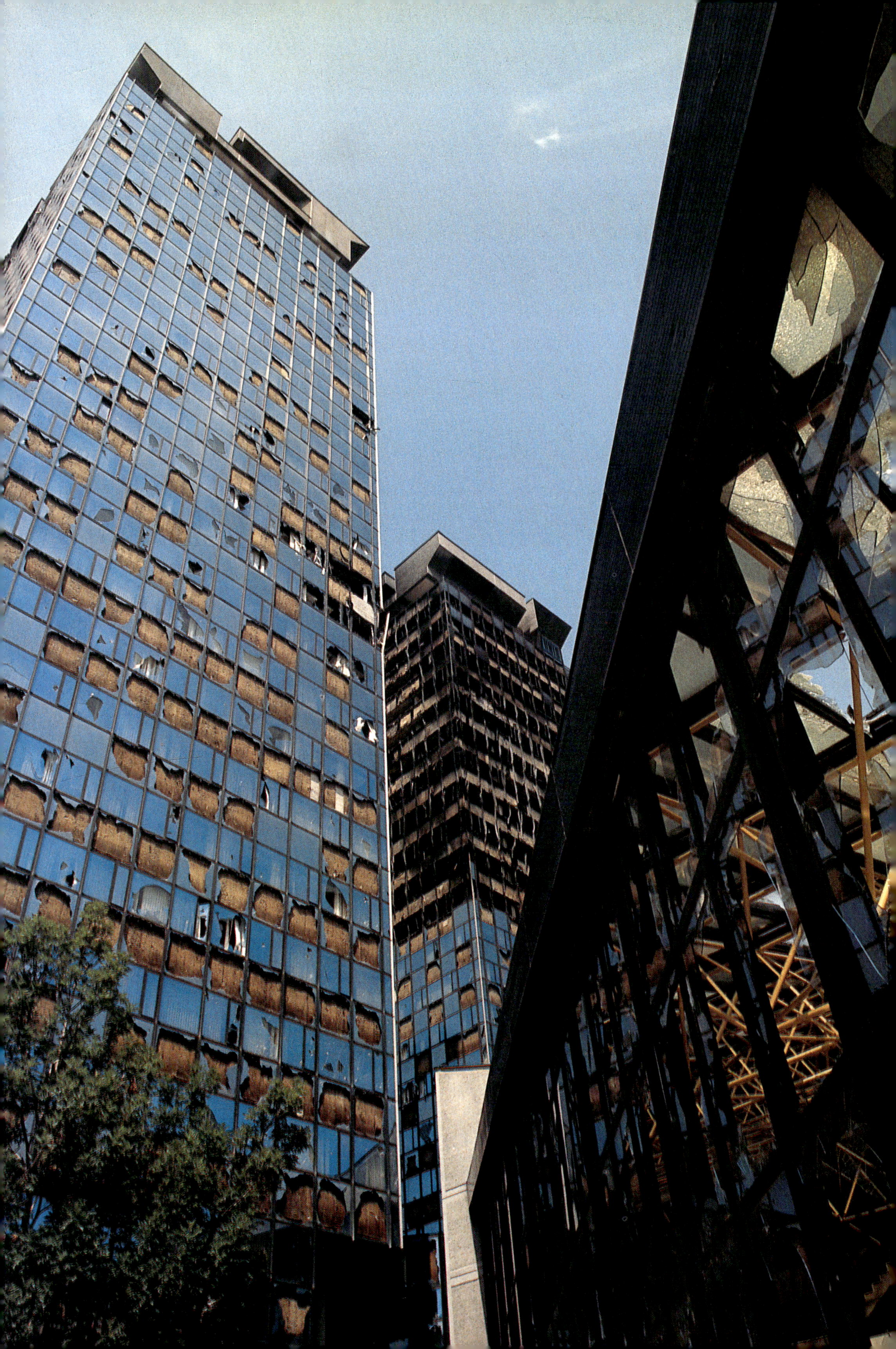

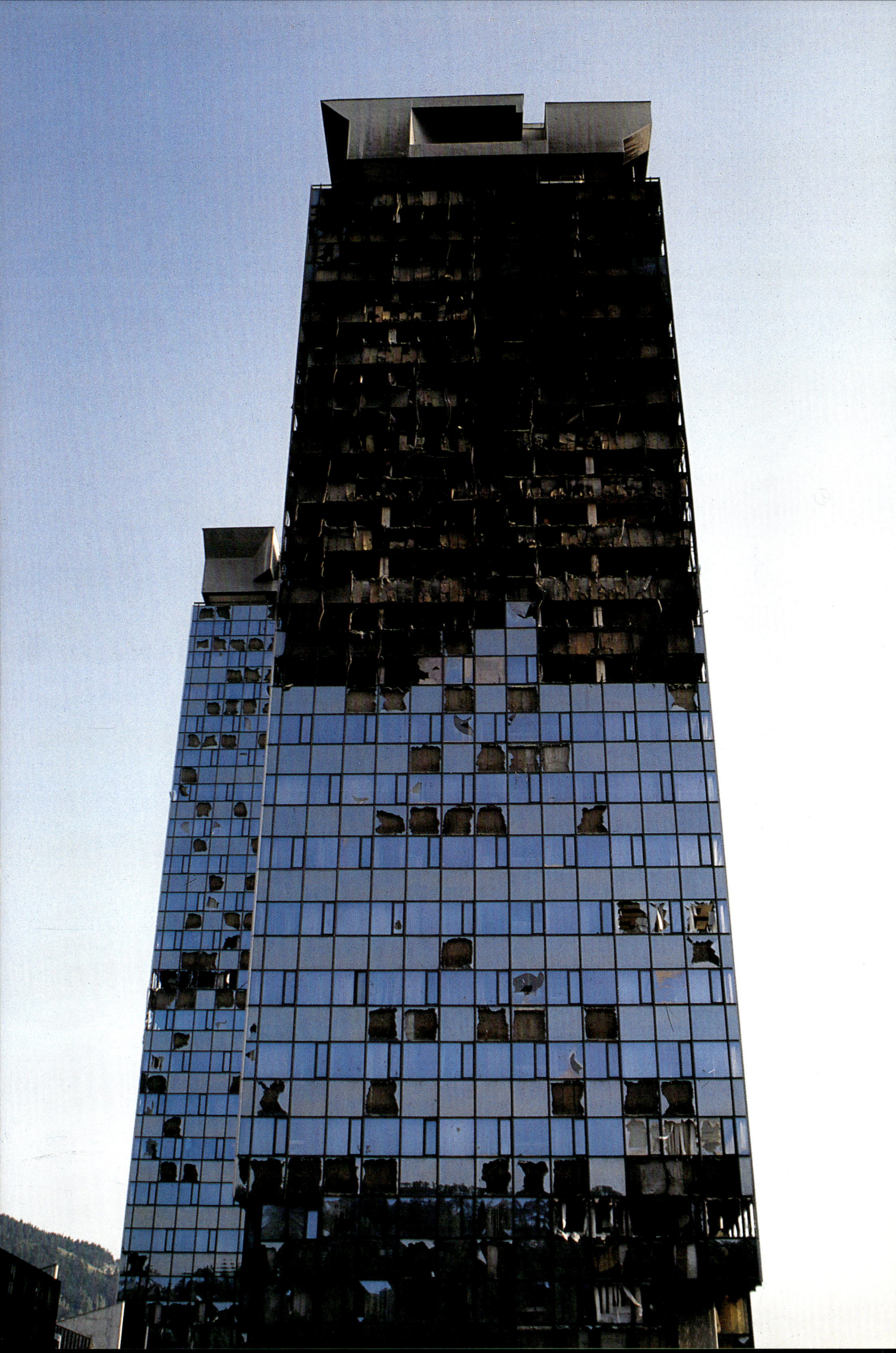

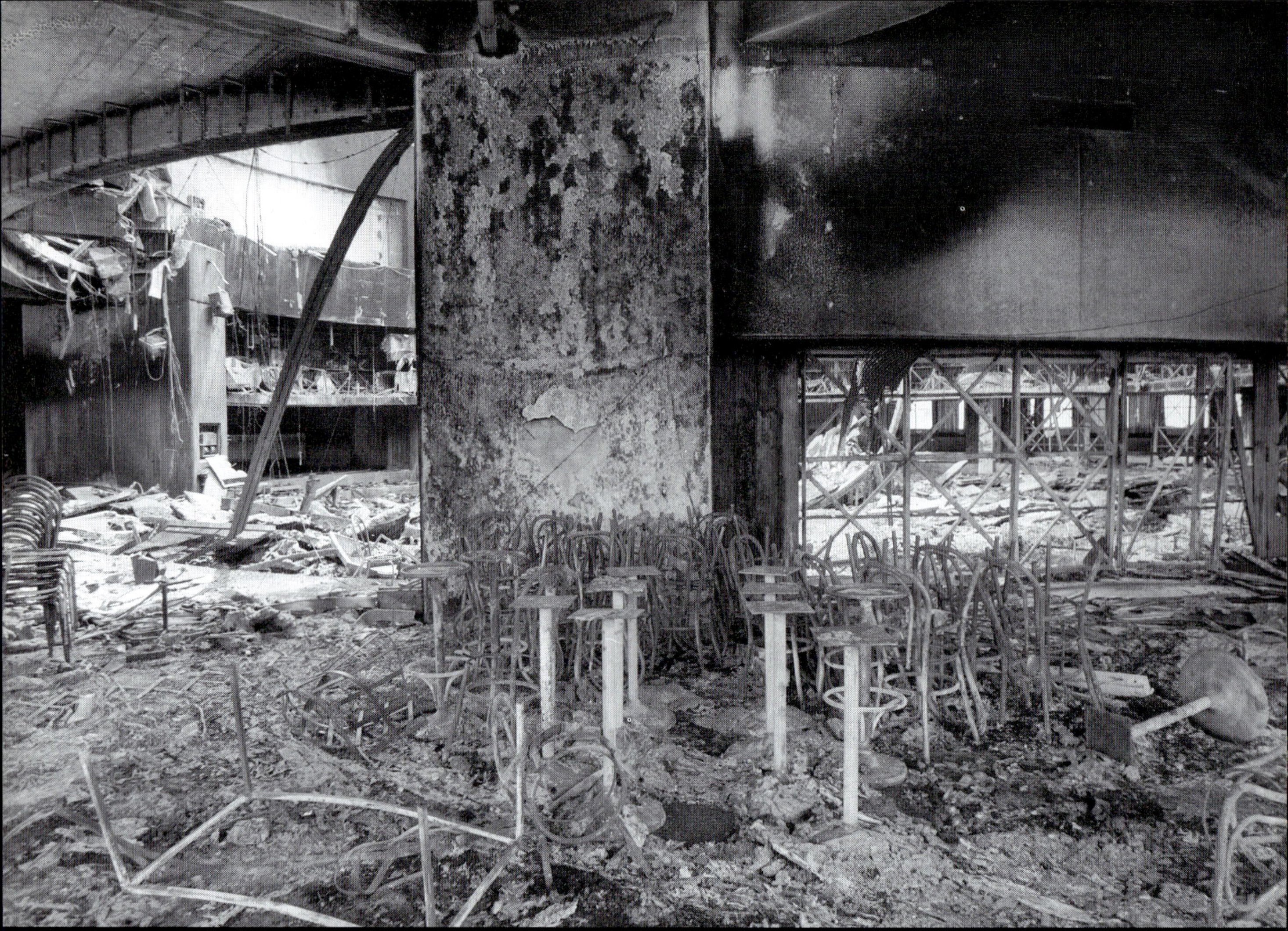

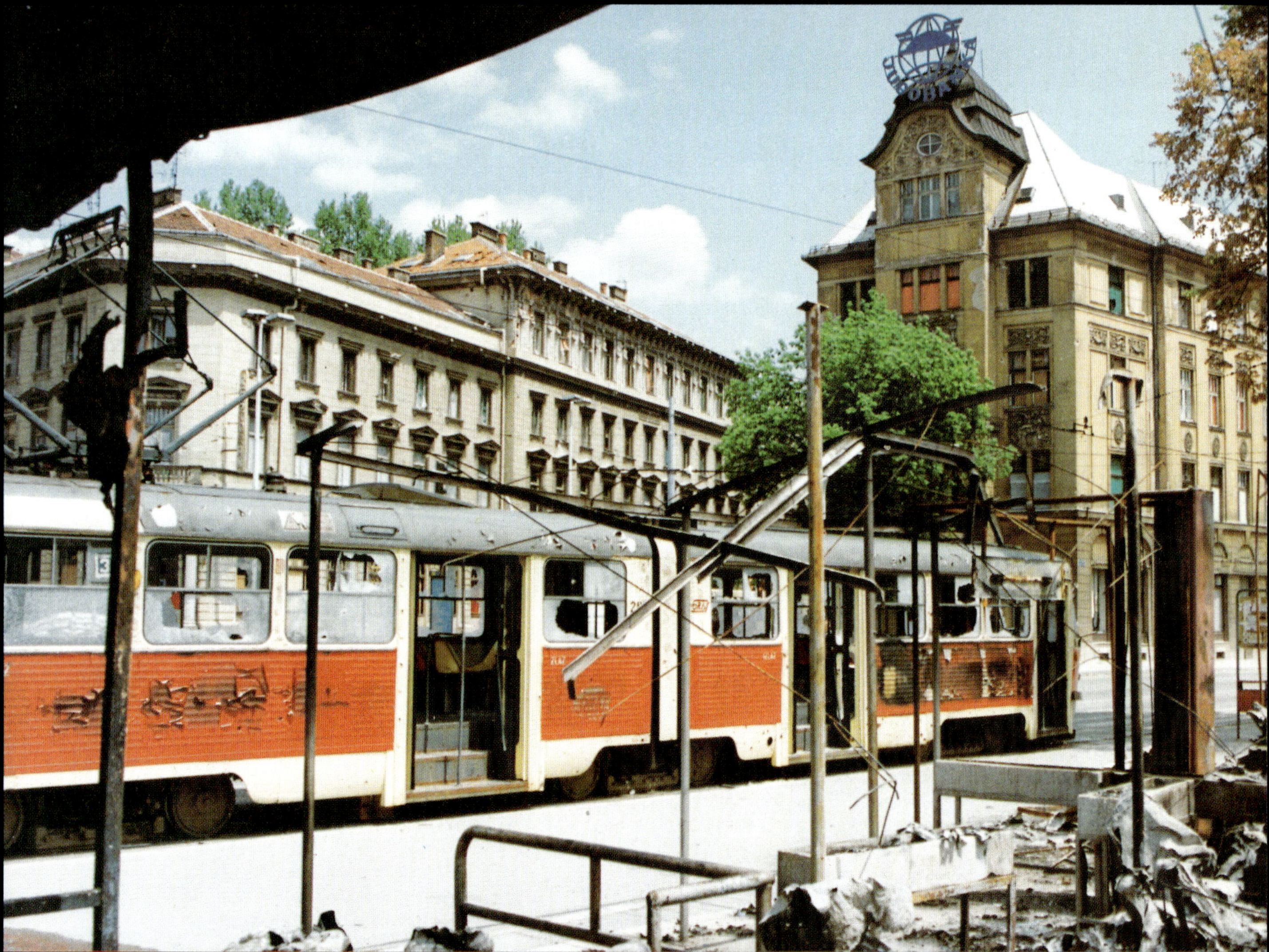

SARAJEVO – THE WOUNDED CITY

1872
1972

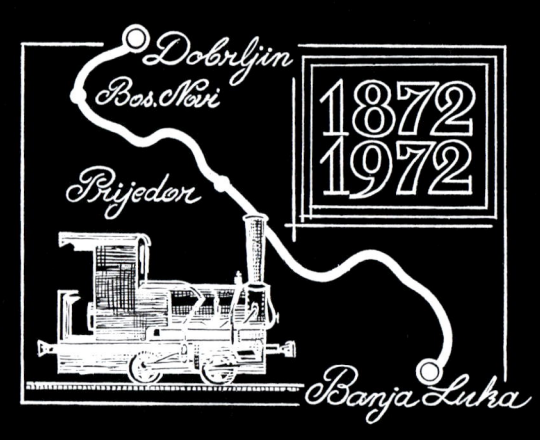

Dobrljin
Bos. Novi
Prijedor
Banja Luka

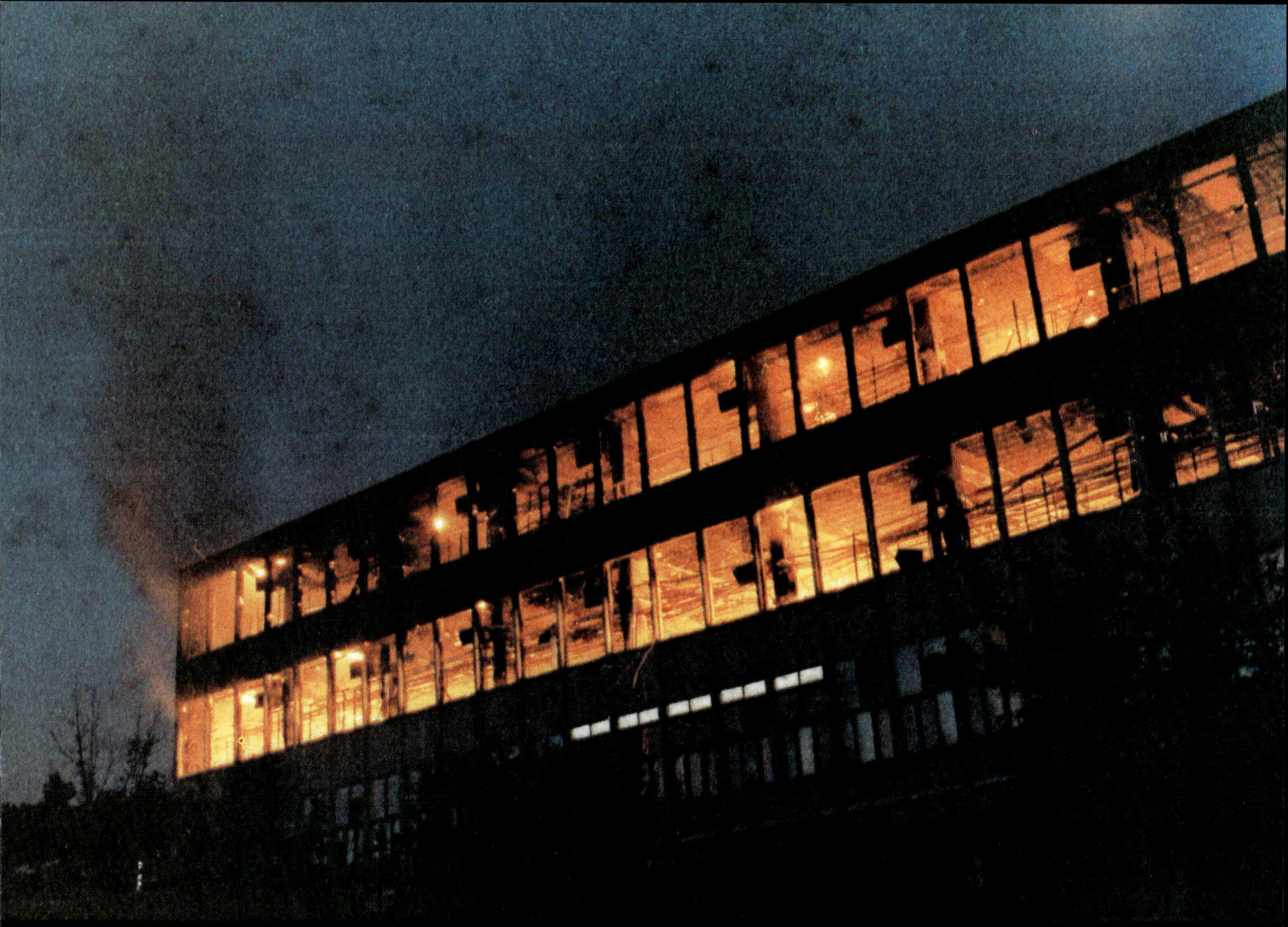

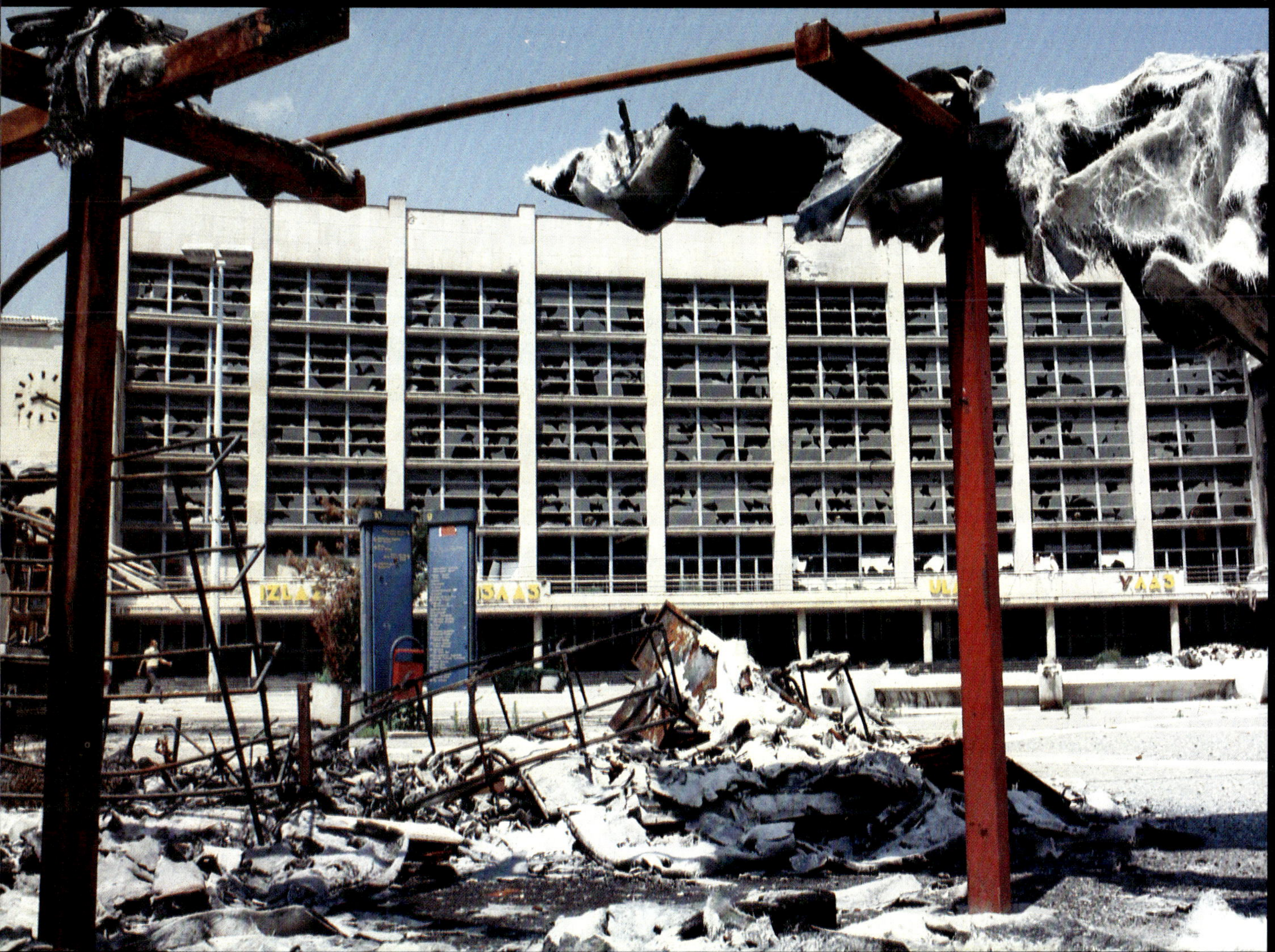

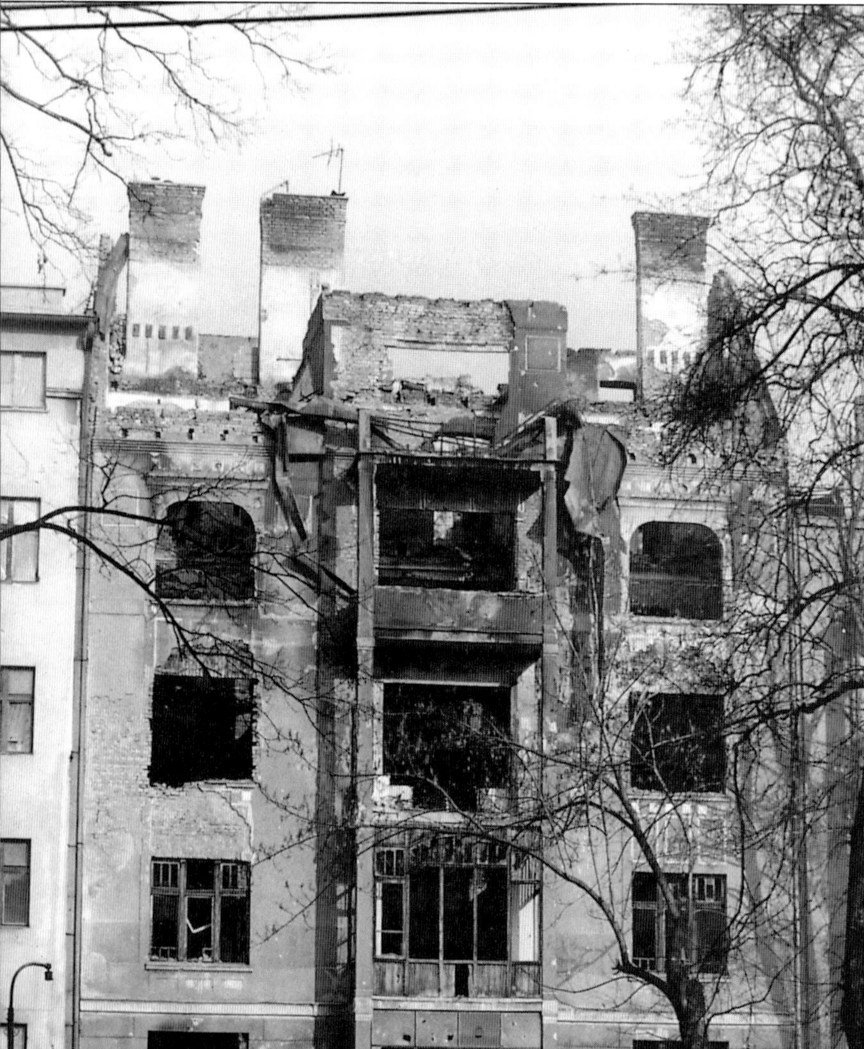

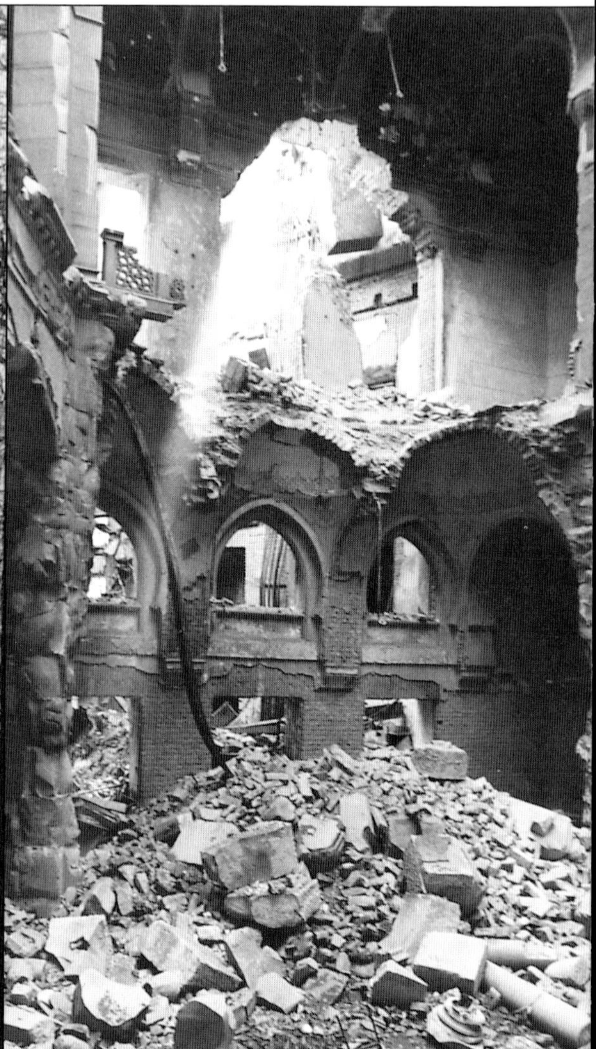

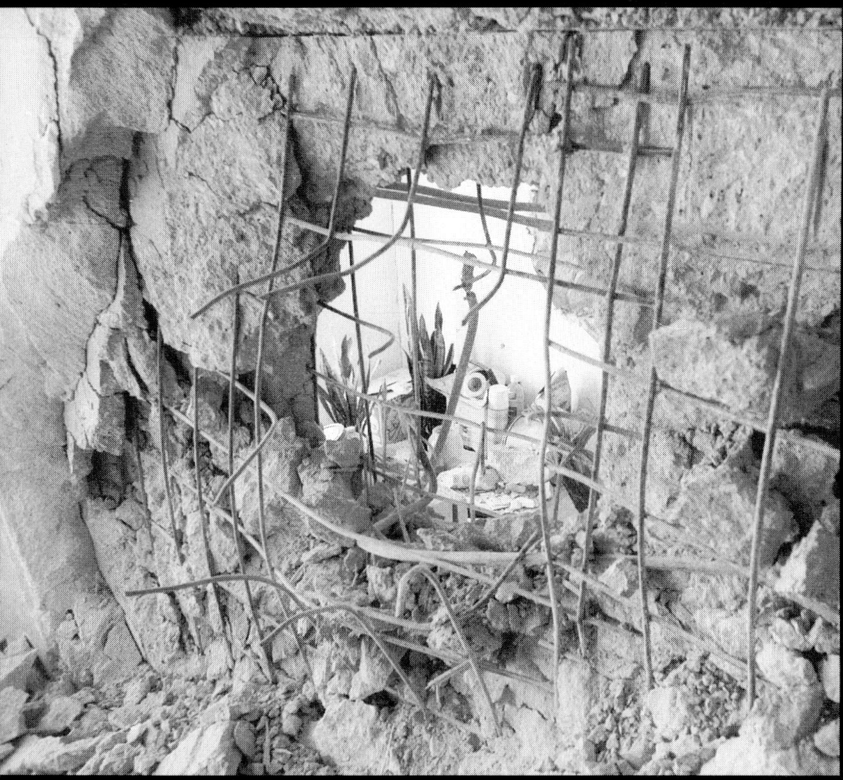

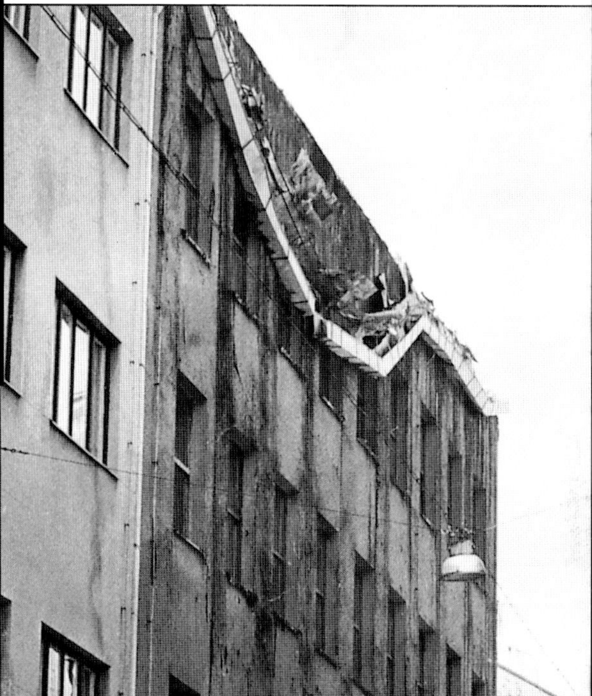

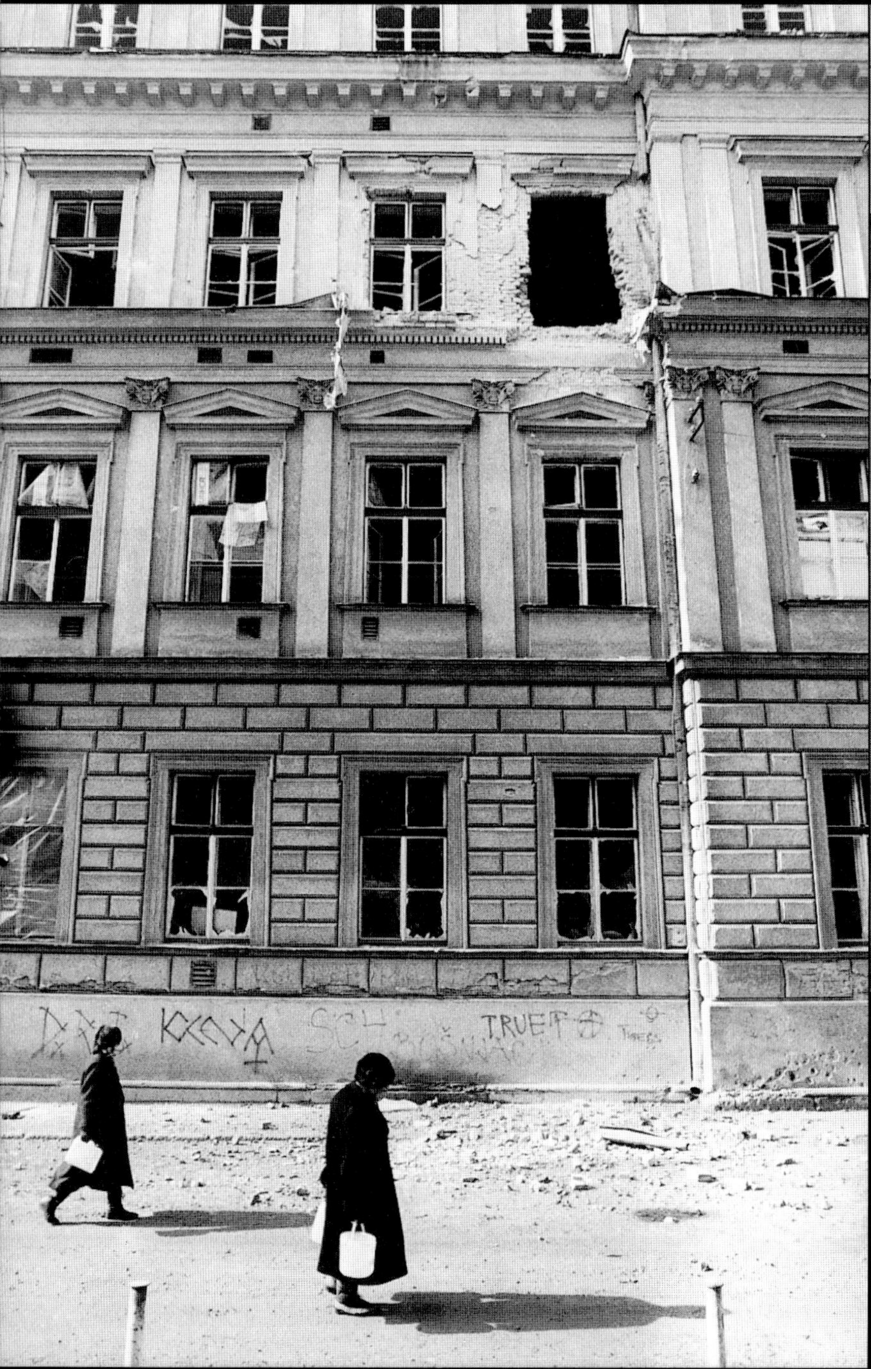

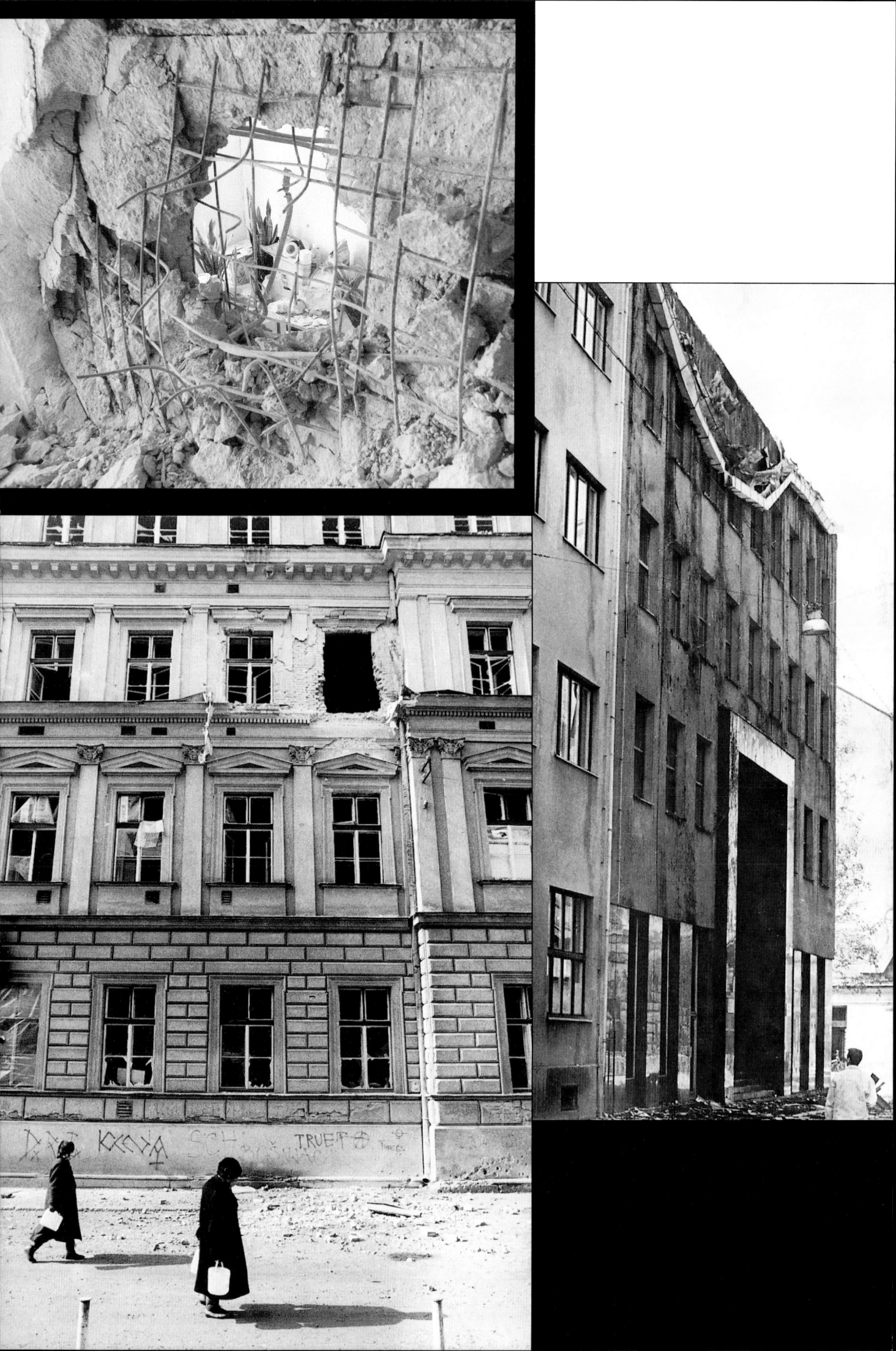

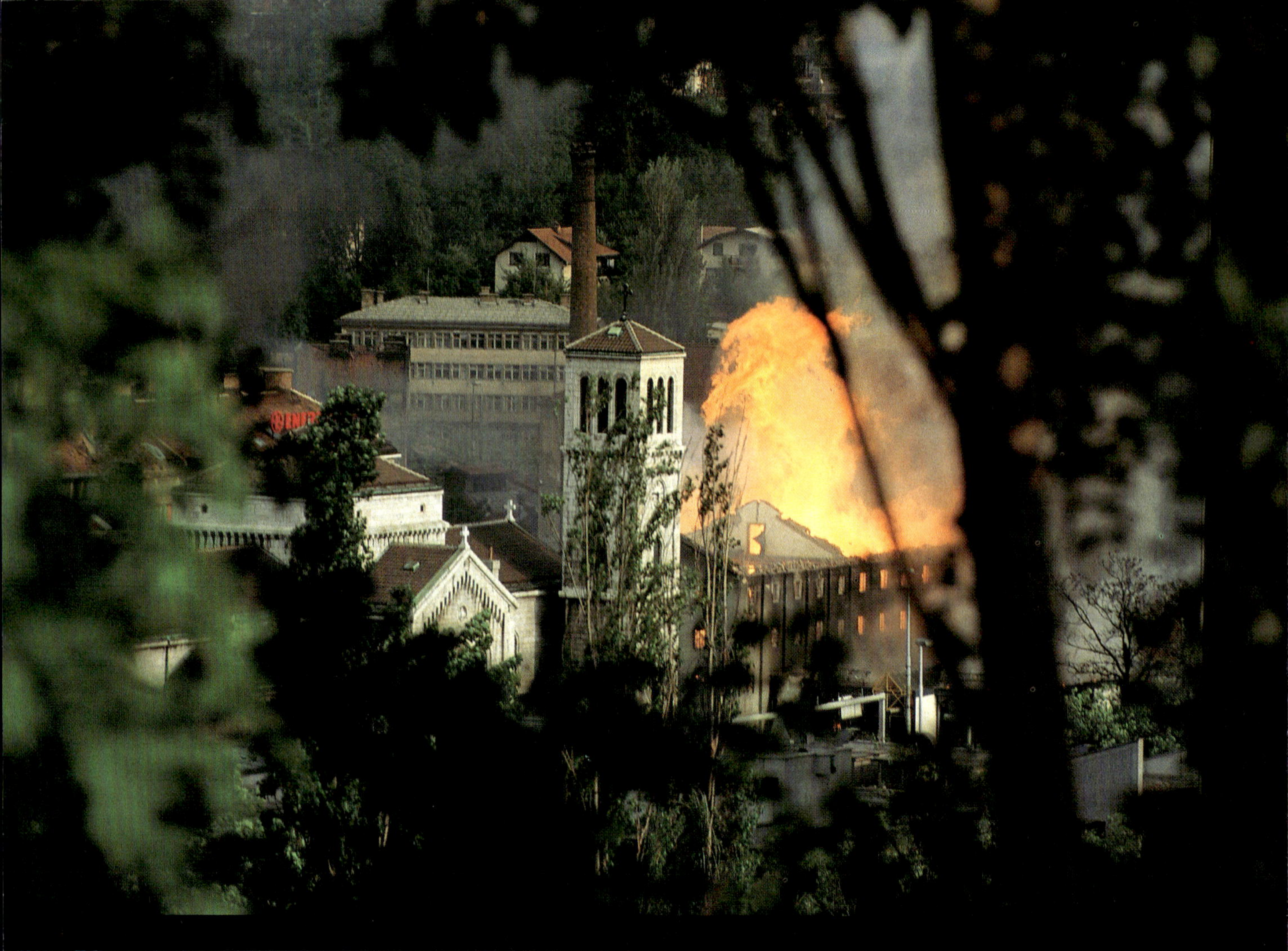

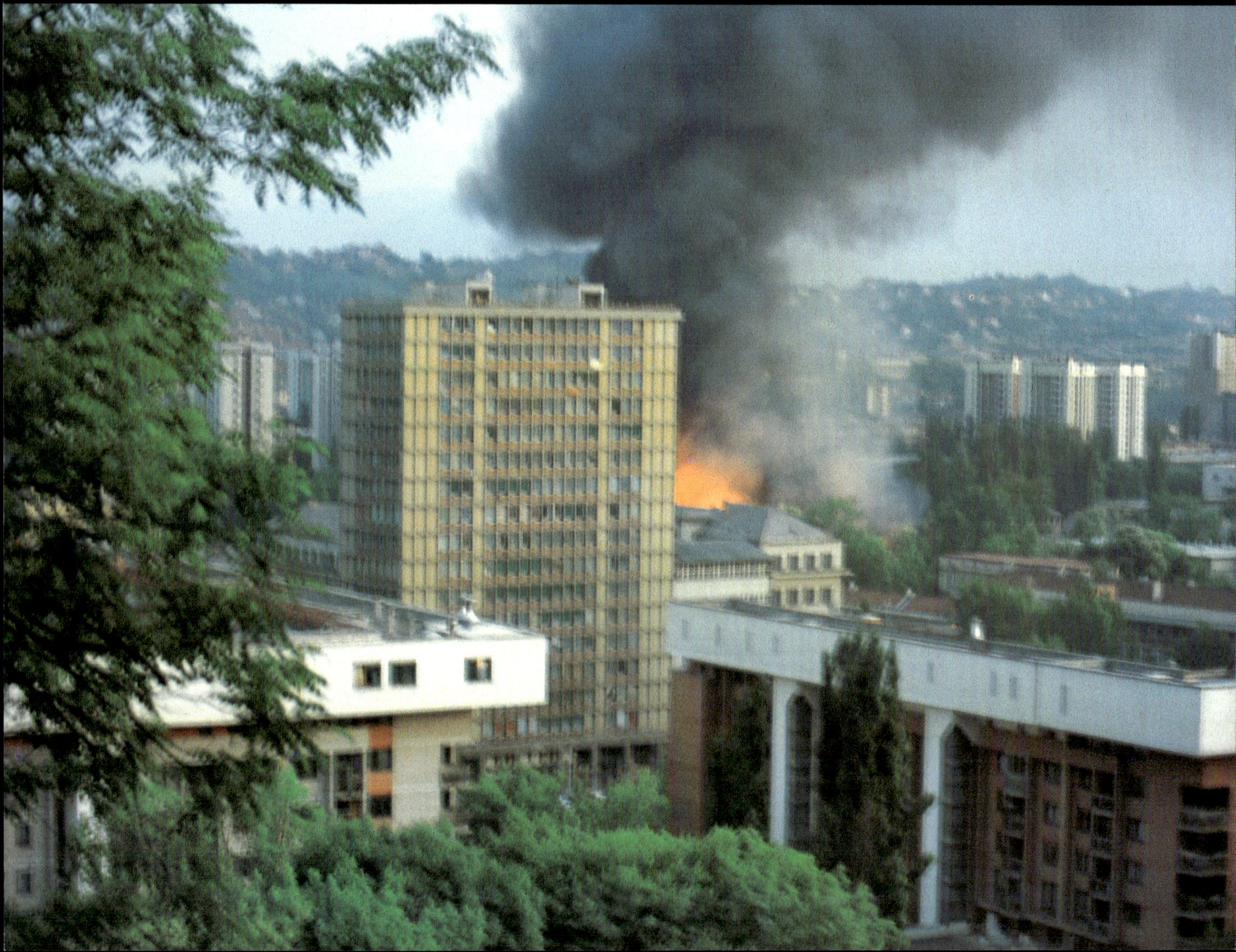

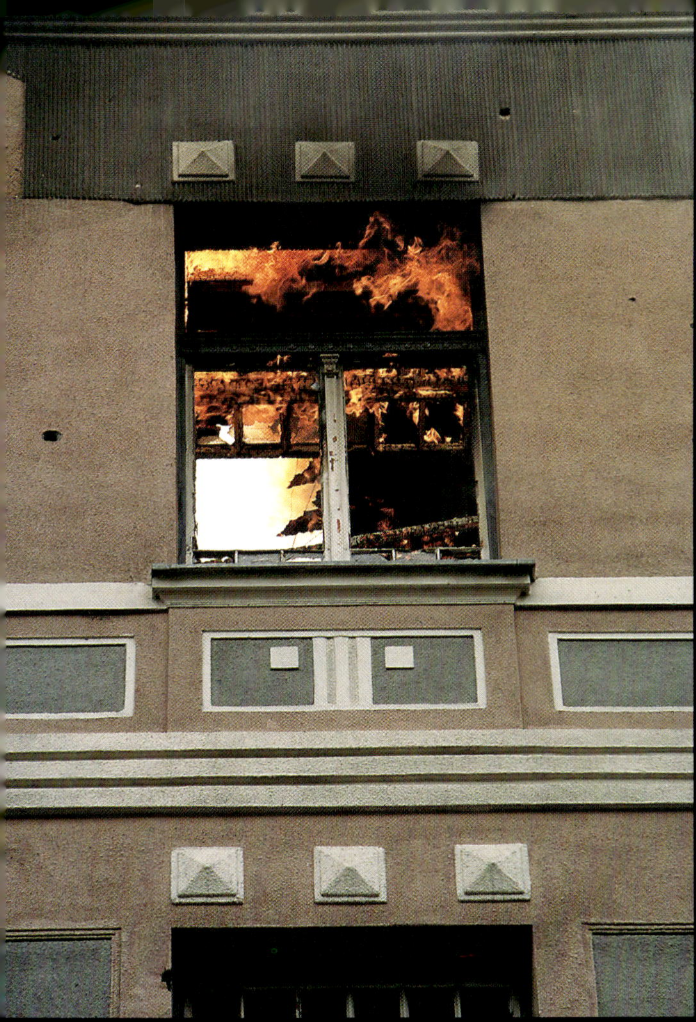
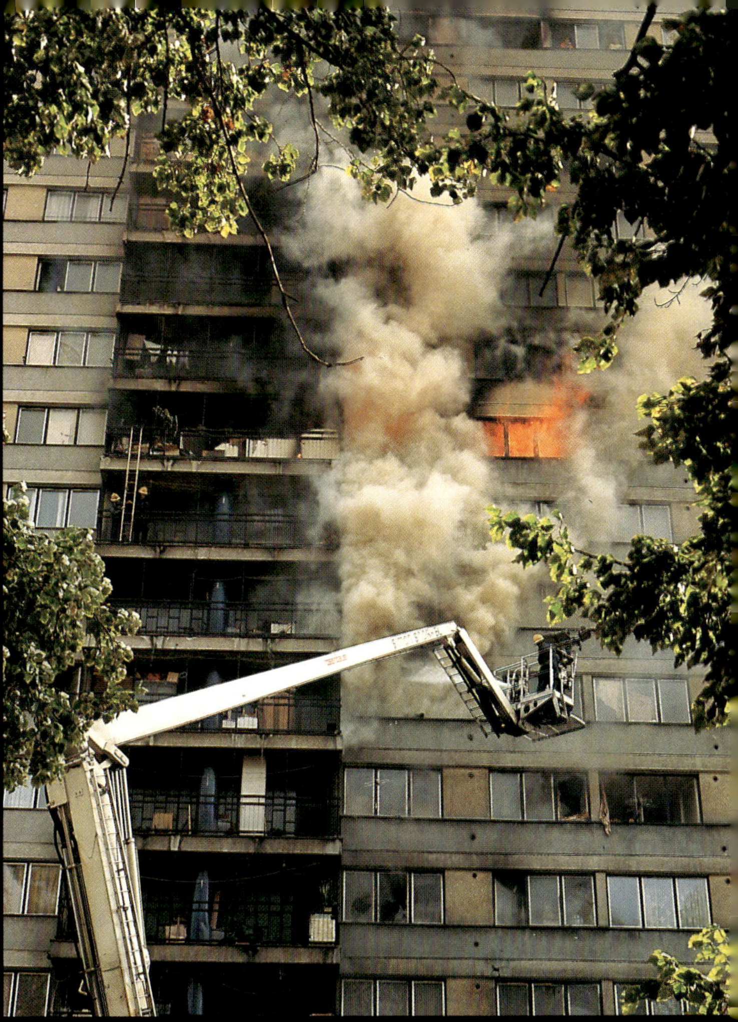
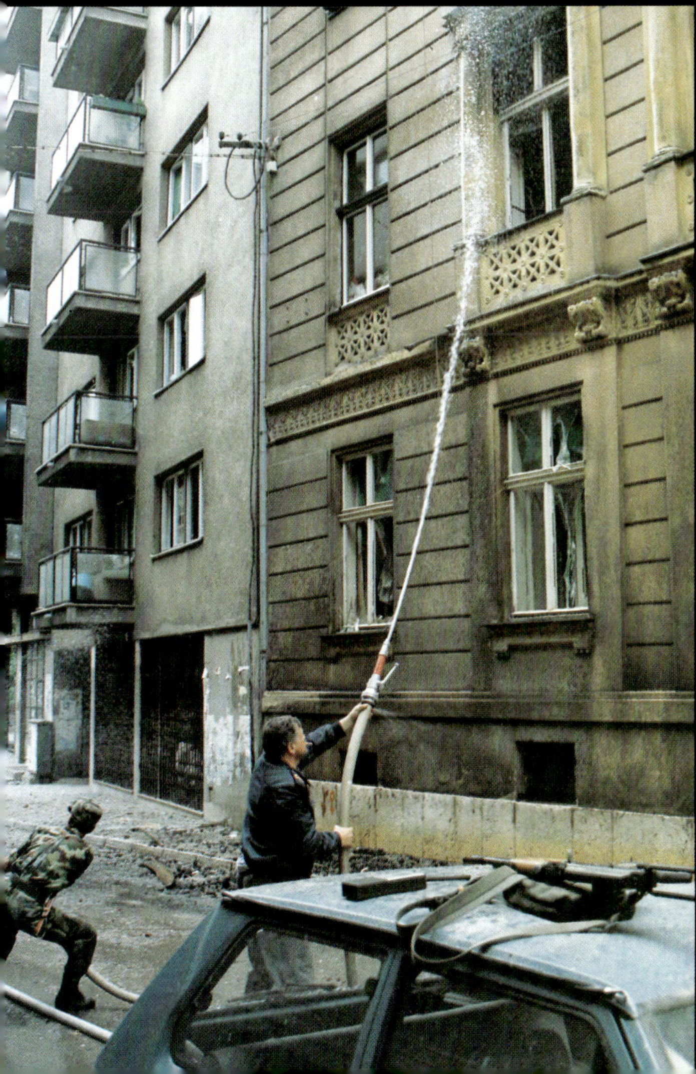
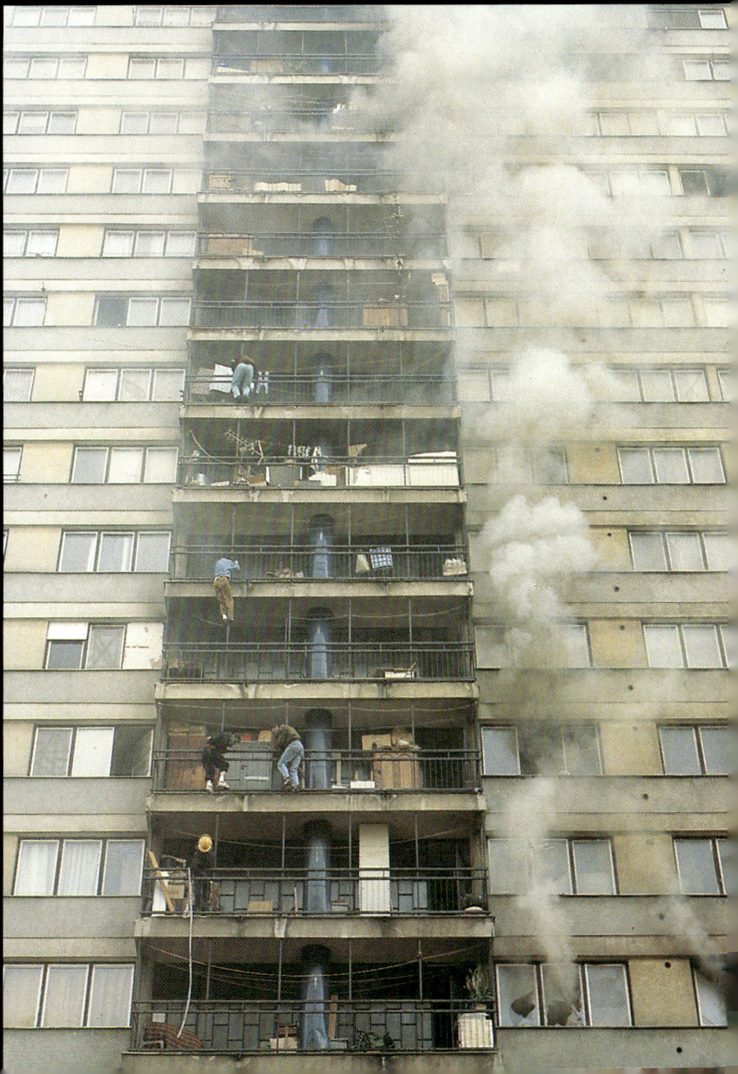

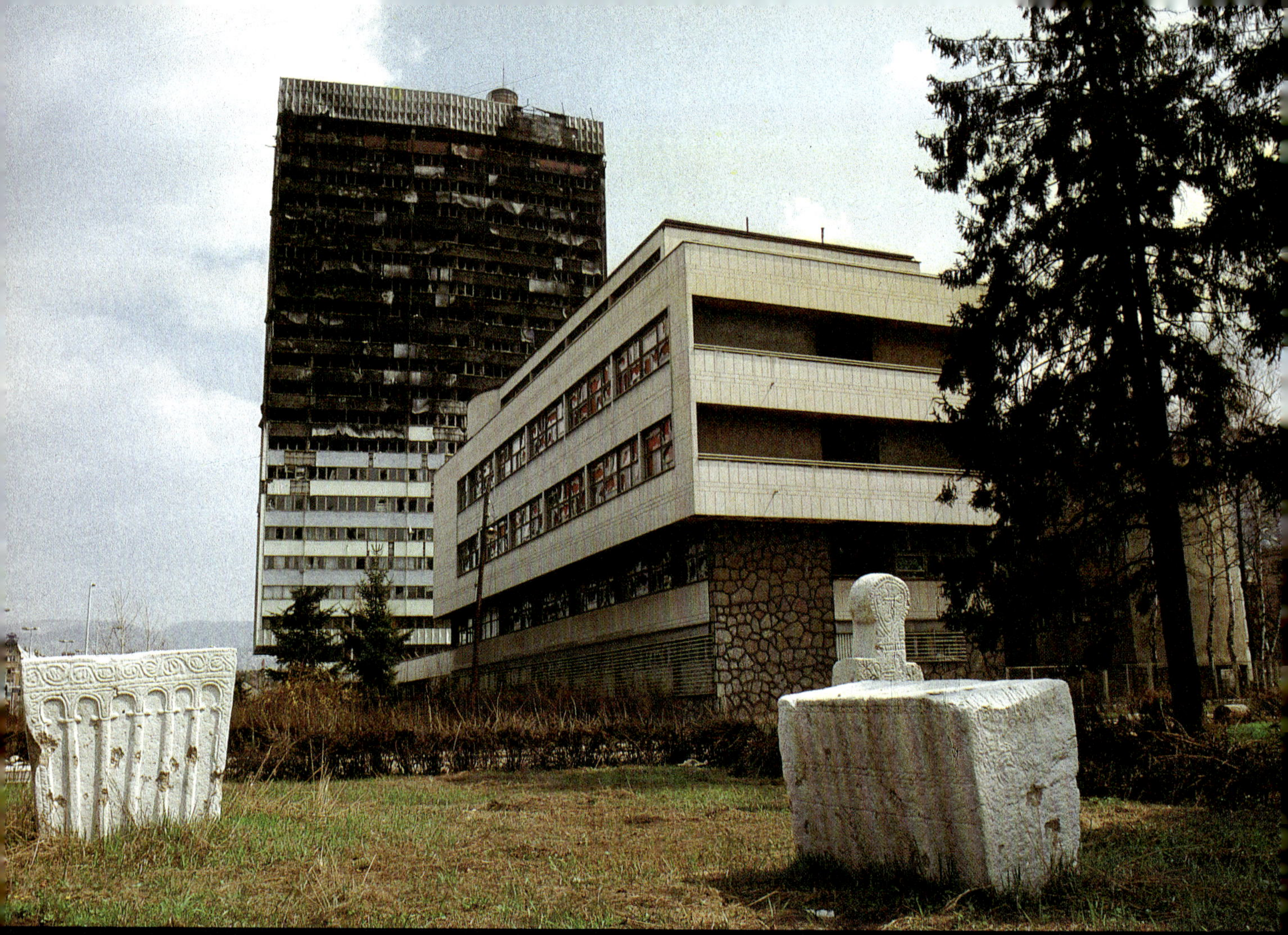

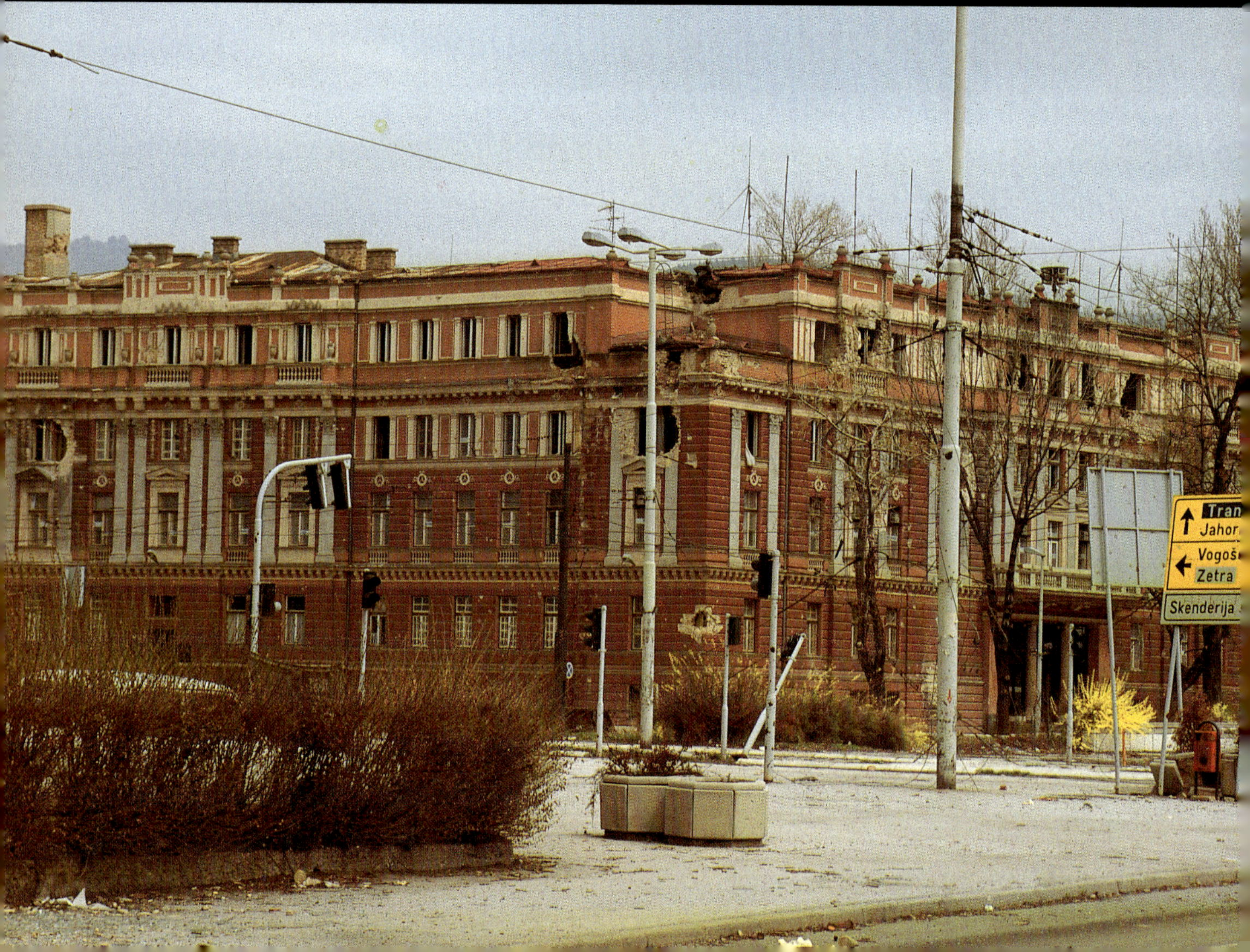
Zetra
Skenderija

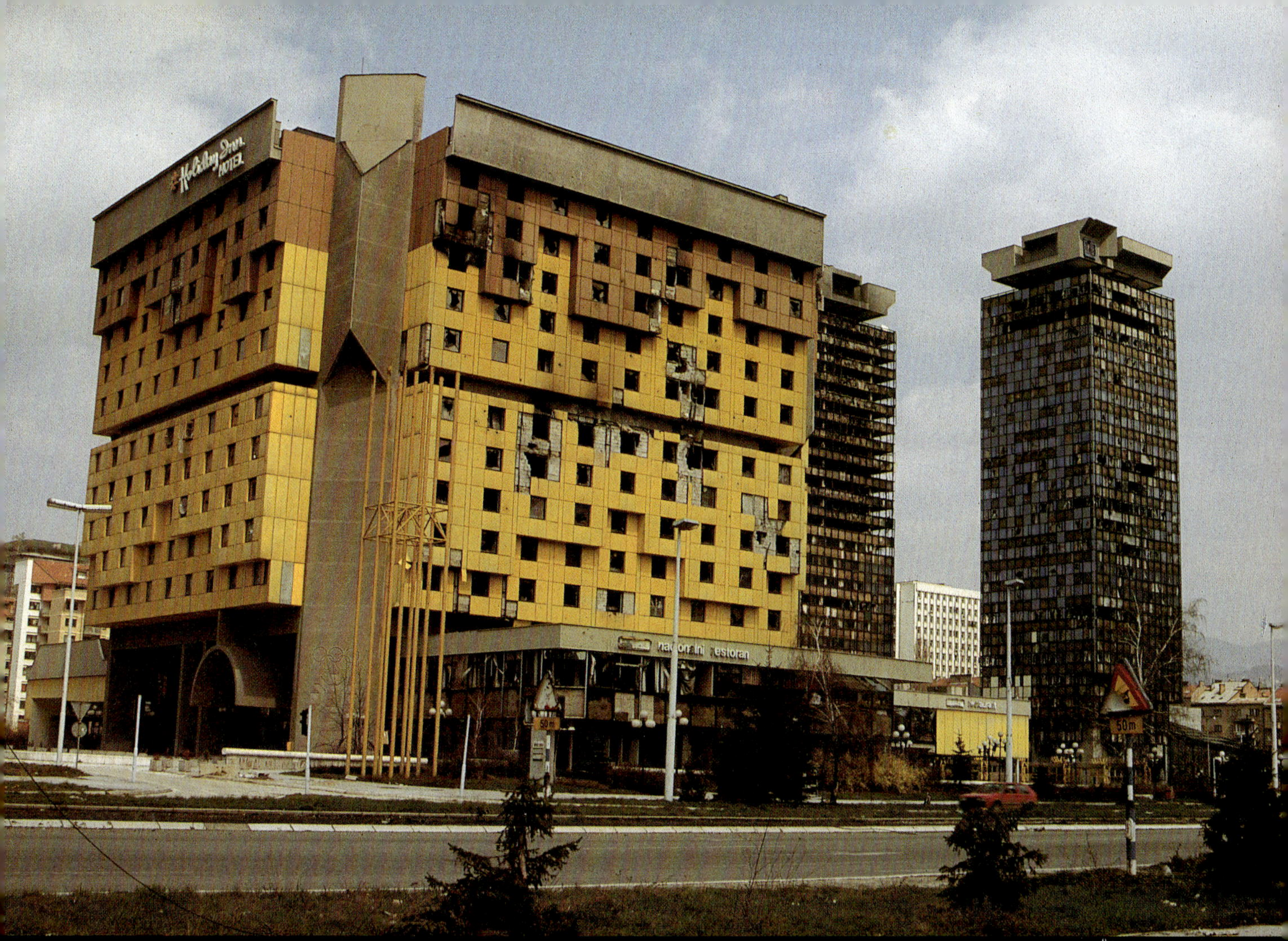
Holiday Inn
HOTEL

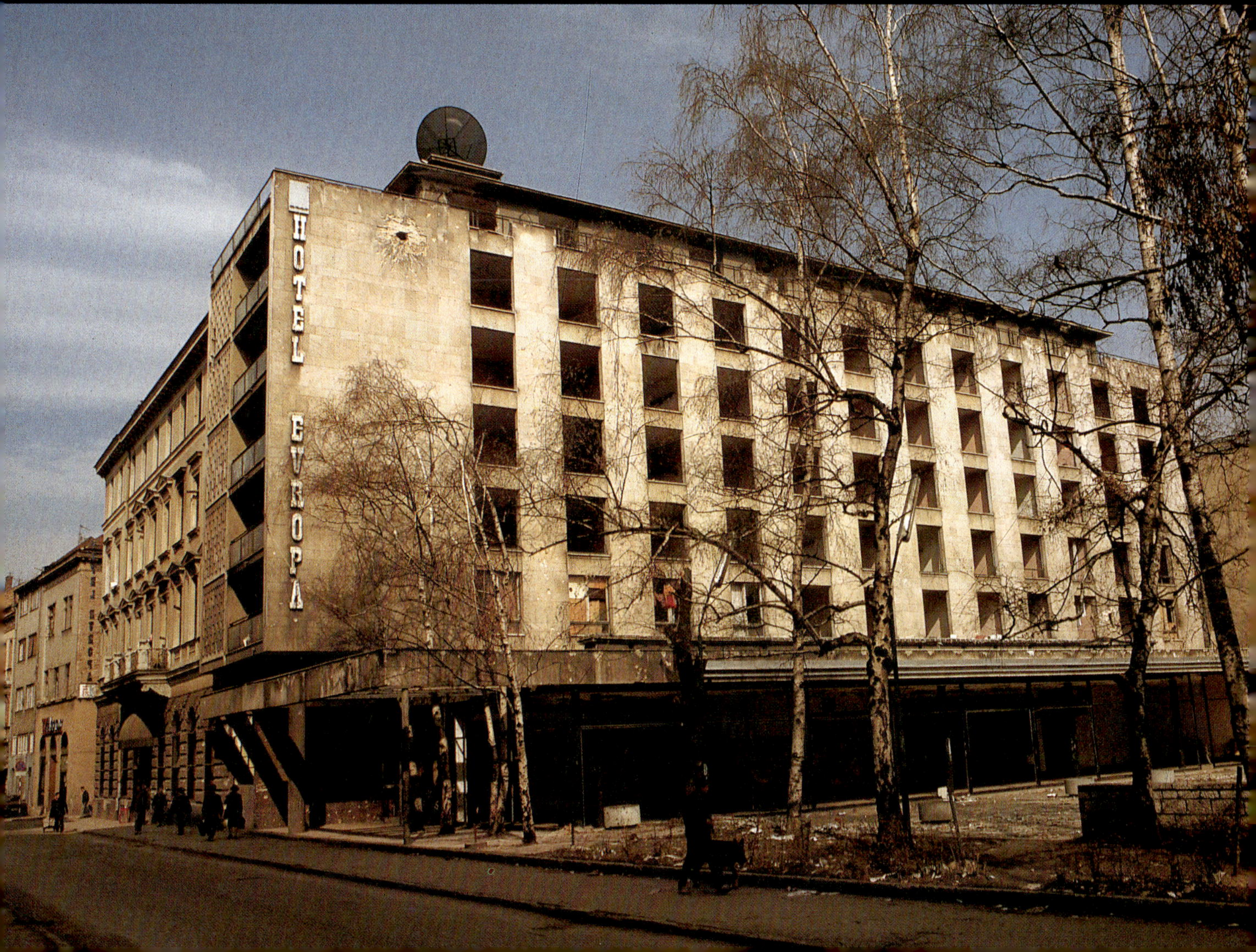
HOTEL
EVROPA

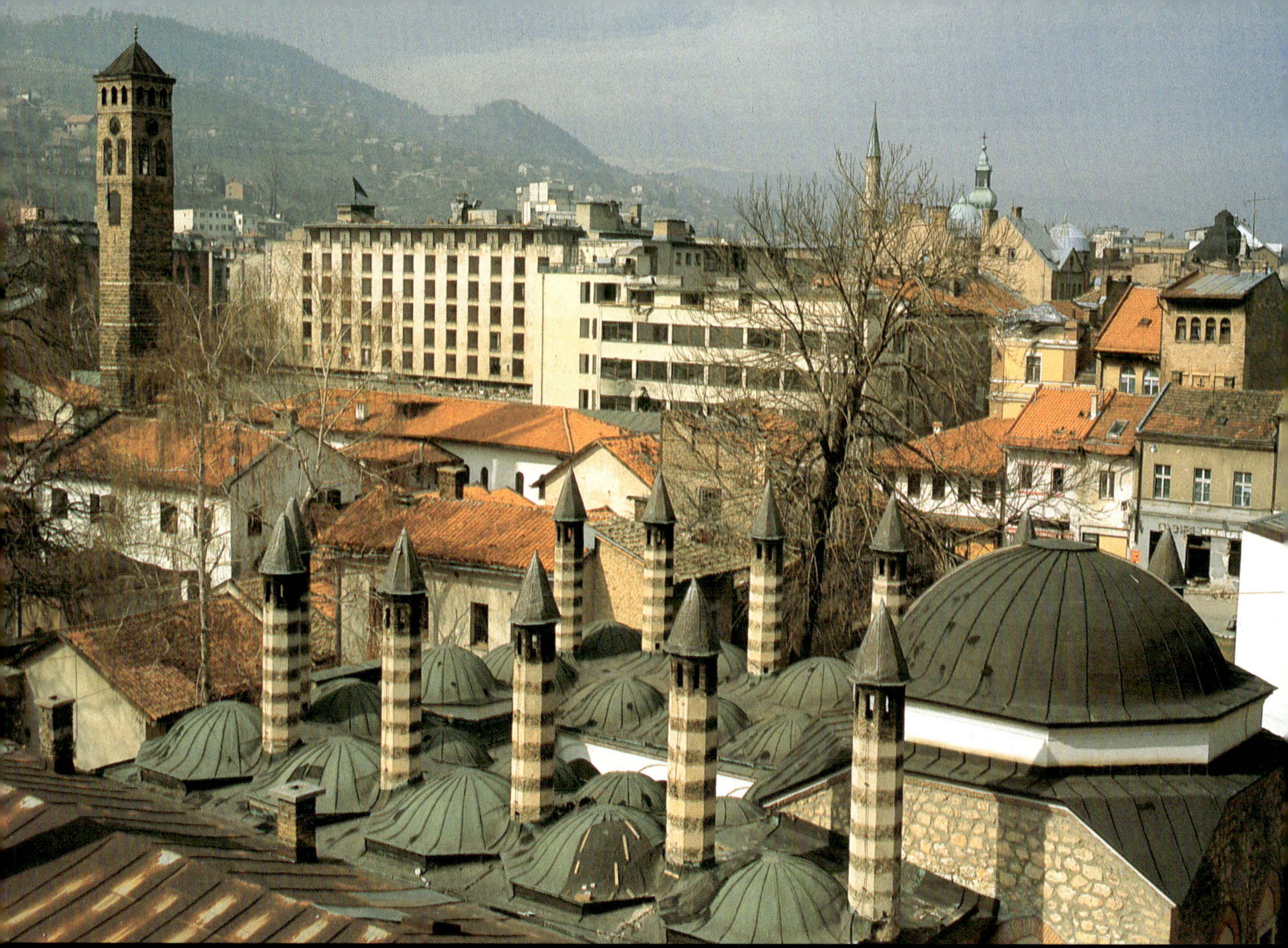

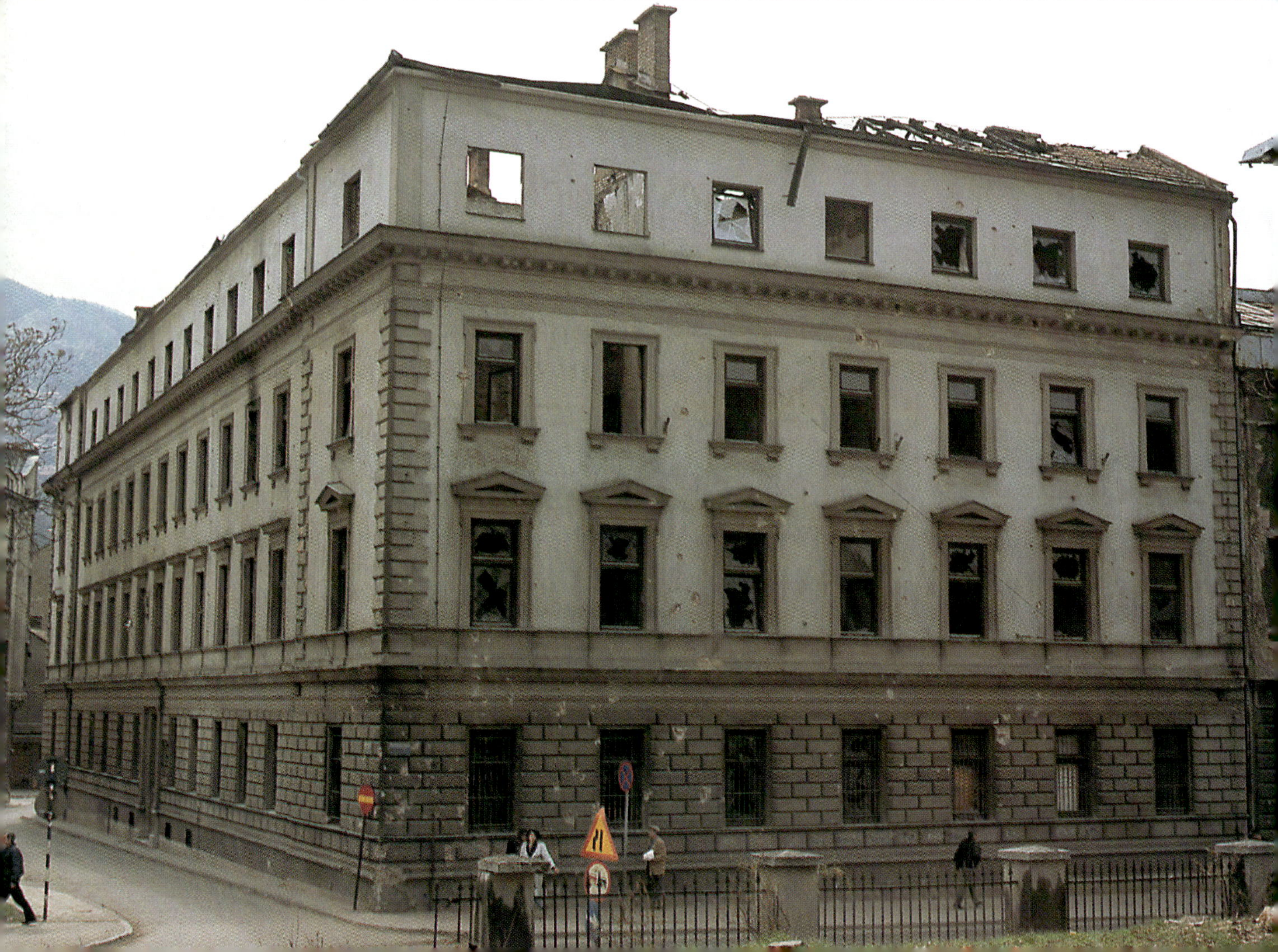

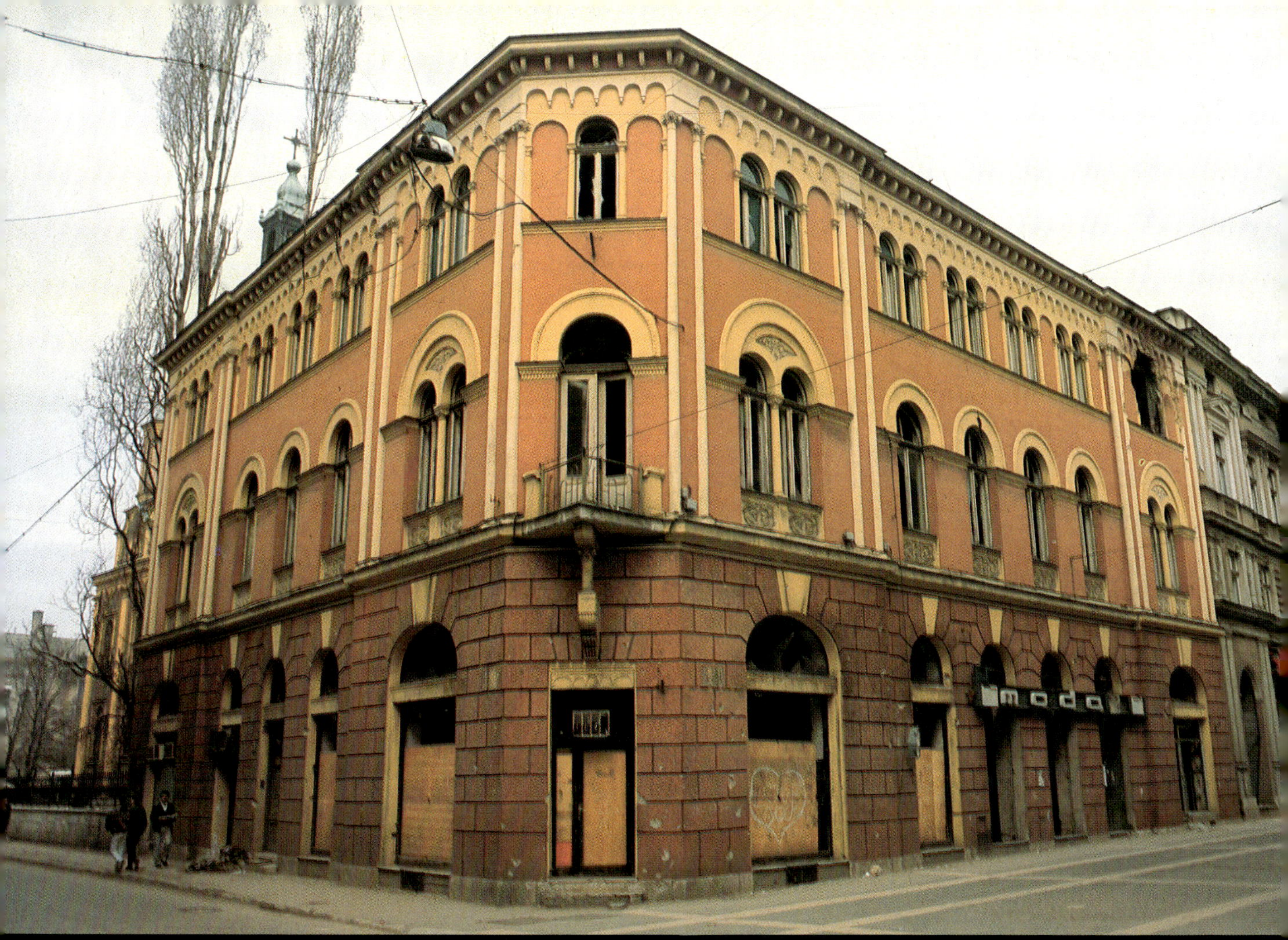
moda

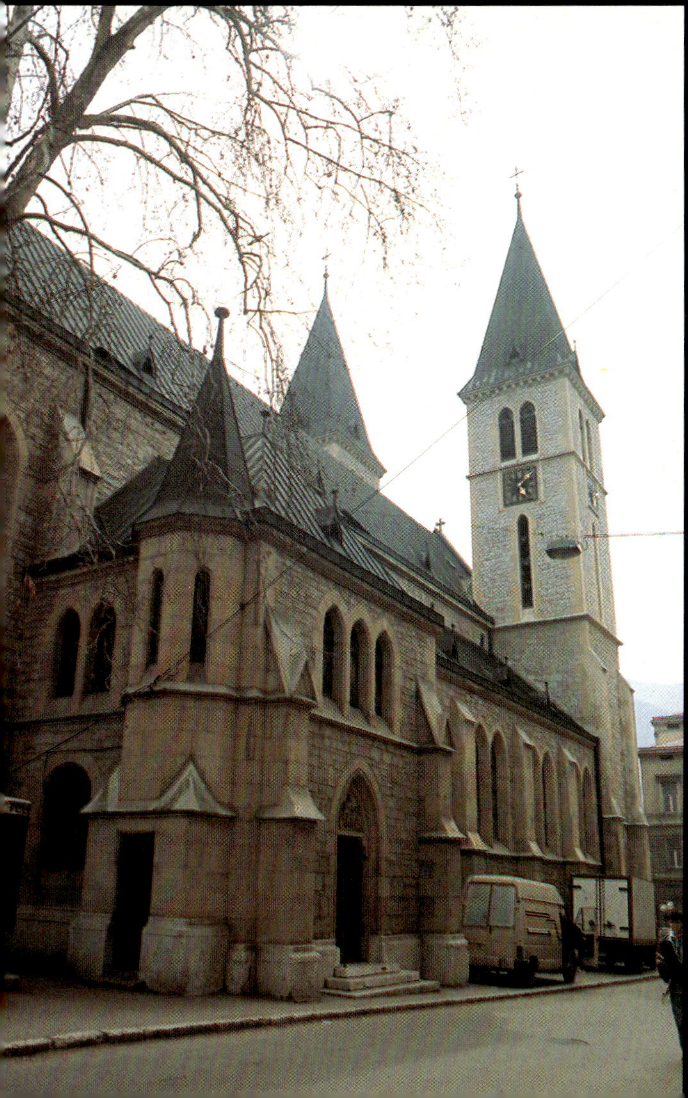

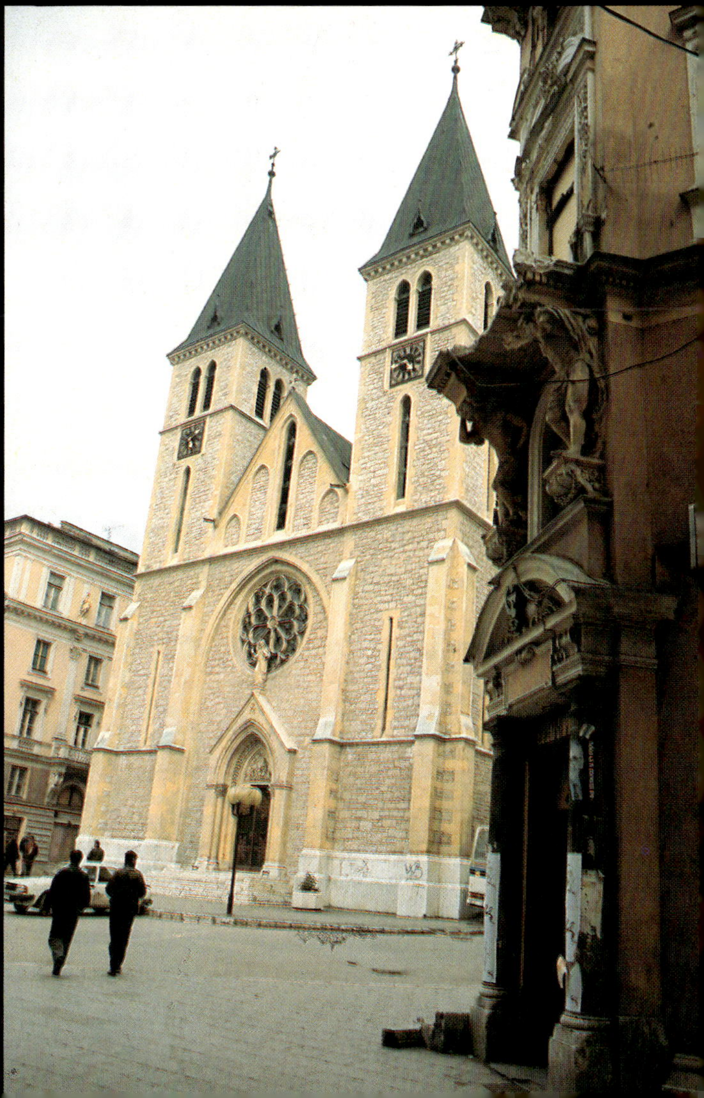

beloved. Who can I write to? I am voiceless. My letters do not go anywhere. Nor can I go myself farther than my slave's shack. The whole city is imprisoned and takes two steps forward, two back, two forward, two back... All our eyes are directed to the holes in the walls, to the broken windows, to the ceilings leaking rain, to the radiators burst with the cold. We wait for the sound of steam in the ducts. No sound. No steam. Everything is cold, dead, everything is halted. The city's "Toplana" (Heating Plant) has been forced to stop working. Thousands of flats have been destroyed by shelling. The radiators and branch ducts burst. The boiler rooms were destroyed. The ducts between the boilers and our rooms were cut. There is no heating. It is impossible to have it. We hope, however, that the cold radiator columns will start heating our rooms. They have always done so. How shall we manage without them? We cannot.

A familiar voice rouses me. My eyes burn with everything I have seen. The world is great. Great is my burden and great is my fatigue. Deep is the night. And one is alone. A friend of mine addresses me. I cannot see him. The eyes, those black, deep eyes follow me. I shut my eyes and mentally listen:

> *"Do deserted parks hide love*
> *Or do two men drink wine,*
> *Bitter wine to the health of the same woman."*

I see the luxuriant fig tree with its ripe fruits again. It invites me to have a rest in the shade. Am I dreaming? Where has this lean, pale man shivering in the snow come from? He presses a bundle of paper under his arm and stamps his feet. It is the beginning of the century. For him too the winters of Sarajevo were hard and long. For whom were they not? He deceives himself with a letter: "Although it's bitterly cold in Sarajevo, I can't make up my mind to buy a coat because I don't think this winter will last long..." I can still hear him, not too loud, taking notes aloud in his dilapidated little room behind the town hall: "Queer is the destiny of this fortunate homeland of ours – Bosnia! Here everybody's wealth has always been safer than an emperor's, so say the old people. What will it be like from now on, God only knows."

Less than a hundred metres away there is a woodpile. The "Bosnische Post" repeats their address to the readership of January 3rd, 1891 about the campaign being undertaken: "Today on the New Road 12 cubic metres of firewood will be distributed to 900 poor people." It is the same street, I now remember, where the writer Petar Kočić shivered with the cold. The dates do not have to coincide. The campaign of the publishers and editors of the Sarajevo newspapers of 1884 is underway. With the donations raised wood was bought for the Sarajevo poor. With the motto "wood for the poor" the better-off made donations. Every week or fort-

tons of flour a day and 3.5 tons of oil. The Conference of Islamic Countries dedicated to the war in B-H is held in Jeddah. "Today, the Republic of B-H, its capital Sarajevo and its other towns, full of historical monuments and products of human diligence, are exposed to shelling by heavy artillery and howitzers that destroy the lives of the people that want nothing else but to live in peace and work in multicultural tolerance" is stated in a letter from the Academy of Science and Arts of B-H, the Jewish Cultural-Educational and Humanitarian Society "La Benevolencia", the Pen-centre of B-H, the Forum of the Citizens of Serb Nationality, the Croatian Cultural Society "Napredak", the Muslim Cultural Society "Preporod" and the University of Sarajevo to the new American President Bill Clinton. In New York Equitable Centre this year's prize for courage in journalism is awarded to Kemal Kurspahić, the editor-in-chief, and to Gordana Knežević, deputy editor of "Oslobođenje". The international women's mass-media foundation awards them for persistence and courage during the war atrocities in B-H. The EC limits the ever increasing number of those requesting asylum.

Wednesday, 2nd: *Heavy artillery fires at the city. The aggressors launch a combined attack of armoured and mechanised units on the western parts of the city (Otes, Doglode, Bare, Sokolje). The "Elektroprenos" manages to restore the electricity system, thus providing workers with electricity for Sarajevo. Nusret Pašić, a painter, sets* *up his exhibition in the ruins of the destroyed and gutted building of the Red Cross of B-H, in the hall of the former "Sutjeska" cinema. The Organization of Islamic Countries passes a resolution at their Foreign Ministers' Meeting demanding that the Security Council stops the aggression on B-H by January 15th. Dr. Hasan Muratović, Minister of Forestry and the Wood Industry declares: "We have planned that 40,000 cubic metres of firewood will be distributed to the citizens of Sarajevo, most probably 1 cubic metre a month per household."*

Thursday, 3rd: *Heavy fighting at Otes, Stup and Sokolje. Sarajevo airport closed "for security reasons" according to a decision by the UNHCR in Geneva. 22 killed and 47 injured in Sarajevo. September pensions increase by 100 per cent. The lowest pensions are 3,633 dinars, the highest 63,607 dinars.*

Friday, 4th: *Severe clashes in the western parts of the city along the lines Doglode, Otes, Stup, Rajlovac and Sokolje. During the night 2,000 shells of 100-mm fall on Otes. Ten killed and 100 injured in Sarajevo.*

Saturday, 5th: *A real drama for Otes citizens: civilians evacuated. Otes is attacked by 19 tanks and powerful infantry forces. Artillery shelling of Žuč, Stup and Kobilja glava. The general alarm is sounded in the whole city. Otes is captured by the aggressors. The whole town is without electricity owing to a power system failure. 11 killed and 131 wounded. Art objects and antiques are sold at auction to raise money for the B-H Armed Forces.*

night about a thousand poor people waited regularly for the help in wood. Thus in winter about 1,000 cubic metres of firewood was distributed. At the same time the under-privileged were given a little money, too. It lasted for decades. The first war winter of 1914/1915 the town municipality took on the obligation to supply the city's paupers. "Sarajevski list" (The Sarajevo Journal) of April 1915 wrote that the Government allocated the municipality six hundred railway freight cars of coal and 2,500 cubic metres of firewood for the city's paupers. The municipality only paid for the freight and cutting costs. And Sarajevo had 26,268 inhabitants in 1885, 38,083 in 1895, and 51,918 in 1910...

The winter whiteness. The same rosy colour as in Gabrijel Jurkić's paintings. He was blinded by that wealth of colours. The painter's eye did not endure nature's beauty, which he transfered onto the canvas with his paintbrush. His winters are and were also cold. As expressive was the winter whiteness of the lady painter Slava Raškoj. Wretched woman, her studio was in a mortuary. She must have been cold, too cold when she left such wonderful winters for us, the most beautiful painter's winters, it seems. She did not survive.

Shall I endure this? Will Sarajevo endure now shackled with ice and bitter winter snow. As if somebody were distorting the truth. The Sarajevo Olympics of 1984 are Sarajevo. We were the world. The city sparkled in the light, abundance, pride of entering the circle of Olympic towns. We remember the flattering compliments to Jahorina, Igman and Bjelašnica, to the opening and closing ceremonies of the Games, to the Olympic hall "Zetra". We walked the world. We were on world's front pages. We were happy.

Today we are back on the front pages. That is not us any more. Misery, blood, death, starvation and cold follow us, show us, perpetuate us in newspaper columns and in the news agencies' reports.

We die of the cold. I envy the Eskimos. They were born on the snow whiteness, in igloos and icebergs. No, I cannot tell you anything today, Mr Eduard Maury. In Paris, a hundred years ago, you published about Sarajevo: "... How beautiful it is to take a rest here, and it is immediately clear that Sarajevo's charms are not the wealth of costumes or oriental monuments, or the contrasts of its population with their so different looks...

"Beggars sit on the steps by the fountain, eating pieces of bread, and all around people pass by... Young girls pass by, laughing... What is the hidden face watching us like? Or, better to say, what thoughts fill those souls sentenced to solitude? The world they see from under their veils must be the world we do not even suspect: sometimes people in the harems of Sarajevo must be philosophizing and building up systems that would be interesting to know. Young girls also wear veils; their fingers painted with henna smear mallow flower pink muslin over their faces and as soon as you glance at them, they run away ashamed, their wooden slippers clattering along the cobbled street..."

Is the comparison important at all? I am cold for most of October, I freeze the whole of November. The joints of my fingers have become swollen. It is difficult for me to write. Movements of the wrists ache. I cannot handle the change while I sell newspapers. This year, money in Sarajevo is not banknotes but paper coupons. I cannot feel my fingertips. It is difficult for me to deal with the change. Two toes of Mrs Riđanović, who started translating my book into English, got frozen in her flat on the fourth floor. The university professor does not manage to read anything. There is no heating. There is no electricity. No glass in the windows. Warm clothes do not help.

It is the same for everybody. The white winter, this bitter, continental winter. The Sarajevo chronicler Mula Mustafa Bašeskija wrote at the end of the 18th century: "The winter was so sharp that there was no one who could remember such a winter... Water froze so that several layers of ice were formed. In brief, this could not be described in words. Children tobogganed throughout the winter and had their fill of it indeed. Eventually, there was no wise one to remember such a winter, as it is said here in Bosnia. In all the storerooms sour cabbage and pickle in jars got frozen so you can see this what the cold was like. Many birds died of the bitter cold, too... Fountains also froze so people fetched water from the Miljacka and from some remote places..."

Does my diary entry of the end of September make any sense?

"The last sunny days slip by. Television pictures from Geneva show the people in overcoats and jackets. We deceive ourselves with the dying summer. People carry some broken off branches over their shoulders, under their arms. A man walks down Moše Pijade Street for the second time carrying a bundle of wood over one shoulder, and over the other an axe on which a freshly cut piece of wood – a large round log – hangs. There, a few hundred metres away from my flat, on no main's land which used to be the entrance to "Bosnalijek", three or four chestnut trees are missing. In April, while rushing along Jukićeva Street I talked to Zec with my eyes set on their treetops in white blossom. Safet's paintings and graphics revealed to me those wild decorative park flowers on treetops that attracted me with the beginning of the autumn. Each new brown and almost greasy nut that fell, each somehow new, attracted me. It cheered me up in that sorrow of dying leaves that rustled and were melancholy at twilight along the street between the two cemeteries at Koševo – Vancaš's Catholic–Orthodox one and the Partisans' one. Faint light through the treetops, now

Sunday, 6th: The damaged transmission line is repaired. The city gets electricity. Fierce shelling of all the city's areas. 30 shells fall onto the Koševo Hospital grounds. Most of them fall on the Surgery and Otorhinolaryngology Wards. Three are killed, four injured. The French Hospital is hit by three shells. 22 killed and 47 injured in Sarajevo. Thanks to the ADRA (Adventists' Voluntary Work) humanitarian organization 1,500 individually sent parcels reach the city.

Monday, 7th: Sarajevo is in the dark. A 110-kilowatt transmission line which supplied the town with electricity collapses as a consequence of the shelling. Heavy clashes take place in the area of Vidikovac and Čolina kapa, also at Otes and Azići, Hrasno and the Jewish cemetery. Artillery fires on the city's residential areas. Chemicals are used in an attack on Pionirska dolina, Hum and Jukić Street. The Koševo Hospital is shelled. A nurse and two visitors are killed, four injured. In the city there are 14 dead and 108 injured. The aggression on Sarajevo has so far claimed 7,579 lives, 2,893 of them being registered in health institutions.
A shortage of paper prevents the printing of "Večernje novine" (The Evening News). It will not come out until further notice. The "Oslobođenje" editorial board decides to let "Večernje novine" publish a choice of articles in "Oslobođenje". Other articles are broadcast on "Studio 99" Independent Radio.

Tuesday, 8th: A particularly hard day for Sarajevo. Shells *fall all over the city. Infantry clashes at Dobrinja, the Jewish cemetery, and around Osmice. Chemical irritants are used in Dobrinja. By an order of the Presidency of the City Assembly all restaurants and cafes in Sarajevo should be closed by 6 p.m. 21 killed and 166 injured. A shortage of medicines and medical supplies threatens Sarajevo hospitals. There is not enough oxygen. Izet Alečković sets up an exhibition of his paintings. A club for people from and friends of Mostar is founded.*

Wednesday, 9th: *The city is without electricity for three days now. There is no water either. Firewood, oil and kerosene are expected to be transported into the city with UNPROFOR help. Bread production in the "Velepekara" is reduced to a minimum. The first issue of the "Front Line", the magazine of the B-H Army, comes out.*

Thursday, 10th: *Ismet Rizvić, a painter, dies at the age of 59. A group of 450 peacemarchers from Italy, Great Britain, Japan and France, called "The Blessed Peacemakers", is still waiting at Kobiljača to be allowed to enter Sarajevo. 13 killed and 110 injured in Sarajevo. Hospitals without electricity and water. A shortage of all energy sources. In Paris, the prize "Reporters without Frontiers" is awarded to Zlatko Dizdarević and the "Oslobođenje" daily newspaper. Those awarded could not attend the ceremony. September pensions start being paid aut.*

Friday, 11th: *Sarajevo is still without electricity. Mirko Pejanović, a member of the Presidency of the Republic of B-H, requests in the name of the B-H delegation that*

I realize, must have reminded me of the Osijek of my primary school days and of the black paths through the parks to Tvrđa and the school with its petroleum-soaked floors or, maybe, of long grammar school and university night walks whose quiet was disturbed by the echoes from pavements of hurried steps along the street, or of that resonant sound of the Požega Tower of St Teresa's Church.

"Now, there are no more chestnut trees of mine and Safet's. The autumn worry about the winter cold took them away with the fast saws of two men and three women who diligently sawed sitting tired on the ground so that the felled trunks could be removed from the slope as quickly as possible. They were only continuing what had already been started. First, one day, some people hurriedly took the slates from the roof of a shack that had already been shifted and had cracked together with two or three valves, probably water ones. Then, when the electricity was cut off permanently, a small tractor with a trailer arrived. Two men with a pickaxe and axes, and six or seven boys climbed onto the roof. At an unbelievable speed they dismantled the rafters, beams, braces and lathes and loaded them onto the trailer. Today the chestnut trees were gone. Tomorrow, the day after tomorrow, but before long, they will remember the bricks as well. They will probably be walling up holes, doors and windows. One must live . . .

"I am here, but I am not in fact. I stand still, stamp my feet, jump and wait. Life's trolleybus does not run. Neither does the desired tram. There are no buses in working condition. Everything stands still and draws us back, back, back. We are without a past. We do not see the future. We cannot bear the present . . ."

How? How long?

Sarajevo first timidly, secretly and then more and more openly guillotined its parks, avenues and three-laned streets. Everything made of wood was taken home. Each shelled flat, shop and house became a source of wood supplies. Window and door frames, beams, roofs, floors of the beech parquet from the old military hospital, the one from the times of the Austro-Hungarian presence here, from the end of the Ottoman rule. How many haversacks were filled with the parquet from the destroyed buildings of the "Marshal Tito" barracks? The trees died at night. Tree-lined streets were mutilated. An acquaintance of mine, the painter Meša, did not know how to teach the woodcutters a lesson. Defending the city's greenery he mentioned the avenue. In their eyes he the saw incomprehension. The avenue? He restrained himself from unnecessary words before the arguments of the axe, the saw, the winter that crept into the hollow homes, into our freezing limbs and bones.

There were more and more felled trees. The tree of life was dying in Sarajevo. There was no electricity. The dark did not annoy us any more. We had got used to it. Prisoners

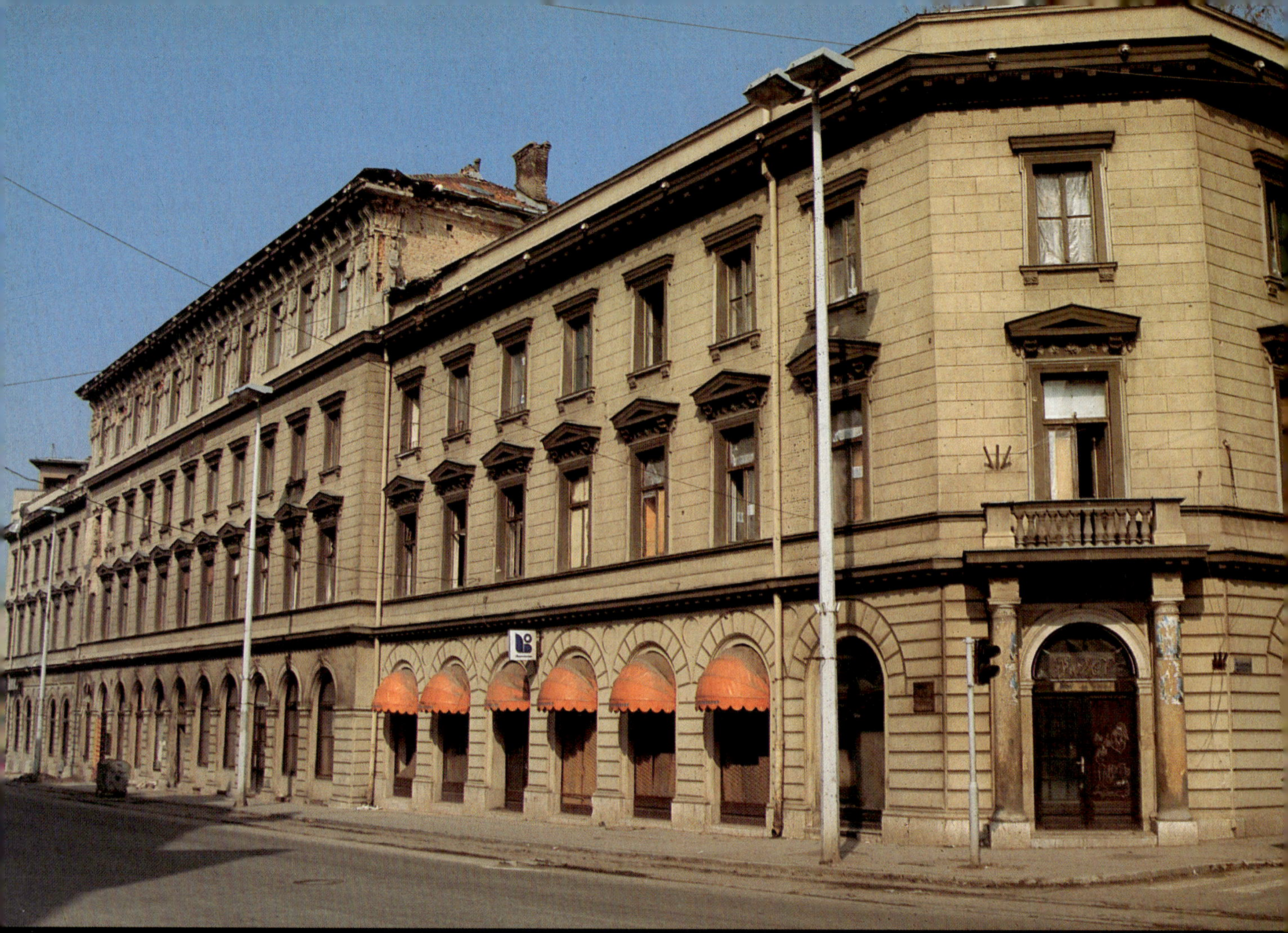

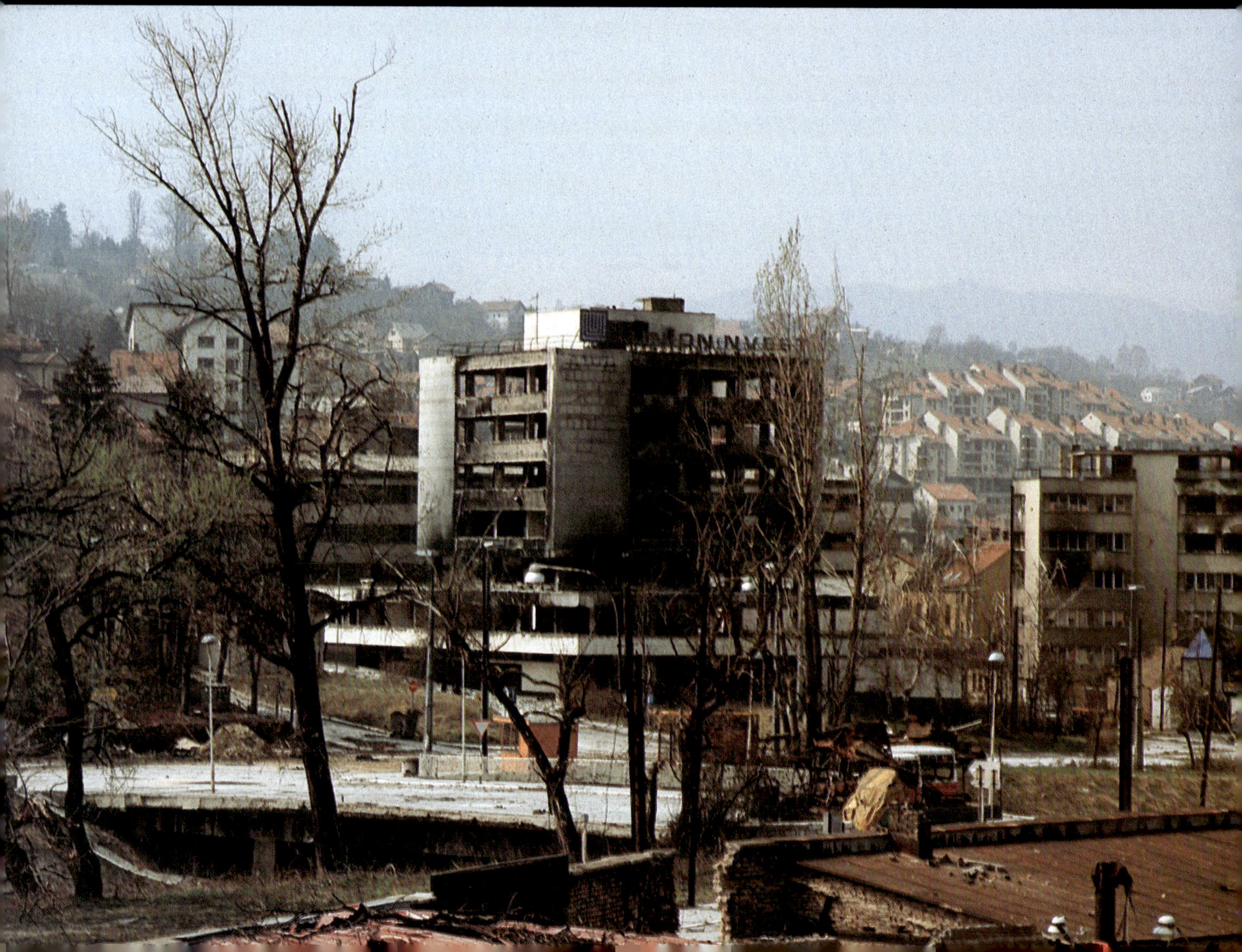

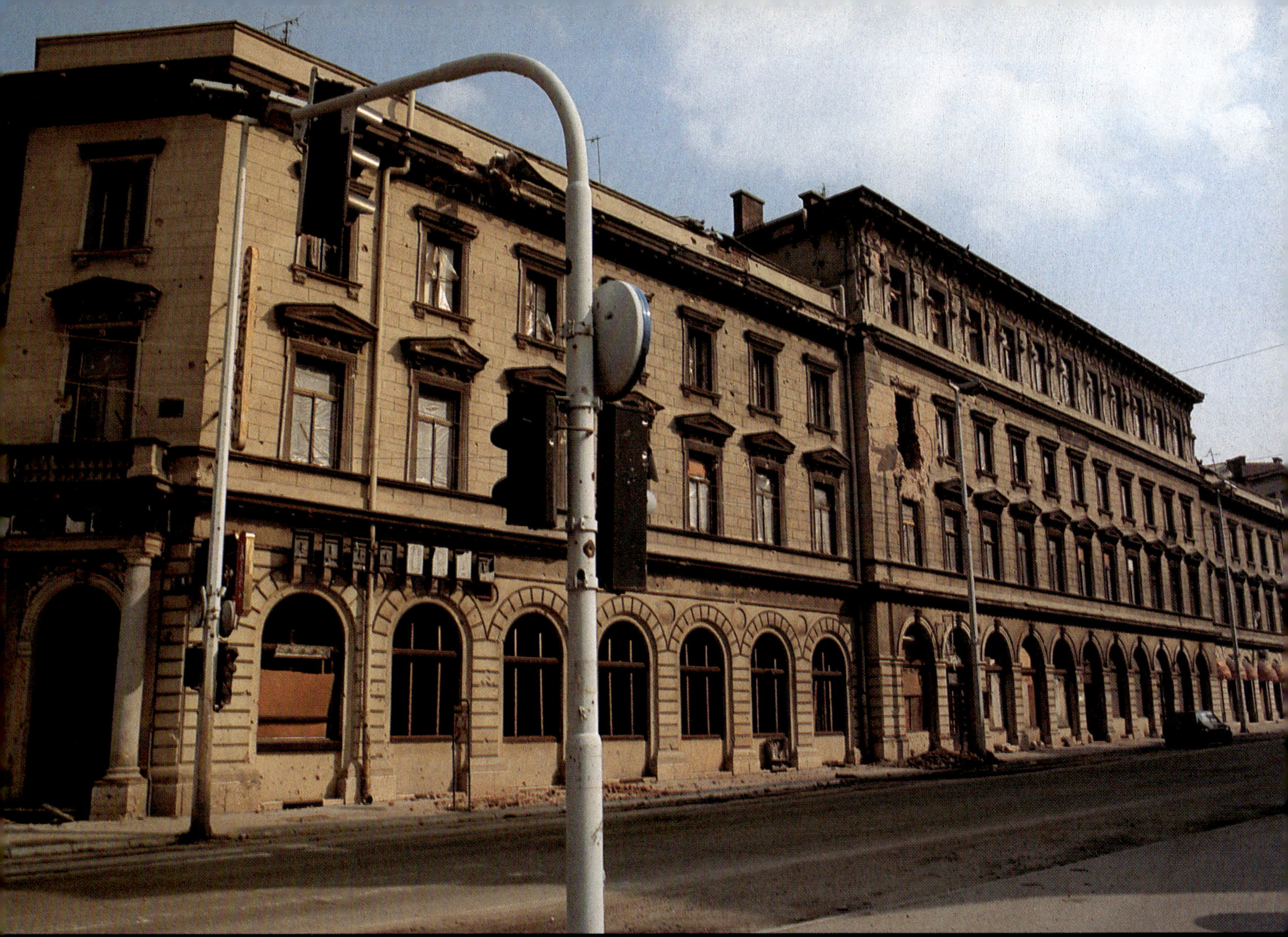

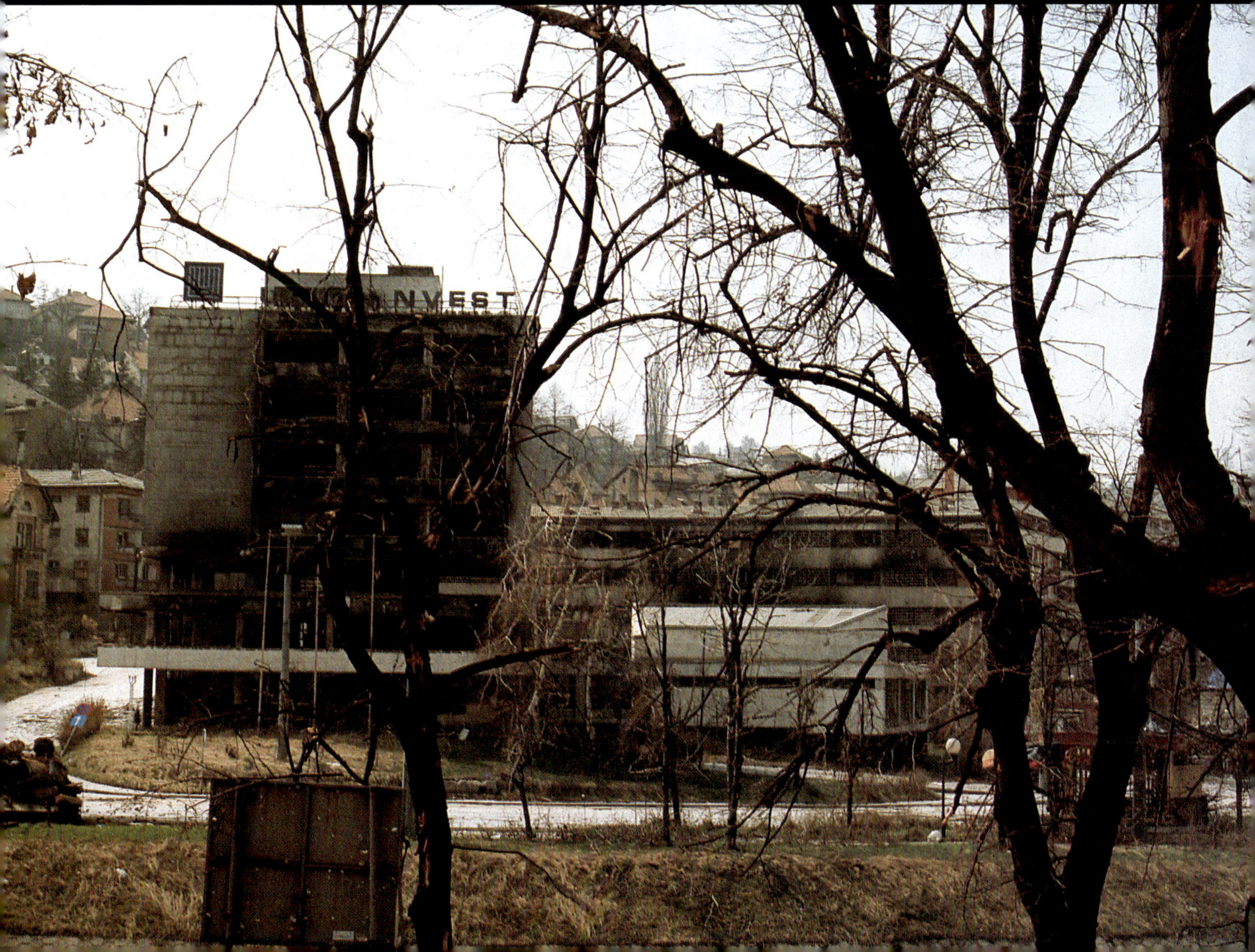

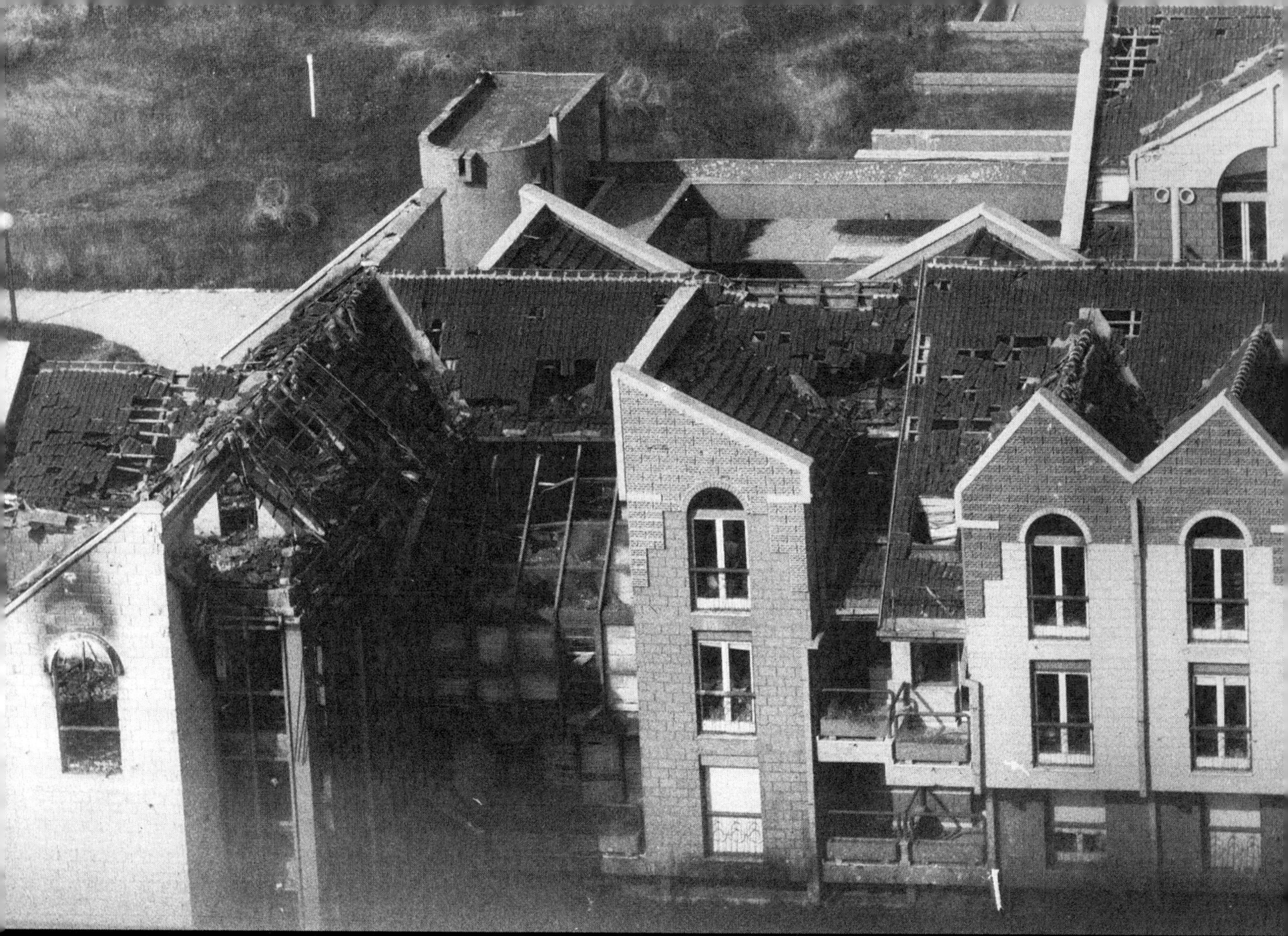

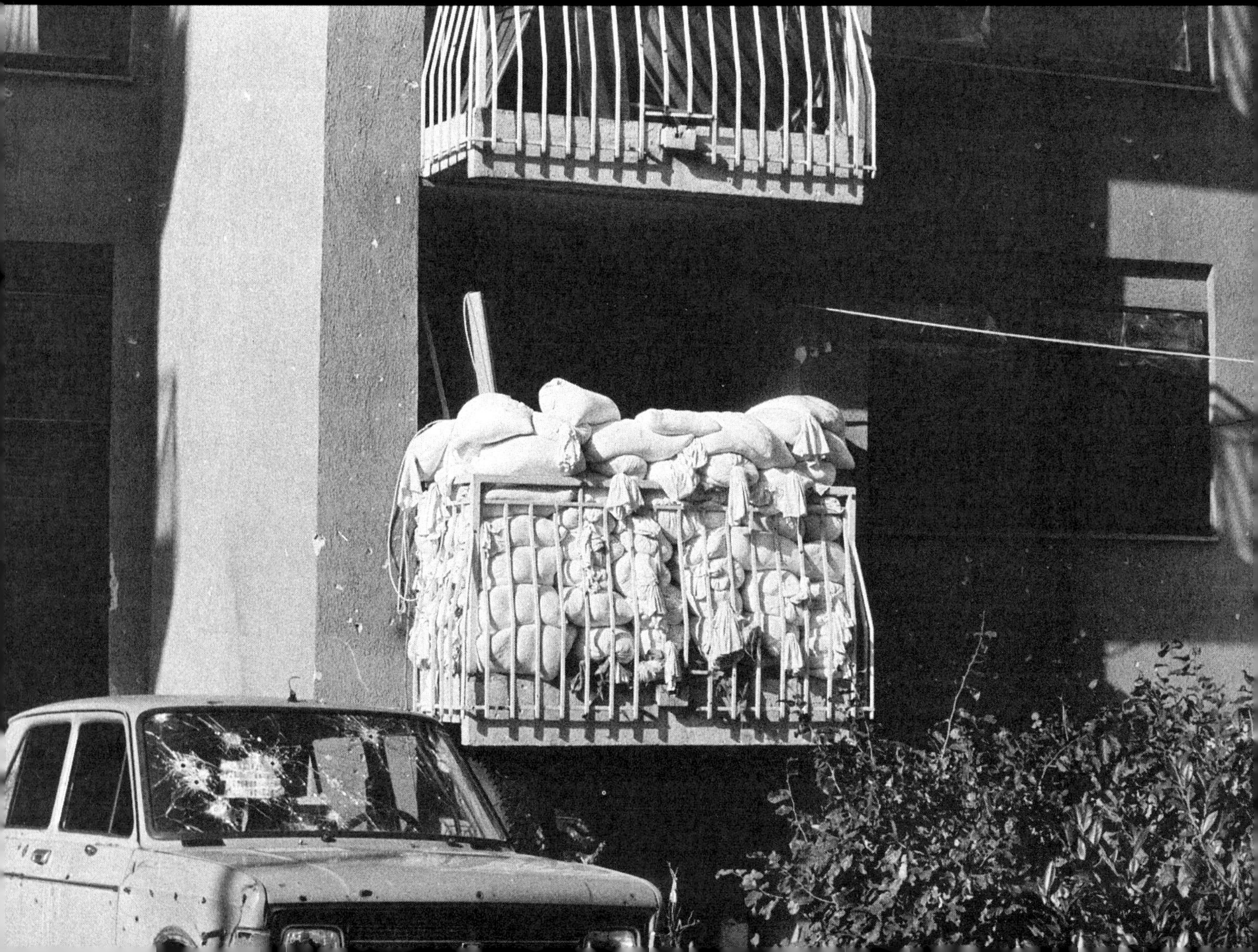

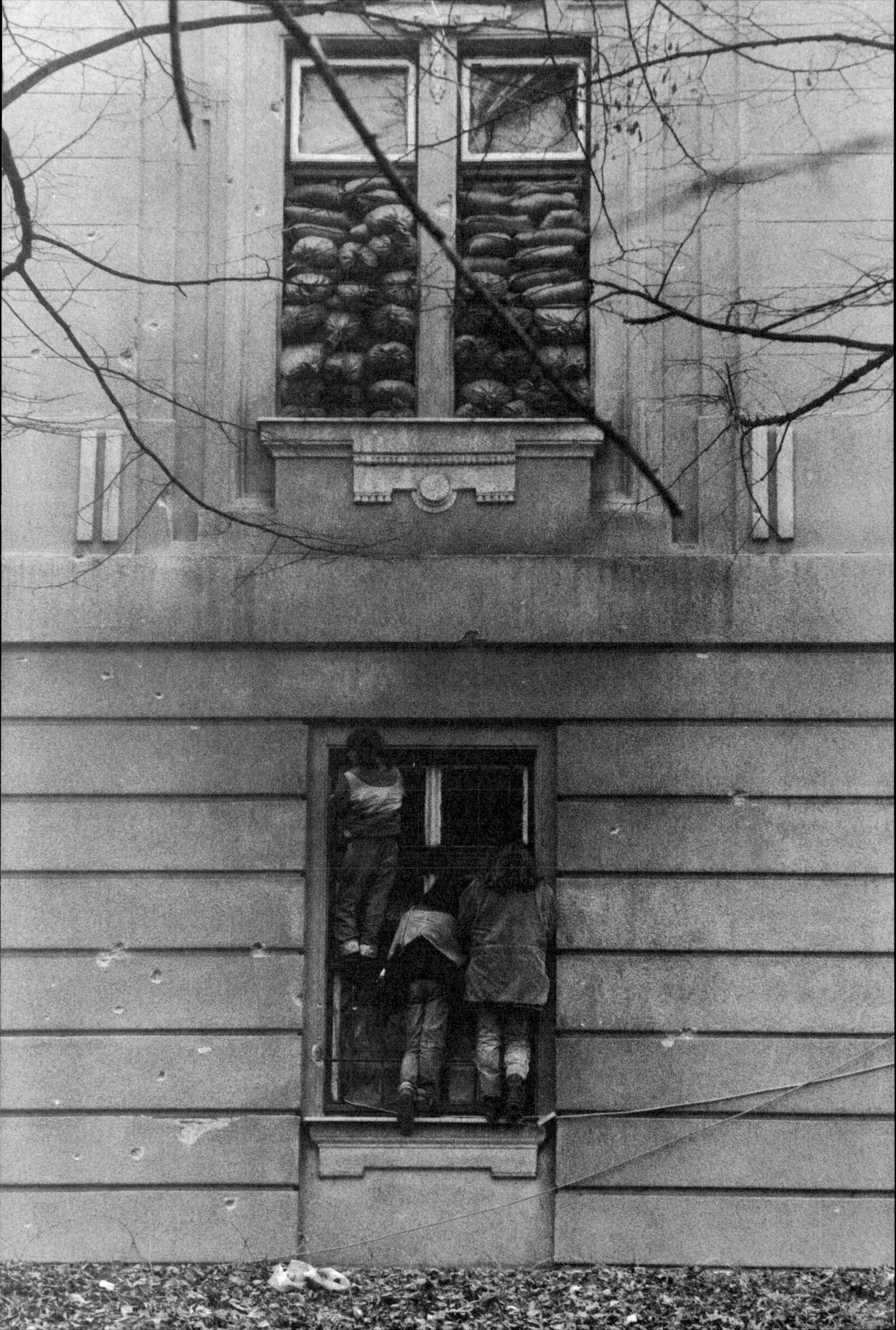

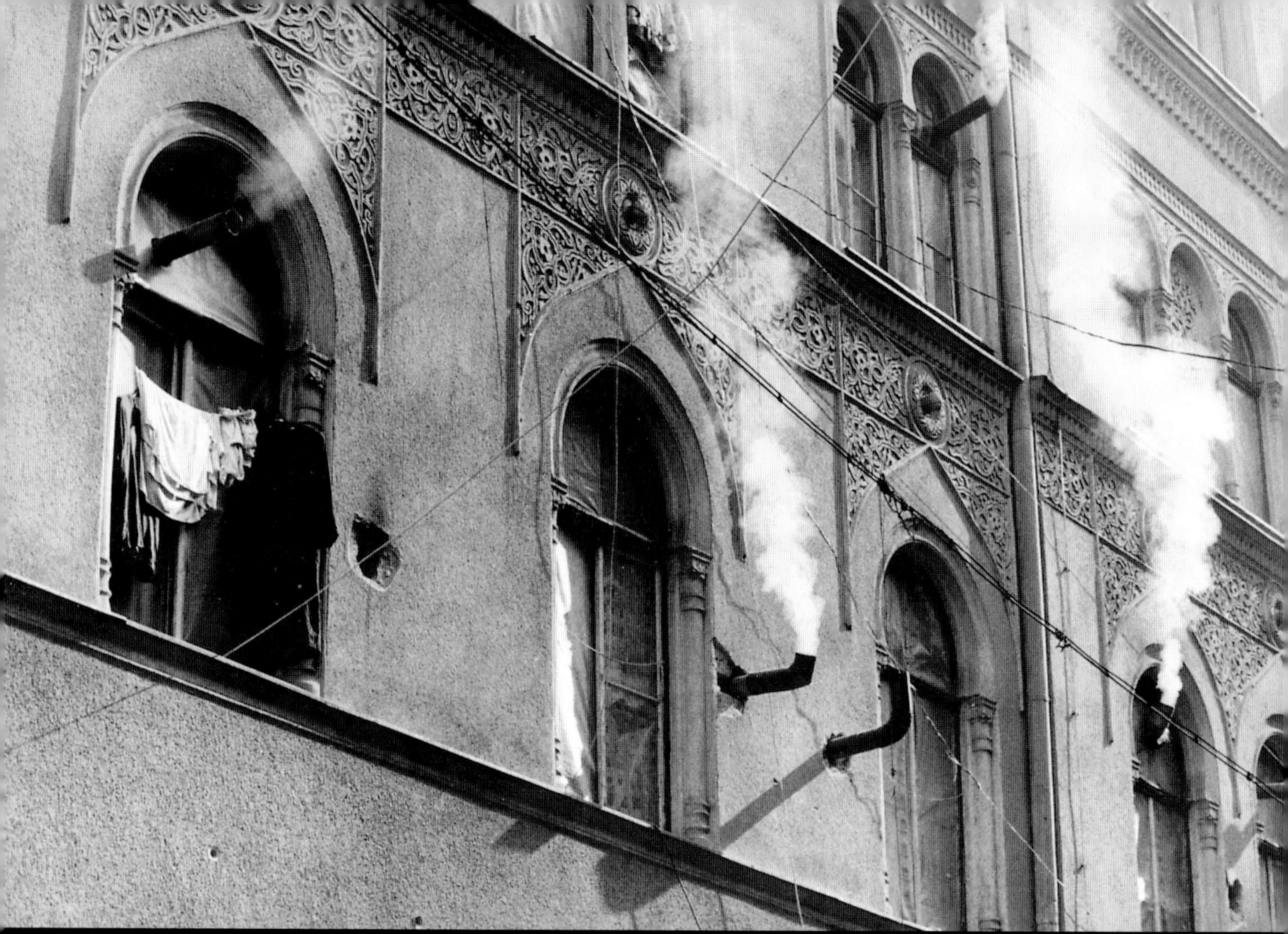
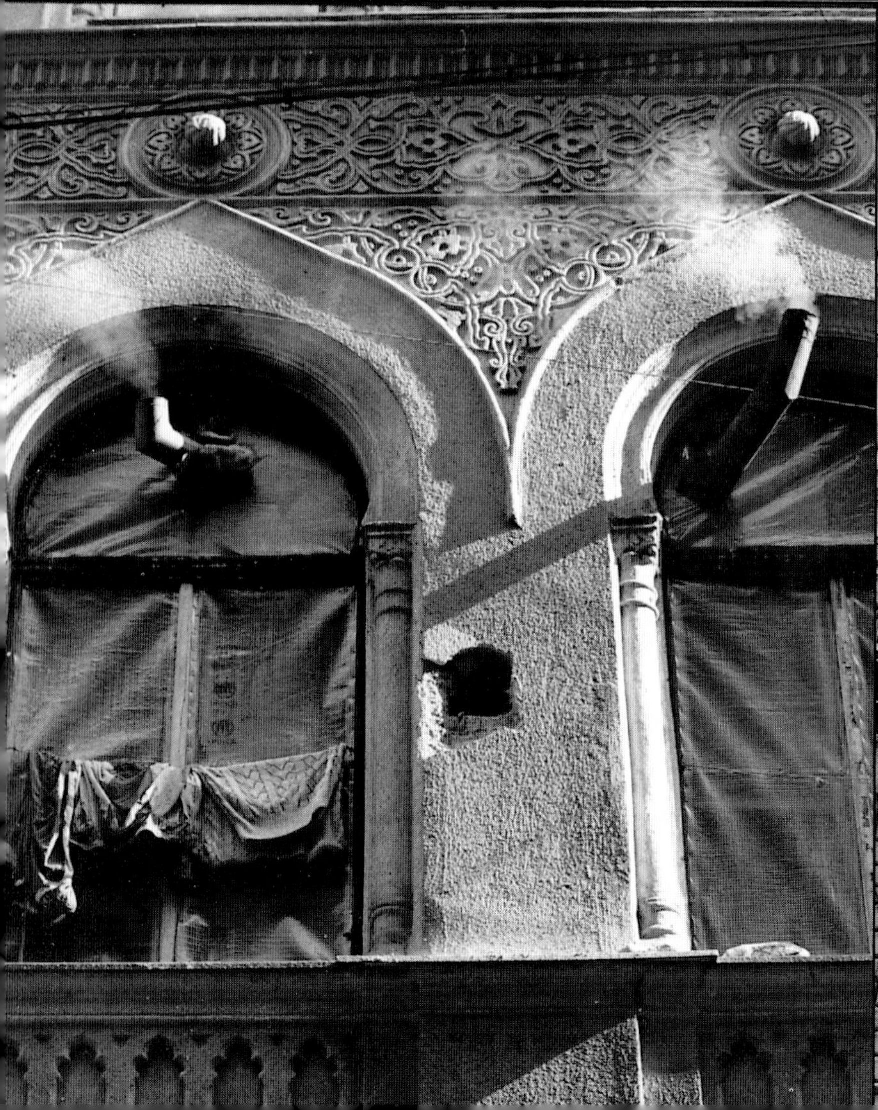
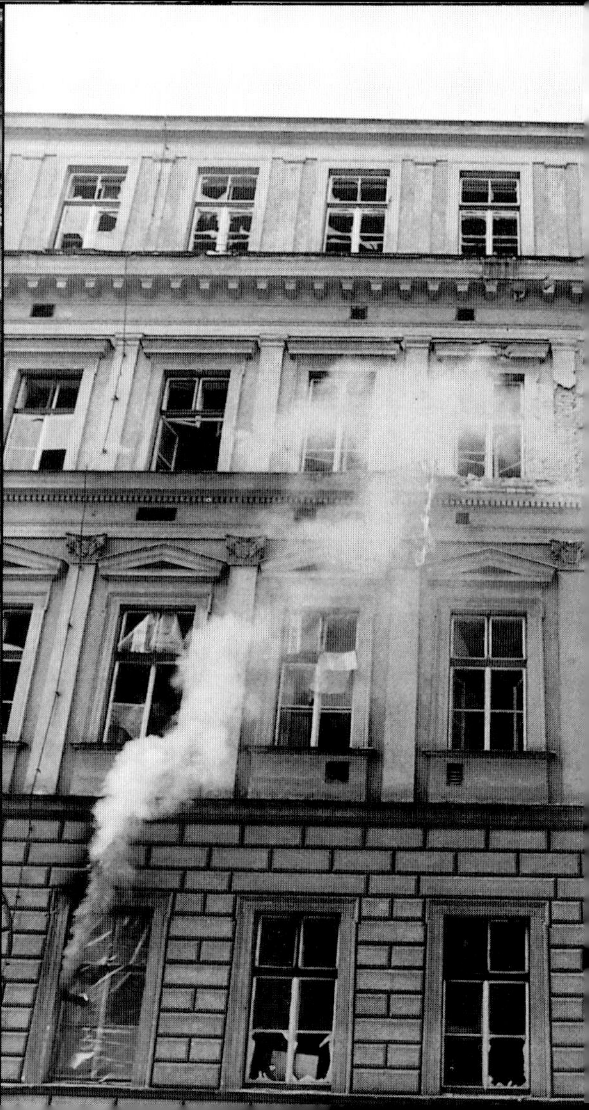

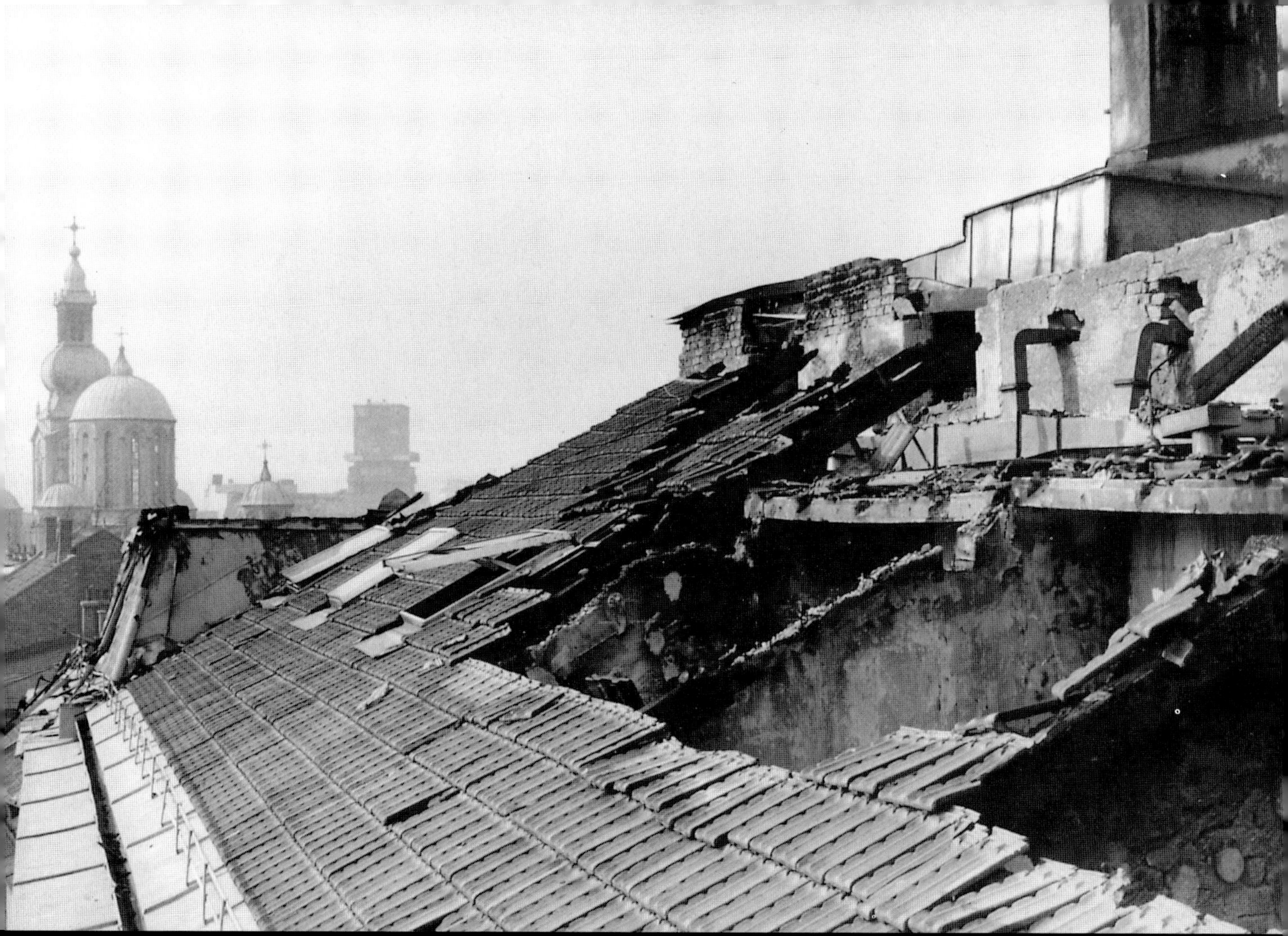
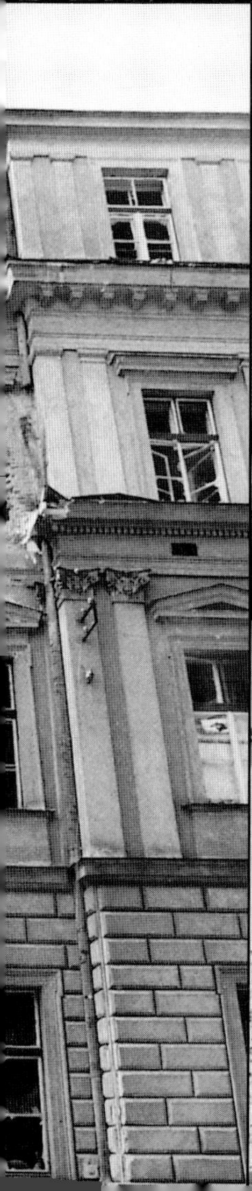
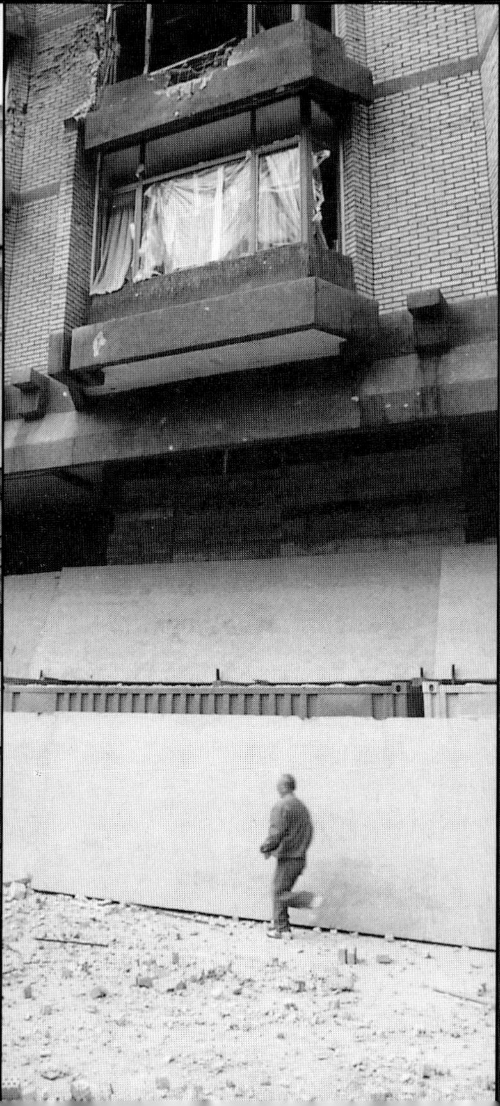
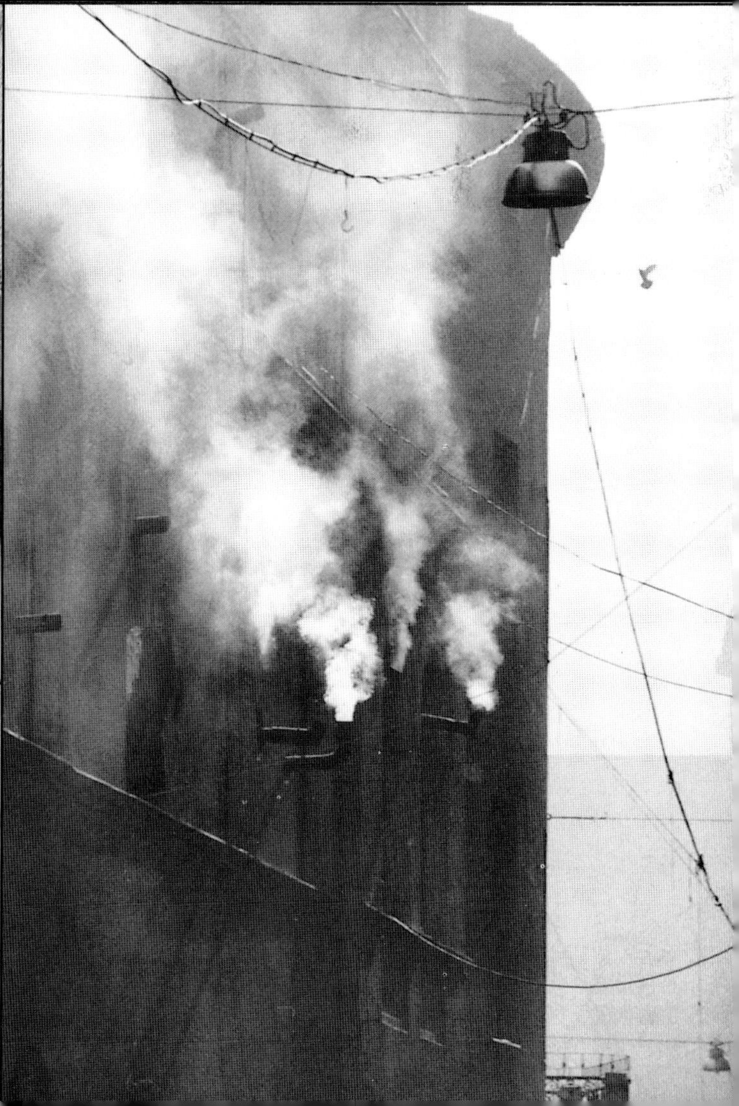

were sentenced to the dark, we knew. There was no firewood. The coal had been used up last winter. The heating plants were helpless. As early as the summer we witnessed, in confusion, the disappearance of the wooden bench backs, seesaws and handrails of staircases from the parks. Our neighbours were then getting rid of superfluous furniture. They were chopping it up in order to survive. Private libraries were getting smaller. Books were burning at the stake of war. Each book that burned meant a few more degrees of heat.

New products appeared at the markets. Old stoves, firewood ranges from the attics and cellars, discarded long ago, were sold. The art of stove making had died out. Old-fashioned ranges of different types: fiacre, boxlike and drumlike ones were being made out of tinplate. Old boilers were being made into stoves. Sickroom night tables were being altered into simple stoves in which a meal could be cooked, bread baked. Everything can be made into a stove. A competition for survival started. Metal beer kegs, big tins, washing machine drums, refrigerators were being used, electric stoves were being altered.

Should I answer Danilo Kiš and his "Street of Wild Chestnuts" when he writes: "Trees, probably, have souls, they get old. Chestnuts, sir, do not die so easily." I believed him, but in Sarajevo, this icy winter, wood has been sold in bags. It has already been chopped up. One bag of damp logs of chopped up park trees is sold at the market for twenty to forty German marks. And people buy them. One lasts for one, or maybe two days for the more economical ones. Coal burns longer, but its price is 50 or 60 German marks per bag. Choose, if you can.

Mr Sken, yes, you James Henry who visited us in 1885. You wrote "The huge number of trees among the houses, of which many are big and lovely, gives the whole town the look of a beautiful, fresh garden and it is no wonder they call it the Damascus of the North." Of course, you can always cite William Miller. He visited us almost half a century later. For him we were, as for many others, only the Balkans and: "Everything is just the opposite of what can be reasonably expected. The traveller enters the realm of romance where all his established ideas turn upside down and he soon begins, like the local population, to see the difference between what is done in the Balkans and in Europe."

No, sir, it has not always been so. It was, I do not deny it. We, in the meantime, ran after Europe. We jumped onto the train of history. We fell off and then again pushed onto it. It seemed to us that we had caught up with you. We may not have been on same train, at the same station. But we were, at least, on the same rails. We were in a hurry.

The tinplate roofs of the new residental quarter was where I found shelter from the cold wail. I warm myself with another refugee family at a friend's. The wind whistles

Sarajevo be declared, by an extraordinary proceeding, an internationally protected zone. Hospitals have no heating because there is no electricity. The book "The State or Fear of Tomorrow" by Prof. Ćazim Sadiković is promoted, published by the "Oslobođenje" public publishing house.

Saturday, 12th: Mortar shells and rocket launcher missiles fall on the city centre and the outskirts of Novo Sarajevo. No aeroplane with humanitarian aid has landed at Sarajevo airport since Tuesday. The city is still without electricity. A shortage of oil halts the city's buses. Promotion of Dženana Buturović's book "Bosnian Muslim Oral Epics".

Sunday, 13th: Sarajevo without electricity and water. 16 killed, 80 injured.

Monday, 14th: Military negotiations continue at the airport. There will be no demilitarization until the artillery is moved to a 30-km radius from the airport tower. 7 people killed and 83 injured in the city. Bread supply becomes increasingly difficult. The main springs at Bačevo are out of service. New car numberplates are presented in public.

Tuesday, 15th: Artillery fires at Žuč and Mojmilo. Sarajevo hospitals again damaged by shelling. Infantry clashes in the Hrasno hill and Kromolj areas. A shortage of bread owing to a shortage of 1.5 tons of oil a day.

Wednesday, 16th: The airport is still closed as a consequence of clashes in its immediate vicinity. Last night 107 persons are prevented from crossing the airport runway. Last week

98 people were killed and 684 injured in Sarajevo.

Thursday, 17th: *Occasional shelling of Stari grad and Novo Sarajevo. A shell kills three boys in Boljakov potok. The city is without electricity, water and heating. Counterfeit banknotes (coupons) of 5,000 dinars are discovered.*

Friday, 18th: *Electricity supply still uncertain. The main springs out of use. The negotiations on peace and Sarajevo demilitarization, held at Sarajevo airport, produce no results. Lord Owen visits Sarajevo. Presenting his credentials, Dr. Zdravko Sančević, the Ambassador of the Republic of Croatia, becomes the first ambassador to come to Bosnia and Herzegovina. 6 people killed, 24 injured. The Journalists' Association is established within the Croatian Culture Society "Napredak".*

Saturday, 19th: *Still without electricity and water. "Velepekara" starts making bread again, but not regularly. There has been enough flour recently, but not enough oil or water.*

Sunday, 20th: *The "Electrical Power Industry of B-H" promises to provide some electricity for Christmas and even more for the New Year. A relatively peaceful day in Sarajevo. The auction of art objects and antiques organized to raise money for the B-H Armed Forces is delayed because of a lack of electricity.*

Monday, 21st: *The winter starts at 3 o'clock and 43.3 minutes p.m. Six aircraft with humanitarian aid land after a three-week break; also, a convoy with food arrives from Metković overland. 9 killed and 53*

through these scabby roofs above the bullet-scarred façades. The smallpox of war marked the faces of the buildings, opened wide the holes in the roofs. Craters made by shells threw pieces of torn off tinplate into the sky. The cold wind whistles over the slopes of the tinplate roofs, and the snowy blanket slowly soaks up the wounds we are under. I can hear it even under the cover pulled over my head. The plastic foil that the world sent us as a gift does not help. Thanks, UNPROFOR, but my windowpanes were warmer. And Mr Zvonko Milas says he cannot endure so many degrees below zero on his twelfth floor. He keeps himself warm by constantly walking outside the house. He is warmer in the street. He does not manage to type one page of text a day on his typewriter with all his warm clothes, blankets over his shoulders and knees, and a woollen cap and gloves on. The academician and professor sacrifices more and more books. He lays them on the tinplate altar called the boxlike stove. His neighbour uses old shoes and cuts up car tyres to warm himself up. He does not want to take part in the cremation of the parks.

Oh, how shall I one day carve somebody's name in a tree? Trees disappear, they are gone without trace. Stripped are even century-old trees near the Alipasha Mosque. Their bark was stripped off by somebody's freezing weak fingers. Some black Sarajevo eyes caress me in the whiteness of Circle Eight. They watch with me all those stoves on the shoulders of doctors, actresses, lawyers and housewives. Only fire can warm up freezing fingers. The soul is warmed up differently. With grief and some pride known only to me, in the park, over a tree stump, I recognize people dear to me. An acquaintance of mine, the poet Valerijan Žujo, with the dignity appropriate to poets, stands near the remainder of a tree stump in the park. He has worn-out leather gloves on. He gathers wood splinters around the tree stump. He thrusts them into a bag, and straightens up again. As if he wanted to tell himself it is not him, that he is, as he really is, far from this humiliating position that we have been pushed into. He is in the park, the park of Sarajevo. The park next to the Austria House, in its centre, had a children's playground with logs, benches and a lazy recess in the shade. Now it is completely bare, its trees are cut down, cleared, taken away; it is deserted. A few people like my poet wander around the tree stumps hardly sticking out of the ground. They meticulously gather branches and splinters. They try to run away from themselves. They do not look farther than the ground and the scarce branches. One must live. Cold inexorably reigns. It is 13, 14, 15 degrees centigrade below zero. "A cold Sarajevo winter..." says my diary. The date is some time this winter.

Yesterday Azra was there, the lady for whom nothing else remained to do. She will not burn books that she has edited. But how will she make tea? Those who are stronger,

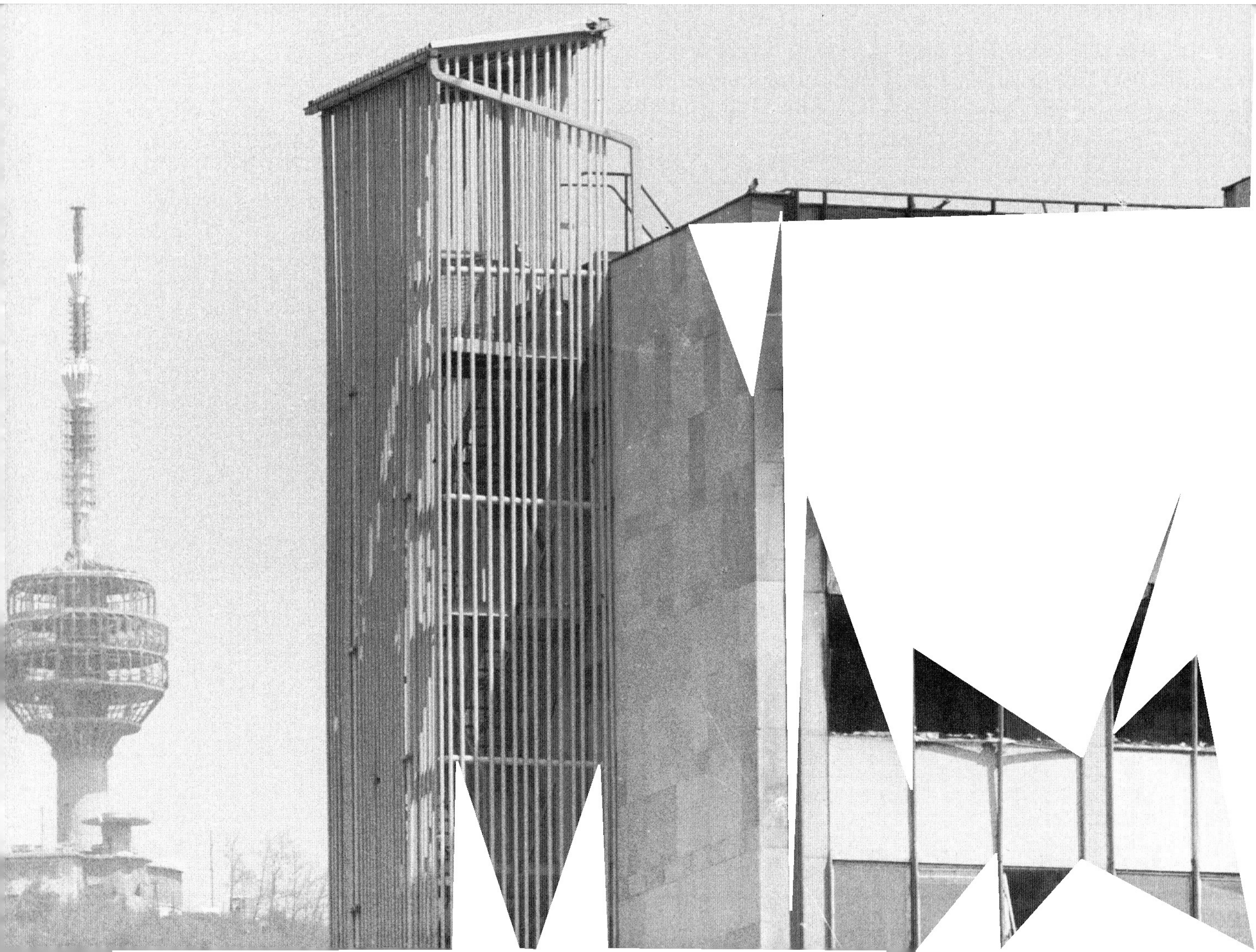

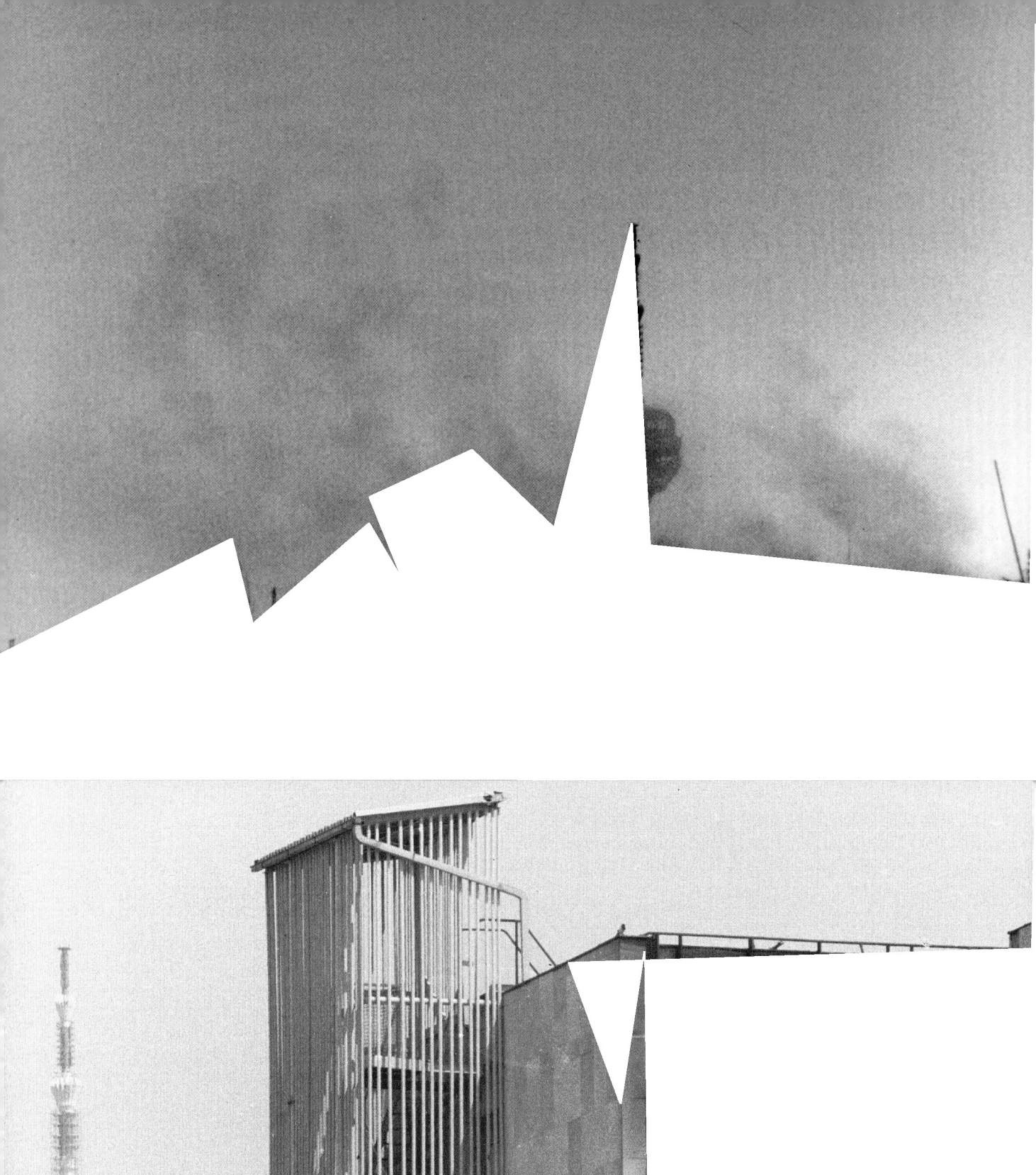

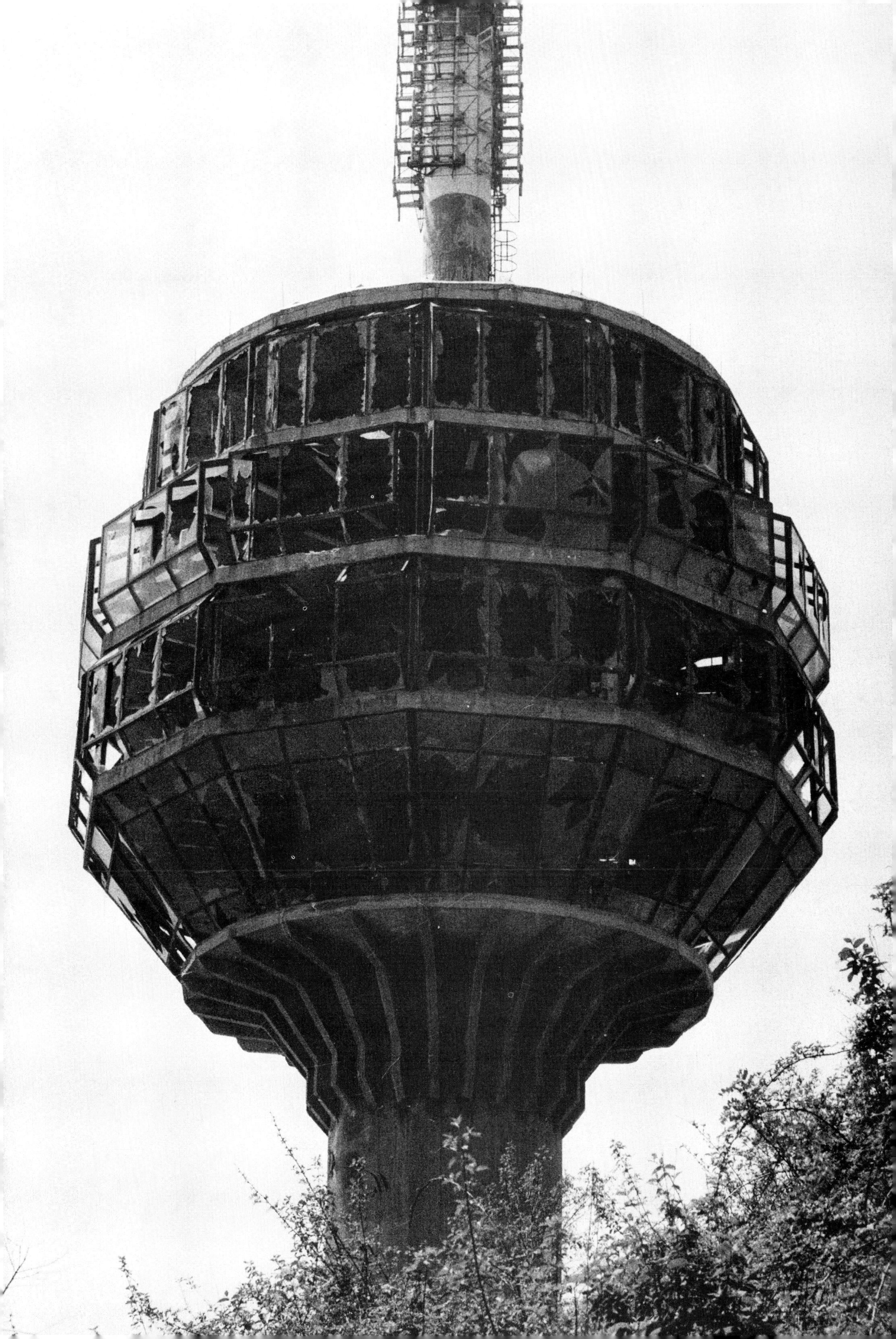

with weapons, younger and more aggresive do not shrink from publicly cutting and transporting trunks any more. They do it hurriedly because the authorities disapprove of killing the parks. Nothing else remains for these weaker, more urbane poor except to be satisfied with the leftovers. The law of justice is broken. Man is only a part of the animal world. The gatherers of firewood are the tame part of the city that shivers, that dies.

Who knows for how long, when everything is over, we shall be ashamed of ourselves? Shall we have enough strength to feel shame? How shall we explain to the birds that we destroyed their homes, the trees with their nests. We magpies settled on the gulters under the roofs of buildings. The Austro-Hungarian architects decorated our façades magpies settled on the consoles under the roofs of buildings. The Austro-Hungarian architects decorated our façades with their hollow-ended beams. This year shrapnel discovered the trick, and the city's birds occupied them. Nothing else was left for them.

We were freezing. We were waiting for the promised electricity, the fuel that should have come into the city. Tragi-comical was the announcement about 5,000 cubic metres of wood. Well, a hundred years ago, the city's poor received that much, and the city was seven, eight or even ten times smaller than it is now.

We were condemned to freeze to death. Shells, bullets, fires, and starvation did not kill us. Why didn't cold push itself among the apocalyptic riders? Did Europe way back last summer, have to warn itself of Bosnia and the winter, and then push us aside mercilessly? They may have been satisfied with caring about us while they were sitting in front of their warm fireplaces with a cup of hot tea. Would you like your tea with milk, lemon, or sugar?

"... Asta kuando?!..."

"... Asta kuando?!..." a hoarse voice repeats for me in the whiteness. I cannot see the whisperer. I can hear:

> "Asta kuando esta indolensia?
> Asta kuando esta apatia dura?
> Asta kuando esta mala egsistencia?
> Asta kuando esta vida eskura?
> Asta kuando esta amargo estado?
> Asta kuando esta suen pezgado?
> ...
> Asta kuando?... Asta kuando?!..."
>
> (How long?!...
> How long?!...

injured. Sarajevo hospitals still without heating. Only one day of oxygen supplies left.

Tuesday, 22nd: George Kelly, a former counsellor to the US President, pays a visit to Sarajevo. "Velepekara" has not enough oil. BH TV becomes a member of Eurovision. The citizens of Žepa, now refugees in Sarajevo, organize a protest meeting in front of UNPROFOR headquarters, because of their failure to provide humanitarian convoys for people from Žepa, Konjević polje and Cerska. Rudo Tomić, a journalist, killed.

Wednesday, 23rd: The city receives electricity (?!). After the Christmas mass in the cathedral, a concert of the Chamber Orchestra of B-H TV and the Female Choir "Gaudeamus" is held, and broadcast direct to ten countries. The Olympic Centre Sarajevo and the PTT Sarajevo distribute New Year greetings cards with the "Vučko" Olympic motif on them to the citizens of Sarajevo free of charge. Out of 18 scheduled flights with humanitarian aid only four aircraft land. The War Congress of the Bosnian Muslim Intellectuals ends its two-day session. The government announces its reconstruction by appointing new ministers.

Thursday, 24th: No electricity, water, bread or, heating. Hunger and cold take their toll. In eastern Bosnia more than a hundred children and old people die of cold and hunger. Heavy clashes on Žuč Hill. The residence of the UNPROFOR commander is shelled. Three lorries with medicines, three lorries with pasta and 3 tons of oil arrive from Scotland for the hospitals. Prof. Tatjana Ljujić-Mijatović and Miro Lasić are appointed new members of the Presidency of the Republic of B-H and Miro Lazović as the President of the Republic Assembly. Curfew is not in force tonight owing to the midnight Christmas Mass celebrated in the cathedral.

Friday, 25th: Clashes on Žuč Hill. Gen. Morillon's headquarters are shelled. Death notices and obituaries sent to the "Večernje novine" ads section are read on the "Studio 99" Independent Radio between 9 and 10 o'clock a.m.

Saturday, 26th: A conference to establish a business association is held. The Association of Muslim and Albanian Friendship – the UMA International – is founded. The Military District Attorney brings charges against Radovan Karadžić and Ratko Mladić based on suspicion of their having committed genocide, crimes against civilians, crimes of destruction of cultural and historical monuments, the criminal act of undermining the constitutional order of the Republic of B-H, jeopardizing the territorial unity and violating the territorial sovereignty of the Republic of Bosnia and Herzegovina.

Sunday, 27th: Fierce clashes on Hrasno hill. The Commander of the UN forces and the Government Vice-President announce that firewood will soon be transported into the city. Electricity and water supply uncertain. The Social Democratic Party of B-H holds a war congress.

Monday, 28th: Twenty planes with humanitarian aid land at Sarajevo airport.

How long this indolence?
How long this apathy?
How long this poor existence?
How long this bitter state?
How long this heavy sleep?
...
How long?... How long?!)

The black eyes whispering translate for me the verses by Isak Altarac. The archcantor of the Great Sephardic Temple in Sarajevo was in the first group of those executed at Vraca in 1941. I do not manage to explain how Sephardic art follows me along my path so much. It helps me overcome all my pain, and then suddenly leaves. On my way, there are not Goran, Blanka, Dodo Danon or Čičak. My Sephardim have abandoned me. Where am I to go? Is there the end, oh my Moorish Lady? Didn't they expel you, too, from Spain? How can you help me? How did I deserve your glance and escort?

Salvation was found in the city's womb. A great ecological project, a decade old, helped us. In the struggle against the unbearable Sarajevo smog natural gas was brought into the city from Hungary, Russia, who knows where else.

Didn't the Austro-Hungarian monarchy try to enrich Sarajevo with gas way back 1879? The Vienna building contractors Lowy and Kohnrat offered to build a gasworks. It was too expensive. Again in 1910 there was the idea of building a gasworks. The Vienna firm Franz Monaschek offered their services. The proposal was ignored from fear of endangering the electrical power plant. The year was 1912. "Sarajevski list" (The Sarajevo Journal) wrote: "The building of the city gasworks is no competition for the city's electrical power plant, but it is only helping the citizenry to meet their needs, because gas lamps can better light the streets in the valley and private premises. So the gasworks was built, near the Paromlin (The Steam mill) at Čengić Vila. The production of gas started on March 21st, 1914, and on April 2nd the first lamps were already burning on Appel Bank. "Sarajevski list" wrote on March 26th: "This is the first gasworks in the Yugoslav countries of our monarchy." In the public lighting 379 lamps burned the whole night, and 282 until midnight. Gas reached households and industries with hard coal from Silesia.

We discovered gas again in this cold war winter of Sarajevo. In the households where gas had already been installed for cookers they started fitting gas heaters. They adjusted them from butane to natural gas. Others used various stoves and ranges they found with burners and fireboxes designed for wood or coal. We started resembling Mexico. Pavements, façades, walls were dug up. Gas was connected whenever it was possible, when it became certain that the promised fuel would not be enough even for the

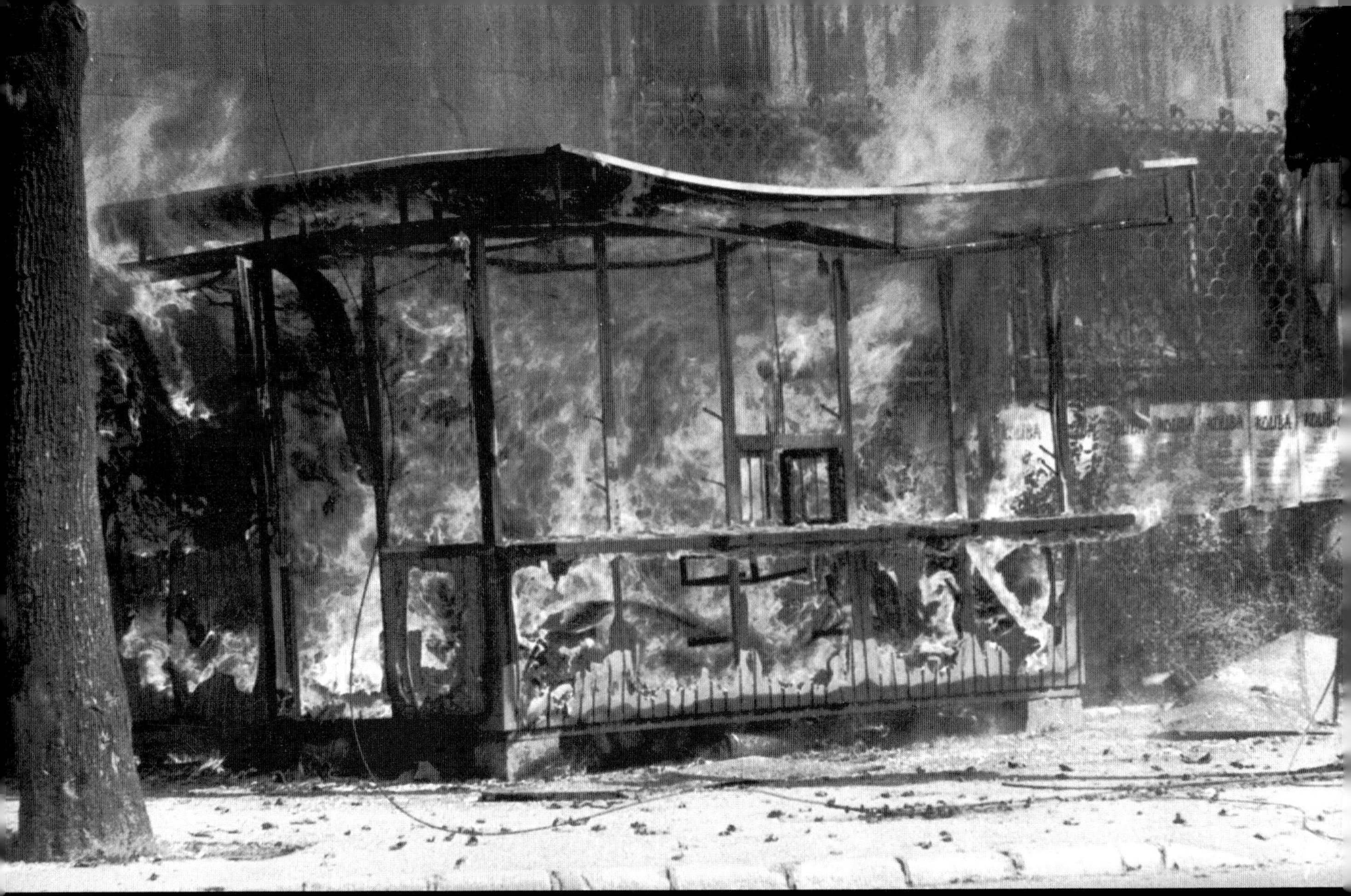

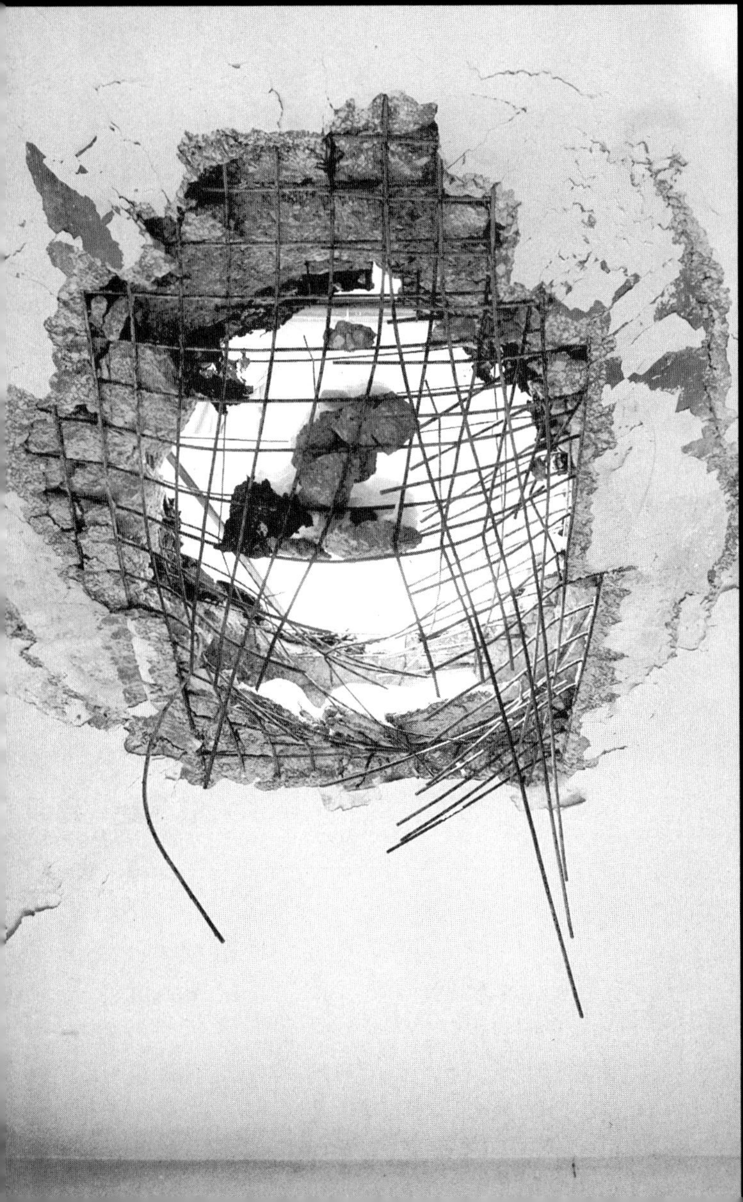

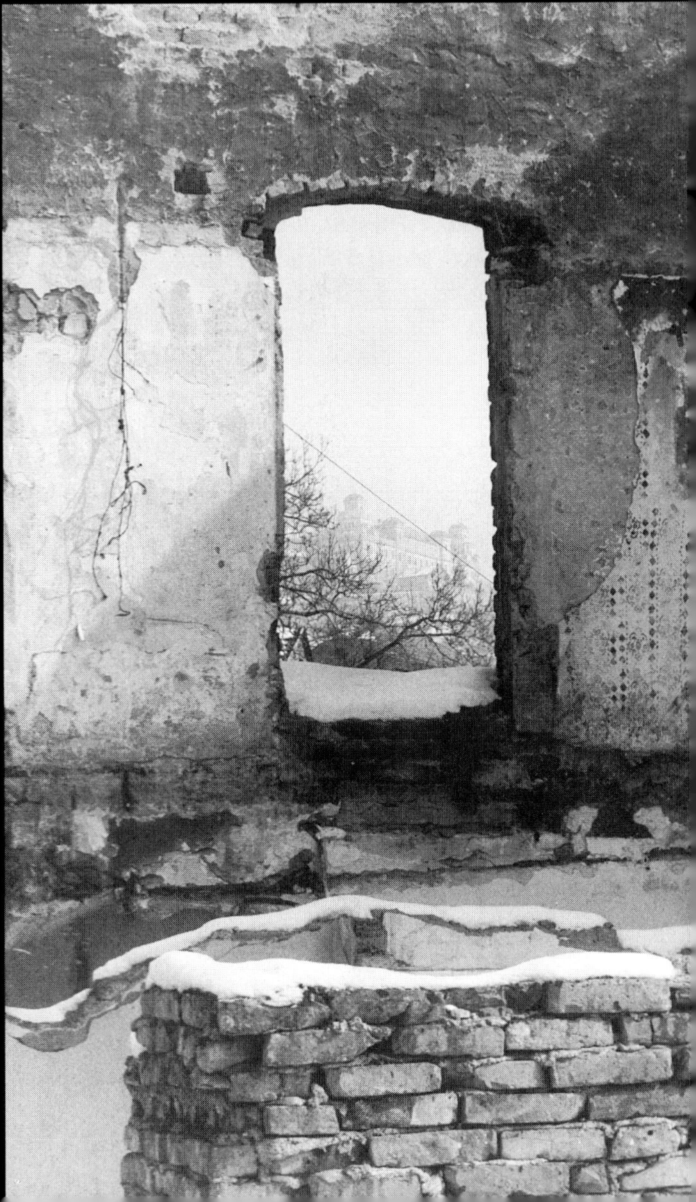

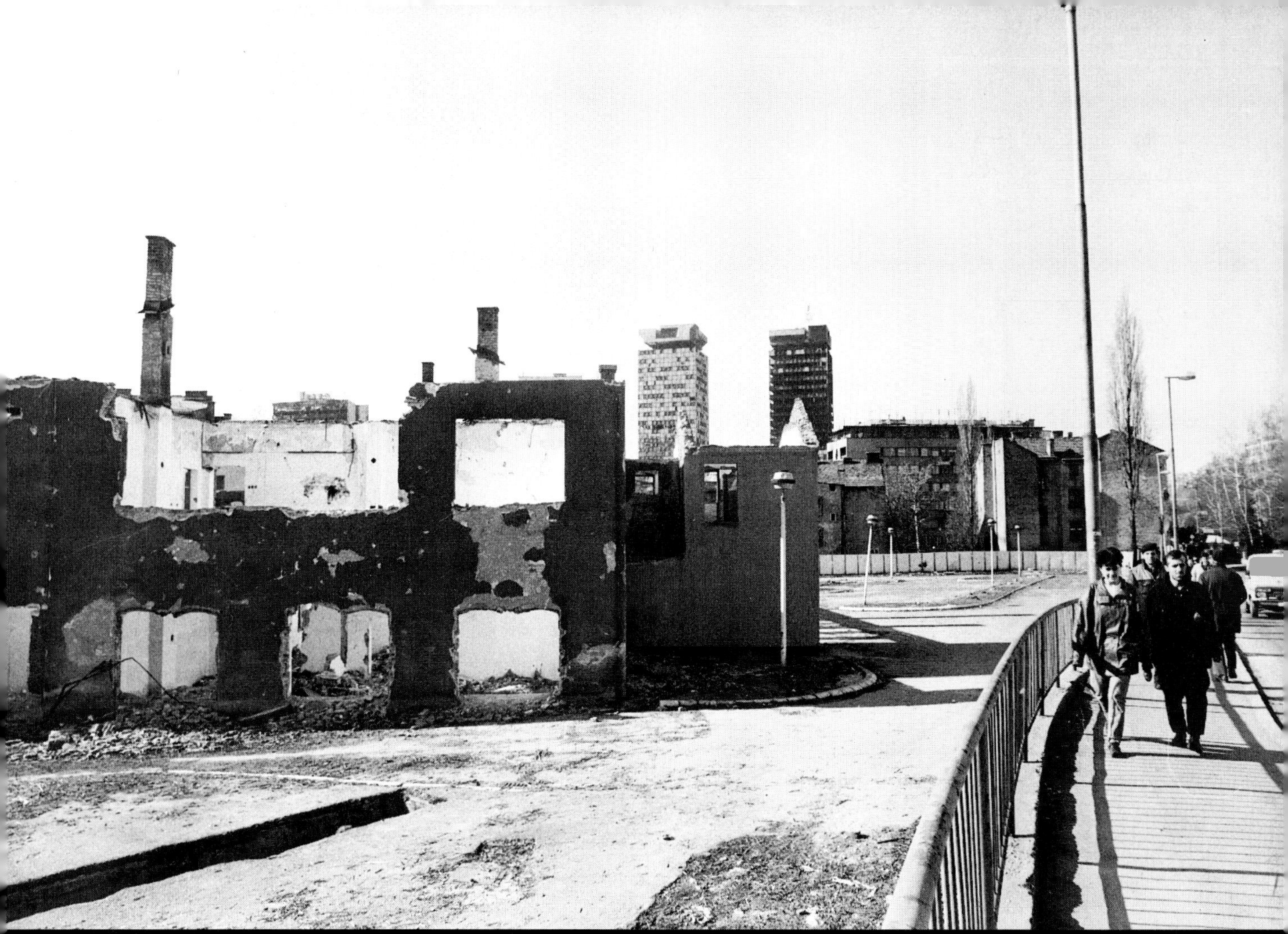

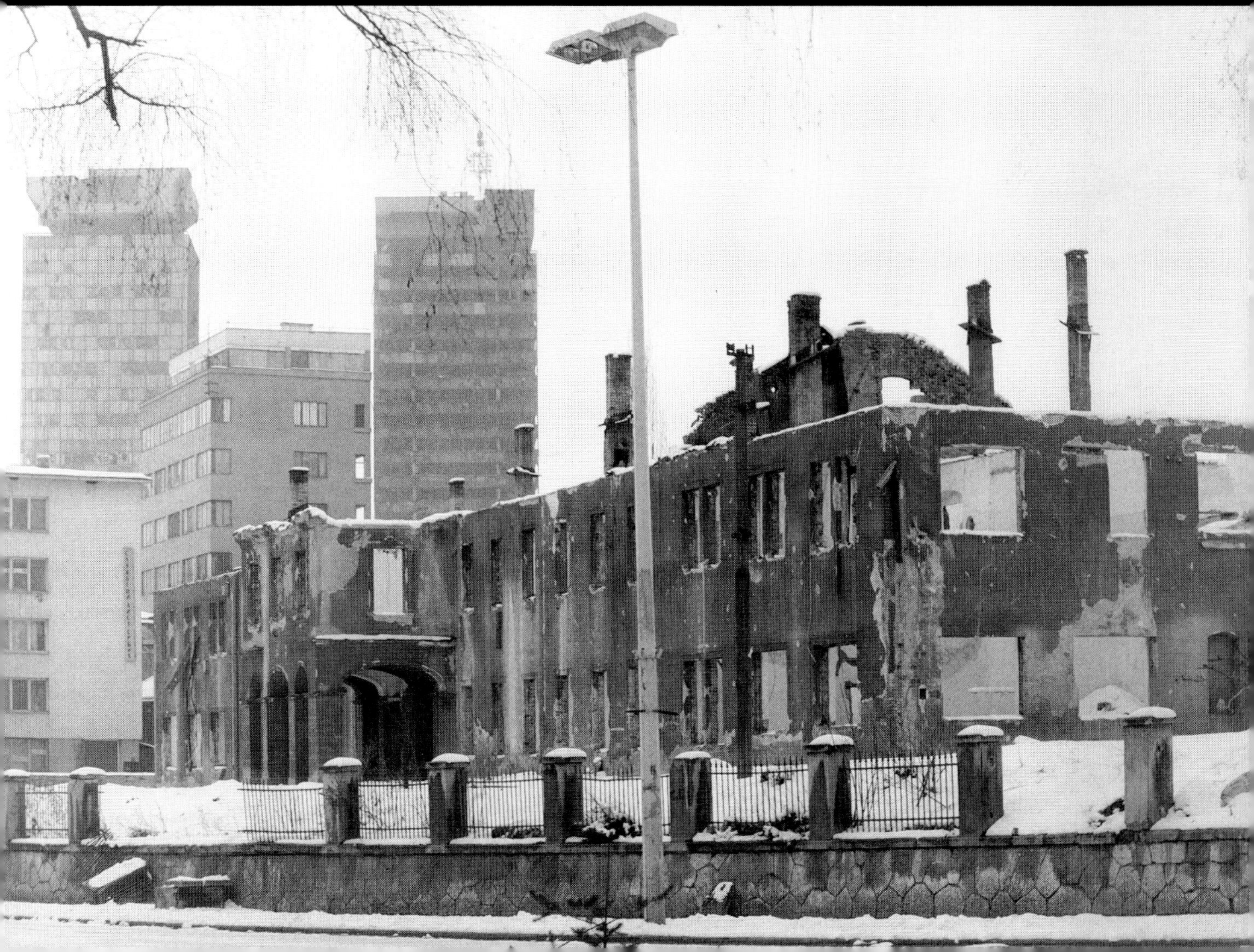

most underprivileged, that it was obvious it would not be available this winter.

Most Sarajevans were bothered by the damp wood, books, shoes and furniture they used as fuel. Out of the city's windows sooty flue pipes showed. They dirtied the façades. They announced life even in the most urbane parts of Sarajevo. We turned the wheel of civilization back a whole century. The official gazette "Bosnian-Herzegovinian News" wrote on October 17th, 1886:

"Since many landlords in Sarajevo, owing to the forthcoming winter, will be installing stoves into some other fireboxes in their homes, the police administration in order to remove any fire danger issues the following orders: 1. Everybody in his home is obliged to fix pipes on stoves and fireboxes if they are not connected to the chimney so that there is a minimum of 75 cm of pipe from any wood in the home. So-called trim collars must be fixed on the necks of pipes. Pipes must be installed in clay bricks but if pipes go through boards or wooden walls, then they must be coated with clay or bricks a minimum of 10 cm thick. 2. In the same way the exhaust pipes of stoves and fireboxes that have already been installed must be prepared by November 10th of this year at the latest. 3. Severe measures will be taken against the landlords and tenants who disobey these orders."

How to put all this together while I am gathering snow in a bucket, taking it to my flat and filling the bath with it? Of a pile of snow in the bath we get less than a fifth of water. To fetch drinking water, we must walk three, four or five kilometres. One can carry ten to twenty litres by hand. Old people and children do not manage to carry even that much. There is no water. No electricity. Around the fountains that are still running there are thick layers of ice. And the regular whizzing of shrapnel. Explosions take away those who come before or after us to the fountains we go to. Blood, punctured canisters, fear and death, façade pieces and ice get mixed. The disabled and dead were in the same queue with us a while ago. The Sarajevo roulette wheel goes round inexorably. Death and life are in the necklace of anno domini 1992.

Shall we succeed in preserving at least the oldest parks. We may survive without them, too. Whom shall I manage to tell about the Big and Small Parks? They are still fairly well preserved. They were built simultaneously with the Land Government Palace, the present building of the Republic's Presidency. The date was October 1st, 1886. A year before that the "Bosnische Post" wrote about the future Town Park. The official of the Land Government Hugo Krvarić designed those first two town parks. The Big Park was arranged on 30 dunams of the old cemetery Čekrekčinica with the still preserved monumental nishans (Muslim tombstones) of Muslihudin Čekrekčija, who left us a mosque

A convoy of 22 lorries with food arrives from Metković. Hospitals are still without heating, electricity and water. Gauze has been supplied in quantities to satisfy 15 days' requirements. One of the largest attempts to cross the airport runway is recorded. 252 people from both directions try to cross to the other side. However, they are all returned. Every night about 130 people on average try to cross over. Temperatures are still low, minus 10° C.

Tuesday, 29th: The ninth round of the humanitarian aid distribution is about to end. Chess Grand Masters Ivan Sokolov and Vesna Bašagić are declared the best sportsmen of B-H in 1992. The most successful teams were: the Marks womens club from Zenica and the B-H National Chess Team. Hakija Turajlić, vice-president of the B-H Government sends a letter to George Bush with a request to deliver humanitarian aid to eastern Bosnia by air. Morning temperatures are about minus 15° C.

Wednesday, 30th: An exhibition of Afan Ramić's paintings opens in the Gallery of the Museum of Literature of B-H.

Thursday, 31st: The UN Secretary-General, Boutros-Ghali, visits Sarajevo, together with Cyrus Vance and General Satish Nambiar. Four people are killed and 13 injured in Sarajevo.

Firewood is expected. 60 cubic metres of firewood should arrive from Fojnica every day. The curfew is not in force during New Year's Eve. The one-man photography exhibition of Senad Gubelić in the PTT Engineering building is visited by the UN Secretary-General, Boutros-Ghali. New Year's Eve in Sarajevo – without electricity, water, telephone, fuel and food, under shelling that continues even in to the last minutes of 1992.

P.S. I leave this detailed chronology of the war in Sarajevo to historians. They should study minutely every day and hour of what we lived through. This is my chronology of events. It is based on data available to me personally and on materials published or broadcast in the Sarajevo mass media: "Oslobođenje", "Večernje novine" and Sarajevo Radio. I have chosen what I thought was important for the life and death of the city. I have maintained the repetitive everyday monotony of localities and events. The data on casualties were obtained from the Republican Headquarters for Health Protection.

below Kovači in 1526. The Waqf administration gave up parts of the old cemeteries Šehitluci and Kemalbeg for the Small Park. The government had pedestrian paths arranged and flowers planted. They also had nursery plants of the rare ginco biloba brought over here. The government bound itself to preserve the nishans and to pay 300 florins a year to the Waqf.

Cold reigns in the city, in Circle Eight of the Sarajevo hell, at every step. The black eyes help me to stop, not to petrify from the cold. I follow them stiffened from the ice, icicles formed on my moustache, I do not feel my hands or feet, my cheeks are numb from the cold, my eyes ache. I slide, slide. I stumble. I do not manage to detach myself from Esad Mekuli. His compatriots, the Šćiptars, the Albanians from Kosovo, used to be the only sawyers in the city. Today the whole city carries saws, axes, and bags with wood. Mekuli repeats for me his verses written in pechalba (while working abroad): "You brother...

"I can see you – with your freezing hands in your armpits, with a wooden saw over your shoulder and a sharp axe on your belt. Its handle shows under your shrunken coat at the back so that it looks..."(Didn't they, perhaps, call us tailed devils because of that?!)

"You cruise the streets of this white city.

"Your ketche (Albanian cap) absorbed the black soot with sweat. Your rubber shoes wore out, they gave up...

"You walk – and you are all ears: won't, now, a door open; won't somebody, from the threshold, call out behind your heels: – Sawyer, come!

. . .

"I saw him on the road – he stared into the distance... Today I saw a panic-stricken pechalbar" (somebody working abroad) – "the victim of misery."

That was in 1936. I see him again in 1992, 1993...

Who knows when and how I will get out of the deadly whiteness? Will I? My good courier Jovanka did not. The winter beat her. The white death (death from the cold) took her away. Death is always black, I know it. Sarajevo draped it with a white icy mantle. All around it is crystal, cold, slippery and steep. How shall we go through all this, my good Moorish Lady? How much of this cold, white road still remains for us to walk? Even your tender fingers do not help me. I plunge downwards.

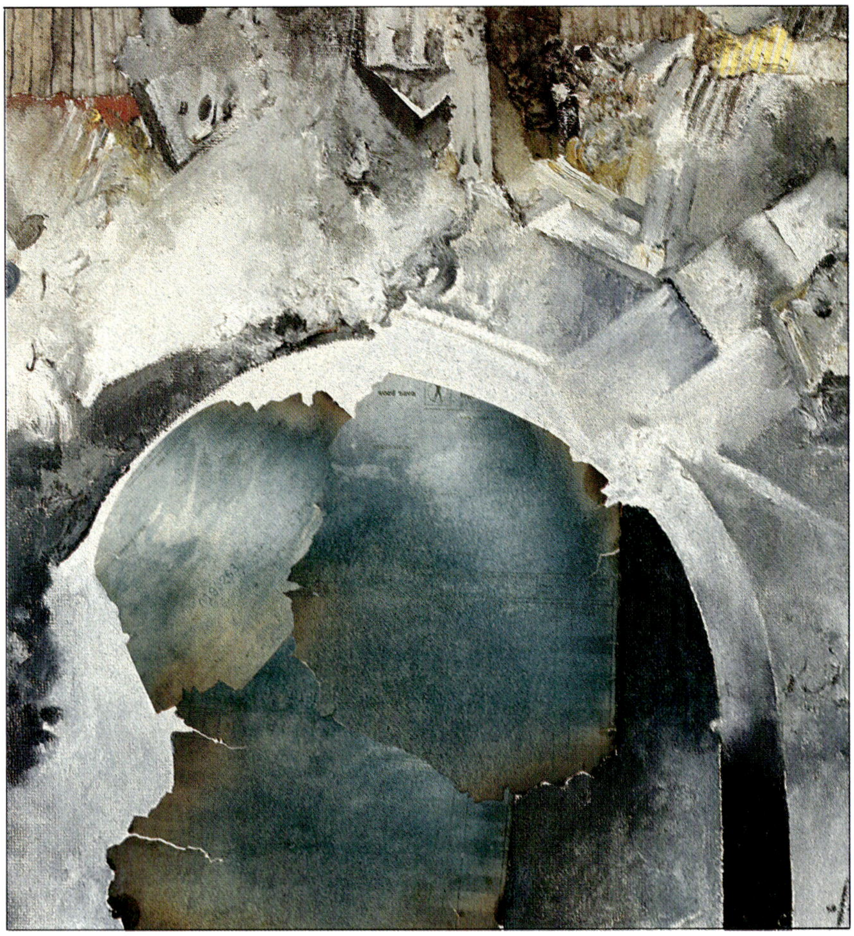

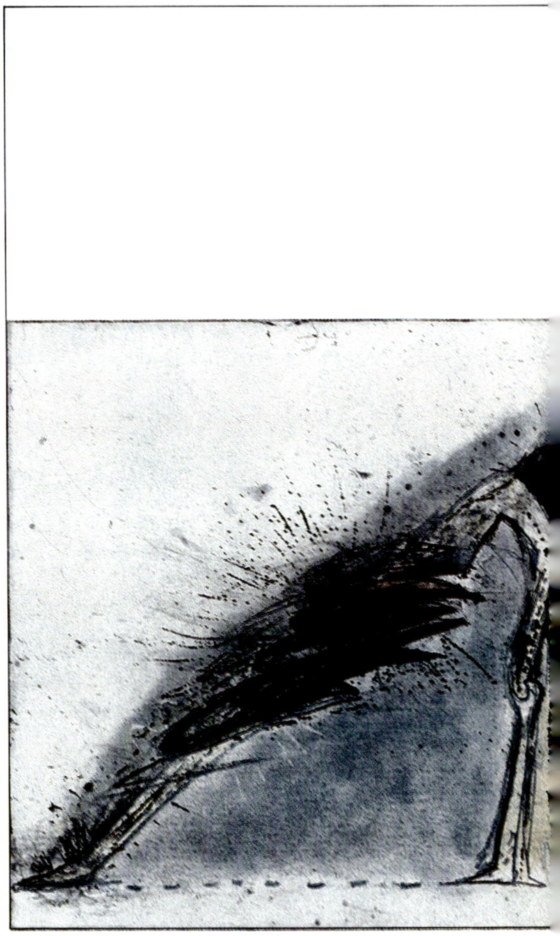

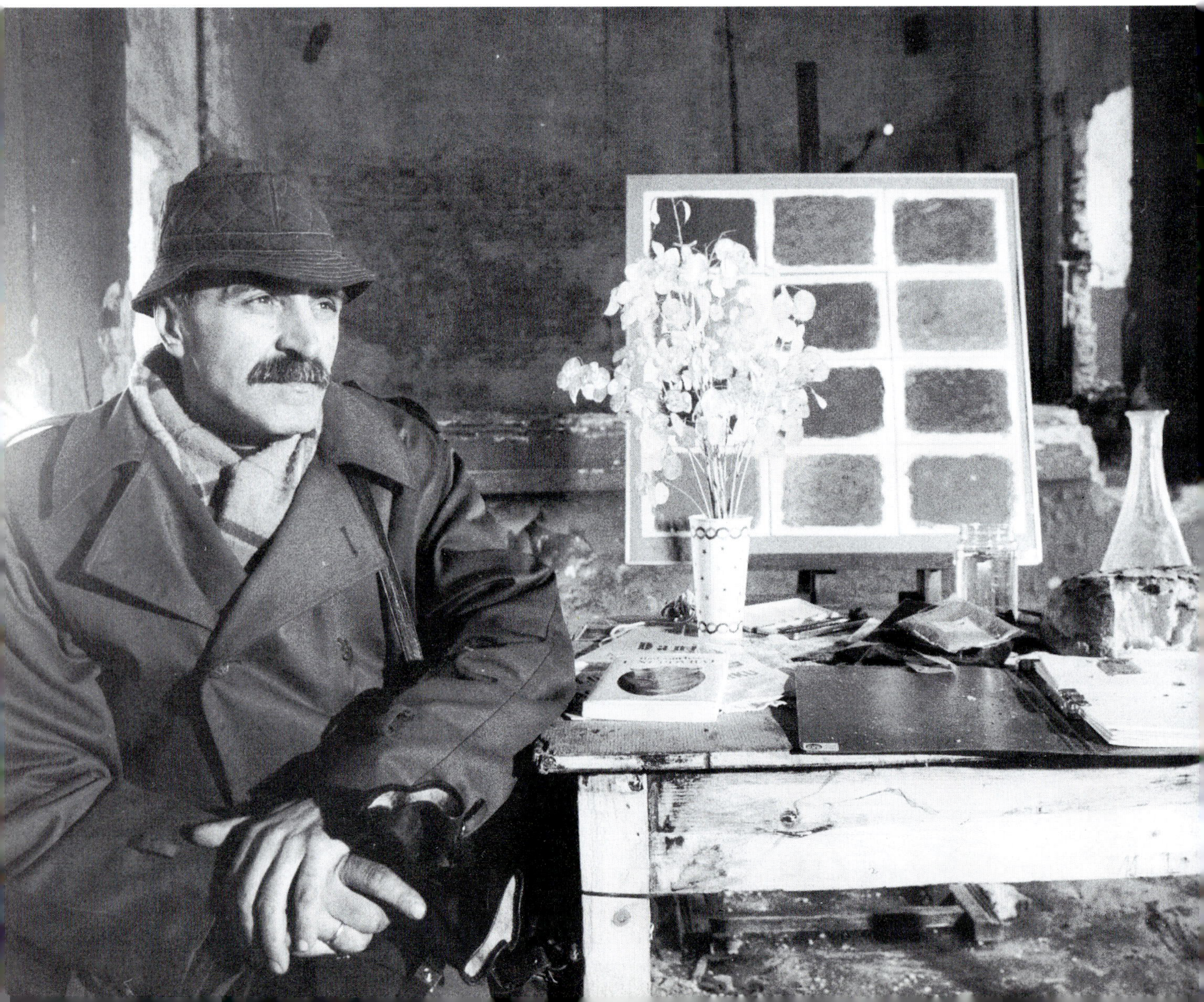

261 SARAJEVO – THE WOUNDED CITY

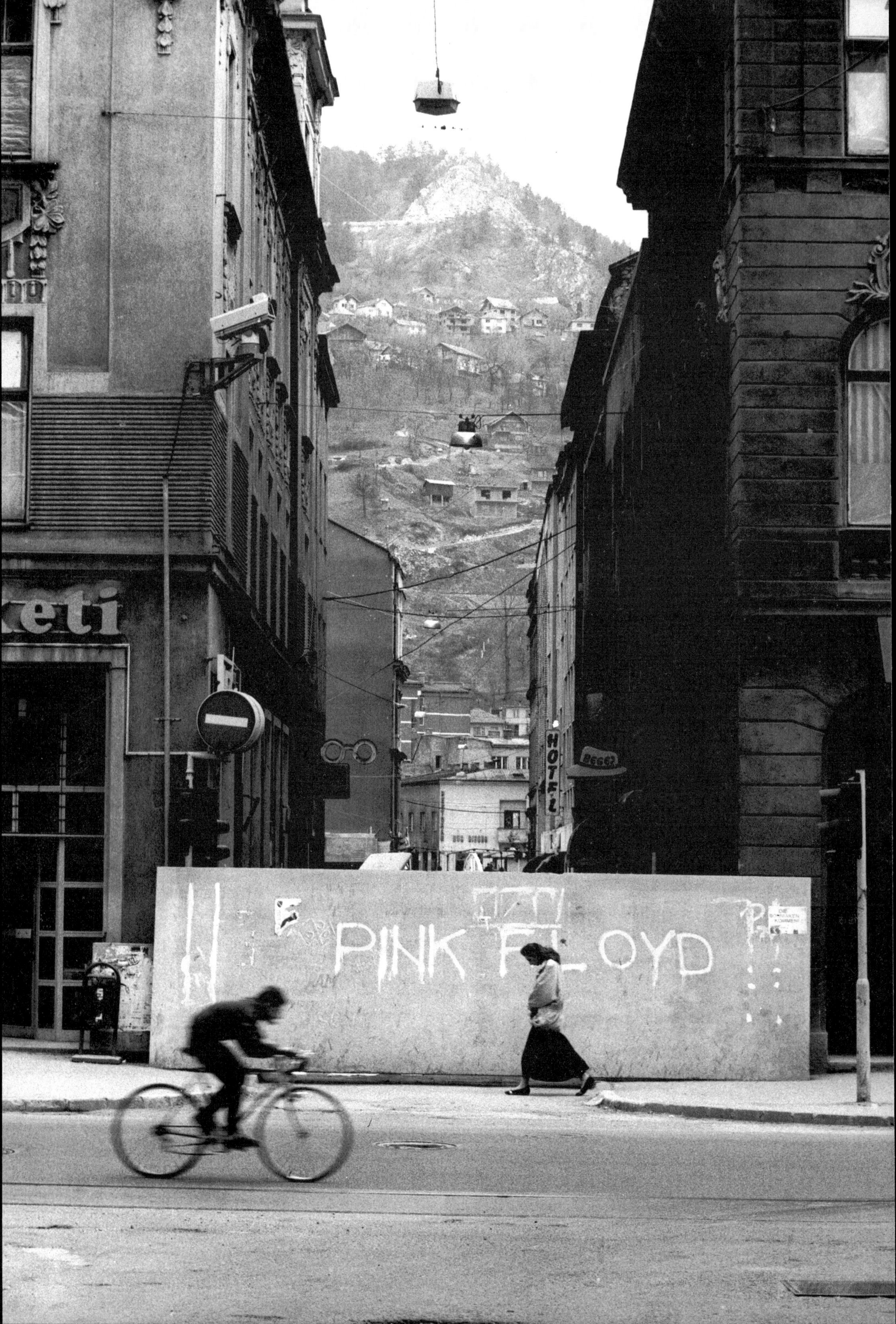
PINK FLOYD
HOTEL

CIRCLE NINE

1993 continues in war, blood and gloom. Its comprehensive chronology brings nothing new. It is all repeated, repeated. It is enough to look back at any random day:

JANUARY,

8th – Hakija Turajlić, the Prime Minister of the Republic of Bosnia-Herzegovina, is killed in an UNPROFOR personnel carrier. He is coming back from the airport, escorted and protected by UN forces. The UN soldiers do not stop the killer at the barricade at Nedžarići.

15th – A massacre near the brewery – eight dead and 19 wounded in a queue for water. Shelling of the entire city. Traumatological clinic shelled as well.

17th – Shelling of Stari Grad, the centre, Novo Sarajevo, Dobrinja and Kobilja Glava. A self-propelled rocket hits a queue for water in Dobrinja – nine wounded. 40 heating stoves arrive. An intense chemical attack at Hrasno hill and Dobrinja. Nine dead, 24 wounded.

Dark. Again I cannot see anything. Has the whiteness blinded me? I cannot manage to warm myself up. I shiver. My teeth are chattering uncontrollably. It is dark.

Did I, perhaps, drown in the dark of her eyes? I wouldn't mind. In that case, I believe, I would not be cold. There are not those luxuriant fig trees here. You promised that with the autumn we would sleep under the fig tree covered with a mantle of a starry sky. There is nothing. Your look has also abandoned me. How can I learn where I have slid?

Bump. Bump. Bump... The monotonous sound of wood hitting something hard. It is approaching. It is being interrupted. Bump. Bump. Bump-bump. Bump. Bump-bump...

I can make out similar sounds in the distance. Some muffled xylophone sounds. Muffled blows of wood on wood. Where is the wood here from? Haven't old Bosnian towns been wiped out in fires? They were built of wood, unfortunately. We did not gather even their ashes. And in the land of Bosnia there has always been at least wood in abundance. Sarajevo, though, is treeless and woodless in this war winter at the end of the twentieth century. Where is, then, the wood for the xylophone from? The bars seem to be made of wood, beech. Here, in Bosnia, beech and oak are highly valued although they are found in abundance. Do I hear the words: Onde esta? Bump. Bump. Bump-bump. Onde esta? Bump. Bump. Bump-bump. Where is it? Bump. Bump. Bump-bump. Where is it now?... Where is it now? Is it the blows of a pickaxe on dried ground? No, it is not that sound. Isn't it the sound of a shovel? Is it an axe? No, it is not. The bumping does not move away. What is it all?

I gradually get accustomed to the dark. I strain my pupils.

Auntie Zejneba, is that you? Are you coming downstairs? I cannot hear your shoe, but only the crutches you are supported by. Isn't there rubber on the tips? Bump. Bump. Bump-bump...

Crutches. I hear the crutches of the disabled on the asphalt, the ground and the parquet. They have not got rubber tips as they touch the ground. The wood they are made of, at least according to the sound, is not new. It is worn out, from striking against the ground.

Crutches. Sticks...

You remind me of your sentence uttered a few years ago. The odour of war, only now I realize it, we smelled in our nostrils. Life taught you many things. You were, between the two world wars, the first Muslim woman to be a barber. At the barber's you got to know the life and spirit of the city, the people, and the habits and pulse of Sarajevo

REPUBLIKA
BOSNA I HERCEGOVINA
РЕПУБЛИКА
БОСНА И ХЕРЦЕГОВИНА
BON - БОН
1000
AD
№ 7034182
TISUĆA DINARA
ХИЉАДА ДИНАРА
HILJADA DINARA
500
PET STOTINA DINARA
ПЕТ СТОТИНА ДИНАРА
NARODNA
BOSNE I HERC
НАРОДНА
БОСНЕ И ХЕРЦЕ
GUVERNER - ГУВЕРН
СТО ДИНАРА
STO DINARA
ПЕДЕСЕТ
1000
НАРОДНА БАНКА ЈУГОСЛАВИЈЕ
NARODNA BANKA JUGOSLAVIJE
НАРОДНА БАНКА НА ЈУГОСЛАВИЈА
Nikola Tesla 1856-1943
1000
ДИНАРА DINARA
DINARJEV ДИНАРИ
1000
AB 943366
NARODNA BANKA
BOSNE I HERCEGOVINE
НАРОДНА БАНКА
БОСНЕ И ХЕРЦЕГОВИНЕ
2

SUGAR
NET WT. 6 G.

NATIONAL PACKAGING CO., INC.
DECATUR, ALABAMA 35603

CREAM SUBSTITUTE, DRY, NON-DAIRY
FOR COFFEE OR
4 GRAMS N
DISSOLVE CONTENTS
IN 1/3 CANTEEN CUP
(8 OZ.) OF BEVERAGE.

NATIONAL PACKAGING CO., INC.
DECATUR, ALABAMA 35603

IODIZED SALT
CONTAINS: SALT, SODIUM
SILICO ALUMINATE,
TRICALCIUM PHOSPHATE,
DEXTROSE, 0.01%
POTASSIUM IODIDE.
NET WT. 4 GMS
DIAMOND CRYSTAL
SALT COMPANY
WILMINGTON, MA 01887

IODIZED SALT
CONTAINS: SALT, SODIUM

500

SFR JUGOSLAVIJA
СФР ЈУГОСЛАВИЈА

БЕОГРАД · BEOGRAD · БЕЛГРАД 1.III 1990

500
ПЕТ СТОТИНА ДИНАРА · PET STO
PETSTO DINARJEV · ПЕТСТ

NARODNA BANKA
SRPSKE REPUBLIKE
BOSNE I HERCEGOVINE

50

50 PEDESET DINARA

FALSIFIKOVANJE SE KAŽNJAVA PO ZAKONU

AA 1190503

BANJA LUKA 1992.

You asked me: "Do these people remember the cripples walking about this city after the war? They were young men then. Do people remember them today?"

I was not able to answer your question. I used to be terrified by a road accident or even a minor injury. I was born after the war. I lived a life of peace. I do not remember the cripples. Some beggar would stretch out his arm or leg stumps from the pavement edges. They were rare. I did not even think those might have been marks of war. There were not too many of those with crutches, with artificial limbs. The world may have looked rosy, more beautiful than the reality of my parents, as it is to every child. In recent years I have been carrying in my mind your question: "Do people remember the cripples after the war?"

You do not have to repeat it with the accompaniment of the old-time wooden xylophone. From the loudspeakers we can hear the monotonous reading of death announcements and thanks. The Sarajevo independent radio station "Studio 99" broadcasts daily newspaper death notices. The newspapers do not print them because of the shortage of paper. The radio here replaces music by the expressions of sympathy, information about deaths, the bereaved, messages that cannot be heard by the dead.

The echoes of crutches, radio death notices, the shell explosions that never stop and the dirge of Ham Mordehaj Konforte from 1948 blend together:

> *"I jo me topo muj asolada*
> *I de toda mi familija dezbarasado*
> *No aj mužer, no aj ižas ni jernos*
> *No aj ermanas, no aj ermanos..."*
>
> *(And so I am lonely*
> *Of all my family deprived*
> *Without wife, without daughters, sons-in-law,*
> *Without sisters and without brothers...)*

He speaks about the destruction of his family, about the war tragedy of auntie Mazaltov. He repeats: Onde esta?... Onde estan?

You go downstairs slowly, Mrs Sušić. Your big old woman's eyes are still cheerful and wise. You are worried about your son and daughter-in-law in distant Mexico. A few years ago you did not want to leave in order to find peace in your old age. You did not want to go to Jerusalem, either, with your granddaughter Amra Berjan and her children. You were invited by Joža and Riska Kabiljo, and Joža's daughter Seka Grinberg, too. You saw others off. You hardly agreed to leave your Grbavica in September. You carry the Medal of the Righteous, one of the highest of Israel's decorations, like an amulet that has protected you, and around ten photographs from a distant country. I know,

23th – Večernje Novine published, after a 45-day-long lack of paper.

29th – Shells fall on Ciglane, Breka, Jukićeva, the Centre, Marijin Dvor, Grdonj, Brekin Potok, Baščaršija, Kobilja Glava and Sedrenik. Poison gas, general air raid and chemical alarm sounded. 26 dead.

30th – General alarm. Yesterday and today, the heaviest shelling of the entire city; 19 dead.

31st – Koševo hospital shelled. Two killed and seven wounded in the intensive care ward. 6 killed, 8 severely and 8 slightly injured...

FEBRUARY,

1st – Peaceful. International observers register 567 shells fired at the city, and 16 from the city at the enemy positions. UNPROFOR turn back 620 citizens trying to cross the airport runway.

5th – International observers yesterday registered 739 shells fired at the city, and 169 fired from the city. Last night UNPROFOR turned back 714 people trying to cross the airport runway.

11th – All parts of the town subjected to shelling. Four French soldiers wounded at the airport. One dies in hospital. City Assembly decides to refuse further humanitarian aid as a sign of solidarity with the population of south-east Bosnia, which has not been getting any aid.

13th – Eight killed, 24 wounded.

18th – No electricity, water or fuel, even for medical institutions.

24th – Electricity provided. Serious accident at the water facilities near Stup.

27th – *No electricity. Telephone connections cut even within the town itself.*

MARCH,

19th – *Shelling started five hours ago. No electricity, no water. The damage to the city's electricity facilities between Reljevo and Buća Potok has not been located as yet.*

21st – *Intense shelling of the entire city, from 4.30 a.m. on. The number of the dead and wounded is increasing.*

22nd – *Electricity restored. Telephone communications restored. Two killed and 18 wounded near a school in Novo Sarajevo. International observers count 2,330 shells fired at the city...*

APRIL

...

MAY

...

JUNE

...

JULY

...

AUGUST

...

SEPTEMBER

...

24th – *The Olympic Committee of Bosnia-Herzegovina accepted into the International Olympic Committee as its rightful member.*

OCTOBER, New government elected – Prime Minister Dr Haris Silajdžić.

26/27th – *Decisive action against criminals and renegade units within the B-H Army – 18 dead and 102 arrested.*

you were there some ten years ago with your sister Nađa at a Sarajevo Sephardic family, the Kabiljo's. You were invited by the state of Israel. You planted a tree each in the Memorial Complex "Jadvašem" (The Hands of Salvation). You did it on behalf of your late father and husband. On that occasion the surname Hardaga was written down in the Memorial Complex. It was the first Muslim name in the shrine in which the Jews express their gratitude for the help during the Second World War sufferings. You hid Joža and Riska in your home near the Theatre and the Great Temple for four long war years. For you, it was normal to do what you did. Now, not only does the family Kabiljo repay you for your care. The Jewish Community as well is grateful to you and they care about you in the misfortune that has struck us. Your family is well, fortunately. You seldom go out with your crutches. Old age has caught up with you. Your muscles are weaker and weaker. What are you repeating in this dark: "Do people remember the cripples who walked about the city after the war?"

Bump. Bump. Bump-bump...

Human oblivion covers many a good deed. It also covers the evil. Why has, just this year, fascism got out of Aladdin's Lamp? Must the names of antifascists be so impatiently wiped off the street plates and school blackboards in Sarajevo, while new and muddy graves spread in the green city parks for which we have not got enough wood to write with dignity the names of the killed on the crosses and pyramids. It is unimportant whether those names were correctly selected, whether they were minor ancestors or whether we forgot some other much more important ones. All this may be necessary, but why this hurry to wipe out the memory of the antifascist struggle when the world still remembers the victims of the world's last cataclysm?

You too ask me the same again, Mrs Sušić. Your friends in Israel repay with love for the former Sarajevo's warmth which you built yourself as well.

Here one lives with death. In the Sarajevo newspapers there is no obituary section. The whole city is an obituary. Everything that made up the life of the city has been shattered, torn to pieces and devastated. Shells have destroyed both people and the city. Some evil worms, under the wing of darkness, ate the city from the inside. The city remained without an obituary. Many things have vanished, been taken away, or hidden. A vulgar witness would call it the plundering of the city. But it was not robbed by the citizens. The war winds hid the coyotes that sullied the hands and honour of us who made up this city, and who continued living a civilised life.

We were worried about the destiny of the city. We lived it. Left, very often, to ourselves we wondered if the future would bear this nonsense of our present. Each new day woke me up with a new knowledge that pushed out the

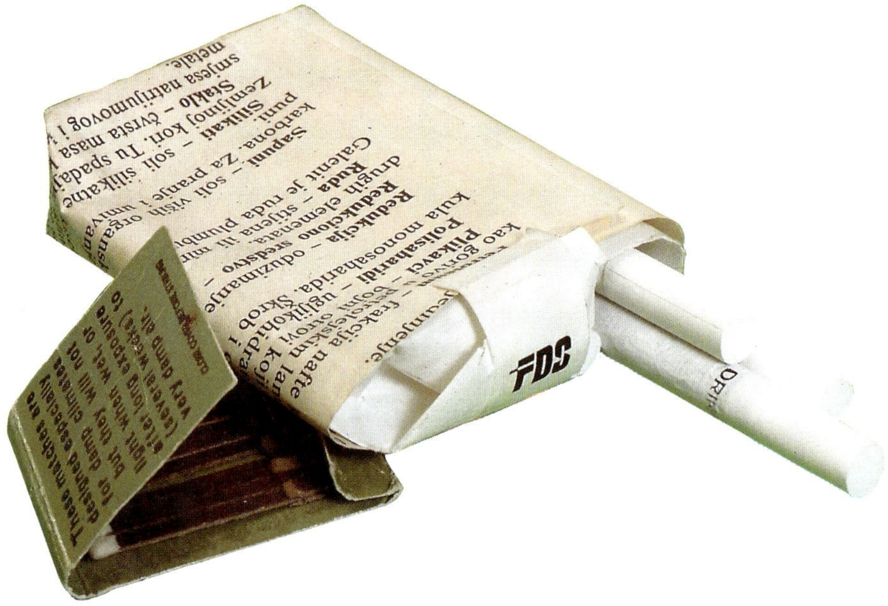
FDS

REPUBLIKA BOSNA I HERCEGOVINA
PTT
100
500
1000
5000
10000
20000
50000
50.000
Sarajevo '84/1994
1994
Plamen
još živi
DESETOGODIŠNJICA
XIV zimskih olimpijskih igara
Sarajevo '84
200 000
100 000
10 godina
poslije
Plamen
još živi

Danielle Mitterrand visits Sarajevo.

NOVEMBER,

8th – *George Soros in Sarajevo. A minimal amount of electricity provided. A convoy carrying 200 old, sick and exhausted people leaves for Serbia. Greek foreign minister, Karolas Papoulias, visits the city.*

9th – *Nine killed and 58 wounded. A shell kills three pupils and a teacher in a school in Alipašino Polje. Thorvald Stoltenberg in Sarajevo.*

26th – *Still no water or electricity.*

30th – *Four grenades hit Koševo hospital – two nurses killed, six patients wounded.*

DECEMBER,

3rd – *A shell kills five and wounds many people near the Careva Mosque.*

6th – *Shells. Five dead and thirty wounded. No electricity, water or gas.*

9th – *Nine killed and 26 wounded, after 150 shells fall on Novi Grad and Novo Sarajevo districts.*

10th – *28 wounded...*

14th – *Shells kill 8 and wound 13 in Stari Grad and the Centre.*

16th – *Heavy shelling of the town – 36 wounded and one dead.*

21st – *Air bridge suspended, after a UN aeroplane is shot at while landing at Sarajevo airport. The "Sarajevo Winter" festival opens.*

27th – *Still no electricity. Six killed and 50 wounded.*

28th – *"A convoy with 900 Croats and Muslims leaves for Split, another with 200 Serbs for Belgrade" (from a newspaper). Pakistan's*

knowledge I previously had. Days overtook one another. I do not know whether we had time to rest, to take a deeper breath, count up to five, or perhaps even to ten, to sum up what we had experienced.

I remember some of last October dates: "We come to Bekir's at twilight. We find Zdenko and Kaća there. They are waiting for electricity to be supplied. It has just gone off. But at Bekir's, electricity is regularly back after being cut off every quarter of an hour. They have brought bread to bake. We learn about a shell that exploded somewhere around in the bushes. It flew into the courtyard. It was about four o'clock p. m. Shrapnel broke the remaining window panes. A shard of glass hit a lady neighbour upstairs. She was sleeping on the sofa in the room like this one.

"And that was the end.

"She is downstairs in the basement. The neighbours took her down. They are waiting for somebody to take her corpse away.

"We are talking about the differences in the language we speak that now has three names: Serbian, Croatian or Bosnian. It used to be Croato-Serbian or Serbo-Croat. We are defining the notions of the words kut and ugao (Croat and Serbian words for "angle"), historija and povijest (the two varieties for "history"). The academic discussion goes on. The electricity is on again. The bread goes into the oven. I ask Kaća how her family in Bačka provided bread during the week. She says that the family was large so bread was baked twice a week. White bread on Saturdays, and on Wednesdays bread made from a mixture of flour, maize and bran...

"A dead woman lies in the basement, below us. A few hours ago she was on the floor above. She had her worries, joys and obligations. The entrance door that is usually locked is now open. On the stairs leading down to the basement an oil lamp made from a jar is burning. It lights the stairs with flickering light. The undertakers "Bakije", they say, do not transport the dead by night. The city mortuary does not have any transport, either. The relatives are looking for some private van to do the transporting. The police were clear: they do not have any transport, either.

"– What are we to do?

"– Wrap her in a sheet, take her out onto the pavement and thumb a lift. Somebody will come by, advises the policeman.

"We have a glass of some old brandy. On the dusty bottle of "Zvečevo" brandy it says: Kovač Gordana 1988. It was kept in the pantry.

"Beki is telling his cousins Belma and Ivona, who have just arrived, that he went to the mortuary this morning. UNPROFOR informed him that they had managed to exchange some bodies – the remains of 16 exhumed people from Grbavica and Lukavica. He was in the mortuary. He was looking for his father. He did not find him. He says that the place smelled terribly bad. His cousin, Dr Zijo, was with him. Even though he is a doctor it was not easy. Beki wonders what has happened to himself, what has happened to us all.

"We have got accustomed to death. Accustomed?!

"What happened to uncle Sudo? He was eighty. Diabetes thinned him over the last two years. They took him away on July 17th. There has been no news about him yet..." (October 30th).

One day at the end of November, another page from my diary was torn out. I read it now a bit later:

"I had to check myself. This morning I went to the central city park where the busts of some writers stand. All our dear ones stood still and quiet in the morning mist. Branko Ćopić leans in a rather decadent manner. Meša Selimović 'wounded in his right shoulder' stares with his eyes popping out. Isak Samokovlija is lonely among the last yellow autumn leaves with branches that almost caress him. Mak looks somewhere far into Bosnia. He is worried. Ročko stands on a dark marble base hit by several pieces of shrapnel, while Veso Masleša covers the whole park with his look. His chin is still dirty after last summer's fall into the dust at the base. Andrić is still absent. The black, marble base is still standing. Last autumn, I still see a vivid picture, Ivo stood here too, with a calm diplomat's look into the distance. He did not care about us. We were only idle walkers or hurrying passers-by, lovingly distressed. Then, on an equally misty morning, the shade of bronze was even darker at least from the mist drops, and one yellow ash leaf was hanging from the left side of his chest, like a high statesman's decoration just awarded.

"Andrić is not there today, either. He has not been there for over a week now. Two rusty screws show from the marble and show that some metal statue stood there. Over the name and the years of birth and death there is a trace of shrapnel, of a stray bullet or some other projectile. The marble was damaged, but not too badly. Down at the bottom, there is a trace emphasized by the fog's dampness and unwashed dust. That is a trace left by urination – somebody aimed and looked for a post on which to relieve himself. I do not know whether he lifted his left or right leg while he was leaving his urine autograph.

"Studio 99", probably because it is independent itself, reported on this. They reported on the desecration of the Nobel Prize Winner's monument.

Others are silent.

Does his experience of Sarajevo through the images of the sounds from the places of worship still remain written on the wall of the Young Bosnia Museum devastated back in May:

"Who ever in Sarajevo spends the night in bed awake can

former Prime Minister, N. Sharif, in Sarajevo.

31st – *Shelling – 5 dead and 40 wounded. New Year's concert by the Sarajevo Philharmonic Orchestra. Valery Giscard d'Estaing, former Prime Minister of France, spends New Year's Eve in Sarajevo.*

THE YEAR OF 1994.
JANUARY,

1st – *A shell destroys a duty-free shop at UNPROFOR headquarters. No gas.*

2nd – *Over one thousand shells fired at Mijatovića Kosa, Zabrdje, Sokolje, Boljakov Potok and Buća Potok.*

3rd – *Six killed and over sixty wounded. Heavy shelling of Otoka, the centre and Boljakov Potok.*

4th – *Nine killed and over 40 wounded. Several shells hit the center and Koševo hospital.*

6th – *An infernal day – nine killed and 26 wounded.*

8th – *Five killed and 31 wounded.*

22nd – *A shell kills six children sledging at Alipašino Polje.*

24th – *General Rose arrives, to replace Briquemont.*

The Prime Ministers of Turkey and Pakistan, Ms Tansu Ciller and Ms Benazir Bhutto arrive in town.

FEBRUARY,

4th – *Twelve killed and 25 wounded; at Dobrinja alone*

8 killed and around 20 wounded.

5th – Two mortars fired at the Markale market-place result in a massacre – 68 dead and 197 wounded.

7th – 90 shells fired at the town – three dead and fifteen wounded.

8th – NATO ultimatum demands withdrawal of heavy weapons to twenty kilometers from the centre of Sarajevo.

16th – Antonio Samaranche visits Sarajevo.

21st – NATO ultimatum expires at 1 a.m. Heavy weapons withdrawn or put under UNPROFOR control, according to official statements from the UN.

28th – School year starts.

MARCH,

8th – First tram, from Čengić Vila to Skenderija.

20th – Football match at the Koševo stadium (UNPROFOR – Sarajevo 0:4).

23rd – First citizens cross the Bratstvo-Jedinstvo bridge, going from Grbavica to town and vice versa, under the supervision of the UN.

26th – Sarajevo bakery produces its 50-millionth loaf since the war started.

29th – Olympic flame lit in Sarajevo.

APRIL,

12th – Branko Mikulić, the veteran politician, the president of the Organising Committee of the 14th Winter Olympic Games, once prime minister of the Yugoslav government, dies in Sarajevo…

hear the sounds of the Sarajevo night. Heavily and unmistakably the clock of the Catholic Cathedral strikes: two o'clock. More than a minute elapses (exactly seventy-five seconds, I counted) and only then does the clock of the Orthodox Church strike with a somewhat weaker but piercing sound; it also strikes its two o'clock. A little after this the clock tower near the Bey's Mosque strikes with its hoarse, distant voice, but it strikes a ghostly Turkish eleven o'clock, according to some strange time measurement of distant, foreign parts of the world! The Jews do not have their own clock that would strike the hours, as it is only God that knows what time it is with them, what time it is according to Sephardic, and what according to Ashkenazic time. In this way even in the night, while everything is asleep, the difference is awake that divides the sleeping people who are, when awake, happy and sad, eating and fasting according to four different, mutually quarrelling calendars, and who send all their wishes and prayers to the same heaven in four different church languages. And that difference, sometimes visible and open, sometimes invisible and perfidous, is always similar to hatred, often completely identical to it."

Now the night sounds are different. The places of worship are silent. A part of Andrić's quotation that has been left out is written in my memory. It does not say that it is from the letter of Max Levenfeld in 1920.

Is what some invisible people are doing today, some suspicious people, done with dedication to Ivo Andrić? He is dead. He has not been alive for a long time. This is not his concern. It does not affect his work, either. He was awarded the Nobel Prize. It was awarded to him by the Swedes. It was awarded to him by the world. They cannot take it away from him here in a Sarajevo park. They cannot destroy his works, either.

This barbarity is a disgrace to the city. It is being done to us.

The city is silent. Nobody has reacted to it for days. They have been occupied by other things. What do a marble base, a bust, or somebody's name and surname mean to anyone any more?

Why all this?

Should I again be amazed at the park between the buildings of the Republic's Presidency and the Municipal Assembly? In it, there is the most beautiful Sarajevo mosque and the one I like best. It was mercilessly shot in the back last summer. It was as if the copper of the dome felt all the murderous pain. It rose towards the sky. Outside the arches of the mosque, a shell pulled down the fountain and stopped the cold water for the refreshment of passers–by and the ablution of believers. Over there, in the shade of the tree, in the eastern part of the park, hardly ten metres from the building of the Presidency, somebody vulgarly desecrated both the park and the beautiful Alipasha Mosque. The cemetery has been around it for centuries. Somebody slapped together a toilet from boards in the park that was erected on the mounds of a cemetery. It has recently been removed from there. Only a square hole remained gaping in the ground. The toilet and faeces spoilt the honour of the city. The hard times that have struck us can hardly be an excuse for us.

What is the meaning of the sentence which is lulling us, that "the dignity with which the citizens of Sarajevo bear the present state is amazing?"

I am still in pitch darkness. A lady gallery owner and a dealer in works of arts and antiques ends her newpaper polemics with a lady art critic with the argument: "If nothing else, the mahala (residental quarter) will appreciate me and I am happy." I choke on the gloom. Mahala is not only a city suburb. More often it is a hamlet, a lane. Whose is it? Must I continuously listen to these dull blows? The crutches, it seems, hit the asphalt, the beaten earth, and set off down the stairs. The cripples march along my life circle. Empty trouser legs and crutches round off the Sarajevo year of 1992. I remember the words of a father who meets his son returning from war in the short literary pages of a military doctor from the last century, Laza Lazarević: "The people will gild it all." He proudly saw off a soldier. He met a disabled one. The wooden leg will be gilded by the people, but it will remain wooden.

Once everything is over and the light overwhelms the dark, what will a walk along the streets of Sarajevo be like? Will the same sound accompany me?

The little boy Kemal Karić was four months old on May 30th. At one o'clock p. m. a shell hit the house at number 10 Šipska Street, a kilometre from my flat. His mother Ifeta was killed. Translated, her name means "Innocent, virtuous." Translated, however, his name means "Perfect". The shell deprived him of his mother's love irretrievably and of his right leg below the knee. At the age of nine months he was still waiting for his artificial leg. He cannot begin to walk without it. Without it he will not be able to walk around Sarajevo. A friend of mine from my university days, the actor Nermin Tulić, was prevented by a shell from coming home to his children. After rehearsals, he called in at the neighbourhood cafe "Cyrano de Bergerac" to have a drink with his theatre colleagues before a meagre summer lunch. He did not manage to reach his staircase. A shell caught him. Both legs were torn off. The actor, all restlessness and nerves, who was never still, stopped. He survived. He accepted his wheelchair with a smile: "Now I can be a radio actor." His name, what symbolism, means "Brave".

The little boy Kemal with a big red dummy in his mouth, the actor Nermin and many others have been waiting for months to go somewhere out into the world for further treatment. My twenty-two-year-old neighbour Irmir

MAY

...

JUNE

...

JULY

...

does not recognize me any more when I pass him by. He has seen little since last July when shrapnel hit him in his temple. He lost one eye, and the other needs to be treated at a clinic somewhere in Europe. He has been waiting for transport and a hospital bed for months. Others are also counting months painfully. There are tens, hundreds and thousands of them waiting for medical help and further treatment. treatment.

The medical staff in Sarajevo are convinced that in this war "injuries are horrible and unrecorded in medical literature". In December Sarajevo needed three to four thousand pieces of prothesis for lower limbs. There was no processed beech, leather, nor metal pieces for them. On the newspaper pages, where not so long ago they printed the names of winners in prize competitions, they give lists of horror. They publish the names of children who are now limbless. "I wanted to catch some sweets that the soldiers were throwing to us over the wire," spoke the tearless boy Alen Šukić. He was playing in the suburb of Alipašino polje outside UNPROFOR's headquarters. The war surgeon, Dr Faruk Kulenović, is haunted by another of his sentences: "Where are my legs, they ache..."

Sanda Jakšić and Svetozar Pudarić do not manage to go out for further treatment, either. The two young intellectuals were mown down by a shell in Đure Đakovića Street. They crowned their love with a wedding in their hospital beds. The smiling historian Sanda lost a leg. The doctors are struggling for the leg of the archaeologist Svetozar, an exceptional young intellectual. Their future baby will bear the knowledge of the Sarajevo shells, of the love of a young couple, and of a registrar from the hospital hall.

I hear again that quadruple wooden xylophone: Bump, bump, bump-bump... bump, bump... A badly oiled wheelchair creaks, too. As if the whole city were on the march supported by crutches. Where are they all rushing to? I cannot hear any sounds. There are no sighs. In the Sarajevo hospital complex, a young man, a student of theatre direction, is in charge of the cremation of amputated limbs in a special furnace. I incessantly hear only: bump, bump, bump-bump... Bump. Bump. Bump-bump... Are we starting a one-way trip!

Where is history driving us?

Is there a bottom at all? Does this path have an end?

I cannot say any more if I am cold. I no longer know where I am. In a rare bit of light I look at my papers. I take them out of my pockets. The dates are December ones.

"I hurry to my news stand. Many journalists have given up selling newspapers. They have given their bags up to others. I am still doing it out of spite, out of a wish to persevere with selling newspapers until the war is over. Across the hospital grounds, where I usually take a short cut to the market, some rare morning passers-by walk. They hurry to work, or return home after their night shifts dulled by the cold winter morning.

"On the recessed stairs leading to the new Diagnostic Centre, there are pieces of façade freshly broken off. Up, above one's head, there is a dark shell hole. It is small. The calibre does not seem to be big. Fortunately. That was yesterday's gift to the hospital, patients and doctors. Somewhere here women who have just given birth and newborn babies lie. Whom do they disturb? Where did it come from? How many times have I walked this way? Convinced this was a protected, recessed corner, I felt safe here. Each time I am amazed anew at the shell impact, at this unexpected shot, at the consequences of the explosion.

"A long queue formed near my smashed news stand at the market. They know that the newspapers arrive at about 8.30 a.m. They patiently stand in the cold, dirty market under the flyover. They are not bothered if they are too early. People wait for one or two hours. This is the only news they can rely on. There is no electricity. Car batteries are empty. Transistor batteries ran out long ago. There is a great scramble for the newspapers when we bring them in our van. Last summer we, the two of us, sold here 600, 700, 800 and even the whole 1,000 copies of "Oslobođenje". Today we hardly get 100 copies. There is not enough paper. We have been waiting to get it since September. It does not arrive. There are 70–80 people in the queue. Sometimes there are even a hundred. I never give anyone more than two copies. Now I have given up that practice as well. One reader can buy only one copy. They all already have their small change ready. All hundred copies are sold in ten minutes. Last summer it took six or seven hours. Now many remain without their copy of the newspaper although they patiently wait. They ask me in vain to give them my copy. They sadly shrug their shoulders making up their minds to come earlier tomorrow to queue up for their paper. I leave the market. I open the newspaper as walk. I leaf through it starting from the back page as usual. On the page next to the last one and the one opposite, there are the death notices.

"At the top of the page there is a photograph of a familiar person. Damjan, the son of Afan, Ramić.

"Killed!? Killed at the age of 27 defending the city. Afan's son?!

"Horrible!

"I do not believe it. I read once again: 'Damjan, the son of Afan, Ramić... Killed at the age of 27 defending the city...' The bereaved daughter Bojana. She is less than a year old.

"This is unbelievable. Today everything is incredible. But everything is possible, unfortunately.

"Death. It walks about with a grinning skull killing people. It does not manage even to dismount from its horse before mowing down new victims with its scythe. It waves it while galloping. Sarajevo is being wiped out by its merciless swathes.

"They did not give the time of funeral. They will announce it later. Why? Is it the father's worry about others or was Damjan's body not removed from the battlefield?

"Did it happen at Otes?

"Who knows? Is it now at all important where? Afan's son has been killed. My friend's only son killed! The war wrote down a new number. Next second, or a few seconds later, it raised its score. War analysts will have in their chronicles for December 6th battles, military units, the position on the battlefield, the number of artillery shells, changes on the front lines, the daily temperature, the wounded, the destroyed, the killed... Will the dead be the first or the last in the series? Who will know that?

"Afan was left without his son. Newspapers hide ominous voices. The desolation of the city's life, all our pain and sympathy, the photographs of our fellow citizens who are travellers without return.

"How much warmth there was on Afan's face when he mentioned his granddaughter Bojana! Can all the pain of the news, for many only a piece of newspaper news, be measured? The whole life, love and future is in this evil message from the top of the page next to the last one.

"During the first months Afan wandered about the city like the majority of us. A man who was always short of hours during the day, drowned in the time which suddenly meant nothing. The painter who at the same time lived in Ston, Počitelj, Banja Luka, Subotica, Mostar, Sarajevo, Dubrovnik and Istria. Now he has remained on some hundred metres of closed asphalted track. Now he needs neither a car nor a watch. He has lost his studio with a view of the river and the Omladinsko šetalište (The Walk of the Youth) – a Sarajevo love walk. In a second he was without his paints, his easel, over two hundred paintings, souvenirs and books.

"Expelled, he wandered about the city without knowing where to spend the night. We talked about the long nights of the south, about the white towns being pulled down, we mourned for Zuko Džumhur, a travel writer and philanthropist, the last of the renaissance talents of our regions.

"And then suddenly Afan vanished. He was not there for days. When I was coldest during last August and September's hot days, when I did not know what to do with my frozen soul, he took me to his mother's place. On the fourth floor in a refined middle-class home with a framed wedding portrait of Afan's parents in brown, trimmed by a large passe-partout of an old-time photographer's atelier, everything was different. His paints, paintbrushes, easel, grounded canvasses, frames and singed boards were in among the armchairs, flowers, sofa and night tables. He

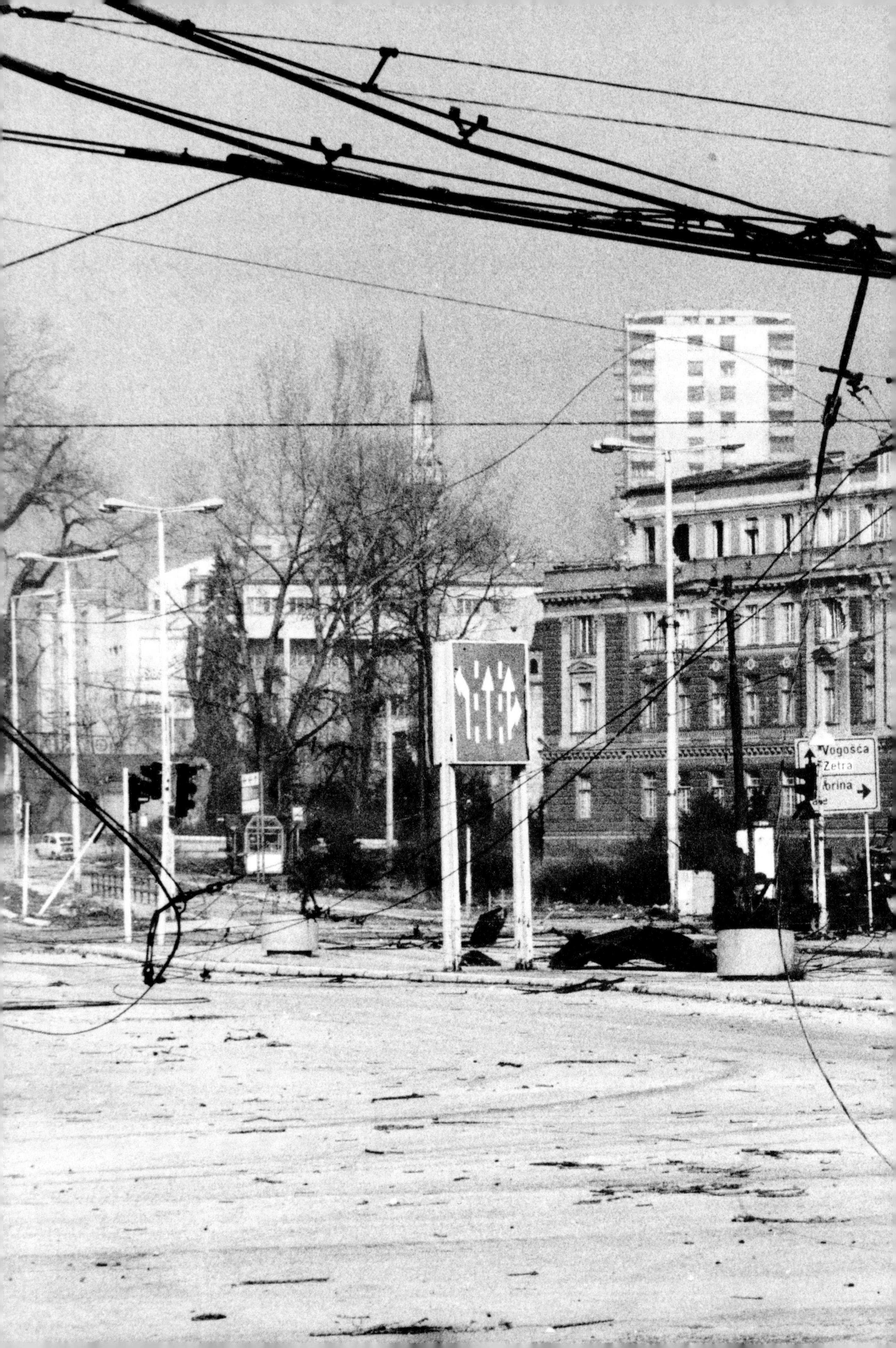
Vogošća
Zetra
orina

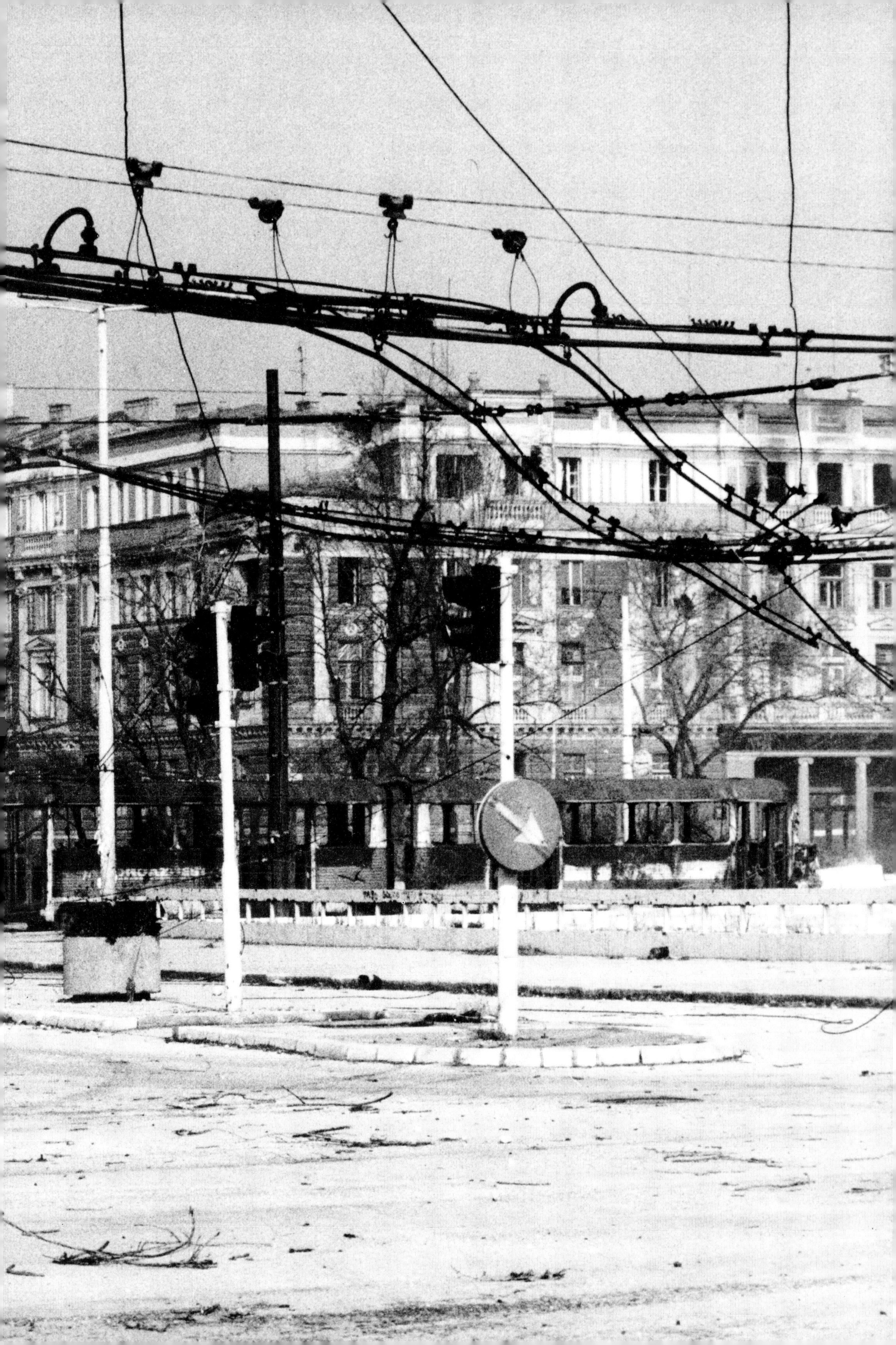

instilled drops of warmth and melancholy into me with his white and grey shades, with the paintings that he was finishing. Afan warmed me and made me bare my soul. Afan's green screen of the Neretva River under the slender stone of Mostar Bridge, with the houses overturned, ash, smoke and heat, struck me. With his colours he revealed the pain of this war. That green screen was such a remote green source of freedom. It was my River Neretva, my Buna, the Trebišnjica, whose waters first bathed me. The artist is entitled to the soul's vivisection. His spirit, imagination and talent talked through his paintbrush strokes, both fine and thick.

"I was grateful to him for that summer afternoon. I wished I had been a stone. In that way I might be built in the whiteness of a town, Ramić's town of course.

"Ominous night sounds repeat themselves. Bursts of fire sing their death sonnets. They are short, long, interrupted... A white winter night lasts a long time. A thin snow blanket rests on grass, roofs and slopes. Nowhere is there light. There, somewhere below the Jewish Cemetery, a house is burning. Somebody's house is vanishing at the stake. The only light in the night are these red flames. I can see them in the distance, in the rectangles of two house windows.

"Ominous night sounds can be heard. Death is singing. We are waiting.

"What for? When?

"How does Afan, somewhere in this city, spend the time until the dawn which never comes?" (December 7th)

"The newspapers say nothing about Afan's son.

"Taša comes with the news that he was buried yesterday.

"We were not at the funeral.

"Afan must have wanted, in his own pain, to spare others. He must have wanted not to multiply death with dangers that call for other deaths.

"Death inexorably makes one ask a question: Why? That 'Why' incessantly resounds. The question hovers. Finding no answer goes arm in arm with it.

"Damjan was killed at Otes. Was he one of some hundred killed, as the rumour goes around the city. A sequel to the rumour is that several hundred citizens were killed. It was, it is said, like Hell. It is not at all important how many deaths there are. It is always one, the only one, individual. It is added to others later.

"This is the death of a son.

"You know, he did not want to admit to me that he was afraid. He told my sister he was afraid, that he went with only a rifle and a few bullets. He confided in her. He did not want to say that to his wife and her parents. He did not tell me, either.

"He was frail, lively, tall and slim.

"I could have had him put somewhere else, not on the

front line. But I did not. I thought he was twenty-six and old enough to make his own decisions. He had his own reasons for going to fight. I had to respect them. A shell might have hit him anywhere in Sarajevo. Even if I had had my son withdrawn from the trenches, his place would have been taken by another young man. Today some other mother could be grieving for her son. Somebody else's brother, father or sisters would be crying with grief.

"I trusted his lucky star. I believed the bullets would spare him.'

"I can see some new wrinkles on his face. He hides them even from his friends. He covers with a smile the hole left for him in the cosmos. His son has died.

"I drink a glass to his soul. This is an ancient custom. I stare at the sooty wall of the room.

"'A hundred things suddenly cease to exist,'" he says.

"An oil stove is on in a cold flat with glassless windows. It smokes. It blackens the white of the doors, too. The blackness penetrates into the lines of Afan's fingers. It mixes with the artist's paints. It builds itself into my friend's tissue. Wounds can, perhaps, heal, but deep scars remain. Mars never rides alone..." (December 17th)

"At twilight I come across Braco Jurišić on the hospital grounds. He says he has been operating on patients until now. He is a neurosurgeon. He is said to be an top expert. A haversack is on his back. He has sports clothes on. He does not look like a gentleman and a doctor. Who in Sarajevo resembles himself any more? He apologizes in front of with our inquisitive looks: 'Water is in the canister. I'm taking it home. I filled it from the tanker that brings water for the operating theatre.'

"A few days ago he told us with a happy smile about his wife. A baby was born to them. It was in Zadar on November 7th. She had a difficult labour. She was in a coma for six hours. They struggled for her life. Now both she and the baby are well. Poisonous gas was found in her blood. She had left Sarajevo in a convoy seven days earlier. They were in a dilemma for a long time as to what to do. Now she feels better.

"'She would not have survived in Sarajevo. There are no conditions here,' he says. He goes off tired after ten hours in the operating theatre. He tightens the belt of the haversack. He waves his hand to us. 'We must live. They found poisonous gas in her blood!? She brought it, then, from Sarajevo. We also breathed it in, without knowing it.'" (December 25th)

"There is a crowd around Pivara (The Brewery). Ice some twenty centimetres thick has formed on the road. This is the only place where there is water. It is poured into tankers, too. It freezes on our fingers, our clothes and the asphalt. Men, women and children push all kinds of carts. They come from all parts of Stari Grad (The Old Town) and

Centar (The Centre) suburbs. They carry jars and canisters, happy to get some fifteen or twenty litres of water. It is for drinking, bathing, cooking und washing. They drag all kinds of improvised carts. It is easier to carry water on them. A few come in their cars loaded with various barrels and plastic containers. They carry water for their neighbours, too. I do not ask even myself where they get the petrol from. I wait, freezing, to fill my plastic containers. I take them up to Breka, to a friend's, three kilometres away. I am happy, like the others, to find water at all. I do not think about the walking or the burden we are carrying any more. I cannot reconcile this with the fact that this city had water supplies at Ilidža as early as in Roman times. Even the floors were heated with spring water. It has had water supplies ever since the mid-sixteenth century. It has had it for over five hundred years. London had its present-day water system built at the beginning of the seventeenth century. Water was brought to Versailles in the second half of the eighteenth century. Here, I am loaded with plastic containers at the end of the twentieth century, happy to get my glass of water.

"At noon Afan's exhibition is opened. One day before the end of the year, Ramić the painter appears in public. He sums up what he has done. The Literature Museum, the old town house of Jeftan Despić, a wealthy merchant, is crowded with visitors who are pushing around the paintings and exhibits. There are many notable personalities: doctors, painters, politicians and professors. And candles. Afan asked his friends to bring candles with them. We have not had electricity for weeks. Nobody knows whether and when we shall have it. We light them exactly at noon. As if we were lighting them as a memorial to Afan's son, as a memorial to all those killed. Afan is in some kind of spasm of grief. The exhibition is a meeting with audiences and critics, a mirror you must look in and bear. This one is dedicated to a son. Less than three weeks have elapsed since Damjan's death. This is at the same time a requiem mass, a memorial and a ceremony. The paintings were painted on singed boards and cardboard stained with war in destroyed city, all in frames punctured by bullets. What else is there in the city?

"Only yesterday there was the twenty-first 'Slovo Gorčina' (The Voice of Gorčin). We were in Stolac, an old Herzegovinan town. It was the warm autumn of 1991. They tried to dissuade us from going there because of the fear of the war that was approaching. I opened Afan's exhibition at the Šarić House, the 'Branko Šotra' Gallery, within a traditional cultural event. That was my last journey to the south. Afan travelled with his paintbrush, his soul and the canvasses of Dubrovnik, Mostar, the rocky ground and the green river. We listened to the roaring from somewhere on the Adriatic coast. We picked up, on the outskirts of Stolac, as souvenirs, empty cartridges of bullets fired by unrely reservists. We felt the hushed misfortune of Dubrovnik and the village of Ravno. We were less than twenty kilometres away from the war.

"It was far from us, too far. We defied it with our presence in Stolac at the empty hotel 'Bregava'. We resisted it with the only things we had: love and art. We drove along empty roads. We encountered frightened looks. We believed we were resisting the war. We spoke a language understood by everybody – the language of love.

"Thirteen months later we are at the site of fire where our illusions were burnt down. Afan, after the distant white towns that he returned to last year, after the crucifixion of Christ and after Dubrovnik, which was attacked in smoke, experienced the destruction of Mostar and the killing of Sarajevo.

"The father and painter, Afan Ramić, dedicates himself and his paintings to his killed son. These are paintings done in war and paintings about war, too. At the end of a brutal year he speaks, through his exhibition, about the inhuman times that have struck us. He builds Damjan and his paternal love into his works. He instills them into us, his contemporaries. He leaves his impression as a fine mark and a message to those who will come..." (December 30th)

Where am I to go? I am tired. There are heaps of rubbish on the pavements around us. The rubbish containers are crowded. There is no place here even for the rubbish. Burning it frequently here in the street, in containers, does not help, either. Rubbish and its stench choke us. It is impossible for us to have it taken anywhere. I am tired, Dante. I am fed up with both you and me. I cannot see Lucifer. The demons are not here, either.

Wasn't Lucifer, too, a rebel angel? You might have interrupted your journey and might not have wanted to go on. You left us with the hope that there were only nine circles of Hell. Dante, how many more circles have I got? Whisper to me, please, how far it is before we reach the bottom. What is down there? How deep can I go and remain a man? Must I, my dear old bard, trudge on further? Shall I be able to?

I passed through 1992. Its nine circles are behind me. I hollowed them out inside myself. I plunged much deeper than I ever thought was possible.

Suddenly, I was not able to pull my feet out of the mud into which I was sinking. After each circle another followed. I was sliding downwards. I was sinking deeper and deeper. Nothing changed at Christmas, which was being announced as a turning point. There were no gifts under the Sarajevo Christmas trees of ours. There were no Christmas trees, either. We had to sacrifice them to the stoves in our cold flats. Only dusty boxes with multicoloured New Year's tinsel ribbons and decorations that became worthless for us remained in the wardrobes. We could not even make a fire

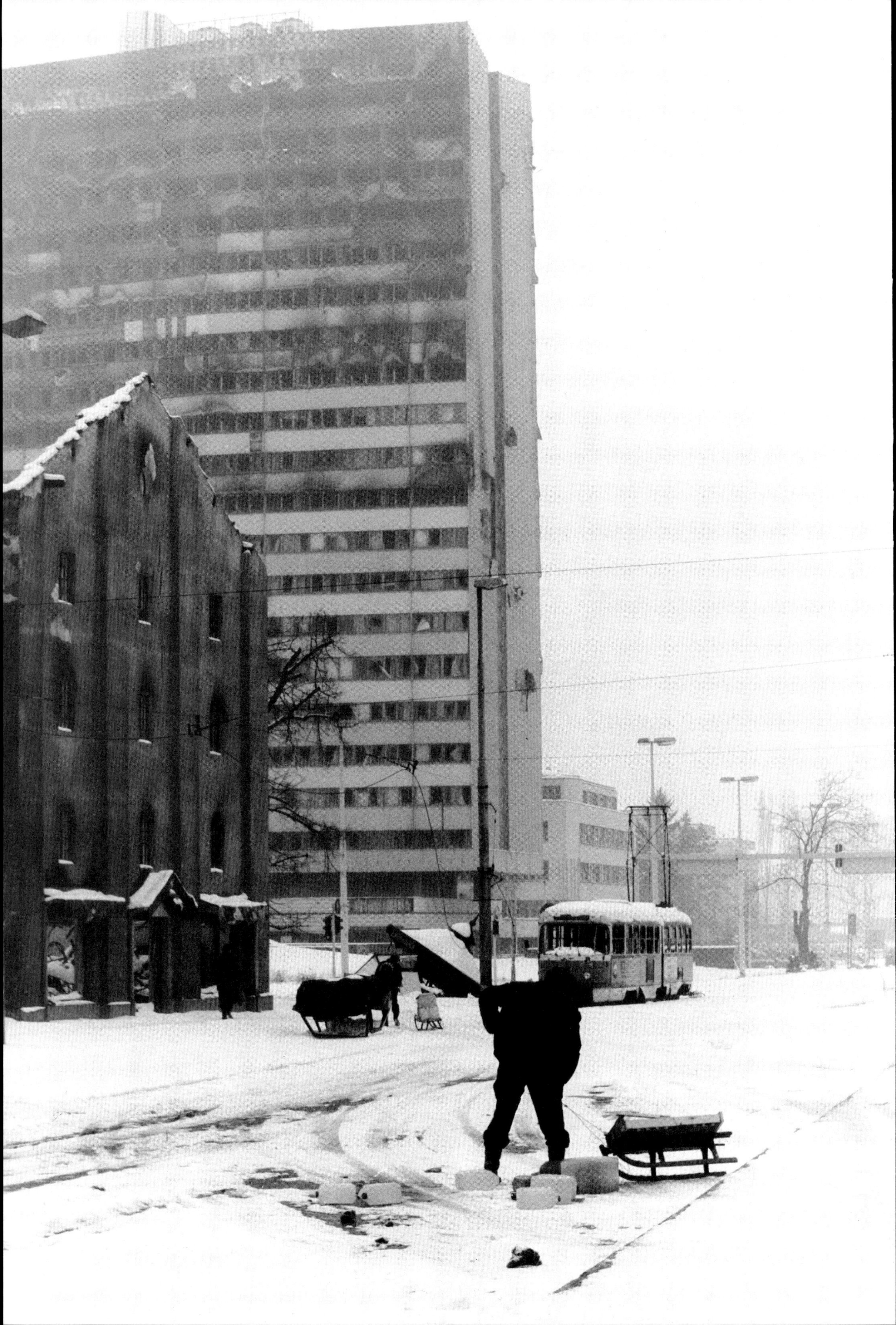

with them, they give off no heat. I cast glances at the wardrobe with clothes more and more often. I calculated how many hours it could heat us. There was no electricity. The firewood they had promised did not enter the city. An increasingly severe winter set in.

I believed we had reached the bottom. But the bottom drew us somehow deeper and deeper. Maro, are you still silent? Do say something. We did not agree that you should take me over to Hades which is endless. Everything is monotonously the same: shells, hunger, ruins, fires, fear, columns of the homeless, detention camps, hatred, dark, hope, cripples, starvation and columns of those who aimlessly go about Europe. Sweating, they press their crumpled plastic bags on distant pavements. Their lives are thrust into them. They hopelessly cast glances towards America, Australia or New Zealand. They leave with mud dried on their shoes and soles gaping with holes more and more hungrily. They do not look back. They murmur between their hunched shoulders the only intelligible words: Non est salus nisi in fuga. (They did not want even to take the keys of their homes with them.)

Aren't the Sephardim of Sarajevo entrusting us with: "Todo pasa por este mundo, guay onda pasa" (Everything passes in this world, alas, but where does it pass)?

Everywhere the same. On every face I meet there is grief. There are marks everywhere. The people in front of me and next to me bear marks. Nor can I be different. It is getting worse from minute to minute. Just when I think that I have already had the worst of it, a new circle opens. And an equally piercing grin from the dark penetrates the bones.

Where could I flee? Shall I ever be able to go back to daylight? I have forgotten its glow. Does light exist at all? Perhaps. It may have been kept in the creases of somebody's memory. I am fed up with all my contemporaries. I do not want, oh, how much I do not want to spend time with them. I have not got too much of it and I have less and less. I have never counted on some other time. I do not hope for anything but everyday routine and what I have to be well deserved. But less and less remains for me. I am fed up with my ancestors. I trip over them so much. There is always somebody to disturb them, pale and yellowed, to wake them up, to move them from the cobweb of the time in which they lived. Remote for me, like a dream, are all those time images. Some such people carry their bones. They have ignored the sacred: May you rest in peace! They dig up their secrets. In some worn-out sieves they sift their dust and search for the gold nuggets known only to them. Out of them they forge their own truths which they do not manage to temper in as much as streams of water. They make everything into politics, the politics of evil and dispute. I am fed up with myself. In my country, in Bosnia, the angels have grown black. I do not remember anyone talking about white

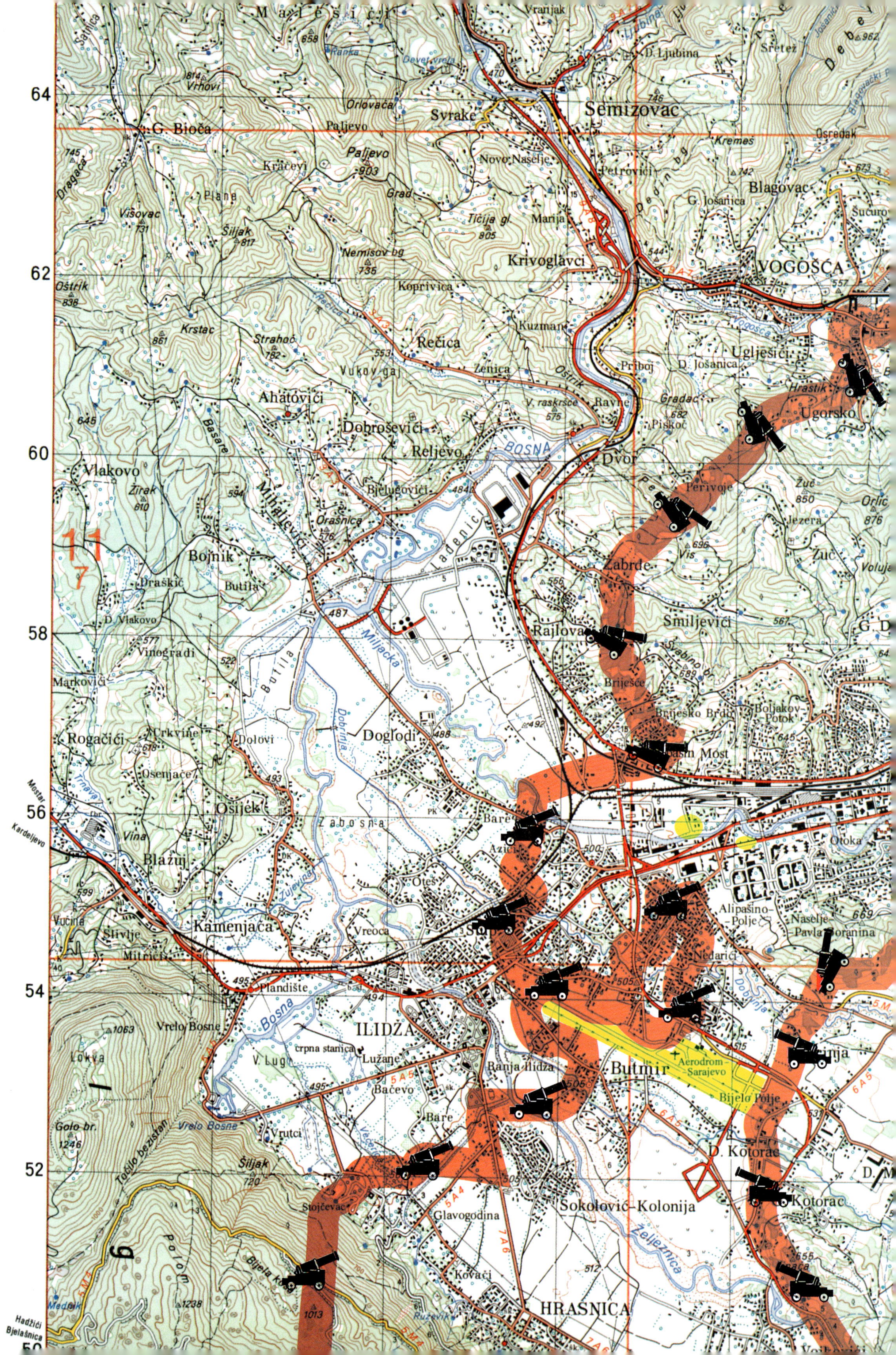
Semizovac
D. Ljubina
Vranjak
Sretež
Svrake
Paljevo
Orlovača
G. Bioča
Vrhovi
Kračevi
Paljevo
903
Grad
Novo Naselje
Petrovići
Kremes
Blagovac
G. Jošanica
Osredak
Šučuro
Dragača
Višovac
731
Plana
Šiljak
817
Tičija gl.
805
Marija
Nemišov bg
735
Krivoglavci
VOGOŠĆA
Oštrik
838
Koprivica
Krstac
861
Strahoč
782
Rečica
Kuzmani
Ugljesići
D. Jošanica
Priboj
Hrastik
Ugorsko
Vukov gaj
Zenica
Ostrik
V. raskršće
575
Ravne
Gradac
682
Piskoč
Ahatovići
Dobroševići
Reljevo
Dvor
BOSNA
Vlakovo
Žirak
610
Basare
Bjelugovići
484
Perivoje
Žuč
850
Orlić
876
Jezera
Oraśnica
594
Mihaljevići
Ladenica
Vis
696
Žuč
Bojnik
Butila
Draškić
Zabrdje
Voluje
D. Vlakovo
487
Miljacka
Rajlovac
Smiljevići
567
G. D.
577
Vinogradi
522
Butila
Markovići
Brijesće
Brijesko Brdo
Boljakov Potok
645
492
Rogačići
Urkvine
Dolovi
Dobrinja
Doglodi
488
Most
Osenjače
Tranava
Mostar
Kardeljevo
493
Osijek
Zabosna
Bare
Otoka
Vina
Azići
500
Blažuj
Otes
Alipašino-Polje
Naselje Pavla Goranina
669
599
Vučine
Kamenjača
Zujevina
Stup
Vreoca
Nedarići
Mitrići
Slivlje
495
Plandište
494
505
Dobrinja
1063
Vrelo Bosne
Bosna
ILIDŽA
crpna stanica
Lužane
V. Lug
Lokva
Banja Ilidža
Butmir
Aerodrom Sarajevo
Bijelo Polje
Bačevo
495
505
Golo br.
1246
Vrelo Bosne
Vrutci
Bare
D. Kotorac
Tešilo bezistan
Šiljak
720
Stojčevac
Glavogodina
Sokolović-Kolonija
Kotorac
Željeznica
Polom
Bijela
1013
Kovači
512
1238
HRASNICA
Medak
Hadžići
Bjelašnica
Ruženik
64
62
60
58
56
54
52
50

Tihovići
Bjelosava
Palež
Močioci
D. Močioci
Rašljevo
Crepoljsko
Gradina
Gvozdarevo
Brestovac
Hadžina k.
Saračevac
Borovac
Strmac
Strmnica
Gladno br.
Brdo
Pjeskovita ravan
Gradac
Drijetina
Pretržanj
Pećine
M. Gradac
Greda
Vukotine
Vratolom
Banderaj
Rudine
Poljine
Kokorevac
G. Hotonj
Izlaze
Mrkovići
Karaula
Radava
Goropec
Bioško
Šiljato br.
Brijeg
Slatina
Barice
Odžak
Crnelj
Kobilja Gl.
Kromolj
Betanija
Faletići
Hladivode
Vrelo Mošćanice
Drumovi
Šip
Sedrenik
Barutana
Grdonj
Emerovića
Bare
Hum
Humsko Brdo
Velešići
Vasin Han
SARAJEVO
Azapovići
Bakije
Pofalići
Hrastova glav.
Ophoda
Klašnja Voda
Odided
Gradište
Kovačevac
Hrid
Lipe
Bistrik
Jarčedoli
Debelo br.
Berkuša
Kozmatica
Miljacka
Sejnovača
Vraca
Grad
Bistrik kula
Ht. Vidikovac
Merdžanov klanac
Santrači
Barjak
Miljevići
Palež
Krnjeginjac
Brus
Lukavica
Turbe
Prljevo br.
Percin
Studenkovići
Gromila
odmaralište
Dobra voda
Ivanići
Petruše
Kadino br.
Energoinvest
Stanojevići
Udež
Uzdojnice
Kozarevići
Blizanci
Meduše
Siljevo br.
Kumansko br.
Rudine
Čelina
Kuburin čanak
Tilava
Sajvoda
Bogdanovići
Bojišta
Bradin Do
Kumane
Petrovići
Krž
Gradina
Bare
Sustići
Kasindolska
Sarajevo
Vučja Luka
Hreša
Sokolac
Jahorina
64
62
60
58
56
54
52

Bosnian angels. Even the icons with their white angels have not been preserved. Frescoes have been scratched off or covered with new layers of mortar, pulled down along with the church vaults.

Only the cemeteries survived. We are proud of stechaks. Nothing else from mediaeval Bosnia has remained. Messages were worn away from these stone blocks by thunder, lightning, rains and winds. Only rare symbols, somehow protected, have been preserved in the stone. The sun, a few swords and a bow and arrow, plant wreaths and a cart silently hover over the remains of our ancestors from the times when the Roman popes strictly, most strictly, forbade dancing at Europe's cemeteries, dancing the kolo over the buried dead. There are also some outstretched hands. As if the spread fingers wanted to touch my face. They welcome me into a world that has disappeared. Or, those hands of my ancestors might be pushing me away from themselves. On those massive stones, I have not discovered stories about caves, rebellious saints, towns or daily bread. Only the scarce sentence "A se vidamo" (And everything is known). Along with the names of the passed away voivodes Miotaš and his son Stipko, on a huge stone coffin, taller than me, there in the hall of the National Museum, a sentence was written in the Bosnian script, the writing known only here and forgotten long ago: "I was long on earth, but nobody died by my hand. I did not want to kill anyone."

Our books by others were taken away, burned and destroyed. It was more difficult with stone engravings. How many nights have I sat up over the notes in the margins of old books and memorized reliefs from bygone centuries? I have been pricking myself with the screams of unanswered questions about the apocalypse. Why have these tombstones remained as my only lesson? My pain and diary message has been: "I did not want to kill him. I did not want to kill him. I did not want to kill him..."

Did everything else have to vanish under the strokes of sabres, fires and horse hooves? Why then that ancient: "And everything is known"? Why must I go back to these unstudied history lessons? We are made to live them. How many times has this ground, with generations which faded away in bygone centuries and those which have not yet been conceived, been anathemized? Where is the secret of our evil fate, our Balkan destiny that we are dragging with us? Might all this be only my part of a bitter morsel which my grandfathers did not digest and perhaps did not even bite into? They, too might have silently brooded over the same questions. The answers may not be in these gorges or the dampness of the scarcer and scarcer Bosnian forests and dried up beds of the green and cold Herzegovinan rivers.

A prayer of the remote twenties drags after me. It was uttered by a thirty-year-old man with round, metal glasses on his nose, in a winding lane of Baščaršija, where small shops and storerooms end, near the town prison: "Lord, Thou who governst the world and know, look, I pray Thee, at this hilly land of Bosnia and at us who from this ground sprang up and who eat its bread. Bestow on us what we pray for day and night, everybody in his own way: bring peace into our hearts and harmony into our towns. Let not foreigners inflict evil on us any more. We have had enough bloodshed and war fire. We long for bread in peace.

"Look at us, Lord, and grant us our prayers, not for the sake of us, who are evil and discordant, but for the sake of..." I do not manage to hear the end. I witness the past and present. I recognize the lamentation of Ivo Andrić, who cannot be seen. He is constantly with us; he disappears but comes back again. I pass by him, but unexpectedly come across him again. I listen to his sentences, and then everything disappears in the dark and strokes of a sledgehammer, a mallet or an axe cutting into a stump. I am not sure, but this could be some kind of our Balkan guillotine. Well, why should Doctor Guillotine have had the honour of introducing his device of execution in democratic France exactly two centuries ago? Must we be the only ones to celebrate that jubilee in such a bloody Bosnian way even though he took over his machine for beheading people from Italy and not from my country?

From the dark a lean man suddenly appears near me with a beret pulled down over his forehead. He paces with his hands crossed behind him like a solitary figure from the graphics by Emir Dragulj, murmuring while passing: "The Lord punished them, He bestowed power on them." I remember him from some steep cobblestoned streets of Bjelave. It was from this poor Sarajevo suburb that the Jews were taken away half a century ago. They were, perhaps, equally peaceful when they were expelled into the unknown. Today we are nailed to our asphalt and city. The world is amazed at the pictures from Sarajevo during those few minutes of television news, and then comfortably sinks into their cosy leather armchairs and woollen slippers waiting for coverage of a tennis match or their favourite serial. My man from Bjelave disappears round the corner. An unuttered sentence remains in my mind: "The Lord punished them, He bestowed power on them."

Where am I to go?

Can anything rescue me? Should I try to obtain indulgence? How? Will I have to pay for absolution for sins committed, for letters preserved, or for all those wrinkles that age has put around her eyes? Even that would not suffice for my salvation. Shall I have to, for absolution from punishment for wrongdoing, give money, preserved letters of all those age wrinkles around her eyes?

They will not suffice to save myself alone. For me it would be even more difficult to be alone. One never accepts

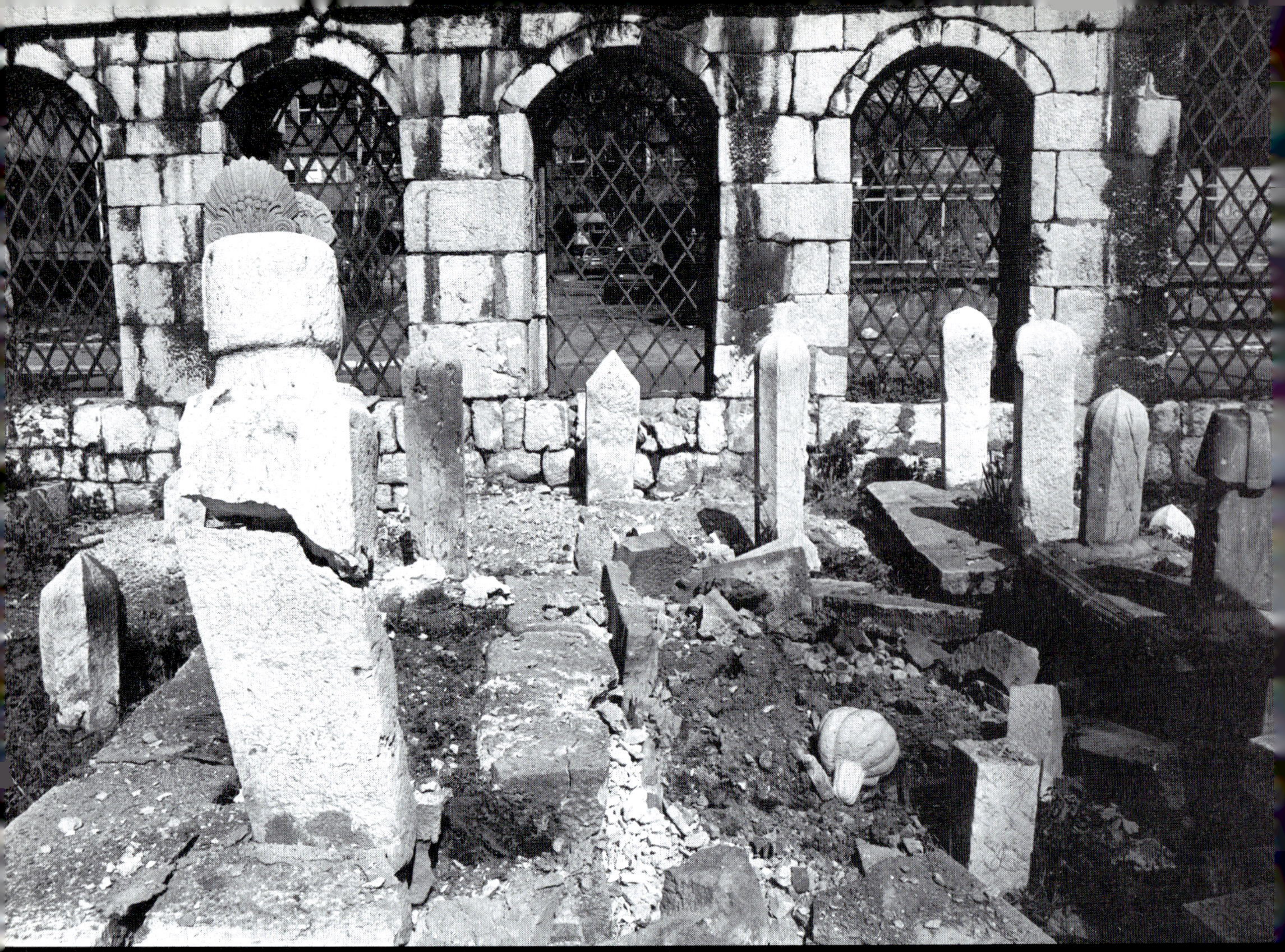

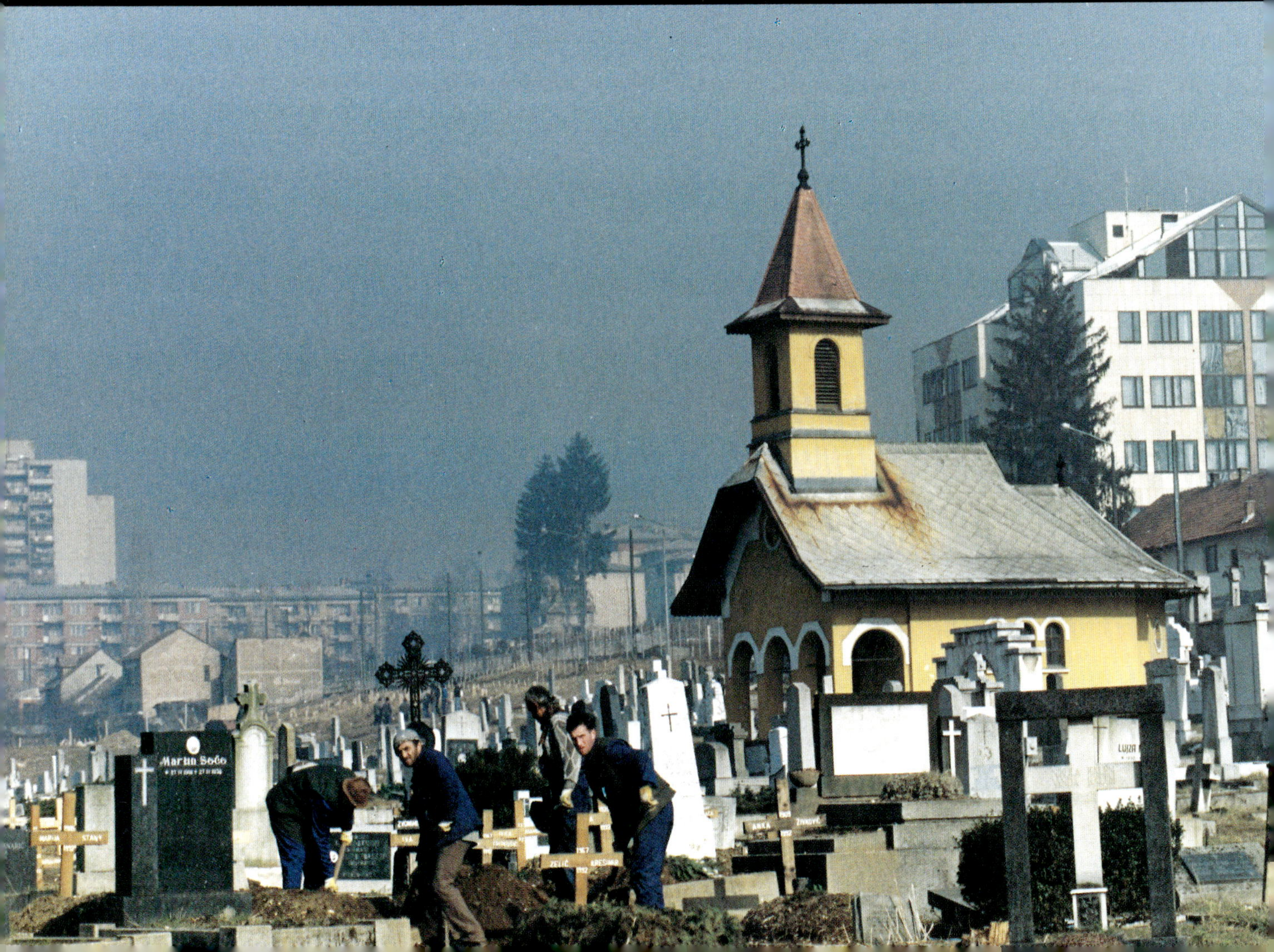

evil or misfortune. One pushes them aside. One flees them. One does not want to accept them. They are never ours. One is convinced, even when one partly accepts them unawares, that they are short-lived, transient, somebody else's evil.

And then that everlasting tormenting of the soul. Good and evil wrestle in the arena. I am somewhere there, in the audience, then on the mat, under the backs of the wrestlers who press me down. My Lucifer and my Dante sit under a fig tree whose fruits have not been picked. They block my view of the big black eyes. They disappear. I feel dizzy. Why now the sleepy Isidora Sekulić: "Bosnia is our Spain. A great friction with inversion terribly alien; friction with inversions between the most opposed faiths; climatic and ground horrors; poverty in everything that can be poor. Monasteries, mosques, cafes and coffee, drinks, conversations, sad songs, and lack of bread and money, 'the Bosnian penury', and then some metaphysical misfortune hovering between this and some other worlds."

Indulgence does not help me. I am already ankle-deep in mud. I cannot manage to get out of it. Some April graffiti flashes in my eyes. Near the hairdresser's "Šanel" in Kranjčevića Street, it was sprayed on the wall: "Whatever this results in, I know we shall never forget it." I wish she were expressing her love for me on the walls. I wish, but much is beyond my scope. I have been through the nine circles of Sarajevo. I have got stuck in circle ten. The following year is here – 1993. How many more years am I to slide towards the bottom?

I am equally tormented by all those dark paths I have walked. I stayed too long in each circle, but so much more has remained for me as a nightmare I have been pushing from myself, but it comes back. And then those letters that arrived at the end of September or beginning of October and that I have been carrying in my pocket all the time. They are already worn out at the edges. They arrived almost simultaneously. They arrived at a time when we had forgotten that letters existed at all. They were written by Tvrtko Forstinger, my university colleague. We did not see each other for years although we lived in the same city, walked along the same streets, sat in the same cafés, were friends with the same people, loved similar things and were angry at the same stupidities. And then, in the whole calvary of Sarajevo, we met several times. Those were chance meetings in the street. We exchanged thoughts and sentences in a hurry and we felt we had not changed, that we had remained as we had been a quarter of a century ago (has so long already passed?) in the university hall or on our graduation trip around Spain.

On an American envelope were my name and surname, and the firm I was employed by: "Oslobođenje". He left a stampless letter at the porter's lodge of the Sarajevo TV building with a request to hand it over to the colleagues from the newspaper so that it might reach me, too. He wrote from Alipašino Polje to me living at the other end of the city, as I had not had a telephone since May 2nd. The town transport system does not work. It is not easy to go on foot because shells and snipers' bullets comb the crossroads of Sarajevo. People do not leave their homes unless in some great need. But the letter reached me:

"It is after 2.00 a.m. on August 22nd in the Sarajevo summer of 1992.

"I came back from Stup for the first time. My friend is alive and well. I brought with me a car battery to get some light for my children and myself, some vegetables and fruit which I had been given as a gift. I convinced myself of what I had known already. There is no electricity. I went to bed reading Pavličić by candlelight and, believing I was tired, I fell asleep.

"But, no.

"I again remembered the letter of 1920. I had to get up again and, for the second or third time during this war, read the great Andrić.

"Max Levenfeld, Bosnia and the hatred...

"Now I can hear distant explosions from Nedžarići.

"And I made a decision.

"I do not regret a bit that my daughters Una (12), Iva (8) and my wife Rasema have stayed here and that we have been through all this together. I am not one who always has a fridge full of food, a reserve of tins and money. We have survived without them and when we had things, others had them, too.

"Positive energy kept us on.

"But, everything has its limits. My family and myself do not want to live with hatred, either now or in the future.

"I consoled my friend at the beginning of the war: keep up your physical fitness and intellectual powers.

"We are leaving.

"I still have to transport the right foot and the base of Gavrilo Princip.

"Miroslav, we would like to see you at our home. Come!"

I was touched by this letter. My friend is tormented by the same problem. He is tormented by hunger, dying, Andrić and Princip. We had met in the city centre back in June. He showed me pieces of the shattered marble plate from the bridge near the Emperor's Mosque, the place where the law student Bogdan Žerajić attempted to assassinate a top Austro-Hungarian employee, the administrator of the annexed Bosnia and Herzegovina of that time, General Marijan Varešanin. It was in 1910, a time when Europe knew only assassinations, including ones that failed, too. That same young man, in that distant June, did not want to shoot at the emperor and king Franz Joseph I of Austria-

Hungary. He gave it up when he saw, at close range, a wrinkled old man in the powerful emperor and king. With the assassination at the bridge he wanted to draw Europe's attention to his country and people, but he hit his target only when he fired the last bullet into his own temple. In a big recycled paper bag full of macaroni, Tvrtko carried pieces of Žerajić's commemorative plate which he had picked up. Now, however, he is writing about Gavrilo Princip, and about his own departure, too.

I did not manage to visit his family home, but two days later another letter arrived. It was dated September 16th:

"My dear Miroslav,

"There is neither you nor news from you. But we live on. If it were not so, we would know about it anyway.

"Miroslav,

"Really, one of the most difficult days for me was August 25th – the town hall was burning.

"On the morning of the 27th, I went to the site of the fire.

"The town hall was burning down. People were still putting the fire out, but fire and smoke were still there. I went inside. The staircase collapsed. The firemen made me go out. Only the outer walls remained.

"The town hall does not exist any more.

"As a souvenir, I picked at random half-burned books: 'Camp inmate 360', 'The Little Great Soldiers (from PLW)', 'Count Sava Vladisavljević' by J. Dučić, along with some bricks and mortar. Enough for me and my daughters.

. . .

"I have been horribly tormented by something for months. Long ago, I was passing by the museum of 'Young Bosnia'. The whole place was smashed. Pieces of the commemorative plaque were scattered over the pavement. Even Gavrilo Princip's footprints were not there. Next time I took a better look, and there it was, the 'foot', although only the right one, but turned face downwards. The rest was crushed and thrown away. I turned it over to see it and decided: I have to keep it. They will perhaps remember that they did not destroy everything.

"The first time I could not take it away since there were many people around, and I did not have any cart, only a bag.

"The second time – the cart broke. But I moved 'Gavrilo' a few hundred metres further.

"And finally, on the Sunday of September 9th I did it. I brought home on a cart my 'Gavrilo' weighing 8 kilograms.

"Well, he is here. One day, he will be back at the place where he used to be. You should know this!

"I wrote in my diary: 'Oh, my Gavrilo, what you experienced. And us?'

"To tell you one more thing. While I was dragging my 'Gavrilo' through the city, I met my principal in Veliki

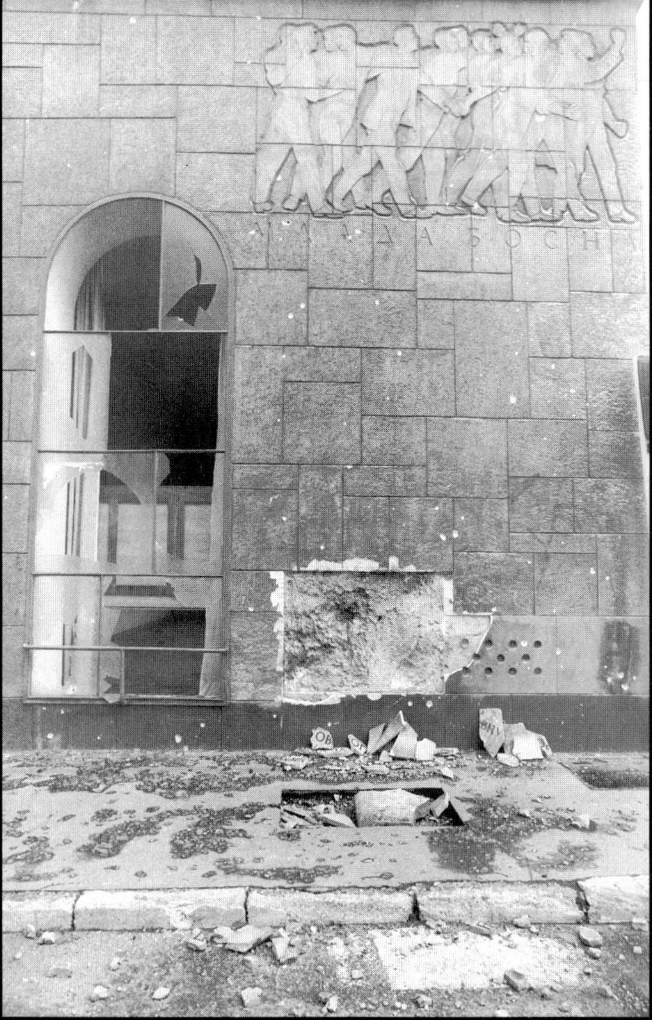

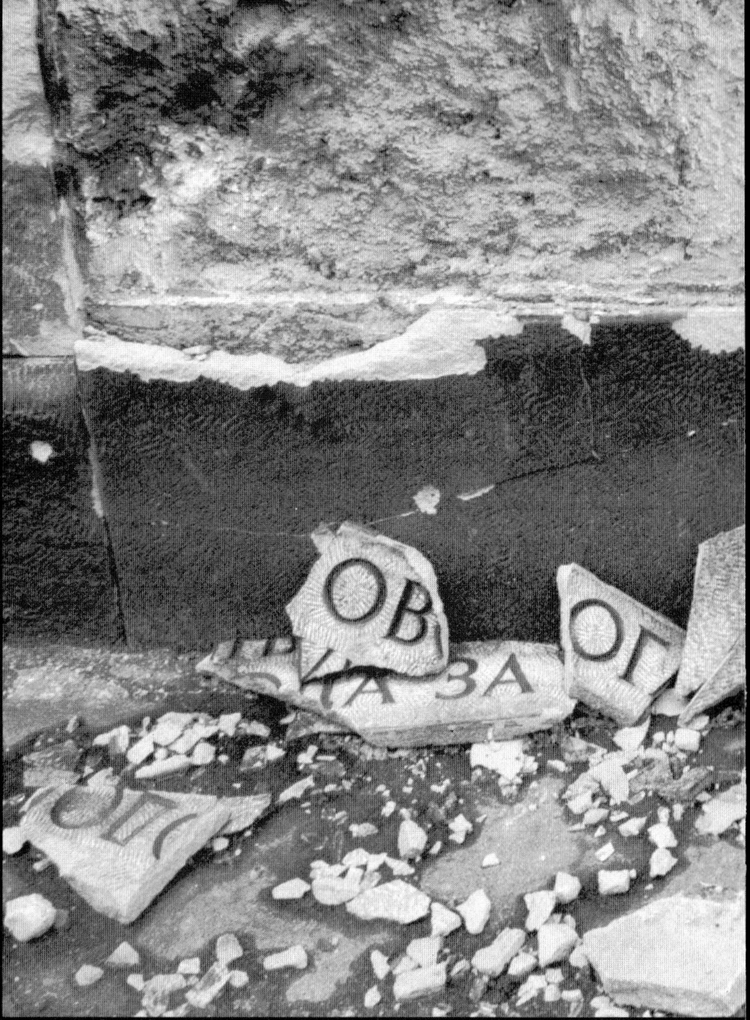
ОВ
ЗА
ОГ

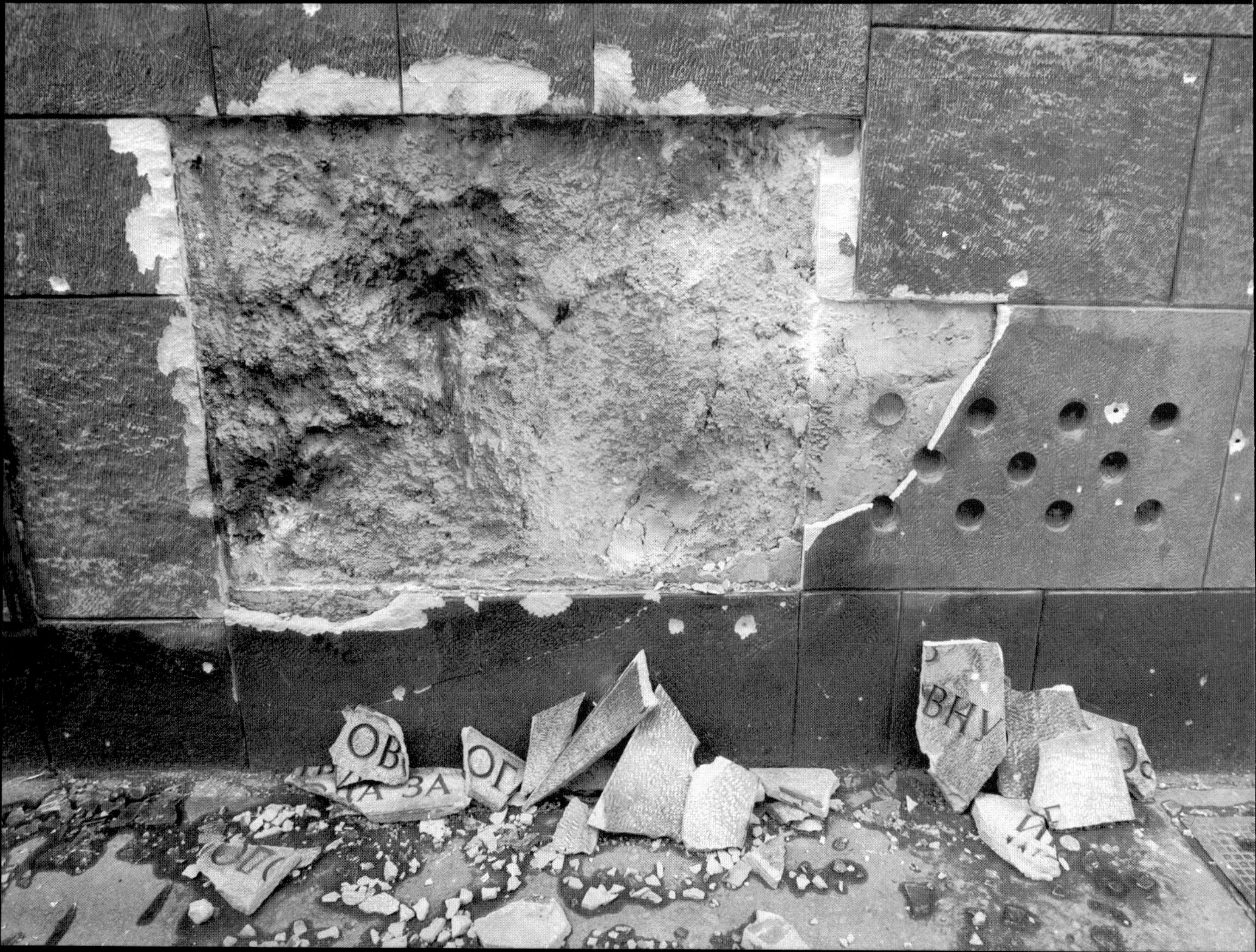
ОВ
ЗА
ОГ
ВНУ

Ćurčiluk Street; he was mending his office. It was destroyed immediately after a shell had hit the Bey's Mosque.

"– What is it you are dragging, Tvrtko?

"– Hush, hush, Gavrilo's right 'foot'.

"– Is it possible!?

"He took off the paper covering the stone. Tears filled his eyes. He was speechless.

"My father – Rainworm, and he – Billy Goat, were scouts together in Sarajevo before World War II.

"He is staying here, and I am getting ready for a trip.

"Miroslav,

"There is one more thing I want to do in Sarajevo. It may be the last one, too. That is why, herewith enclosed, I send you letter addressed to the politicans in power. I regret that I did not do it myself, for the sake of the poor people who got killed in Vase Miskina Street, but for the sake of all of us who are still alive, too.

"I know that the sculpture is valuable. It radiates goodness and optimism and good vibrations, too, for those who feel them. I am not concerned with others.

"So, I ask you to take it and keep it in case it is not removed and if I am not here. The design is a souvenir, and there will be time for the sculpture, if not here, perhaps then in some other place.

"Tomorrow I am going to look for some food. Apart from flour and rice, I have got nothing. I suppose that tomorrow's bag will be enough till our departure.

"However, I will not remember all this as bad, but as a precious experience for all my life. This also goes for my daughters Una and Iva and my wife Rasema.

"A great and undeserved misfortune. We did nothing to deserve it, and we suffer so much. We are neither alive nor dead, we are out of time, less and less sensitive to other people's, and even our own, misfortunes.

"I do not want myself to lose a chance to laugh, especially not my children.

"Miroslav, I would like to see you...

"Oh, my Gavrilo, you died for nothing there in Teresien!"

At the bottom of the letter, by his signature, he drew an irregular asphalt square with a foot impressed in it. It was that foot from the pavement near the museum of "Young Bosnia and Gavrilo Princip", and it marked the spot where the young assassin was standing when he shot the heir to the throne, Archduke Franz Ferdinand.

He killed a woman, a mother. Ferdinand's wife, and thus committed a double murder.

How deep are the furrows ploughed by assassins in the fields of history? Can a hut under the sun, not to mention a house, be built with blood and death? How much chauvinism is there in every national feeling, and how much more in the shots fired throughout Europe? How much hatred, misery, and passion gone mad is there in everything being plotted in the Balkans? And the eternal query: who was behind the assassin, the assassination, the murder? The thesis and the hypothesis, being plotted throughout Europe. There could have been more than a few interested parties. When kings fall, gallows rise. The blood does not stop with drops. An entire river flows. It is hard to stem the flow. Impossible. According to the laws of nature, torrents have to rush through, to wash out the rubbish from the banks, to rip out the century-old trees, to flatten whatever stands in their way. History does not lack torrents. These bloody rivers separate the banks, and move them ever further from each other. They make them steeper. The bridges which rise above the rivers mudded by blood, the rivers carrying human corpses, the rivers swollen with blood, are fragile.

Who knows which are and whose are the truths dragged around by pale, Bosnian travellers, escapees, dreamers, the unfortunate, the enslaved, the humiliated, the humble and the proud.

Oh Bosnia, with your wounds crusted over but never healed, your bags empty, tears unwiped, doors and windows broken, beams burnt, gallows high, axes, rapes, exodus...

Can murders speed up the hour-glass of history? What is loftier – to kill or to consent to remain a victim? Why do we have to prove to others that not all of us are assassins, that we are not gripping a gun-handle in our pocket, but merely crumpling a wet handkerchief which we have just taken away from our faces?

Why is it, anyway, that Tvrtko, the Austrian and the Sarajevan, writes letters to me in particular? Doesn't he bear the name of the best-known and the most powerful Bosnian king, crowned by the Pope, the King of Bosnia, Serbia and Dalmatia? What does he need those 48 kilos of broken asphalt for? After all, his assasin did not stand on asphalt! The assassins pace through their own dreams, and wear black rings under their fatigued eyes, in the dungeons in which they perish.

We happened to neet in the main street a few days later. We were in a hurry. Shell explosions cut our sentences short. He was carrying some ten books he had just bought at ridiculously low prices. I did not manage even to apologize for not coming or to explain to him that I had received his letters with considerable delay. He talked to me about the sculpture he had made, about Gavrilo Princip's foot which he had preserved, and about his uncontrollable need to leave. He was hurrying to Austria to his cousin who had offered to accommodate him, to provide for him. We did not manage to say goodbye to each other.

I still have the two letters of his. I think of him and his little girls, our university days and the city which is poorer for a dear lean, tall, bearded man with glasses. I go back to the public address of a city's politician: "May he be damned who forgets all these sufferings and the blood of the fighters for the freedom of their city, of innocent civilians, women and children." Not a single victim, a shed tear or a destroyed house should be forgotten. Must we be made by a curse to remember it? Is there in all this some indicated and inevitable revenge, some war cry for mutual extermination, for collective emotions? Dante, I know those verses of yours, you do not have to remind me of them: "Charges from the masses/will always accompany the party harmed/as usual, but revenge/must be truth-founded." Is Max Levenfeld not to return? How can we flee the folk verse about ourselves? "Krajina is a bloody dress/It lunches with blood and has dinner with blood/Everybody chews bloody bites/Never is there a peaceful day or rest."

Where could I place Count Josef Freiherr von Schwegel, the delegate to the Berlin Congress, where the fate of the Balkans was determined: "To me it looks like the cock's first crowing at the dawn of a new day full of bloodshed, which will cause deep sorrow to mankind. Culture and morality will disappear and give up their place to power and greed. We may not be witnesses to it, but it will come sooner or later."

The historical continuity of the city is being cut. The bridges over the Miljacka, that backbone of the city, have ceased to be passable. The banks were separated. They moved away from each other. Suddenly, too distant is the beautiful Kozja ćuprija (Goat's Bridge), across which people had entered and left the city for centuries. Thus the eastern gate to the city was locked. Thus, they stole the east from us. The town hall, near Šeher-ćehaja Bridge, was irretrievably destroyed by shells and fire along with hundreds of thousands of books. The National Library of Bosnia and Herzegovina is not there any more, the greatest accummulation of books in this miserable country where towns and people have been burned. The wounded Žerajić Bridge again became imperial, and Princip Bridge has lost its name because the neighbouring museum of "Young Bosnia" and the unfortunate Gavrilo has also been destroyed. In the vicinity of these bridges, Tabački mesđid, the Imperial Mosque, the shops of Baščaršija – the core of the old part of the city has also suffered damage. Ćumurija or Zrinski Bridge is seriously damaged. Around it, destructive shell flowers were planted. Drvenija, the bridge of grammar students in love, is under treacherous sniper fire. No different is Tomo Masarik

Bridge, better known as Čobanija Bridge. By it, ghostly still stand the blackened walls of the main post office that burned to the ground. And so on. The two bridges at Skenderija are targets of gunners from the Jewish Cemetery. Only the brave and fools cross them in mist or in the evening. Around them badly wounded are the Home of Youth and the old electrical power plant where Energoinvest's "Iris" branch was located. The buildings of the Municipal Assembly and the Presidency of the Republic of Bosnia and Herzegovina were hit by shells. People do not cross Vrbanja Bridge, either, the bridge where the girl student Suada Dilberović was killed. Hundreds of shells have destroyed the magnificent structures of the Republican Assembly and Government, burned the "Unioninvest" office building, the old Tobacco Factory and modern skyscrapers of the economic giant "UNIS". Shells left their devastating imprints on the new multi-storey Military Hospital (today called the State Hospital), the Holiday Inn hotel, and the National Museum complex. The Institute for Oriental Studies also vanished at the stake of devastation. The railway station, and the majority of the boxlike buildings of the "Marshal Tito" barracks... The front line is on Bratstvo-jedinstvo Bridge, too. By it, the new building of Vodoprivreda BiH (Water Management of B-H) has also burned. Equally dangerous to cross is the bridge near "Elektroprivreda BiH" (Electrical Power Industry of B-H). Blackened with soot of the destroying fires are also the "Bristol" hotel, the skyscrapers on the Miljacka's banks and the "Shopping" skyscrapers, then the buildings of Social and Old Age Insurance, of the Electrical Power Industry of B-H, the residential skyscraper called "the matchbox" and a number of multistorey buildings in the Hrasno suburb.

The apocalyptic riders compete on the banks of the Miljacka while over our houses, streets, citizens and rooms the metal excrement from the iron war machines, which have put their deadly arms round the city, has been deposited.

The bridges in Ilidža over the Željeznica and the Bosna rivers are out of our reach. I do not know what the mediaeval stone bridge near Plandište looks like without walkers and picnickers. So they have stolen the west from us, as well. My south ends under Zlatište while the north ends at Kromolj.

We are confined to the centre of the city. We are imprisoned. We do not know what is going on at Grbavica, Ilidža, Vogošća, Vraca, Lukavica, Trebević, Osjek or Reljevo. And once they all were within the city. From there only the expelled and beaten up, humidiated and robbed arrive. And they witness the misfortune that has befallen us. We do not know anything about the cemeteries in those other areas now so distant.

The iron street "hedgehogs" (tanktraps) and barricades were only, as we now know it, children's games. War is something different. We resisted it for a long time. We were deceived. We pushed it from ourselves. We did not take it as a war, but it mercilessly drew us into itself. Its evil boot did not sow only death, devastation and destruction. A chasm opened between neighbours. The war planted doubts into our souls. It produced dilemmas in the heads of desperate people as to the aimlessness of life, wiping out centuries of living together in the same suburbs, newly-built settlements, cobble-stoned lanes, houses, flats with different but the same people. Who ever asked the dweller of the Miljacka valley if he was a follower of Orthodoxy, Islam, Catholicism or the Torah scrolls with the reading of the Haggadah, whether he was Muslim, Serb, Croat or Jew? Here lived only the inhabitants of Sarajevo. They were simply Sarajevans. They withstood many temptations, but they were and have remained citizens of the city they love, where they were born or which they chose.

Then one of the apocalyptic riders came and polluted the air, water and souls, maimed the city, blocked its bridges, cut off some of its parts and sentenced it to death.

Life became purposeless.

The youngsters do not go courting any more around their "aunt with her outstretched arms".

Larger and larger was the number of those who grew discouraged, who wanted to flee Sarajevo, the life they lived, themselves. The cemeteries were growing larger. They spread to the edge of the football stadium and its stands, too. Any moment it could be recorded in the city chronicle, with the name, surname and the year of birth, just another Sarajevo clay pigeon. There remained only the question: Who is next? There were many of us. And there still are. There were more and more shekhids on the city's slopes, and the shekhid in Islam means "witness", someone who manifests his belief, but it also means one who is killed defending his faith, homeland, family, property and honour. A shekhid is a martyr, one who will have many privileges in heaven. There were more and more of them in Sarajevo, regardless of whether they were called Ahmed, Jusuf, Rabija, Hasan, Nikola, Josip, Milovan, Zvonko, Salomon or Šefket. The forgotten and dilapidated sculpture of the wounded lion by Josef Urbany from 1917 at the Military Cemetery at Koševo was revived on its seventy-fifth anniversary. The green grass around it, which in the meantime had levelled the tombs of World War I and World War II soldiers, gave in to more and more new graves in the yellow clay. And the poet Silvije Strahimir Kranjčević, who rests in peace in the Koševo valley, at the foot of a crouching angel, does not know that new residents are arriving at the graves next to his, denying his verse: "The old cemetery is silently still, like an old woman in the lower corner."

What is in store for me, for this city, for all my beloved

ones, my acquaintances and friends? It is true that in this city today there are no "dressed up, good-looking women, expensive perfumes, good drinks and foreign cigarettes". Here, the theatre actress Jasna Diklić, who was born and grew up in Tršćanska Street at Marijin Dvor, has had, like others, no water, no electricity and no heating for months. And when she leaves her flat to go to the "Holiday Inn" hotel a hundred metres away, where foreign journalists and war reporters from the battlefields of Sarajevo and the country of Bosnia and Herzegovina stay, in the interval of the concert of her friend from the opera, she slips into the staff bathroom to take a quick shower and happily rub herself dry with paper napkins.

We need so little here to be happy. What should I write to that young woman with a four-year-old boy who wrote from Vienna? She sent a letter which reached me in December:

"Good Lord, I've started thinking how much the life of a human being costs now winter comes.

"Will you, please, write to me and tell me how much money is necessary for four people somehow to survive for one month, at least to get some idea.

"I miss you terribly. I can't put it into words. I more and more lose any hope of coming back home soon.

"I'm writing these lines but I'm not at all sure whether you'll read them. We're so far from each other. This lack of communication drives me crazy."

I've mixed up everything. Yesterday, today and tomorrow have merged, been stirred and shaken up. For us, time has stopped. Only the seasons change. Fewer and fewer things have any importance. We are happy with a third of a loaf per day and queueing up for it. It is uncertain to arrive. Every day is the same. In some city suburbs there is not even any bread. Here the citizens have had to reconcile themselves to their 0.174 kg of flour a day. A newspaper article started with the sentence:

"It is as if the life in Sarajevo were from a folk tale in which a little gypsy boy receives a slap on the face from his father, who also is hungry, for eating too much of a pie that exists anyway only in his imagination."

We were becoming poorer and poorer from day to day.

I had to dress the wounds caused by the words of this desperate painter, who had plunged them into me like a knife...

Lovers meet in dark places and achieve new conquests. We were sinking into poverty. We did not even notice that our lives had sunk to the level of hardly being able to buy bread and of the humanitarian aid crumbs we looked forward to. And when we were given beans all weevil-eaten, our question about it was answered from Geneva: "To be boiled before use!"

At the same time, in the packages of medicines we got as aid there were some with small letters and numbers distinctly showing that they had passed their expiry dates. They were thrown away so as to be useful for us.

Unfortunately, we were still literate.

We have had, ever since the 16th century, a library with manuscripts and books in Turkish, Arabic, Persian, our mother tongue and other languages. Under the roofs of the Old Orthodox Church, the Jewish Synagogue "El kal grande" and St. Peter's Cathedral from the 13th century and in other of the Lord's temples we kept and read books in Spanish, Greek, Latin, Hebrew, Old Church Slavic, German and Russian. It has gone on for centuries. In this city, four out of five of the world's great religions have existed next to one another and together with one another. We also knew about beans (Phasolus vulgaris) after they had been brought from America, as well as about many delicious dishes and sweets, either in our homes or in public kitchens, inns, restaurants and hotels. A whole century ago, William Miller wrote of Sarajevo: "You can take a walk around the town and imagine you were in a real oriental town before the shops in Franz Joseph Street, within five minutes' distance, take you back to an Austrian town." Whose fault was it that we were not aware that we burdened, like parasites, the world with ourselves? We took it as normal to be supported and fed by others. A whole, big European city had become a hungry beggar who is not able to help himself. The story about beans full of weevils is appropriate for a beggar. At the end of the year we were given the ninth batch of humanitarian aid by the UNHCR. The whole year was put into six lunch packets, two litres of cooking oil, 1.5 kg of sugar and lentils, a kilo of cheese, beans, potatoes, 4.2 kg of rice, sixteen tins (of meat paste, fish and corned beef), 1 kg of flour, three small packets of biscuits, a bar of soap and half a kilo of detergent, soya and maize flour. In nine months, nine batches of aid fell into my hat. On the pavement's edge, I did not get in one week enough to survive.

I am constantly facing the fact that a war is going on in my city, that I am going through it cruelly, that I can go nowhere, that I have to forget about travelling, that I have not seen my mother for a year, that I could not go to the funeral of my grandmother having learned about her death six months later. The news took six months to reach me. In a letter form that arrived through the Red Cross, a boy of my daughter's age wrote to his parents that he often saw her. I do not get any letters from her. They do not arrive although I know that she writes and sends them. My fifteen-year-old daughter has always liked writing, but I have had only one letter during all this time. Some of my friends do not even know where, out in the world, their children are.

Bojana's friend writes that they meet on the steps of the Horse, a bronze monument in memory of the grand duke and they weep. They weep together...

On some other steps, river banks and bridges, the same is done by some other people's sons, some other people's daughters, some other people's wives, mothers and sisters.

Letters do not arrive. There is no telephone. Carrier and other pigeons were killed or we ate them. The swallows did not return this summer, my friends persuade me. No, they did not, and we did not even notice they were not here. I cannot remember seeing them. We must have killed them, too. Our communication with the rest of the world is not normal any more. The only news is sometimes granted to us by means of radio hams' microphones and headphones. Our feelings are reduced to:

"I miss you... Don't cry... I can't speak... I dream of you... I dream of you every night. I was worried about you... The flat is all right. Only one shell flew in. Don't worry... Be good. Study hard. Hold on just a bit longer... Look after yourself..."

For days after that we feel, deep in our hearts, scraps of inhaled happiness after hearing one another after so long, after establishing any communication whatsoever. Broken fragments of speech, sentences of listening followed one another.

Unintelligible words were repeated for us by the radio hams to understand what we were told by our dear one from afar. Weeping interrupts us: "I have nothing more to say". And we wanted to say so much and had silently repeated so much for days. We do not manage to mention even birthdays. We forgot congratulations. University professor Medo Kantardžić confided in us that in Makarska, as his wife, a jobless doctor in exile, writes to him, children are classified into those who go and those who do not go to school. His nine-year-old son told him, holding tight his mother's hand in November: "Look, Mum, that boy's got a schoolbag."

We continue living fragmentally. Thousands of images are composed into a film which is continously being shot. Some small new images are added. A time document which will outlive us grows bigger. It seemed comical to me a sentence uttered in April by an eight-year-old girl, the daughter of Adela Mičić, as an answer to her mother's question why she trembled so much during the first night's shooting that they experienced in their groundfloor flat in Grbavica:

"Mum, this is my first war."

The girl trembled and crouched in the bathroom. Her mother and she discovered the most hidden part of the flat. They felt safest if crouched on a rug laid between the bath and the washbasin. The child's exaggeration had seemed witty until we realized we were sinking into a long, dirty and for many of us the first war.

Wars are never short. Nor are they clean. It is not easy to live in their cruelty.

I wrote in vain on my sheets of paper: "Some dreams, loves and hopes are being ruined... Sad is this country of mine."

The horizon outside the windows is dull.

It is gloomy in my room.

I feel anxious. I still do not succeed in looking at myself in the mirror which did not crack but which is growing duller and duller. Will my neighbours be able to, will they dare do the same?

Dante, I believed that the restless Bosnian teacher Vaso Pelagić would come by somewhere. From this city he was expelled to Asia Minor. All his life he was expelled, imprisoned and hungry, and died undiscouraged in the humidity of Požarevac prison almost a century ago. So we constantly sink back into the past, touch the present, sink again, swallow the air and painfully dive into the time which is behind us. Is history teaching us or are we repeating some lessons which we never learned? I wanted to apologize to Mr Pelagić for his knocked down bust in the park between the Municipal Assembly and the Republican Presidency buildings. It has been lying for months looking at the sky. Now it is covered with snow. He may be lamenting over his books which ended at the public stake in one of Belgrade squares in 1890. What symbolism there was in that fire while the pages of his book "People's Rights or Our Urgent Needs" were burning! A shell hit him this September summer and knocked him down to the ground. It came from the slopes of

Trebević looking for people. In its hatred it found a man who immeasurably loved his country Bosnia and Herzegovina and its people, and who wrote so long ago, but so familiarly: "Today people do awful harm to everybody generally and to everybody individually. This barbaric national hatred often brings about wars and countless misfortunes."

He is not here probably because he did not want to wade through the mud, which sucks me in more and more. He would not be able to drag around here his prison chains but I believe that he is fed up with the darkness of his cell and of our shelters. Is he daily repeating for me what was written down long ago, while from the wall of my burned out editorial office the good Miroslav Krleža is smiling: "When books are burned, then, as a rule, human bones break." What would he add if he saw, in addition to the Old Slavic Prayer Book from the library of the Metropolitan's residence set alight by a shell, and singed old manuscripts from the Institute for Oriental Studies, a Sarajevo exhibition of dozens of wounded paintings by the masters of the brush, broken off mortar with al-seco arabesques of the Gazi Husrev-bey's Mosque, the sculptures and crucifixions of St Vinko Paulski and Mary's Ascension churches at Stup, and paintings lost for ever by Mica Todorović, Roman Petrović and Vojo Dimitrijević. It is unnecessary to add the burned out studios of Branko Popovac, Afan Ramić and other robbed studios in Grbavica belonging to Ibrahim Ljubović, Milorad Ćorović and Ljupko Antunović.

I beg you, Dante, let me catch my breath. Here, I can see that the date of the beginning of the next circle has remained unchanged:

"Today seems to be the coldest. The radio announces that it is 20 degrees below zero according to the scale of the Swede Anders Celsius. There are doubts in the city about the exactitude of the temperature data. It seems to us much colder. The snow under our feet squeaks. There is some hoar frost on the black hair of a girl I meet. The vapour she breathes out crystallizes white and sticks onto the locks falling over her forehead. Tiny icicles form on my moustache, too.

"Freezing while waiting for the newspapers, which do not arrive because of a breakdown of the printing press, I gave up going to my flat as I had planned...

"Jasmina arrives. She is freezing as well. She is stunned by the knowledge that we have been reduced to the level of cavemen. She was in our flat. Our neighbours who stayed in their flats are freezing. They heat their meals on some improvised stoves in which they burn damp wood or car tyres cut up into pieces, old shoes and plastic crates for mineral water bottles. Almost anything we can find around us can be used as fuel. The temperature in the rooms heated by these stoves does not go over eight degrees Celsius. Rooms have been turned into kitchens, woodsheds, storerooms, laundries and rooms for drying laundry. Dishes are washed in melted snow. In the crystal whiteness, only after the snow is melted are deposits of soot found. They sift that water to use it for cooking, washing and meagre bathing. My neighbour Konstantin from the first floor flushes the toilet with the hot water he gets by melting snow. He does so two or three times a night to prevent the drainpipe from freezing.

"Despair has settled in our home. The drainpipe has burst on the third or fourth floor. Brown faeces pour down the walls. It immediately gets frozen. Stinking brown icicles, like stalactites, hang from the ceiling over our bed or run down the wall. There is no water yet. There is no electricity, either. There is no central heating. Our neighbours shiver from the cold with layers of clothes on. They are, most often, some old, discarded rags. Now they are welcome. Sad and poor the people look who used to dress in the latest European fashions, wore soft Italian shoes, used choice French perfumes and drove shiny new cars."
(January 6)

Nothing is better two days later:
"Again shells and bullets around my flat. My neighbours warn me not to call in after 4.00 p.m.. At that time our three eight-storey buildings and small neighbouring houses are targeted from Kromolj. Low-calibre projectiles are used, they tell me. I do not know what this means, but they makes holes in the walls, they wound and destroy.'

"I have moved within my flat for the third time. I replaced some furniture from the bedroom brought earlier from the unsafe sitting room. I took the clothes and bedlinen out. I removed some of those stinking icicles, threw away the burst bottles in which I kept water reserves now frozen with the cold, I roamed around the rooms with a sorrowful lump in my throat and locked the door behind me. I did not have the feeling it was my door.

"I can do nothing. My neighbour Konstantin goes down to the ground floor every hour. In the demolished business offices he heats the main drainpipe before it gets frozen. He advises me to do the same. I thank him for his concern. I leave exhausted and with a bitter taste in my mouth. I spit in the street, blow my nose strongly and wash my hands in snow.

"I can smell the stench of urine in the bedroom. It may have spread through the whole flat. It has permeated my clothes, hair and moustache.

"I have lifted my manuscripts and some more important papers from the floor up on top of the wardrobe. I hope to save them. I still hope that incendiary bullets and the fires will miss me."

I could not go on. I cannot. Everything is the same. Everything is worse than the worst, and the darkness does not stop, does not settle down, does not go anywhere. Where is the end? In an ancient book, which was quoted to me on the eve of this journey to Hades, it was written, it is said, that the cosmos falls to pieces when a letter is disturbed. Could it also be my fault that in some dear people's books which I edited, some misprints disturbed the whole universe. I will have to be careful enough while writing about all those destinies and stories which make up this sad saga about my city, even before the final full stop is put at the end of the experience.

Maro, would you mind taking me back, please?

Dante, give my regards to all our acquaintances. Will you excuse me for not being able to go further with you? Remember, you did not feel like going on, either.

And to finish – an ordinary war greeting of Sarajevo!
TAKE CARE OF YOURSELVES! (We have no instruction how to.)
Am I ending?

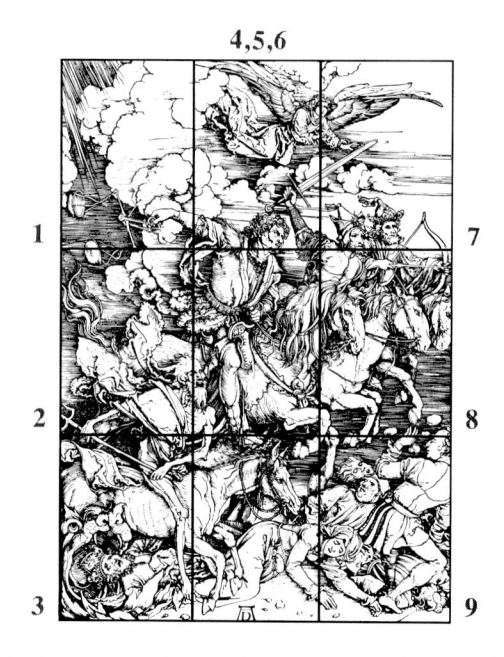

4,5,6

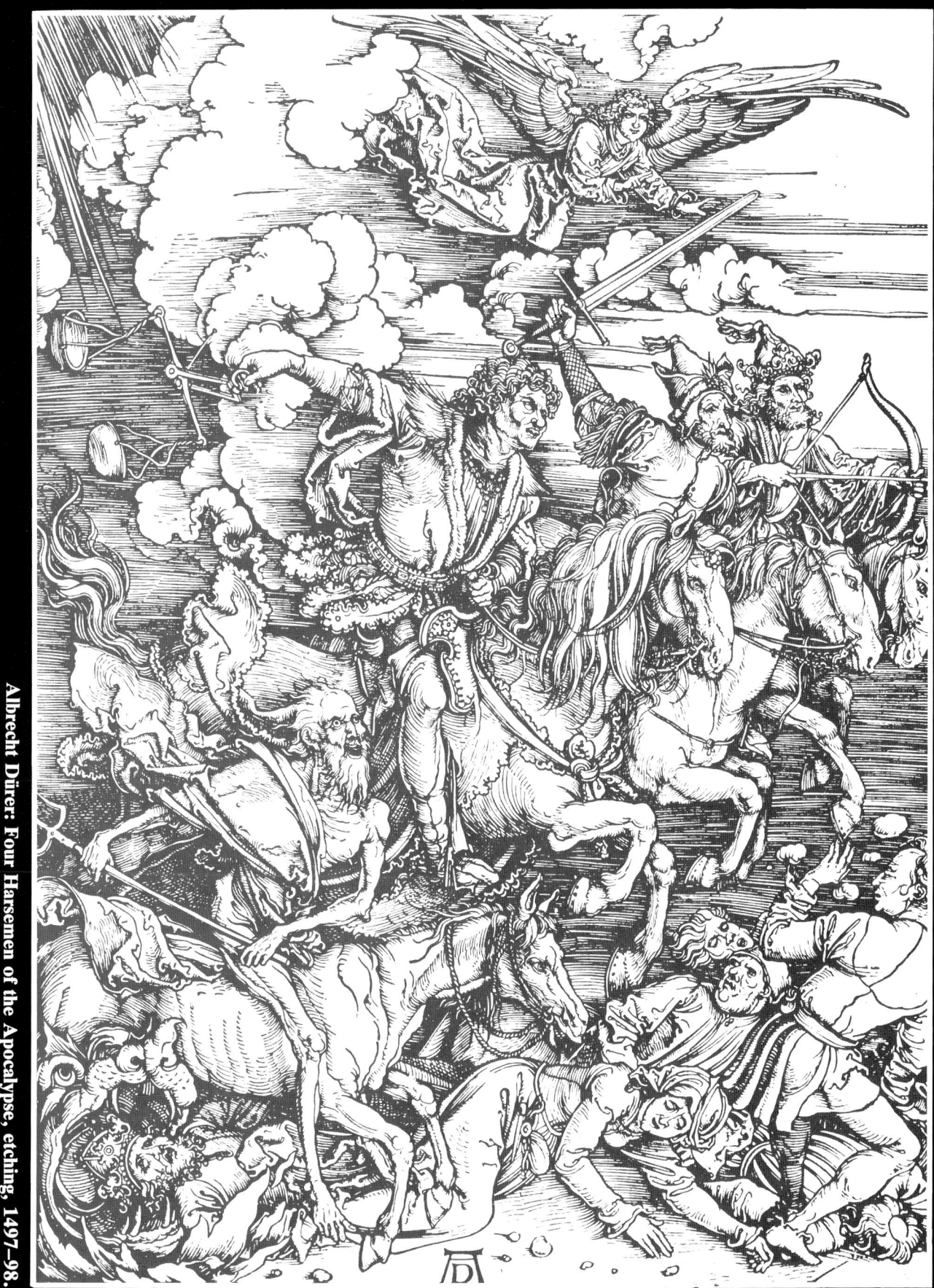

Albrecht Dürer: Four Horsemen of the Apocalypse, etching, 1497–98.

Instead of an epilogue

By the end of 1992 there had been 8,037 killed and 47,116 wounded in Sarajevo. The figures do not include those killed or injured at Grbavica, Nedžarići, Vogošća and other parts of the city forcibly cut off from the rest of it. According to Ministry of the Interior information, more than 800,000 shells of various types were fired at Sarajevo from the surrounding hills. The weight of iron, steel and explosive fired onto the town was about 20 million kilograms. If the shells were linked into a chain (the average length of a shell is 50 cm), it would be 400 kilometres long, which is exactly the distance between Zagreb and Belgrade. About 30 kilograms of explosive was fired at each Sarajevan.

Of 20,000 cubic metres of firewood and 80,000 tons of coal promised to the citizens, not a single lorry of fuel for households arrived.

The city saw in the New Year weighing at least 5,700 tons less than before. Namely, if each Sarajevan had lost 15 kg on average and at least 380,000 citizens remained in the city, it means that the load on the city's pavements was that amount less.

All of Sarajevo was without electricity (read: light) for 81 days: from August 10 to September 8, from September 21 to October 16, from November 5 to 8, from December 7 to the end of the year (and longer). In spite of the UNPROFOR soldiers' presence, 21 workmen were killed and 76 injured while repairing damaged lines. Throughout the war, the areas in and around the city were supplied with electricity from only one, sometimes two, sub-stations of 110-kilowatts of the existing ten, thus reducing electricity (when there was any) to 20% of requirements. Before the war the city had 962 km of water pipes, 213 km of gas pipelines and 6,210 km of low-voltage electricity lines. It had 90 trams, 257 local buses, 100 trolleybuses and 71 minibuses, which ran along 111 lines in the city.

In 1988 there were 81,436 motor vehicles in the town, 62,803 of which were passenger cars. In the same year, there were 205,895 people employed. We had four major department stores and 2,120 shops of various kinds.

Sarajevo University has 19 faculties, three academies, three high schools and 42 scientific research institutes with 32,126 students.

The city boasted twenty cinemas with 8,798 seats, six museums with annexes and three professional theatres; in peacetime 80 newspapers and magazines were published with an annual circulation of more than 50 million,

Twenty hotels in Sarajevo and its surroundings had 2,590 beds with more that a million visitor-days per year.

In about a hundred health institutions (hospitals, medical centres and chemist's shops) there were 30,147 doctors and other medical staff in the month of March. By the end of the year, the number had been reduced to 19,600, while overall damage to health structures is estimated at about DM 190 million.

Out of the 52 elementary schools 38 were damaged to some extent and 2 completely destroyed. The buildings of twenty-two secondary schools out of 32 were seriously damaged. Sarajevo is surrounded by 14 rocket launchers with 32 tubes, 59 howitzers, 101 heavy guns, 50 recoilless guns, 113 82-mm and 90 120-mm mortars, 51 armoured personnel carriers, 51 tanks and a huge number of anti-aircraft guns, anti-aircraft machine-guns, hand-held rocket launchers, machine-gun nests (according to a statement by the chief of the General Staff of the B-H Armed Forces on July 25). The official army magazine stated at the end of the year that more than 2,100 barrels were pointing at Sarajevo along a 60-km long front line, meaning that there were 35 weapons for each kilometre of the front. Military records show that during the battle for Berlin there was a record number of 25 weapons per kilometre of front line. The same source mentions that Sarajevo had been attacked by 5,600 artillery weapons, 110 tanks and 180 personnel carriers and that half of these had been destroyed.

The UN passed about 20 resolutions on Bosnia and Herzegovina, most of them being nothing more than dead letters.

By the end of 1992 UNPROFOR had 1,598 soldiers and 100 civilians employed in Sarajevo. There were 413 Egyptians, 837 Frenchmen and 348 Ukrainians. In Bosnia and Herzegovina as a whole UNPROFOR had 7,983 soldiers and 39 civilians (988 Spaniards, 2,621 British, 1,884 Frenchmen and 1,347 Canadians) and 152 military observers. UNPROFOR had three Spaniards, two Frenchmen and one soldier each of the Egyptian, Ukrainian and Benelux battalion wounded and one member of the BH Command.

The costs of the engagement of the UN and its bodies in Sarajevo calculated in US dollars will be neatly written down one day in one of their reports...

In the Sarajevo Maternity Home, 1,867 new Sarajevans were born in the first months of the war...

P.S.
At the end of 1993, according to official data, 9,662 people have been killed and over 56,000 wounded in Sarajevo. Without any data referring to those parts forcibly amputated. Just in the time of the Christmas cease-fire, which had been agreed upon, 39 Sarajevans are killed and 200 wounded.
On the last day of January 1994, the number of those killed is already 9,842. In Bosnia-Herzegovina, in those parts where data are available, the number of dead reaches 142,165 and wounded 161,142. At the end of 1993, those numbers are 135,000 killed and around 155,000 wounded.
The number of shells of various calibres fired at the city exceeds two million. There are different estimates as to their weight.
No coal or wood entered the town in 1993.
The town went on starving. Every ten days another round of humanitarian aid was distributed, which was all one had to live on. There was no other food, nor could anything else enter the town. So, before Christmas 1993, each Sarajevan received: one kilo of flour, 400 grams of beans, 3.3 dcl of oil, and a 125-gram can of herrings. Twenty days later, in January 1994, he received half a kilo of flour, 3.3 dcl of oil, and 800 grams of beans. The crumbs on the empty dining tables of Sarajevo are ever tinier. The aid is not enough for survival.
There was generally no electricity for days, for weeks, for months, almost throughout the whole of 1993. The city was forced to get used to darkness and privation. Because of the damage to electrical installations, and because of the deliberate cutting off of electricity supplies, the city was without any electricity whatsoever on 140 days in 1993, the longest period being from June 21 until August 13, or 53 days. Of the ten power stations which had supplied the city with electricity in times of peace, electricity now came to the city through only one power station (110/10 KV), and from Oct 13 through another one (110/35 KV).
UN soldiers were coming, going and getting killed. The cost of their deployment rose to 1,650 billion US dollars, to 79, 80 ... dead. Commanders, with new general's ribbons and new decorations, succeeded one another, honourably or less honourably, as the heads of UN troops in Bosnia-Herzegovina. After the Canadian Lewis MacKenzie, the Frenchman Phillip Mourillon came, then the Belgian Francis Briquemont (who, helpless, proudly resigned), then the Englishman Michael Rose. They came, they went, and the Sarajevans remained where they were.
The number of Security Council resolutions on the situation in Bosnia-Herzegovina exceeded thirty...
Etc. Etc. Etc.

Why is it that sad eyes always gaze at the sky?

10, 11 **THE PEOPLE'S PARLIAMENT** – Sarajevans responded to the barricades and weapons of April 5 by going into the streets. Shots fired from Vraca at demonstrators in Bratstvo-jedinstvo Street (Brotherhood and Unity Street) and the first victims on Vrbanja Bridge who were in a peace demonstration created the People's Parliament. The citizens of Bosnia and Herzegovina chanted against division, for peace, for life...

Photo: *Danilo Krstanović*

14 **WALK** along the Miljacka bank past a tank trap is only the beginning of anxiety, but also of the city's protection.

Photo: *Danilo Krstanović*

24, 25 **BARRICADES** intersected the town. Tank traps at Bendbaša protected Sarajevo against unwanted tanks and personnel carriers. Flower boxes on the Bratstvo-jedinstvo Bridge stopped cars, gradually separating Grbavica and consolidating the border that nobody crossed, and barricades near Mojmilo cut off the residential areas Aerodrom and Dobrinja for months. Later on, passage was possible here only at one's own risk. Masked terrorists stopped the peace demonstration by shooting from the courtyard of the "Chimney sweeps-'house". Blood was shed on Vrbanja Bridge. The first of the war victims were murdered by bullets from the masked terrorist on the right, while the one on the left fired into the air.

Photographs: 1 and 4: *Kemal Hadžić*
3: *Emil Grebenar*
2: *Danilo Krstanović*

26, 27 **CAGE** has become a synonym for Sarajevo. With a parrot inside, it could have found a buyer until the moment when no more bird food was available.

Others are waiting for hours in the deserted railway station hall for trains without a timetable, squatting next to their bags, suitcases and cardboard boxes tied with rope.

Three generations are going somewhere, but only the boy's face has a smile, not knowing that only tomorrow a gun or a crutch could end his carefree joy.

In long queues people patiently wait for food. Something may come. Maybe. A dog has found a bone. Lucky him!

Photographs 1, 2 and 3: *Emil Grebenar*
4: *Danilo Krstanović*

30, 31 **BRIDGES** – Dramatically twisted bars of Žerajić's Bridge railings near the Emperor's Mosque tragically chant the Sarajevo poem of '92, in which singed roof beams "on four waters" witness the hundreds of homeless of this country, while bookshop windows in the main street, smashed by explosions, imply that the time for reading books will come later. Here life and war are just ending their dramas, leaving the tranquillity of the deserted shelves of a supermarket only to a stray cat.

Photographs 1–3 and 5: *Kemal Hadžić*
4: *Emil Grebenar*

34 **PLACES OF WORSHIP** were mercilessly shelled. No matter whether it was the Old Orthodox Church, a Catholic Church in Novo Sarajevo, the Old Jewish Temple or a New Mosque at Kobilja Glava, the minaret of which collapsed.

Photographs: *Milomir Kovačević*
Kemal Hadžić

40, 41 **LONG QUEUES OF HUNGER** – On the market stalls, once full of fruit and vegetables, only small heaps of nettles can now be seen. A man selling tomato nursery plants in a box walks around, and in a doorway seemingly sheltered from shells a crippled man is standing waiting for alms. Which of the two will get more money for bread?

Maybe something will come to the market; how can one return home with an empty shopping bag? People wait patiently for hours. Our daily bread must come.

Photographs 1: *Emil Grebenar*
2, 4 and 20: *Rikard Larma*
17: *Kemal Hadžić*

44, 45 **TURRETS** of the architect Karlo Paržik on the former villas of Nikola Mandić, a lawyer, and Heinrich Reiter, one of the Sarajevo Brewery directors, date from 1903. The roof and the interior of the Museum of 14th Winter Olympic Games have been burnt down together with part of the archives and documentation of the Olympic Games.

The City Transport Company was among the first structures shelled. Trolleybuses and buses do not work. Neither do the electric trams which have been circling around Sarajevo since 1895.

Photographs 1–5: *Kemal Hadžić*
23: *Miki Uherka*
7: *Rikard Larma*

48 **MAY 2, 1992. TIME OF THE DAY 6 p.m.** The main street of Sarajevo – Marshall Tito Street. A calm sunny Saturday turned into an infernal cauldron, a little after mid-day – with shells, rifle fire, fire barrage. I never thought, running away from the Main Post Office all in flames, while being protected by a policeman we used to know, that we were running into a war we had never wanted. My colleague, Milomir Kovačević, sent this photo of ours out into the wide world, to the front pages of the newspapers. We could not stop, as the murderous shells were falling all around us, rifle fire echoing, entire façades collapsing, the dead lying, the wounded groaning, the pools of blood... No, this is no carefree little photo for a family album. It is for me an ineradicable print of war on celluloid.

52, **POST OFFICE** – Shells and fire destroyed the
53 Military Post and Telegraph dating from 1913. There remains only sorrow, sooty walls and a wish to have again our old Post Office which was designed by the architect Josip Vancaš.

Photographs 1–3: Emil Grebenar
4: Kemal Hadžić

THE TOWN'S EYES – Shelling from the hills, the murderers drove us down into our cellars. Windows, these eyes of a town, did not wipe off boys' smiles, girls' curiosity or the melancholy looks of elderly women. At times one has to have a look at tomatoes grown in balcony flower pots, a naked mischievous child behind bars, a youth peeping behind collapsed beams, or simply to stop near a flower vase made of shell fragments.

Photographs 11 – 139: Rikard Larma
10: Emil Grebenar

58, **DECORATIONS** of the town façades from the
59 Austro-Hungarian period are damaged. Also damaged are the impressive caryatides above the chemist's shop in the residential-business block from 1894 which belonged to a well-known merchant, Mihailo D. Babić. Its architect, Josip Vancaš, is wounded himself in this way. Wounds gape open on the "ZEMA" Department Store at the corner of the main street, and on a relief on the building of the National Bank of B-H.

Photographs 1–3: Emil Grebenar
4: Kemal Hadžić

60, **FLAMES** consumed 600,000 books, publications
61 and magazines of the National and University Library of B-H in the building of the former Town Hall. Behind the sooty architectural ruins remain arabesques, stained-glass windows, a staircase of Hungarian marble, columns from Tyrol and the beautiful red-black marble from the quarry in Koševo valley and bricks with initials I. M. of the Merhemić's brick kiln.

Photographs 1–4 and 6: Kemal Hadžić
5 and 7: Rikard Larma

68, **THE PANORAMA OF SARAJEVO** with the
69 UNIS tower blocks, a block of flats at Hrasno, the Holiday Inn Hotel and the demolished roof of the old military hospital is dimmed by smoke, blood-like fire reflections, but there are also stripped beams that can be still used.

Photographs: Rikard Larma

72, **FIRE** caused by shelling consumes the work of
73 the architect Ivan Štraus, a modern building of "Elektroprivreda B-H" (Electrical Power Industry of B-H), and the upper floors of the Assembly of the Novo Sarajevo Municipality. The electricity company of B-H with 18,000 employees had one of the most modern systems. Their fixed assets were 7,688 million US dollars and their total income was 1,360 million US dollars on December 31, 1991.

Photographs: Kemal Hadžić

76, **MOSQUES** have not been spared in this war
77 either. Most frequently shelled were those from the 16th century. The Gazi Husref Bey's Mosque bore the brunt of the artillery fire, hit by 94 shells of various calibres. Damaged are its walls, the large dome and fence of the balcony, as well as the minaret. Seriously damaged are cupolas with the walls of two turbeh (mausoleums) next to the mosque – those of Gazi Husref Bey and Gazi Murat Bey Tardić, and ornate names of notables buried around the mosque.
Shells pierced the dome and destroyed the fountain of the Ali Pasha Mosque, for me the most beautiful Sarajevo mosque. The Emperor's Mosque had its dome, portico, walls and minaret damaged. The White Mosque was mercilessly shelled. Damaged are the roof and minaret of this splendid mosque at Vratnik, built by hajji Hajdar, Gazi Husref Bey's secretary.

Photographs 1–3: Kemal Hadžić
4: Miroslav Prstojević
5 and 6: Rikard Larma

78 **THE DESTRUCTION** of the town did not spare even the 17th century clock tower which measured the time "a la turca". Fire destroyed the interior of the mosque, Tabački masjid as well.

Photographs: Milomir Kovačević

80, **MAGRIBIJA** or Sheikh Omer Effendi Magribi's
81 Mosque is badly damaged. This mosque, dating from the middle of the 16th century, had its minaret destroyed to its very foundation and its roof structure and interior wooden vault seriously damaged.
The decorations on the top of the minaret of the Ferhadija Mosque show only a slight damage to the dome and the minaret.
The situation is no better with the many other mosques of Sarajevo. They are damaged no matter whether they were built a few centuries or only a few years ago.

Photographs 1: Danilo Krstanović
2 and 3: Kemal Hadžić

82, 83 **THE CLOCK-TOWER** still shows the passing of time, even of the evil time that is oppressing Sarajevo together with all the blows it has experienced in the past. Damaged are also the large domes and minarets of the Muslihudin Čekrekčija's Mosque below Kovači and the Havadža Durak's Mosque, also called the Baščaršija Mosque.
A characteristic minaret of the New Mosque at Kobilja glava and many shops in Goldsmiths' Street were destroyed by about thirty tank and mortar shells.

Photographs 1–4 and 6: Kemal Hadžić
5: Emil Grebenar

88, 89 **SNIPERS** – Crossroads have become places of dying. Instead of collapsed traffic lights, warning signs are being written: BEWARE SNIPERS! The way out is to run across a street. It is not so easy for those on crutches.

Photographs 1–3: Danilo Krstanović
4: Emil Grebenar
5: Kemal Hadžić

92, 93 **CHILDREN,** unfortunately, have not been spared in this war. Father's gun and helmet are only an effort to imitate the grown-ups. Gasmasks are a preparation for survival, but shrapnel wounds are an everyday event.

Photographs 1: Senad Grubelić
2: Danilo Krstanović
3: Didije Torše

94, 95 **GAMES** – Children have always taken adults as their models. Games have become warlike, with bullet-proof jackets made of cardboard boxes with the address on them UNHCR FOR UNHCR, Sarajevo. Sorrow for destroyed property has to be shared with father, and a wounded dog protected with a toy gun.

Photographs: Senad Grubelić

100, 101 **RUINS** – Murdering citizens is not the only objective. Red-hot artillery barrels have turned Sarajevo into a modern Carthage, Guernica or Warsaw. Homes disappeared under shells and in the fires they caused. What is a woman watching from the balcony of the house that does not exist any more?

Photographs 1 and 4: Rikard Larma
2, 5, 6 and 7: Kemal Hadžić
3: Emil Grebenar

104, 105 **SARAJEVANS** – A mortar shell ended up in the bark of a hundred-year-old tree. Unlike the Sarajevans, the tree survived. There are no empty chambers in Sarajevo roulette. Deep and lethal are the holes in tissue made by red-hot pieces of shrapnel, no matter whether the victim is hit in the main street, or a fashionable residential area like Ciglane, or somewhere on the outskirts of the town. Sarajevans have become statistics that increase the death rates. The luckier ones are marked by zero which does not disturb the sum, but continues life.

Photographs 1: Kemal Hadžić
2–5: Rikard Larma

106, 107 **DYING** – Death mowed us down while we were walking or riding our long-forgotten bicycles. It found us with water canisters, or armfuls of wood, or in queues to pay electricity bills. It did not discriminate according to sex or age. The taxi-driver Mile Plakalović, a humanist, who did not stop his car for a single day during this war in spite of 7 bullets and numerous pieces of shrapnel which pierced his new Audi 80, was at hand even when no help was needed any more, when the only help was to take away the man whom a shell stopped forever in front of the "Sarajka" Department Store, at 9.30 on September 29th.

Photographs 1, 3 and 4: Emil Grebenar
2: Kemal Hadžić
5: Danilo Krstanović

108, 109 **NEWSPAPERS, BLOOD AND BREAD** – Queues for bread and ice-cream soaked the asphalt with blood in Maxim Gorki Street on that fateful May 27th. Two shells left behind mess, deaths and invalids. We were left with unhappiness, obituaries, flowers and daily newspaper with a headline: WAR AND PEACE.

Photographs 1 and 3: Emil Grebenar
2: Rikard Larma

112 **STAINED-GLASS** fragments on the "Ognjen Prica" Grammar School are witness to the killing of beauty and youth of Sarajevo.

Photographs: Kemal Hadžić

116 **THE GREAT DEMAND** for daily newspapers was an effort to get to know more, while long queues in front of shops envied a stray dog for having found a bone.
Wherever did he find it?

Photographs: Danilo Krstanović
Emil Grebenar

118, 119 **IN THE STREETS OF MY TOWN** there are destroyed traffic lights, broken electric lines and containers that protect against the killers from the hills; trams and burnt cars are there as well, while citizens try out all their acrobatic skills to cross Ćumurija Bridge.

Photographs: Kemal Hadžić

120, 121 **AN EXPENSIVE TARGET** – Having been shelled, this Golf burnt up, and it was worth DM 30,000. Sarajevans' salaries in this war are hardly DM 10, which means that patiently saving for 250 years one could buy a Golf again, provided that all the salary can be saved. Gradually, shells turned private cars into scrap heaps.

Photographs 1 and 6: Danilo Krstanović
2 and 3: Emil Grebenar
4 and 5: Kemal Hadžić

122, 123 **CEILINGS** look into the sky in most residential areas. Recorded on camera are houses at Kromolj, Nedžarići and Aerodrom, as well as "Palma", the most beautiful cake-shop in town, with its fountain.

Photographs 1: Kemal Hadžić
3 and 4: Emil Grebenar
2: Danilo Krstanović

124, 125 **ROAD SIGNS** – A clock at Marijin Dvor stopped at 8 o'clock (and four minutes); it is near a road sign pointing to the Assembly and the Government of B-H, hotels and exchange-offices. How far these things are now from us, and how near are the destroyed office blocks of the UPI, "Energoinvest", the military hospital, the post office and residential buildings!

Photographs 1–4 and 6–8: Kemal Hadžić
5: Miroslav Prstojević

132, 133 **"MARSHAL TITO" BARRACKS,** one of the largest military complexes in the Balkans, was a thorn in the town's flesh. In time it became a main target of the artillery, with fires that took hold of some of the buildings, where flames "pressed" sheet metal gutters, and where the former JNA (Yugoslav People's Army) had left behind what they no longer needed: a crumpled Yugoslav flag, Marx's "Das Kapital", and damaged tanks.

Photographs 1: Emil Grebenar
2 and 3: Rikard Larma
4: Danilo Krstanović

136, 137 **ZETRA** – The Olympic Sports Hall Zetra was burnt down by incendiary missiles. It was built in 1982 according to the designs of Ludimil Alikalfić and Dušan Djapa with the purpose of being used for many sports and cultural events. Closely linked to it is the question: DO YOU REMEMBER SARAJEVO? The "Borba" news agency had awarded ZETRA the highest recognition for architecture in former Yugoslavia.

Photographs 1: Rikard Larma
3–5: Kemal Hadžić
2: Emil Grebenar

140, 141 **BLUE HELMETS** – Sarajevans expected salvation from UNPROFOR and UNHCR. In time they got to know their work which ranged from elementary town needs (water, electricity, food, oil) to airport control, mediation in exchanges of prisoners of war and also of captured women, children and old people. The first Hercules brought the first crumbs of relief to the starving city.

Photographs 1: Emil Grebenar
4 and 5: Kemal Hadžić
2: Rikard Larma
3 and 6: Danilo Krstanović

142, 143 **WATER** – In spite of the fact that Sarajevo had a water supply system in Roman times, and the city itself since 1461, it is thirsty in these war days. We could not be consoled by the knowledge that 120 years ago there were as many as 143 water supply systems and 156 public drinking fountains in Sarajevo, because we had to walk for miles to get some water.

Photographs 1 and 4: Kemal Hadžić
2 and 3: Emil Grebenar

144, 145 **REFUGEES** – The whirlwind of war drove people from their homes. In some places the exodus was a result of fear, in others of shells that destroyed homes, but often it was brutally carried out by the policy of ethnic cleansing, rape and murder. People became goods used for exchange – thirsty, hungry and scared.
Most frequently the exchanges took place on the front line, near the "Bristol" Hotel and "Palma" cake-shop a few hundred metres away. A girl and her father dramatically run to the side of the town, while the mother and the other daughter stay in Grbavica. Divisions of the town have separated families, they even go through their bedrooms.

Photographs 1, 3, and 6: Danilo Krstanović
2, 4 and 5: Kemal Hadžić

148, 149 **THE TREE-LINED PATH** in Đuro Đaković Street gradually disappeared. Not even a month had passed from the moment when the first tree was cut down until the moment when not a single tree could be seen. From the same place the view was quite different. Other tree-lined paths, parks and surrounding woods have disappeared without a trace. The woodcutters do not know that the first Sarajevo parks were designed in 1886 by Hugo Krvarić, an official of the Territorial Government. The Small and Big Parks were made on old graveyards of Kemalbeg, Šehitluci and Čekrćinica. Trees are cut down from two parks behind the 2nd Grammar School, designed by Smiljko Klaić.

Photographs 1–3: Emil Grebenar
4: Kemal Hadžić

150, 151 **BOSNIAN STEW** is a culinary specialty. It is made of various kinds of vegetables and at least two kinds of meat which are stewed for a long time over a gentle fire. But it has been relegated to some far-away memories. The reality consists of old stoves of the most varied forms produced by some new craftsmen. The main objective is: to have a spoonful of hot soup or some other dish.

Photographs 1 and 5: Senad Grubelić
2: Emil Grebenar
3: Miroslav Prstojević
4: Danilo Krstanović
6: Kemal Hadžić

152, 153 **FUEL** is a **sine qua non** of survival in a mountainous town with a severe continental climate at 535 m above sea level. Parks died to the woodcutters' smiles; on the "Austrian gift house" from the period of the Olympic Games in 1984, a sign of traditional culture has remained: Sarajevo Winter '92. There disappeared even the bark from hundred-year-old trees, and a new Rodin's Thinker is smoking, tired, on the snow, while children drag home anything that can heat them.

Photographs 1 and 4: Kemal Hadžić
3, 5 and 6: Rikard Larma
7: Emil Grebenar

156, 157 **BAŠČARŠIJA** is deserted. Shells injured it day after day. Even its square with Sebilj (a drinking fountain) and pigeons were not spared. Shops are closed in the usually very lively Kazandjiluk; the notices "Painless ear-piercing", "Goods can be purchased with cheques","Express repairs" sadly witness the past throngs in the old Goldsmiths' and Coppersmiths' Streets.

Photographs 1: Miki Uherka
2 and 5: Miroslav Prstojević
3, 4 and 6: Rikard Larma

160, 161 **CEMETERIES** – Even the dead could not rest in peace. At Dobrinja, lawns are turned into cemeteries, at Koševo a football stadium is used for burials. Those killed are buried on former grass-covered slopes that were used as stands, and soldiers and the youth of Sarajevo on sports grounds.

Photographs 1 and 2: Rikard Larma
3: Kemal Hadžić
4: Miroslav Prstojević

162, 163 **FUNERALS** – We buried dozens every day. Life moved to the town cemeteries, it got reduced to burials and funerals, and became a target not only for camera lenses but of shells as well. We were killed by shell fragments and bullets while saying our last farewells to our friends, fathers and children; at the same time Jana Schneider, Milomir Kovačević Strašni and others did their job as photographers with courage and caution.

Photographs 1: Kemal Hadžić
2–5: Rikard Larma
6: Emil Grebenar

164, 165 **THE RED CROSS** has been spared in all other wars. Here, targets were ambulances, the Red Cross building, lorries with medicines and white flags, the Maternity Home, and even new-born babies like little Kemal Karić.

Photographs 1, 3, 4, 6 and 7: Kemal Hadžić
5: Emil Grebenar
2: Rikard Larma

166, 167 **FIRE** has swallowed up many homes. Destroyed is Tabački masjid from the 16th century, covered with tiles, hit by 8 missiles. The interior and roof structure of this mosque without a minaret were burnt away. Similar things happened to houses in modern residential areas.

Photographs 1: Emil Grebenar
3: Kemal Hadžić
2 and 4: Rikard Larma

168, 169 **ROOFS** – The shrapnel was merciless. Roofs, façades and buildings are destroyed. Life goes on, but it is necessary to patch up a window of the "Napredak" palace in which Frangeš's sculpture "Force" with a mace in hand has been damaged. Luckily, the second sculpture ("Knowledge") has remained intact.

Photographs 1: Kemal Hadžić
3 and 4: Emil Grebenar
2 and 5: Danilo Krstanović

172, 173 **RUBBISH** stayed in the streets for months. We could not take it anywhere. It was burnt on the pavements. Photographs, however, cannot convey the stink. The rubbish blocked both the main street and the parks. A man and a dog compete for looking for food even there, especially at dumps where UNPROFOR disposed of their rubbish.

Photographs 1: Emil Grebenar
3 and 4: Rikard Larma
2: Kemal Hadžić

176, 177 **SERIOUSLY DAMAGED** were roof structures of the St Anthony of Padua Church and Monastery, St Joseph's and the Holy Trinity churches. Seldom were stained glass windows not either destroyed or badly damaged.

Photographs: Kemal Hadžić

180, 181 **THE CENTENARY** of the Church of the Assumption of the Virgin Mary was commemorated by its destruction. Incendiary shells mercilessly destroyed God's temple at Stup.

Photographs: Kemal Hadžić

182, 183 **HOPE** has not deserted the nun Benedicta who is collecting broken pieces of the altar in St Vinko's Church. Religious statues like the top decorations on minarets equally bear witness to the intention to destroy Sarajevo completely.

Photographs 1–3: Kemal Hadžić
4: Danilo Krstanović

184, 185 **PLACES OF WORSHIP** cannot remember such devastation in their eventful centuries-long existence. Many mosques are destroyed. The Hadji Sinan Tekke (monastery), a place of spiritual life of the town, masjids, the Reis-ul-ulema residence and the Waquf buildings have not been spared either.

Photographs 1, 2, 4 and 5: Kemal Hadžić
3: Emil Grebenar

"OSLOBOĐENJE" has endured. Several times it was on fire and the office block collapsed – a skyscraper with the editorial offices of weeklies and journals, publications for children and businessmen, the publishing house "Oslobođenje Public", the marketing agency "OPRESA" and the agency for market communications "OSSA". War demolished the building from 1982, designed by Mladen Gvozden, Ahmed Kapidžić and Kenan Šahović, and also the "OKO" printing shop machines (2 four-coloured offset machines, one two-colour offset machine, photo-typesetting computer installations with 69 MB of memory, a laser colour scanner, a bookbinding machine, programmatic–cutting press...). Nevertheless, the typographers and journalists never stopped working through these war days.

Photographs 1 and 3: Danilo Krstanović
2: Senad Grubelić

FIRE consumed flats, houses, skyscrapers and office blocks. Shells were accompanied with incendiary bullets and other phosphor bombs. The modern building of the "Energoinvest" economic giant was destroyed over months by various missiles until fire swallowed up its 6 floors. Out of the 2.200 employees that used to work there, only 375 of them work now, under continuous firing from Grbavica. In 80 factories of the "Energoinvest", engineering and commercial departments, there were 40,000 employees in ex-Yugoslavia and abroad, 22,000 in Sarajevo. When the war is over, will even 5,000 of them have jobs?

Photographs 1: Rikard Larma
2: Danilo Krstanović
3: Kemal Hadžić
4: Emil Grebenar
5: Didije Torše

THE MARIJIN DVOR AREA has been exposed to the most severe destruction. An industrial symbol of the town is the old Tobacco Factory which sent into the world even a century ago packets of Herzegovinian and Bosnian tobacco and cigarettes under the names "Damen", "Hercegovina", "Bosna", "Guslar", "Drina", "Sarajevo", "Mostar", "Norenta", "Štefanija", "Foča", "Flor", "Posavina" and "Vrbas" ...

Photographs 1 and 3–6: Kemal Hadžić
2: Rikard Larma

THE LIFE OF THE TOWN continuously moved from one place to another. We sheltered from snipers' bullets behind concrete slabs in Kranjčević Street or patiently queued for hours to buy two packets of cigarettes (if there were any left by the time our turn came).

Photographs: Kemal Hadžić

OBITUARIES – Newspapers are full of death notices every day. Obituaries attract our attention in streets as well; in lists of those who have received parcels we eagerly look for our names.

Photographs 1: Emil Grebenar
2: Kemal Hadžić

PAVEMENTS – The beloved town has changed its face. Ship containers are used to protect us at pedestrian crossings. Even the post for the display of public notices is hit. On the river bank, full of broken glass, trams are stopped and the shells take the lives of cyclists as well.

Photographs 1, 3 and 4: Kemal Hadžić
2: Emil Grebenar

THE STREETS OF MY TOWN are sad, too sad. Fog and snow have comitted our wasteland to memory.

Photographs 1 and 4: Kemal Hadžić
2 and 3: Danilo Krstanović
6: Rikard Larma

A MOMENT – The speed of a Golf saves a passenger from fragments of a shell that has just fallen near the "Casino" restaurant, while the expediency of passers-by will probably help the injured man to have his leg saved. For the old woman and the car with flat tyres, moments have lost their significance, but not for the man with a crutch who is hurrying somewhere with a bunch of flowers.

Photographs: Rikard Larma

The new **VODOPRIVREDA** building on the left bank of Miljacka is burning by the Bratstvo-jedinstvo Bridge. It used to house the republic's water fund, the public water works company, and the Institute for the Water Industry of Bosnia-Herzegovina. The flames swallowed the modern computer center that was worth one milion US dollars, the powerful printing works with the book-bilding machinery, the documentation the value of which is hard to establish, the library with rare manuscripts, the data base. The damage in rough terms is $ 10 milion.

Will the bridge by the building continue to carry the old name even after the UN checkpoint was established there as a link between Grbavica and the rest of the city? The bridge and the river have become the world's new wall in the division of the city, as our own Berlin vision of the present and the future.

Photograph: Kemal Hadžić

SHOPS – Everything has become dark and futile, and a sentence spoken in 1886 by Consul James Minchine sounds very distant nowadays: "And as for the citizens of Sarajevo, they seem to be industrious and frugal people: they open their shops at dawn and do not close them until sunset."

Photographs: Emil Grebenar

THE MAIN STREET has changed its appearance. Wounded are the National Bank, the "ZEMA" department Store and the house with the "Dekor" shop in which nuns stay as well. Near the Ljubljanska Banka and the popular cake-shop "Oloman", there is a doll dressed in the uniform of a former JNA officer, with a notice pinned on it which says: AGGRESSOR. The broken window of the chemist's shop is replaced by boards and turned into a market for cars, firewood, fur coats, water pipes, gas stoves, kitchen ranges and everything else that can be bought or sold. Together with it goes that autumn wish "I'm looking for a woman to live with through the winter".

Photographs 1–3: *Emil Grebenar*
4: *Kemal Hadžić*

216, 217 HITS have changed the entrance to the building of the Interior Ministry, they have turned balconies into staircases at Dobrinja (too much shooting on the other side of the building), they changed the functions of cafés and made tall pedestrians stoop while going along the wall of the "Vaso Miskin Crni" factory, which is the only reasonably safe way towards the western parts of the city.

Photographs 1, 2 and 4: *Emil Grebenar*
3: *Danilo Krstanović*

224, 225 OUR INTERIORS have changed. Bread is burnt in a devastated kitchen, our favourite coffee-drinking ritual is interrupted, only the windows remain of our homes, overlooking the "Jajce" barracks, and refugees who are without any shelter have moved into the School of Arts.

Photographs 1 and 2: *Rikard Larma*
3: *Danilo Krstanović*
4 and 5: *Kemal Hadžić*

226, 227 THE UNIS tower blocks used to be our pride standing out from low houses on the hills of Sarajevo. The office block of the Associated Metal Industry is badly damaged. Many other factories are destroyed as well. The production of VW cars, Golfs and Jettas has also been halted.

Photographs: *Kemal Hadžić*

228, 229 THE YOUTH HALL, designed by Živorad Janković, has been demolished. The dancing hall does not look very appealing or other facilities of the cultural, sports and economic centre "Skenderija".
The tram at Marijin Dvor reached neither the City Assembly nor the "Elektrotehna" building near the Cathedral. This beautiful old residential and business block of the Racher-Babić firm from 1913, designed by Carl Kueschanrek, was on fire destroying the rich archives of the Tourist Association of the City and the republic there.

Photographs 1 and 5: *Kemal Hadžić*
2 and 3: *Rikard Larma*
4: *Miki Uherka*

230, 231 NERO'S LAUGHTER echoed menacingly in the Sarajevo nights. The "Gumitehnika" and the "Alhos" ready-made clothes factory are on fire. Burnt out is the railway station built in 1954 according to designs of the Czech architect Bogdan Stojkov. The clock does not work any more, but why should it, when 1,034 km of railway network in B-H are without trains? Of that number 850 km used to be equipped with modern signalling, safety and telecommunication devices. The B-H Railways had 87 electric locomotives, 40 diesel locomotives and 147 for shunting locomotives, 24 sets of electric trains, 370 passenger carriages and 9,525 goods waggons of various types and series. When all the war damage on railroads, bridges and structures is taken into account, the loss for the B-H Railways amounts to 350 million US dollars.

Photographs 1 and 2: *Rikard Larma*
3–5: *Kemal Hadžić*

232, 233 WAR SCARS – Many houses have burnt down to their foundations. Out of 62,268 flats in the housing sector in the four city municipalities, 37.42% have been completely or partly destroyed. Out of 70,000 private housing units 25,000 have been, according to the estimates, damaged and 7,000 completely demolished.
The First Grammar School, the oldest and most renowned secondary school in Sarajevo, gave shelter to displaced people, while the City Savings Bank built from 1929–1932 according to Mate Baylon's design lost its upper floors.

Photographs 1–4: *Kemal Hadžić*
5: *Emil Grebenar*

234, 235 TONGUES OF FLAME licked and bit by bit swallowed up the city. The Tobacco Factory at Marjiin Dvor could not be saved. Fire destroyed the studio and paintings of Branko Popovac in the house on the corner of Daniel Ozmo and Kralj Tomislav Streets. Part of a skyscraper called "a box of matches" disappeared in flames.
Firemen equipped with guns and radios extinguished fires under fire. In spite of their superhuman efforts in Daniel Ozmo Street, only the doorbells at the entrance remained: Peje Aleksandar, Topuzović, Šipek D., Greda E., ring 2×, Kovačević A., ring 2×, Gerin.
In Salom Palace in M. Tito Street a piano with the metal structure of the well-known firm Evdokia Dulizky from Vienna was literally cooked under jets of hot water that flowed down the burning beams.

Photographs 1 and 4: *Miki Uherka*
2, 3 and 6: *Kemal Hadžić*
5: *Rikard Larma*

236, 237 A STEĆAK (MEDIEVAL TOMBSTONE) was not spared either. It got its share of hits just like the National Museum in which the Natural Science collection situated in the pavilion closest to the River Miljacka bore the brunt of the shelling. Considerably damaged were the remaining three museum buildings. The roof with its glass domes was destroyed by 30 direct hits. More than 50 shells fell into the Botanical Garden, and the façade took about fifteen.
The skyscraper of the Government of the Republic of Bosnia and Herzegovina, the work of the well-known architect Juraj Najdhart, was several times on fire owing to continuous bombardment by dozens of various calibre shells. The City Assembly and the Holiday Inn Hotel withstood all the attacks. They never stopped work. The Holiday Inn has been full of foreign journalists since June, but the oldest hotel "the Europe" did not have such luck. In that distant 1894 Robert Munro wrote about it: "... On the ground floor there is

a large café and a billiards room with a view onto the main street, while the restaurant and the kitchen are opposite the entrance. In summer, the interior courtyard is used as a dining hall, and when nicely decorated, as the case is, with large exotic plants, it makes a very pleasant place for lunch. Before we finished our lunch, the owner came and told us with a smile that he had already prepared for us a very nice room. That was a truthful description and we found out that the room was indeed both comfortable and elegant." Today, pipes hang out of the hotel rooms, and the devastated ground floor smells awful.

Photographs: *Miki Uherka*

238, 239 **THE GAZI HUSREF BEY'S MEDRESA** (a religious secondary school) dating from the 16th century was damaged on the roof. The Oriental Sciences Institute with its invaluable manuscripts disappeared in flames. Mere walls cannot replace the burnt heritage. The same happened to the residence of the Serbian Orthodox Church Metropolitan designed in 1898 by the imaginative Rudolf Tönnies, with part of the roof structure and the second floor consumed by fire. Ugly marks remained on the Cathedral as well, with damage to the stone skirting, the walls, the entrance staircase, the stained-glass windows and a rosette above the portal...

Photographs: *Miki Uherka*

244, 245 **THE INDUSTRIALIST** August Braun, son of Franjo Ksaver, using bricks from his own brick kiln built in 1895 a large residential building with flats to let and named it after his wife Marija. He gave her this court as a present in 1912, and the whole of the western part of the town got its name from it.
Not far away is Vrbanja Bridge, the recent Suada Dilberović Bridge and the view of Kovačići and Grbavica, the left bank of the River Miljacka, the suburb cut off by this war, a view of it accessible only to the brave. And there is a destroyed tank, the skeleton of the business block of "UNIONINVEST" and corpses of citizens that nobody dares to approach.

Photographs: *Miki Uherka*

246, 247 **A NEW RETIREMENT HOME** has never received its old people. Its first residents are UNPROFOR personnel. It is in no man's land. One cannot go further owing to trenches, shells and bullets.
In Dobrinja's residential areas, the balconies are full of sandbags. The same is true of the windows of the former Command of the Sarajevo area where UNPROFOR soldiers are deployed.

Photographs 1: *Didije Torše*
3: *Emil Grebenar*
2: *Kemal Hadžić*

248, 249 **SMOKES OF SALVATION** gush through stovepipes that jut out of the once beautiful Ajas Pasha Court or the "Central" Hotel designed in 1888 by Josip Vancaš.
Winter has done the same to the windows of the First Grammar School. The flames of destruction made holes in the roof of the "Europe" Hotel with a view of the Synod Church on whose dome tambours are damaged.
We find warmth and fear by running across bricks from the façade of the "Svjetlost" publishing house.

Photographs: *Kemal Hadžić*

252, 253 **THE RELAY** station on Hum was targeted by tank shells and rockets fired from warplanes. Hundreds of shells have fallen on the Radio and Television Centre of B-H. Relays and repeaters all over the Republic have been destroyed or captured, journalists and reporters killed, but the television pictures and words from Sarajevo have not been halted.

Photographs 1: *Rikard Larma*
3: *Danilo Krstanović*
2: *Emil Grebenar*

255, 256 **ON FIRE** is a kiosk hit by a shell near the Institute of Hygiene. We are surrounded by ruins; the old Military Hospital built in 1864 in the period of the Ottoman Empire speaks of its own sorrow.

Photographs 1: *Didije Torše*
3–5: *Kemal Hadžić*
2: *Emil Grebenar*

260, 261 **CULTURE** could not be killed. Artists resisted the war through their art. Afan Ramić painted **"Mostar"**, Petar Waldeg presented his impressions of war destruction in a map of graphics "Sarajevo '92", and Edin Numankadić exhibited his **"War traces"** with installations in the "Obala" Gallery – the burnt out interior of a former cinema. Dževad Hozo was finishing his oil painting "M... rat" (**"M... war"**), and a restless contrabassist Vedran Smajlović played his music even at places where everything looked ghostly and devastated. Kemal Monteno, Slobodan Vujović, Davorin Popović, Dino Merlin... sang of their sorrow.

Photographs: *Kemal Hadžić*

262 The war seems to have stifled the **ART OF GRAFFITI**. They have been reduced to swear words or simply: PINK FLOYD – written as a graffito on a concrete slab which protects passers-by in the main street against snipers' bullets from Osmice, while in a corner, written in green chalk is hardly visible: DON'T PANIC.

Photographs: *Kemal Hadžić*

264, 265 NUMISMATISTS of the world will include the year of 1992 in Sarajevo among their curiosities. As many as five currencies were valid here. At the beginning of the year the money of the SFR Yugoslavia was in circulation. Then the money withdrawn into the depots of the National Bank in 1991 was back in circulation in blockaded Sarajevo and the independent Republic of Bosnia and Herzegovina, but hand stamped by the National Bank of Bosnia and Herzegovina, the five-pointed star from the coat of arms being scraped off with a razor blade. The part of the city under the army and power of the SDS (Karadžic's Serb part, had money from the Serbian National Bank in Banja Luka. It is interesting to note that the watermarks on the 50-dinar banknote with a girl's portrait had been used on the 10-dinar banknote issued by the National Bank of Yugoslavia and that format, paper quality, patterns, colour shades and printing are identical to the technological process of the former Institute of the National Bank of Yugoslavia.

Then Bosnian-Herzegovinian money was introduced, in a computerized creation by Istok Hozo, with the trademark lyrics of Mak Dizdar, seen only through a magnifying glass: *"Bosnia, a country obstinate with dreams"* which reached Hrasnica, Butmir and Sokolović-kolonija, while the town itself had to be satisfied with money coupons, designed by Alija Hafizović and Darko Skert.

All these kinds of money quickly los their value. The German mark was the basic currency, and Sarajevans survived by means of ration coupons for bread and the bare necessities of life, and the charity of the world and combat rations with sachets of coffee, sugar and salt in them.

268 The first Bosnian-Herzegovinian STAMPS are a hope that letters will, nevertheless, somehow get through. People waited for a long time for the post office to print the stamps. The fact that they lacked the customary perforations was of no importance. The first series is a philatelic attraction in the world of collectors, but it also represents resistance to destruction. Then there are Olympic stamps, as a commemoration of the Sarajevo Olympics exactly 10 years ago, but also as a greeting to the Norwegian Lillehammer with the message: THE FLAME LIVES ON. It was not put on them that the war damage to the Olympic facilities was estimated to amount to some 65 million US dollars.

There was nothing. There is nothing. The town in hungry, thirsty, and also craving for CIGARETTES. One could somehow do without all the rest. Look, even those who have never tried smoking have now started.

The Sarajevo tabacco factory FDS manages to make cigarettters. There is a lack of paper for the packets. There is not enough white paper. Pages of unbound books can very well serve for packing. On the cigarettes, DRINA is written. Of course there are no other brands; it doesn't matter either. What matters is to draw in the smoke, to light it with a match from an UNHCR lunch-parcel.

276, 278 THE CITY ASSEMBLY with empty streets around, moved its main entrance to the back of the building.

Photographs: *Kemal Hadžić*

282 SLEDGES AND CANISTERS with water were a part of our winter scenario, our turmoil and the slow disappearance of the city and its inhabitants.

Photographs: *Kemal Hadžić*

284, 285 Topographical map of THE SIEGE of Sarajevo, scale 1:50.000

288 The centuries-old PEACE of the harem of the Emperor's Mosque has been disturbed. Destructive shells have not spared the old stone nishans. Grave in a grave – nothing remains worth the dignity of human life. Space for the burial of the dead soon ran out. Old graves were dug up. In the cemeteries of St. Josef and St. Mark the dead were buried in old graves. The old inhabitants did not mind the new ones.

Photographs: *Milomir Kovačević, Rikard Larma*

292 THE SARAJEVO ASSASSINATION of Franz Ferdinand has been included in history text-books all over the world. The broken plaque on the Museum of "The Young Bosnia Group and Gavrilo Princip" and footprints broken off from the pavement witness a new assassination attempt in Sarajevo.

Photographs: *Kemal Hadžić*

319 SALVATION for our souls and bodies was expected from the world. Hopes for peace were placed in the UN and its specialized organizations. Without them we could not have survived, but even with them it was difficult. Quite understandable is the protest of a small group of women in front of the frequently shelled building of the Presidency of the Republic with a sign which reads "EUROPE, YOU TRAITOR".

Photographs: *Kemal Hadžić*

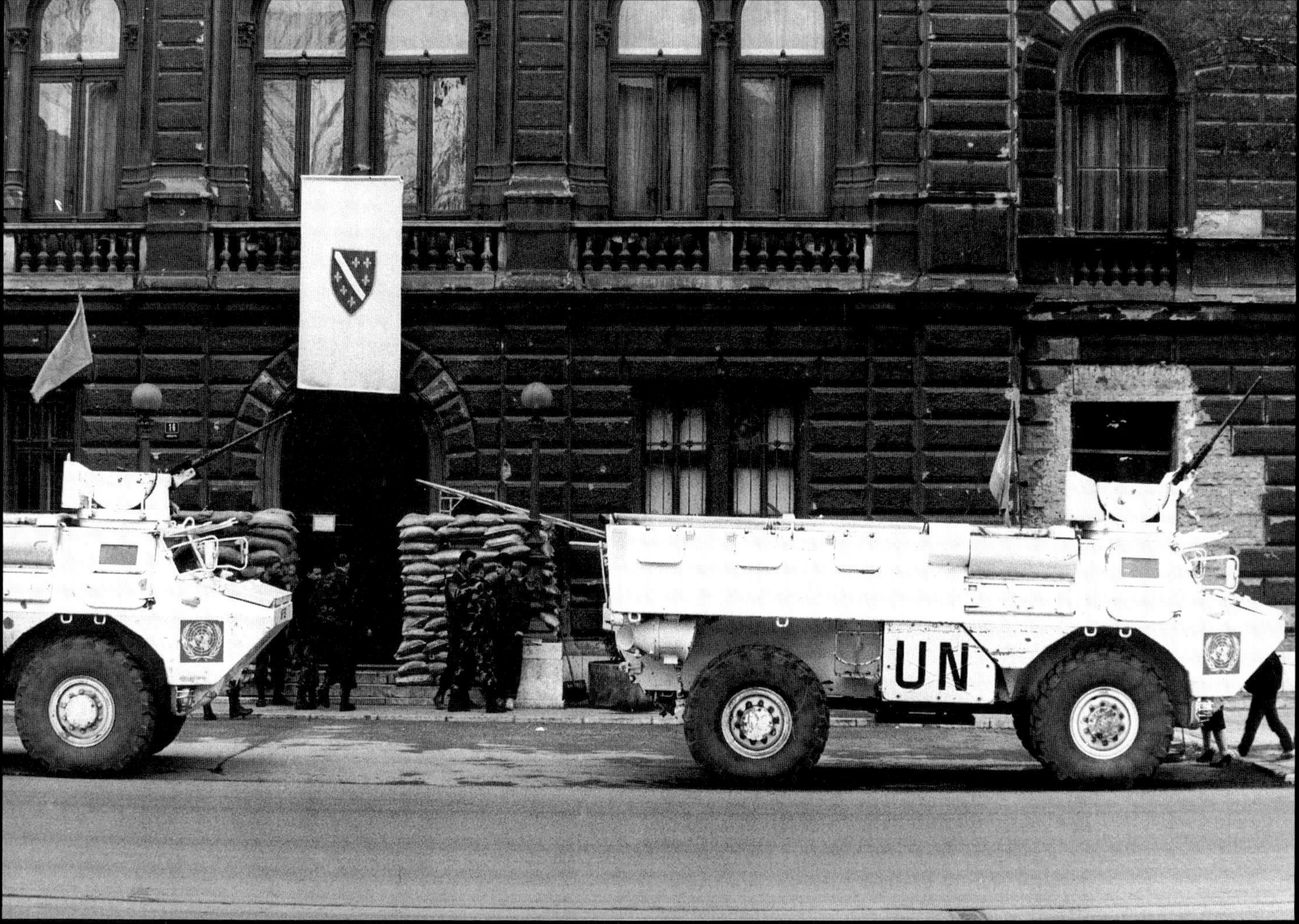
UN

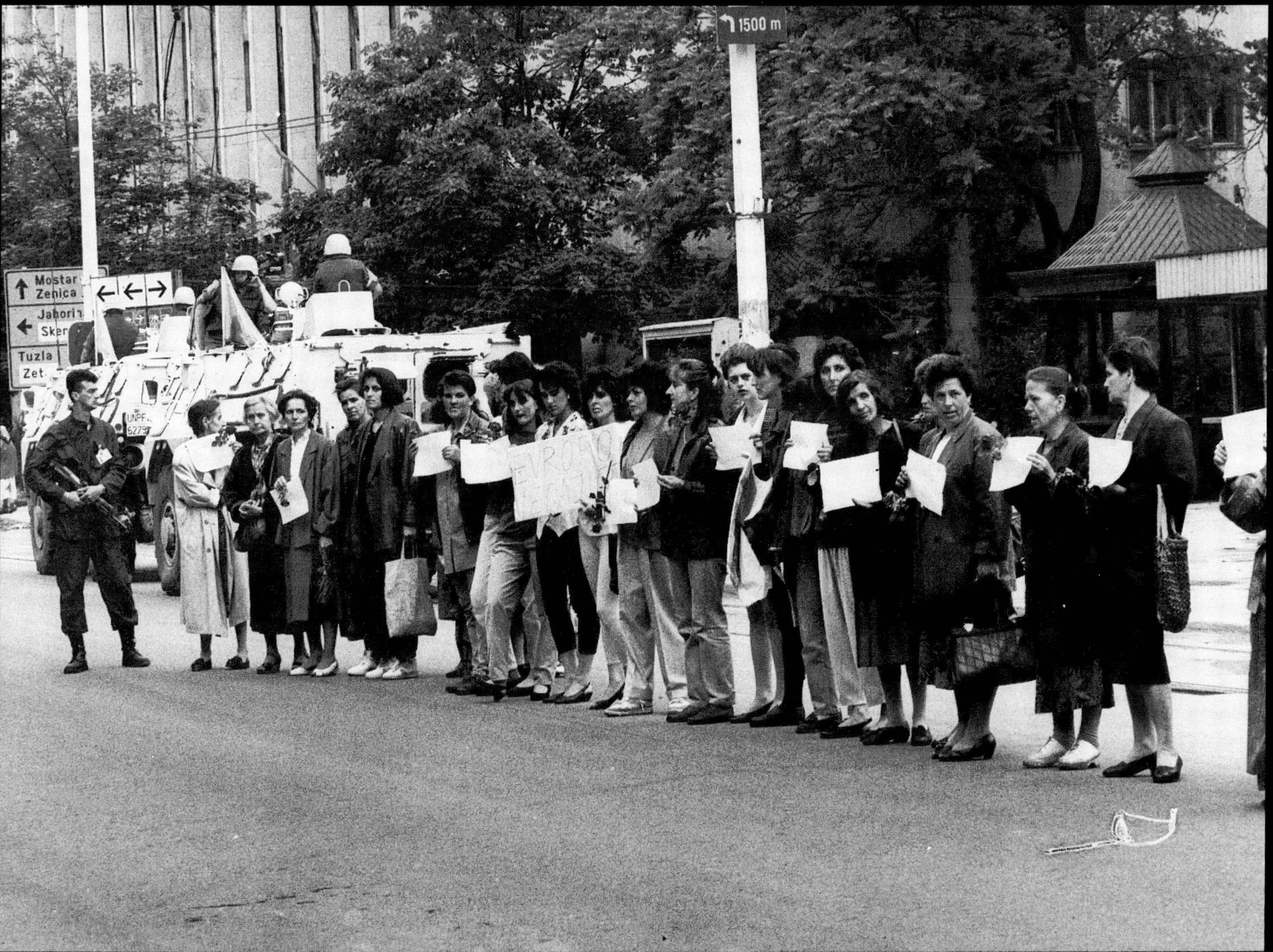
1500 m
Mostar
Zenica
Tuzla

This book does not aspire to explain why all of this happened to Sarajevo and to its people, why it was and is so. I had no political intentions either. I know, everything is politics and one cannot possibly escape it. It compels us, restrains us, chokes us.

This is, simply, my story about my city in a war which none of my people, no-one sane, ever wanted, ever wished for.

And all the time I naively hoped that it had come to an end, that the world would not allow further misery, that there was some sort of power, away from the Bosnian mountains and the Balkan madhouse, that would say: ENOUGH! I hoped it would be said in a strong enough way not to leave any doubts about what was said, not to leave any time for waiting.

No, nothing happened. Nobody managed to speak out, in a convincingly loud voice, that long wished for "STOP!"

And the days were becoming alike, crammed with the odour of gunpowder, with the roaring of shells flying over and exploding, with death, blood, and then shells again, splinters hitting hospital beds, schoolyards and babies. Death is all around us, we are in the reach of its fingers, and the blood, thick, red and sticky, prophesies ever new misery.

This book was completed in March 1993 in Sarajevo. I had intended to stop with the first year of the war.
The second year of war passed.
The third year of war in Sarajevo, in Bosnia-Herzegovina came.
Nothing changed in the incessant killing of the city, in its destruction, its annihilation.
There are more and more of those who are weary of its misery, who simply decided to go away, flee, vanish from the city they'd believed they would never leave, who are going away to look for a new sun and a new place of their own. Yet another immense misery of Sarajevo is being born, that ot those who leave and of those who remain.

I got out of Sarajevo, out of war. Others could not. My friends from Austria helped me with their persistence and the trouble they took, believing in my testimony, in my need to go away. Friends made it possible for this manuscript to get out of Sarajevo. It was not easy, but they did it.

Does anybody need this book?
Do you need my testimony, you madam, you sir, you my friend? You are Europe, the world, and the Balkans, the Balkans are somewhere down there, far, far away... That Sarajevo is, less than an hour's flight from Vienna, two and a half hours from Frankfurt, three hours from London...
The door to the hell of Sarajevo has remained open, sir.
And what, once it is all over?
The Golgotha of Sarajevo goes on and on...

The number of citizens killed in 1993 is shown on the last page of the book and the first pages shown the number of those killed in 1992.

CIP – Kataložni zapis o publikaciji
Narodna in univerzitetna knjižnica, Ljubljana

355 (497.15 Sarajevo) »1992/1994« (084)

PRSTOJEVIĆ, Miroslav
    Sarajevo, the wounded city / Miroslav Prstojević ; photos Emil
Grebenar ... [et al.] : [translation into English Dževahira
Arslanagić, Gordana Kisić]. – Ljubljana : DAG Grafika ; Sarajevo :
Ideja, 1994

Izv. nasl.: Sarajevo, ranjeni grad
ISBN 961-224-001-9

42384384

Publisher
DAG GRAFIKA, Ljubljana
PP "IDEJA", Sarajevo

Editor
Darko GRKINIĆ

Reviewrs
Prof. Dr. Hanifa KAPIDŽIĆ-OSMANAGIĆ
Željko IVANKOVIĆ

Editor-in-Chief
Dževad TAŠIĆ

Design
Prof. Dževad HOZO

Translation into English
Dževahira ARSLANAGIĆ,
Gordana KISIĆ

Lektor
Nick van der Bergh

Printed by
Ljudska pravica, Ljubljana

First published
1994

Cover page
Kemal Hadžić

Photograps of Sarajevo before 1992 on the first eight pages of the book are from the documentation of the Tourist Association of the City of Sarajevo and the Republic of Bosnia-Herzegovina

Sponsors who helped with the publishing of the monograph "The Wounded City": ROGIK "HIDROGRADNJA" and the Bosnia-Herzegovina Headquarters for the Protection of Cultural Heritage, the institution and the people who work in it.

Rješenjem Ministarstva za kulturu Republike Slovenije broj 415-607/94 od 11. 8. 1994 knjiga je proizvod za koga se plaća 5% poreza na promet.

DAG – Grafika
Medvedova 24
Ljubljana, Slovenija
tel. 00386 61 329 326
fax 00386 61 271 684

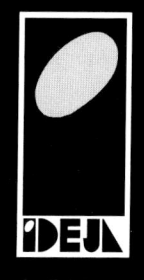

COPYRIGHT © DAG Grafika, Ljubljana & PP „IDEJA" SARAJEVO

9662